D1287289

A PARADISE OF BLOOD

A
PARADISE
— OF —
BLOOD

The Creek War

— *of* —

1813–14

Howard T. Weir, III

WESTHOLME
Yardley

TO:

James Dickey, Richard Dillard, Glenn Eaves, George Garrett, Stuart Harris, Lillian Hellman—Teachers

Howard and Emma Frances Weir—Parents

Howard IV, Lisa, and Emma—Children

Anne—Everything

Westholme Publishing, LLC

904 Edgewood Road

Yardley, Pennsylvania 19067

Visit our Web site at www.westholmepublishing.com

First Printing December 2015

10 9 8 7 6 5 4 3 2 1

ISBN: 978-1-59416-193-3

Also available as an eBook.

Printed in the United States of America.

CONTENTS

❖

PART TWO

PART THREE

MAPS

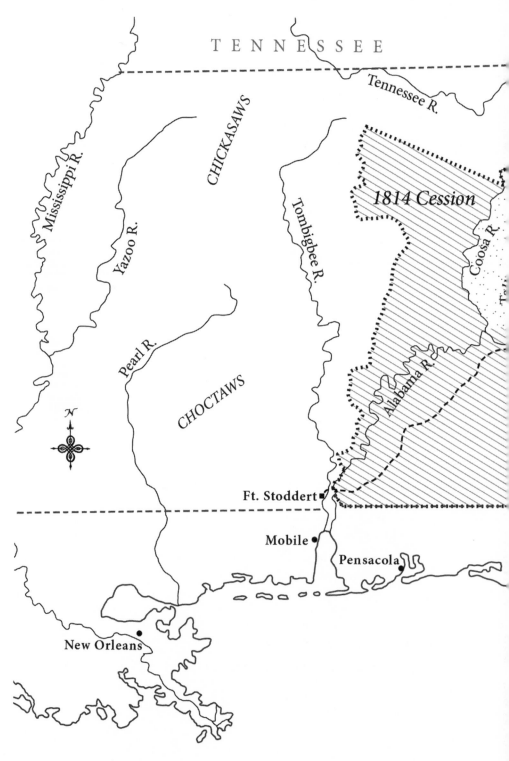

Creek Land Cessions, 1733–1832.

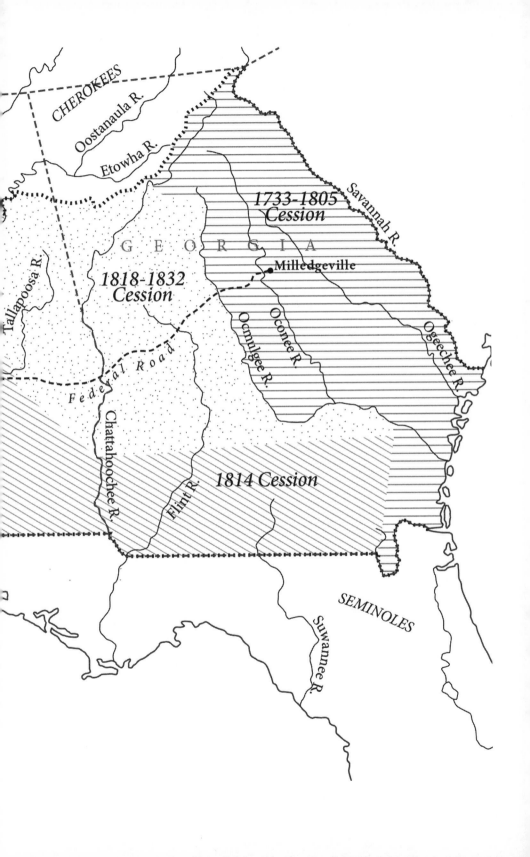

PROLOGUE

The Spanish Entrada

In the year 1535, the Spanish conquistadors gazed upon thousands of miles of ruined Native American civilizations from Mexico to Peru and decreed the work good.[1] Preternaturally restless, they turned an inventive eye north and east, particularly to the Indian chiefdoms that dotted the fertile landscape of the southeastern part of what would one day be the United States. It was a land largely untouched by violence and unwatered by serious effusions of blood; a land ready to be visited with unnatural mischief.

Spain's chosen instrument was a proven dealer of death on an industrial scale, one Hernando de Soto (the anglicized version of his actual name, Soto). His birth date is uncertain, but he appears to have been born around 1500, the scion of minor nobility from the hardscrabble province of Extremadura, Spain. Like so many other impoverished but ambitious young Spaniards in those days, the young de Soto came to the New World to seek his fortune. He was a small man but a furious fighter who had honed his skills in Indian fighting against the natives of Central America. There he had had the exceptionally good luck to cast his lot with the infamous conquistador Francisco Pizarro. Against tens of thousands of battle-tested Native American warriors, Pizarro, along with de Soto and several hundred companions, cut and lanced their way in great torrents of blood through the enormous Inca Empire that sprawled from Ecuador to Chile. The tale beggars belief but is nonetheless true. Pitting a deadly brew of European technical advances in weapons and armor, the terrifying creature known as the horse, impossible bravery, heartless cruelty, and diabolical cleverness against a loosely woven polity of conquered native states then in the midst of a dynastic civil war, the Spanish clawed the guts from the Inca Empire in a matter of months. For de Soto, who had become a leading captain under Pizarro, this success meant he need never work again; now in possession of gold and silver by the ton and rich lands by the square miles, he could settle in Peru or even in Spain and live like a great European prince.

But it was not to be. De Soto was so pathologically ambitious and competitive that he was willing to risk his personal comfort, considerable wealth, and indeed his life, not to mention the lives and fortunes of every-one (family, friend, and, of course, foe) with whom he came into contact to conquer an empire to rival those won by his master Pizarro in Peru and that greatest of all conquistadors, Hernando Cortes in Mexico. To his ambitions de Soto also married in his person a feral cunning with unwa-vering courage and a transcendental cruelty; the perfect satanic instru-ment for the task ahead. De Soto's greed also made him the perfect butt of the satanic joke played out on the conquistador during the course of his creation of a southeastern hell. It was the age of Don Quixote, and like a Don Quixote from the Pit, de Soto embarked on a diabolical quest through unknown lands and unprepared peoples after a mirage of gold.

De Soto left Peru for Spain in 1535, driven by a vision that held complete dominion over his wretched soul. After the standard long months and headaches of dealing with Spanish officialdom, he secured from the crown bureaucracy an appointment as governor of Cuba and *adelanto*, or gover-nor, of Florida, as the lands north of the Gulf of Mexico were then known. The crown, of course, was delighted to allow de Soto to spend his fortune and to bleed off from Spain some of its impoverished and troublesome young bloods on an adventure aimed at acquiring for the Spanish Empire vast new lands, fabulous riches, and numberless human beings whose bodies could be exploited and whose souls could be saved.

In 1536, de Soto's expedition sailed from Cuba for the largely unex-plored lands north of the Gulf of Mexico. Included among its approxi-mately seven hundred members were soldiers, some Aztec warriors, lay priests, friars, artisans, and general hangers-on and ne'er-do-wells. A key component of the Spanish flotilla, along with packhorses and mules, were around two hundred of the warhorses that had so terrified the Mexicans and Peruvians and would have the same effect on other Native Americans as well. Almost as terrifying to the natives as the Spanish horses were the packs of war dogs the Spanish brought with them and allowed, to further encourage their enthusiasm for combat, to feast on Indian flesh. More mundane, but more biologically significant than any of these creatures, were the hundreds of omnivorous Iberian swine that accompanied de Soto's expedition. In time, these would grow as big as young Muria bulls, just as quick, more nimble, and armed with savage, scimitar-shaped tusks. With their extraordinary ability to proliferate and survive in the worst conditions, these animals would in time transform the biological land-scape of the region.

The expedition landed in the Tampa Bay area and promptly began mur-dering, enslaving, and burning its way through the native communities of what are now Florida, Georgia, and South Carolina. In invading the coun-try, de Soto applied the tried and true methods he and his colleagues had perfected in Central America and Peru. He feigned friendship toward the chiefs, or *caciques*, as the Indians called them, of the native towns he encountered and then, when the opportunity arose, took them hostage. Through them he imposed his wishes on their subjects. When he reached the next chiefdom he repeated the process, but generally released his current hostage.

As if bewitched, the Spanish horde, accompanied by the legion of swine and long lines of impressed Indian porters and female slaves, chained together from iron collars around their throats, steadily chased the carrot of Indian tales of golden cities that lay just beyond the next horizon. Handed off by its Indian guides from petty chiefdom to petty chiefdom, whose capitals centered on palisaded temple mound complexes, the expedition finally reached the Appalachian Mountains, whose pale resemblance to the mighty Andes gave hope of gold to de Soto and his comrades. Modest deposits of gold were there for the finding, but the Indians had yet to locate them and the Spaniards never did, at least not in any meaningful quantity.

Unfailingly, however, news came to de Soto from the local Indians of a fabulously wealthy kingdom known as Coosa within an easy march to the south down the upper Coosa River valley in what is now northwestern Georgia. Having previously arranged to rendezvous with a Spanish supply fleet under Captain Diego Maldonado at the Bay of Auchuse (Pensacola Bay) on the Gulf of Mexico, de Soto and his motley army headed toward the fabled Coosa in the direction of Auchuse Bay. First, however, the conquistador extracted an array of female slaves from the populace and impressed more of the local Indians as porters. Once assembled, the expedition marched off down the Coosa River valley accompanied by the competing music of the tinkling little bells the Spanish attached to the horses' saddlery and the jangling chains draped from the porters necks, ominously heralding the sounds of African slave coffles two hundred years later, as they made their doleful way from the played-out farmlands of the mid-Atlantic to the rich soils of the Deep South.[2]

On July 16, the army arrived at the beautiful province of Coosa, along the northern reaches of the river of that name. One of de Soto's soldiers, a Portuguese known as the Gentleman of Elvas, declared: "The land was heavily populated and had many large towns and planted fields which reached from one town to the other. It was a charming and fertile land, with many good cultivated fields stretching along the rivers. In the open fields were many plums, both those of Spain and those of the land, and grapes along the rivers on vines climbing up into the trees."[3]

On reaching the chief town of the province, de Soto seized the *cacique*, evicted the natives from their homes, and lodged his men in them. De Soto and his army remained at Coosa for several weeks, devouring the natives' abundant food supplies, but the Spaniards found no gold. During his sojourn there the Coosa lured him from their town with news of another rich province to the southwest known as Tuscaloosa. On August 20, with the Coosa *cacique* and a replenished retinue of chained bearers and female slaves in tow, de Soto marched the expedition toward the capital of that province. Along the way he picked up additional porters at the town of Tallassee. After remaining some days at Tallassee, he released the *cacique* of Coosa, for whom he had no further use, and continued on his way in easy marches down the heavily populated valley of the Tallapoosa toward Tuscaloosa's capital, Athabuchi, which lay several days' journey to the southwest on the Alabama River south of present-day Montgomery, Alabama.

Apart from several nasty fights with some very tough Native Americans in the Florida swamps, de Soto encountered Indians that mostly complied with his demands in his expedition from Georgia into Alabama. Based on that experience, he had no expectation that the natives' current tame response to his invasion would not continue as he moved on. But awaiting him at Athabuchi was a *cacique* the likes of whom he had never encountered. The chief's name was eponymous with his province—Tuscaloosa—which means Black Warrior. By all accounts, Tuscaloosa was a giant of a man and well proportioned, with an imperious, shrewd, and bold nature. De Soto entered Tuscaloosa's town on October 10. There he found the chief seated on the veranda of a two-story structure built on a low mound. A retainer holding a large feathered fan above the chief cooled and shaded his master from the sun. At the chief's side was his equally large son. As usual, de Soto feigned friendship. Undeterred by all the Indian pomp and circumstance, at his first opportunity the conquistador seized Tuscaloosa and demanded the usual women and porters. This time de Soto's tried and true practice toward the natives failed him disastrously—he had made a captive of the wrong man.

Initially, Tuscaloosa grudgingly submitted to his captivity. But de Soto was not the only one who could dissemble. Tuscaloosa immediately dispatched his lieutenants to organize a trap designed to exterminate the entire Spanish army. Meanwhile, he responded to de Soto's demand for porters and women by filling only part of the Spaniard's quota, explaining that they would have to travel to Maliba, a town several days' march south, to find sufficient porters to fill the remainder of the Spaniards' needs. At Maliba, Tuscaloosa had assembled a horde of warriors from his own and allied chiefdoms to destroy a common evil.

The expedition left Athabuchi on October 12, 1536. Tuscaloosa, at his request, was mounted on one of the fearsome horses, which, because of the *cacique*'s great size, was actually a pack animal. Two days later they reached the town of Piachi, believed to be located where White Oak Creek empties into the Alabama River.[4] On October 16, the army crossed the river for Maliba on rafts it had constructed of cane and timber, the Indians disingenuously claiming they had no canoes available. Along the way to Maliba, the Spanish encountered numerous Indian settlements, where they took great delight in looting and in generally abusing the populace. This sport, however, had the effect of dispersing the strength of the army about the countryside. Thus it was that when de Soto finally reached Maliba on October 18, 1536, his immediate retinue was greatly diminished.

Maliba sat on a large plain with a sizable lake nearby. The town was small, only several acres, but strongly fortified. Its walls were made of thick tree trunks, as well as living trees that had been incorporated into the palisade; all were bound together with cross-ties and plastered over with clay. Towers were built along the wall, and loopholes for bowmen had been cut through the structure. It had two gated entrances and was filled with large houses, also pierced with loopholes, built around the typical plaza. Ominously, the ground surrounding the fort had been cleared of houses, which created an open field of fire for Indian bowmen in the fort.

Some of de Soto's lieutenants sensed danger as they approached the town and urged the conquistador to remain outside its walls. He replied that he was weary of sleeping outdoors, and, accompanied by a small personal guard of eight or so infantrymen and several cavalrymen, along with Tuscaloosa and his retainers, the imperious conquistador entered the town. There, concealed within the cluster of houses, waited several thousand of Tuscaloosa's warriors and allies. Just inside the walls, the exhausted Indian porters lay their burdens on the ground and squatted in their chains beside them. Meanwhile, de Soto and his small retinue gathered in the square, the cavalrymen dismounting and tying up their mounts.

The Indians had arranged refreshments for their guests and entertainment that from sad experience they knew would distract the Spanish: a troupe of comely dancing girls. During the festivities, and before de Soto could even commandeer a house for his headquarters, Tuscaloosa preemptorily announced to de Soto that he would go no farther and advised the Spaniard to leave his province. An argument ensued between the two men, and before de Soto could act, Tuscaloosa stalked off and entered a nearby house. When the *cacique* refused de Soto's commands to come out, the Spaniard ordered several of his men to drag the chief from his refuge. This attempt touched off an immediate attack on the Spaniards by the thousands of heavily armed Indians hiding within the houses. Garishly painted, they rushed toward the little band of Spaniards with bows drawn and notched with arrows. Among the first to die in the Indian assault were several of the dreaded horses, which the Indians had wisely chosen to be among their initial targets. De Soto ordered his men to head for the open gate and out of the fort. Amid the deafening cries from thousands of

Indian voices, flights of arrows flew thickly from Indian bows toward the fleeing Spaniards. De Soto and all of his men were hit, and the commander fell to the ground several times before reaching the gate. So heavy was the arrow storm that one of de Soto's guards, the chronicler Rangel, had twenty arrows jutting from his armor of quilted cotton as he rode onto the field outside the fort looking much like a gigantic hedgehog.

As the Spanish retreated out of arrow range, the porters shouldered the Spanish baggage they had been transporting and entered the fort. Once inside its walls, the Indians quickly rifled the baggage of its contents and derisively brandished myriad Spanish possessions from the walls of the town at their former owners. Even then, however, de Soto was sending messengers to bring in the bands of Spanish soldiers from their looting forays about the surrounding countryside. Once he had his total force together, de Soto determined to destroy the town and its inhabitants. First he ordered his cavalry, with its long lances, to surround the town to prevent any Indians from escaping to the safety of the nearby forests. Next he formed four companies of infantrymen equipped with axes, as well as the deadly halberds and swords the soldiers typically wielded. Each company was assigned to a side of the fort and ordered to make simultaneous assaults on the walls with the object of chopping passages through them to the town inside. Once inside, the men were to fire the buildings and slaughter the inhabitants for their treachery.

Spanish chroniclers report that Indian boys as young as four years old fought the Spaniards as the Malibans contested the Spanish assault on the town walls. The fight raged for hours, and many Spaniards and their horses were killed or wounded by the defenders' accurate arrow fire. By late afternoon, after much suffering on both sides, the Spanish managed to gain passage into the town. With fire and steel, the real slaughter began as the Spanish were at last able to come to grips with their adversaries. In the hand-to-hand combat that ensued, the Indians' bows were of no use, and their wooden and stone-headed war clubs were insufficiently lethal against the tempered steel of the Spaniards' swords, broadaxes, and pikes. Fires set by the Spanish also began their work, and those Indians who were not driven out by the flames to be slaughtered in the dirt yards of their own homes were horribly consumed by them.

When the battle was over, several thousand Indians lay dead within the smoking ruin of the town. The bodies that were not destroyed in the flames carpeted the open spaces of the settlement in all manner of gruesome contortions and dismemberments. Above the desolation hung the forlorn, limp signpost of a single Indian. When the warrior had run out of arrows, he twisted one end of his bowstring around his neck, the other around a stout limb of one of the living trees incorporated into the wall, and jumped. Not one Indian surrendered, although it is said that in the first stages of the battle, at the insistence of his advisers, Tuscaloosa had escaped from the town and disappeared into the countryside.

As for de Soto, the Battle of Maliba was an utter disaster. Accounts vary, but it appears that from twenty to twenty-two of his men and seven of the irreplaceable horses had been killed. An additional 148 men—one account says 250— and 29 horses had been wounded. With an almost Teutonic precision, the Spanish tallied 760 arrow wounds among the soldiers. Almost all of the precious baggage of the Spaniards had been destroyed by the very fires set by their owners, including some two hundred pounds of freshwater pearls the Spanish had seized from Indian temples in their trip through South Carolina. More critically for the numerous wounded, the Spaniards' medical supplies had also been lost to the flames. They were, therefore, forced to harvest the yellowish fat from the dead citizens of Maliba to treat their wounds.

Strangely, although Maliba was the bloodiest encounter between Europeans and Native Americans in North American history, after much searching by archeologists over more than one hundred years, the site of the town has never been discovered. The battle also marked the beginning of the end of de Soto's expedition. After his army had recuperated sufficiently to once more take up the march, de Soto led it northwest out of the Alabama country toward lands he hoped could feed his army. He had puzzlingly discarded his plan to meet the Spanish supply ship at Auchuse, perhaps because his army lacked sufficient supplies to reach that place. Or it may have been that de Soto sensed that once his men reached the coast they would never turn back to face the unrecompensed dangers of the interior. Like his predecessor, the great Cortes, who burned his army's ships at Vera Cruz to prevent its retreat, de Soto's turn away from the coast may have been his way of burning his ships behind him.

Bereft of even the items necessary for the army's priests to conduct mass, the disintegrating expedition slogged and fought its way to the lands well beyond the Mississippi River. De Soto's army's encounter with that massive stream gained the conquistador a sliver of immortality as its discoverer (actually, Spanish sailors had certainly cruised by its mouth years before)—or rather, as is taught today, its first European discoverer—but it also became his grave. Following months of wandering in the western lands, de Soto returned to the Mississippi River. By that time, with a feverish de Soto still at its head, the army had been reduced to a force of several hundred souls clad in skins and the rags of their former proud attire. De Soto soon thereafter died of his illness. His companions sank his body into the Mississippi so the Indians might not learn that the conquistador was not the god the Spanish had portrayed him to be. The remainder of the army constructed boats and made its way down the Mississippi to the Gulf of Mexico and onto the Mexican coast. Only three hundred miserable adventurers from the original *entrada* survived. In its tailings, an unknown number of captured Indians also survived. At least four of them—women—were taken to Spain. Behind them de Soto and his companions left a wasteland.

As the result of de Soto's quixotic campaign, the Mississippian people had been wiped almost clean from the land, swept away by Spanish arms, horses, dogs, famine, and the wave of diseases that followed in the expedition's wake. Twenty years later, when a second Spanish expedition entered the "far famed" province of Coosa, those in the Spanish retinue who had been there with de Soto did not recognize the place. They must have been bewitched, they exclaimed, for when they first beheld the countryside it appeared a "rich and populated" province. Now the land they gazed on was sparsely populated and little cultivated. "There was much forest but little fruit," and where fields of grain had been all was now "full of thistles and weeds."[5] To the hungry Spaniards, the once grand place about which they had heard so much was only wilderness, and they never founded settlements there. Shorn of its human inhabitants, the land lay untouched and waiting for a Native American rebirth, a blank slate upon which other tragedies would be written.

Part One

1. A Rope of Sand

The Birth of the Muskogee Confederation

I N the two hundred years that followed the *entrada*, in the slow way a clear-cut forest regains its former glory, Native Americans gradually began to repopulate the vacant land. They settled in a region covering tens of millions of square miles of terrain that rose and fell in ancient mountains that eased, fingerlike, from the north on to the piedmont and coastal plains before the land finally reached the famous white sand beaches and turquoise waters of the Gulf of Mexico. The diverse topography of this wild country was etched with large and beautiful rivers of astonishing clarity and melodious names that matched their beauty and mimicked the sound of flowing water. Across the north central part of Alabama, the Tennessee River hung from each corner of that state in a ragged arc. In what is now Georgia, which in colonial days was a tenth of its present size, the white citizens were largely confined to a strip of land between the Atlantic Ocean and Ogeechee River to the west. The rest of Georgia was occupied by Indian tribes—mostly Creek but also Cherokee who inhabited the northern mountainous region of the state. Moving west, the next major river system was the Oconee, and farther west the Ocmulgee River. These rivers came together in the lower eastern third of Georgia to form the Altamaha River, which flowed into the Atlantic Ocean. Even farther west ran the Flint, and beyond that the Chattahoochee, the mightiest river in Georgia, which now forms much of the border between that state and Alabama. The Chattahoochee met the Flint's waters in the lower western third of Georgia to form the Apalachicola River near Georgia's southwestern border with Florida. That river in turn flowed into the Gulf of Mexico, providing the European states access to the Muskogee towns in the lower part of the Muskogee Confederation, which the whites commonly referred to as the "Nation."

Fifty miles to the west were the Coosa and Tallapoosa river systems. These large streams forked south from the mountains of east Tennessee, dropping loudly from the highlands in tandem until they met to form the great Alabama River. The area making up this great river system was the heart of the Upper Creek settlements. Farther to the west, near the border of present-day Alabama and Mississippi, woven from innumerable bright streams spilling out of the western foothills of Alabama, flowed the Black Warrior River. Not far to its east, the Tombigbee River, whose Choctaw-derived name means coffin-maker, flowed south out of the Mississippi hills.[1] Just above the as-yet-to-be-built town of self-exiled Napoleonic officers, called Demopolis, the Tombigbee gathered in the waters of the Black Warrior River. Farther south, the Tombigbee and Alabama met thirty miles above the Spanish town of Mobile to form the Tensaw and Mobile rivers. From there these streams wrestled south with each other toward the Gulf of Mexico, leaving in their wake an enormous swamp of thousands of square miles that is difficult and dangerous to penetrate to this very day.

Five Indian nations coalesced within this enormous wilderness and along its many beautiful rivers and streams. The Cherokee people settled in the ancient mountain valleys of eastern North and South Carolina, northwestern Georgia and southeastern Tennessee. On the eve of the Creek War in 1813, the Cherokees had a history of roughly one hundred years of incessant conflicts, both large and small, with the whites. Over those years, because of the relentless white incursions into Cherokee land and the multiple pathogens that marched in unpredictable step with the invaders, the strength of this once formidable tribe was greatly diminished. Although the Cherokees still retained a significant military capability, the long years of warfare with the whites had sufficiently tamed them so that by 1794, the governor of Tennessee, William "Willie" Blount, felt so confident of white dominance of the tribe that he wrote the secretary of war, Henry Knox, that he could "in short time, induce [them, as well as the Choctaws and Chickasaws] . . . to aid the United States in the total destruction of that nation [the Creeks]."[2]

The Chickasaws were scattered about the rolling hill country of northwestern Alabama and northeastern Mississippi. This tribe was sadly diminished in numbers and power from its glory days in the eighteenth century, when it defeated every French expedition sent against it.[3] Estimates vary, but at the time of the Creek War, the Chickasaws numbered around three thousand people, of whom about six hundred were warriors. To their immediate south were the Choctaws. This tribe populated two-thirds of Mississippi's piedmont and a sliver of western Alabama bordering on the Tombigbee and Black Warrior rivers. Their numbers approached twenty-five thousand souls, of whom about four thousand counted as warriors. The Choctaws were noted for their practice of molding the skulls of their infants to a fashionable shape and for their inability to swim. They were a powerful tribe but proud of the fact that they had always been at peace with the whites.

Several hundred miles to the southeast of the Choctaws, the Seminole tribe occupied the low piney woods of southeastern Georgian and the panhandle of Florida. They were a wild people and loosely allied with the

Indian nation to their north that is the principal Native American actor in this story, the Muskogees, or—as the whites called them—the Creeks. The Seminoles were a small but warlike tribe; its population in the second decade of the nineteenth century ranged between four thousand and five thousand.[4]

Of all the Five Nations, the Muskogee Confederation was the dominant polity in the region. Among whites it was known as the Creek Nation, the name apparently being an Anglo abbreviation of the name Ocheese Creek Indians, whom the English first encountered living along the stream of that name.[5] By the mid-eighteenth century, the Muskogee Nation, with a population about the size of the Choctaw Nation, ruled the choice lands bounded by the Ocmulgee River in western Georgia, the Tombigbee River in western Alabama, the Tennessee River in northern Alabama, and the Spanish province of East Florida that ran along the Gulf Coast from Saint Augustine to Mobile. But to speak of the Creek Nation, as most whites did (possibly because "nation" was a concept with which they were familiar), was wrong. The Muskogee were actually a confederation of tribes, some of whom spoke different languages and whose uneasy alliances were reminiscent of the inconstant alliances formed by the city-states of the Italian Renaissance. Years later, Theodore Roosevelt would accurately liken the attempt to govern these unruly tribes of the confederation to an attempt to manage "a rope of sand."[6]

The tribes of the Muskogee Confederation were largely made up of the survivors of the *entrada* and of tribes that had sought refuge in Muskogee territory from white expansion and conflict with other tribes. The heart of the confederation was in the fertile river bottoms where the Coosa and Tallapoosa rivers flowed together to form the broad Alabama, and in the large towns along the central Chattahoochee. The mound-building cultures were now long gone, and the great heaps of sculpted earth, long covered with trees and brush, were slowly returning to their origins. In their shadow arose neatly ordered towns of dwellings made of wood and daub, with chimneys made of the same materials, and cypress-shingled roofs. The towns were constructed around a square courtyard of public buildings, a precursor of the white towns with their courtyard squares that would emerge across the Southern landscape in the wake of the Indian diaspora beyond the Mississippi River.

A prominent scholar, with some diffidence, claims that from a linguistic standpoint and the age of occupation of the land, the true Muskogee were the Kashita, Coweta, Coosa, Abihka, Holiwahali, Eufaula, Hillabee, Wakoka, Atasi, Tuckabatchee, Kolomi, Pakana, and Okchai tribes.[7] The Abihka, known as the door shutters because they guarded the nation's northern borders, lived on the upper Coosa Valley along its borders with the Cherokees. Their chief town, Aubechoo, was located among the limestone hills of the Talladega Valley on Nauchee Creek, five miles from the Coosa River. The town was known for an ancient brass drum it possessed that was said to have come from Hernando de Soto's expedition. Nearby a renowned and sacred cavern twisted through the inner dark of the mountains. Long ago, Native Americans had enlarged its chambers and conducted burials by torchlight there.[8] Among the bones later found there were those of an overcurious and undercautious white man. Incised in the cavern wall above these relics was the unintended *memento mori* "I.W. Wright, 1723."[9]

South of the Abihka were the Coosas. They had migrated downstream from their homes on the upper Coosa River after the *entrada*. By the end of the eighteenth century, they had settled on the eastern bank of the middle course of that river where the mountains met the piedmont.[10] The tribe was much diminished from its pre-Columbian salad days. But the mother town had spawned sturdy and redoubtable offspring who settled mainly about the upper Tallapoosa. Foremost among these in population and military prowess were the Okfuskees. Their principal town, Okfuskee, was on the west bank of the upper Tallapoosa River. From this mother town, smaller satellite towns ranged up and down the Tallapoosa. In the middle of the eighteenth century, the British established a tiny fort and trading post at Okfuskee to counter influence among the Creeks of the French Fort Toulouse, located at the forks of the Coosa and Tallapoosa.[11]

The most famous of the Coosa sibling towns was Ocheaupofau, or the Hickory Ground, situated on a lovely plain on the east side of the Coosa just below its last and greatest falls. During the coming war with the Americans, this town, a place of deep and sacred importance to the Muskogee Nation, became the prime objective of the American armies. Thirty miles to the west of the Hickory Ground, on the east bank of the Tallapoosa River, was another important sibling town known as Big Tallassee. This large town was the home to one of the intellectual leaders of the war against the Americans, Hoboheilthle Micco, a venerable chieftain, now in his nineties, known variously to the Americans as the Tallassee King or Tame King. During the Revolutionary War, he had sided with the Americans against the British—an act he would later regret.[12]

Between the middle reaches of the Coosa and Tallapoosa rivers lay a country of low hills and numberless pretty creeks where three groups of Muskogee made their homes. These people lived in a collection of settlements allied with the towns of Hillabee, Wakoka, and Eufaula. Hillabee was on a creek of that name, about a mile from the Tallapoosa River, and had several satellite towns nearby. Eufaula lay on the west bank of the Tallapoosa about five miles below the mouth of Hillabee Creek in a region of piney hills. Farther west, built on the bank of a creek that ran into the Coosa, was the town of Wakoka, which means heron breeding place. The area was famous for the salt moss that grew on the stony banks of its creek. It was said that horses taken from Wakoka to other parts of the nation were so addicted to this moss that if able to escape from their owners, they would travel great distances to return to the creek to feed on this succulent vegetation.

On the bottom land of the lower Tallapoosa, a few miles below the river's fall line, three of the most prominent Muskogee towns sprawled over the rich soil for twelve miles along both sides of the river. The northernmost of these towns, and arguably the most prominent town in the Creek Nation, was Tuckabatchee. It was situated in an enormous, hairpin-shaped bend of the Tallapoosa, just across the river from Tallassee. Tuckabatchee, in the years just before the Creek War, was the largest town in the nation. Fittingly, its chief, known to the whites as the Big Warrior, was a gigantic man, with character flaws that matched his impressive physique. He and Hobotheliethe, the *micco*, or chief, of Tallassee town, had been political rivals for many years. Their struggle soon morphed into a national catastrophe.[13]

Five miles below Tuckabatchee, just downstream of the mouth of Calebee Creek, on the east bank of the Tallapoosa, was the ancient town of Atasi, which in the Muskogee tongue means war club.[14] De Soto and his expedition had passed through this place on their way to Mabila, and the remains of a mound from that earlier time flanked the river by the town. During the Creek War, the town and an American military encampment just upstream of Calebee Creek were the scenes of two major and viciously fought battles. Many of the Indian participants in those battles came from a town known as Hoithlewaulee, five miles downstream from Atasi on the opposite shore of the Tallapoosa. Hoithlewaulee was a "war town," meaning it had the responsibility of declaring war for the nation and sending out that decision to other towns; for this reason its name meant to share out war.[15] Farther downstream from Hoithlewaulee was a string of important Muskogee towns running almost to the junction of the Tallapoosa with the Coosa: Fusihatchee, or bird tail, with its ancient and abandoned fortifications; Coolome, with its abandoned conical mound; Ecanhatke, or white ground; the Shawnee town of Sausanogee; and finally the little town of Muckklassa.[16]

The towns of the other division of the Muskogee Confederation, known as the Lower Creeks, were situated along the middle stretch of the Chattahoochee River, a name that means marked or flowered stone and comes from the rocks of that description in the river's bed. The principal towns of the Lower Creeks were Coweta and Cussetah. The Cussetahs were the largest Muskogee group in the Lower Nation. Their principal town was on the east bank of the Chattahoochee below its falls near the mouth of Hatcheethlucco Creek. In the cornfields upstream from the town were two flat-topped mounds, one conic and one oblong. They had long been abandoned and were covered with trees and brush.

The Cussetahs were friendly with the whites, although their chiefs complained that their young warriors had become so corrupted by their association with their Anglo neighbors as to be largely ungovernable. On the opposite shore of the Chattahoochee lay the Lower Creeks' war town of Coweta, peopled by the tribe of that name. Coweta lay three miles below the falls and two and one-half miles upstream from Cussetah. It shared a fishery in the rough waters below the falls with Cussetah. One of Coweta's principal leaders at the time of the Creek War, William McIntosh, had a large plantation just north of the town. [17]

The most important non-Muskogee members of the Creek Confederation were the Alabamas, the Uchee, the Natchez, and the Shawnees. The most numerous and powerful of these confederate tribes were the Alabamas. This tribe's towns were located along the upper reaches of the Alabama River. During the two years leading up to the Creek War, these people were at the center of the prophetic movement started by the famous Shawnee chief Tecumseh and his followers. The Alabamas' leading prophet, Josiah Francis, had established a new town, known as the Holy Ground, in a remote area on the Alabama River twenty miles below what is now Montgomery, Alabama. The Uchee were located on the west bank of the Chattahoochee, a little over ten miles below Coweta. Renowned fighters, they were also notable because the roots of their language are distinct from other eastern Native American Indian tribes. Thus, the Uchee were virtually incomprehensible to their Muskogee allies.[18] Their laws and customs were also strikingly distinct from their Creek neighbors. One of their most influential leaders prior to the opening of the Creek War was an Indian countryman named Timothy Barnard who worked for the United States as an interpreter and assistant Indian agent for the Creeks. Barnard was married to an Uchee woman, and their eldest son, Timopochee, played an important role as an ally of the Americans during the war.

The Natchez people, who settled in the northeastern part of the nation, were originally refugees from a disastrous revolt they had attempted against the harsh rule of the French colony of Louisiana in the early eighteenth century. After some initial successes, they were soundly defeated by the French. The remnants of the Natchez people that the French did not kill or transport to serve as slaves on the hellish plantations of the French colony of Saint Dominguez (present-day Haiti) fled north from their Mississippi homeland to the Chickasaw Nation. A number of the refugees were also given sanctuary by the Abihka tribe of the Creeks and allowed to establish a home near the Abihka in the Talladega Valley.[19] Years later, during the Creek War, the Natchez would repay the Abihka's kindness in false coin.

Finally, in the mid-eighteenth century, a group of the peripatetic Shawnees, who established settlements throughout the eastern United States, made their home among the Creeks in the string of Creek towns on the lower Tallapoosa. Their primary town was Sauwanogee, the home of a man known as the worst white man in the nation, the trader John Haigue, nicknamed Savannah Jack.[20] Like the Uchee, the Shawnee members of the confederacy retained their old language and customs. The parents of the most famous of all Native Americans in North America—Tecumseh— lived here along the lower Tallapoosa River before their relocation to the Ohio River Valley where Tecumseh was born. His dramatic return to his parents' homeland in 1811 was a triggering factor in the uprising of the Creeks against their American neighbors.

Benjamin Hawkins, Lord of the Muskogees

FOR over fifteen years prior to the political and social implosion of the Creek Nation, a single employee of the US government, with virtually proconsular powers, oversaw all of the Indian tribes in the vast area south of the Ohio River. He was army colonel Benjamin Hawkins, and the Creeks gave him the honorific title "beloved man." Now little known, Hawkins was one of the most remarkable, consequential, and tragic figures in American history.

Born into North Carolina landed gentry in 1754, Hawkins enjoyed a distinguished military and political career prior to his appointment as Indian agent by his friend, President George Washington. Well educated and fluent in French, Hawkins attended the College of New Jersey (now Princeton University). There, he lost his right eye when a fellow student, on a lark, snapped Hawkins's own pistol off in Hawkins's face, not knowing the gun was charged with mustard seed shot. Notwithstanding this injury, Hawkins served in the colonial army during the American Revolution as a member of General Washington's staff. After the war, he entered North Carolina politics and, in 1789, was elected to the US Senate from that state, where he served until 1795.

In 1796, Hawkins served as a commissioner to the landmark treaty negotiations with the Creek Nation at Coleraine, Georgia. During these negotiations, if not before, Hawkins became fascinated with these people, particularly their women.[21] Casting aside his promising political career, Hawkins obtained an appointment from President Washington as temporary US agent for the Southern tribes, a position later made permanent. The office was one of great power, covering the tens of thousands of Indian people and tens of millions of acres of Indian lands south of the Ohio River from Georgia to the Mississippi River. The Washington administration charged

Agent Hawkins with implementing its plan to civilize the Indians of this region and, thereby, opening up a vast territory to white settlement.

Hawkins was a stern and magisterial looking man, with the visage of the predatory bird with whom he partly shared a name. But his outward appearance and demeanor were deceiving. The agent had a depthless sense of responsibility toward, and compassion for, his Native American charges. On the eve of the Creek War, he lived at the Creek agency located near present-day Macon, Georgia. He had built this establishment on the east bank of the Flint River on eight thousand acres of land provided to him by the Creek Nation. One might think Hawkins would have wanted to be nearer to the nation's center, rather than over one hundred miles away on its eastern border. But the Flint River location gave him and his family more ready access to the nearby white settlements and the educational and cultural advantages they provided to a non-Indian family. The Lower Creeks, in whose territory the agency was located, were also certainly more congenial and more receptive to Hawkins's plan of civilization than their colleagues in the interior. The agent and his family were also safer here, but the place of his residence left him out of close touch with the critical events taking place deep in the nation among the Upper Creeks early in the second decade of the nineteenth century.

Whatever his reasons for choosing to situate the agency on the Flint River, by 1809, in what was clearly a labor of love, Hawkins had established at the new agency a model plantation complex that was largely self-sustaining. The government underwrote the operation, and Hawkins used it as an educational institution devoted to transforming his Indian charges into yeoman farmers.[22] The plantation contained shops for weaving, blacksmithing, hatmaking, tanning, and carpentry. There was also a water-powered mill on the property that Hawkins used to saw lumber, grind corn, and gin cotton. The homes and shops on the place were constructed in two parallel lines, with most of the houses built as residences for the seventy-odd black slaves who worked at the agency. Indeed, Hawkins's own home was next door to one of his slave cabins. A tavern for the entertainment of the frequent Indian visitors sat six doors down from Hawkins's home, and for the general entertainment of all and sundry, a bear pit lay next to the stables. On this vast establishment, Hawkins lived with and eventually married, on what all incorrectly believed was his deathbed, a white woman named Livinia Downs, with whom he had six children.[23] His children were home schooled by a "respectable gentleman from the Northward" in "reading, writing, arithmetic and Geography and lectures in Botany." Hawkins even had his offspring attend dancing school in the new state capital of Georgia, nearby Milledgeville.[24]

Despite the racial prejudices that had been instilled in people of Hawkins's generation, Hawkins genuinely liked the Indians and was a steadfast proponent of a plan sponsored by the US government to preserve the Indian nations from the rapidly growing white population, which was fast encroaching on the last of the Native American lands east of the Mississippi River. The essence of this plan was to wean the Indians from their traditional way of life as hunter-gatherers toward a culture based primarily on agriculture, both farming and stock raising, and cottage industries, such as cloth production. In short, the Native American population of the United States would be transformed by men such as Benjamin Hawkins into a red version of Thomas Jefferson's yeoman farmers. As such they would have no need for the vast forest lands necessary for their traditional occupation of hunting deer and other animals. This surplus land could then be settled by the land-hungry and clamorous white population of the United States. Hawkins described the program of "civilizing" the Creeks to Secretary of War Henry Dearborn in a letter dated July 15, 1802, signed by Hawkins and General James Wilkinson, commander of the US 7th Military District within which the Creek nation lay:

> [W]e believe a solid foundation has been lain for a salutary reform in the habits and manners of this people, and we have no doubt, that, by due perseverance in the system which have prevailed, the great work of their civilization may be accomplished: The philanthropist and the friend of humanity will rejoice to hear that the Creek nation, which six years since (excepting a morsel of corn and a few vegetables raised by their women) lived entirely by the chase, and dissipated their hard earned skins for Rum and Gimjaws, have recently appropriated one thousand dollars for axes, hoes, and salt, the last article principally to cure their domestic meats in the proper season and to nourish their stock.[25]

This, in essence, was the US plan for transforming the powerful Creek Nation into a polity that would present no threat to the Americans' expansionist interests. For Hawkins personally, this plan was not an exercise in hypocrisy. He understood very well that the government's intent was to use the plan to peacefully divest the Indians of a great majority of their lands over time. Nonetheless, Hawkins also truly believed that the only way to save the Native American peoples was by transforming them through education from hunter-gatherers to farmers.

Hawkins's sympathy for the Native Americans' dilemma, and his untiring efforts to promote his program of civilization, earned him a significant following among the Creeks, particularly the Lower Creeks living near the Georgia border with whom he cultivated good relations. Under the influence of their chiefs, many of them took up in a serious way the raising of stock and agricultural products such as corn, rice, rye, barley, oats, wheat, flax, and, of course, cotton.[26] Hawkins's white assistants taught the women to spin and weave, and they produced their own cloth for their people. Even some of the men joined in the work. As one prominent old chief of Coweta who was engaged in making cloth put it, "I am old . . . and as such according to our old ways useless but according to the new way more useful than ever."[27]

The majority of the Upper Creeks, however, were not as receptive as the Lower Creeks to the US plan to civilize them. The men feared the loss of their masculine identity and their freewheeling way of life and did not wish to incur the indignity and effort involved in doing what they considered women's work. As Hawkins observed, "The plan is not relished by the men, they are apprehensive that the women by being able to clothe themselves will become independent and compell the men to help them in their labour."[28] Somewhat surprisingly, many of the women also were not comfortable with this new way of life being steadily and insistently thrust on them. Their primary fear was that with their men around the household, they would lose their dominant and unassailable sway over domestic matters. [29] Thus, Hawkins's efforts to implement the government's plan of civilization made him many enemies among the Upper Creeks.

But they made him even more enemies among the Americans. His earnest attempts to civilize the "savage" (a word white North Americans commonly applied to their Native American neighbors) Creeks had engendered great animosity among the growing population of Georgians, Tennesseans, and Mississippi Territory settlers pressing on three sides of the nation's borders. For example, in June 1812, Ferdinand Claiborne, a brigadier general of the Mississippi territorial militia living near the town of Natchez, wrote to his associate, Colonel James Caller, a notorious swindler, land speculator, Indian hater, and all-around villain living along the western borders of the Creek Nation. Claiborne's letter was written in response to a letter from Caller warning Claiborne of the menace that the Creeks presented to the frontier settlements. From his comfortable home in Natchez, which he called Soldiers Retreat, Claiborne voiced his opinion to Caller that the Creeks, whom he called "pests," should be "confined to some distant & secluded tract of country," and that one barrier to ridding the territory of this menace was Colonel Hawkins. According to Claiborne, "The recent conduct of the Creeks is not so astonishing, when it is known that Col Hawkins (our agent) is a principal chief of that nation."[30]

Likewise, the governor of Tennessee, Willie Blount, was particularly notorious in his attitude toward Hawkins and his Indian charges. It was a family tradition. Blount's elder half-brother was William Blount, a prominent land speculator and Tennessee political kingpin. This Blount was a rascal of the first order in a land overrun with such characters. The elder Blount saw politics, of which he was a master, as the best means to further his true passion: land speculation on the grandest of scales. Indeed, among the Creeks, William Blount's insatiable hunger for land earned him the sobriquet the Dirt King, and among the Cherokee that of the Dirt Captain.[31]

William Blount was a Revolutionary War soldier from North Carolina. After the war, he served in the state legislature and in the Continental Congress. In 1790, with the backing of fellow North Carolinian Benjamin Hawkins and other well-connected politicians, President Washington appointed Blount territorial governor of Tennessee. Governor Blount also was the US agent for Indian affairs in the region. In 1796, Tennessee was admitted to the Union as the fourteenth state, and Governor Blount soon found himself appointed to the US Senate. Meanwhile, he had embarked on a now little-known and breathtakingly audacious scheme to divest by force the Spanish of their North American territories from Florida to the Mississippi River and to turn the Spanish lands over to, of all nations, his former enemies, the British.[32]

Reasoning on a global scale, Blount's plan, which anticipated Aaron Burr's conspiracy by almost ten years, was to take advantage of the national rivalries and alliances presented by the Napoleonic War to gain control of millions of acres of Indian land. Spain, the reluctant ally of France against Great Britain in that conflict, held sovereignty over the vast lands south of Tennessee that Blount wanted. Under Blount's scheme, Britain would finance a filibuster, or unauthorized invasion, by Blount's white partisans and their Indian allies to seize the Spanish lands. Blount would then effectively transfer sovereignty of the conquered territories to Great Britain. In return, Great Britain would deed vast tracts of the former Spanish lands to Blount and his clique. In order to enhance the value of these lands, Great Britain would also open the Mississippi River and the critical port of New Orleans to free trade.[33]

Senator Blount was particularly fearful that his old benefactor, Colonel Hawkins, who had recently been appointed agent to the Creeks, should not discover his plan to employ the warriors of that nation to attack the Spanish, because Blount knew that the upright colonel would attempt to stop it. To prevent this, Blount worked to have the Creeks request that President John Adams remove Hawkins as agent.[34] Unfortunately for Blount, the federal government discovered his traitorous scheme, and on July 8, 1797, he was expelled from the Senate, bringing an ignominious end to what would have been his greatest land deal.

Willie Blount shared his half-brother's lust for land and power and despised Hawkins for the agent's support of Indian land claims. When he became governor, the younger Blount continued his older brother's machinations against Hawkins. In 1812, Governor Blount pushed the Tennessee legislature to order the state's congressional delegation to attempt to persuade the federal government to remove Hawkins from his post.[35] It was all to no avail. The politically well-connected Hawkins remained in his position long enough to see his life's chief aim destroyed.

Hawkins had also made numerous enemies among Georgians—high and low—by enforcing US laws against their attempts to snooker the Indians out of their lands. The Georgians were particularly incensed by Hawkins's conduct during the negotiations among the Creeks, Georgians, and the United States in connection with the Treaty of Coleraine. These negotiations took place in June and July 1796, at the US military post at Coleraine, located on the Saint Mary's River, thirty miles by land and sixty miles by water from the town of Saint Mary's in the lovely Sea Islands region of the southern coast of Georgia. Hawkins was one of three commissioners representing the United States and took the leading role for the federal government during the negotiations. Georgia also sent three representatives. The Creeks had 435 of their people in attendance, of whom 22 were "kings."[36] The large number of Creeks who attended is probably due to the fact that many poor and "nearly naked" Creeks had come to Coleraine "in expectation of 'gitting a blanket.'"[37] Hawkins placed the Creeks in a camp near the river and a spring, and he restricted access to the place in order to keep the Indians from being fleeced by the usual group of vulpine undesirables who flocked to a gathering of Indians.[38] By the end of the treaty negotiations, not only would these petty miscreants, whose schemes for fleecing the Creeks Colonel Hawkins thwarted, hate him, but also the more high-toned thieves, draped in the grand mantle of Georgia commissioners.

Thus, on the eve of the Creek War, the Creeks' best friend among the Americans was roundly despised by Indian and American alike.

The Treaty of New York

FROM the perspective of the United States and the Creeks, the purpose of the meeting at Coleraine was to negotiate the implementation of the Treaty of New York entered into by those nations in 1790. This significant treaty was largely the product of the efforts of the Creek leader Alexander McGillivray and President George Washington to secure peace in the Old Southwest.

McGillivray was the most remarkable figure in Creek history and indeed was one of the great political and diplomatic minds in a century filled with them; he was the Talleyrand of Alabama, as the antebellum historian Albert James Pickett called him.[39] McGillivray was born in 1750 at Little Tallassee, a small town on the east bank of the Coosa River just above the enormous drop of a waterfall that the whites called the Devil's Staircase.[40] His father was the trader and plantation owner Lachlan McGillivray. Lachlan McGillivray had been born into a prominent Scottish merchant family that lived near the town of Inverness, of Loch Ness monster fame. As a teenager he moved to South Carolina to make his fortune and eventually did so in business ventures in the southern colonies. Alexander's mother was a mixed-blood Muskogee beauty named Sehoy Marchand, an aristocratic woman of Creek and French ancestry who belonged to the nation's most prominent clan, the Wind Clan. Her mother, the first Sehoy, was a famous Creek beauty who had married a captain in the French army named Marchand, who commanded Fort Toulouse when the French held the gulf coastal region in the days before the French and Indian War. Alexander McGillivray's Indian blood was so diluted by his white ancestors that he even looked like a white man.[41]

A frail, sickly child, McGillivray grew into a tall, sickly man, constantly oppressed by a variety of illnesses, the most frequent of which appear to have been gout and rheumatism. He was said to have been something of a dissolute youth, which was reflected in his appearance.[42] At some point in the astonishing trajectory of his life, McGillivray contracted a venereal disease, probably syphilis, which severely impaired his health. His constitution may also have been affected by a deep love of wine and spirits that lasted until the end of his life. Unlike many Creek leaders, given his physical condition, he was never much of a warrior. But, as if in compensation, the young man possessed a formidable intellect that legend has it was presaged by a dream his mother had of paper, pens, and ink shortly before McGillivray's birth. At age fourteen, McGillivray was sent to Charleston for schooling and in his later teens worked for two Charleston merchant houses, one of whose owners became a governor of Georgia. Although he learned to speak and write in perfect English, his mastery of the Muskogee tongue was wanting, and he relied on interpreters to communicate with his own people on important occasions.[43]

When the Revolutionary War began, McGillivray's father sided with the British. His son followed suit and became a colonel in the British army and Britain's commissary to the Muskogee Nation. In 1782, the Creeks' famous war chief Emistisiguo was killed at the Battle of Savannah trying to break through the American siege lines.[44] In May 1783, McGillivray, who at one point in his military career managed to cross the American lines into Savannah, was appointed to succeed Emistisiguo. By then peace was only a few months away, and McGillivray's military duties were largely confined to keeping the land-crazed Georgians at bay.[45] He did lead a Creek contingent in support of the British defense of Pensacola. There he met a young Maryland Tory with the impressive-sounding name of William Augustus Bowles who purportedly was serving as a captain in a British regiment. Some years later, McGillivray had good cause to remember young Bowles, who, in one of his many incarnations, made the last years of the chief's life a misery and roiled the political waters of the Creek Nation into the opening years of the next century.

With the American defeat of the British, Lachlan McGillivray's considerable properties, valued at over $100,000, were confiscated by the states of South Carolina and Georgia. The new American government also forced him to leave the country, and he returned to the ancestral lands in Scotland. True to Creek social mores, Alexander McGillivray remained in the nation with his mother's family and, because of the family's prominence, became a lesser chief among the Muskogee.[46] That status was soon to change.

The negotiations at Coleraine had their genesis in the political crisis that arose within the Creek Nation at the end of the Revolutionary War. On September 3, 1783, the day the signing of the Treaty of Paris ended that war, Great Britain signed a treaty with the United States' ally Spain. Under the terms of that treaty, Britain agreed to return Spain's former Florida territories to Spanish control. With the departure of the British from these lands, a power vacuum opened in the Old Southwest. Spain, its former power exhausted by three centuries of European warfare, attempted to replace the powerful British in its former Florida dominions. With Great Britain gone, however, Spanish control of the Floridas (as the present state of Florida and a narrow strip of land running from its Panhandle to New Orleans was called), was now threatened by the restless power of the young American republic. The Muskogee and other southern Indian nations provided the ideal buffer between the Spanish and American frontiers, if the Spanish could just control the allegiance of the inconstant tribes. For the Indians' part, the departure of the British left them without a protector against American schemes, already being implemented, to take Indian land. In particular the Indians needed a dependable source of weapons and other trade goods that was independent of US control. Into this political vacuum slid the young and ambitious Alexander McGillivray.

In the coming conflict with the Americans, McGillivray saw an opportunity to employ his talent for intrigue. During British rule, the Scottish merchant firm of Panton, Leslie & Company enjoyed a trade monopoly with the Creek Nation, one it was eager to preserve under the new Spanish rule. As the former British commissary for the Creeks, McGillivray was well acquainted with William Panton, the head of Panton, Leslie. Panton introduced the chief to several Spanish authorities: Estevan Miro, the governor of West Florida, Arthur O'Neil, the commandant of Pensacola, and Marin Navarro, the intendant general of Florida.[47] McGillivray, Panton, and the Spanish soon worked out a modus vivendi that addressed everyone's interests. Panton wished to continue its trade monopoly with the southern Indians. The Spanish crown wanted a credible Indian counterweight to its new American neighbors. McGillivray, for his people, wanted a European power to protect the nation's lands from the Americans and a dependable trading partner. He supported Panton's candidacy, Panton promoted McGillivray to the Spanish as the leader of the Creeks, and the Spanish promised to accommodate the ambitions of McGillivray and Panton in return for their loyalty to Spanish interests in the Floridas. Their agreement was formalized in the Treaty of Pensacola of 1784 between the Spanish and the Creek Confederation. A key but unwritten part of the arrangement provided McGillivray with enormous power among his people: Indians wishing to receive supplies from the Spanish government had to present written authorization, signed by McGillivray, before they could draw such items.[48] Young McGillivray was on his way.

Not surprisingly, the Georgians, hemmed up in their narrow strip of territory along the Atlantic coast, precipitated the crisis that McGillivray then rose to exploit. Over several years following the Treaty of Paris, there was no effective national American government to bridle the individual states' constant schemes to rob the Indians of their land. The Georgians took particular advantage of the weakness of the national government under the Articles of Confederation to seize Creek lands along the state's frontier. The signatures on the Treaty of Paris were barely dry when the Georgians inveigled several Creek chiefs to sign the Treaty of Augusta (1783), the Treaty of Galphinton (1785), and the Treaty of Shoulderbone Creek (1786).

The treaties were each and every one laughably illegal. The Georgians were so confident they could act with impunity that they did not even bother to vary their methods of fleecing the Creeks of their lands. Their method was to arrange negotiations with two chiefs whom they knew to be friendly toward Americans: Hoboheilthle, or, as he was known to the whites, the Tallassee King, or, even more wonderfully appropriate given his pliability, the Tame King; and the chief of the Cussetahs, known equally descriptively as the Fat King. The Tame King, who favored the Americans over the British in the war, led the opposition to McGillivray in the nation and pronounced his rival to be a mere "boy and a usurper."[49] Improbable as it sounds, the kings seemed to fall for the same ploy time after time. They met with the Georgians at a negotiation ground where the Georgians entertained them and their followers. After the requisite pleasantries, the Georgians intimidated the chiefs by prominently stationing armed troops at the negotiations, getting them to sign away the nation's lands. As the chiefs of only two of many Creek towns, they and their hosts well knew the men had no authority to act on behalf of the entire nation.[50]

Perhaps the Tame King and the Fat King were playing their own venal game with the Georgians. The Georgians would give the chiefs presents, and in return the chiefs would sell them lands everyone knew they had no power to sell. As McGillivray derisively said of the Tame King, he "is well known to be but a roving beggar, going wherever he thinks he can get presents." Whatever game the two chiefs may have been playing, their cozy relationship with the Georgians finally backfired on them. In fall 1786, the Georgians assembled an army on the Oconee River to invade the nation. When they heard that the Creek warriors were gathering in large numbers to repel the invasion, the Georgians decided to take hostage, as security for their own safety, "their good friends the Tame King & Neah Mico (the Fat King of Cussitah)" who had foolishly gone out to meet them.[51] McGillivray describes what happened next: "[T]he Tame King for once in his life time behaved like a Man. When he found that he & [his] people were to be detained he thundered out a furious Talk & frightened the Georgians from their purpose of keeping them, & made them some presents & bid them go home. The Americans & the Indians parted from each other at Oconee & each returned home."

But the Tame King's surprising resistance to the Georgians' latest land scheme brought no peace to the frontier. In 1787, the crisis that had been percolating along the southern frontier for some years finally spewed over the borderlands with extreme violence. In late spring 1787, McGillivray and other Creek chieftains met with representatives of twenty-five nations of the northern Indian confederacy, including the Shawnees, Iroquois, Hurons, and Wyandots. The attendees agreed "Jointly to attack the Americans in every place wherever they Shall pass over their own proper Limits, nor never to grant them Lands, nor Suffer Surveyors to roam about the Country." And the Creeks fulfilled their promises to their Indian brothers with a vengeance. Over the next six months, "after repeated & obstinate attacks," they drove settlers from Virginia and North Carolina out of the Cumberland Valley lying in what would become the state of Tennessee. The Creeks devoted special attention to the troublesome Georgians, who were, according to McGillivray, at the Indians' "Mercy" after several months of fighting.[52]

The string of Creek victories over the Americans was made possible by their Spanish allies who supplied the arms that fueled the Indians' assaults on the American frontiers. As Creek successes mounted against the American interlopers, however, the Spanish grew more concerned that they had created a monster that, for Spain's own safety, must be reined in. The Spanish needed the Creeks to act as a buffer against American intrusions into Spanish territory. But the Dons, as the Spanish were colloquially called by the Americans, had no desire for war with the United States. As long as the Indians simply maintained the status quo, the Spanish were happy to keep supplying them with arms. However, now that the balance of frontier power was tilting in the Indians' favor, the Spanish determined to curtail that supply lest they ignite an unwanted conflict with the United States.[53]

In the meantime, the United States was anxious to end the bitter skirmishes along the Creek frontier that were fueled by the settlers'—particularly the Georgians'—ravenous appetite for Creek lands. The fiscally weak federal government had no desire to waste its meager resources in prosecuting a war against the Creeks to advance Georgia's land-grab schemes. But the US government did want to establish the principle that it alone had the authority to treat with the Indian nations—a power the states believed they had over Indian lands within state jurisdiction. Thus, McGillivray now found his people caught between the weakness and inconstancy of his Spanish ally and the growing power and national ambitions of the federal government for supremacy over the unruly thirteen states.

Among the most troublesome states was Georgia, which, despite the obstinacy of the Creeks and the protestations of the federal government, persisted in its attempts to rob the Muskogee people, as well as the other southern tribes, of their lands. In 1789, Georgia launched the so-called Yazoo sale—its most audacious swindle to date and one that would have made the old Dirt King, Senator William Blount, proud. Someone, probably a too-clever-by-half lawyer, exhumed a charter issued to the former Georgia colony by Charles II. That legal instrument granted Georgia sovereignty over land running between 31 and 35 degrees of latitude from the Atlantic Ocean all the way to the Mississippi River. Ignoring the fact that Spain, as well as four Indian tribes, claimed sovereignty over this same territory, the Georgia legislature approved the sale of over fifteen million acres of this land to various companies of land speculators: the Virginia Yazoo Company, the South Carolina Yazoo Company, and the Tennessee Company. The federal government considered the non-Spanish portion of this territory federal land and issued a decree invalidating the sales. The Tennessee and South Carolina companies ignored the decree. Fortunately for near-term federal-state relations, all the land companies ignored their contractual payments to the state of Georgia, which promptly nullified the sales.[54]

The Georgians' scheme was just one of the frontier headaches that President George Washington's government faced that year. Aside from the Creeks' ongoing conflicts with the Cumberland Valley and Georgia settlers who clamored for federal military action against the Indians, a more acute Indian problem had arisen in the Ohio Valley. There, in spring 1789, an Indian confederacy led by the militant Shawnees determined to remove the white settlers pouring into Indian lands north of the Ohio River. In June they sent a delegation to Detroit, still illegally occupied by the British, to obtain munitions for an attack on the Americans. The British happily and fulsomely complied with the Indians' request. The ensuing result was a dramatic uptick in Indian raids on the white settlements along the frontier. Atrocities on both sides mounted, and by fall 1789, the violence associated with back-and-forth raids on white and Indian communities reached such a crescendo that the federal government felt compelled to step in and try to obtain mastery over a situation that was fast spinning out of control.[55]

Faced with this serious northern Indian threat, the United States, with its limited resources, had decided in 1787 to attempt to secure its southern border against war with the Native American tribes that ruled those lands. Over the next two years, the United States made several attempts to convince McGillivray and his people to negotiate the land question with US representatives. In summer 1789, McGillivray finally agreed to a meeting with US negotiators at Rock Landing on the Oconee River in Georgia. He arrived there with nine hundred chiefs and warriors and set up camp on the west bank of the river in the fashion of Creek towns around a hollow square. There they awaited the arrival of the treaty commissioners appointed by the United States: Benjamin Lincoln, a renowned Revolutionary War general; Cyrus Griffin, a former president of Congress; and Colonel David Humphreys, a former aide-de-camp to General Washington and budding, but arrogant, young diplomat.[56] The commissioners, accompanied by four hundred troops, set up camp on the east bank of the Oconee opposite the Creek encampment.

Prior to the departure of the commissioners for the treaty grounds, President Washington issued a lengthy set of instructions to the delegates regarding the negotiations. The primary issues the commissioners were to address were the land cessions claimed by the state of Georgia under the treaties of Augusta, Galphinton, and Shoulderbone Creek. Washington rightly saw that this issue was the source of the escalating violence between that state and the Creeks. Accordingly, he instructed the commissioners to ascertain whether the treaties were valid and, if so, to insist that the Creeks honor them, using threat of force if necessary. If, on the other hand, the commissioners found that Georgia did not fairly obtain the disputed lands, the commissioners were not to attempt to persuade the Creeks to agree to the cessions. Washington recognized, however, that with the backing of Georgia officials, the state's citizens had already "settled and planted on [these] lands in great numbers." Therefore, it would be "highly embarrassing" to Georgia if the federal government required the state to abandon these lands to the Creeks. If the federal government insisted that Georgia do so—and this was Washington's real concern—it would probably undermine Georgia's attachment to the national government. Therefore, the president ordered the commissioners to employ their "highest exertions" to convince the Creeks to sell the disputed territory to Georgia—minus, of course, the amounts the state had already paid the Creeks for the lands.[57]

McGillivray's objective regarding the disputed lands was diametrically opposed to Washington's. He wanted the Georgians to relinquish every parcel of what he considered Indian land taken via the fraudulent treaties with the Tame and Fat Kings. His resolve was strengthened by a recent promise from the Spanish to supply the Creeks with arms if, during the treaty negotiations, the Americans made unreasonable demands on the Indians.[58] Bad-faith conduct by the Americans would give the Spanish the cover they needed to support their Indian allies in any conflict with the United States.

The treaty negotiations began late on the morning of September 24. At McGillivray's insistence, they were held in the square of the Creek encampment. Following the traditional ceremony of the black drink, in which the commissioners participated, Lincoln addressed the Indians. After a tiresome boast of the power of the United States, he delivered the proposed treaty terms. Without having even inquired into the validity of the three treaties between Georgia and the Tame King and Fat King, as Washington had instructed, Lincoln recited Article II of the US draft of the treaty, which declared that the boundaries between the Creek Nation and the United States be established as set forth in the prior treaties with Georgia. McGillivray provided a curt but polite response the following morning: Article II was unacceptable, and given that hunting season approached, the Creek delegation would be leaving camp. The commissioners were obviously astonished by this response, and in a grave error of judgment sent the self-important young Humphreys to McGillivray's camp to speak with the Creek leader.

The discussions between the sensitive McGillivray and the young diplomat did not go well. McGillivray described Humphreys as "that puppy" and as "a great boaster of his political knowledge" from treating with various European powers.[59] McGillivray, who was well-versed in diplomatic protocol, obviously resented, and was perhaps even insulted by, the absence of the senior commissioners at these private discussions. Over the course of several meetings with the chief, Humphreys tried all sorts of approaches: "flattery, ambition and intimidation"—to convince the wily McGillivray to continue the negotiations. His efforts failed, each and every one. Finally, McGillivray sent Humphreys a message informing the young man that he would not have the proposed treaty crammed down his throat.[60] The chief then gathered his men and departed for home. Some of the more accommodating Creeks remained behind and attempted to conciliate the commissioners. But the Americans knew that the real power in the nation lay with McGillivray and sent messages after him complaining of his abrupt departure and trying to persuade him to return and continue the negotiations.[61] These attempts all failed, and McGillivray returned home.

In winter 1790, frustrated by McGillivray's obstinacy, and with the northern Indian threat growing, Secretary of War Henry Knox tried another tactic. He sent the chief a personal letter from Senator Benjamin Hawkins, who had long developed an interest in Indian affairs, setting forth in what Knox hoped were persuasive terms the reasons why it was in the Creeks' interest to treat with the United States. To underscore the importance of the matter, the letter was hand-delivered to McGillivray by a distinguished veteran of the Revolutionary War, Colonel Marinus Willett. In his instructions to Willett, Knox stressed that the purpose of the colonel's mission was to prevent a war between the United States and the Creek Nation by persuading McGillivray to participate in peace negotiations to be held in New York City, then the seat of the federal government.

Following the maxim "Pray for peace, but prepare for war," Knox had already ordered three companies of US troops stationed at West Point to leave for Georgia. They were expected to arrive in the area about the time Willett reached McGillivray. If the appearance of these soldiers proved an insufficient assist to the colonel's persuasive talents, Knox instructed Willett to advise McGillivray that they were simply advance units of a larger force that the United States would send depending on the Creeks' desire for peace. Again betraying US ignorance of Indian governance, Knox instructed Willett to concentrate his efforts to set up peace negotiations with the Upper Creeks but informed the colonel that he had leeway to invite a few of the Lower Creek chieftains to the negotiations as he saw fit.[62]

On March 15, 1790, Willett set out for the nation bearing Hawkins's letter for McGillivray. He took a ship from New York Harbor and fourteen days later reached the lovely harbor of Charleston, South Carolina, with the island where Fort Sumter would later stand, looking like an egg between a serpent's jaws. He set out from Charleston several days later with his servant. Willett rode a horse while his servant drove a surrey filled with their luggage. The servant shortly grew afraid to continue the journey, and Willett sent the man back to New York, replacing him with a German of dubious character. Along the way he stopped at the South Carolina plantation of Revolutionary War general and hero and South Carolina congressman Andrew Pickens. After enjoying Pickens's hospitality, the colonel then plunged into the nearby wilderness.

On April 30, Willett arrived at the Hillabee towns. There he met an English trader named Scott, whose son over twenty years later appears to have been one of the Creek leaders in the Battle of Talladega against Andrew Jackson. Scott escorted Willett to the Hillabee town where a Scottish trader named Grierson had a flourishing plantation at which McGillivray was staying. When Willett met McGillivray at Grierson's, he delivered Hawkins's letter to the chief. The two men then enjoyed dinner together. Willett found McGillivray to be "a man of an open, candid, generous mind, with a good judgment and very tenacious memory." Likewise, McGillivray found Willett to be an agreeable man and an appropriate envoy from the US government. From Grierson's, the two men traveled to McGillivray's home at the Hickory Ground some thirty miles southwest. On arriving, McGillivray arranged for a council of the nation's leaders to be held at the prominent Lower Creek town of Coweta on the Chattahoochee River. There Willett delivered a talk inviting the chiefs to New York City to negotiate a treaty "which shall be as strong as the hills, and lasting as the rivers." The talk was well-received by the Lower Creeks, and they agreed that McGillivray and an entourage of chiefs and warriors should go to New York for the treaty negotiations.

Having obtained the assent of the Lower Creeks to address their Upper Creek brethren, Willett and McGillivray traveled sixty miles west to Tuckabatchee, which Willett found to be "a most agreeable settlement." His talk there was also well received by the Upper Creeks, as was his address at Autosse just downstream on the opposite bank of the Tallapoosa River.[63] So it was that McGillivray came to travel the long miles to New York to meet the most famous living American.

The party, which included Willett and his German servant, left Little Tallassee in the late morning of June 1, 1790. McGillivray was accompanied by his nephew, David Tate, son of the British army officer and spy David Taitt, and McGillivray's sister, Sehoy III.[64] McGillivray also took with him the young mixed-blood Indian Sam Moniac as an interpreter, an African American slave named Pardo, two servants, and eight Upper Creek warriors. On June 9, they arrived at what is now Stone Mountain, Georgia, the future Mount Rushmore of the defeated Confederacy, with the gigantic likenesses of Robert E. Lee, Stonewall Jackson, and Jefferson Davis chiseled into its beetling granite face. Eleven Lower Creeks from Coweta and Cussetah greeted their arrival. Like many a tourist after him, Willett could not resist climbing to the summit of that enormous stone.[65]

On June 14 the party reached the plantation of the hospitable General Pickens, who had hosted Willett on his outbound journey. There the colonel's party was joined by the Tallassee King, the Natchez King, and their respective entourages. On June 18, a remarkable cavalcade of personages departed Pickens's plantation. Twenty-six of the Indian delegates were loaded into three wagons. McGillivray, his nephew, and two servants were on horseback. Willett now drove the surrey while his servant rode on horseback.[66] The colorful and novel party, to the delight of the populace along the journey, proceeded on its slow way north through the Carolinas and into the Commonwealth of Virginia. On July 3, the watchful Knox wrote Willett, reminding him that one purpose of the Creeks' journey to New York was to impress them with "our numbers," and toward this end he had written the governors of Virginia, Maryland, and Pennsylvania to "extend civilities" to the party on its journey north.[67] Thus, the Creek delegation was well-entertained by the local dignitaries at Richmond,

Fredericksburg, and Baltimore. Best of all, on July 17, when the travelers reached Philadelphia, they were royally feted by the city's kingpins and treated to the sights. Once the Philadelphia festivities concluded, Willett arranged for water transport for the party from nearby Elizabeth Town, New Jersey, to New York City. On July 21, around noon, the Creek envoys arrived at the landing on Wall Street, where, as a Spanish official sourly remarked, "they were received hardly less highly than royal persons." Among the reception committee was an improbable group of whites who, to the Indians' utter astonishment, were mirror images of themselves.[68]

This improbable part of the welcoming committee hailed from a newly constituted political organization called Tammany Hall, after a long-ago Delaware chieftain who had dealt with William Penn, the white saint of fair negotiations with the Indians. Tammany Hall purportedly was formed to promote true American values, and thus, as an emblem of their sincerity, its members dressed as Native Americans. They were pale imitations of the real thing who disembarked somewhat unsteadily onto the firm stone of the wharf dressed in wildly colorful attire, tattooed, and with elaborate silver piercings dangling from their ears and noses—all but McGillivray. He was dressed in a suit the bright scarlet color of fresh arterial blood, like a Creek painted for war.[69]

The Tammany Hall members had undoubtedly just renewed their acquaintance with the lively grape, and the Indians soon followed suit. A seemingly impromptu parade was organized, and the Creeks and the Tammany delegation began marching along a street lined with astonished spectators, most of whom had never seen an Indian before. From the ranks of the true Indians, the unfamiliar and unnerving whoops of the Creeks rang out as the procession made its way toward Federal Hall, where Congress was in session. As the noise of the parade announced itself, congressmen stopped what they were doing and came out on the balcony of Federal Hall to gawk at the unearthly spectacle. The parade marched on to President Washington's house, where the Creeks were introduced to the great man. From there the raucous but merry group strolled along the city streets for visits with Secretary of War Knox and New York governor George Clinton. The delightful journey ended at the City Tavern, where the Creeks were elegantly entertained.[70] McGillivray was then housed at Knox's home, and his companions camped just outside the city.

The long trip from the nation and the day's activities on the Creeks' arrival at New York City took their toll on McGillivray's delicate constitution. Shortly after he reached the city, he fell seriously ill, delaying the pace of the negotiations.[71] Meanwhile, the Americans provided no shortage of entertainment to their unusual but important visitors. During the course of their stay, a number of the Creeks visited the nearby home of Vice President John Adams and his wife, Abigail. Mrs. Adams had never seen a "savage" before but found her novel visitors to be "very fine looking Men" with "placid countenances & fine shape, and well-behaved."[72] Indeed, her observation is borne out by the portraits of five of the Creek delegation, purportedly including Hoboheilthle in a US military coat (who, given that the appearance of the individual portrayed is much too young to be the elderly chief, is perhaps Alexander McGillivray), that artist John Turnbull surreptitiously sketched in pencil. To cap all the revelries, a somewhat recovered McGillivray was also feted by the Society of St. Andrew at the City Tavern and, as a nod to his Scottish heritage, was made an honorary member of that organization.[73]

In leading the negotiations on behalf of the Creek Nation, McGillivray found himself pitted against some of the finest minds this country has ever produced. Many, such as Washington, Jefferson, and Hamilton, were founders of the United States. But the sickly *mestizo* (as the Spanish referred to people of mixed blood) from the southern woods was more than a match for his more celebrated adversaries. McGillivray realized that recent events had combined to provide the Creeks with an ideal position from which to negotiate. The infant US government was beset with serious issues along the length of its frontier and lacked the financial capacity to address them all at the same time. The Indian confederacy roiling the Ohio Valley settlements had to be pacified and the Indian lands of that region secured to accommodate the country's expanding population. In addition, the various Yazoo speculators had to be stopped in order to prevent a war with the southern Indians, whose lands were being sold out from under them, and the principle established that this territory was the property of the whole United States.

McGillivray clearly understood that the US interest in arriving at a treaty with the powerful Creek Nation proceeded not from "principles of justice and humanity" but to prevent the Georgians from luring the United States into an Indian war over the Yazoo lands, which "if successful after much loss of Blood and Treasure Georgia would reap the whole advantage." His subtle mind divined that sectional rivalries between the North and the South underlay the federal government's push for a treaty; that the Northern states resented greatly paying and dying to implement Georgia's land schemes. All of this state-federal turmoil made it a propitious time for the Creeks to negotiate, while they still could, a peace with the Americans on terms most favorable to the Indians. As McGillivray put it to Governor Estevan Miro of Louisiana, the promises floated by President Washington before the Creeks proceeded not from eleemosynary impulses but rather from the federal government's current "poverty & Inability to Support & Maintain a Vigorous Contest to reduce us by force. It is better to treat with an enemy under Such circumstances than a more powerful one."[74]

McGillivray's negotiating position with the Americans was unintentionally strengthened by the meddling of Spanish and British agents assigned to monitor the Creek treaty negotiations. The Spanish agent, Captain Carlos Howard, traveled to New York on the laughable pretext that he did so for his health—as if anyone then or now spends July and August in New York City for their health. McGillivray pretended to accept this explanation but was well aware that Howard was there to prevent the chieftain from violating the Treaty of Pensacola with Spain. The Americans were also well aware that Howard was not visiting New York for his health. On July 3, Knox wrote Willett that the Spanish had dispatched Howard, whom he described as an able man, to monitor the treaty negotiations. Knox advised Willett that Howard had already reached Baltimore, and perhaps even Philadelphia, and ordered him to watch the captain. Nonetheless, the capable Willett was unable to prevent Howard from handing McGillivray some letters from the Spanish authorities during the Creek delegation's stopover in Philadelphia.[75]

In regard to the British, their agent, Major George Beckwith, purportedly wanted to meet with McGillivray to ascertain whether one William August Bowles, an old acquaintance of McGillivray's from the Revolutionary War and a con man extraordinaire, was an impostor. Bowles, like a bad penny, had recently turned up in Canada with some Creek and Cherokee Indians. Bowles and his Native American companions were well decked out in odd finery, and Bowles claimed to the British officials to be an authorized representative of the southern Indian nations on an important mission to Great Britain. Beckwith's real aim of the meeting, however, was to obtain intelligence from McGillivray about the course of the peace negotiations. The Americans, in this primitive game of espionage, tried but failed to prevent McGillivray from meeting either Howard or Beckwith.[76]

For his own part, McGillivray played the role of the coquettish belle at this dance of spies and flirted with all three nations. He kept the Spanish Captain Howard informed, but not completely, of the progress of the negotiations, and also reassured him that nothing to which the Creeks agreed would violate the Treaty of Pensacola. In regard to the British, despite the best attempts of Secretary of the Treasury Alexander Hamilton to prevent a meeting between McGillivray and the British agent Beckwith, the major still managed to meet with the chief. Aside from probably assuaging British concerns regarding an American-Creek alliance, McGillivray surely informed Beckwith that Bowles was indeed an impostor—not, as we shall see, that this intelligence had any effect on the course of Bowles's latest scheme.

Well apart from his dance with the British and Spanish, McGillivray's main and immediate objective in the negotiations was to retain as much of the land as possible that the Tame King and Fat King had supinely ceded to Georgia in the three fraudulent treaties with that state. In 1790, the territory of the state of Georgia was confined to a roughly forty-mile-wide strip bordered by the Atlantic Ocean, the Savannah River (which formed Georgia's border with South Carolina), and the Ogeechee River to the east. The disputed territory lay in the east-central part of the state, roughly between the Ogeechee River and the Oconee River and Altamaha River systems to the west, and from the forks of the Oconee and Oakmulgee rivers to the Saint Mary's River near the Spanish Florida border. This tract of land was shaped somewhat like Florida, with the panhandle to the north, and ran from between twenty miles in its northern neck expanding up to fifty miles at the tract's southern end.

The problem facing the negotiators was that over the intervening years, a large portion of the disputed land, which the Americans considered "the most valuable," had been settled by the Georgians, and it would take a war to remove them. The remaining portion of the contested acreage extended from the juncture of the Oconee and Oakmulgee rivers southwest to the Saint Mary's River. This territory constituted some of the Creeks' most important winter hunting grounds, and, as President Washington advised the Senate, this land the Creek negotiators "absolutely refused to yield." After some days of back-and-forth discussions, the Creeks and the American negotiators compromised. The Creeks would cede a portion of the land claimed by Georgia that ran east from the Ogeechee River to the Oconee River in return for a payment of $10,000 worth of merchandise and $2,000 annually, but would retain their hunting grounds. President Washington was content to relinquish the government's claims to this country because, as he informed Congress, "This land is reported to be generally barren, sunken, and unfit for cultivation, except on the margins of the rivers, on which by improvement, rice might be cultivated; its chief value depending on the timber for the building of ships, with which it is represented as abounding."[77]

This treaty, which included a number of less critical provisions, did contain a sleeper cell of a clause, inserted at the insistence of the United States, in which lay encapsulated a germ of the Creek War to come. Numbered Article XII, the clause provided that in order to promote the civilization of the Creek from a nation of hunters to a nation of herdsmen and cultivators, "the United States will from time to time furnish gratuitously the said nation with useful domestic animals and implements of husbandry."[78] This article was intended to advance the American government's plan to peacefully and cheaply separate all of the Native American tribes from their hunting lands by turning them into farmers who did not need the vast acreage required by hunting for their subsistence.

But this public treaty was not the only one being negotiated between the Americans and the Creeks. Unknown to all but McGillivray and the principal chiefs of the nation, a secret treaty between the parties was also in the works. This treaty arose out of the United State's desire to make inroads into, and eventually to supplant, the current trade arrangement between the Creeks, the Panton, Leslie firm, and the Spanish. This objective was a critical one for the president because that old Indian fighter had recognized that control of "the trade of the Indians is a main mean of their political management."

However, during those negotiations, it became apparent that it would take time for the United States to secure from the Creeks any commitment that threatened the Creeks' current trade relations, because—and this sounds like McGillivray's words—"the present arrangement cannot be suddenly broken without the greatest violation of faith and morals." Accordingly, on August 4, 1790, President Washington reported to the Senate that although the parties were close to concluding their treaty negotiations, it was necessary to carve out from those negotiations a "secret article" addressed to the trade question. That article, as eventually formulated, simply provided that if the Spanish obstructed its current trade with the Creeks, the United States would be allowed to commence trade with the Creek Nation. However, the article also allowed the United States to trade on a regularized basis with the nation if, by August 1, 1792, the parties could agree to such an arrangement.[79] As McGillivray reported, the trade issue was so difficult to resolve that he thought it should be deferred for a couple of years. This treaty accomplished that objective.

The secret treaty that was eventually signed also included some sweeteners for McGillivray and the principal chiefs. The chiefs of the towns of Okfuskee, Tuckabatchee, Tallassee, Coweta, Cussetah, and the Seminoles each "should be paid annually by the United States, one hundred dollars each, and be furnished with handsome medals."[80] McGillivray, reflecting his preeminent role in the negotiations, was appointed a brigadier general in the US army with a salary of one hundred dollars per month. This appointment required him to take a standard loyalty oath to the United States, which, unknown to his Spanish allies, he did.[81] Further underscoring the importance of the treaty to the president, and McGillivray's critical role in bringing it about, Washington presented the Creek leader with a number of valuable gifts.

The most valuable item was a beautiful silver pocket watch. But this was not just any watch. On appropriate occasions, the president was in the habit of gifting watches to individuals, but the instruments given out were usually engraved on the back with Washington's title—"President"—as well as his name.[82] What made this watch unique among Washington's presentation watches was that the engraving on its back cover did not contain the president's title but rather the simple personalized inscription "George Washington."

Along with the pocket watch, Washington also presented McGillivray with a set of gilt-edged books that the chief later proudly displayed at his home. But the gift from Washington that McGillivray prized most, which if authentic must also have been one of Washington's most prized possessions, was an epaulet the general had purportedly worn throughout the Revolutionary War.[83] Moreover, the secret treaty contained a gift to the Creek Nation, most likely made at McGillivray's suggestion, requiring the United States to educate several Creek children a year. Thus, when McGillivray departed New York City, he left behind his adolescent nephew, whom he had brought to the negotiations, to be the first of his nation to enjoy the advantages provided by this article of the secret treaty.[84]

On August 6, the president reported to the Senate that the negotiations with the Creeks, which, as planned, had proceeded in an informal manner, had advanced to such a stage that a more formal approach was required to finalize the document. For this purpose, Washington nominated, and the Senate approved, Henry Knox, who had been the lead US negotiator all along, to be the government's official representative to the Creek delegation.[85]

The following day, the public treaty was signed by Knox, McGillivray, and twenty-three other Creeks. The only Creek to sign the secret treaty was McGillivray. That night the Creeks, no doubt amply fueled by free rum, celebrated the treaty by building a great bonfire, and they "danced around it like so many spirits hooping, singing, yelling, and expressing their pleasure and satisfaction in the true savage stile."[86]

The Senate ratified the treaty on August 13, 1790, at Federal Hall with great pomp and ceremony amid a galaxy of American luminaries, including President Washington and Vice President John Adams. But the star attraction must have been the alien-looking Creek delegation led by a tall, well-dressed but sickly looking white man. The public treaty was read aloud and translated for the Indians' benefit. Then around noon, Washington rose from his chair and made some brief remarks about the treaty and how the instrument was fair to all. These remarks were also translated for the Indians, who voiced their assent. The president, along with Secretary of State Thomas Jefferson and Secretary of War Henry Knox, then signed the document. Washington also handed McGillivray a string of beads and a sheaf of tobacco as a symbolic commemoration of the event. McGillivray then said several words in response, and congratulations were exchanged all around. The treaty was a singular and significant achievement for the young chief, and it largely preserved the peace between the Creeks and the Americans for over two decades. However, the adventurer Bowles, currently attempting to hoodwink the Canadians into sending him to Great Britain as an emissary for the southern tribes, would make sure that McGillivray never saw the treaty put into effect.

On August 19, the Creeks left New York City on a schooner for the Saint Mary's River, which empties into the Atlantic off the southern Georgia coast. Accompanying their original party was an American army officer named Caleb Swan. McGillivray thought the man a spy, and Swan was certainly sent by the American authorities to monitor McGillivray's activities regarding the Creeks' implementation of their duties under the recent treaty. He also appears to have been sent to cultivate the favor of the Creeks toward the Americans. The party reached the Georgia coast September 1 and was almost fatally shipwrecked. After a rough land journey through the eastern part of the nation, McGillivray reached Little Tallassee on October 8. There he spent almost a year resting, as best he could, from his political and diplomatic labors, enjoying the life of a gentleman planter, seemingly oblivious to the chaos now swirling around him.[87]

The Prince of Liars

WHILE Alexander McGillivray rested from his labors, a serpent of a man slipped into the garden of the Creek leader's life. His name was William Augustus Bowles, the same Bowles who had turned up in Quebec masquerading as a representative of the southern Indian nations during McGillivray's treaty negotiations in New York. Bowles was one of the great rascals of this or any age and seems to have been fashioned by some devilish imp to plague the Creeks, Spaniards, and Americans. Among other things he was described by his enemies as a "villain," "a vile, infamous character," a "Prince of Liars," a "Scoundrel." His friends among the Lower Creeks, however, called him "Our Beloved Friend & Father."[88] Whatever his contemporaries' personal views of the man, Bowles was highly intelligent, brave, and audacious, with the nerves of a daylight safecracker, cleft-jawed, movie-star handsome, true to his own peculiar sense of honor, and possessed of the hypnotic charm serpents are said to have over their prey. The hard facts of his life are not easy to come by. He is said to have been born in 1764 into a prosperous family then living in Frederick County, Maryland—a scenic land of neat, small farms at the base of South Mountain, a land that, in 1862, at nearby Antietam Creek, would see the single most horrific day in the Civil War. As a teenager during the Revolutionary War, Bowles joined the American troops loyal to Great Britain, and in 1778, sixteen-year-old Bowles found himself posted to Pensacola, Florida. There he met Alexander McGillivray, who was leading a contingent of Creeks assisting in the defense of that town. McGillivray later described Bowles as a "Captain in the Loyalist Corps," but the chief may have been one of many of the victims of Bowles's impersonations, for the Spanish governor of Saint Augustine wrote McGillivray years later that

Bowles was never a captain but merely an ensign in a Maryland Loyalist regiment.[89] Whatever his military rank, it appears that Bowles, not surprisingly, got on the wrong side of a superior officer, which made it necessary for him to leave Pensacola. He would return.

From Pensacola, Bowles joined up with a party of Seminoles who had come to that town for presents, and he returned with them to their homes in the Lower Creek Nation. There he spent several years learning the language and cultivating powerful friends among the Indians. He even married into the powerful Perryman clan. Thereafter, having gained a following among the Indians, the restless Bowles returned to Pensacola leading a party of warriors in support of the embattled British. The British-held town was threatened by the Spanish who had recently seized Mobile, and in 1780, the British called on their Indian allies for assistance in meeting this threat.[90] In the contest for the town that followed, Bowles distinguished himself, even collecting several Spanish scalps. His performance against the Spanish caused the British to reinstate him in his old Loyalist regiment. When Pensacola finally fell to the Spanish, Bowles's regiment was repatriated to New York City. After the war ended, Bowles, like many Loyalists, immigrated to the Bahamas, where he ended up in the capital of Nassau on New Providence Island.

For a time the enterprising Bowles made a living as a successful portrait painter and—something he was particularly good at—acting. He also taught himself to play the flute and violin, and in order to obtain colors for his portraits, he learned just enough chemistry to almost blow himself up.[91] But Bowles's true métier was deviltry. Following that instinct, he applied his charm to gain the attention of John Murray, Earl of Dunmore and governor of the Bahamas, and the governor's business associate, John Miller, a principal in the trading house of Miller & Bonamy. Dunmore and Miller were scheming to break the monopoly on the southern Indian trade that Panton, Leslie had been granted by Spain. With Bowles's fluency in the Muskogee tongue and his contacts among the Lower Creeks, Lord Dunmore and Miller decided he would be the ideal accomplice to assist them in their scheme.

It is said that timing is everything in life, and Bowles's timing in approaching his Creek friends on behalf of his new employers was excellent. The Spanish had recently reduced their military assistance to the Creeks, so the Indians were ready to welcome a new source of such aid. In late spring 1788, outfitted with a ship and a modest amount of munitions, Bowles sailed from Nassau to the lands of the Seminoles and Lower Creeks. In the course of his regular tour of the towns, McGillivray met the Indians' unknown benefactor, who had made his way to Coweta. There he found his old acquaintance "Captain" Bowles. At this particular moment, Bowles was posing as an agent for a secret charitable society that had learned through the British newspapers of the Creeks' desperate need for military assistance and had dispatched Bowles to provide it.

Whether McGillivray really believed Bowles or not, he seized the opportunity to obtain the badly needed supplies, and more importantly to gain leverage with the Spanish to reopen the flow of munitions to the Creeks. On his return to Little Tallassee, McGillivray wasted no time in informing the Spanish authorities in Pensacola and New Orleans of the arrival of Bowles and his military supplies. As the chief explained to the governor of Louisiana, Esteban Miro, about the incident, he did not think himself "warranted" to refuse Bowles's gift because the Creeks had many enemies and, adding a subtle dig, because "you do not furnish me with Means of defence untill You have orders from Court, & before which could happen an enterprising enemy might overrun our Country."[92]

Bowles's arrival in the nation soon had the Spanish authorities and the Creek Nation itself in an uproar. McGillivray's enemies claimed that Bowles's arrival heralded a plan by McGillivray to drive the Spanish out of northern Florida. The Tame King and his allies took advantage of this rumor in a futile attempt to alienate the nation from McGillivray. More significantly, the governor of West Florida, Arturo O'Neill, also fanned the flames of this ridiculous rumor. He even persuaded McGillivray's unscrupulous brother-in-law, Charles Weatherford, to spy out support for O'Neill's paranoid delusion about McGillivray.[93] Weatherford apparently held a grudge against McGillivray for failing to promptly free him from jail in Pensacola where the Spanish had placed him for one of his various misdeeds. In any event, his report to O'Neill about McGillivray was innocuous.

In pursuit of the commercial objectives of his employers, Bowles returned to the Gulf Coast in November 1788, with a small supply of munitions for the Indians and a contingent of 30 or so riffraff from Nassau. With these men, and with the backing of his Indian friends, Bowles apparently planned to raid the local Panton, Leslie storehouse. But the men deserted to the Spanish, and the Indians, unhappy with the scanty munitions Bowles had brought, failed to support his scheme. By the following year, Bowles was back in Nassau reinventing himself and dreaming up an even more ambitious scheme against the Spanish in Florida.[94] When Bowles returned to the Creek Nation, it was with a vengeance.

Taking advantage of some elaborate uniforms he scavenged from a so-called shipwreck, Bowles, who may also have included piracy among his various talents, made his way by boat to Canada. With him were some Indian cronies of the Creek and Cherokee nations. He and they dressed up in the finery Bowles had salvaged from the wreck. Posing as an ambassador of the two Indian nations, Bowles convinced the governor of Canada, Guy Carleton, Lord Dorchester, of Bowles's potential importance to British interests in southern North America. Apparently Major Beckwith's report of his interview with McGillivray about Bowles's bona fides did not reach the governor in time, because Lord Dorchester arranged passage for Bowles and his Indian cronies to England to meet with British officials there.

Bowles and his party were well received by Crown officials in London and sent back to New Providence to implement a scheme to undermine the Treaty of New York. In September 1791, backed again by Lord Dunmore and Miller, Bowles landed on the Gulf Coast of Florida in a schooner laden with supplies for the Indians.[95]

The scheme, which involved great personal risk, required enormous charm, boldness, and enterprise, all of which Bowles possessed in spades. His idea, which was breathtaking in its audacity, if not its insanity, was no less than to weld the unpredictable Muskogee tribes into the core of a small empire that Bowles would eventually expand, with British aid, up to Canada through the incorporation of other tribes. Of course, Bowles would be the ruler of this Indian empire, which he styled the State of Muskogee and over which he gave himself the title of director general. In the scope of his vision, the self-aggrandizing Bowles was something of a Tecumseh.

With the tacit blessing of his London contacts, who were intrigued at the prospect of a pliant ally replacing the Spanish in the southwest and in the opening up of Spanish ports for British trade in Spanish Florida, Bowles launched his venture as an Indian trader along the Gulf Coast of Spanish Florida. This time masquerading as an official British agent instead of a representative of a charitable organization, Bowles quickly made inroads among the tribes in that area, especially the unruly Seminoles, by playing on their resentment of the commercial predations of the British trading house of Panton, Leslie, and the land cessions attributed to McGillivray and his adherents in the Treaty of New York. In order to win Creek loyalty, Bowles made all sorts of extravagant promises to the Creeks, including British military aid in his schemes against the Americans and, more immediately dearer to the Indian's hearts, cheaper trade goods that Bowles claimed were on their way from the British West Indies. He soon gained a substantial Creek following, particularly among the Lower Creeks, who had long been partial to the British, to add to his legion of Seminoles.

Strangely, McGillivray was slow to act against his new rival. Initially, the astute McGillivray appears to have been somewhat seduced by Bowles's impersonation of a British agent and more importantly the supply of munitions Bowles had brought for the Creeks; despite Bowles's last fiasco, perhaps the freebooter could still be of use to him. McGillivray was soon disabused of such notions but still appeared not to take the impostor seriously. Perhaps McGillivray was alarmed by the resentment of a number of the Lower Creeks to the land cessions that would come from their territory as required by the Treaty of New York, and the chief decided to reduce his profile as a target of that resentment. The US Creek agent, James Seagrove, thought McGillivray's apparent indifference to the threat that Bowles posed to the chief's power was a ruse that masked a sinister plot by McGillivray against US interests. As Seagrove wrote to Secretary of War Henry Knox: "I never could scan the General's [McGillivray's] motives in affecting to treat Bowles' usurpation, and the confusion his country hath been in for near a year, with such indifference; there must be a hidden cause, but which cannot long lie dormant. I am again impelled to repeat my want of faith in this man's integrity to our country; the whole tenor of his conduct is a flimsy appearance of friendship, but not one pointed or spirited exertion in favor of the United States."[96]

From secret information Seagrove received from an unnamed member "of McGillivray's own family" (perhaps the self-styled Great War Chief LeClerc Milfort, who was in Spanish pay, or the unscrupulous Charles Weatherford), the agent believed that to the detriment of both the United States and the Spanish, McGillivray planned to "re-establish the English with the Creeks."[97]

Ironically, the Spanish believed McGillivray was scheming to replace them with the Americans. More likely McGillivray, never in the best of health, was worn out with managing his unruly and inconstant people, many of whom had turned on him in favor of the unscrupulous outsider Bowles, and simply needed a break from the relentless stress of managing the affairs of the nation. McGillivray may also have calculated that Bowles's own considerable character flaws would destroy the man without any need for McGillivray to exert himself. In addition, jealously may have played a part in McGillivray's inaction. He complained that the Indians had "admitted the talks of a stranger and thrown his aside." Now they could find someone else to do his job: he was leaving the nation. He also reminded his countrymen that when the British ruled the colonies "with all his people, and had besides the aid of all the Indians who wished to come, the Americans had expelled [the British]." Then he uttered a prophecy that would be echoed by his successor over two decades later: given the Americans' defeat of the British, "what could they (the Indians) expect to do with only a handful of men against the United States; that he, Mac-Gillivray, had preserved them for a long time in peace, but that they would not experience this in the future."[98]

Whatever his reasons for withdrawing from the political life of the nation, in January 1792, McGillivray suddenly up and moved his family and slaves from Little Tallassee to his plantation along the Little River in the Tensaw country. From there he left for nearby Mobile, where he took ship for New Orleans.[99] That spring he started to burn down his house at Little Tallassee but was prevented from doing so by the Spanish agent,

Captain Pedro Oliver, who was living there while he spied on McGillivray.[100] McGillivray was no doubt distressed about his people's acceptance of Bowles's lies, but McGillivray was also not without thespian talents himself. A good judge of others, as his survival and prosperity among the volatile Muskogees attests, McGillivray knew that Bowles's own worst enemy was Bowles. Given time, Bowles would light the fuse to the powder that would blow his latest scheme apart.

And that is exactly what Bowles did. If he were to realize his goal of becoming the ruler of the Creek Nation, he had to quickly deliver on his promises to the Indians. First and foremost was the matter of the large shipload of British goods that Bowles had assured the Creeks would soon arrive. As Bowles well knew, however, no substantial amount of trade goods would be landing on the Florida coast, courtesy of Bowles, in his lifetime, much less in the near future. But this fact did not deter the enterprising Bowles. He simply gathered a group of his most loyal Indian followers, along with some other white adventurers who had joined his motley outfit, and on January 16, 1792, attacked Panton, Leslie's well-stocked warehouse at Saint Marks.[101] The manager of the post fled to the nearby Spanish fort for safety. But as the fort was manned by only fifty soldiers, he could not prevail on the commander to challenge Bowles's superior forces.

While Bowles and his confederates happily distributed the riches of Panton, Leslie's warehouse among his Indian allies, the new Spanish governor of New Orleans, the Baron de Carondelet, dispatched twenty-three soldiers to Saint Marks under the command of an enterprising ensign, Jose de Hevia.[102] Hevia persuaded Bowles to accompany him to New Orleans to discuss peace with the Spanish. Bowles, all too confident of his charm and powers of persuasion, decided to accept the ensign's offer under his promise Bowles would be given safe conduct to and from the governor's headquarters.

And indeed for a time Bowles did manage to charm Carondelet, at least to the extent that he turned the governor against Panton and McGillivray by persuading him that the two had alienated the Creeks through their sharp business practices and McGillivray's cession of the Creek lands under the Treaty of New York.[103] The governor was less enamored of Bowles's grandiose scheme to create an independent Indian state in America, for although it might counter American expansion, given Bowles's British connections it might also create an entry for the British into Spain's North American possessions. Rather than substitute one problem for another, the governor decided to remove Bowles from the North American political scene altogether. Slyly convincing the strangely trusting Bowles that he should continue these discussions with Carondelet's superior in Havana, Captain General Luis de Las Casas, the governor arranged passage for Bowles to Cuba. For a time the Spanish hoped to use him as a tool to further their own interests in Florida, and even as a counterweight to McGillivray.[104]

But the ever-surprising and complex Bowles demonstrated his own peculiar brand of integrity and resisted the Spanish attempts to turn him to their side. After some months of dealing with the stubborn Bowles, the frustrated Spanish eventually shipped him to imprisonment in their Philippine colonies. There he spent his ample spare time devising new schemes for Spanish Florida and fashioning a plan of escape. With Bowles out of the country, McGillivray returned to Little Tallassee and to power. As the chief of the Natchez tribe put it with a metaphorical flourish shortly after the Spanish deported Bowles to Havana, "Bowles laid our beloved man, Gen. McGillivray, on the ground, and made him of no more consequence than a child, but we will raise him up again; and, from the talks we have now heard, we are convinced he is right; we will therefore put his enemies under him."[105]

Upon his return to power, the chief found himself assailed by an old friend and older enemy, and his own people, over the Treaty of New York. For several years prior to the signing of the treaty, the Spanish had supplied the weapons that enabled the Creeks to push back the advance of the American settlements in Georgia and Tennessee and thereby secure the borders of Spanish Florida. The success of those attacks prompted the Americans to turn their focus on the Creeks' Spanish patrons as the source of their troubles with the Creeks. The Spanish in Florida were too feeble to take on the United States even with the help of the Creeks, and they quickly performed an about face, reduced their supply of arms to their Creek proxies, and encouraged them to make peace with the Americans. The result was the Treaty of New York, which the inconstant Spanish now wished the Creeks to disavow, lest through its terms they grow too close to the United States. But McGillivray, their old ally, stood in their way. Spanish interests required that he be removed. To that end, the Spanish clumsily placed a spy in his home: the French-born Captain Pedro Oliver. His mission was not only to spy on McGillivray but to attempt to reduce the chief's influence among his people.[106] McGillivray was not fooled for long, if at all, by this ham-handed maneuver, nor was he concerned about its prospect of success. Instead of rebuking the Spanish for their attempt to undermine his power, he welcomed Oliver into his home and let him act out his charade beneath his host's contemptuous but watchful eye. Eventually, realizing that McGillivray had become wise to this scheme, Oliver's superior, Governor Baron de Carondelet, wrote the chief in October 1792, confessed to the nature of Oliver's mission, and laid it off to Carondelet's fear, since assuaged by McGillivray, that the chief had sided with the Americans against Spain.[107] Carondelet assured the chief that going forward he would forbear from interfering with his governance of the Creeks, and the parties reconciled.

Like the Spanish, the Georgians hated the treaty as well, but for a different reason: it clawed back from them a substantial portion of their fraudulent land grab of Creek territory.[108] Some Creeks, particularly those from the lower towns, were also unhappy with the treaty because it ceded land from their territory. This discontent had been a major source of Bowles's power.

Of all the powers interested, only the United States wanted the treaty fully implemented. Secretary of War Henry Knox believed the best way to cultivate the friendship of the Creeks was (as the Spanish had done) to have a representative stationed in the nation: "Were an agent, of respectable talents, present with them at their general meetings, administering to their convenience on all occasions, by means of artificers, husbandmen, and physicians, and always evincing himself their impartial friend and protector, with adequate means to their end, such an arrangement appears to me would be attended with more efficacy than all external applications, through bad interpreters and doubtful friends."

Presciently, the wise Knox predicted that unless the United States could establish a "conciliatory system" for dealing with the Indian nations, as the federal government's ad hoc national policy now stood,

> hostilities will probably ensue, and be continued until the Indians are driven beyond the Mississippi, which may require a period of twenty-five or thirty years. But in case of corrosive measures, not a single particle of benefit will result to the United States generally, either in a pecuniary or moral view; but instead thereof, a black cloud of injustice and inhumanity will impend over our national character during the above period, and for many years after the extirpation of the Indians shall be effected.[109]

But of course, no such policy was yet in place, and no such person had arisen among the Americans capable of residing among the Indians to implement it. The vicious little border wars continued, and the Treaty of New York's boundary line remained unrun. Then, at this critical national juncture, the only real leader the Muskogee Confederation ever had passed from the scene.

In February 1793, McGillivray traveled from his plantation on Little River, where one of his wives also lived, to Pensacola to visit his friend and business partner William Panton. During the cold and damp journey, the chief became ill. This time the illness was fatal. Eight days after arriving in Pensacola, on February 17, 1793, the forty-three-year-old McGillivray passed away at Panton's home. Panton reported that he died of inflamed lungs and gout on the stomach. The Spanish authorities, whom McGillivray had served so well, would not permit the non-Catholic chief to be buried in the town cemetery, so he was interred in Panton's garden with Masonic rites.[110] At the time, a number of Creeks happened to be in Pensacola on business and they accompanied their Beloved Man's internment with a loud and mournful dirge as the ancient Egyptians are said to have done on the death of a pharaoh.[111]

The Treaty of Coleraine

W ITH the death of Alexander McGillivray, history drove yet another nail into the coffin of the Muskogee Confederation. It now found itself without the one man with the wisdom, political skills, and intellectual gravitas to keep the American wolves from its tribal lands. As the US agent for the Creek Nation, James Seagrove, put it in a letter dated July 29, 1793, to his colleague Timothy Bernard, "That the nation is convulsed, and their counsels distracted, is evident, the cause of which rises, in a very great degree, for want of some person to direct them, in whom they can place a confidence."[112] Implementation of the Treaty of New York remained in limbo, and in its place were constant and violent conflicts between the Georgians and Creeks on the lands that were the subject of the treaty. As Charles Weatherford wrote to Seagrove on March 22, 1793, since the death of McGillivray, chaos reigned within the nation.[113]

Implementation of the treaty was also complicated by the visit to the nation of a delegation of ten northern Shawnees, who were attempting to convince the Creeks to make war on the white settlements along the Georgia frontier. Their task was facilitated by the constant stream of white depredations against the Creeks by the Georgia settlers. These Americans constantly drove their livestock onto Creek land to feed and hunted out the game—from deer to turkeys to bear—on Creek lands.[114] The Creeks in turn, sometimes egged on by unscrupulous white traders, stole the Georgians' horses and slaves, sold them to the traders, which the traders then resold at a sweet profit. From time to time both sides engaged in murder. Seagrove, who for fear for his life stayed out of the nation, conducted his work through his surrogate Timothy Barnard, who soldiered on despite repeated threats against his life. Even with Barnard's assistance, Seagrove's attempts to stop the violence, much less run the treaty line, were ineffective. The conference at Coleraine, therefore, was intended by the United States to end the incessant skirmishes between the Indians and Americans and to establish the boundary line between the Creeks and the state of Georgia that had been agreed on six years earlier in the Treaty of New York.

The Georgians had other ideas. They viewed the conference at Coleraine as an opportunity to undo the work of Washington and McGillivray and to obtain title to all the disputed lands settled by the Treaty of New York. What ensued was a conflict between the United States and Georgia over the scope of the rights of the individual states versus the national government—a conflict that grew exponentially among the United States and all the southern states in the coming decades. This friction manifested itself from the outset of the Coleraine discussions, starting with the Georgians' unsuccessful attempt to land a party of armed militia there. In prior treaty negotiations between the Creeks and Georgians, the Georgia treaty negotiators had been accompanied by a militia force. According to the Creeks, the presence of the Georgia militia at these negotiations had intimidated the Creek representatives into signing unfavorable treaties with the Georgians.

Former senator Benjamin Hawkins was well aware of this situation and realized that the Georgia militia's presence at Coleraine would scuttle the treaty negotiations. Thus he and the other US commissioners were unbending on the intimidating presence of the militia; they wanted it gone. Their position caused a weeklong exchange of acrimonious correspondence between the federal and state commissioners. In what would later be a constant refrain from the southern states, the Georgians claimed that the federal position on the militia impinged on the state's rights and constituted an insult to Georgia. The US commissioners replied that the contents of the Georgians' letter was "absurd" and paid little regard to the "truth."[115] They would not even allow the militia to disembark from the ship that had conveyed the soldiers to Coleraine. Eventually, after much protest, the Georgians backed down and their militia escort stayed away. But this minor tempest was a bad prologue to the actual negotiations and boded ill for future federal-state relations at Coleraine.

Over the coming weeks, the Georgia delegation complained incessantly of numerous instances of federal infringement by Hawkins and his colleagues on state prerogatives—they even compiled a list of such transgressions that they handed to the federal representatives at the end of the conference. But the main rift between the parties was the Georgians' attempt to impose the terms of the three illegal treaties on the Indians. The lands ceded to the United States by the Creeks pursuant to the Treaty of New York were significantly smaller than the land cessions claimed by Georgia pursuant to its treaties with the Indians. The Creeks argued that the chiefs who signed the treaties with Georgia had been intimidated into signing by the presence of the Georgia militia, and that in any event they were a minority of the nation's leaders and had not been authorized by the whole nation to cede the lands. To complicate matters further, the Creek leaders, while arguing that the Treaty of New York governed the scope of the lands they were willing to cede, also contended that the nation had not agreed to the extent of the land cessions contained in the language of that treaty.

Caught between the Creeks and the Georgians, Hawkins and his colleagues did not waiver. They ruled that Georgia's treaties with the Creeks were illegal. Following the states' ratification of the Articles of Confederation, Hawkins explained, the sole governmental power to make treaties with the Indian tribes was vested in Congress. Because Georgia had made its treaties with the Creeks after the ratification of those articles, the treaties were invalid. As for the Creeks' argument, the federal commissioners agreed with them that the terms of the Treaty of New York governed the scope of the Creeks' land cession. However, as they correctly pointed out, the plain language of that treaty did not support the more limited land cession that the Creeks claimed they had made. In response, the Creeks argued that Alexander McGillivray, whom they contemptuously described as a "half-breed," had advised them on his return from New York that the delegation had only agreed to the more limited land cession.[116]

Hawkins, who was one of the US senators who had ratified that treaty, replied that the United States did not care what McGillivray had told his people, the language of the treaty, which he and over twenty of their other leaders had signed, said differently, and the commissioners had no power to alter it.[117] Hawkins pointed out that the United States had placed copies of the treaty in tin boxes for safety and sent them to the nation, where McGillivray "was directed to promulgate it throughout all your land." The federal commissioners also pointed out to their Creek counterparts that Secretary Knox had a given the Tallassee King, upon the chief's departure by boat from New York City to the nation, ten copies of the treaty for delivery to the commander of Fort Saint Mary's, just downriver from Coleraine. Nonetheless, the Creeks insisted that McGillivray had not advised them of these treaty terms and further charged that he had defrauded them.[118]

Thus, although it is likely that many of the Creek attendees at Coleraine were ignorant of the scope of the land cession in that treaty, it is also certain that their principal leader at the time, McGillivray, and many, if not all, of the other Creek leaders who participated in the New York negotiations and were now attending the Coleraine conference were well aware of what lands were being given up under the public treaty. Other than McGillivray, the other Creek participants in the secret treaty were still alive and receiving their annuities from the United States provided under that treaty. The Creek leaders of the secret treaty also betrayed their knowledge of that treaty during the Coleraine negotiations when they protested the implementation of one of its secret, unpublished provisions—that the United States would educate up to four Indian children a year. Several Creek parents took advantage of this opportunity to obtain a white education for their children; McGillivray's nephew was the first to enter the program. But despite McGillivray's good intentions, in its implementation, this treaty provision backfired on the Creeks. Some of these little scholars, for instance, like Dixon Bailey, the son of Richard and Elizabeth Bailey of

Autosse, returned home with an undisguised contempt for their Indian heritage. For this reason and others, the Creeks were unhappy with the educational arrangement provided under the secret treaty, claiming that it turned the children into worthless, mischievous, troublesome characters. Similarly the Indians rejected Hawkins's suggestion that to ensure the Indian children received proper guidance, they be educated by whites in Indian towns. Hawkins's suggestion was received with "such dislike by the Indians" that he tabled it.[119]

Finally, on June 26, 1796, after much grousing about the fraud McGillivray had perpetrated on the nation, the Creeks, probably influenced in their decision by the chiefs on the US payroll, acceded to the Americans' demand that they honor the 1790 treaty as regards their land. However, the chiefs refused to sell the Georgians the additional lands claimed by them under their three treaties with the nation.[120]

The treaty negotiations at Coleraine were concluded on June 29, 1796, thanks primarily to the skills and firmness of Hawkins. Neither the Georgians nor the Creeks were satisfied by the outcome—the hallmark of a successful negotiation some would say. The Creeks believed they had given up too much; the Georgians believed that the Indians had given up too little.[121] So unhappy were the Georgia commissioners with the outcome of the negotiations that before they departed for home on June 30, they left a document with the US commissioners setting forth in detail seven complaints they had with the conduct of those commissioners.[122] Hawkins and his colleagues left Coleraine about a week later.

All the participants in the negotiations were probably delighted to leave the steam bath of a summer in the interior of southern Georgia. Given the results of Hawkins's evenhanded treatment of the Indians, the touchy Georgia delegation could not have been too happy with the commissioner. This unhappiness was doubtless exacerbated when they learned later that year that George Washington had appointed his friend Colonel Hawkins temporary agent for all the Indian tribes south of the Ohio River, perhaps as a reward for his achievements at Coleraine. In any event, the timid and ineffectual agent Seagrove disappeared, and upon Hawkins's appointment as agent, Creek and American relations entered a new era. For the first time since Alexander McGillivray's death, the Creeks, in the person of Hawkins, had a leader with the political skills, courage, and personal integrity to thwart the schemes of the Americans and Europeans against his Native American charges. From the federal government's perspective, Hawkins was also a sincere patriot who had the ability to carry out the objectives of the United States. Thus, President Washington and Secretary of War Knox believed they had found the man to implement their "conciliatory" policy toward the southern Indians. For his troubles, the great and good Hawkins would become the butt of one of history's cruelest jokes.

Hawkins received a taste of what was to come when, in fall 1799, like a bad penny, the freebooter Augustus Bowles once again turned up on the Seminoles' doorstep in Spanish Florida. After spening seven years in Spanish custody in the Philippines, the Spanish governor there had had his fill of Bowles and arranged to have him shipped to prison in Spain, where he could become some other poor soul's problem. During the voyage to his new home, the intrepid Bowles managed to escape from his maritime captivity. While his ship was docked at the African port of Gorée, a British frigate attacked the port hoping to capture one of the Spanish ships docked there. In the confusion, Bowles squeezed himself through the port-hole of the French ship on which he was imprisoned and jumped into the harbor. From there he swam to a nearby American merchant ship docked in the port. The captain of the ship allowed him on board, then hoisted sails and fled the melee. The Americans dropped Bowles off at the British colony of Sierra Leone, and from there he made his way to London.[123] With the help of friends there, Bowles secured passage to the Bahamas. There he renewed old acquaintances and was soon on this way back to his Indian friends in Spanish Florida, nursing a particular hatred for the Spanish and planning further schemes against Panton, Leslie and the perfidious dons.

Bowles was particularly cheered to learn that his old adversary, Alexander McGillivray, was long dead, and he saw an opportunity to realize his ambition to become the leader of the southern Indians. Bowles did not know that the vacuum in Creek leadership left by McGillivray's death had been filled by the Creek agent Benjamin Hawkins. He soon learned that, however, and spent several frustrating years butting his persistent head against the stone wall of Hawkins's power. During this time, the self-styled director general of a great Native American confederacy was reduced to leading a small band of no more than sixty warriors, whom Hawkins claimed were "more interested in frolicking than fighting."[124] But Hawkins also recognized that even with these limited resources, Bowles and his gang, if not stopped by the weak Spanish, could "destroy or ruin all the inhabitants of East Florida without the walls of St. Augustine." The Spanish governor of Pensacola eventually offered the substantial sum of $4,500 for Bowles's capture, but none of the coastal tribes, no matter how poor, attempted to recover it. Bowles even convinced the old Tallassee King and the Little Prince of the Lower Creeks to assist him in his failed attempt to capture Saint Marks.[125] But eventually, as was his nature, Bowles overreached himself.

In May 1803, Benjamin Hawkins called a council of chiefs from the four so-called civilized tribes at the Hickory Ground. The subject of the meeting was further Indian land cessions in Georgia. Forbes and Estevan Folch, the son of the governor of West Florida, Vincente Folch, were also there, hoping to capture Bowles and take him into Spanish custody. The over-confident and overambitious Bowles, along with his Seminole supporters, decided to attend. It appears that Bowles, by opposing any further Indian land cessions to the Americans, hoped to gain leadership of the four tribes. If so, as Hawkins reported to Secretary of State James Madison: "It was inconceivable to me that Bowles who understood a good deal of the Indian language, had been here formerly and visited with General McGillivray, should not have been able to make the necessary determination between past and present. He must have seen a material change in the manners of the Indians."[126]

Bowles's miscalculation, suggested by Hawkins, proved to be fatal. Bowles and his Seminoles reached the Hickory Ground, where numerous Indians from the "civilized" tribes had congregated. Beforehand, Hawkins had arranged with the Upper Creeks to take Bowles prisoner.[127] As part of this scheme, Bowles was allowed to address the council on May 24, 1803. He fulminated against white encroachment on Indians lands and urged the Indian leaders not to sell the Americans any more of their territory. The next day, Hawkins led a group of mixed bloods, among whom were Sam Moniac and Charles Weatherford's son, William, into Bowles's camp and seized him amid his supporters. He was bound and taken to the old French fort. There he was held captive until a blacksmith in Hawkins's employ fashioned iron handcuffs for the prisoner. Then Estevan Folch placed them on Bowles's wrists.[128]

The plan was to transport Bowles by pirogue down the Alabama River and deliver him into Spanish custody in Mobile. But Bowles's bag of tricks was not yet empty. Four days into the journey, while captors and captive camped on an island for the night, Bowles somehow managed to slip out of camp unnoticed, seize the pirogue, and propel himself to shore. Then, perhaps unhinged somewhat by his ordeal, Bowles made an uncharacteristic mistake. Rather than riding the boat down the river or concealing it in the brush on the shore, he abandoned the vessel in plain sight on the riverbank and fled into the forest. His furious—and embarrassed—captors, the $4,500 reward vanishing before their eyes, picked up Bowles's trail near the boat. They captured the fugitive and transported him, without incident, the rest of the way to Mobile. There they turned him over to the Spanish for the reward. Taking no chances, the Spanish sent Bowles to Havana, where he was incarcerated in the formidable Moro Castle. Out of tricks, Bowles died in captivity several years later.[129]

With the departure of Bowles from the scene, Benjamin Hawkins oversaw, aside from small acts of localized violence, a decade of relative peace between the Indians and their American neighbors. During this period he managed to convince the Creeks to cede the land between the Oconee and Oakmulgee rivers to the United States and to allow a mail road to be built through their territory from the Georgia settlements to Fort Stoddert on the Mobile River. At this point the American demand for Creek territory abated until 1811, the year of the Great Comet and of the New Madrid earthquake—a year that came to be called the Year of Miracles. Though dealing with the independent-minded Creeks was often like trying to herd cats, Hawkins was afforded a fair window of time to make his program of civilization work. Indeed, in 1807, the agent wrote:

> Our plan of civilization is progressive and has taken such strong hold of the Indian mind that it is not in the power of our enemies to render it abortive. Spinning and weaving, attention to stock raising, settling out from their old towns [to obtain unexhausted soil], fencing their settlements, planting fruit trees, a friendly attention to the rights of their neighbors with good will to the human race has extended itself over one half of the agency [the Lower Creeks]. The ancient habits of the natives begin to yield to the force of truth and ere long will spread itself over the other half [the Upper Creeks].[130]

Given such sentiments, it is not surprising that when the storm finally broke over the Creek Nation, Hawkins was probably the most astonished of all its inhabitants.

The Creek Nation on the Eve of Its Fall

To the Creeks, their culture and the land, in all its manifestations and its wonderful variety of flora and fauna, were one and the same. The concept of property, in the capitalist sense, was foreign to them before the coming of the Europeans. To the puzzlement of men like Benjamin Hawkins, even their chiefs beggared themselves by giving away their possessions to members of their tribe. Indeed, it was only in the decades prior to the Creek War that padlocks came into use among the Creeks to secure what they now viewed as personal property. Thus it was that the nation had much more to lose to the whites than just its land. If it followed Hawkins's well-meaning plan of civilization, it stood to forfeit its identity, and even its soul, in exchange for a life fattened by the material but stripped of the spiritual comforts. In this way the Muskogee found themselves boxed in between the choice of two forms of extinction. This Hobson's choice between an ancient but unmaintainable identity and a white-centric identity is essentially what divided the nation on the eve of war into factions whose composition otherwise made no sense. The fact that many of the most prominent Creek leaders of the anti-American party in the nation—such as William Weatherford, Menawa, and Peter McQueen—were also wealthy mixed bloods (also called Métis) who had adopted many facets of white planter life goes a long way in explaining the incongruity.

Apart from the Muskogee, like a growing fire beneath the kettle of Indian life, were the unruly frontiersmen, the criminal class, the simple settlers hungry for land, and the rising class of ambitious planters. This coarse collection of men and women, far removed from the Tidewater gentry of Maryland and Virginia whom they would come to emulate, were creating what one contemporary observer described as a "new era of credit without capital and enterprise without honesty," a budding frontier society characterized by "vulgarity—ignorance—fussy and arrogant pretension—unmitigated rowdyism—bullying insolence."[131]

Also stoking this fire were the British in Canada and their Spanish allies in Florida. The powerful British, emerging victorious from the Napoleonic Wars, wanted to recover control from the United States of the Ohio River Valley territory that it had lost to its former colonists. The feeble shell of the Spanish Empire wished to hang on to its remaining possessions in Florida. Both nations were finishing their joint campaign to evict the French from Spain and would soon have the ability to turn more attention to these objects. As they had done repeatedly in the past, they intended to use Native Americans as cat's-paws to achieve their objective of gaining control of the Mississippi Territory.

Although the Indian population had rebounded robustly since the Entrada, by the first decade of the nineteenth century, the five Indian nations of the Old Southwest were a sparsely populated island in the steadily rising sea of white settlement. In 1810, Tennessee had an estimated population of around two hundred sixty thousand whites. Its principal towns were Knoxville, hard by Cherokee country in the northeast part of the state, and Nashville, in the state's central hills near the Chickasaw lands. For that same year, the American population of the Mississippi Territory numbered just over thirty-one thousand. The famous city of Natchez, on the Mississippi River, was its main town; the nearby town of Washington was the territorial capital. And on its eastern borders was the little town of Fort Saint Stephens, on the high limestone bluffs of the Tombigbee River, which soon became the administrative hub of land ceded by the Spanish and the Choctaws to the Americans. As for the state of Georgia, by 1800 its slave population alone—sixty thousand—exceeded the number of Native Americans living in the whole of the Old Southwest. Its new capital of Milledgeville had recently been established near the Creek frontier, making plain the direction in which Georgia believed its future lay.[132]

Given these figures, for the southern Indian nations, even collectively, to go to war against the more numerous, technically superior, and vastly better armed Americans required a mental state of utter desperation and despair. For the Creek Nation alone—divided internally among war and peace factions—to rise up against the Americans would first require that the Muskogee people be rendered mad. And that is what occurred in 1811.

2. Rise of the Prophets

The Man from the Northern Lakes

A veteran director of Hollywood Westerns could not have staged it better. Near sunset of September 19, 1811, a band of eighteen or so horsemen rode out of the east toward the setting sun and down the low western hills overlooking the plains of the Tallapoosa River valley in the direction of the capital of the Upper Creek Nation a few miles distant. The group was an ecumenical representation of several Indian tribes, predominantly Shawnee but also warriors from trans-Mississippi tribes such as the Kickapoos. But any onlookers could not tell from their attire that the riders were from different tribes, because each of the men dressed alike as if making a silent pronouncement: we are one Indian people.

All the riders wore buckskin hunting shirts and leggings gartered below the knees. A square of cloth dangled from their hips, and ornate moccasins beaded with multicolored porcupine quills covered their feet. Their skulls were bound with a band of red flannel overlain with a narrower band of silver, from which three braids of jet-black hair fell to their waists. Bands of silver encircled their brown arms, and silver rings hung from their ears. They had painted red crescents beneath each eye, a red dot on each forehead, and a circle of red on their chests. Each man carried a new British musket as well as the traditional tomahawk and scalping knife—essentially a simple kitchen knife mass produced in England and modified by the Indians for more specialized work. All but one—a particularly handsome man— wore the long feathers of birds of prey in their hair. As for that singular personage, his head was crowned with the delicate stems of two crane feathers: one the bird's natural white color, the symbol of peace, the other painted red, the symbol for war. This man was their leader, the famous Shawnee known to the whites as Tecumseh.[1]

Tecumseh and his companions had traveled far: first, one thousand miles from the Great Lakes region near Detroit to the Choctaw Nation in the Mississippi Territory; from the Choctaw lands, the party journeyed three hundred miles to the sacred Creek settlement the Hickory Ground on the east bank of the unruly Coosa River; from that important town, Tecumseh traveled about sixteen miles west to the small spine of land overlooking the fertile Tallapoosa River valley where he now found himself. When these warriors had first crossed the western border of the Creek Nation several days earlier, they fought, together with their Choctaw hosts, a fierce skirmish against a band of Creek horse thieves living on the Choctaw borderlands who had raided their camp. In that fight, men were killed on both sides. This incident was put aside, however, and Tecumseh and his entourage arrived safely among the Muskogees to enlist that nation in a great Indian confederacy against the Americans.

As he descended to the plains of the Tallapoosa River valley, Tecumseh could see in the distance, growing ever larger at his stately approach, the large and famous town of Tuckabatchee, grown far larger now from the thousands who had gathered there for the great council of the Creek Nation called by Benjamin Hawkins, purportedly to discuss the US request to expand the postal trail through the Creek Nation into an actual road. Here was the land of his mother and father set among the coils of the Tallapoosa River, whose clear waters he could see just beyond the town, refulgent with light from the falling sun. In the sky above, like a guardian beast, traveling with him was something no living man at this assemblage had ever seen: a spectacular comet with a one-hundred-million-mile tail and a head half again as big as the sun; a prop beyond the inventiveness of a Hollywood screenwriter; a phenomenon to which everyone could bear witness, and a portentous sign of great events to come that the superstitious Muskogee could hardly fail to ignore.[2] After a long and perilous journey, Tecumseh arrived, heralded by the comet, at the place on which all his hopes for the southern Indian people most depended. His unflagging confidence had grown even stronger as he entered his ancestral homeland. Here at Tuckabatchee, here where enemies abounded and where his very life was in danger, here Tecumseh would not fail. The hunter was home from the hills.

Tecumseh's Southern Odyssey

TUCKABATCHEE was an ancient town. Several hundred years earlier, the energetic Mississippian culture had lived here, and it left behind like a mystery on the northwestern side of the river two of its characteristic mounds. The present town stood on a level plain that fanned quickly and broadly out from the mouth of a hairpin bend in the Tallapoosa River some two and a half miles below the last and greatest falls of that river. At those falls, the river dropped its now turbulent waters forty feet through two channels of pale grey masonlike blocks of stone to the southern plains of Alabama. Losing its energy over several miles of shoals, the stream slowed to a quieter flow just above the town.[3] In the summer months, when the waters shallowed, the stony bed of these shoals grew thick with salt-rich moss on which livestock, wild animals, and waterfowl fed. In these shallower waters, the Tuckabatchees hauled up numerous species of fish in great skeins and wrestled their catches to shore. In the gray of late fall, when the waters grew cold and heavy with rain, all manner of waterfowl descended from the north in great noisy clouds to feed in the surrounding fields of recently harvested corn.

Beyond the town, fields of corn, cotton, sweet potatoes, pumpkins, and watermelons stretched out for several miles toward the low hills to the southwest. The Tuckabatchees had fenced off other land from the croplands for horses, cattle, and swine to feed. Chickens ran loose among the cabins and gave sport to small children. Peach orchards, introduced by various Europeans, bloomed white and fragrant in the spring. Tart muscadine grapes, from which the Indians made a paste, grew wild and plump in the nearby woods. Downstream of the town, or *talwa* in the Muskogee language, several chiefs and white traders owned prosperous plantations. It was a land of easy plentitude and, to the eyes of white officialdom, native indolence.

Tuckabatchee was laid out in the traditional manner of Creek towns, around a central area containing a large square of beaten earth.[4] On each side of the square stood a single-story building forty feet long, sixteen feet wide, and eight feet high framed with timber supported by heavy wooden posts carved in the shape of alligators, the town's predominant clan. The buildings were roofed with wooden shingles or the bark of the cypress tree, and the walls were plastered with clay and painted in bright colors. The interiors of each building were divided by low clay walls, which promoted circulation, into three rooms. One building served as a council house, another as a banqueting house, the other two as accommodations for the populace during public festivals. Just outside the square, off one of its corners, lay an octagon-shaped structure thirty feet across with a conical roof twelve feet high at its crest. Inside the structure, an earthen mound on which fires were made rose in a spiral. The inner walls of the building were lined with several rows of benches, like theater seating, made of cane and laid with reed matting. Known as the rotunda, this building was used as a council house in the cold months.

Beneath the earthen floor of the rotunda the Tuckabatchees had secreted two copper and five brass plates. For reasons beyond modern memory, this tribe had become the objects' custodians. Some unknown artisan— God, the Tuckabatchees believed—had worked the conjoined Roman letters *AE* on the objects' metal faces. Of ancient and forgotten origin, the plates were displayed once a year at the nation's most important religious event. Known as the busk ceremony, the event lasted from four to eight days, depending on the traditions of each town. The ceremony was a mixture of harvest celebration and cleansing of the old year's sins. It largely

consisted of the performance of various dances and purifications cere-
monies that involved the ingestion of powerful emetics. At one of these
dances, Tuckabatchee's religious leaders displayed the ancient copper and
brass plates to the townspeople.[5]

The town's residences spread out from the square, mimicking on a
smaller scale its arrangement of four buildings around a central square.
Each building in this compound served a different function. One was a
winter dwelling and kitchen, one a summer house, one a storehouse of two
stories with a corncrib on the upper story. The fourth building was a warehouse for storing deerskins and meeting with traders—the Creeks did not
allow whites inside their living quarters. Not all family groups, which were
matrilineal, were prosperous enough to own a complete complex of four
buildings, but their dwellings had at least some elements of this arrangement.

Part of the town, like many other Creek settlements, was set aside for
lacrosse games, what the Creeks referred to as the "little war." The game
was played on a large field between warriors from two towns. The contest
was incredibly violent. During the course of the game, broken limbs and
serious maimings were common, and deaths were not unheard of. Among
the spectators, gambling on the game's outcome reached insane proportions. In some cases people wagered everything they owned. As a sporting
event, it resembled in its violence and high-stakes gambling modern
American football more than modern-day lacrosse. A prominent Creek
town, such as Tuckabatchee, also had a playing field flanked by a low earth-
en embankment that was devoted to an ancient game called chunky. This
contest involved a beautifully rounded and polished stone about the size
and shape of a hockey puck. The stone was rolled across smoothed and
level ground, and the contestants flung spears at the spot on the course
where they calculated the chunky stone would come to rest. The contest-
ant whose spear landed closest to the spot won.[6]

The national council began in the latter half of September beneath what
is known to history as the Great Comet of 1811. With the enormous ball
of its brilliant head framed by a thinner veil of light and an estimated 110-
million-mile tail of light streaming behind it, the Great Comet enchanted
and frightened the people of the Northern Hemisphere. For the greater
part of human history, comets had been viewed not only with wonder but
with terror as well: omens of the coming of a momentous, often terrible,
event. Even after the Enlightenment, and in particular after the great Isaac
Newton stripped off their supernatural trappings, the big comets
remained objects of astonishment to even the most sophisticated
Europeans.[7] William Blake painted the Great Comet; Leo Tolstoy, in perhaps the greatest novel of all time, *War and Peace*, made it an omen of disaster for Napoleon's invasion of Russia; and, on a more pleasant note, the

French vintners of Bordeaux named the outstanding vintage grown that year as the Comet Year. Yet surely none of the Native American attendees at the Creek National Council, and perhaps none of the whites, had read the latest scientific treatises on astrophysics. Although, as the most educated man there, Benjamin Hawkins probably had sufficient knowledge of celestial phenomena to at least have attempted to explain the unexplainable to some of the friendly chiefs. However, most of the Native Americans in attendance, like the pre-Enlightenment Europeans before them, would naturally have viewed this otherworldly sight with wonder and trepidation. Tecumseh, who almost certainly had learned the true nature of the comet from his British allies in Detroit and who also knew how deeply the superstitions of the Indian people ran, employed this celestial wonder to his advantage.

A French astronomer first sighted the Great Comet on March 25, 1811. Months later, as Tecumseh rode through the Creek Nation in September, the comet had not yet reached the apogee of its brilliance.[8] It would have been closer to the horizon and thus less spectacular than when it reached its apogee a few weeks later in October, when its effect on the Creeks, as far as Tecumseh's visit was concerned, would have been more profound. On the other hand, the longer Tecumseh stayed among the Creeks, the greater the comet grew. But when he finally left the nation some weeks later, its brilliance began steadily to decline as if, like a fierce but tamed beast, it was somehow tethered to the arrival and departure of its master, thus reinforcing the association of the supernatural with the man.

When the object finally emerged in the sky like a beast of fire unleashed by God across the heavens, it took no great stretch of the Indian imagination, and little prompting from Tecumseh and his companions, to associate Tecumseh's appearance among the southern Indians with the comet's spectacular arrival. To the Indians at Tuckabatchee, it must have seemed no coincidence that the man who had traveled a thousand miles from the Detroit region to the land of his father and mother had been named at birth the Panther across the Sky or Shooting Star.[9]

Along with the Great Comet, Tecumseh came with an idea that burned just as brightly: to unite the Native American peoples in a great confederacy against the motley hoard of Americans invading their lands. Tecumseh's idea was not a new one. In the late seventeenth century, Metacomet, or King Philip, as he was known to the whites, cobbled together a great tribal confederacy against the Massachusetts Bay Colony that rocked the foundations of the whole of colonial New England. But in the end, the confederacy was defeated, and New England was never threatened again by tribes living within its boundaries. As for King Philip, for his troubles, he ended up with his head on a spike above Plymouth Town, a white settlement that his father, Massasoit, had made possible.

Almost a century later, following the close of the French and Indian War, another Native American visionary, an Ottawa chief known as Pontiac, created a confederacy of northern tribes in the Great Lakes and Ohio River Valley area to drive the British from their lands. After repeated successes against the British troops and colonial militia, the movement known as Pontiac's conspiracy was finally defeated, and the British moved farther west. Nonetheless, after Pontiac's defeat, stubborn bands of northern Indians, principally Shawnee, periodically visited the Creeks to enlist them in a war against the people of the new United States. However, nothing memorable came of these desultory efforts. Until Tecumseh.

Already, he and his brother, a nativistic religious leader known as the Prophet, had brought together a great confederacy of dozens of northern tribes stretching all the way into the vast territory west of the Mississippi River. Now, Tecumseh set out to bring the southern tribes into his confederacy, thus creating an Indian barrier to white expansion from the Canadian border to the Gulf of Mexico. To effect this plan, in August 1811, Tecumseh decided to visit the tribes inhabiting the Old Southwest and trans-Mississippi region and, relying on his considerable personal charm and martial reputation, convince them by reason of the need to unite with the northern tribes against the American menace before it was too late. Although Tecumseh's concept of a Native American tribal confederacy was not new, he was far and away its most famous advocate. Perhaps it was the scope of his vision, perhaps his undeniable charisma, or perhaps the weed-like proliferation of newspapers in every little town that could afford a printing press from which his fame grew. Surely all of that. But just as surely was the grand, quixotic nature of his doomed quest to unite his people against the whites.

Tecumseh left Vincennes, Indiana, on August 6, 1811, with about eighteen to twenty-four companions, mostly Shawnee, but also men from other northern tribes such as the Kickapoo.[10] They traveled by boat down the Wabash River to its juncture with the Ohio River, and on down that river to southwestern Tennessee. Tecumseh's first objective was the so-called civilized tribes in the southeastern United States: the Chickasaws, Choctaws, and Cherokees, and the powerful Creek Confederation.

In late August or early September 1811, having now obtained horses, Tecumseh and his party crossed the Tennessee River into the Chickasaw Nation just south of what is now Memphis. The Chickasaws were led by George Colbert, who, among his many ventures, operated the ferry that Tecumseh used to cross the Tennessee River into that nation. Colbert was another product of a mixed marriage between an Indian woman and a white man. Through his mother's influence and his own considerable business and political skills, Colbert had risen to a position of power in the Chickasaw Nation. He was a good friend of the Americans, who had placed him on their payroll in the form of a one-thousand-dollar annuity. Out of naked self-interest, he and his large family had grown wealthy adopting white ways of agriculture and trade.[11]

When Tecumseh and his party arrived among the Chickasaws, Colbert immediately made it known to Tecumseh and the Chickasaw people that the Chickasaws had no interest in Tecumseh's plan of Indian unity against the Americans. He even appears to have promptly notified the American authorities, no later than September 9, 1811, that Tecumseh was traveling through the south seeking allies among the southern tribes for an attack on the "frontier settlements."[12] Quickly seeing that he would have no success among the Chickasaws, Tecumseh crossed over into Choctaw country to the immediate south.[13]

Tecumseh cannot have been greatly surprised or even dismayed at his reception among the Chickasaws. They were a weak and scattered people largely enthralled to the avaricious Colbert family who saw no profit in crossing the rising American power along their borders. Rather, the Colberts viewed the stream of American travelers along the Natchez Trace that ran through their lands as an opportunity to enrich themselves and their associates. There was also bad blood between the northern Indians and the Chickasaws that stretched back to President Washington's administration. In the seemingly endless struggles between the whites and the Indians for the Ohio River country, the Chickasaws had sided with the Americans at the Battle of Fallen Timbers in 1794, in northern Ohio. In that battle, a young Tecumseh had bravely led a small party of warriors in a fighting retreat; casualties were light and about even on both sides, but the Americans drove the greatly outnumbered Indian confederation from the field. Given the present political situation in the Chickasaw lands, it was probably sufficient for Tecumseh's purposes that he obtain passage through that nation unmolested. In any event, a far bigger prize lay directly to the south, in the numerous and powerful Choctaw Nation.

Tecumseh prudently sent the customary messengers ahead of his party to prepare the way for entry into the Choctaw lands. In early September, he forded the Oktibbeha Creek, which formed the boundary between the Choctaws and Chickasaws, near its junction with the Tombigbee River. Here, just below the mouth of the Oktibbeha, near present-day Columbus, Mississippi, lay the flourishing plantation of John Pitchlynn, the US interpreter for the Choctaw Nation. Pitchlynn's was a well-known stopping place on the trail south, and it is most likely that Tecumseh was met here by the Choctaw delegation assigned to convey him into the nation.

For several days the Indian party traveled down a path known as the Six Towns. It halted at a town governed by Moshulitubbee, the amiably crafty chief of the northeastern division of the Choctaw Nation. Tecumseh and his companions enjoyed Moshulitubbee's hospitality for several days while the Choctaws made arrangements for convening a council of Choctaw notables to hear the message Tecumseh had brought. The council was planned for a town farther south ruled by a chief known as Hoentubbe. Tecumseh and Moshulitubbee appear to have become friendly and traveled to Hoentubbe's town together. Tecumseh charmed this *micco* as well, and when he left Hoentubbe's town to go even deeper into the Choctaw Nation, he presented the chief with a silver gorget, probably of British manufacture. This object became a treasured possession of the Choctaw chief's and remained in his family for many decades until destroyed in a house fire.

But it was at the council held at Hoentubbe's town that Tecumseh's visit to the Choctaw Nation began to sour. The cause was a stout, moon-faced, fifty-one-year-old Choctaw, about five-feet-ten-inches tall, named Pushmataha. This hard-fighting and harder-drinking man was the leader of the southeastern division of the Choctaw Nation and a great friend of the Americans. True, Pushmataha was on the American payroll, but this happy arrangement did not alone explain the chief's steadfast attachment to the troublesome whites. At the time, groups of American frontiersmen were clustered in a few small settlements along the Tombigbee River and spread out on isolated farms in the Tensaw Delta to the southeast. Should war come, the settlers' closest succor was the Mississippi River town of Natchez and its satellite towns and villages some two hundred miles to the west. Caught between the powerful Creek and Choctaw nations, in a land of dense forests and impenetrable swamps, these scattered white outposts would be quickly raked from the landscape if the Indian nations combined forces. But for some reason, Pushmataha liked his white neighbors and took special pride in the fact that the Choctaw and American people had never been at war. His personal predilections aside, however, the personally brave chief plainly realized that the Americans were too numerous and too strong, materially and technologically, for any combination of Indians to defeat them permanently. Pushmataha no doubt believed that if the Choctaws were to survive as a tribe, they must learn to coexist with this incalculably more powerful people, and that Americans of goodwill, like Benjamin Hawkins, had shown the way.

Over the next few weeks, as Tecumseh and his party moved farther south and west into the Choctaw Nation, Pushmataha shadowed the northerner. When Tecumseh traveled to a new Choctaw town to give his talk, Pushmataha was there to counter it. The denouement of this back and forth between the two men came at Moshulitubbee's second home, near present-day Brooksville, Mississippi, about fifteen miles from the Tombigbee River. There a council was held, attended by the principal chiefs of the three Choctaw districts—Pushmataha of the southeastern district, Puckshenubbee of the western district, and Moshulitubbee of the northeastern district—and other Choctaw notables. Unfortunately for Tecumseh, also in attendance were the US interpreter for the Choctaws, John Pitchlyn, and the mixed-blood Choctaw David Folsom, both of whom worked assiduously to undermine Tecumseh's influence at the council.

The council lasted two days and was held under an enormous red oak on the property. Tecumseh spoke first, giving his standard lengthy talk about the need for all the Indian nations to unite against the white menace. Pushmataha spoke the following day. He reminded his audience that the Choctaws and the whites had long been friends and had never gone to war against each other. He probably also emphasized the danger to the Choctaws of joining with Tecumseh in such a war. He ended his oration with a vow he did not forget in the coming years: if any Choctaw should join Tecumseh in a war against the Americans and survive that war, upon that warrior's return to the nation, Pushmataha would have him executed. This threat appeared to create a sensation among the other chiefs, who quickly rushed to follow Pushmataha's lead in denouncing Tecumseh. Although not all the chiefs agreed with Pushmataha, in particular the younger chiefs and younger warriors living nearest the Creek Nation, they remained silent in the face of the animated majority of their leaders.

Following the close of the council, the principal chiefs held a private council to which the Shawnees were not invited and at which the Choctaws decided to advise Tecumseh that he and his companions must leave their nation immediately or be killed. The council assigned David Folsom the task of escorting the northern Indians to the Choctaws' border with the Creeks. The Choctaw chief Hoentubbe and several whites also accompanied the party.

Even though not unexpected, the council's formal decision must still have been a terrific psychological blow to the aspirations of Tecumseh and his companions; the powerful Choctaw Nation was a key part of the confederacy he hoped to form against the Americans. Nonetheless, although the news was hard, Tecumseh remained undaunted. Perhaps he thought the future might bring a change in the Choctaws' attitude toward the concept of a Native American confederacy as a bulwark to white expansion. Certainly Moshulitubbee and Hoentubbe had shown friendship toward him, and the Little Warrior was clearly in his camp. And when the powerful British joined him against the Americans, the Choctaws might reconsider their position. Momentarily thwarted but unbroken, Tecumseh headed east with his Choctaw guides toward his greatest prize. What shortly followed illustrates perfectly one of the foremost obstacles that Tecumseh and Native Americans over the centuries before him faced in devising a solution to the threat to the Indian posed by the white man.

Traveling east by horseback, the party stopped in the afternoon at the Tombigbee River to construct rafts for the crossing. These the men built from logs bound together with the strong vines of wild grape. They finished the rafts shortly before dusk. With some men paddling the ad hoc craft and the others holding the reins of the horses swimming alongside, about half the party, including Tecumseh, crossed the river. Folsom and the others, among whom were some of Tecumseh's Shawnees, remained on the western shore and made camp for the night.

Watching these activities from concealment were scouts from a large raiding party from the nearby Creek settlements along the Black Warrior River to the northeast. When the leader of the Creek party learned that the Choctaws had divided their party, the Creek raiders crossed the river below Folsom's camp to engage in their favorite sport of horse stealing. Several of their men crept up silently through the dark woods to the Choctaw camp and located its unguarded horses. They then made off undetected with a number of mounts, both Choctaw and Shawnee, in preparation for another favorite Creek sport—the ambush—making no effort to conceal their trail.

When Folsom's men awoke that morning, they discovered the theft. They also took the Creek bait, and a group of Choctaws and Shawnees were sent in pursuit of the thieves. The Creeks were lying in wait a few miles downstream, concealed in a canebrake growing beside the thieves' trail. When Folsom's men came within range, the Creeks opened fire on their pursuers, killing some and wounding others. The survivors fled back to their camp pursued by the triumphant Creeks. One Shawnee had his horse shot out from under him but, along with his companions, was able to make it back safely to camp.

The pursuing Creeks stopped short of the Choctaw camp and assembled on the crest of a small hill overlooking the place, waiting for battle. The furious Choctaws and their Shawnee guests quickly obliged the Creek raiders and assembled their forces in a canebrake at the bottom of the hill. A seesaw fight ensued, with the Choctaws trying to drive the Creeks from the hill and the Creeks trying to drive the Choctaws from the canebrake. At the sound of the firing, Tecumseh's party recrossed the river and joined the battle, which proceeded in fits and starts for much of the day. Finally, around sunset, the Choctaws were able to drive the Creeks from their hilltop position. Both sides suffered a number of killed and wounded in this senseless affair. Among the wounded was Folsom, who had been shot in the shoulder. Despite his wound, the determined young man made it a point to cross the river into the Creek Nation with Tecumseh's party and thus fulfill his mission. For his part, Tecumseh must have been struck by the ironic nature of the fight with the Creeks—the gratuitous battle between the two tribes was exactly what he had been preaching to the Choctaws against.

It is not known if any of Tecumseh's party were killed or wounded in the fray, but given the length and ferocity of the contest, it seems unlikely that every man in the party escaped unhurt. It is also unknown if the Creeks, amid the smoke and confusion of the fight, knew that Tecumseh's men were fighting with the Choctaws. Certainly, as Tecumseh's party made its way east up the Alabama River valley toward the heart of the Creek Nation, it does not appear to have been molested by anyone. It is more likely that Tecumseh's Creek-born interpreter, Seekaboo, had been in touch with his acquaintances among the Creeks concerning Tecumseh's visit and its purpose and that the Creeks had sent men to guide the northerners to their destination.

The Creek Nation at the Crossroads

A T the time Tecumseh entered the Creek Nation in September 1811, he was truly a man in full, nearing the apogee of his fame. He was about forty-three years old, markedly handsome, five-feet-ten-inches tall, and had an athletic build and an aura about him that commanded respect and loyalty. But, as if the gods felt they had bestowed too many gifts on the chief, he was slightly lame from an injury to one leg, and the otherwise unblemished white of his teeth was marred by a tooth with a bluish cast. Already his exploits as a war leader and gifted hunter had spread throughout the nation and he had become, particularly to the young people, a hero and a man to emulate.[14] Tecumseh's celebrity status, however, did not make him welcome to all. Powerful forces within and without the nation resented and felt threatened by his presence. However attracted to him, and even overawed by him, as some people were, the poison of self-interest and legitimate concerns as to what his visit might portend for the welfare of the Creeks overrode the temptation to follow his plan for unity among the Indian nations.

When Tecumseh rode into Tuckabatchee, the life of the Muskogee Nation had come to a critical crossroads, with no unanimity among its people as to which direction to take. In one direction lay the continued and comfortable path of their ancient culture, in the other a new and frightening path toward the adoption of a European mode of living. On these choices the nation was divided into two factions. On one side were what the Americans called the old chiefs. These were men who favored accommodation with the Americans and their plan of civilization as the only way the nation could survive, and they themselves could continue to prosper. On the other side were the more nativistic chiefs who deeply resented the Americans' intrusion into the Indians' lands and into their ancient way of life.

The most prominent leader of the old chiefs was a Tuckabatchee, and the current speaker of the nation, called Tustannugee by the Creeks and the Big Warrior by the whites. The Big Warrior's name had nothing to do with his prowess at war; he was a politician, not a fighter. His name came from his great size; he was said to be the largest man among his people and weighed around three hundred pounds. Unfortunately, his great body was afflicted with a horrible skin condition that rendered him spotted like a leopard. As if in compensation for this disfigurement, the chief adorned himself with silver ornaments and beaded leggings. The appellation "Warrior," however, was a misnomer. The chief was a timid man—some said a coward—who, during a fight with another tribe, ignominiously fled the battleground in fear.[15] But he balanced his timidity with great cunning and powers of persuasion, fueled by an inordinate appetite for wealth and power. Although the Big Warrior had no love for the Americans, he had even less love for anyone, like Tecumseh, who threatened the chief's comfortable and powerful position in life. Benjamin Hawkins, who would use and coddle the giant through the deadly months ahead, described him as "avaricious, ambitious and intriguing."[16]

Like almost everyone who met Tecumseh, the Big Warrior was impressed by the Shawnee leader, he was also afraid of him. More importantly for the Muskogee Nation, however, the Tuckabatchee chief was even more afraid of the destructive consequences on his own fortunes and those of his people that Tecumseh's plans portended. The Big Warrior had long been close to the Americans and had greatly profited by Hawkins's plan of civilization, becoming a wealthy planter with extensive lands, a number of black slaves, and many head of cattle. He also had experienced firsthand the Americans' unslakable and unprincipled thirst for land, and he had seen their power grow in proportion to their rapid increase in population and mastery of technology. Thus, the Big Warrior was all too sensible about the inevitable outcome of a war with the Americans. Even with the promised aid of Britain, he feared that the Creek Nation would be destroyed.[17]

Although the Big Warrior was an Upper Creek, he had few supporters among the upper towns. His primary allies were the Lower Creeks led by such men as the Little Prince and William McIntosh. The Upper Creeks were somewhat insulated from the Americans by the Cherokees to the northeast, the Chickasaws to the northwest, the Choctaws to the southwest, and the Spanish to the south. The lands of the Lower Creeks, however, lay between the Chattahoochee and Flint rivers hard against the nation's border with Georgia and its unremittingly rapacious and aggressive citizens. Situated thus, the Lower Creeks would be the first to suffer if war broke out with the Americans.

Josiah Francis: Self portrait of the Alabamas' leading prophet drawn in London where he was soliciting British aid. (*British Museum*)

Benjamin Hawkins: Creek agent charged by the US with "civilizing" the Creeks.

William Augustus Bowles: The flamboyant Maryland-born Tory and freebooter known as the "Prince of Liars." (*Museum of Early Southern Decorative Arts*)

Alexander McGillivray: Creek political and diplomatic genius whose machinations kept the Creek Nation intact against American aggression. (*Fordham University Libraries*)

Pushmataha: Choctaw chief who opposed Tecumseh and fought with the Americans against the Creeks. (*Alabama Department of Archives and History*)

John McKee: Tasked by Andrew Jackson to convince the Choctaw and Chickasaw nations to join the Americans against the Creeks. (*Alabama Department of Archives and History*)

William McIntosh: Wealthy Lower Creek leader who distinguished himself in battle against the Upper Creeks. (*Library of Congress*)

Menawa: Upper Creek leader who years after the Creek War oversaw the execution of William McIntosh for treason. (*Library of Congress*)

The Lower Creeks, among whom Hawkins had built his agency compound, were also more receptive to Hawkins's program of civilization than were the Upper Creeks. Accordingly, they were less receptive than the Upper Creeks to Tecumseh's message that the Indians should return to their old way of hunting, subsistence farming, and abstinence from alcohol. One of their principal leaders, thirty-three-year-old William McIntosh, another product of a marriage between a Scotsman and a Creek woman, was particularly taken with the white ways. His half-brother was a Georgia politician, and McIntosh had become a wealthy planter and important Creek leader with a fine plantation outside the important Lower Creek town of Coweta on the Chattahoochee River.[18] Unlike the Big Warrior, McIntosh was a true warrior, a courageous and fierce fighter. Like the Big Warrior, however, he was an opportunist who had been seduced by European ideals of money and personal power. McIntosh was a great friend of the Americans and a better friend to himself.

Much of McIntosh's prominence flowed from the political support of an elderly Lower Creek chief known as Tustennugee to the Creeks and the Little Prince to the whites. In the American Revolution, the Little Prince and an Upper Creek named Davy Cornells led 250 Creek warriors against the Americans during the colonists' siege of the British forces at Augusta, Georgia. In this successful affair, the Little Prince earned a reputation for hard fighting, but that reputation was tarred by the atrocities his warriors committed on American prisoners after the Americans broke off the siege. After the war, the Little Prince entered politics and rose to become speaker of the Lower Creeks. Despite his prior allegiance to the British, he had now become a fast friend of the United States.

The opposition in the Muskogee Nation to the Big Warrior's clique was led by an ancient and complex character called Hoboheilthle Micco by the Creeks and the Tame King or Tallassee King by the whites. As one of his white names suggests, he was chief of the town of Tallassee, located directly across the Tallapoosa River from Tuckabatchee where Uphapee Creek empties into the river. At the time of the great council, Hoboheilthle was over ninety years old, but he was mentally sharp and physically vigorous. Unlike the Little Prince, during the Revolutionary War, Hoboheilthle had been one of the few Creek leaders to side with the Americans.[19] At their instigation, he had driven the British agent, David Taitt, from old Fort Toulouse and had expropriated or destroyed all the British possessions there.

Since that time, his career had been checkered. He was, as we saw earlier, played by the Georgians during the negotiations of the disastrous treaties of Augusta, Galphinton, and Shoulderbone. A few years later, however, according to Benjamin Hawkins, the old man was instrumental in bringing to fruition the monumental Treaty of New York, which largely overturned those treaties. Hoboheilthle's image, like Alexander McGillivray's, as a disinterested advocate for his people was somewhat tarnished, however, by the pension he was given by the United States in the secret articles of that treaty.

Ironically, the Treaty of New York became the Tallassee King's undoing. Following that treaty, the United States appointed James Seagrove as its agent to the Creeks. After the great McGillivray's death, a struggle for leadership of the nation ensued. Seagrove's primary task was to oversee the implementation of the terms of the Treaty of New York. Seagrove, who was afraid of the Creeks and lived outside the nation near the Georgia coast, interjected himself in this internal power struggle on the side of Hoboheilthle's rivals, the Big Warrior and the Little Prince.[20] Ultimately, Hoboheilthle's rivals prevailed, and Seagrove's officious intermeddling in the nation's affairs turned Hoboheilthle's friendship for the United States into enmity, and he withdrew from any involvement in Muskogee politics.

When President Washington chose his friend Benjamin Hawkins, in 1797, to replace the timorous and bumbling Seagrove as agent to the Creeks, Hawkins determined to win Hoboheilthle back into the American camp. As a member of the generation of young men who gained US independence from Great Britain, Hawkins had a deep appreciation for the old chief's support of the colonial cause. After several years, Hawkins's persistence paid off, and the old chief returned to the nation's political arena. Before long he had won control of the nation's political leadership. This triumph, however, lasted only several years. The Big Warrior and the Little Prince joined forces to replace Hoboheilthle's faction as the nation's leaders.

Even after this political defeat, Hawkins retained his fondness for the old chief. The agent also found him useful in countering the endless schemes of the Big Warrior.[21] In spring 1810, the Big Warrior conceived the notion of a league of the southern tribes under the leadership of the Muskogee Nation—meaning the Big Warrior. Whatever his motivation, the Tuckabatchee chief's stated reason for this coalition was sound: to prevent the sale of Indian land to the whites. But Hawkins, whose loyalties were first and foremost to the United States, was determined to derail the Big Warrior's plans. To that end, Hawkins, who knew that Hoboheilthle was dismissive of the Big Warrior's enterprise as "visionary," enlisted Hoboheilthle's aid to sabotage his hated rival's designs. [22] The two men succeeded in thwarting the Big Warrior's ambitions.

In his opposition to the rapacious Americans, Hoboheilthle's principal henchman was the rabidly anti-American Peter McQueen. McQueen was the leading warrior of Tallassee, a brave man but with a pronounced vicious streak. He was the son of a Creek woman and a Scottish deserter from the British navy, James McQueen. The elder McQueen, who was said to have been born in 1683, had reached the incredible age of 128 when he died in 1811. The father had arrived in the nation in 1716, and over the years had prospered in trade with the Indians. His son, Peter, had apparently inherited his father's business acumen, for he also had become a successful trader and planter, owning substantial holdings in land, livestock, and slaves.[23]

Thus, on the eve of the most important national council in Muskogee history, the nation was fatally divided into two factions that hated each other. Following Tecumseh's appearance at that council, and thanks to Tecumseh, a third and more dangerous faction would soon spring up in the Creek Nation to vie for the leadership of its people.

The Great Council of the Creeks

I T could hardly have been coincidence that Tecumseh timed his appearance at Tuckabatchee with the opening of the Nation's great council. This event brought together some five thousand people: warriors and their families from all over the nation and from neighboring nations—Cherokee, Choctaw, and Chickasaw. Also in attendance was a motley collection of non-Indians: American and British traders, many with Indian wives; African slaves and free Africans; and people from a wildly variant mixture of racial and national origins—Indian, African, British, French, Spanish, white, and black—so that a virtual Babel of tongues lashed the air like disparate flocks of raucous birds. All these peoples had a variety of motives for attending this hybrid legislative conclave, sports festival, and outdoor party, not the least of which were political power, money, land, and a good time fueled by ample supplies of the fiery, rotgut trade rum known as tafia.

Although a number in the crowd at Tuckabatchee had come for a rollicking frolic or to make an easy dollar, the subject of the council meeting was one freighted with great danger for the Muskogee Nation. Over many centuries, the abodes of the Indian peoples in the Old Southwest had been connected by a network of paths large enough to accommodate not only foot traffic but horses and cattle as well.[24] Indeed a major pathway known as the Wolf Path was the primary artery of trade connecting the nation with the Spanish town of Pensacola, and its British trading house John Forbes & Company, successor to Alexander McGillivray's old firm of Panton, Leslie & Co. Along this path the Creeks led trains of the small but sturdy Indian packhorses loaded with bales of deerskins and other animal pelts, barrels of honey, containers of bear oil and hickory-nut oil, and a constellation of other Creek commodities. The Creeks also drove herds of cattle to the coastal markets. When the Indians returned home, their horses were laden with household utensils, clothing, blankets, and colorful fabrics, items of personal adornment such as beads and silver jewelry, salt, and most important of all guns, powder, and ammunition. The American government had now decided that this pathway was to be enlarged to form with other Indian paths a road running from the capital of Georgia at Milledgeville to New Orleans.[25]

For the Americans, however, the roadway they sought to build through the nation had little or nothing to do with trade with the Spanish and British merchants at Pensacola and the nearby town of Mobile. The Americans' initial objective was to facilitate communications with their military facilities in Louisiana and Mississippi in anticipation of a coming war with Great Britain. To achieve their military objectives, the Americans required a road wide enough and stable enough underfoot to accommodate legions of marching soldiers, heavy supply wagons, and artillery trains. A secondary objective, at least for the moment, was to provide potential settlers a more convenient route to the isolated island of American lands lying between the Creek and Choctaw nations at the fork of the Alabama and Tombigbee rivers.

The American interest in a right-of-way through the nation was not new. Under the 1805 Treaty of Washington, the Creeks not only ceded a section of their lands in north central Georgia to the United States but gave the United States the right to construct a "horse path" for the transportation of US mail between the American settlements in middle Georgia and those in the Mississippi Territory. Construction on the path began in 1806.[26] The objective was straightforward, the task was anything but. For several hundred miles, a four-foot right-of-way had to be cut through dense forests and canebrakes, and bridged over the frequent swamps and numerous streams, that lay between Fort Hawkins in Georgia and Fort Stoddert in the Mississippi Territory. Following its completion in 1806, and until 1811, the path was principally used for postal delivery and trade, although it became most famous for its use by the US military to transport former vice president Aaron Burr, who had been charged with treason, from southwestern Alabama, where he had been captured, through the Creek Nation to his eventual trial in Richmond, Virginia.

By 1809, as the result of rising tensions with the British and the increasing possibility of war, the post road came to the attention of military planners in Washington, who soon envisioned enlarging the narrow horse path into a military highway to New Orleans.[27] The Americans also wanted to build a second road from the Tennessee settlements to Mobile to facilitate access to that port for trade. Initially the Creeks were consulted, cosmetically as it turns out, at the presidential level about the proposed military road through their nation. But the Creeks flatly rejected President James Madison's proposal as well as a separate one for a "water path" along the

Coosa-Alabama River system to Mobile. In a lengthy letter to the president dated May 15, 1811, Hoboheilthle (who ironically was still receiving secret payments from the Americans for his role in selling Creek lands) eloquently set forth the reasons why his people objected to the road being built. He first thanked Madison for seeking the Creeks' permission to build the road "without doing it first." The old chief then told the president that the "little path" through the nation was already causing conflict between the young Creek warriors and the whites and that the construction of a military road would only increase that conflict. The Indians, he said, "have a little sense yet"; God had given his people their lands "to walk on," and for them to relinquish their ancient right to control traffic through the lands or on the waters of the nation "would not do." The "chiefs and warriors now present will never say yes," he told Madison, and the whites should not mention the road again.[28] Some months later the whites did mention the road again to the Creeks, but by then it was already being constructed.

By late summer 1810, Lieutenant John Luckett of the 2nd US Infantry had already quietly conducted a survey through Creek land of several hundred miles of the proposed road. Over many arduous days through rough country he had pursued his task all the way from the Tensaw River to a creek near present-day Montgomery, Alabama. There his work was abruptly stopped by a party of Creek warriors—remarkably, without bloodshed. However, in July 1811, two months after Hoboheilthle had written Madison that the road was unacceptable to the Creeks, the federal government ordered the commander of the Southern Theater (or the 7th US Military District as it was officially known), Brigadier General Wade Hampton, to begin immediate construction of a wagon road through the nation.[29] Hawkins was tasked by his government to deliver the bad news to the Creeks and quietly went about organizing a national council at Tuckabatchee in which to do so.

In late August, the Upper Creek chiefs invited Hawkins to a council to be held at Tuckabatchee on September 15, 1811. The council was to include not only Creeks but Cherokees, Choctaws, and Chickasaws as well. The Choctaws and Chickasaws were principally there because a second road that the United States planned to run from Nashville to Fort Stoddert on the Mobile River would run through their lands as well. Thus, the main subject of the meeting was to be the roads, although the Cherokees also planned to discuss boundary issues with the Creeks.[30]

As a US senator from North Carolina, Hawkins had been a distinguished member of a Congress that contained some of the most intelligent and politically talented members in US history. It was also a Congress whose members, under the Articles of Confederation, represented individual and competing states within a polity that in some respects resembled the Creek Confederation of separate and distinct tribes. Thus, the former senator understood what he was about when he approached the problem of reconciling the leaders of the Creek Nation to the de facto decision of the United States to build the hated road. Knowing the temper of the Upper Creeks, Hawkins wisely did not dare broach at the council the equally obnoxious subject of American river travel through the nation. That would come later. As Hawkins explained to General Hampton, his plan was to use the council to secure the chiefs' official blessing for the roads: "I shall do whatever depends upon me to obtain their assent to the just expectations of the government, and if they refuse their assent I shall let them know the determination of the government that the thing must and will be done."[31]

Hawkins also cynically, but realistically, recognized that the construction of the road was merely one piece in the expansion of American territory at the expense of Indian lands. As he wrote the governor of Georgia, David B. Mitchell, about a month before the great council: "I know the United States are bound to extinguish the claims of the Indians to the lands [in Georgia] as far as Chattahoochee for the accommodation of Georgia when it can be done peacefully and for a reasonable price."[32]

The council actually assembled on September 17. Beforehand, Hawkins had skillfully lobbied his allies among the chiefs to support the US government's "request" to build the road. Although it appears that Hawkins did not provide the chiefs with direct monetary inducements for their support, he did point out to them the nice fees they could earn from travelers by operating ferries and rest stops along the way. He also probably utilized the carrot of the government subsidy already paid to certain chiefs, and the stick of its discontinuation. Nonetheless, prior to the opening of the national council, only a Coweta chief had openly given his assent. The others awaited the council debate because at this time they thought it "impolitic to give their public assent."

Ultimately, the council was a sham, staged by Hawkins and his Creek allies to give the pliant chiefs political cover. For while Hawkins was busy lobbying the old chiefs for their support, not only had the federal government let contracts for the road's construction but, back in Georgia, the road was already being built.[33] Indeed, the opportunistic William McIntosh had already begun scheming to have the road run by his plantation.[34] Nonetheless, on September 17, Hawkins convened the council for what the chiefs not in the know thought was an honest debate among the leaders of the nation whether to authorize or reject the building of the road.[35] Thus Hawkins had to stage manage a sham debate to mask the fact of the chiefs' prior understanding with Hawkins that the road would be approved.

The bogus debate raged for three days in the great council house of the Upper Creeks just off of the town square. Hawkins opened the affair through his mixed-blood interpreter Alexander Cornells, who was also one of Hawkins's subagents and a Tuckabatchee chief as well. Through Cornells, he advised the assembled chiefs that the president of the United States had read their May 1811 letter to him and found it "unreasonable and unsatisfactory." The president, Hawkins explained, viewed the Indians and the whites, at least for the purpose of free travel, as one people. Just as the Indians had the right to travel freely through the white lands, so should the whites have the right to free travel through the Indian lands. The issue of the road came down to a matter of fairness, he told them.

At that point in his talk, Hawkins switched from the carrot of reason to the stick of coercion. As the Indians well knew, he reminded them, the Americans had troops along all the Indian borders. They had been placed there, he told them, at great expense to the United States to prevent the whites from encroaching on the Indian lands. Hawkins's not so subtle message was that the troops could easily turn their coats from protectors to adversaries. Then, switching back to the carrot, he explained that the road was for the benefit of the Indians as well as the whites. Once the road was in place, the Indians would have the right to charge travelers tolls for the use of its bridges and ferries over the numerous rivers and myriad creeks along the way. The Creeks could also make money by establishing inns beside the road for the rest and refreshment of weary travelers— meaning, of course, that the entrepreneurial and self-aggrandizing chiefs like the Big Warrior and William McIntosh and their associates could grow rich from the traffic of the whites on the roads.[36]

No doubt Hoboheilthlee expressed, loudly and at length, outrage at Hawkins's proposal. Other chiefs, mostly Upper Creeks, would have added support to Hoboheilthle's objections. The dissenters probably even included the hypocritical Big Warrior, and perhaps some of Hawkins's Lower Creek friends, as a way of covering their role in the conspiracy with Hawkins to build the road. A primary and forceful argument marshaled by Hoboheilthle and the antiroad faction was that the road would create a serious source of conflict between the Americans and the Indians. The temper of their young warriors about the road was such, Hoboheilthle argued, that the chiefs would have great difficulty in protecting the lives and property of the travelers from these young hotheads. Such incidents could easily give rise to war.

On the evening of September 19, into the turbulent midst of the road debate, Tecumseh and his party entered Tuckabatchee. The next day the council resumed its deliberations. Along with the numerous Creek chiefs in attendance there were nineteen Choctaws, forty-six Cherokees, and several Chickasaw representatives.[37] The latter tribes were involved because the Americans also planned to construct a second road in the region running from Nashville to Mobile. As Hawkins explained to these three western tribes, the people of Tennessee "must have a road to Mobile" to transport their goods to market, and the United States required a thoroughfare to expedite travel of its military forces from "post to post."[38] This road would run through the territory of all these tribes.

Tecumseh and his companions were allowed to attend the council. Hawkins counted among their party sixteen Shawnees and several Indians from unknown tribes who, for lack of an interpreter, Hawkins was unable to identify.[39] For some unknown reason, Hawkins made no protest at their attendance at a council among the southern tribes to debate a critical issue in which these northern Indians had no legitimate interest. Undoubtedly, Tecumseh's friends among the Creeks, probably some powerful chiefs such as Hoboheilthle and Peter McQueen, and the hotheaded chief known as the Little Warrior, had advised Tecumseh of the council and briefed him of its proceedings before the Shawnee chief ever left the Hickory Ground for Tuckabatchee. They probably also used their considerable influence to arrange for him and his companions to be admitted to the deliberations. Hawkins cannot have been pleased at the sudden appearance of these utter strangers, but he was also so confident in his ability to control the outcome of the debate that he decided not to make it an issue with Tecumseh's powerful friends.

Hawkins did not have to wait long to regret the northern Indians' intrusion. Some of these northerners from two tribes living far up the west bank of the Mississippi, perhaps the unidentified Indians, brought an elaborate war pipe to the council. They wanted the Creeks to smoke from the pipe as a seal on a promise to ally with them in a war against the Americans. One of the party raised the pipe aloft to the crowd around them as a silent token of their purpose. The northerners then began a lengthy harangue to the assembly, enumerating the wrongs the Indian people had suffered at the hands of the Americans and the threat the Americans posed to the Indians' very existence. The only way left to the Indians to counter this threat, they told the Creeks, was for all Indian people join in an alliance against the whites. At the end of their talk, one of the northerners, gripping the lit pipe in both hands, dramatically extended it to the assembled chiefs. In a loud voice he invited them to smoke the pipe as a seal on their promise to join the northerners in an alliance against the Americans.

With Hawkins looking on, the Creek chiefs one by one refused the pipe. To Hawkins's great satisfaction, a number of them denounced the very idea of war against the whites. Through all these back-and-forth speeches, Tecumseh remained silent, taking the temperature of the proceedings. He had obviously known beforehand of, and may even have orchestrated, the pipe-smoking presentation. He now saw for himself the extent of the influence Hawkins and his allies had over the Creeks. Evening had arrived when the northern war pipe was placed in its case and its humiliated custodian fell silent. It was then that Tecumseh rose, with Seekaboo at his side to interpret his words. Artfully dissembling, Tecumseh reassured his audience that although he had traveled with the far western Indians who carried the pipe, the plan it symbolized should be rejected. He believed strongly, he said, that the Indians should unite, but they should unite in a peace that eliminated the constant internecine warfare among the tribes. As for the Americans, there must be peace with them as well.[40]

Although it appears that Tecumseh attended the debate about the road and made the conciliatory talk reported by Hawkins, Tecumseh refused to address his real message to the nation while Hawkins was present. Instead, he and his companions bided their time, mingling with the delegates and building support for Tecumseh's plan of unity. At night, Tecumseh and his men performed in the town square what was known as the Dance of the Lakes. The dance mimicked the events of a successful battle between Tecumseh's party and their enemies. This performance was unusually well acted and was a novelty for the Creeks, who customarily danced after, not before, a war had been fought. During the daylight hours, however, the northerners remained secluded in the residential quarters of the town.

The desire among the crowd at Tuckabatchee to hear Tecumseh speak grew more pronounced by the day. Tecumseh, however, did not wish to make his talk until Hawkins had departed the town. To excuse his delay in delivering his speech, Tecumseh came up with a somewhat implausible ploy. At the close of each afternoon, Tecumseh would announce to the crowd that the sun had traveled too far in the sky to give him sufficient time to present his speech. Still the debate over the road continued, and still Tecumseh continued to make his excuse to the crowd.

Hawkins understood the Creeks' love of a spirited argument and let the debate continue for three days before he finally lost patience with the council. Rising from his seat, Hawkins, through his interpreter, quieted the chiefs. When he had their attention, he told them flatly that he had not come before them "to ask their permission to open a road but to inform them that it was now cutting."[41] Hoboheilthle and his adherents must have been stunned by Hawkins's betrayal and utter bad faith, and furious at the way Hawkins had duped them. Nonetheless, Hawkins's peremptory announcement did not end the council. For it was not until September 26 that the Creeks signed the road convention Hawkins drew up. But even the signing did not end matters. Opponents of the road forced the council to reconsider its acceptance, a process that took two days. Finally, the power of Hawkins's allies among the Lower Creeks and the power of Big Warrior and his adherents prevailed. On September 28, 1811, the road convention was reconsidered and unanimously ratified by the council. Satisfied with his achievement, Hawkins left for home that day. By September 30, he was back at the agency.[42]

Hawkins's mission had ended "happily." As he boasted to Madison in a letter dated October 13, 1811, permission from the Creeks to build the road and to allow the Americans to pass unmolested along its course had cost only a "mere tith, considering the extent of territory thro which they are to pass and the wildness of our people."[43] That "tith" consisted of a promise by the United States to provide the Creeks with one thousand spinning wheels and one thousand pair of cotton cards to comb the cotton strands over the next three years, along with delivery of a ton and a half of iron to the Upper and Lower Creeks respectively. The Creeks were also to enjoy the right to charge reasonable tolls for ferries and bridges to travelers who used the road. Finally, the United States would provide two blacksmiths to work in the nation.[44] In signing the road convention, the Creeks had essentially signed the death warrant of their nation

With Hawkins's departure, Tecumseh felt free to expand his audience from private meetings with sympathetic chiefs to a wider Indian public. Already he appears to have cultivated relationships with powerful chiefs such as Hoboheilthle; McQueen; Menawa, the famous Okfuskee leader; and other chiefs who bitterly opposed the federal road and were furious at the high-handed way Hawkins and his Indian allies had imposed its construction on the nation. At the same time, Seekaboo was doubtless finding allies among the Creek religious leaders. Nonetheless, Tecumseh still had to take care to conceal his plans from the general public. Scattered among the thousands of Indians at Tuckabatchee were a number of Americans who had come to the great council for trade and a frolic, and who would report to the authorities any threat against their country. Also at Tuckabatchee were agency employees such as Alexander Cornells, who was also a chief of that town, not to mention members of rival tribes such as the Cherokee, and Lower Creeks sympathetic to Hawkins's plan of civilization. Thomas Woodward, a participant in the Creek War and author of a series of letters describing the conflict, says that William McIntosh, speaker of the Lower Creeks, was Hawkins's spy.[45] Confident of his influence over the nation and that he would receive a full report from his informants of any further council proceedings—and strangely ignorant of Tecumseh's true influence and power among the northern Indians and of the Shawnee's unequalled leadership abilities and persuasive powers—Hawkins left for his comfortable home well content that he had succeeded in his mission to persuade the chiefs to concede a further piece of the nations' sovereignty to the Americans.

Although the accounts are conflicting, it appears clear that Tecumseh had decided to deliver at Tuckabatchee two talks, each tailored to a different audience. One talk he would make in the town square, under the open night sky, beneath the streaming banner light of the comet, to the thousands attending the council. The other talk he would make to a select audience of Creek miccos and leading men within the guarded confines of the town's rotunda.

Both of Tecumseh's talks shared two common threads: the Indian people should return to their old customs and way of life—although neither the least sophisticated and most isolated among his audience could remember a time without the white men and their enticing trade goods— and the Indian nations should unite to preserve their remaining lands from the Americans. The key difference between the two talks was how the native peoples would achieve those goals, through passive or active resistance.

Whatever he might say to the masses, Tecumseh was under no illusions that the Indians could preserve their land and achieve an idyllic cultural purification without considerable help from the white man's technology, and a large dose of severe violence, including a widespread war. When he began his journey south, Tecumseh was well aware that war between the Americans and Great Britain was looming. He had already obtained from the British somewhat nebulous promises of British aid in his own plan to stop American expansion. But timing was critical. On the southern frontier, ambitious and rapacious Americans led by men such as Governor Willie Blount and Andrew Jackson of Tennessee, Governor Mitchell of Georgia, and a group of Mississippi planters and politicians centered on the town of Natchez and led by the Claiborne brothers were looking for any excuse to help themselves to the rich Indian lands abutting their respective settlements.

The Indians' putative allies—the British—were engaged in a vicious struggle with Napoleonic France in Spain. Until the British were ready for a North American war, the Indians were isolated against the powerful Americans. Thus, Tecumseh had to proceed carefully to maintain a delicate balance between unifying the Indian people against the Americans without prematurely provoking war with them.

Tecumseh's public talk in the great town square was his usual piece of spectacular showmanship and oratory.[46] It took place late at night and began with the entrance of Tecumseh at the head of his twenty-some companions into the middle of a throng of thousands massed cheek to jowl around the square. The Indians in the crowd dressed in their fantastical finery of brightly colored cloth, silver ornaments, and feathered headgear; the whites in drabber attire of cloth shirts and buckskin leggings. Many in the crowd, Indian and white alike, were no doubt severely drunk on cheap rum from Pensacola, and to them, at least, the temperance part of Tecumseh's speech would be unwelcome. Nonetheless, however raucous the expectant throngs gathered around the perimeter of the square might have been, they went eerily silent when Tecumseh and his companions entered.

The northern Indians were almost naked, painted black, and armed with tomahawks and scalping knives. With Tecumseh at their head and Seekaboo right behind him, they marched single file into the square with great dignity and no expression on their faces. Once they reached the square's center, they stopped and gathered behind their leader. There in the warm Alabama night, with the firelight around and the comet's strange light above, Tecumseh stood quiet and motionless, milking the expectant silence of several thousand men, women, and children of all races. Finally, a studiously composed Tecumseh delivered his oration—forcefully, eloquently, and at great length. Although he spoke through the interpreter Seekaboo, his delivery was as expressive as his words. As in all the talks he gave during his travels, Tecumseh emphasized from the start that his words were those of the Master of Breath, directed through him, to all the Indian peoples. He spoke of the great danger facing the native people from the growing power of the Americans and their insatiable hunger for the Indian lands. He traced for his audience the first coming of the whites to the continent. The Europeans were weak then, he said, but under kind treatment by the Indian people they grew strong, like a serpent warmed by the sun. And like a serpent, once they had grown strong, they repaid the Indians' kindness with the serpent's sharp tooth of death and destruction.

Tecumseh also pointed out that the Indians had allowed themselves to be so seduced by the white man's goods and culture that they had become risible imitations of the whites. Tecumseh advised his audience that if the Indians were going to stop the avalanche of white settlers onto their lands, they must cast off white ways and abandon the very program of agriculture and textile production that Hawkins was attempting to foist upon them. Tecumseh urged his Native American listeners to toss away the hoe and spade, the cotton cards and spinning wheels, and return to their traditional methods of feeding and clothing themselves. To the discomfort of the many drunks in the crowd, the teetotaler Tecumseh urged the Indians to cast off their love of the liquor that white men had introduced among them; alcohol was the poison the whites employed to destroy the Indian soul. What Tecumseh did not counsel in this talk was war with the Americans. Nor did he reveal to the crowd promises of British and Spanish aid in that war. Instead, he advocated peace with the Indians' white neighbors.[47]

Tecumseh's public speech, which was calculated to allay white fears, was followed by his private one. That speech was delivered at midnight in the great rotunda to a select crowd of Indian leaders. The audience members seated themselves according to rank and tribe along the three tiers of benches lining the walls. The building's interior was lit only by its central fire mound, with the bowls of the Indians' pipes winking in the dark along the walls, leaving the air thick with the smoke and the bittersweet smell of tobacco. The sources are not all in agreement as to the exact text of Tecumseh's speech to this assembly, but its principal elements are not in serious dispute. It was here, outside the presence of the Americans, that Tecumseh fully revealed his plans for an Indian confederacy aimed at driving the Americans from Indian lands. His talk was said to have been a masterpiece of oratory and showmanship, delivered with great force and eloquence but with an underlying dignity much appreciated by an Indian audience.[48] In it he counseled not only the need for Indian unity but also for all-out war by a confederacy of all Indian people against the Americans. Their old fathers the British would help them defeat the Americans, but even more importantly, if the Indians threw off the corrupting mantle of white ways, the Master of Breath would cause the earth to swallow up any armies the Americans sent against them. Although not reported by the chroniclers of this speech, a man of Tecumseh's cunning would also have undoubtedly played to the powerful Hoboheilthle and his faction in the audience and woven into his talk a red thread of outrage at Hawkins's imperious manipulation of the Creeks in connection with the Federal Road issue.

Probably all in the crowed rotunda were moved by Tecumseh's eloquence and that of Seekaboo, who followed him with a talk of a new religion that simply required the people to return to the ways of their ancestors. Not all among his audience, however, were convinced of the advisability of going to war against the Americans. The entrepreneur Sam Moniac confronted Tecumseh and told him that his war talk was wrong, that the Americans were too strong for even a united Indian people to defeat.[49] As for Tecumseh's promise of British aid, Moniac pointed out that over a quarter of a century ago, when the Americans were far weaker than they were now, the Americans had defeated the British and drove them over the sea. The Coosada chief, Captain Sam Isaacs, was even more confrontational. Ever the blowhard and bully—at least when safely surrounded by a coterie of his henchmen—he told his listeners that Tecumseh was a bad man and urged them not to regard the Shawnee's counsel.

William Weatherford, destined to be the most famous of the Creek leaders during the war, echoed his friend and kinsman Sam Moniac's sentiments. Weatherford was yet another of the Métis who had risen to prominence among the Creeks. As befitted the son of the rascally Charles Weatherford, William Weatherford was somewhat of a Creek Prince Hal and had enjoyed a dissolute youth. He had gained fame among the Creeks as a captor of Augustus Bowles and was now renowned among the Creeks for his physical and martial prowess. At six feet two inches, he was taller than Tecumseh and had the latter's athletic build and handsome features. Also like Tecumseh, he was fearless. Although not a chief at the time or ever, he had risen to prominence as a leader among the Muskogee Nation.

As evidence of that status, he now dared speak at this critical council among the nation's leaders.

Like his friend and former brother-in-law Moniac, Weatherford had ample appreciation of American power. Take no side, he advised the Creeks, in the war that was coming between the British and the Americans. The Muskogee people should well remember that when the British were in power, they treated the Indians as badly as or worse than the Americans. Like Moniac, he reminded his audience that the Americans had beaten the British when the Americans were much weaker. The second time around would be no different, Weatherford predicted. If the Creeks sided with the British in this second war, he warned, the Americans would exact a terrible revenge against the Indians. Indeed, Weatherford counseled, in a war between the two white nations it would be better for the Indians to support the Americans.[50]

The Lower Creek leaders almost certainly echoed these sentiments. The Big Warrior, however, was too sly to take sides at this time. Like Moniac and Weatherford, he believed that war with the Americans would bring the destruction of the nation and, more importantly, an end to the power and prosperity the Big Warrior enjoyed under the status quo. Tecumseh was a compelling figure, and the Big Warrior had no love for the Americans, but upon reflection, the Tuckabatchee chief became so afraid of the danger Tecumseh posed that he and his intimates discussed assassinating Tecumseh. However, unlike Pushmataha, the Big Warrior was not politically powerful enough, and certainly not courageous enough, to move against Tecumseh on his own. Thus, when the Big Warrior's cronies advised him not to murder Tecumseh, because of the terrible dishonor that would fall upon the whole nation for murdering their guest, he abandoned his assassination plan. He soon came to regret this failure of will.

For his part, Tecumseh immediately saw through the Big Warrior's dissembling, and it enraged him. Either during Tecumseh's speech in the rotunda, or more likely sometime later in the Big Warrior's cabin, Tecumseh faced his spotted host and accused him of double-dealing. You have a white heart, Tecumseh told the cowering giant, and for all your feigned friendship, you are an enemy of the Indian people. Tecumseh is said by most sources to have threatened the Big Warrior: "You do not believe the Great Spirit has sent me. You shall believe it. I will leave directly and go straight to Detroit. When I get there I will stamp my foot upon the ground and shake down every house in Tookabatcha."[51]

Notwithstanding his threat to the Big Warrior, Tecumseh did not "leave directly" for Detroit but spent some more weeks traveling among Creek towns politicking for an Indian confederacy. When Tecumseh left the Creek Nation he rode north in a futile attempt to persuade the Cherokees to join his confederation. When he finally departed for home in December,

Tecumseh left behind with the Creeks Seekaboo and several Shawnee prophets. Their task was to recruit followers and turn the Creeks' minds toward war with the Americans. In this task they were both aided and used by men like Hoboheilthle. With the Americans' road-building treachery fresh on his mind, Hoboheilthle needed no further convincing from any Shawnee prophets about the American threat to his people. But the old warrior recognized that he could use the prophets to mold the disaffected and superstitious Creek masses into a serious party in opposition to those Creeks friendly with the Americans.[52]

Nonetheless, despite the converts won by Tecumseh's speeches and politicking, and the anger of many Creeks about the road, the prophets had much work to do before the majority of the Creeks were ready to risk war with the Americans. It would take the most violent natural event to strike the North American continent in recorded history, and a subsequent train of human violence, to help them reach that disastrous state of mind.

A People Gone Mad

T HE ancient Greeks poetically said that before the gods destroy a man they first render him mad. The great twentieth century historian Barbara Tuchman described this condition in political entities as the perverse "pursuit by governments of policies contrary to their own interests."[53] Benjamin Hawkins, neither a poet nor a historian, simply called it fanaticism.[54] Whatever the condition was called, in the months following Tecumseh's visit to the nation, many of the Muskogee people and their government were fast tumbling into that state. The superstitious would say that the hell that followed was heralded by the earth itself going mad.

Four hundred miles northwest of Tuckabatchee, on the western plain above the Mississippi River, not far downriver from Saint Louis, Missouri, lay a little town of four hundred souls. Known as New Madrid, the town was founded in 1789, in what was then Spanish territory, by a Kentucky entrepreneur and Revolutionary War notable named John Morgan. Morgan had politically named the town for the capital of Spain, and for a time the place prospered, situated as it was between Saint Louis and New Orleans on a great waterway forming the border between two empires. However, by the time Tecumseh spoke at Tuckabatchee, New Madrid was in decline. The Louisiana Purchase had erased its border advantage. And its fading fortunes were further hurried along by the river, which during every flood season gnawed out house-sized chunks of the high banks on which the town was built. On December 16, 1811, about the time Tecumseh should have reached Detroit, the town was down to four hundred residents and steadily disappearing into the Mississippi River. On that day, New Madrid also lay upon what was then the most dangerous patch of earth on the planet.[55]

Morgan had had the bad fortune of situating his new town over one of the fault lines that loosely stitch the tectonic plates of the Earth's crust together. This fault was unusual, however, in that it existed as a weak spot within a single plate known as an intraplate fault. Around 2:00 A.M. on Sunday, December 16, 1811, the geological stitching holding the plate together unraveled, the edges of the rip in the plate slipped, and an estimated 7.2 to 8.1 of Richter scale hell opened beneath New Madrid and the surrounding countryside. To the accompaniment of sounds erupting in the black of night like the boom of cannon signaling the onset of battle, or trumpets sounding the beginning of the Apocalypse, the ground beneath the town began to undulate like the deck of a storm-enveloped ship. People were tossed from their beds and even out of their homes, chimneys fell, and houses were torn apart. The cries of tens of thousands of terrified birds came out of the darkness, and the poor creatures fell from the sky and landed on the heads and shoulders of equally terrified human beings as if to seek a little comfort there. As the earth ripped apart in crevasses that ran for miles and shot columns of sand into the sky like oil from a blown well, clouds of sulfurous air rolled over the tormented earth. Where there had been land there was now water, and where water had lain there was now dry earth. And most amazing of all, the Mississippi began to writhe in its bed like a serpent whose head has been crushed beneath a farmer's heel. At one point along the river's length, the land beneath it rose so high that its tremendous waters ran backward.[56]

Immediately, the first shock waves reverberated outward through the Earth's frame from the epicenter of the quake, as if struck by the clapper from a metal bell, and radiated out at supersonic speed from the epicenter around New Madrid for hundreds of miles. Minutes after the first quake shook New Madrid, it traveled through the hard stone of the Atlantic plate into the Creek Nation. Around 2:30 A.M., the first of the New Madrid earthquakes struck Tuckabatchee, reportedly damaging much of the town and shaking the earth all the way to Charleston to the east, Mexico to the south, and Canada to the north.[57] A report from Milledgeville, Georgia, the nearest American town to Tuckabatchee and about 150 miles to the east, described an event that lasted several minutes, shaking the ground beneath the little town of fewer than two thousand, violently agitating the houses, throwing open doors, and, in some instances, tossing furniture from the houses.[58] While terrified citizens fled into the streets, above the uproar and confusion, the bell at the statehouse clanged maniacally, as if signaling the advent of Judgment Day. A second violent temblor hit the region at 7:00 A.M., then a third at 10 and a fourth around noon the following day.

To the west of Tuckabatchee, in what must have been a typical experience, a young girl named Margaret Eades was traveling from Tennessee with her family to the settlements in the Tensaw River delta, known to the frontier people as the Forks, when the temblors first hit. Years later, Miss Eades, then married to Jeremy Austill, penned a memoir of her adventures during her early girlhood in the wilds of Alabama. She had survived the Creek War and married one of the American heroes of that war. Among the most memorable of her adventures was the quake: "One night after a fearful day, the Indians had followed us for miles, we camped in an old field. Just as supper was announced, a most terrific earthquake took place, the horses all broke loose, the wagon chains jingled, and every face was pale with fear and terror. The Indians came in numbers looking frightened, and grunting out their prayers, and oh, the night was spent in terror by all but the next day some of the Indians came to us and said it was Tecumseh stamping his foot for war."[59]

On New Year's Day 1812, Benjamin Hawkins fell ill with what he called pleurisy. His condition so quickly and seriously worsened that by the end of the week it was thought that he could die at anytime. He rallied on the seventh, but by the night of January 9, Hawkins was so ill that he took (for him) the drastic step of making a will and marrying Livinia Downs, his common-law wife and mother of his six daughters (the last daughter, Jeffersonia, was born after his will was made). These acts appear to have bestowed some measure of grace on Hawkins, for almost like a sign from Providence, on the night of the tenth, a peaceful foot of snow descended from the heavens, and soon thereafter Hawkins began to recover. On January 12, he was well enough to write a letter to Secretary of War William Eustis describing a recent discussion he had had with Tustannugee Hopei of Tuckabatchee concerning that warrior's interview with "the Shawnee deputation," which was proselytizing among the Creeks. As Hawkins informed Eustis, Tustannugee was a young warrior of high rank among the Creeks who administered the functions of the nation's executive council. One day, after listening to the preaching of the Shawnees and their descriptions of their conversations with God on Indian affairs, Tustannugee decided to interview them "to discover the meaning of what they heard as to detail it to [Hawkins]."[60]

Some of Tustannugee's associates accompanied him to the interview, and collectively they came away with the opinion that the prophets' leader, the mixed-blood Creek Haujo Haugee, formerly known as Josiah Francis, was both a madman and a liar and was best ignored. This opinion and advice, from a respected Creek leader, coincided with Hawkins's own, and to the great peril of his life's work and the future of the nation, he and the Creek leaders foolishly followed the course recommended by Tustannugee.

But war with the Americans was not yet at hand. Even after the terrible first temblors struck, and even after equally strong quakes persisted through December and into January and February, many Creeks resisted Tecumseh's call to war with the Americans. Indeed, not long after the earthquakes had ceased, Hawkins wrote on March 30, 1812, to Eustis that the Creeks were busily occupied in such peaceful pursuits as agriculture, spinning thread, weaving cloth, settling new lands, and improving old lands.[61] Thus, the prophets still had much more work to do before the nation would be wedded to war. Nonetheless, the quakes had no doubt greatly increased the base and ardor of the prophets' followers. And several months after Hawkins's letter to Eustis, the situation became even more complex and perilous among the Creeks. On June 18, 1812, a woefully unprepared United States declared war on Great Britain.

When Tecumseh left the Creek Nation, he left behind him the seeds of its destruction in the form of a mysterious figure known as Seekaboo. Seekaboo was a Creek related through his mother to Tecumseh's mother. Seekaboo's father was a white man, perhaps with Creek blood. By the time he appeared with Tecumseh at Tuckabatchee, Seekaboo was around forty. He was of average height and was considered a great warrior and a brilliant orator and linguist; in addition to Shawnee, he spoke English, Muskogee, Choctaw, and perhaps several other Indian dialects. When and how he met Tecumseh is unknown—perhaps through family, perhaps as part of the Creek contingent under Little Warrior, who had lived among and fought with the Shawnees for years. However the two men met, by the time of Tecumseh's journey to the southern tribes, Seekaboo was a trusted companion, serving Tecumseh as an interpreter and a spiritual adviser.[62]

After spending time among the Creeks, Tecumseh decided that Seekaboo should remain with them and spread through the nation the religious teachings of Tecumseh's brother, the one-eyed prophet and former drunk Tenskwatawa (meaning the Open Door). Seekaboo's talk at Tuckabatchee had made him well known among the Creeks, particularly the young men and women but also the older leaders, such as the disgruntled Hoboheilthle and his war chief, Peter McQueen. These two men cynically supported the prophets' movement in order to foster their own ambitions to unite the Creeks against the Americans and to destroy such enemies as The Big Warrior and the Lower Creek chiefs.

The prophets cleverly exploited the peoples' distaste for Hawkins's program of civilization and their hatred of the rapacious Americans to promote their nativistic religious movement. Like a virus, that movement spread quickly through the Creek Nation. Seekaboo found his first and foremost adherents among the Alabamas. It was he who probably convinced that tribe to establish a center for the new religion at a remote place on the upper Alabama River that came to be called the Holy Ground.

Seekaboo certainly was aware of a precedent for this type of town, for his mentor, Tenskwatawa, was living with his adherents at such a town he had founded on the Tippecanoe River in Indiana.

Among the Alabama tribe, Seekaboo found his greatest acolyte. Tecumseh had sent additional Shawnee prophets to the Creek Nation to assist Seekaboo in his work. However, Seekaboo wisely knew that for Tecumseh's plan to succeed, he needed to orchestrate the rise of influential prophets among the Creeks. Foremost among the men he chose was Josiah Francis. Like so many Creek leaders known to the whites, Francis was the son of a white trader of Scotch/Irish extraction and a Creek woman. The father's name was David Francis, and he operated a trading house at the town of Autauga on the upper Alabama River. He was also a silversmith, crafting various silver ornaments for his Indian customers. His son Josiah took up this trade, but as Creek and American relations deteriorated, he found a higher calling in the coming conflict.[63]

Mention of Josiah Francis is found in the Spanish records as early as 1793, in connection with saving the life of a runaway black female slave from the vengeance of a machete-wielding wife of an Indian whom the slave had murdered.[64] It appears Francis's motives were not altruistic: he saved the slave to obtain the 100 pesos offered by her owner for her capture. The only visual image we have of Francis is one by his own hand. While in England after the Creek War, seeking assistance to continue the Creeks' struggle against the Americans to get their lands back, he sketched a full-length portrait of himself. Crudely drawn, as if by a child doodling in his free time, it depicts a tall, thin man with a long, thin face ornamented by a sliver of a mustache and smoking a long-stemmed pipe. The portrait could have been one of a country schoolmaster instead of the clever huckster and vicious politician into which Seekaboo's machinations transformed the raw clay of Francis's character. But apparently Seekaboo saw something in the timid artisan that he could mine for his cause.

One day among the Alabamas, Seekaboo isolated Francis in a cabin and began conducting a wild dance, punctuated with nerve-shattering howls. For ten long days and nights Seekaboo danced, announcing to the astonished Alabamas that Francis had been struck blind by the Master of Breath in order to transform him into a great visionary. At the end of the ten-day ordeal, Seekaboo led Francis from the cabin. Like one who was truly blind, Francis stumbled out into the yard, blinking at the painful sunlight, supported by the solicitous Seekaboo—a charade made easier for Francis because of his ten-day confinement in the dark cabin.[65]

For the rest of the day, the apparently sightless Francis tiptoed about the town under Seekaboo's close care. When night fell, Francis's eyes suddenly went wide with sight to the delight of Francis and the astonishment of the townsfolk. In honor of this miracle, Seekaboo anointed Francis with the name of Hillis Hadjo, meaning the New Made Prophet. From that time on, Francis grew in reputation and power as a prophet until he became the most famous in the nation.

Perhaps Francis, in some part of his superstitious soul, particularly after the ordeal of the cabin, believed he had been transformed into a higher being. George Stiggins, the only Native American to write a history of the Creek War, tells a wonderful story about how Francis learned to write in Spanish. Each day, for some days, Francis disappeared into the forest. When his acolytes questioned him about these disappearances, Francis solemnly explained that he had gone off to commune with the Master of Breath who was tutoring Francis in the reading and writing of several languages. In this way, Francis said, he would soon be able to conduct his business with the outside world without the necessity of paying for an interpreter.

Finally the time came for Francis to demonstrate his divinely learned literary skills. In order to conduct the war with the Americans that Francis soon hoped to begin, the Creeks needed additional arms and ammunition. The best source for these commodities was the Spanish town of Pensacola. Accordingly, Francis called for paper, pen, and ink and began to compose a lengthy letter to the Spanish governor requesting arms. When the letter was completed, Francis selected some of his people to deliver the letter to the governor. First, however, he took the precaution of reading the contents to his men.

On arriving in Pensacola, Francis's emissaries went to the governor's office and presented the letter to the Spaniard. The governor, in his official dress and seated behind a large desk, impressed the Indian envoys with his authority and apparent power. He looked over the letter for a moment then burst into a rage, demanding of the terrified Indians what trick they were trying to play on him. Francis's letter was not in Spanish or in any other language the governor recognized. In fact, it contained not even one letter in any writing known to man, but was nothing more than a mass of scratchings on the paper. The governor's anger soon turned to amusement, however, when the frightened Indians collected themselves sufficiently to explain the source of the document. The governor replied that he was tempted to answer Francis's letter in kind but settled for turning the men away without the weapons and munitions for which they had come.[66] The abused Creek emissaries were not amused.

This setback for Francis's reputation was only a momentary check on his prophetic career. Explaining away failed miracles was part and parcel of the prophet's repertoire. Building on the terrifying New Madrid earthquakes, the undaunted Francis convinced many in the nation that the Maker of Breath had provided him with an arsenal of weapons to wield against the Americans that were far more powerful than any the Spanish governor could provide. He could invoke thunder and lightning or the sun or the earth to his aid. He could turn the ground about him into a sucking quagmire through which whites could not pass and draw magic circles about a place that would kill nonbelievers if they tried to step through them. Creek towns that opposed the prophets would be sunk by earthquakes or have hills turned over on them.[67]

Soon Seekaboo, Francis, and their adherents transformed the political and social landscape among the Alabamas. According to a letter Hawkins wrote to Secretary of War John Armstrong dated June 28, 1813: "The Alabamas were the most industrious and best behaved of all of our Indians. Their fields were the granary of the upper towns, and furnished considerable supplies, by water, to Mobile. But this fanaticism has rendered them quite the reverse."[68]

By the time this letter was written, many of the Upper Creek towns were with the Alabamas. However, as Francis and his disciples grew in influence in the nation, a rival prophetic power rose to challenge their religious leadership. He was Captain Isaacs, the Coosada chief and all-around troublemaker who spoke out against Tecumseh at the great council. He was not a man to miss an opportunity: a contemporary described him as "one of the most cunning, artful scamps I ever saw among the Indians."[69]

Isaacs decided to seize on the new religion of the prophets as a means to power. He began his prophetic career as a minor conjurer. In a short while, he claimed to have undergone an experience so fantastic that even Seekaboo and Francis might blush to recount it. According to Isaacs, one day he dove into the Coosa River near his home and swam to its bottom. There he encountered a gigantic serpent who befriended him; it was a curious choice of creatures, given that the serpent was preeminently evil in Creek lore.[70] Isaacs remained with his new friend beneath the water for several days while the accommodating reptile instructed him in the prophetic arts. Upon rising from the Coosa, Isaacs recounted his adventure to his people. Like ripples from a stone tossed into water, the story began to spread from Isaacs's town to every town among the nation. Without question, Isaacs's astonishing experience trumped Francis's ten-day confinement to a cabin, and Isaacs's fame grew to overshadow Francis and Seekaboo's prophetic movement.

In response to Isaacs's newly finagled power, Francis and his adherents began to plot Isaacs's downfall. They quickly spread the story among the ever-credulous Creeks that Isaacs's serpent friend was actually a diabolic spirit and that at the bottom of the river the serpent transformed Isaacs into a witch. The Creeks were terrified of witches, who they believed would take flight in the evening and cause all sorts of terrible mischief. Accordingly, if they caught a witch they burned it. Stiggins reports that popular opinion now turned against Isaacs, and he and his followers had to flee to the Big Warrior at Tuckabatchee for sanctuary. Prudently, some months earlier, Isaacs had purchased a significant amount of munitions in Pensacola. Now his train of packhorses laden with those much-needed munitions gained him prompt entrance into the Big Warrior's town, where, for the moment, he was safe from Josiah Francis and his men.[71]

In spring and summer 1812, the prophets' movement, which Hawkins and the friendly chiefs continued to ignore as mere superstitious foolery, turned deadly serious. Although its leaders were older males, its shock troops were the young men and women whom Hawkins's program of civilization threatened to disenfranchise from their centuries-old mode of existence. The Creeks' matriarchal society, which imposed many burdens on women but also gave them great power, was being eroded by the patriarchal model pushed by the Americans. The male warrior society, although it derived its power through the mother's bloodline, was a paradise for the men. It combined the noble arts of warfare and the chase, and manly games like lacrosse, with lounging about in the shade when the weather grew hot and in a snug council house when the weather grew cold, swapping tales, smoking their pipes, gambling, and getting violently drunk. The numbing drudgery of tilling the soil, managing livestock, and manufacturing cloth, which Hawkins sought to impose on these warriors and hunters, held no attraction for them—or, for that matter, the white men living in the nation—and, as generations of Creek males had been taught, it was suitable only for women or slaves. Fittingly, one of the first murderous outbursts from the prophets' party was organized by an eighteen-year-old prophet named Lectau from the town of Aubeccoche in the lower Coosa Valley.

3. The Red Clubs

The Year of the Little Blood

As Hoboheilthle had predicted, serious troubles between the Creeks and Americans soon began on the Federal Road. The floodgates through which Americans of all stripes immigrating to the Mississippi Territory poured opened in mid-October 1811. Benjamin Hawkins noted that by mid-March 1812, three thousand seven hundred of them, with their attendant wagons, carts, sedan chairs, and livestock had trooped along the road as it passed the Creek agency into the nation.[1] Given this heavy traffic, the enterprising Sam Moniac had seized on the economic possibilities the new thoroughfare presented and opened an inn along the road near Pinchony Creek, about ten miles southwest of present-day Montgomery, Alabama.[2] The first trouble between the Creeks and the Americans traveling on the road started close to Moniac's new establishment.

In early spring 1812, sixty-two-year-old Revolutionary War veteran Thomas Meredith, his wife, Abigail, their extended family, and their slaves were traveling west along the Federal Road from Georgia to the lower Alabama and Tombigbee river lands. On March 26, 1812, the Meredith party had all crossed the high-running Pinchlong Creek except for Meredith, his nine-year-old son, Thomas Jr., and an unidentified man accompanying the party.[3] As these travelers were waiting their turn to cross the stream, a group of five Creeks headed by an elderly, well-known chief called Maumouth strode heavily up to them. The Indians had probably been drinking at or had obtained liquor at Moniac's tavern just up the way. Maumouth was drunk; his companions were not. Words were exchanged with the whites; perhaps the Creeks wanted a fee to permit the crossing. Whatever the white men said, it was the wrong thing. The Creeks suddenly began to assault them with sticks and knives. Meredith and his elderly companion attempted to escape across the creek by canoe but were caught by the Indians. While his family looked on, the Creeks murdered Meredith and mortally wounded his companion.[4]

The Creeks quickly fled the scene, and the whites gathered up their dead and injured and took them to Moniac's inn. The innkeeper, although no friend of the hostiles, called it an accident, perhaps because Maumouth was drunk and the Creeks had a different view of personal responsibility than the whites of a man under the influence of alcohol, ascribing the fault to the drink rather than the man.[5] But Thomas Meredith Jr., not surprisingly, saw the death of his father as simple cold-blooded murder. Meredith was buried in the yard of Moniac's home, and the incident was reported to Hawkins by letter from the son. Hawkins, who personally liked Maumouth, demanded the Creeks render justice, which in Maumouth's case arrived slowly.[6]

Although the Meredith incident was indicative of the resentment most Creeks felt toward the white settlers moving through their lands, nothing about the incident indicates that the attack on the Meredith party was premeditated. Even Meredith's son pointed out in his description of the incident that Maumouth was drunk. Certainly Hawkins thought it an isolated, albeit serious, incident, because in his report to Secretary of War Eustis about the attack, he assured Eustis that no other American travelers on the road had since been molested. In fact, Hawkins said, the "road is crowded with travelers."[7]

The murder of Arthur Lott (whose first name is sometimes mistakenly given as William)[8] on May 23, 1812, was an altogether different matter; at least one contemporary historian, Thomas Woodward, believed that the murder even triggered the Creek War.[9] The prominent mixed-blood Sam Moniac believed the same.[10] The location of the murder is at issue. Hawkins says Lott was killed about eight miles from the Creek agency. Woodward says he was killed along the Federal Road by warriors from the Tallassee tribe near Warriors Stand, about six miles southeast of present-day Tuskegee, Alabama. A report by one of the Moravian missionaries living at the Creek agency, Johann Christian Burckhard, lends support to Woodward's story. Burckhard was traveling along the Federal Road the same day Lott was murdered and passed Warriors Stand on his way to the home of Alexander Cornells, the Creek subagent and Tuckabatchee chief. About fourteen miles from Cornells's home, which was a short distance outside of Tuckabatchee, he met several travelers who informed him of Lott's murder. When he reached the Cornells's residence, he found Lott's son there. The son gave him details of the murder and informed him that Lott had just been buried on the grounds of Cornells's plantation. Given that the Tallassees' chief town was several miles away across the Tallapoosa River from Tuckabatchee, it is reasonable to assume that they murdered Lott near their lands and not deep into Georgia near the Creek agency.[11]

What is not in dispute is the fact that Lott was traveling with some companions through Creek territory when his party was fired on by a group of four Indians belonging to a branch of the Tallassee tribe. One of the warriors fired a shot at an elderly member of Lott's party but missed. Another warrior fired at Lott and killed him. The post rider happened on the scene and rode off to alert Alex Cornells, the agency's interpreter for the Upper

Creeks, of the murder. Cornells promptly set off to investigate. One of Lott's companions took Cornells to the scene of the murder. From there the interpreter bravely tracked the murderers to their town, then reported their location to the agency.

Plainly alarmed, and feeling betrayed by Lott's murder, Hawkins complained to Secretary Eustis that the Creek leaders had solemnly assured him that the Creeks were friendly to the Americans and would make every effort to restrain their young warriors from harming the white people traveling on the road and their property. With an urgency he did not display in reaction to the Meredith killing, Hawkins ordered the chiefs to immediately convene a meeting at Tuckabatchee to discuss the apprehension and punishment of Lott's murderers. Not hearing anything from the chiefs promptly enough to satisfy him, Hawkins dispatched assistant agent Cornells and an ensign from the US Army to Tuckabatchee to hurry the chiefs along in their deliberations. As Hawkins wrote Eustis, the murder had greatly alarmed the Indians, particularly the Lower Creeks, who were determined to assist the Upper Creeks in punishing Lott's murderers.[12] Although unsaid by Hawkins, the Lower Creeks were closest to the white settlements and knew they would be the first to feel the settlers' anger.

After the visits from Hawkins's men, the old chiefs acted quickly. They assembled a posse of warriors from the Upper and Lower Creeks and placed them under the command of the Coweta chief William McIntosh. By the second week of July 1812, McIntosh and his men had killed all of those responsible for Lott's murder. In its pursuit of the killers, the posse took the radical step of following the leader of Lott's murderers to the sanctuary town of Tallassee—Hoboheilthle's town. The killer had fled to that place assuming that under Creek law the traditional status of the town would protect him from harm. Instead, contrary to Creek law—and to the astonishment of the fugitive, whom the war party found seated in apparent safety on a bench in one of the public buildings on the square—the posse killed the unresisting man with gunshots through the head and body.[13] This killing in a sanctuary town shocked ordinary Creeks and put an end to whatever self-restraint Hoboheilthle had managed to exercise from acting against the Big Warrior and his clique. The prophets also lost no time in exploiting the killings of the Tallassee warriors as evidence that the old chiefs were mere lackeys of the Americans.

In May 1812, hard on the heels of the execution of the Tallassees who murdered Arthur Lott, came a far more serious problem for Hawkins to address. Several hundred miles north of Tallassee, near the mouth of the Duck River, not far from the small but fast-growing town of Nashville, Tennessee, a band of Creek warriors launched, seemingly unprovoked, an exceptionally vicious attack on a group of settlers who were, with but one exception, women and children. The attack so terrified and outraged the citizens of Tennessee that but for Hawkins's political skills, war would have started then and there. The old chiefs attempted to portray the incident as the product of an unfortunate misunderstanding. According to their story, a prominent Creek warrior had been told that whites from Tennessee had murdered his aunt and her companion while the Indians were out hunting. Unaware that the report was untrue, the young man assembled a war party and headed north to the Tennessee frontier in search of retribution.[14] What actually occurred, however, appears to have been a first flexing outside the nation of the muscles of the newly risen party of the Creek prophets.

Early Tuesday morning, May 12, 1812, frontierswoman Martha Crawley was in her cabin going about her daily routine. Her husband was away on business, but she was not alone. With her were her three children and a woman named Manley and her three children. Manley and her brood had been there several weeks. Her husband had gone off on business, leaving his very pregnant wife and their children with the Crawleys to await the birth of their latest child. The child had been successfully delivered in that hard wilderness and was now little more than a week old. Also present at the Crawley home was a young man named Hays, who was out in the cabin yard with one of the Crawley children as a war party crept silently through the dark piney woods toward the Crawley home. Suddenly, the morning stillness cracked open and Crawley her family and friends were blown out of their workaday world as some eight to eleven Creek warriors, howling at the limits of their breath, crashed out of the forest and sprinted toward the open cabin door.

With great presence of mind, Crawley slammed the door shut and dropped the bar. She then grabbed her two youngest children by their arms and shoved them into a shallow potato cellar hacked out of the earth beneath the cabin floor and shut the lid. The Indians were now at the door. Crawley raced back to the door and threw her weight against it while the Indians thudded against its outer wood. From her bed, where her infant nestled in her lap, a frantic Manley screamed at Crawley to give up her struggle because the Indians were going to get in anyway. Crawley ignored the woman and pressed against the door with all her strength. Despite her efforts, as Manley had predicted, the Indians soon broke the bar. The door swung open into the cabin, slamming Crawley behind it and against the wall. While she was pinned between the door and the wall, four of the Indians went to work. One of the intruders snatched Manley's child from her and slung it fatally against the nearest wall. The other Indians butchered her remaining children and two of the Crawley children—one in the cabin, the other in the yard—as well as Hays. Mrs. Manley received a full dose of Indian terror tactics. The warriors fired one bullet through her jaw and another through her knee, scalped her, and, as if to punctuate their message, shot arrows into her privates. Incredibly, the tough young frontierswoman remained alive for several weeks after her ordeal before succumbing to her horrible wounds.[15]

Crawley's ordeal, however, was just beginning. When the Creeks finally discovered her behind the cabin door, she somehow managed to retain her presence of mind amid the utter horror surrounding her. At once, she threw her arms around the nearest warrior and begged for her life. Apparently sated with killing, the Creeks took her south with them to a village at the falls of the Black Warrior River, where the town of Tuscaloosa, Alabama, lies today. They didn't harm her on the journey other than tying her up at night, and they forced her to cook for them.[16]

The attack on the Crawley settlement sent Governor Willie Blount and his fellow Tennesseans, most notably and most vocally a middle-aged militia general and planter named Andrew Jackson, into paroxysms of outrage that reached new heights of the colorful, opportunistic rhetoric of the times. Both men virtually scrambled over the other to incite the federal government and their fellow citizens to immediately launch a military expedition into the Creek Nation. A pursuit by the local militia was organized, but none of the war party was killed or captured. In the course of that pursuit, the militia did manage to scoop up a lone Creek male, whom they made a prisoner. But before any connection with the Duck Creek murders could be established, he was killed while trying to escape.[17]

A report quickly circulated among the whites of the unspeakable ordeal Crawley was enduring at the hands of her savage captors. It was said she was being dragged by her captors from town to town as a living trophy of war. On reaching a town, the savages would strip her naked and then shove her into the center of the public square. There, for the entertainment of the townspeople, they performed lengthy dances about the terrified woman.[18] With lurid, sexually charged stories such as these circulating among his constituents, Blount redoubled his efforts to convince Secretary of War Eustis to take immediate action against the Creeks. The set-upon Eustis, in turn, ordered Hawkins, by dispatch of June 22, 1812, to free Crawley and deliver her captors to the United States for punishment.[19]

Already faced with the ambiguous murders of Meredith and Lott, Hawkins cajoled the old chiefs into convening a council at Tuckabatchee to deal with the murders. If they did not, as Hawkins informed them, he would "call in warriors of another color" to do the Creeks' job. The council finally met on June 11. Representatives from twenty-one towns took part. After intensive deliberations, the council informed Hawkins that it had organized three war parties to pursue the murderers. One party would go after old Maumouth, the second after Lott's killers, and the third after the Duck River assailants. The Big Warrior and his friends had skillfully portrayed themselves to Hawkins as "perplexed" about the recent murders and ascribed them to "ungovernable young men." In fact, although Maumouth's violent outburst may have been an aberration, the old chiefs knew very well who was responsible for the other attacks. This discovery had left them not perplexed but terrified, particularly the Big Warrior.[20]

Credible evidence exists that the Lott and Duck River killings were not the product of some young bucks' frolic but the considered plan of the prophets. The Duck River attack required the assailants to cross through Chickasaw territory to get at the settlement. On its way back home through the Chickasaw lands, the Creek war party, with Mrs. Crawley in tow, met up with George Colbert, one of the leaders of the Chickasaw Nation. The Creek leader of the war party, whom Colbert identified as one Ellipohorchew, boasted to the Chickasaw leader of the murders and informed him that he was going to take his prisoner and the booty back to the nation and, if the headmen disapproved of his actions, he would do to them what he had done to the whites, particularly to the Big Warrior. According to Colbert, the man informed him that his party had joined the prophets and for that reason had committed the murders. Although the Creeks allowed Colbert to speak with Crawley, he claimed he did not have the power from his government to free her.[21]

After meeting with the war party, Colbert wasted no time in attempting to extricate the Chickasaw Nation from the middle of what promised to be a deadly struggle between the whites and the Creeks. To appease the whites, he sent letters to the local paper explaining that the Chickasaw people had nothing to do with the Duck River murders. He also sent a letter from the Chickasaw leaders to the Creek leaders asking the Creeks to disavow the rumor that the nation "had joined the Shawnee prophet & his party against the whites."[22] Colbert also had this letter published in the paper.

As for Crawley, through a strange set of circumstances, she was by now safe at Saint Stephens in the home of the US factor for the Choctaw Nation, George Gaines. Gaines was a handsome young man of twenty-seven from a distinguished North Carolina family. His soldier brother was famous throughout the Alabama frontier as the captor of the fugitive Aaron Burr near Saint Stephens in 1809. The story goes that during her captivity, Crawley had been befriended by the Creek woman into whose custody she had been placed. One evening, Crawley's friend informed her that the Indians had decided to execute her that morning and that a grave had already been dug for her corpse. Waiting for dark, the woman helped Crawley escape the camp and then left her to fend for herself. Let loose in the trackless woods, the distraught Crawley wandered for several days toward starvation, her clothing and flesh torn by brambles and her mind slipping steadily into madness. Her sufferings ended when some young warriors, dispatched by the chief of the village where she had been held captive, found her and brought her back to the village.[23]

Oceochemotla, the chief of the town where Martha Crawley was held captive, noted for his guile and likely hedging his bets with the whites against the coming war, changed his mind about her fate. He sent word downriver to his friend Tandy Walker that a white woman was held captive in his village and had been dropped off there by a Creek war party that had moved on without her.[24] For many years, Walker had worked for Hawkins as a blacksmith in the Creek Nation. He spoke fluent Muskogee and was well-liked by the Indians, particularly by Oceochemotla. Some years earlier, Walker had retired from blacksmithing and become a planter in the Tensaw region. There he and George Gaines became close friends.

Through his family, Gaines also had connections to the leading men of Tennessee, such as Andrew Jackson, Willie Blount, and General James Robertson, the US agent for the Chickasaws, as well as, and more near at hand, the governor of the Mississippi Territory, W. C. C. Claiborne. Gaines liked and trusted Tandy Walker, describing him as one of the few "good and honest" men in the area. And with good reason. The previous fall, Walker had helped saved Gaines's life when Oceochemotla had attempted to extort a one-hundred-dollar credit from the factor during a visit by the chief with forty of his warriors ostensibly to conduct business at the trading post. Fortunately for Crawley, the former blacksmith had kept up his contacts with the very Creeks now holding her captive.[25]

As soon as Walker received the message from Oceochemotla concerning Crawley, he went to Gaines's home to give him the news. At home with Gaines was his seventeen-year-old wife, Ann. After hearing Walker's sad story, she begged Walker to rescue Crawley. Walker agreed, and, on the pretense of visiting his good friend the chief, he traveled up the Tombigbee and Black Warrior rivers to the Creek town at the falls of the Black Warrior. Two weeks later, he returned by canoe with the bedraggled and mentally unstable Crawley. On the former captive's arrival, Ann Gaines gave the traumatized woman a "tepid bath," fresh clothes, and a room in the Gaineses' home. For a week, the kindly Ann Gaines nursed the woman back to health. When Crawley had sufficiently recovered to travel, George Gaines organized a party to carry her back to Tennessee. There she enjoyed a bittersweet reunion with her husband and her two remaining children, whom she had last seen hiding in the potato cellar.[26]

Despite this happy turn of events, Governor Blount, in a letter to Secretary Eustis, lashed out at Hawkins for failing to free Crawley and seize her captors. Nonetheless, Crawley's remarkable deliverance gave Hawkins a little breathing space with Eustis in which to apprehend the band of kidnappers and murderers. For unlike the killers of Meredith and Lott, the members of the Duck River war party were not so easy for the old chiefs to find.

Finally, after some weeks' maneuvering, on August 31, 1812, the old chiefs managed to lure the leader of the Duck River outlaws, Hillaubee Haujo, to the council house at the Hickory Ground. Perhaps he thought the sacred nature of the town would protect him. If so, he was terribly wrong. Once he was there, the old chiefs' war party killed him and tossed his corpse into the Coosa.[27]

The actions of the old chiefs, which Eustis characterized as prompt, satisfied him but not the disappointed Blount, who had just had an excuse for war snatched from his hands. When Eustis politely informed the governor that in view of those actions, he hoped there was no longer any need to mount a campaign against the Creeks, Blount sourly replied that Eustis's view of the old chiefs' solution to the matter and his view "widely differ."[28] But given Eustis's opinion, Blount swallowed hard and bided his time until the next Creek depredations occurred on the American frontier. They would not be long in coming.

Winter 1813 was unusually hard and long in the nation. Hawkins had taken ill with a chest cold and "rheumatism." White travel through the nation on the Federal Road that winter had been without incident other than petty theft. In fact, the road was considered safe enough for US dignitaries, such as generals and congressmen, to travel to and from the Mississippi Territory. Nonetheless, white animosity toward the Creeks continued to fester, and rumors of Indian misconduct, perhaps spread by unscrupulous whites, roiled the frontier settlements. Then, with the coming of spring, the killings began anew, and this time there was no let up until blood had washed over the entire nation.[29] It started with a journey north.

In October 1812, ten Creek warriors led by the Little Warrior of Wewocau and Stimmauligee of Tuskegee passed through the Chickasaw Nation on their way to visit Tecumseh and his British allies. While Tecumseh had been away on his trip through the south in fall 1811, his brother the Prophet, against Tecumseh's express orders, had engaged in a battle with an American army led by William Henry Harrison, the governor of the Northwest Territory. Harrison had assembled his army to disperse the coalition of northern Indians tribes that had gathered at the religious center established by the Prophet on Tippecanoe Creek in northern Indiana. Harrison marched his command just outside the town of Tippecanoe and camped for the night.[30]

The Indians could not ignore this provocative maneuver and decided to launch a night attack on the Americans' camp. The attack surprised the Americans and nearly succeeded, but they rallied at dawn's first light and drove off the assailants. The whole town fled, and the Americans looted and burned the extensive dwellings and surrounding fields. Of far greater consequence, this event gravely tarnished the Prophet's reputation as a religious seer and dismantled the tenuous coalition of tribes Tecumseh had worked so hard to build. After the setback at Tippecanoe, Tecumseh laboriously managed to rebuild his tribal confederation. He was now alongside the British, leading those forces in the field against the Americans.[31]

Already Tecumseh's Indian forces had achieved considerable success against the Americans.[32] On January 22, 1813, the British and Indians surprised an American army of about nine hundred soldiers, largely Kentuckians, commanded by General James Winchester. The Kentuckians had advanced to a small British settlement known as Frenchtown on the river Raisin thirty miles below Detroit and had driven off the defenders, who were to their rear. To their front lay open, snow-covered ground.

Early that morning, about six hundred British soldiers and seven hundred Indians, commanded by a chief known as Roundhead, and among whom was probably the Little Warrior's party, fell on the exposed Kentuckians.[33] General Winchester's men initially met the attack with a deadly stream of gunfire that ripped apart the charging British infantry. But the Americans were too badly positioned to resist the determined assault of their enemies. The Indians broke the right flank of the American lines, and a terrible rout began. When the battle ended, virtually every Kentuckian had been killed or captured. Worse, as his army marched off, the British general left behind in Frenchtown about eighty Americans too disabled to travel. They were to remain there purportedly until the British could arrange transport by sleds. Inexplicably, however, the British left the American prisoners without a guard of British soldiers. The next day, after the British departed, some fifty Indians who remained behind got drunk and massacred every one of the prisoners.

Later the next month, after consulting with British general Henry Proctor, Tecumseh apparently dispatched Little Warrior and his men south with a letter from the British general for the Spanish governor in Pensacola at the time, the recently installed Mateo Gonzalez Manrique. No copy of the letter has been found, and it was probably burned by the Spanish governor, who later described it as a letter of "introduction." However, a number of reports of its contents exist that indicate the letter instructed the Spanish governor to supply the Creeks with arms, powder, and ammunition for use in a war against the Americans. There is also evidence that Tecumseh was careful to instruct the Little Warrior that after the Creeks acquired the Spanish munitions, they were to quietly bide their time, committing no violence against the whites, particularly those traveling on the Federal Road, until Tecumseh ordered them to war. That war was planned for autumn 1813, when the British would have troop and supply ships off the southern Gulf Coast.[34]

Leaving Tecumseh, the little band of Creeks traveled southwest down the Ohio River valley. All were bedecked with new pipe hatchets and with the gleaming silver half-moons of British military gorgets dangling from their necks. Near the end of February 1813, they reached the mouth of the Ohio River. There they encountered a tiny white settlement. After the usual scout to ascertain its strength, they attacked the place in a calculated act of terrorism. When they were done, seven families lay slaughtered. As if to punctuate the slaughter and send an obscene and unforgettable message to the whites, Tuskegee Warrior slit open the belly of a woman well advanced in her pregnancy and ripped out her living child. He then impaled the fetus at the entrance to the settlement on a long stake he had fashioned for the purpose.[35] Its brutal work completed, the Little Warrior's band passed through the Chickasaw Nation for home, bearing scalps and rumors of the British general's letter to the Spanish. Like some malignant being, after many travels and strange vicissitudes, the rumored letter would finally help spark the Creek War.

Because of the proximity of the massacre to the Chickasaw lands, the American authorities initially accused the Chickasaws of the Ohio River massacre. On March 1, 1813, General Robertson, the Chickasaw agent, received a letter from a Lieutenant Anthony, commanding at Fort Pickering, where Memphis, Tennessee, now stands. In that letter, Anthony advised Robertson of the massacre and pointed to the Chickasaws as the most likely culprits. Robertson, however, immediately realized that the Creeks had committed this terrible crime, but he knew that unless he could quickly exonerate his Chickasaw charges, they would become the targets for every white with a gun. He promptly sent news of the massacre to the Chickasaw leaders. These chiefs at once dispatched a war party in search of Little Warrior and his party of killers. Although the Chickasaws were unable to overtake the Creeks, who were at a Creek town on the Black Warrior River, one of the Chickasaw leaders, George Colbert, did learn their identity. On March 4, he informed Robertson that as the general had expected, the killers were Creeks, led by Little Warrior and Tuskegee Warrior. Robertson relayed this information to Benjamin Hawkins, who in turn forwarded it to the Big Warrior at Tuckabatchee, along with a demand that the old chiefs take swift action against the Little Warrior and his party.[36]

Little Warrior was not in the least concerned about the possibility of tribal retribution for the Ohio murders. After he returned to the nation, he boldly informed the Creek leaders that he had brought from the north important talks from the British and the Shawnees. The principal chiefs then convened a council at Tuckabatchee on March 24 to hear Little Warrior relate these talks. Little Warrior's message from the north was simple: the Creeks should ready themselves for war against the Americans, in which they would be assisted by British power. The old chiefs were outraged that Little Warrior would propose such a dangerous course of action for the Muskogee Nation. He was "severely reprimanded" for daring to support war with the Americans and driven from the council house. Shortly thereafter, the chiefs pronounced the Little Warrior an "outlaw" and dispatched warriors in pursuit.[37]

By April 18, 1813, the old chiefs learned that Little Warrior and a nephew had fled to a Creek town on the Black Warrior River. The Big Warrior and Alex Cornells prudently wrote the clerk of the court at Saint Stephens, Thomas Malone, and warned him of the presence of Little Warrior's fugitive band in the region and the dangers he presented to the "weak" settlements established there. The two Tuckabatchee chiefs also urged Malone to notify the Choctaws and Chickasaws that the Little Warrior was abroad near their lands and to request that they kill or capture him. However, the Little Warrior, as well as the Tuskegee Warrior, were apparently confident that their stature in the nation and the power of their clans would keep them safe from reprisals from their people. For rather than fleeing to a place of safety, they simply returned to their homes near the fork of the Coosa and Tallapoosa rivers.[38]

At the time the news of this latest Creek massacre reached him, Hawkins was recovering from yet another bout of the various chronic illnesses that plagued his daily existence; this time it was rheumatism and a bad cough. At once the agent recognized that this latest Creek incident was of a different order and magnitude than the previous depredations with which he had dealt. Little Warrior and the Tuskegee Warrior were not renegade young men out on a scalping spree or purportedly seeking revenge for the killing of family or friends. Little Warrior had been a chief for twenty years. Nor were the Ohio River killings the result of an isolated encounter on a public road or the result of a drunken Indian frolic. Like the Duck River killings, the massacre of the Ohio River settlers had been swift and well-planned, and the killers had punctuated their attack with a particularly vicious atrocity that the Creek war party must have known would cause an uproar in the white frontier community. Most importantly, the murderers were led not by some hot-headed young warriors whom the old chiefs could easily cast as renegades, but by two senior chieftains, one of whom had personally committed the atrocity on mother and child. Indeed, Hawkins surmised that the murders were done to "hurry on the war."[39]

The Ohio murders by Tecumseh's Creek allies also flew in the face of his plans, as well as his history of compassion toward noncombatants and prisoners of war. The southern war was not to begin until the British forces were in place along the Gulf of Mexico, and that event was six months or so away. Why hurry the war on before essential arms were secured by the

Creeks and the British troops, and supply ships were anchored off the gulf coast? The attack on the Ohio settlements served no military objective other than to terrorize the frontier whites. Indeed, so senseless were the Ohio murders that it has been speculated that they were carried out to satisfy demands for retribution by Creek clans for the execution of their clan members responsible for the Lott and Meredith murders.

Tecumseh's reaction to these events can only be imagined, but it must have mirrored the rage he felt toward his brother the Prophet for the debacle at the Battle of Tippecanoe Creek. As for Hawkins, he made plain in a letter to the Creek leaders dated March 25, 1813, that he saw his work of sixteen years among the Creeks on the verge of being swept away. Reminding them that during the Revolutionary War, when the Americans were vastly weaker than now, the Americans had defeated the British and their Indian allies, the old soldier, drawing on his military experience, warned them: "Our country is an open one; armies can come among us, any season of the year. They can bring their cattle and hogs for food with them; can find a great many cattle among us; will establish their forts at all suitable places, and keep the country: and what are we to do?"[40]

Forty years earlier, British Indian agent James Adair had made the same observation about the vulnerability of the Muskogee Nation to invasion: "Their land is generally hilly, but not mountainous; which allows an army an easy passage into their country, to retaliate their insults and cruelties."[41]

In 1813, with the rapid growth of the white settlements along the nation's borders, Adair's observation was truer than ever.

The Old Chiefs Render Justice

I N early spring 1813, seeing his life's work unraveling before his eyes, Hawkins immediately set the old chiefs to the task of apprehending the Ohio murderers. The chiefs were well aware of the significance of this latest attack on the settlers. Hawkins described them as "more alarmed than I had ever known them to be before." That alarm was no doubt further heightened when, just before the chiefs were scheduled to hold a council to discuss the Ohio killings, a report came in that many miles down the Federal Road, unknown assailants had murdered one white traveler and wounded another.[42]

Within a week of writing officials at Saint Stephens, warning of the Little Warrior's presence in the neighborhood, the old chiefs learned that he and his murderous band had returned home and were within a short ride from Tuckabatchee. The response of the old chiefs to this discovery was swift and deadly. On April 25, 1813, a war party was assembled at Tuckabatchee comprising Upper and Lower Creek warriors. William McIntosh from

Coweta commanded the Lower Creeks, and the ever-useful Tustunnuggee Hopoie of Tuckabatchee commanded the Upper Creeks. As witnesses to their good faith toward the Americans, the old chiefs prudently had an employee of the Creek agency, Nimrod Doyle, and two prominent mixed-blood Creeks friendly to the Americans, James Cornells and David Tate, accompany the war party.[43]

Initially, the war party expected to find the hostiles at the village of Kohowlaw. That evening, however, they learned that the hostiles had split up: some went to the Hickory Ground, the others went to the town of Hoithlewaulee some eight miles downstream of Tuckabatchee on the south bank of the Tallapoosa River. On receiving this information, the war party split in two and set off in pursuit of the hostiles.[44]

After marching all night, one war party arrived at the Hickory Ground at dawn. In short order, that town once again became a killing ground. The Tuskegee Warrior and four others (two of whom were his younger brothers) had barricaded themselves inside a house and refused all demands to surrender. Between volleys of gunfire, the Tuskegee Warrior taunted the attackers by boasting that while with the Shawnees he had dined on white flesh. He also bragged to them about his role in the Ohio River murders, particularly his part in eviscerating and killing the pregnant woman.

It was a hard fight. William McIntosh's nephew was one of the attackers and was badly wounded. A rifle ball broke his left arm and "entered his side." James Cornells's son, Washington, was wounded in the hand. The Tuskegee Warrior was also badly wounded but continued to defy the attackers. To drive the hostiles from the house, the attackers set it ablaze, immolating the Tuskegee Warrior. The chief's two young brothers were also badly wounded in the fracas, but unlike their older brother, they begged the attackers to save them from the fire.

Their assailants granted their request and allowed them to crawl to the door of the house. Once the wounded men arrived at the threshold, their attackers seized the brothers and dragged them twenty yards from the burning house. There in the yard, away from the flames, they dropped their prisoners to the ground and tomahawked them to death. The remaining two hostiles managed to rush from the house toward the Coosa River. One was wounded as he fled to the river, but he managed to escape his pursuers. The other, a man named Hocolen, was not so fortunate. Before he could reach the safety of the Coosa's broad waters, he was overtaken and killed.

When the attack at Hickory Ground occurred, the Little Warrior was in a house on the opposite bank of the river where the fields of the town lay. Upon hearing the attack on his allies on the opposite shore, he bolted for the swamps that lay thick and extensive nearby. Captain Isaacs, Ispoakoke Haujo, and Talosee Fixico were tasked with apprehending him. That evening they found the Little Warrior hiding in a swamp about a quarter of a mile from the Coosa River. He was heavily armed with a gun, pistols, a bow and arrows, and the usual tomahawk and scalping knife. Like the Tuskegee Warrior, he was determined not to be taken alive. Shortly before 10:00 P.M., Ispoakoke Haujo was able to lure the Little Warrior out of the swamp and onto a killing zone. Ispoakoke Haujo and his three comrades moved carefully toward the Little Warrior, all four of them rattling their shot pouches to unnerve their quarry as they approached him. Two others in the war party attempted to shoot the Little Warrior, but their guns misfired. The snap of the misfires, however, was fortuitously hidden from the Little Warrior by the sound of the rattling pouches, giving a third warrior the opportunity to fire his gun and kill the renegade.

The second war party found two members of the Little Warrior's band sheltering in the town of Hoithlewaulee. One was accompanied by his brother, a man who was not involved in the Ohio murders. Both brothers resisted and were killed. The other murderer escaped but was not pursued because the chief of the town advised the war party that the killing of the two brothers (even though one was innocent) had satisfied the nation's debt to the whites. At this, the war party returned home. The opinion of the chief of Hoithlewaulee, however, was soon reversed by the old chiefs back at Tuckabatchee. Agent Doyle, who had been in the armies of Generals Arthur Saint Clair and "Mad" Anthony Wayne in the battles with the Indians of the Ohio country, reported the chief's ruling to the old chiefs. At the same time, he reminded them that Hawkins had ordered the chiefs to punish all the murderers and said the life of an innocent man would not suffice for the life of a guilty man.

The old chiefs, who by now were ready to do anything to satisfy the American's demands for justice, promptly dispatched another war party from Tuckabatchee to apprehend the fugitive. When they caught up with their quarry, he refused to surrender. This warrior was a tough, experienced fighter, seasoned in many combats over the course of his five years living with the northern tribes. As his pursuers came within range, he fired a shot from his gun that narrowly missed the head of one of the attacking party. He then dropped the gun and went at his enemies with a tomahawk in one hand and a knife in the other. He managed to wound one of the war party before they put three bullets through his body. Incredibly, he managed to live another day, coolly amusing himself through terrific pain with boasts about getting fat on the flesh of the whites he had eaten when up north with the Shawnees. He also warned his captors that those who sided with the Americans would be destroyed. He died calling out the name of Tecumseh.

While these executions were taking place, General Thomas Flourney, newly appointed to replace the notorious brigadier general James

Wilkinson as commander responsible for the 7th Military District, was traveling through the Creek Nation to his headquarters in New Orleans. Passing along the Federal Road just outside of Tuckabatchee, Flourney announced himself to the chiefs and was given an escort of warriors through the nation. During his stay, the old chiefs assured the general that the United States had nothing to fear from the Creeks, because they had put to death Arthur Lott's murderer and all but one of the Ohio River murderers. The old chiefs went on to assure Flourney that they wanted only peace with the United States and would kill any Creek who violated that policy.

On reaching Fort Stoddert on the Mobile River, Flourney dashed off a letter dated April 26, 1813, to Governor David Mitchell of Georgia, informing him of the general's conversation with the old chiefs so Mitchell might be "informed of the real state of our affairs with Creek Indians" and urging him to control his constituents from mistreating their Creek neighbors. There were "many evil disposed persons," Flourney warned the governor, "ever ready to misrepresent the Indians, & the Conduct of Col. Hawkins, respecting Indian affairs."[45]

Thus, on June 7, 1813, a much relieved Hawkins was able to report to the new secretary of war, General John Armstrong, that between April 16 and April 26, the old chiefs had "put to death" eleven warriors responsible for the murder of Americans. Hawkins also reported that the rumor that the British at Pensacola had a supply of armaments for the Tallassee people was a "bubble." The Tallassees who had traveled to that town had found no British soldiers there, no arms there, and not even the Spanish governor there; he was in Cuba. Hawkins, therefore, informed Armstrong that at present "there is nothing hostile to be apprehended from [the Creeks]." He also assured Armstrong that he, Hawkins, as the Creek agent, was the person who best knew the Creek mind and that if he detected "any symptoms of hostility among them," he would inform the secretary immediately.[46]

When a deluded Hawkins wrote this letter to his superior, the first battle of the Creek War was less than two months away. A bitter and bloody civil war among the Creeks themselves, however, was already beginning beneath Hawkins's very nose.

Civil War among the Creeks

Unlike Benjamin Hawkins, the Georgians immediately understood what was happening in the Creek Nation and what it portended for the fate of the Creeks. An article in the *Milledgeville Georgia Journal* of April 14, 1813, knowledgeably summed up the situation and the golden opportunity it presented for the Georgians:

The Creeks are divided into two parties and it is yet uncertain which will prevail. Most of those who own property (and some of them have large plantations and many negroes) are anxious for peace as they have everything to lose and can gain nothing by war. The more indigent Indians, and particularly the young warriors, are eager to display their prowess in war and to acquire property by plunder. It is supposed by some, that a civil war will break out among them, and save us the trouble of chastising their insolence and violence. The commencement of war with us, will be the signal for their destruction. Our frontier is thickly settled with a brave and hardy population who wait only for the word to strike a blow, which if it does not exterminate, will drive them forever from the territory they now occupy.[47]

For some reason, with all of his intelligence, with all of his military and political experience, and with all of his sixteen years in the nation, Hawkins did not see, or perhaps refused to acknowledge, what even a small-town newspaper saw was coming and coming fast. The antebellum historian Albert James Pickett described Hawkins's conduct during this critical period before the war as "strangely benighted."[48] This otherwise meaningless phrase may unintentionally adumbrate an underlying truth. Certainly from the end of 1811 onward, Hawkins was continually disabled with various illnesses whose etiology suggested he had in the past contracted malaria, a common but severely debilitating and incurable illness in the South into the twentieth century.[49]

Within two weeks of Hawkins's upbeat report to Secretary of War Armstrong of June 7 on the success of the old chiefs in handling the renegades, the prophets began murdering the friendly Creeks. The executions ordered by the old chiefs of the renegade Creeks involved in the Ohio River, Duck River, and Federal Road murders had gained the prophets' movement powerful support from the murdered Creeks' outraged immediate families and clans and had put pressure on the prophets' party to revenge those executions. The old chiefs had dismissed the prophets and their followers as a lunatic fringe group confined to the superstitious, the fanatical, the opponents of Hawkins's plan of civilization, and some of the unruly and restless young. In late spring 1813, the prophets' adherents strode out of the shadows of the old chiefs' inattention and into the light of the nation's consciousness as a deadly threat to the old chiefs' power and very existence.

In June 1813, the Big Warrior and his allies were assembled at Alex Cornells's farm several miles downriver from Tuckabatchee. They were preparing for a journey to the Creek agency on the Flint River for a June 16 meeting with Hawkins. On the eve of their departure, however, a rumor reached the chiefs that immediately caused them to postpone their trip.

Word had come that the venerable Old Medal Chief, Hoboheilthle, and his lieutenant, Peter McQueen, had joined the prophets. Realizing the danger at last, the Big Warrior immediately dispatched Tustunnuggee Hopoie to Tallassee to ascertain the truth. The Tallassees denied any involvement with the prophets, but the Big Warrior, his keen instinct for self-preservation now fully aroused, confirmed the rumor of the Tallassees' defection to the prophets through other sources.[50]

Returning from Cornells's farm to nearby Tuckabatchee, the Big Warrior called his allies to council to discuss how best to handle the situation. Eventually the council decided to send a delegation of chiefs to the prophets within twelve days. Their choice of messenger to inform the prophets of this decision and to personally deliver a verbal warning to them underscored the old chiefs' ignorance of a primary source of the storm that was about to descend on them. The unfortunate man chosen to deliver the chiefs' message had been a member of one of the war parties sent by the old chiefs to execute the Ohio River murderers, and the message he was to deliver was not one that improved his standing with the hostiles. As instructed by the old chiefs, on arriving at the Alabama town, the messenger informed the prophets of the coming visit of the old chiefs; then, on behalf of the old chiefs, the messenger admonished the prophets, saying: "You are but a few Alabama people. You say that the Great Spirit visits you frequently; that he comes in the sun, and speaks to you; that the sun comes down just above your heads. Now, we want to see and hear what you say you have seen and heard. Let us have the same proof you have had, and we will believe what we see and hear. You have nothing to fear; the people who have committed murders have suffered for their crimes and there is an end of it."

As he finished uttering the last of this talk, the prophets put him to death, scalped him, and sent his scalp upriver to a town at the fork of the Coosa and Tallapoosa. The murder of the messenger seemed calculated as a signal for the prophets' party to unleash its plan to take control of the nation and go to war with the Americans.[51]

Within days of the man's death, adherents of the prophets plundered Captain Isaacs's house of its goods, burned it to the ground, and put to death two of the warriors whom Isaacs had led against the Ohio murderers. Several days later, Sam Moniac's plantation on the lower Alabama River was destroyed and his slaves carried off by a party of hostiles led by his brother-in-law, Josiah Francis. The divisions among the Creeks ran deep: Moniac's son, as well as his brother, who along with Moniac's daughter had joined the prophets' party, assisted Francis in this arson and theft.[52]

Soon thereafter came the news that the hostiles had burned to the ground the friendly village of Hatchechubbau in the piney woods on the west bank of the Tallapoosa, fifteen miles above Tuckabatchee, and ravaged the surrounding countryside, senselessly killing all the cattle, hogs, and horses they could find and destroying any corn they found. The rebels also turned their violence on the old chiefs and their adherents. By July 4, 1813, they had killed at least nine people, one a woman, and probably more. In the ancient town of Autosse, just below Tuckabatchee, a prominent Autosse warrior and opponent of the prophets named Fooscehaujo had disappeared. A search was conducted, but all that was found was blood in one of the missing man's houses.[53]

At last the long-gathering storm had finally exploded on the nation. Too late, the old chiefs awoke to the prophets' plan and to the terrible danger they and the nation now faced. The chiefs were confident that their execution of the Duck River and Ohio River murderers had demonstrated their power to the prophets' movement, which they had viewed "as a sort of madness and amusement for idle people," when all the while "it was secretly gaining strength and converts."[54] Equally surprised at the strength of this movement was Hawkins, and particularly that it sprang from the Alabama tribe. As Hawkins wrote Secretary of War Armstrong on June 28, 1813, "The Alabamas were the most industrious and best behaved of all our Indians. Their fields were the granary of the upper towns, and furnished considerable supplies, by water, to Mobile. But this fanaticism has rendered them quite the reverse."[55]

Hawkins and the friendly chiefs soon learned, however, that the prophets' movement was only the initial manifestation of a more ambitious plan that had been conceived during Tecumseh's visit to the nation. Not long after the Great Council of September 1811, Hoboheilthle, in consultation with Tecumseh, had begun plotting the destruction of the Americans from the frontier settlements in Georgia all the way to the Atlantic Ocean. That plan now quickly took shape. First, aided by the supernatural powers that Tecumseh had already amply demonstrated, the prophets intended to kill those Creeks responsible for the execution of the various murderers of the whites over the past year. Once they had dispatched those offenders, the prophets would next kill all of the friendly chiefs who followed Hawkins's commands, particularly the Big Warrior and Alexander Cornells. Then, if Hawkins had not fled out of their reach, the prophets planned to kill the old agent—the fountainhead of the civilizing process they so detested. However, even if Hawkins managed to escape, it was of little moment. After the prophets' party had eliminated the friendly chiefs, Hawkins would have no one to translate his talks into the Creek language; his influence over the Creeks would be gone. With the nation cleansed of Creeks friendly to Americans, the poisonous tools and ideas of the white civilization, and their apostle, Hawkins, the prophets would turn their attention to ridding the Creek lands of the Americans.[56]

Hoboheilthle's stated plan to achieve this goal was first to destroy the Big Warrior and his adherents at Tuckabatchee. Once that task was completed, he planned to march his forces to Coweta and destroy all the Lower Creek leaders residing there who had participated in the execution of the warriors who had murdered the American settlers. That accomplished, he would then attack the American settlements in western Georgia from the borders of the nation to Ogeechee, the Creek name for the Okmulgee River in north-central Georgia. There he would halt his campaign to rest and regroup his army. With his northern flank secured by the British, he would then launch an attack on the Georgians eastward from the Okmulgee and drive them into the sea. The no longer "Tame" King would accomplish this great undertaking with the assistance of Tecumseh and his confederacy, aid from the British, and, most of all—or so Hoboheilthle told his superstitious people—the prophets' God-given command of the earth below and the sky above.[57]

However, not all the prophets were pleased that war among the Creeks had broken out at this time. One of their parties, with the sinister-sounding and intriguing name of Captain Snake, who had been captured on an ill-concealed spying mission among the friendly Creeks, exclaimed in dismay when he realized the friendly Creeks now knew of the prophets' plan, "the prophets of Alabama had begun prematurely. They were to go on with their magic until Tecumseh arrived, who was to put the plan in motion, and he would come when his friends the British were ready for him."[58]

That time was not scheduled for at least another five months. And now, without British aid and Tecumseh's unifying presence and leadership, the prophets' party had to defeat not only the Big Warrior and his followers but the far more formidable and ably led forces from the many Lower Creek towns friendly to the Americans.

Civil war spread rapidly among the Creeks. Over the coming weeks, the prophets' faction was strengthened by contingents of Shawnees sent by Tecumseh. By June 22, seven of the Upper Creek towns nearest Tuckabatchee went over to the prophets, including the important towns of Tallassee, Autossee, and Fusihatchee. By the end of July 1813, twenty-nine Upper Creek towns and villages, marshaling an estimated two thousand five hundred warriors, had allied with the prophets. Only five smallish Upper Creek towns remained loyal to the old chiefs.[59]

With this support, the prophets' party now began attacking not only the old chiefs but anyone and everything associated with the Americans and Benjamin Hawkins. Not only did they make war on their human enemies but also on every material manifestation of Hawkins's program of civilization. Foolishly, the prophets' fanatic adherents began destroying "cattle, hogs and fowl," even those of their own towns, as well as the implements of the hated farming and manufacturing practices that Hawkins had introduced into the nation: spinning wheels, cotton cards, hoes, and the like.[60] Observers reported that for fifteen miles around Tuckabatchee, the awful stench of slaughtered farm animals hung above the land. In time, many thousands in the nation would come to regret this destruction of a major food source. Faced with the growing defection of the Upper Creeks, the Big Warrior forted himself behind a simple wooden stockade built across the mouth of the Tuckabatchee Peninsula and turned to the Lower Creeks and the Americans for his deliverance.

Around June 26, to the irritation of Hawkins, who believed all things Indian were solely within his province, the Big Warrior cleverly dispatched Cornells to Milledgeville, Georgia, to seek aid from Governor Mitchell. Concurrently, the Big Warrior, who was well aware of Hawkins's sensitivity to encroachments on his authority, also began lobbying Hawkins for American troops. The Big Warrior, however, had heard that US troops were tied up on the Gulf Coast in anticipation of the arrival of the British, and helpfully suggested to Hawkins that if the army could not spare the necessary troops, Hawkins should ask the governor of Georgia for six hundred to eight hundred mounted men to join with the two hundred friendly Creeks the Big Warrior would raise. Together the friendly Creeks and Georgians would attack the hostiles and defeat them. In addition to raising warriors, the Big Warrior generously offered to compensate the Georgians for the cost of this military expedition against his own people out of the lands of his conquered enemies.[61]

Not one to leave a stone unturned, the Big Warrior also sent an emissary to the nation's sometimes adversaries, the Cherokees, for help against the rebellious Creeks. The Cherokees responded favorably. On July 30, John Ross, a Cherokee chief who had visited the friendly chiefs and learned of their dilemma, wrote Colonel Return J. Meigs, the US agent for the Cherokees, recommending that the United States support the Big Warrior and his allies. Civil war among the Creeks had erupted, Ross explained, when the friendly chiefs executed the Creeks responsible for the murders of the white families at the mouth of the Ohio River. The civil war also proceeded from the fact that the friendly chiefs would not join the rebels in hostilities against the United States. The rebellious Creeks, Ross informed the agent, were "said to be very numerous," and without help from the United States there was a good chance that the friendly Creeks would "be conquered from the superior force of the rebels."[62] Thus was laid the groundwork for the spread of the Creek civil war into intratribal warfare. The letter also put US officials in Tennessee on notice that an important faction of the Creek Nation contemplated war against the Americans.

Into the midst of this violence rolled one of the most fascinating and unscrupulous figures in US history: General James Wilkinson. He was descended from impecunious Maryland gentry but surmounted that shortcoming through his wits and considerable charm to gain a position on George Washington's staff during the Revolutionary War. These credentials enabled him to marry into a wealthy and well-connected Philadelphia family. After the war, Wilkinson used his wife's family's connections to obtain a brigadier generalship in the western department of the army during Washington's presidency. In that position he served as second in command to General "Mad Anthony" Wayne at the famous Battle of Fallen Timbers, which ended a string of Indian victories over the United States in the Ohio Valley. The victorious outcome of that engagement, however, did not muffle General Wayne's opinion of his subordinate as "the worst of all bad men." Since General Wilkinson expended as much energy seeking to undermine General Wayne's reputation as a commander as he did fighting the Ohio Indians, Wayne's opinion of Wilkinson is understandable. And as events proved, Wayne's opinion of the man was not far off the mark.[63]

Wilkinson's failure to destroy his commanding general's career did not stop his incessant scheming. Taking further advantage of his position, Wilkinson managed to secure a lucrative sinecure on the Spanish payroll to spy on his own countrymen and to become a key figure in Aaron Burr's plot to carve a personal empire from the southwestern lands of the United States. Thereafter, having betrayed his partner Burr and weathered rumors of spying for Spain, Wilkinson somehow managed to obtain command of the US 7th Military District, which covered Louisiana and the Mississippi Territory. In that position he then turned on his Spanish paymasters. In April 1813, the general orchestrated a bloodless victory over the Spanish garrison in Mobile. To the anger of the Spanish authorities, whose country was not at war with the United States, Wilkinson convinced the hapless Spanish commander that Mobile was part of the Louisiana Purchase. Thus, because, according to Wilkinson, Mobile was now a US possession, he was not attacking Spain. He was simply relieving the commander of the unnecessary expense and trouble of further protecting an American city.[64]

Not long after Wilkinson secured this important port for the United States, President Madison promoted him to major general and ordered Wilkinson to report to Washington City. From there he was to proceed north to command the American forces being assembled for the latest invasion of Canada. This change in command also quelled a growing revolt among Louisiana's political nabobs who despised the general, whom they thought incompetent and corrupt. The locals' opposition to him, however, did not prevent the widowered general from recently marrying the wealthy, twenty-two-year-old daughter of a prominent Creole family from New Orleans. Delighted with his good fortune in love, and unwilling to be parted from his young bride, who was now pregnant, the fifty-two-year-old Wilkinson decided to take his new wife on the long and rough overland journey from New Orleans to Washington.[65] This trip involved a journey along the Federal Road through the entire breadth of the Creek Nation. Nonetheless, even the rapidly deteriorating relations between the Creeks and the settlers in the Mississippi Territory did not deter the besotted general from taking his sweetheart, as well as her sister, along with him.

The town worthies at Saint Stephens had warned Wilkinson that trouble with the Creeks was fast developing. In a letter dated April 17, 1813, the US factor for the Choctaw Nation, George Gaines, and several citizens of Saint Stephens, including two men who would figure prominently in the opening battle of the war, Colonel William McGrew and Major James Woods, warned Wilkinson that they feared an impending attack of the Creeks on the Tensaw settlements and requested that he station in the region the volunteer cavalry under his command.[66] The general ignored their request and their warning. In early June 1813, as civil war among the Creeks began, the Wilkinson party embarked from New Orleans on an overland trip across the nation for Washington City.

Not entirely heedless of his retinue's safety, Wilkinson prudently arranged for an escort of some twenty armed men to accompany the party. Twenty civilians, including Wilkinson's family, made up the remainder of the travelers. John Weatherford, William's brother, was engaged as an interpreter.

The general's years of self-indulgence, which included an addiction to laudanum taken for his nerves, had by now rounded out his military figure and decorated his neck with additional chins.[67] Thus it was perhaps as much by necessity as by choice that he traveled with his family by coach while the rest of the party went by horseback. However, Wilkinson's apparent advantage in comfort was a dubious one, even when fortified by laudanum. The route they traveled was the former postal path between Georgia and Saint Stephens, now grandiosely called the Federal Road. Although the horse path had been widened and numerous streams bridged, the new construction had merely created a broader hellway for travelers; over ten years later, in the 1820s, an experienced traveler described it as "the very worst road."[68] Even for a bad road, however, it was strangely deserted. When the Wilkinson party first encountered fellow travelers, the event was not a happy one.

According to mixed-blood James Cornells, who had joined the Wilkinson party as it passed by his plantation along the lower Alabama River, the travelers met a band of hostile Creeks on the road. The Indians were confrontational and arrogant and identified themselves as enemies of the Big Warrior, all his supporters, and the United States. They boasted that they were friends of the British and would fight at their side against the United States. In fact, their leader, who sounded like the bombastic Josiah Francis, even demanded to know from the general when the

Americans would be prepared to go to war with them. The situation along the route did not improve. Around June 22, the weary Wilkinson party reached Sam Moniac's inn ten miles outside present-day Montgomery, Alabama. By now the general was fully alerted to the perilous situation in the nation, describing himself as "surrounded by dangers."

On arriving at Moniac's modest establishment, Wilkinson found that Moniac and his friend John Ward were living in the woods outside the inn, too fearful to stay inside. The general learned from them that Ward's wife and family had been kidnapped by the hostiles under the leadership of the prophet Josiah Francis, who, they told Wilkinson, claimed to meet periodically with God to discuss the elimination of the Americans. It was not a good place for Wilkinson to tarry. Only fifteen miles away, on the east bank of the Alabama, at a remote location called the Holy Ground, Francis had recently established a stronghold of three hundred rabidly anti-American hostiles.

Alarmed by this intelligence and already fearful for his own safety, Wilkinson dispatched his interpreter, John Weatherford, to federal Judge Harry Toulmin at the Tensaw settlements with a warning of the potential for attack by the prophets' party and advice to call up the "volunteers" for defense. Venal, but no fool, Wilkinson also astutely informed the judge that he feared "that Hawkins' government will be found too feeble to bind a herd of savages, unless the arm of the Union is interposed," advice Toulmin would later conveniently forget he had been given.[69]

That done, the general and his by now equally fearful party, in carriages and on horseback, rattled and rode on as quickly as possible to Tuckabatchee. There Wilkinson met with the Big Warrior, who had importuned him for military assistance. The general had more important duties awaiting him to the north, such as the invasion of Canada, and most likely referred the chief to his successor as commander of the 7th District, the irascible, self-important, and incompetent General Thomas Flournoy. Wilkinson then continued on his way to Hawkins's plantation at the Creek agency, 150 miles to the east on the Flint River. There James Cornells left Wilkinson's party and returned home. After refreshing himself at the agency, Wilkinson rolled on northward with his caravan into further infamy.[70]

Fortunately for the Big Warrior, Hawkins had meanwhile come closer to reaching the same conclusion as Wilkinson about the need for US troops. In early July, in accordance with Hoboheilthle's plan, the prophets' men had attacked Tuckabatchee and now had the Big Warrior and his followers penned up in the town. With the Big Warrior awaiting rescue in his capital, Hawkins's response was to mobilize military assistance. At the same time, he belatedly decided to convince those chiefs who had gone over to the prophets to abandon those evildoers. On July 6, 1813, Hawkins wrote a message to be delivered by four "great chiefs" of the Lower Creek town of Cussetah to the prophets as well as to the Upper Creek chiefs who had "taken part with the prophets."[71] Among these were the Tallassee King, old Hoboheilthle, and his ally, Peter McQueen, both of whom had finally emerged from the shadow of the prophets' movement as leaders of the civil and military arms of the prophets' crusade against the Americans.

The tone of Hawkins's message to these men was that of the stern but fond parent to the Creek child. The agent expressed hurt and surprise that after all he had done for the nation, they would turn on him with threats of war against their brother Creeks and the neighboring Americans. "You know who I am," he wrote, "I have been long among you. My talks have been always for peace, and they have been the saving of your country." Hawkins tried to reassure the rebellious chiefs that the Americans were their friends and all but pleaded with them to settle the dispute now, while Hawkins was still their friend, and before "you see me with an army." He also warned them against harming any of his Creek friends and singled out his interpreter, Alexander Cornells, the man Hawkins had long ago admonished to mend his drunken behavior, as one they must not touch. As for the supposed powers of the prophets with which they had threatened other Creeks, Hawkins warned the Red Clubs that these boasted powers "cannot frighten the American soldiers. . . . [T]he thunder of their cannon, their rifles, and their swords will be more terrible than the works of your prophets." A "war with the white people will be your ruin," he prophesized as he concluded his message.[72]

Making this talk was one thing, delivering it to the hostiles another. The Cussetah chiefs knew where many of the hostile chiefs were: they and their warriors had the Big Warrior, his warriors, and their women and children trapped in the Big Warrior's Tuckabatchee fort, along with the chiefs and warriors of three other towns. With limited food and powder sufficient only to meet an attack on the fort itself, the Big Warrior could not hold out for long. Given the situation, Hawkins promptly sent his message to Tuckabatchee with an escort of just over two hundred well-armed Lower Creek warriors, who were ordered to fight their way through the hostiles into Tuckabatchee, if necessary.[73]

The Cussetahs, led by Joseph Marshall, the son of an Englishman and a Cussetah woman, arrived at Tuckabatchee in the midst of the siege. There on the hot July plains before the fort, the Lower Creek contingent met with Yauflco Emauthla Haujo, chief of the nearby Autossee town, and one of the hostile chiefs to whom Hawkins's talk was directed. Yauflco, who within the year would be on the run for his life, haughtily refused to even hear Hawkins's talk—"I am done with him and his talks," he announced—or the talk from any American for that matter. He then attempted to bar the Lower Creek warriors from entering the fort, but he let them pass when they threatened to fire on him.[74]

Within days of this confrontation, the hostiles launched an early morning attack on the fort, and although they suffered heavy losses, some of them managed to reach the forts' pickets. But the fire of the defenders was so fierce that several warriors were forced to stretch out on the ground and play dead. The more valiant among them rolled along the ground to the pickets to close with the defenders. Eventually, however, their losses (around thirteen killed) forced even these warriors to retreat.[75]

The fort's defenders were also in distress. Although their casualties were minimal—Joseph Marshall, the Coweta chief, lost an eye to an enemy bullet; one woman suffered a broken arm; and a horse was killed—their ammunition was largely spent, their food supplies were cut off, and they were burdened with numerous noncombatants to protect and feed. So perilous was their situation that they decided to embark on that most difficult of military maneuvers, even without a large group of civilians to care for: evacuation of a besieged position.[76]

On the day of their departure, the friendly Creeks had already been under siege for seven days and nights. In a scene that would be repeated many times during the coming months, as they looked out from the fort that morning, they could see a prophet chanting magic incantations and gesticulating spasmodically with his entire body as a prelude to opening the earth and swallowing the fort whole. From the fort, a young Tallassee warrior put a sudden end to the prophet's antics with a well-placed rifle ball to the head.[77]

The escape from the fort to the Lower Creek towns fifty miles to the east involved the crossing of the Tallapoosa River by hundreds of men, women, and children of all ages, burdened by whatever few possessions they could manage to carry. The river was low this time of year, facilitating the refugees' movement to the other bank. The chiefs, even the wounded Joseph Marshall, organized their people in a single line for the crossing. Warriors were intermingled with noncombatants, and a group of naked warriors, their bodies painted red or white or black, acted as a rear guard. Surprisingly, the river crossing, when the party was most vulnerable to arrows or gunfire, went unopposed, nor did the hostiles mount a pursuit during the friendly Creeks' long, slow march to Coweta. Perhaps the hostiles held back because, as the Creek historian George Stiggins speculates, they had sustained painful losses from their siege of the fort and needed to regroup. It may also be that they did not wish to engage in a fight that would surely kill many of their own innocent people. In any event, the prophets' party was not reluctant to plunder and then burn Tuckabatchee to ashes.[78]

The attacks by the prophets against the friendly chiefs spread. In late July, an eighteen-year-old prophet named Letecau sprang a particularly treacherous trap on the chiefs of his own town of Aubeccoche. Aubeccoche was along the banks of the Tallushatchee Creek where it empties into the Coosa. It was built on the ruins of the famous old town of Coosa, which had existed at various locations along the river from before de Soto's *entrada* in 1538. In its present incarnation, Coosa lay six miles upstream of Aubeccoche opposite the mouth of Kelly's Creek.[79]

Letecau initiated his plot by spreading the word among his townspeople that he and his band of eight brother prophets were planning to travel to Coosa town to display young Letecau's magical powers. In particular, they issued an invitation to the chiefs of their town of Aubeccoche to travel upriver to Coosa to witness the spectacle. The credulous chiefs accepted. A crowd of young men and women gathered, and the whole group followed the prophets and the chiefs to Coosa.

Following his arrival at Coosa, the treacherous Letecau arranged his fellow townsmen on a flat stretch of ground along the riverbank and instructed them to sit. Letecau took a stick and drew a circle in the dirt at their feet. He and his gang of prophets then began to dance within the circle the Shawnee dance of the lakes, brandishing their red-painted war clubs and making all manner of unearthly sounds. The teenaged prophet and his acolytes gradually worked themselves into a frenzy. At that point, Letecau suddenly voiced the war whoop, and he and his men attacked their chiefs. The young prophets killed three of them and wounded a fourth, but the remainder leaped into the Coosa River and swam to the safety of the far bank. The fugitives then made their way down the shore to a point opposite their town, where they crossed over to arm themselves and to gather their warriors.

When they returned to Coosa town, Letecau and his men were still there, dancing away in their magic circle, believing themselves immune from harm. One of the Aubeccoche chiefs stepped boldly into the magic circle, whereupon the prophets interrupted their dance, clubbed him to the earth, and shot arrows into him. In response, the murdered chief's companions killed Letecau and his men in their not so magic circle, scalping Letecau in the bargain.[80] The already fragile fabric of the Muskogee Nation was everywhere fast unraveling.

Colonel Hawkins's War

BY the first week of August 1813, the Creek Nation had firmly split into pro- and anti-American factions. Among the Lower Creeks, sixteen towns remained friendly to the Americans and still under the influence of Colonel Hawkins. These were mostly located among the Muskogee settlements in the Chattahoochee and Flint River valleys.[81] Among the Upper Creeks, the number of pro-American towns was considerably smaller. In the valley of the Coosa, near the nation's border with the Cherokees, only the towns of Coosa, Aubeccoche, and Nauchee remained loyal to the Americans. The prophets' threats, however, had prompted the inhabitants of all three towns to flee for safety to Turkey Town, a Cherokee settlement sprawled along forty miles of the Coosa River between modern-day Gadsden and Centre, Alabama. Also siding with the Americans were the Big Warrior's people from Tuckabatchee and several allied towns upstream. In total, the friendly Creeks could muster around one thousand warriors.[82]

The hostile Creeks were almost all concentrated in the upper part of the nation, along the banks of the Coosa, Tallapoosa, Black Warrior, Cahaba, and Alabama rivers in twenty-nine towns and villages.[83] At the beginning of August, the Big Warrior estimated their strength at roughly two thousand five hundred warriors. The anti-American party, now known by the whites as Red Clubs or Redsticks for the color they had painted the war clubs many carried,[84] was a loose and volatile mix of traditional Creeks, such as Hopoleithle, Menawa, and Peter McQueen, and a group of converts to the Shawnee religious movement led by Josiah Francis and Paddy Walsh, the diminutive but vicious Alabama tribesman. In late May or early June 1813, following the execution of the Little Warrior and members of his war party, a plan for confronting the American menace began to take shape among the hostile Creeks. The executions of the renegade Creeks ordered by the old chiefs had outraged much of the nation and turned a substantial portion of the populace against their faction. Thus, the hostiles Creeks' first order of business in their plan to remake the nation was to eliminate the pro-American chiefs and unite the nation in war against the Americans. To achieve that vital goal, the Red Clubs hoped to persuade the members of the Muskogee Confederation shielding the friendly chiefs to hand them over to the Red Clubs and to join their movement. At the same time, the hostiles undertook to cleanse the nation of all manifestations of Hawkins's program of civilization.

In response to the attacks by the prophets' party upon the friendly Creeks, Colonel Hawkins quickly organized a defense from those Creeks in the nation still loyal to him: the Big Warrior and his followers and the majority of the Creeks from the lower towns. Hawkins made the town of Coweta on the eastern bank of the Chattahoochee River the headquarters of the resistance. There, after the skirmish at Tuckabatchee, five hundred friendly warriors had gathered. On August 4, 1813, Hawkins convened a meeting with the friendly chiefs to discuss strategy. The old soldier advised that they should conduct a proactive defense. Strong parties of friendly Creeks, under leaders such as William McIntosh, would be sent out from Coweta to attack nearby Red Club settlements one town at a time. These raiding parties were to burn the hostile towns and carry off their produce and livestock. Hawkins hoped that the steady pressure of these raids would restore the general population of Creeks to their senses and that they would abandon the prophets' party.[85]

The friendly chiefs were in no hurry to implement Hawkins's plan. They wanted American soldiers, arms, and ammunition, and for Hawkins to accompany the strike against the hostiles, as he was "appointed to have the care of the Indians." In a line deliciously dripping with irony, the Big Warrior invited Hawkins "[t]o let your heavy baggage come along, as you have a public road to come in our nation."[86]

Weeks passed and the aid from the Americans never came. Eventually Hawkins was able to persuade the friendly Creeks to act. On August 18, 1813, a detachment of 375 friendly Indians under the command of McIntosh left Coweta to attack McQueen's town of Chattucchudfaulee.[87] This settlement lay several miles upstream of the prominent town of Tallassee itself, on a branch of Uphapee Creek. At the time of McIntosh's attack on McQueen's home, McQueen and his followers were most likely down in the Alabama River country organizing the attacks on the American settlements in the Tensaw region, which began at the end of August, for when McIntosh's forces approached McQueen's town, they found it recently deserted. Most of the inhabitants' possessions, including kettles, pots, and hides, had been left behind, indicating they had detected the approach of their enemies just in time to organize a hurried evacuation of the remaining women, children, and old men. A large quantity of salt, which along with alcohol had been proscribed by the prophets, was found in the town's deserted houses. After McIntosh's men completed looting the place, they burned the town, its fort, and the town's cornfields and rustled fourteen head of cattle.[88]

Another raiding party captured four of the luckless McQueen's slaves, while a third such party took prisoner "one of his family," a twelve-year-old boy. Thirty-five miles or so north of McQueen's town, near a town called Newyauca on the Tallapoosa River, a famous lower Creek warrior known as Itchhoo Haujo, or Mad Beaver, and his raiding party of twenty-three men killed three hostiles and "badly wounded" a fourth. The scalps of the unfortunate men were ripped from their skulls and carried back to Coweta, where Mad Beaver triumphantly displayed them to the people in the town square.[89]

By September 1, Hawkins's friendly Creeks had captured "two hundred cattle and some horses" from the Red Club settlements. However, as Hawkins ruefully noted, the success of his campaign against the rebel Creeks was compromised because the parties of warriors he sent against them were more interested in plunder than war.[90] In the months that followed, while Hawkins waited for Georgia to assemble an army to attack the hostiles, his campaign against them dwindled into petty incursions into the Upper Creek territory that accomplished nothing.

As the hostile party ranged violently about the nation, attempting to unite the Muskogee people, the Americans on the nation's borders woke to their danger and began mobilizing their amateurish local militia companies.[91] Ironically, the catalyst cited for setting these ill-trained soldiers and the war into motion may have never existed. It has long been received dogma among contemporaries and historians that British general Proctor gave the Little Warrior a letter authorizing the Spanish governor of Pensacola to supply the Creeks with arms to use against the Americans, and that the hostile Creeks presented this letter to the governor expecting that he would obey its directive.[92] Whatever the truth, enough key people on both sides of the coming conflict believed in the letter's existence to transform what may have been a fiction into a dangerous fact on which people on both sides acted. As the civil war among the Creeks continued its desultory progress in the east, the toxic document was reportedly being grandly escorted west toward Pensacola by McQueen, the leading prophets, and hundreds of warriors. Not long thereafter, reports of Creek depredations in the fork of the Alabama and Tombigbee rivers—as well as two white scalps—reached the friendly towns. Infinitely worse news was to follow.

Peter McQueen in Pensacola

WHILE his compatriots were besieging the Big Warrior in Tuckabatchee around July 19, 1813, Peter McQueen set out for Pensacola, reportedly armed with the well-traveled British general's letter authorizing the Spanish governor to furnish military supplies to the Creeks. Accompanying McQueen was the Autosse chief High Head Jim, the prophet Josiah Francis, and several hundred warriors, including a vocal contingent of Shawnees, along with numerous pack horses to haul the anticipated Spanish munitions back to the nation. The letter was a matter of common knowledge among the Creeks and the Americans. After Little Warrior's death that April, it had become the subject of much searching by both. Unfortunately for the whites, the Little Warrior's nephew reportedly had managed to get his hands on the letter and it was now on its way with McQueen to the Spanish at Pensacola.[93]

The trail was a familiar one to the Indians, who had been trading up and down it for decades. Nevertheless, in the heat and humidity of an especially hot southern summer, the journey was a long and arduous one. Although the hostile Indians' primary objectives on this visit were arms and ammunition, they took advantage of the trip to wreak gratuitous havoc on their anointed enemies along the way. They burned Sam Moniac's inn on the Federal Road and his nearby plantation on the Alabama River, and when they reached the Tensaw Delta region, they destroyed Moniac's plantation there along with the plantations of Leonard McGee, a prominent metis (mixed-blood) planter, and James Cornells.[94]

In the course of the raid on Cornells's place, they scooped up Cornells's wife, Betsy Coulter, and a white man named Marlow who lived at Moniac's place and added them as prisoners to their caravan to Pensacola, where they planned to sell them as slaves. Fortune turned to the better for the two captives when they reached Pensacola. There a kindly married Spanish woman named Barone saved them from McQueen and his people by purchasing them from the hostiles and promptly freeing them. It was well that she did, particularly for Marlow. Before leaving Cornells's plantation, the brutal McQueen had beaten the helpless Marlow half to death. A black man also found on the property received similar treatment from the hostiles.[95]

McQueen's party would have inflicted more damage on the settlements farther down the road but for the escape of several of Cornells's slaves. These men raced on foot to give the alarm to the nearest settlers. Unfortunately, the first settler they encountered responded to their warning by frantically packing up his family and taking to the woods. They had better luck at the next farm down the road. At the slaves' report of McQueen's depredations, the owner of that place promptly mounted his horse and, Paul Revere style, gave the general alarm to the families farther on down the way.[96] Nonetheless, the hostiles were later able to ambush a post rider, shooting off his hat, killing his horse, and capturing a bag of mail bound for Mobile. Contrary to later reports, the Creeks were apparently not trying to kill the man, only to capture the mail and have some cruel fun with him. Otherwise it is highly doubtful that he could have escaped his attackers and made his way on foot safely to Mobile, as he eventually did. The Indians took the mail pouch with them to Pensacola, where they handed it over to Spanish officials for inspection.[97]

Earlier in July, Moniac had had a narrow escape from the hostiles, and he appears to have sounded the first alarm in the settlements of McQueen's expedition to Pensacola. Around July 11, 1813, while traveling along the Federal Road to check up on his inn, he happened on an Autossee chief he called High Head Jim and a party of Autossee warriors. (Some sources conflate High Head with a man named Jim Boy, and confusion stills reigns as to whether they were the same man.) The Autossees were camped out near the inn on their way to join McQueen's expedition to Pensacola. Before Moniac could get away, High Head Jim saw him and approached. High Head Jim, in addition to being an accomplished warrior, was also a disciple of the prophet Josiah Francis and instructed in the prophets' ways. When High Head Jim reached Moniac, he applied the test his master had taught him for detecting traitors to the prophets' cause. The test involved a prophet's reaction to his subject after shaking his hand. If the subject was not a true believer in the new religion, the prophet would go into convulsions. As Moniac described his encounter with High Head Jim in a deposition given to Mississippi teritorial federal judge Harry Toulmin, "He shook hands with me and immediately began to tremble and jerk in every part of his frame, and the very calves of his legs would be convulsed, and he would get entirely out of breath with the agitation."[98]

When his convulsions subsided, High Head Jim asked Moniac whose side he was on. No fool, Moniac replied that he was with the hostiles and volunteered that he planned to sell his property and use the proceeds to buy them ammunition. At least pretending to be convinced of Moniac's sincerity, despite Moniac's having failed the test by sending High Head Jim into convulsions, Jim outlined for Moniac the hostiles' plans for war—how once they had sufficient military supplies and had united the nation by killing the friendly chiefs, the Creeks, with the Choctaws' assistance, would launch simultaneously a three-pronged attack on the surrounding white settlements: Indians from the Coosa, Tallapoosa, and Black Warrior towns, as well as the Choctaws, would attack the Tensaw Delta settlements; Indians from the northern towns would attack the Tennesseans; and the Seminoles and Lower Creeks would attack the Georgians. But first, he told Moniac, the hostiles needed to secure a large supply of munitions. They planned to obtain these from the Spanish in Pensacola on the strength of the infamous letter Little Warrior had been given by the British authorizing the Spanish to supply the hostiles' needs. Already the hostiles had organized an expedition to Pensacola to obtain the promised munitions, and it would shortly be on its way.[99]

As soon as the hostiles departed, Moniac hurried away to the Tensaw settlements to warn the Americans. On July 13, 1813, Moniac arrived in the region, where he happened upon the noted frontiersman Sam Dale. Dale was already on his way to becoming a legend and would be known by future generations as the Daniel Boone of Alabama. He stood just over six feet tall and weighed around 175 pounds of muscle and gristle. His weathered features bore the scars of his many brawls. As his friend Thomas Woodward described Dale:

> [H]e was honest, he was brave, he was kind to a fault, his mind was of the ordinary kind, not well cultivated, fond of speculation and not well fitted for it; a bad manager in money matters and often embarrassed, complained much of others for his misfortunes; was very combative, always ready to go into danger; would hazard much for a friend and was charitable in pecuniary matters, even to those he looked upon as enemies. . . .

He knew very little about Indian character, and entertained a good feeling for that persecuted people. So soon as he had an enemy in his power he was done, and would sympathize with and for him and at times would cry like a child.[100]

Early in his career, Dale had been a trader, and sometimes smuggler, in the nation. But at the time Moniac found him, Dale was engaged in guiding prominent settlers from Georgia to the wilds of the Mississippi Territory. In spring 1813, it seems that Dale had run afoul of the Georgia authorities because of his smuggling activities. These activities included the importation of slaves and other contraband from Spanish Florida into Georgia for sale. If caught and convicted, the wilderness-loving Dale stood a good chance of spending substantial time confined within prison walls. Thus it was that Dale wisely decided to change professions to one that would take him far away from the Georgia authorities. He took a job guiding the families of a Judge Stafford and a Colonel Phillips, prominent planters from the Georgia frontier, to Point Jackson on the lower Tombigbee River near Saint Stephens. He had just finished that task when Sam Moniac found him. Moniac immediately relayed the story of his encounter with High Head Jim to Dale and Dale's companion, John E. Myles.[101]

Alarmed, Dale and Myles hurried to the local militia commander, Colonel James Caller, and informed him of their conversation with Moniac. Caller relayed Moniac's news of the Creek expedition to Judge Toulmin. Among other things, they decided to dispatch three men to Pensacola to spy on McQueen's expedition: the wealthy planter David Tate; William Peirce, a cotton mill owner; and William Hollinger, another wealthy planter and ferry owner. Tate was William Weatherford's half-brother and the son of James Taitt, the British agent for the Creeks during the Revolutionary War. Peirce and his brother, John, owned one of the earliest cotton gins and presses in the Tensaw Delta. On July 19, the three amateur spies left for Pensacola, where they arrived the night of July 20.[102]

The judge had been busily collecting evidence of Creek hostility toward the settlers. In the course of this work, he obtained the depositions of Cornells and Moniac, and a statement of Tate's that reported that the Creeks were preparing to attack the American settlements. Toulmin gave these three documents to Colonel Caller, who forwarded them to his superior and good friend, Brigadier General Ferdinand Claiborne, commander of the Mississippi territorial militia.

Toulmin's efforts were unnecessary. By the time Caller had sent the packet of documents collected by the judge to Claiborne, the general was already coming to the rescue. He had raised, and personally financed with other Americans in the Natchez area, an army of militia to protect the

Tensaw settlers from a rumored Creek attack. Claiborne and these soldiers were now on the march from Baton Rouge to the frontier. The frontier community was already on edge, and these latest revelations collected by Toulmin of the Creeks' plan to attack further roiled the fears of the American settlements. Particularly disturbing to the settlers was the news of Peter McQueen's expedition to Pensacola.

On July 20, McQueen's party of several hundred heavily armed warriors, their terrified captives Betsy Coulter and Marlow, and dozens of the small horses the Creeks used to transport trade goods emerged from the forest to the north and into the little town of Pensacola. When the large party of fantastically dressed Creeks entered the sleepy coastal town, it must have seemed like a nightmare. Pensacola was the capital of Spanish West Florida. Established by Spain in 1698, the town lay along the northern shore of Escambia Bay, whose western end opened onto the turquoise waters of the Gulf of Mexico. Pensacola was laid out in about thirty squares arranged around a large plaza on a plain between the bay and the surrounding piney hills. On either side of the town lay swamps that almost joined at the rear of the town. Between the swamps two roads, guarded by blockhouses, ran into the town. On a hill behind the town the authorities had constructed a small bastion of wood and sand grandly named Fort Saint Georges. The town itself consisted of five principal streets running parallel to the bay and several cross streets running toward the hills. Many of the homes were situated among enormous and gnarled live oaks. Most were built in the Creole style: one and a half stories set up on brick piers, gabled roof, tall windows to catch the breezes off the gulf, and a gallery porch out front. The large square in the heart of the town was commanded by a blockhouse of sand and wood construction and mounted several cannon. A frame barracks of three stories and a verandah lay off the town square along with other public buildings. The governor's house lay between the barracks and the bay.[103]

Perhaps the grandest structure in the town was the home of John Innerarity Jr., the John Forbes & Company agent in Pensacola. The building was originally constructed in 1797, as the headquarters of Forbes's predecessor company, Panton, Leslie. In 1809, Innerarity converted the building into what passed for a mansion in Pensacola. It was a gable roofed structure of two and a half stories located on the bay. The bay side of the building was pierced with floor-to-ceiling windows to open and gather in pleasant breezes from the bay, flanked by heavy shutters to shut the house off from foul weather. A large, covered verandah of two stories, supported by simple, squared-off wooden posts, with stairways at either end, ran across the entire front of the house. Innerarity's impressive dwelling would soon gain the unwanted attention of Peter McQueen.[104]

The Spanish governor of the town, Gonzales Manrique, was newly appointed to his post. With the arrival of McQueen's party, he suddenly found himself caught between a hoard of veritable devils and the deep blue sea. On the one hand, Spain was not at war with the United States and had no wish to be. On the other hand, his town was now all but overrun with hundreds of Indians so fanatical that to the Spaniards' surprise they would not even touch alcohol and demanded that the governor furnish them with all the military supplies their pack horses could carry. To complicate matters, on the Creeks' arrival, a close friend of Manrique's advised him against giving the Indians any munitions beyond what was customary because he believed they intended to use them against the Americans.[105]

McQueen wasted no time in arranging a meeting with Manrique. It took place the same day the Creeks arrived in Pensacola, July 20. Attending on the Indian side were McQueen, twenty-four chiefs, and three hundred warriors. Manrique received them, at least the chiefs, in his audience room. Through the Spanish interpreter, McQueen advised the governor that the Creeks intended to make war on the Americans and that they hoped the Spanish, as the British had done, would join them in that fight. McQueen also demanded that the Spanish furnish the Creeks with a substantial amount of military supplies. At this point he apparently handed Manrique the notorious letter that the British had given the Little Warrior, purportedly authorizing the Spanish to provide the Creeks with these supplies. Manrique put the letter aside to have it translated later into Spanish. He went on to explain to McQueen that he had no authority to make war on the Americans, much less to give the Creeks the military supplies they wanted, and that to do so would be in violation of Spain's treaty with the United States.[106] In order to mollify the Creeks, however, he promised to provide them with the "customary" presents of food, clothing, and munitions. The Creeks concealed their disappointment, apparently hoping that with time, or the influence of the British letter, Manrique would change his position, and they left his audience room without incident.[107]

The following morning, six of the chiefs requested another meeting with the governor, which he granted. At that meeting, once again these chiefs repeated their desire that the Spanish join the Creeks in a war against the Americans and provide them with the full amount of the arms they had requested. Manrique informed them once again that he did not have the power to declare war on the Americans or to provide the Indians with the requested arms; like a lesser chief, he had to obey his superiors. As for the Little Warrior's letter, it is difficult to believe, particularly because the prophet Francis's Spanish-language skills had deserted him, that the hostiles had never had this important document translated from English to the Muskogee tongue. Thus the Creeks were now in for a nasty surprise. To the chiefs' astonishment, Manrique informed them that the precious letter did not authorize the Spanish to deliver the much-anticipated military supplies. Instead, the document merely recommended the Creeks to the Spanish as good friends of Great Britain.[108]

The chiefs became furious. Through the interpreter they accused Manrique of deceiving them. One the one hand, they said, he pretended to support the Indian cause, while on the other hand, the Spanish remained friends with the Americans. At the conclusion of their harangue against the Spaniards' perfidy, the incensed Indians began uttering loud threats against the Spanish, vowing that if they did not get their way they would kill every Spaniard they found outside Pensacola. Alarmed, the governor stalled the chiefs with the promise of a later meeting. In high dudgeon, the Indian leaders stalked out of the room, promising that their next stop would be the trading house of John Forbes & Company, the nation's principal trading partner for decades. Indeed, McQueen and Francis each owed Forbes significant sums of money.[109]

The person in charge of Forbes's business in Pensacola was the thirty-year-old Innerarity, a native of Scotland and the nephew of William Panton, one of the founders of Forbes' predecessor company, Panton, Leslie, in which the great Creek leader Alexander McGillivray was a silent partner. Innerarity and his elder brother, James, were brought over from Scotland by their father to work in the family business of trading with the southern Indians.[110] The merchant bore some resemblance to Andrew Jackson. Innerarity had the same thick shock of hair as Jackson, and the same long face. He also possessed a good measure of Jackson's fearlessness, personal integrity, and ability to manage men, as well as a stern and steel streak of Scottish rectitude.

Shortly after the Indians arrived in Pensacola, Innerarity received a letter from his brother, who was head of the Forbes establishment in nearby Mobile, just down the coast to the west. James's letter warned his brother of the Indians' intent to attack the American settlements north of Mobile after obtaining arms from the Spanish authorities in Pensacola, and it urged him to persuade Governor Manrique not to sell such supplies to them. So panic stricken about these developments was James's messenger, a man named D'Olives, that the moment he delivered James's letter to John Innerarity, the man fled to the countryside, not even affording Innerarity time to pen a reply.[111]

On receiving this letter from his brother, Innerarity immediately went to Manrique's house to speak with him about the matter. When he arrived, he found that the Creeks were already there in conference with the governor, their second visit to him in as many days. Innerarity cooled his heels in Manrique's secretary's office waiting for the meeting to end. When the Indians departed, Manrique called the Forbes agent into the audience room. With the governor was the parish priest, a Father Coleman.

Manrique described to Innerarity his difficulties with the Indians and warned him that they planned to visit the Forbes trading house in an attempt to extort military supplies from him.

The following day, Innerarity heard a commotion outside the house and went to the verandah, where he looked out on a disturbing sight. McQueen was there with his entire party of warriors, who were painted and fully dressed for battle. Some of the men squatted on the building's outside stairs and galleries, the others crowded thickly in the yard of the house—plainly there to intimidate him. Striding toward the merchant were McQueen, his interpreter, and a "shaker," probably the Autossee chief, High Head Jim, whom Moniac had encountered on the Federal Road several days before. Jim's convulsive antics, rather than terrifying Innerarity, only annoyed the merchant, who instructed the interpreter to order the prophet to leave the house. The interpreter, who had doubtless seen High Head Jim's act many times before, advised Innerarity to ignore the agitated chief.

These preliminaries over, McQueen strode forward and started to harangue Innerarity about the Indians' need for military supplies. Innerarity quickly interrupted McQueen's rant and calmly but firmly, and with great indignation, began a harangue of his own. Manrique had already told me what you all are about, he said to McQueen, but your threats will get you nothing from me. Well aware that McQueen and Josiah Francis were in debt to Forbes for substantial sums of money, the merchant threw in McQueen's face the fact the Creek Nation itself was currently deeply in debt to his trading house. McQueen repeatedly tried to interrupt the Scotsman, but Innerarity ignored the chief and continued berating him. Finally McQueen got the floor, and he denied all that Manrique had told Innerarity. Then, joined by another chief, McQueen and his coadjutor directed another lengthy and bombastic speech at Innerarity. In that speech, the Red Clubs described their unprecedented rise to power within the Creek Nation, and they boasted of the great Indian confederacy stretching from the Great Lakes to the Gulf of Mexico to which they belonged and which was about to descend on the Americans, and of their close acquaintance with the Great Spirit, who had personally commanded them to wage war against the United States. After a great expenditure of breath, the hostile Creeks closed their more-than-hour-long speech with an iteration of their demand for military supplies.

Innerarity was not impressed. But crowded about as he was by armed men whom he believed had gone "stark mad," he decided to exercise a measure of caution by pleading the poverty of his trading house and blaming the company's poor financial condition on the Indians' failure to pay their debts. All he could offer them, he said, was some clothing and salt. The Indians saw this offer as a weakening of Innerarity's position, a crack in his defenses that they could exploit, and they feigned pleasure at the offer, even shaking his hand before they departed some two hours after the conference had begun. Meanwhile, the canny Scot ordered his employees not to sell the Indians any of the munitions he had prudently secreted in the magazine of the town's main fort.

Around 11:00 A.M. the next day, the Indians gathered in the town plaza to receive Manrique's and Innerarity's presents. Innerarity had sent over eight damaged blankets, 100 pounds of tobacco, 110 pounds of beads, some vermillion, and three barrels of salt. He would have been better off sending nothing. For when these paltry items were laid out on the packed sand of the square, the Indians exploded with rage, pouncing on the blankets, beads, and vermillion, angrily tossing the gifts into the air, and trampling them into the parade ground when they landed. Then, in a clamorous fury, a group of them, led by McQueen, set off for the Forbes company trading house. There they burst into the house and rummaged through it, looking in vain for guns, powder, and ammunition. Frustrated in their search, they confronted Innerarity and demanded munitions—they were sure the agent had ample supplies stored somewhere in the town. With great courage, Innerarity still refused to provide the incensed warriors with what they wanted; he knew that meeting the Creeks' demands would mean the deaths of many innocent people, and he did not want their deaths on his conscience.

With Innerarity in tow, the enraged Creeks hurried back to the town plaza, where their attention was diverted to those items the Spanish had laid out in the sand of the square. Although these presents were "very considerable"—foodstuffs, clothing, and household items, and more importantly, one thousand pounds of gunpowder and proportionate shot—the Indians were not satisfied, and a number of them began to ransack the town. In particular, they were looking for Americans, some of whom had already fled to the governor for protection. It was probably during this fracas that High Head Jim rescued a friend, Zachariah McGirth, a wealthy planter married to a Creek woman, from the excited warriors.[112]

Before the Indians could get far in their depredations, Manrique called his soldiers to arms under the loud and insistent tumult of beating drums. As some soldiers took their posts in the fort and blockhouses, and others assembled in their ranks in the plaza, part of the Indians formed a line of cavalry at their end of the square, while their comrades began loading their guns. The Indians' composure soon vanished at the sight of the Spanish troops setting up the dreaded cannon at the Spanish end of the square. Within moments everyone became friends. The Indians accepted Manrique's offer of presents, and in response to the governor's pleas, Innerarity sweetened his original offer with more cloth, a barrel of sugar, and a barrel of coffee. To the end, however, Innerarity kept true to his original resolve not to furnish the Indians with any implements of war, even when the head of the Shawnee contingent begged Innerarity to a least fill the chief's powder horn as a gesture of friendship. Innerarity adamantly refused, "determined that even this sin should not lie on my head."[113]

Although the Red Clubs did not receive all the munitions they had hoped for, the day's events aroused their martial spirits and, as the terrified citizens of Pensacola looked on, they began to conduct the frightful Dance of the Lakes in the town square, uttering oaths as they danced to make war on the Americans, starting with the Tensaw settlements.[114] Shortly thereafter they left Pensacola, headed for the nation with pack trains of horses loaded with the supplies they had managed to cajole from Manrique and Innerarity. Before they attacked the American settlements, however, the Red Club leaders wisely deemed it essential to finish their civil war with the old chiefs and unite the nation. With their new military supplies, that should not take long.

The Battle of Burnt Corn Creek

While Peter McQueen and his people were negotiating with the Spanish governor in Pensacola, utter panic seized the inhabitants of the sparsely populated Tensaw region fifty miles or so to the northwest. Reports of the Indian depredations along the Federal Road started the panic. Judge Toulmin's amateur spies, David Tate and William Peirce, had returned to Fort Stoddert from Pensacola on July 22 and July 23 respectively. When their reports about the military supplies the Spanish governor had given the hostile Creeks spread through the settlements, the entire region became unhinged. Thousands of people—white, black, red, and mixed-blood, from all walks of life, from the wealthy planters and their slaves to the small farming families to the lawyers and doctors and government officials and merchants in the small towns that had sprung up in the region—abandoned their homes, buried all their possessions they could not carry, and streamed for the lands on the west side of the Tombigbee River. Some hardier souls remained behind, but on July 23, 1813, Toulmin reported that nine-tenths of the population had fled west behind the barrier of the Tombigbee's waters.[115] Once there, they began constructing stockades, as did those who remained east of the river. By the end of August, the broad area was studded with stockades of all sizes ranging from Mobile on the Gulf of Mexico to the wild lands several hundred miles north.[116]

The panic also spread to the civil and military authorities of the Mississippi Territory nearest the Creek terror. They had petitioned their superiors farther west in Baton Rouge and New Orleans for aid, but they also realized they could be dead before that aid arrived. From the reports of Tate and Peirce, from the prominent but calculating Choctaw chief

Moshulitubbee, from John Pritchlyn, the influential US interpreter for the Choctaws, and from the frontiersmen Sam Dale and John Miles, the authorities had learned that McQueen's party was moving up the road from Pensacola with pack trains of military supplies. The hostiles were reportedly bound for a rendezvous with a force of some seven hundred other hostile Creeks at a place called Whetstone Hill, one hundred miles from Fort Stoddert. There, according to what the spies had heard, the two groups of Indians planned to unite, divide the Spanish supplies among themselves, and head off to exterminate the white inhabitants of the Tensaw Delta.[117] According to the spies' information, the hostiles had no designs on the mixed-bloods in the area. As long as these people joined with their brother Creeks in the war against the whites, all would be well. If, on the other hand, the mixed-bloods supported the whites, they would be exterminated along with them.[118] Notwithstanding these assurances, the mixed-blood Indians in the Tensaw area wisely decided not to trust the hostiles and, like their white neighbors, fled in terror for the dubious safety of the frail stockades mushrooming about the countryside.

The panic that seized the settlements was due, in good measure, to their utter isolation from white civilization. But it was also stoked from within by unscrupulous wealthy land speculators. With the influx of immigrants streaming down the newly opened Federal Road into the Mississippi Territory, the speculators were fast running out of land on which to speculate. But tantalizingly, just beyond their grasp, in whatever direction they turned, were millions of acres of some of the finest land in North America. The fact that it belonged to the Creek, Choctaw, Chickasaw, and Cherokee tribes, not to mention the Spanish to the south, was a mere detail to these ambitious men. A good war with one or more of these declining nations was all it would take to pry a bonanza of salable acres from their current occupants.

When something is feared, it is also hated; the settlers feared the Native Americans surrounding them. By 1812, the Tensaw speculators considered the time ripe to turn the local community's fear of the Creeks into a racial war. Some of the most strident advocates among the speculators for military action against the Creeks were two brothers from North Carolina, John and James Caller. The elder brother, John, had arrived first in the new territory, around 1797, bringing with him his large family and an ample contingent of slaves. In 1802, he was joined by his brother James, who also brought along his family and their indispensable slaves.[119]

As a near contemporary observed, "It is good to be shifty in a new country."[120] The Callers were nothing if not shifty, and this attribute had been good to them. On their arrival in the territory, it quickly became apparent to the brothers that land was the coin of the realm in this wilderness kingdom and that the keys to unlocking these riches lay in the offices of the land commissioners, the register of the land office, and the receiver of public funds. The Callers themselves did not seek these positions; cleverly, they sought to place their own "creatures" in these important public offices. For themselves, the Callers aimed much higher in the social pecking order of the community. John became a judge, and James became a colonel in the local militia. Although they specialized in land fraud, the Callers also dabbled in theft, concealment of stolen goods, filibustering, and even murder.[121] As one scholar neatly put it, "As for the brothers Caller, there simply seems to have been no end to their energies for participation in corrupt schemes."[122]

Over the past decade, the nemeses of the Callers and their ilk had been the federal judges Ephraim Kirby and Harry Toulmin. Kirby was a Connecticut lawyer and politico who had been gravely wounded in the Revolutionary War. His true profession and love, however, was land speculation on an audacious scale. That love, however, jilted him, and he lost his fortune in a Virginia land transaction. Desperate for income, Kirby called in a Republican Party political chit, and in 1803, President Thomas Jefferson appointed him land commissioner in the wilds of the Mississippi Territory east of the Pearl River. He soon parlayed that position into a federal judgeship, which gave him appellate jurisdiction over the decisions of the local justices. From there he moved into foreign affairs, inserting himself into relations with the United States' Indian and Spanish neighbors.

Within a year, Judge Kirby's wide-ranging duties brought him into conflict with the Caller brothers. In summer 1804, Kirby got word that these gentlemen and their confederates were planning an attack on Spanish West Florida. Given that the United States was not at war with Spain, the Callers' scheme was not only highly illegal but also dangerous for their fellow citizens in the Mississippi Territory. The judge initiated an inquiry into the Callers' activities and reported that the witnesses who testified against James Caller in the proceedings "prove him guilty of almost every possible enormity," including the assassination of a Mobile merchant who had somehow run afoul of him. In retaliation, Caller initiated his own investigation of Kirby in a local court as to the judge's "conduct since you have been in this country." Conveniently, his brother John was a judge on that court. The conflict between Kirby and the Callers ended when Kirby died at Fort Stoddert, probably of a malarial fever. The Callers' filibustering scheme was, however, thwarted for the moment.

Kirby's replacement as federal judge, Harry Toulmin, was a former citizen of Great Britain. Toulmin, the son of a radical Unitarian preacher, himself became a follower of the famous chemist and political thinker Joseph Priestley. Priestley's radical political views eventually drew the ire of the British establishment, and he and his acolytes, including young Toulmin, decided to immigrate to the United States. Toulmin ended up in

Kentucky, where he served for some years as secretary of state and as an administrator of Transylvania College. In 1804, President Jefferson appointed him to replace the late Kirby as federal judge in the eastern portion of the Mississippi Territory. Soon thereafter, Toulmin assumed the virtually proconsular duties that Kirby had enjoyed as the principal representative of the federal government in the territory.

For some years after Toulmin assumed his duties in the territory, he and James Caller were on the best of terms. Toulmin owned a large tract of land on the west bank of the Mobile River near property Caller owned and appears to have speculated in land in the region. The two men also served on a board responsible for the construction of a road between Natchez and Saint Stephens. Plainly, from the moment Caller learned of Toulmin's appointment to Kirby's office, he determined to draw Toulmin within the circle of public officials with whom he had influence. Later ruefully describing Caller's methods, Toulmin said he was a man "who always knows how to adapt his language, his sentiments and his apparent feelings to those of the men whom he means to influence."[123]

The break between the two men did not come until 1810, and, like the trouble between Judge Kirby and the Caller brothers, it was occasioned by another, but more ambitious, filibustering expedition against the Spanish in Mobile. The filibusterers' objective was to establish a new nation called West Florida in the lands currently ruled by Spain.[124]

In July 1810, Judge Toulmin informed the territorial governor, David Holmes, of plans by the local citizenry to attack Mobile and free it of Spanish rule, thereby freeing themselves of the hated customs duties the Spanish imposed on goods traveling through their territory. Holmes instructed Toulmin to use his influence to quell such an expedition. Ironically, Holmes also wrote to James Caller, whose brother was a leading filibusterer, and other militia commanders, alerting them of the plot against Spain and the possibility that their troops might be called on by the "civil authority" to suppress it.[125]

Over the following months, Toulmin watched as the filibusterers' preparations to attack the Spanish matured. By December 1, the judge had gathered sufficient evidence about the plot that he felt legally justified to act. On December 6, 1810, he issued an arrest warrant for one of the conspirators, a Dr. Pollard, but stayed its execution until Pollard recovered sufficiently from a gunshot to the chest by a fellow conspirator, Dr. Thomas Holmes.[126] On Sunday evening, December 9, 1810, John Caller and Ruben Kemper foolishly entered Fort Stoddert, where Judge Toulmin was waiting for them with a warrant for their arrest. Caller at least had an excuse for this rash behavior—he was thoroughly drunk. The arrogant Kemper appears to have presumed that no federal officer would have the nerve to arrest him. Both men gave testimony (which they later claimed was coerced) that implicated them in the plot against Spain in violation of federal law.

Over the succeeding days, Toulmin courageously continued his investigation into the conspiracy; one of the conspirators' leaders, a Captain McFarland, whom the judge had arrested and who subsequently escaped, vowed to "have [Toulmin's] blood."[127] Unfortunately, all of the judge's hard work proved insufficient to stop the Kemper party's invasion of Spanish Florida entirely. The filibusterers achieved that end by their own lack of discipline and downright idiocy. A few hundred of them had managed to assemble on the western bank of the Mobile River, not far above the town, where they waited for reinforcements and supplies. That night they decided to while away the time with a frolic. Bonfires were built, fiddles uncased, and kegs of whiskey uncorked. A traitor, however, had informed the Spanish authorities of the Americans' situation. So while the company of now inebriated filibusterers made merry, Spanish troops stole upon their camp. When the surprise Spanish attack ended, four Americans lay dead, a number were wounded, twelve were taken prisoner, and the remainder had fled into the night. Among the prisoners was a local judge and Revolutionary War veteran, Major William Hargrove. He and his fellow captives spent the next five years in the dungeons of Morro Castle, in Havana Harbor, the former hard lodgings of that king of filibusterers, William Augustus Bowles.[128]

Thus the attempt by the citizens of the Mississippi Territory to take Mobile from the Spanish ended in ignominy. The commander of the US 7th Military District headquartered in New Orleans, General James Wilkinson, would achieve that objective a few years later without the loss of blood. The attempt, however, underscored the frustration of the local citizens with the federal government, which had made little, if any, attempt to remove the iron yoke of Spanish custom duties on American commerce through Mobile. The federal government's role, and particularly that of Judge Toulmin, in thwarting the filibuster also increased the antipathy of the local citizens toward their masters in faraway Washington City. This feeling was made manifest in grand jury proceedings in the local court system organized by the Caller brothers and their cronies against Toulmin. This proceeding resulted in a long list of charges against him, including "having holden a Court of Examination in the Garrison of Fort Stoddert and examined Witnesses at the point of a Bayonet."[129] These charges, known as a presentment, were forwarded to Congress by the speaker of the Mississippi territorial House of Representatives. Nothing, however, came of them—Congress wound up praising Toulmin's exercise of his judicial authority. Of more immediate concern to the local and federal authorities, however, it also demonstrated the dangerous weakness of the present militia system in the Mississippi Territory.[130]

As for the Callers, their leviathan appetite for infamous deeds was undiminished. The grand jury proceeding they had instituted against Toulmin appears to have momentarily checked the judge's enthusiasm for grappling with them. They now turned their rapacity on a much bigger prize than the little town of Mobile, and they were willing to once again set their local government against the national government to get it. That prize was the same one that a generation ago the Dirt King, William Blount, had risked his fortune and reputation to obtain: the millions of acres owned by the southern Indian tribes. The Callers were not as smart or as clever as the Dirt King. Where Blount employed a scalpel, these lesser scoundrels wielded a sledgehammer; they and their fellow speculators engineered a war with the Indians that opened a golden age of speculation in the lands of the dispossessed southern tribes. This latest audacious enterprise placed the Callers and Judge Toulmin at odds again.

In early March 1812, Colonel James Caller set the people in the Forks in an uproar over information he claimed to have received from an anonymous source in the Creek Nation that the Creeks were planning an immediate attack on the settlements. The quick-thinking colonel promptly obtained for himself all the arms and ammunition stored at the Choctaw factory in Saint Stephens, purportedly to use against the Indians. Toulmin, however, was not impressed. As he wrote Secretary of State John Graham in Washington City, "I suspect that the dangers are greatly magnified. A part of the reports and circumstances connected with the leading fact,—I know to be false, from information, which I think may be relied upon." In a dig at Colonel Caller, Toulmin also expressed the concern that the federal government promptly receive information about the situation with the Creeks in order to "check the exercise of illegal power" and to place the necessary power "in discreet & judicious hands." Interestingly, the judge did report that he deemed "it very probable that a troublesome chief called Cap[tain] Isaacs may be brewing mischief" and that if he had the means "would endeavor to exterminate this settlement." [131]

James Caller and his associates kept up the drumbeat of an impending Creek attack on the community. In June, probably taking advantage of the Lott murder, Caller, Colonel Joseph Carson, and Colonel William McGrew wrote to territorial governor Holmes about the impending threat by the Creeks to the settlements. An anxious Holmes promptly wrote to William Eustis, the US secretary of war, requesting troops. Later that summer, Colonel Caller implemented more radical steps to bring on an Indian war. [132] As Toulmin reported: "A party of rangers have been sent out by Col. Callier, without any occasion,—& whose avowed design is to murder indians:—two companies of militia were ordered out by him on a groundless, idle rumor;—a party of indians were wantonly & without provocation fired upon by others,—and some peacable Choctaws were almost beaten to death in Washing[ton] County."

Toulmin's assessment of the situation was that "[o]ur militia officers here, have been extremely anxious . . . to bring on an indian war."[133]

Other than a letter to General James Wilkinson in April 1813, requesting that he station troops in the Tensaw region, Caller's bellicose cries for action against the Indians were muted. It was not until July 1813, when the alarming reports of Peter McQueen's expedition to Pensacola reached the settlements, that Caller and his cronies stirred themselves. He and Toulmin set aside their differences in the face of the purported Creek threat, and even before their spies returned from Pensacola, the local worthies met to discuss how to address what they perceived as an imminent assault on their community by the savages. As a result of that meeting, they precipitously decided to launch a preemptive strike on the Creek pack train on its return from Pensacola. On July 20, 1813, Colonel Caller wrote his friend General Claiborne, outlining his plan. Caller informed Claiborne that it was essential to attack the unsuspecting Creeks in order to prevent McQueen and his men from breaking up the "infant" settlements in the Tensaw region. In support of this course of action, Caller sent Claiborne the various statements gathered by Toulmin attesting to the holocaust about to descend on the settlements. The heroic Caller lamented to Claiborne that his command was "badly provided" but said the men were nonetheless "well disposed" and would depart on Thursday morning, before the general could arrive to assist them, to engage the Indians in battle.[134]

Notwithstanding Caller's martial title and airs, however, some in the tight-knit frontier community questioned the colonel's military abilities and even his courage. Nonetheless, at the news of the impending Creek attack, the locals flocked to his questionable standard. He brought his forces together in the booming river town and territorial capital of Saint Stephens. The town was located, by water, 120 miles north of Mobile, on a magnificent limestone bluff that rose steeply above the eastern shore of the Tombigbee River just below the head of navigation. The land on which the town was built had once been owned by Spain who had maintained a fort on the site. The United States acquired the land from Spain in 1799 and, in 1802, established a post for trading with the Choctaws in the old Spanish fort. The town of St. Stephens (renamed Saint Stephens from 1811–1815) was laid out in 1807 and grew rapidly thereafter.[135]

At this new town, Caller assembled within three days three militia companies of about forty men each. The tiny force was a motley collection of untrained and undisciplined planters, farmers, lawyers, merchants, and mechanics. They were armed with an equally motley collection of firing weapons—rifles, muskets, and even shotguns, the latter deadly effective but only at close range—as well as the usual array of cutting weapons—swords, knives, and hatchets. All the men were mounted on their own or borrowed horses. As an exemplar of their ecumenical attire, the large and portly Colonel Caller wore a calico hunting coat, a high bell crowned hat, and top boots and was mounted on a large and magnificent bay.[136]

Surprisingly, given his scorn for the Callers, the principled Judge Toulmin nonetheless permitted his seventeen-year-old son, Theophilus, to join Caller's command. He was the youngest soldier among that ill-assorted band of brothers. Fortune rewarded the judge's rectitude. He was later gratified to hear from Holmes that the young man had fought bravely in battle.[137] To Caller's credit, he also brought his son Robert along on the expedition. The father later reported to General Claiborne that Robert had behaved bravely.

Not everyone in the community thought Caller's motive for the campaign against the Creek supply train was simple patriotism. Some shared Toulmin's opinion that Caller and his confederates were after Creek land. Unfortunately for Caller, one of those people, Lewis Sewall, wielded a poison pen. Sewall was the register of the land office, a man Toulmin described as a "mere creature" of Caller and his gang.[138] But before the Creek War there was a falling out among thieves, and Sewall revenged himself against his former boss by publishing a satire, in iambic pentameter, of the colonel's expedition against the Creek pack train. Near the beginning of this work, in which Caller is the Falstaffian hero, the poet suggests the colonel's true motive for the expedition:

> *Roused by a zeal which fertile lands inflames*
> *And vainly hoping for a war like name*[139]

Many others in Caller's little army probably were motivated by the same desires.

On the evening of July 24, the expedition crossed the Tombigbee River and marched east to the small town of Jackson, where it camped for the night. The men arose early in the morning of the twenty-fifth, and by that evening had reached Sizemore's ferry on the Alabama River. There they were joined by the much welcomed frontiersman Sam Dale. Dale had brought with him a company of fifty men. He was the company's captain. His second in command was twenty-three-year-old Lieutenant Girard Creagh. The unwelcomed news was that there was no ferry with which to cross the river. The ferry operator had apparently joined the local population's exodus to the west and, beforehand, had destroyed the ferry to keep it from the Indians. As a result, Caller's reinforced but still-tiny command had to cross the Alabama by canoe and by swimming the horses. Once across the river, the army rode southeast. That evening it arrived at some cow pens owned by William Weatherford's half-brother and erstwhile spy, David Tate, where they camped for the night.

While camped, Caller's army enjoyed further reinforcements. Sometime between nine and ten that night, a company of mixed-blood Creeks arrived on the scene. They were commanded by another remarkable man, Captain Dixon Bailey. Like many prominent settlers in the Tensaw territory, Bailey was the son of a Creek woman and a white trader. He was raised on the family farm outside the important Tallapoosa town of Autosse. While Bailey was still a child, his parents took advantage of the secret provisions of the Treaty of New York and sent him away, at an early age, to Philadelphia to be educated among the Quakers. At school, he absorbed the white ways with a vengeance. After returning to the nation, he grew to be a stout man of between five feet eight and five feet ten inches. He was dark skinned, intelligent, and of unquestioned courage, a ferocious fighter who once, armed only with a hand spike and assisted only by his sixty-year-old mother, defeated Captain Isaacs and his gang of Coosada warriors when they attacked Bailey's ferry operation (almost beating ferryman Linn McGee to death) after Bailey refused to pay Isaacs protection money for the privilege of operating the ferry.[140] Presently, Bailey owned a prosperous plantation on the Alabama River just upstream from Samuel Mims's plantation and ferry. Here, Bailey also operated the ferry that had drawn Captain Isaacs across the Alabama River, from which he realized a lucrative income. He was married and was the father of several children.[141]

The following morning, July 26, 1813, the reinforced army rode out of Tate's property toward the southeast. Several hours later, the Americans struck the intersection of the Wolf's Path and the Pensacola Road. There they took the Pensacola road south. Along the way, Sam Dale and some of his troop rode ahead to scout for the Creek pack train.[142]

Around 11:00 A.M., the main column was halted by a message from Dale advising that a large party of Indians, with several hundred fully loaded pack horses, had stopped for a leisurely lunch not far ahead. The unsuspecting Indians, about sixty of them (although accounts vary) under High Head Jim, had halted their journey for a late morning meal and to rest the pack animals. They had selected the only flat patch of ground in the area, a lightly wooded acre that would accommodate their caravan. Their campground lay in a semicircle formed by a curve of low hills to the north and the line of Burnt Corn Creek opposite. A swamp spread south from the far side of the creek. The swamp was largely composed of thick reeds eight feet high, affording a man excellent concealment. A small spring at the base of the hills gave rise to a narrow stream that fed into the creek and provided welcome fresh water on that summer's day, particularly with the pack animals muddying the creek as they watered. It was a fine and pleasant choice for a rest stop—had not almost two hundred armed men anxiously intent on killing them been on the heights above. Amazingly, the Indians had neglected to take the simple precaution of placing sentinels on those heights; perhaps because, as High Head Jim later remarked, "the war had not fairly broken out." [143]

While the Creeks were lounging around their smoking cook pots, or moving about preparing their meals, or tending their animals, the Americans gathered in a council of war on the other side of the low, pine-covered hills above, debating how best to destroy their unsuspecting foe. Some of the officers, including Captain Patrick May (later general of the Alabama militia), were for sending their mounts to the rear and ambushing the Indians as they were strung out along the road riding toward home. The majority of officers, however, wanted to launch an immediate attack on the Creeks and thus surprise them at their meal. That plan was agreed on, and the Americans began to stage their attack behind the sparsely wooded hill.[144]

The settlers decided to simultaneously hit the Indians with three columns of men led by Colonel Caller. Captain Bailey was to command the left column, Captain Dale the center, and young Captain Smoot the right. Colonel William McGrew, commanding the remaining one hundred or so men, would follow. Evidencing a lack of strong, central command, even for so small a body of men, the troops were left to decide for themselves whether to attack on horseback or on foot; the majority of the men, in the best Cavalier tradition, chose to stay mounted.[145]

The task facing the militiamen must have appeared to them a simple one. In order to reduce the chances of losing the entire lot of the critical supplies they had obtained in Pensacola, the Creeks prudently decided to divide the supplies among several groups for the journey home. Thus the group of warriors led by High Head Jim and taking their ease below the waiting Americans was less than one-third the size of the American force and unaware they were about to be attacked.

The attack jumped off around noon. A combination of swift but careful movements by the American vanguard up the curve of hills and the noise issuing from the Indian encampment itself must have masked the Americans' advance because the Indians were caught in utter surprise as dozens of American troops rushed down the hill above their campground. Fortunately for the Creeks, the ill-trained militiamen fired before they were in range and did no great damage. Nonetheless, the surprised Creeks panicked, and a general and confused melee began as the Indians rushed in consternation for their weapons and the Americans advanced somewhat blindly through the thick smoke of their own guns.[146]

Running at the head of his men, Dale stopped and fired his gun, blowing away the Indian in front of him. But as Dale paused to reload, he was shot in the chest, the ball "ranging" around his ribs and coming to rest against his spine. At that very instant, the man alongside Dale, Private Elijah Glass, whose twin brother, David, was also in the fight, was fatally shot. But Dale, after vomiting a copious amount of blood and feeling "easier," took up his gun, which one of his men had helpfully reloaded, and returned to the fight.[147]

The outnumbered Indians shook off their initial panic and put up a dogged resistance, their efforts probably assisted by the fact that a number of the Americans had turned their attention to the coveted pack animals. Lieutenant Creagh of Dale's company, who years later provided Albert Pickett with a written account of the fight, watched as an arrow flew just above his head and through a kettle fixed to the back of a horse, while his comrades ran, insensible in their greed, to and fro about the field, amid Creek bullets and arrows, chasing the panicked pack horses. Before long they had some eight to ten of the little animals in hand. With such antics going on among their undisciplined troops, it took the Americans almost an hour to drive the Creeks into the swamp. In all that time, and contrary to the image of the dead-eyed shooting skills of the American frontiersmen, Caller's troops had managed to kill only several individuals. These included a Creek woman and a black male slave. These two probably thought that as noncombatants, they had no need to flee. Unfortunately, they had not counted on the military incompetence of the American militia, which, in the noise and smoke and confusion of battle, shot two innocent people, including, in the slave, the most valuable prize on the field.[148]

When the routed Indians disappeared into the tall reeds, they got a break from the dangerously inexperienced and arrogant Colonel Caller. Dixon Bailey had implored Caller several times to order his troops to charge the swamp, but the colonel ignored the captain's advice.[149] In fairness to Caller, perhaps he thought that the Americans had the Indians on the run and that in entering the swamp, where horses were of little or no use, he risked snatching defeat from the jaws of an apparent victory. Certainly many of the white troops were not unhappy with this decision. Their focus, particularly those just coming up to the fight, was in catching one of the pack horses and their valuable cargo, not in risking their lives in an attack on an enemy concealed in a swamp.

While the Americans chased, or squabbled over possession of, the crazed pack animals, or milled about waiting for orders, their opponents regrouped. Although they had only about thirteen guns among them, some of which had defective firing mechanisms, the Creeks used them, as well as their bows and arrows, to good effect. Soon arrow points and lead shot flew toward the Americans from invisible assailants hidden among the reeds of the swamp.[150] Groups of Indians began to steal around their flanks. Another group of warriors, painted scarlet, brandishing tomahawks, and firing their weapons, came howling out of the reeds toward the startled Americans. Alarmed at this unexpected turn of events, Caller dispatched Bailey to the inexplicably tardy McGrew with an order for him to immediately bring his company of one hundred men up to the fight.

McGrew's men refused. They had lagged about a half mile behind the initial advance and were, by this time, busily engaged in catching the Indians' pack animals.[151] Any interest the militiamen once had in fighting Indians had since disappeared.

Unfortunately for the Americans, before anyone could restore a semblance of order to blunt the Creek assault, an American officer or officers shouted retreat. Some participants in the battle say Caller issued the command after McGrew was unable, or unwilling, to get his men to stop wrangling horses and join the fight; others blame an unknown officer. Caller wrote Governor Holmes several weeks after the battle that McGrew and his subordinates, Major Zachariah Phillips and Major J. Farland, had uttered the fatal command.[152] Whoever issued it, Dale later wrote, with wry understatement, that the command to retreat was not a wise one to give raw and untrained troops caught up in the confused melee of combat.[153]

Predictably, the ill-advised order immediately caused the untrained Americans to stampede for the shelter of the nearby hills. Despite the danger, however, among many of the retreating soldiers, greed overmastered their understandable fear. For while their terrified comrades fled toward the crest of the low hill, these more intrepid or avaricious souls retained sufficient presence of mind to take the time to drive or drag the captured pack horses up the hill with them.

Other militiamen stayed and fought and died, and it is to these few brave souls that many of their fleeing comrades owed their lives. Captain Patrick May was one such man. While the bulk of their unhinged comrades scrambled up the semicircle of hills, he, Captain Benjamin Smoot, Lieutenant Creagh of Dale's company, a Private Miles, and others ignored the cry of retreat and stood to face the onrushing Indians. Fifty yards in front of May, an Indian materialized from the green wall of reeds and raised his rifle. May instantly did the same. Both men fired simultaneously. The ball from the Indian's gun hit May's gun just in front of its lock, and the Indian disappeared into the reeds. By this time May and his companions had had their fill of combat and decided to join the retreat.[154]

As the men ran for their lives, a ball from one of the few Indian guns hit Creagh in the left hip. Providentially, before the fight, Creagh had stuffed a silk handkerchief and a pair of buckskin gloves in the left pocket of his top coat. The Indian's ball struck Creagh's coat at just that point, pierced the gloves but stopped against his hip joint, knocking Creagh to the ground and painfully deadening the joint.[155] Creagh cried up to the nearby May, "Save me Lieutenant or I am gone." Under fire from the approaching Indians, May tried to lift Creagh to his feet, but Creagh was unable to stand. May was about to throw Creagh over his shoulder when he spied a riderless horse running toward them. May grabbed the animal's bridle and pulled the terrified beast up short. While Private Miles held the animal, May threw Creagh on its back, mounted behind the injured soldier, and galloped off at once up the hillside toward a group of appreciative onlookers.[156]

Sam Dale was also one of the American officers who had not panicked. Badly wounded in the chest, he had by now moved away from the fight but kept his eye on what was happening around him. In so doing, Dale spotted a group of Indians chasing two soldiers, Private Robert Lenoir and a man named Ballard, up the hill. Lenoir was pulling away from his pursuers, but Ballard, who had been shot in the hip, was falling behind. Against the advice of his companions, Dale decided to attempt a rescue. He cried out to Private David Glass, whose twin brother, Elijah, had earlier been killed at Dale's side, to help him save their comrades. Dale then plunged down the slope on foot toward Ballard and the oncoming pack of shrieking warriors.[157]

Glass, who was mounted, quickly reached Lenoir. Lenoir at once vaulted behind Glass onto the horse, and the two raced to safety. Poor Ballard was not so lucky. Dale was about fifty yards from the fleeing private, but one of the pursuing Indians was only ten yards behind. As Dale ran toward the private, he saw Ballard suddenly step to one side, turn, and shoot the nearest warrior. The other pursuing warriors paused momentarily as their comrade dropped to the ground, then they fell upon Ballard. The young private tried to defend himself by swinging his empty gun by its barrel at the warriors. But the Creeks quickly overwhelmed the luckless man, and Ballard went to the ground. At that, one of the warriors swiped his knife across Ballard's skull and, with his other hand holding a twist of Ballard's hair, ripped Ballard's scalp from the bone and held the smoking object up to the onlooking Americans. Enraged by this horrible sight, Glass, some fifty yards away, took Lenoir's gun, which was charged with buckshot, and fired at the warrior. Dale saw the warrior fall to the ground. Then, wasting no more time, he turned and made his way up the hill with the remaining Americans.[158]

When May reached the crest of the hill with the injured Creagh, he paused to catch his breath and let others see Creagh to safety. As he looked about him, he saw Captain William Bradberry, in civilian life a lawyer from the little town of Jackson, attempting to rally the fleeing men and put them back on the attack. May stopped to assist Bradberry, whom he saw was wounded, but both men quickly realized their efforts were futile. Their panicked comrades were so intent on escaping with their lives, and the prized pack horses, that they ignored the two officers' commands to stop and fight. At this point in the retreat, May's greed overcame his prudence. In the midst of disaster, he grabbed the bridle of a loose pack horse and made his escape, gleefully leading his prize to the rear.[159]

What had started out as an American victory became a disgraceful rout with every man for himself. The Indians pursued the fleeing Americans for almost a mile through open woods before finally breaking off the chase. Sometime between two and three that afternoon, no doubt when the word spread that the Indians were no longer pursuing them, several junior officers got control of their winded men and horses. Lieutenant Creagh took over command from the badly wounded Dale of the captain's company. They decided to return the way they had come, in hopes they could cross the Alabama River to safety before the savages descended on them.[160]

The wounded—about fifteen men—were placed at the head of the ragged column of terrified militiamen, and Smoot's company provided a rear guard. A number of men were now on foot, or riding double, because the Creeks had captured their horses. By eleven that night, the army's wounded could go no farther, and the exhausted and bedraggled little caravan, the prized pack horses still in tow, halted and made camp along the roadside for the night.[161]

Colonel Caller was not among this group. He and Major James Woods, one of McGrew's officers, had lost their horses to the Creeks and were now forced to precede on foot, joined by twenty-four-year-old Private Abner Lipscomb, the son of a Revolutionary War soldier. The colonel, however, did not stop to share the hazards of the night with the army that he at least still technically commanded. As he informed his two comrades, he knew the Indian mind, and they would surely attack the Americans' encampment at dawn. Their best course, Caller advised, was to continue down the road past the army's encampment, thereby placing the army between their three-man party and the Indians. It was probably at this point in the retreat that the ever resourceful Caller hit on an unorthodox stratagem that would not have fooled an Indian child. With his knife, he cut the leather of his boots and reversed the soles back to front. In this way he expected to fool any pursuing Indians as to the direction of his travel. His companions did likewise, and the three of them hobbled down the road past their army's bivouac.

When Caller decided they had gone far enough to be safe for the night, they made a solitary camp in the concealing woods. Exhausted, the three men, who had unaccustomedly been traveling for many hours on foot, slept so soundly that the following morning the entire army passed by their camp without waking them. When the three finally awoke, it was to the sound of guns firing. Believing his prediction of an Indian attack had come to pass, Caller urged his companions to flee through the woods. But because the sound of the firing was coming from the banks of the Alabama River ahead, Lipscomb insisted that the sound they heard was their own men firing in celebration at reaching the river, and that they should join them. Caller and Wood were so terrified that they lacked the wit to discern the true state of affairs. They rejected Lipscomb's proposal and urged immediate flight. Trusting his own ears, Lipscomb, who later became chief justice of the Alabama Supreme Court, volunteered to investigate the source of the firing if his companions would wait for him at the camp until he returned. Caller and Wood agreed.

Cautiously approaching the river, Lipscomb spied the army preparing to cross. As he had suspected, the sound of firing had come from some soldiers who spontaneously discharged their weapons in celebration of reaching the river with their scalps intact and the prized pack horses in hand. Hurrying back to give Caller and Woods the good news, Lipscomb found that they had deserted him and vamoosed into the forest—a very unwise decision as it turned out.[162]

While Caller and Woods fled into the dubious safety of the wilderness, their defeated and disconsolate little army slunk home in embarrassment. After a two-day journey, it finally reached safety on the west side of the Tombigbee River, and the soldiers peeled off for their homes. But Caller and Woods's ordeal was just beginning. For nine or more days, buffeted by heavy rains, they wandered lost through the green and black hell of an enormous summer swamp, the ground beneath the skin of water a thigh-deep suck of stinking mud, the air around them ablaze with clouds of biting insects and so thick with humidity that a person could almost lean against it. Some days later, on arriving from Baton Rouge at the US military post known as cantonment Mount Vernon with his exhausted men, General Claiborne dispatched the experienced woodsmen Dixon Bailey, Sam Moniac, and David Tate to search for his friend Colonel Caller and Major Woods. After much hard searching they found the lost men starved, all but naked, and deranged from almost two weeks of wandering aimlessly through the vast swamps of the Tensaw Delta.[163] Caller was also suffering from a dangerous fever, from which he was some time in recovering.

Thus ended one of the most ill-conceived, ill-led, and ill-executed military expeditions in US history, one that was truly unique in that unlike other military disasters, the Battle of Burnt Corn Creek was remembered not as a tragedy, or even a tragicomedy, but (perhaps because only two privates had died) as an utter farce, an ever-refreshed fountain of amusement for a generation of south Alabamians. As Thomas Woodward aptly summed up the affair: "I have seen many of those that were in the fight, and they were like the militia that were at Bladensburg [Maryland]—they died off soon; you never could hear much talk about the battle, unless you met with such a man as Judge Lipscomb, [companion of Caller and Wood in their flight from the field] who used to make a laughing matter of it."[164]

In the battle's aftermath, a deflated James Caller was the principle target of much criticism and cutting backwoods ridicule. His family and friends worked hard to rehabilitate his reputation and were somewhat successful.

He was portrayed in letters just after the battle, sometimes with a sotto voce sigh of relief from their authors, as performing bravely in the fray and having been deprived of victory by undisciplined and unruly troops.[165] As General Wilkinson's son James, a regular army captain commanding at Fort Charlotte in Mobile, wrote General Claiborne a week after the battle, "It gives me sincere pleasure to learn, that Colonel Caller acted with much bravery:—for it was currently rumored in Mobile, that he drew off the Militia in person from the battle Ground."[166]

Aside from Lewis Sewell's local and long-forgotten lampoon of Caller's role in the Burnt Corn Creek battle, the colonel's conduct in that affair has escaped the judgment of history. Whether he called for a retreat during the battle will almost certainly remain debatable. What is not debatable is his conduct during the Americans' helter-skelter retreat from the battlefield. Although the antebellum historian Albert J. Pickett had the reputable Patrick May's written account of Caller's infamous conduct in that retreat, that account never found its way into Pickett's history of the battle. It is unlikely that Pickett believed May an untrustworthy witness, because in his history of Alabama, Pickett relied heavily upon May's account of other incidents in the war. It is even more unlikely that Caller and Woods lost their entire army, particularly because it was slowed by its wounded, during the retreat from the battlefield. More likely Pickett, a fellow member with Caller of the planter/politician class that ruled Alabama, remained silent for the sake of the colonel's family. This was not the only time in his book that Pickett overlooked or glossed over James Caller's intolerable behavior.

The true villains of the Burnt Corn Creek debacle by more than a nose, however, appear to be Callers' second in command, Colonel McGrew, along with officers in McGrew's command. Patrick May reported that while he did not observe McGrew's conduct during the battle, "it was said by all I heard speak of him, that he acted cowardly and disgraced himself." Likewise, Dr. Thomas Holmes places responsibility for the rout on McGrew and his "cowardly party."[167] And of course Caller, although hardly a disinterested observer, also claimed that McGrew and his officers ordered the retreat.

Certainly there was plenty of blame to go around for this disgraceful affair. Some of the targets, however, took it better than others. Not surprisingly, the toadyish Caller, with the reptilian hide of the born politician, eventually managed to rise above public obloquy and mirth and continue his career as a prominent member of the community. His daughter even married a future governor of Alabama and US senator, Gabriel Moore. [168] To Caller's credit, however, when he finally recovered from his ordeal in the swamps, he wrote a letter to General Claiborne dated August 25, 1813, in which he recommended for promotion several veterans of the Burnt

Corn Creek fight, including Captains Smoot and Bailey and Lieutenant May (as well as his own son, Robert). Strangely conspicuous in its absence from Caller's letter was any mention of the extraordinary heroics of the badly wounded Sam Dale. Interestingly, Caller also did not mention the battle by name, or, indeed, at all. The Battle of Burnt Corn Creek must have been for Caller so painful a subject that he was reluctant even to utter its name. He certainly did not return to active military service, but he did engage in further infamous schemes and even murder.

On the other hand, Caller's companion in flight, Major Woods, came to a sad end. Lacking Caller's thick skin, the sensitive Woods, who also never returned to military duty, was forced to armor himself with spirits against the slings and arrows of his neighbors and washed away the remainder of his life in strong drink, suggesting that there was more than some truth to the reports of his and Caller's behavior during the retreat after all.[169] Ironically, several months after the Burnt Corn Creek affair, the well-traduced Colonel McGrew found at least partial public redemption in death in combat with the hostiles.

Beyond its farcical overtones, this obscure fracas between the Creeks and the Tensaw settlers had ramifications far disproportionate to the numbers engaged and the casualties suffered. In strictly military terms it was, as High Head Jim described it, "a light affair." Still, this "light affair" started a war that many wanted—but none were ready for. Contrary to frontier rumor greatly fueled by Judge Toulmin and his depositions, the Red Club leaders had no intention before, or even weeks after, the Battle of Burnt Corn Creek of mounting a near-term attack on the Tensaw settlements. As Benjamin Hawkins correctly predicted, before the hostiles attacked the whites, their leaders first wanted to end the Creek civil war and unite their nation. Caller's knee-jerk assault on the unsuspecting powder train ultimately removed that option from the Creek leaders' plans.

The competent Colonel Joseph Carson, the senior commander left in the region after the battle, recognized what was coming. On July 30, four days after Burnt Corn Creek, he reported the battle's outcome to the newly arrived General Claiborne. While he acknowledged that Caller's "[Powder] Expedition . . . took about two hundred pounds of powder and Some lead," Carson also understood that the consequences of the expedition were worse than a mere failure. "I think as soon as these Indians find themselves in a Situation," he wrote, "they will endeavor to revenge themselves on our frontier."[170]

Part Two

4. Run Up to Tragedy

The Establishment of Fort Mims

O N July 30, 1813, General Claiborne of the Mississippi territorial militia and approximately 650 twelve-month volunteers arrived from Baton Rouge at cantonment Mount Vernon. Mount Vernon lay fifty miles north of the town of Mobile and was built on the high ground back four miles from the western shore of the Mobile River. The post had been erected there because the place enjoyed a healthier climate than its neighbor, the hot and pestilential military establishment called Fort Stoddert. That fort had been built several years earlier, in 1799, principally to collect custom duties on goods traveling by river between US and Spanish territory.

When Claiborne's army arrived at Mount Vernon it was exhausted and at the extremes of misery. Heavy and incessant rains had swollen the many water courses in its path and turned the road into a quagmire. Consequently, it had taken Claiborne's army thirty long, hard, rain-sodden days to reach Mount Vernon and the threatened Tombigbee and Alabama river settlements.[1] As Colonel Caller had predicted, Claiborne's army arrived too late to reinforce the ill-begotten powder expedition. Now his friend Claiborne's worn-out soldiers were faced with addressing the threats that bungled affair had called down on the frontier.

Ferdinand Claiborne was a member of a well-connected and talented Virginia family that had immigrated to the Mississippi Territory. The Claibornes flourished in that new world. Ferdinand's brother became governor of the territory, and Ferdinand became general of its militia, speaker of the territorial legislature, and a planter with a home known as Soldier's Retreat in Natchez on the Mississippi River. The name of his beloved home fit the man well. He began his career as a professional soldier in Virginia in 1793. That year, President John Adams appointed the twenty-year-old Claiborne to the regular US Army as an ensign in the 1st Regiment. Young Claiborne soon found himself under fire at the famous Battle of Fallen Timbers in northern Ohio, in which a young Shawnee warrior named Tecumseh also distinguished himself.

At that fight, an army commanded by the Revolutionary War hero known as General "Mad Anthony" Wayne defeated an Indian confederacy led by the famous Little Turtle of the Miami tribe. As a reward for his gal-

lantry at the Battle of Fallen Timbers, Claiborne was promoted to lieutenant. In the coming years, he served in a number of campaigns against
the northwestern Indians, eventually rising to the rank of captain. He
resigned his commission in 1802 and moved to the Mississippi Territory,
where his brother William was governor. He quickly prospered in that new
land as a planter and businessman. By the end of 1804, young Claiborne
was described by a contemporary as "a gen[tle]man of Considerable
wealth and influence in this Country."[2]

On March 8, 1813, as the war with Great Britain continued in the north,
the notorious general James Wilkinson, the commander of the US 7th
Military District, appointed Claiborne brigadier general of volunteers for
that district and ordered him to Baton Rouge, Louisiana. On June 28, the
newly appointed and militarily inexperienced General Thomas Flournoy,
who succeeded Wilkinson as commander of the 7th Military District,
ordered Claiborne to the cantonment at Mount Vernon.[3] From there,
Claiborne would be in position to protect the Tensaw frontier from possible Indian attack or to reinforce the troops at Mobile should the Spanish
and hostile Creeks attempt to retake that town.

During his dreary slog through heavy rains from Baton Rouge, with sick
men falling constantly by the wayside, Claiborne was well briefed on the
uproar on the eastern frontier, the flight of the settlers, the Indian expedition to Pensacola, Caller's plan to intercept the returning party, his disastrous defeat, and his disappearance with Major Woods into the unforgiving depths of the Alabama swamps.[4] As we have seen, one of Claiborne's
first acts on arriving at Mount Vernon was to dispatch some competent
local woodsmen to search for the missing officers. Of far greater importance than the rescue of his missing friend, however, was the need to
promptly organize a defense of the threatened frontier. This Claiborne set
out to do as a stopgap measure until he could gain permission from his
superior, General Flournoy, presently stationed in Bay Saint Louis,
Louisiana, for an invasion up the Alabama River into the Creek heartland.
From his experience in the northern Indian wars, Claiborne had learned
that the best way to defeat the Indians was to attack them in their towns.

When Claiborne arrived at cantonment Mount Vernon, he surveyed the
state of the defenses of the region he was ordered to protect. If anything,
these defenses were worse than he had been told. He found the citizens disorganized and panicked by the Burnt Corn Creek debacle. For the most
part, they had fled their exposed farms, abandoning their ripening crops
as well as personal items too large to transport and penned themselves up
in a foul and motley collection of structures they grandly called forts;
these, in fact, were nothing more than flimsy and indifferently constructed stockades where the only thing that flourished was disease.

These refugees ranged from the town of Mobile and up the Tombigbee and Alabama river valleys. The port city of Mobile itself was guarded by Forts Charlotte and Bowyer. Some miles up the Mobile River, on its west bank, just below the confluence of the Alabama and Tombigbee rivers, stood Fort Stoddert and, several miles to its west, cantonment Mount Vernon. Farther north, on the western bank of the Tombigbee, stood the oldest fort in the region, Fort Saint Stephens. It had been built by the French, under Bienville, in 1714. Courtesy of the European wars that occupied the remainder of the eighteenth century, it passed, like a political ping-pong ball, to Spain in 1763, then to Great Britain, back to Spain, and finally, in 1799, to the United States.[5] Perched on a high, whitely gleaming limestone bluff overlooking the Tombigbee River, it was in little danger of attack, much less of being taken by the Creeks, although few of its current residents were confident of that.

Of more pressing concern to General Claiborne were the smaller posts that had sprung up on the eastern side of the Alabama River in the rich bottomlands at the fork of the Alabama and Tombigbee rivers. Unlike the older forts, these were isolated in the piney woods and swamplands of the river delta; many were still under construction, and by amateur fort builders at that. Under the crowded and unsanitary living conditions at these poor refuges, sickness broke out among the inhabitants, particularly dysentery.[6] Grasping at once their vulnerability, Claiborne immediately dispatched several detachments of soldiers from his command to reinforce the garrisons at these places.

One of the largest of these forts, and one to which many of the mixed-bloods of Dixon Bailey's company and their families had repaired, was on the farm of Samuel Mims, an old and wealthy Indian countryman who had settled in the region at the end of the last century. Mims's plantation was near the Federal Road, about fourteen miles east of Fort Stoddard. The enterprising Mims had greatly supplemented his farm income by operating a ferry transporting travelers on the road across the Alabama River. The old man was famous for his hospitality, and many a guest reported a lively evening of dance and drink at the Mims family home, including the handsome and fun-loving William Weatherford, captor of Augustus Bowles.[7] Around Mims's main house were the outbuildings typically found at a prosperous, self-sufficient farming operation of the day: a kitchen and smokehouse, a spinning house and a weaving house for cotton, stables for Mims's twenty-one horses, corn cribs, and a blacksmith shop. Among the domestic animals Mims owned were at least 100 sheep, 200 hogs, and 415 cattle.[8]

Mims's plantation was on a slight rise about one quarter of a mile upland from a body of water known as Tensaw Lake or the Tensaw Boatyard. The lake was a remnant of an ancient channel of the ever-changing course of the Alabama River, and its appendix-shaped waters extended a mile northeast from the river. The land around was low and flat, largely unredeemed from the swamps, with immense canebrakes and piney woods that spread to the horizon. It was a land where the settlers let their hogs and cattle run wild, a land still inhabited by deer, bears, wolves, panthers, and, in the swamps and rivers, alligators of monstrous size (in 2012, one was hoisted out of the upper Alabama River that weighed around 830 pounds). And everywhere there were several species of poisonous snakes, some up to ten feet long and as large around as a man's lower leg. Even today it is a wild land, with confusing topography, visited, at some peril, mostly by hunters and fishermen.

The local residents of all ages and races—black, white, mixed-blood, and Indian—flocked to Mims's plantation from their outlying farms during the month of July. There they began construction of a fort, known locally as Mims Blockhouse, around Mims's plantation buildings. The construction of Fort Mims would have resembled Margaret Eades Austill's contemporaneous description of the early stages of construction of a neighboring fort at Carney's Bluff on the Alabama River: "When we arrived at the river it was a busy scene, men hard at work chopping and clearing a place for a Fort, women and children crying, no place to sit down, nothing to eat, all confusion and dismay, expecting every moment to be scalped and tomahawked."[9]

In the steamy heat of early August 1813, the area around Mims's plantation houses must have resembled an enormous country fair run amok. Dozens of families were there, with adults and children of all ages. With them, by wagon, horse, or human foot, they had brought their considerable personal possessions. These included English crockery, kitchen implements, furniture—from feather beds to sideboards— farm tools, clothing, and large quantities of corn and cotton. Then there were the animals— thousands of them. In addition to Samuel Mims's large quantity of livestock, the mixed Randon family had brought 300 head of cattle, 15 horses, 50 hogs, and 100 sheep; Dixon Bailey, who had so distinguished himself at Burnt Corn Creek, had brought 260 head of cattle, 6 horses, and 60 hogs; his brother James had brought 40 head of cattle, 50 hogs, and two horses; Josiah Fletcher had come in with 7 horses, 20 sheep, 12 goats, and 75 hogs; and James Earle had appeared at the place with 24 horses and 50 hogs. The list of large farm animals, not to mention swarms of chickens and the ever-present dogs, goes on and on. And of course, with all the well-heeled families that flocked to Mims's place came their most valuable possessions of all: their slaves. In a good market, two healthy young African American males could fetch the price of Samuel Mims's substantial dwelling house. This valuable human property numbered approximately one hundred individuals of both sexes and ran the gamut of ages. In sum, the place was

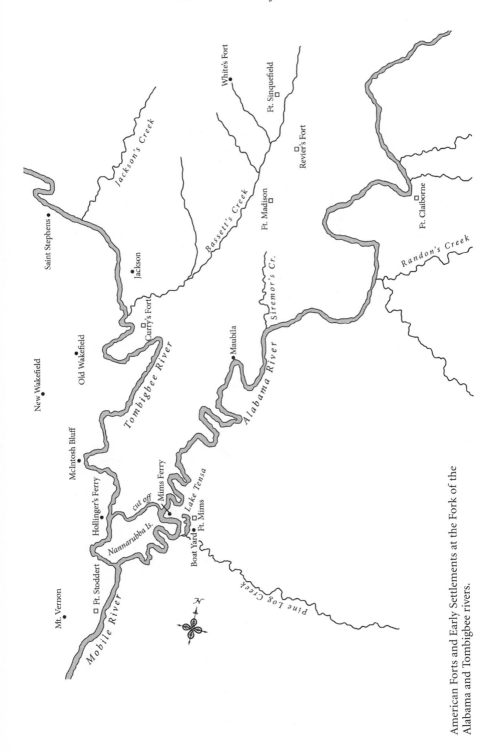

American Forts and Early Settlements at the Fork of the Alabama and Tombigbee rivers.

an unsanitary and noisome bedlam, but as time dragged on without incident, it took on even more the manic atmosphere of a hurricane party.[10] And a storm of sorts was not long in coming.

The local authorities, such as they were, tried to bring a modicum of order to this chaos. During the last week in July, Colonel Joseph Carson, who had preceded General Claiborne to Mount Vernon, ordered a young, baby-faced lieutenant from North Carolina named Spruce Osborne and twenty men to Fort Mims to reinforce the fort. On July 28, 1813, Lieutenant Osborne, who was also a physician and budding poet, wrote Carson, declaring that "this stockade is in good condition."[11] Not long after he arrived at Mount Vernon, Claiborne, who was apparently dissatisfied with young Osborne's evaluation of the fort's condition, dispatched his good friend and political ally, Major Daniel Beasley, to take charge of the post. With Beasley came 160 officers and men.

The choice of Beasley to command this post was a fateful one. Beasley had immigrated to the Mississippi Territory from North Carolina. Trained in the law, he was forty-five and handsome, about five feet ten inches tall, with dark eyes, dark hair, and a dark complexion.[12] Like that of so many young men on that frontier, his nature was an odd and volatile mix of short-tempered violence, intelligence, and a sensitive and romantic nature. Like many southerners, particularly of his class, Beasley had imbibed a stubborn arrogance and a twisted sense of personal honor from the prevailing culture in which he found himself. He had prospered in that new land, settling in the delta town of Greenville, Mississippi, where he started what quickly became a flourishing law practice. In short order, he was elected sheriff and apparently opened a tavern with a friend, potentially a very profitable venture. He found a beautiful young woman from a fine family, and they planned to marry.[13]

The pleasant arc of his life was interrupted, however, by a dispute with a man over an utterly trivial matter involving sponsorship of a dance. After the customary exchange of insults in the local paper, a duel was arranged between Sheriff Beasley and a lawyer named Frye. It took place at a local dueling ground in Spanish territory, on a sandbar along the Mississippi River. There, American antidueling laws enacted to prevent the local aristocracy from decimating itself did not apply. Pistols were the weapon of choice. When the duel was over, Frye lay dead on the sand.[14]

In that age of deadly and ill-considered honor, for Beasley, and for far more prominent men than he—Aaron Burr, Alexander Hamilton, Andrew Jackson, Stephen Decatur, Thomas Flournoy, and even Beasley's friend, Ferdinand Claiborne—dueling was not only an accepted but an expected and laudatory way for gentlemen to settle disputes. Because Beasley had fought his duel outside the jurisdiction of the United States, he went free, his honor intact, his courage esteemed by his peers. Some reports claim that afterward, Beasley was struck with an all-consuming remorse for his opponent's death, lost his lady, and decided to ask his friend General Claiborne for a commission in the territorial militia. In that profession, he hoped to find in battle a socially sanctioned end to his sufferings.[15]

The story is romantic but untrue. It is unlikely that a professional soldier like Claiborne would have supported the award of an officer's commission to a man in such personal distress. More likely, Beasley saw a commission as an officer in the militia as a way to advance his standing in society. In any event, shortly before the War of 1812 broke out, Beasley received a commission in the territorial militia signed by President James Madison. Initially, Beasley served as a captain on Claiborne's staff, but in February 1813, on the retirement of a line officer, Major Wood, Beasley, on Claiborne's order, was promoted to succeed Wood as a major. A brave man, perhaps even a fine sheriff, Beasley nonetheless had no experience in Indian warfare and, thus, little respect for his opponents.[16]

When Beasley arrived at Fort Mims on that hot and stifling August 2, he found twenty volunteer militia under the young Lieutenant Osborne already on hand. Also present to defend the fort was a volunteer company of the tough mixed-bloods who had fought under Dixon Bailey at Burnt Corn Creek. Beasley ordered the volunteers to elect their officers, and Bailey, not surprisingly, was their unanimous choice for captain. The election for ensign in the volunteer company was somewhat complicated, because one of the potential candidates, a man named Plummer, had disgraced himself at the Battle of Burnt Corn Creek, and even though he had no opponent, he did not receive a majority of the votes. Eventually, a man named Crawford was convinced to stand for election. Although he was "untried," he received the necessary votes and was elected. Several days later, Beasley discovered that Crawford was a deserter from the US army and dismissed him. Peter Randon, a local mixed-blood from a prominent family, was elected ensign in Crawford's place.[17]

Immediately after his arrival at Fort Mims, Beasley put his men to work improving the fortifications. By August 7, the major was writing General Claiborne, at nearby Mount Vernon, that he needed more whiskey because the extra gill, or half a cup, he was distributing to the work party was exhausting the supplies on hand, and the men expected that extra ration. Beasley also asked Claiborne to send a drum with the whiskey, because he had discovered a man among his militia who had served as a drummer for five years in the regular army and was quite adept at playing that instrument. The drum and a barrel of whiskey were sent and received; both became instruments of the garrison's destruction.[18]

That same day, Claiborne showed up at the fort to inspect its progress. He did not like what he saw. What progress had occurred since his last visit was indifferent. Claiborne therefore instructed Beasley in writing (politically prudent for Claiborne, as it later turned out) to strengthen the pickets and to construct two, and perhaps even three, blockhouses. In his letter to Beasley, Claiborne also advised the major that, "To respect the Enimy & to prepare in the best possible way to meet him, is the certain means to ensure success."[19]

Claiborne also soundly advised Beasley to frequently dispatch scouting parties from the fort into the surrounding countryside to discover any approaching hostiles. To this end, Claiborne detached from his command Cornet Thomas Rankin, a sergeant, a corporal, and six dragoons to Fort Mims to serve Beasley as scouts.[20] The general had chosen Rankin for this important task because he lived on the frontier and was familiar with the Tensaw region. It remained to be seen whether Beasley would use this valuable asset wisely.

Work on the fort proceeded such that on August 12, at least in Beasley's estimation, as he wrote Claiborne, even though his men were short of tools, he expected they would complete the "stockade" by the next day. Less encouraging was his report that many of his men were sick and one had died "the night before last," although none of the surviving men were seriously ill. Beasley also complained to Claiborne that Captain Benjamin Dent's company was being detached from his command and sent to the small stockade at nearby Peirce's Mill, "as it weakens my command very much." Beasley further informed the general that an Indian, apparently belonging to Captain Bailey's company, had deserted, and that he had instructed Bailey to capture him.[21] There is no evidence Bailey captured the man. Thus, if the deserter made his way to the hostiles, they now had solid information about the defensive capabilities of the fort.

Two days later, Beasley again wrote Claiborne and asked for twenty to thirty muskets because eight to ten men of Bailey's company and some "citizens" at the fort at Peirce's Mill were without arms. More ominously, Beasley reported that some Indians had been seen by a young slave of Samuel Moniac's while searching the nearby swamp for his lost horse. Beasley sent a party to investigate the slave's report, but all they found were marks on the riverbank where a canoe had been dragged into the river. The horse was found, and Beasley cavalierly dismissed the matter as a "mistake."[22]

As for General Claiborne, ensuring that the frontier was prepared for the Indian attack that everyone felt sure was coming was not his only concern. He was also engaged in a campaign to convince his superior, Brigadier General Flournoy, of the seriousness of the Indian threat and of the need to meet it head on with an immediate military expedition up the Alabama River into the nation's heart. Flournoy was born in North Carolina in 1775, and had moved to Georgia, where he practiced law. Like Major Beasley, and so many other prominent white "gentlemen" of the age, by the time Flournoy was twenty-nine, he had killed a man in a duel, held in 1804. The loser was a man named John Carter Walton, whose uncle, George Walton, was a former chief justice of the Georgia Supreme Court, a governor of the state, a signer of the Declaration of Independence, and a US senator. The duel was fought over a ruling by Judge Walton to which Flournoy took exception.

Under the southern code of honor at the time, this extrajudicial murder had no lasting effect on lawyer Flournoy's career and may have even promoted it. For without any prior military experience, on June 18, 1812, Flournoy was appointed brigadier general in the regular US Army in command of an infantry unit responsible for protecting the border with Spanish East Florida. When that old rascal general Wilkinson was transferred to a northern command, General Flournoy was selected to assume command of Wilkinson's 7th Military District, headquartered in New Orleans.[23]

Two days after he arrived at Mount Vernon, General Claiborne wrote General Flournoy of the importance of invading the Creek Nation as soon as Flournoy's command joined Claiborne's. Claiborne assured Flournoy that by such action they could not only achieve peace with the Indians but, more importantly, grab for the government "any portion of the Creek country they please."[24] Having received no permission from Flournoy to invade the Creek Nation, Claiborne decided to go behind his superior's back. On August 14, 1813, Claiborne wrote Governor Mitchell of Georgia, succinctly explaining his reasons for urging this course of action:

> I sincerely hope that I may then be ordered by Genl. Flournoy under whom I act, to penetrate into the Creek Nation. More could be effected now; by one thousand men, than could be accomplished three months hence by double that number.
>
> If I am ordered to act on the defencive much serious injury will be done on the Frontiers. The best mode of fighting Indians is to penetrate into the heart of their settlements and to give them battle at the threshold of their doors.[25]

That was excellent advice, born out of Claiborne's hard-won experience gained while serving under General Wayne in the northwest. Governor Mitchell did nothing, however, and Flournoy was in no mind to take military advice from Ferdinand Claiborne. Despite the fact that Flournoy was no Indian fighter, or even an experienced soldier for that matter, he had a low opinion of Claiborne's abilities to command the territorial militia. In fact, only days after Claiborne conducted his inspection of the military construction at Mims's plantation, Flournoy wrote Claiborne and chastised him for being "too loose in the management" of his officers. After listing Claiborne's shortcomings in managing his command, such as permitting men going absent without leave, Flournoy admonished the easy-going Claiborne, "My Dear General these things will not do. Believe me, you will render yourself more popular as an Officer, & as a man, by making every man in your Service attend to his duty & by demanding Courts Martial from me in every Case of delinquency."[26]

As a former officer in the regular army, with an outstanding combat record, Claiborne must have been rankled by the inexperienced Flournoy's patronizing advice. Nonetheless, at least as regards men such as his friend Beasley, with whom Claiborne had perhaps too cozy a relationship, it was good advice.

Regardless of the friction over command styles, the issue of strategy was the more serious one separating the two men. In summer 1813, the war with Great Britain was entering its second year. Flournoy's main concern was defending the critical port cities of Mobile and New Orleans, not defending some backwoods region sparsely populated by Indians, half-breeds, and the worst sort of whites.

By the time Claiborne wrote his letter to Governor Mitchell, Flournoy, who had been ill, had made his way from his headquarters in New Orleans to Port Saint Louis on the Gulf Coast. From there, Flournoy continued his exchange with Claiborne about strategy. Claiborne wanted Flournoy to send the 7th Regiment of regulars, currently under Flournoy's command, to Claiborne at Mount Vernon for a strike into the Creek Nation. On August 10, Flournoy sent a message to Claiborne dashing these hopes: "I shall send the 7th regiment by water to Mobile. I fear that it is the design of the Spanish government to draw our force to the upper country by playing off the Indians against us there, and then to make an attempt to retake Mobile. To guard against this, Major Gibson will be directed to remain with the 7th at Mobile till further orders."[27]

Flournoy, who was clearly afraid that Claiborne would take some action on his own, took care to admonish Claiborne not to let his "zeal for the public good" drive him into "acts of indiscretion." Claiborne's invasion plan, "with a view for commencing the war," was not acceptable, and to make sure his position left Claiborne no room for a different interpretation, Flournoy once again informed Claiborne that "our operations must be confined to defensive operations." Flournoy also immediately quashed Claiborne's alternative proposal that Flournoy authorize Claiborne to call up the local militia, curtly informing him that military regulations gave Flournoy no such authority.[28]

Unfortunately for the local frontier people, the relationship between Claiborne and Flournoy was one in which a superior officer clearly did not trust his subordinate officer, whether out of jealously of Claiborne's military accomplishments, insecurity concerning his own abilities, fear that

Claiborne was headstrong and would unnecessarily start a war with the Indians, or simply because Flournoy felt that his primary responsibility, as he had stated, was to keep the Spanish and their British allies out of the key port city of Mobile. Flournoy was also no doubt influenced by his recent trip through the nation and his meeting with the Big Warrior, during which that powerful chief assured Flournoy of the nation's intent to remain friends with the Americans and to refuse to enter the war on the side of the British. After all, as evidence of its good faith, the nation had just put to death a number of its warriors for attacking whites. Even more important than the Big Warrior's assurances, Flournoy trusted in Benjamin Hawkins's evaluation of the temper of the Muskogee people. What American could claim to have more experience with them than the colonel? As Hawkins had recently written to Flournoy in a letter, which he passed on to Claiborne on August 26, the Muskogee Nation was not now and may never be a danger to the Americans. "[T]hey must finish their civil war," Hawkins explained, "before they can go to war with us. And it is by no means certain that the war party will succeed in overpowering the party friendly to us."[29]

As it turned out, despite the blizzard of recriminations and finger pointing that would begin in several weeks, neither Hawkins's nor Flournoy's position was unreasonable from the particular perspective of the other. But such were the times that even Claiborne, whose proposed strategy was later vindicated, nonetheless found himself fighting for his military reputation before the war was done.

While Flournoy and Claiborne squabbled over strategy, and the Tensaw settlements forted up, the Creeks continued their civil war. But, like the Americans, the Red Club leaders also engaged in some heated debates over military strategy. As the Creek civil war ground on with petty raids and skirmishes, some in the hostile party, bent on revenge for the Americans' surprise attack at Burnt Corn Creek, began eyeing the Tensaw settlements and their traitorous mixed-blood community as their next target.

The Massacre at Fort Mims

THE Battle of Burnt Corn Creek had gone surprisingly well for the Red Clubs. Although poorly armed and facing three times their number, they had forced the Americans to skedaddle from the battlefield. It was true that the Red Club losses in men were somewhat greater than for the Americans: probably five killed, not counting one slave, and ten to fifteen wounded. They also lost a good amount of the supplies they had extorted from the Spanish in Pensacola.[30] But all in all, their victorious outcome against a numerically far superior force of American soldiers seemed to support the prophets' insistence that the Red Clubs had God on their side.

Nonetheless, the loss of the supplies captured by the Americans presented a serious problem. To address that loss, before returning home, the leaders of the expedition to Pensacola decided to divide their forces. One group was sent back to Pensacola to replenish their lost supplies; the other, with the remaining pack horses and their wounded, returned in triumph to the nation. They arrived home by August 3, considerably puffed up with an exaggerated victory. As they filed into their respective towns and villages, they enjoyed a favorite Creek pastime of regaling their neighbors with tales of a monumental victory: how a small band of warriors defeated an overwhelming and treacherous American host, driving them like frightened game from the field of battle. To punctuate their boasts, they waved, whooping with delight, sections of the dried and treated scalps of privates Ballard and Glass. In order to make these valuable trophies go farther, they divided them into strips and parceled them out among the war leaders. As additional, and more useful, emblems of their triumph, they also distributed Spanish powder, lead, and trade goods among the towns.[31]

Old Hoboheilthle, Peter McQueen, and the other Red Club leaders were naturally pleased with the enthusiasm for war against the Americans that they had kindled among their followers. But their concerns ran manifestly deeper regarding the direction the nation should now take in response to the holocaust that the Americans would surely attempt to visit on it. After some consultation, the wisest among them decided that before they could effectively confront the Americans, they must first unite the nation by destroying the leaders of the friendly Creeks. They had these traitors and their reluctant supporters penned up at Coweta. If they could destroy the friendly chiefs, the Red Club leaders believed that the other Creeks, who constituted many hundreds of warriors, would join their movement.[32]

Accordingly, they planned to attack Coweta in twenty days. Following their traditional method of marking time, the Red Clubs handed out bundles of sticks among their towns. Each day a stick would be broken. When all twenty were broken, the warriors in the various towns knew it was time for the assault. Once the Creek leaders friendly to the Americans were killed and the nation was united, the Red Clubs planned to turn their attention to the Americans. Their plan was audacious in its scope. They would commence three coordinated assaults against the Americans: one on the Georgians, one on the Tennesseans, and one on the settlers in the Mississippi Territory.[33]

But many among the hostiles did not agree with McQueen's plan. They were the relatives of the warriors who did not return from the Burnt Corn Creek battle, or whose kinsmen were badly wounded in that fight, or warriors who were angered at the Americans' unprovoked attack on High Head Jim's pack train and the theft of the goods given to the Creeks by the Spanish governor. This relatively small group of Indians, doubtlessly backed by their respective clans, wanted revenge for these wrongs, and they wanted it immediately—revenge on not only the treacherous white settlers in the Tensaw Delta region but, in particular, revenge on their neighbors, the wealthy and traitorous mixed-blood elites, like Dixon Bailey, who had joined the whites in the surprise attack on the Creek pack train and who had for years, separated by several hundred miles from established Muskogee towns, figuratively thumbed their noses at traditional Muskogee society. The seeds of resentment sown by these elites, who over a decade ago had removed themselves from their countrymen to the lower Alabama country, were about to ripen into bloody fruit. Many influential Creeks believed that these traitors, in particular, owed their fellow Muskogees a debt that must promptly be paid.[34]

But McQueen's strategy clearly gave the Creeks whatever small chance they had to preserve their lands. Once the friendly chiefs forted up at Coweta were eliminated, their considerable followers were likely to join the winners. As things now stood, the Red Clubs' greatest threat came from the Georgians. They had a large number of citizens near their border with the Creeks and the new Federal Road to provide them ready access to the Red Club strongholds along the lower Tallapoosa River. The friendly Creeks' bastion at Coweta also gave the Georgians an excellent staging point for an expedition to these strongholds, which were only fifty-five miles west of Coweta.

In contrast, along the nation's western border, the Tensaw settlers were few, no more than ten thousand souls, according to Judge Toulmin. They were also disorganized and forted up in isolated, diseased-ridden, and indifferently built stockades. Several hundred warriors waging a guerilla campaign could easily keep the Tensaw people in check. And there was still the possibility that the Red Clubs, whose emissaries were already abroad seeking support from their fellow Native Americans, could enlist in their cause at least a part of the Choctaw Nation on the western border of the Tensaw settlements. William Weatherford and another Creek warrior, Ochillie Hadjo, reportedly visited the Choctaw chief, Moshulitubbee, who was the head of the Middle Division of the Choctaw Nation, on just such a mission.[35] Their success with the crafty Choctaw leader was minimal at best. However, Moshulitubbee did report to the Americans that by mid-July, thirty Choctaw warriors had joined the hostile Creeks at the Black Warrior River towns.[36]

Finally, there were the Tennessee settlements to the north. As a matter of logistics, it was one thing for the Tennesseans to send raiding parties against the Creek settlements in the rugged country to their south but yet another thing altogether to mount a large assault against these places. The Tennessee settlements lay a hundred miles north of the Upper Creek population centers. The country between Tennessee and the main rebel towns consisted of ridge after ridge of rough, heavily forested hills, without a Federal Road through them to facilitate transportation of an army. The Americans would also have to pass through the Cherokee lands that lay between Tennessee and the northern border of the Muskogee Nation. At the very least, the Tennesseans would have to negotiate with the Cherokees for safe passage through their territory. Then there was the possibility that if the hostile Creeks could win a significant victory over the Americans, they could convince the Cherokees to join their movement.

The debate among the rebel Creeks over the issue of strategy must have been long and fractious, for it was some weeks before a decision was reached. But in the end, all of the Red Clubs' military power and their success at Burnt Corn Creek did McQueen's party little good against the Muskogees' long engrained code of revenge. Perhaps McQueen and the ancient Tallassee King, Hoboheilthle, had lost some measure of influence over the prophets' movement. With the prophets' support, their strategy would likely have prevailed; without that support it had little chance of success. The upshot of the debate was a decision to send a party of approximately seven hundred warriors into the Tensaw settlements to sweep the Americans and the traitorous mixed-bloods from the land. After that was accomplished, the Red Clubs could turn to the old chiefs hiding in Coweta. Historian Barbara Tuchman's "march of folly" was on.

At this point, a new and reputedly reluctant Creek war leader emerged to direct the Red Club offensive into American territory: William Weatherford, son of the old reprobate Charles Weatherford, the wealthy Scots plantation owner and famous horse breeder, and his aristocratic wife, Sehoy, a member of the prominent Wind Clan.[37] William Weatherford's maternal uncle, Alexander McGillivray, was said to have instilled such a dislike of Americans in his nephew that in later years, Weatherford was heard to boast that he had no "Yankee blood in his veins."[38] Ironically, he did not have much Indian blood either. Weatherford was only one-eighth Creek, but he considered himself a full member of the nation nonetheless.

By all accounts, even hostile ones, Weatherford was a handsome man, with a pale yellow complexion that earned him the Indian nickname Billy Larney or Yellow Billy.[39] His eyes were black and crowned by heavy black eyebrows. He wore his black hair short, in the style of the whites. He was well built, powerful, and a noted athlete and brawler, a little over six feet tall and about 165 pounds of hard muscle. At this point in his life he was a wealthy and cultured planter, "received into the first class of white society—even that of white ladies," though he could neither write nor read.[40]

When in his planter mode, Weatherford wore a black suit of broadcloth, a black hat with a beaded band, a beaded girdle, silver-buckled shoes, and a richly distinctive ring on his hand. He loved the fiddle and fine horses. In his younger days he was something of a Prince Hal, rich, handsome, and the leader of a band of dissolute young men. He had gained renown among the Creeks as one of the captors of William Augustus Bowles at the Hickory Ground. He, his brother John, and his half-brother, David Tate, had plantations along the lower Alabama River, and William also had a home near Josiah Francis's newly built town on the upper Alabama River known as the Holy Ground. Weatherford was thus a man with the proverbial foot in both worlds, and as such, his allegiances were suspect by both.

Weatherford's married life reflected the close and complex relationships among the inhabitants of the nation. He was married three times. His first wife was Mary "Polly" Moniac, the sister of his friend Sam Moniac. By her, Weatherford had three children. After Polly died in 1803, William did not marry again until 1813. His second wife was his first wife's niece, the daughter of Sam Moniac's brother John. Her name was Sopoth (Raney) Thlaine. She was reputedly a great beauty who closely followed the traditional Creek ways and had joined the prophets' party. She had one son by Weatherford, named after his father, but in March 1816, the couple separated, and Sopoth and her son returned to the Creek Nation.[41] In June 1816, William married Mary Stiggins.[42] Her brother, George Stiggins, was a prominent member of the Natchez tribe and among the earliest historians of the war. This Mary and William had four children and made their home in the Little River community, once the second home of Alexander McGillivray.[43]

How and when Weatherford joined the Red Club party is unclear. The best sources agree that around mid-July 1813, Weatherford and his former brother-in-law, Moniac, who seemed to have a knack for unpleasant encounters with his Creek relations, returned home from a business trip outside the nation to find that the hostiles were holding their families hostage near the fork of the Coosa and Tallapoosa rivers. The hostiles had already stripped Moniac of his slaves and other property at his plantation on the Alabama River; now they did the same to Weatherford at his plantation on the Alabama. At this point the accounts depart. One author, General Thomas Woodward, who fought in the Creek War and knew Weatherford personally, writes that Weatherford and Moniac had just returned from selling cattle to the Chickasaws when they learned of the kidnappings of their families.[44]

According to Woodward's account, the two men immediately rode to the hostile town where their families were being held. Upon their arrival, the Red Club leaders gave the men a choice: either join the hostiles or die. Moniac refused their offer, jumped onto his horse, and was about to ride away when Josiah Francis, his sister's husband, grabbed the horse's bridle. Reacting quickly, Moniac snatched Francis's war club from the prophet's other hand and smashed it against him. The injured Francis dropped the bridle, and Moniac galloped off amid a hail of bullets, leaving his family behind. Weatherford, whom no one disputes was the bravest of the brave, agreed to join the hostiles, telling them that although he did not approve of their course of action, he had been brought up among them and considered them, not the Americans, his people. Thereafter, he began to consult with them on a strategy for the coming war.[45]

The other author, Creek historian George Stiggins, writes that Weatherford returned home from a business trip to find his family and possessions held hostage by the prophets' party. But Stiggins writes that the trip was to Pensacola, and was taken by Weatherford alone to obtain supplies and to avoid the coming conflict. As in Woodward's account, Weatherford hurries to the town where his family is being held captive, Hoithlewaulee, on the north bank of the Tallapoosa River some ten miles downstream from Tuckabatchee.[46]

Faced with the fact that his family was being held hostage by religious fanatics of the most vicious stripe, Stiggins says Weatherford decided to dissimulate, pretending that he was with the prophets, all the while awaiting an opportunity to spirit his family to safety. James Caller's surprise attack at Burnt Corn Creek on the pack train from Pensacola ruined that plan. Now, even if Weatherford and his family managed to escape the hostiles, they had no place to run. For as Weatherford learned from several slaves who had escaped from their masters to the Red Club town, the embarrassing American defeat at Burnt Corn Creek has so incensed the settlers in the Forks that some seriously dangerous men among them, probably Dixon Bailey for one, had vowed to take Weatherford's life.[47] With that, as in Woodward's account, Weatherford entered into the war councils of the hostiles.

Weatherford's motives for joining the Red Clubs were plainly complex. Certainly concern for his family entered into his decision. But to what degree? Sam Moniac left his family in the hands of Josiah Francis and joined the Americans. In contrast, Weatherford seemingly entered wholeheartedly into the war on the side of the hostiles, figuring prominently in several campaigns and, although never a chief, rising to the rank of war leader of the Creek forces. In so doing, Weatherford not only risked his considerable property but, on several occasions, his very life. In the end, it may well be that he had been raised a Creek and, for all of his white blood and his white planter ways, had over the years completely absorbed a Creek identity. As Weatherford once explained, these were his people, and he could not abandon them, particularly to the hated Americans.[48]

On entering into the war councils of the Red Clubs, Weatherford learned that clan vengeance had triumphed over military principle and that the primary target in the Red Clubs' proposed expedition to the Tensaw region was the rough-hewn stockade with the grandiose name of Fort Mims, which had been built around the homestead of the hospitable old countryman Samuel Mims where the fun-loving Weatherford had spent many an enjoyable evening with the local gentry. Weatherford and his new Red Club associates had learned that forted up in the stockade were Dixon Bailey, his extended family, and other wealthy mixed-bloods and their families. These were people the Red Clubs considered traitors because their men had participated in the treacherous attack at Burnt Corn Creek. As such, they became the primary object of the Red Clubs' plan to attack the Tensaw settlements. Further crowding the small fort were local white settlers and their large broods of children, some pure-blooded Creeks, and a large number of slaves and over one hundred militia.

Toward the end of August, despite Major Beasley's assurances to General Claiborne, Fort Mims was still a far cry from the bastion Claiborne had ordered the major to construct. Over a month's time, made miserable by heavy rains, the settlers had leisurely enclosed an acre of ground around Mims's plantation complex with fifteen-foot-long pine pickets. The logs were split lengthwise and set butt end down, in the ragged line of a ditch that had been excavated to receive them. The builders placed them so that the rough-barked exterior of one half of each split log alternated with the smoother yellow-white interior of the other half, giving the fort a striped appearance.[49] Horizontal wooden stringers stitched the logs together, and numerous portholes for small arms were cut along the walls, three feet off the ground and several yards apart. For some unknown reason, the builders failed to provide firing steps behind each firing hole. This simple measure would have allowed the portholes to be placed higher off the ground and out of easy reach of any attackers.

Within the fort were a number of structures built around Mims's home. The house bespoke its owner's wealth. It was a frame home with a shingled roof, verandas on either side, and an internal chimney; one authority of the period described it as a Creole-style dwelling.[50] Hard by the southwest side of Mims's house was his kitchen. This structure, built near a tree, was set away from the main house, as was typical in those days, for fear of fire. A woodpile for fuel lay nearby. In a northwestern diagonal from Mims's house lay four houses: the Dyers's home was the nearest, the small Steadham home next; then two nameless houses stood close to the northwest corner of the fort.[51]

The fort had two entrances. The western entry was protected by two gates. The outer gate was set in the wall of a shallow rectangle of pickets that had been tacked on to the fort's original west wall. This feeble structure was about twenty-five feet deep and half the length of the original wall. A second gate was set in the center of the original west wall. A guard-house stood within the south side of the enclosed area between the outer and inner gates. Bailey's family's house stood on the enclosure's north side. Two water wells, lined with cypress wood, lay near the western gate.[52]

Two-thirds down the south wall, another rectangular enclosure jutted out from the main wall. The station of one of Beasley's company com-manders, Captain William Jack, was set within this rectangle. Not far down the south wall from Jack's station stood an inner wall of pickets that ran south to north. These pickets formed the original east wall of the fort. Major Beasley's men had extended the pickets fifty yards to the east, form-ing a separate compound. Inside this compound stood Beasley's small house and the tents of Captain Jack's and Captain Hatton Middleton's companies.[53] A gateway had been centered in the outer wall of this com-pound. It was kept constantly open, probably to let a breeze into the reek-ing confines of the fort. Unnoticed by Beasley or anyone else in the garri-son, the open gate had become fixed solid in the soil, which had been soft-ened by the heavy rains that had recently passed through the area. This bastion, tacked onto the fort's original east wall, was probably the work that Beasley mentioned in his August 12, 1813, letter to General Claiborne as nearing completion.

Behind the inner east wall of the compound, starting from its southern corner, lay a small house next to a large tree. On the other side of the tree was a row of tents belonging to Captain Middleton, Lieutenant Peter Randon, Ensign George Gibbs, and Ensign William Chambliss. This line of tents ended at the gate cut in the original wall. On the northern side of that gate two small houses stood. Completing the circuit of the fort, to the west of those houses, along the upper expanse of the fort's northern wall, stood the home of John Randon, Peter Randon's father. From the middle of that wall a bay of pickets protruded toward the forest. Within this enclosure stood a large structure called Patrick's loom house or the "bastion." Bailey's militia company was stationed just outside this bay.[54]

The fort's defenders had good fields of fire. In the land beyond the fort's walls, the men had pushed the boundaries of Mims's fields into the piney woods until some six to eight acres had been cleared around the fort. This work left the newly cleared ground studded with resin-bleeding pine stumps and, against the edge of the forest, piles of freshly cut trees. About eighty yards from the south wall, along the edge of a sweet potato patch, were log stables with haylofts where Mims stabled his horses. To the north-east, along the Federal Road, near the intersection of the road to Pensacola and the road to the fort lay Mrs. Benjamin O'Neal's substantial house. Beyond the western gate a long stretch of open ground ran from the fort to the lake. Three buildings lay along the west shore of the lake near its juncture with the river. The one nearest the fort was a cotton gin owned by the Peirce brothers, where thousands of bales of ginned and unginned cotton were stored. The other structures were cabins owned by the Peirces and Moses Steadham. A small potato patch lay about fifty yards outside Captain Jack's station, and beyond that a row of what were labeled on a map as three "Negro Cabins" stood near the tree line.[55]

There were two other fortified places nearby. The Peirce brothers had erected a small stockade at their mills, about two miles southeast of Fort Mims. On the night of August 14, at the request of Weatherford's half-brother, David Tate (whose wife and her family were at Fort Mims), Major Beasley sent a small detachment of men to reinforce that stockade.[56] Beasley also sent another detachment of troops to Hinson's and Kennedy's sawmills ten miles south on the east bank of the Tensaw River. These mills were purportedly critical to the federal government because they supplied the lumber used in the improvements being made to Forts Bowyer and Charlotte in Mobile.[57] Although this dispersal of troops from Fort Mims materially weakened that garrison, by August 24, 1813, an attack on Fort Mims appeared so unlikely that Lieutenant Osborne, the young soldier-physician, wrote General Claiborne requesting a transfer to Captain Scott's command at Saint Stephens because there was little or nothing for him to do at the fort. Only one man was seriously ill, the other sick were convalescing well, and those on duty were healthy. Osborne expected the command to remain healthy because of the "lightness of their duties"—an ominous assertion given that not one of the blockhouses Claiborne had instructed Beasley to build had even been started, while the first stood unfinished.[58] Moreover, working heavy construction in that August heat and humidity, as the men were supposed to be doing, could hardly be described as light duty—if indeed the men were even working.

Following the explanation as to why his services where not needed at Fort Mims, the young lieutenant came to the real reason he wanted a transfer from this backwater post: he had entered military service because it offered the prospect of promotion and glory (no small advantage when he entered private medical practice) and there was none of either to be had at Fort Mims. Unfortunately for Osborne, Claiborne never acted on the young man's request, and the lieutenant was probably already dead before the general even had time to consider it.

Osborne's apotheosis was near at hand, and yet, as if Providence itself could not bear the horror fast approaching Fort Mims, its defenders were favored with several last and definitive warnings of the coming Red Club attack. Seventy miles north, on August 21, 1813, a well-known Choctaw warrior called Bakers Hunter entered Fort Easley with alarming news. The fort was situated on a precipitous bluff overlooking the western shore of the Tombigbee River. Several miles downstream from the fort was a

Choctaw settlement known as Turkey Town.[59] As the highly agitated Choctaw told the fort's commander, a Captain Cassity, about four hundred Creeks were camped twelve miles or so north, preparing within six days to sweep through the forts and settlements to the south. When the Creeks were in place outside Fort Easley, the Choctaws at nearby Turkey Town would be given the signal to join the attack. So confident was the Choctaw in the accuracy of his information that he offered to let the Americans cut his throat if he were proved wrong. Bakers Hunter's story was soon seconded by a white resident of the Choctaw Nation who had recently arrived at Fort Easley, where his brother was staying, to give a similar warning.[60]

Captain Cassity's statement was taken down by Colonel Joseph Carson at Fort Madison on August 23, 1813, and immediately forwarded to General Claiborne at Saint Stephens, who received it that same day. The following day, not far behind the report, fleeing in terror from Fort Easley, one hundred settlers and all but six of its garrison of soldiers reached Saint Stephens. In response to Cassity's intelligence, Claiborne sent an express rider to Beasley at Fort Mims summoning the major to Mount Vernon for a conference of war. When the two men met, Claiborne advised Beasley of the latest intelligence from Fort Easley, "impressed upon him the certainty of an attack upon Fort Mims," and urged him to employ the utmost vigilance against an attack.[61]

In light of Cassity's report, Claiborne reconsidered the disposition of his troops among the forts in the region. Expressing confidence that Beasley could handle an attack on Fort Mims, the general improbably concluded, even though there were no settlers there to defend, that Fort Easley was the post in greatest danger. Accordingly, Claiborne hastily cobbled together a force of eighty men and headed upriver to defend a remote post from which almost everyone had fled.[62] In arriving at this bizarre decision, Claiborne apparently did not question whether, by the skillful dissemination of false information, the Creeks were actually attempting to decoy him away from their real targets. Nonetheless, Claiborne did take the time during his Fort Easley adventure to write Beasley on August 28, 1813, and warn him that a large force of hostiles was in the area, and that Fort Mims was a potential target.[63] While at Fort Easley awaiting attack, Claiborne wisely took the precaution of sending scouts into the surrounding forest, but they found no signs of hostiles. In the end, the only casualty suffered by the Americans at the fort was a slave of Samuel Easley's who was killed by a tree felled during the fort's construction.[64]

On August 29, a messenger from Claiborne rode into Fort Mims with news for Beasley of the unsettling report from Cassity of the Creek threat to that fort. That report was partially confirmed by two slaves that very day. The Indians generally did not harm slaves. The primary threat slaves faced from the Indians was a change in masters. From the slave owners' perspective, it was wiser to risk the loss of their property to the Creeks than their own lives. Thus, from stockades throughout the region, masters would send their slaves out into the hostile countryside to look after their plantations.[65]

On the morning of August 29, two young slaves, whose owners had sent them on just such an errand, came running breathlessly back to the fort's open eastern gate with tales of Indians in the nearby woods. One slave was owned by John Randon, whose son was a lieutenant in Beasley's command; the other was owned by the popular planter Josiah Fletcher.[66] Their masters had sent them to Randon's plantation just over two miles west of the fort directly across the Alabama River to tend Randon's cattle.[67] On the way they spied a troop of painted and howling warriors racing toward nearby Peirce's Mill. They hurried back to Fort Mims to tell what they had seen.[68]

The young men's report was not the first time slaves had claimed to have seen Indians on their excursions outside the fort. The prior day a slave belonging to Zachariah McGirth, a planter who was married to Alexander McGillivray's second wife, Vicey Cornells, unexpectedly showed up at Fort Mims in great agitation.[69] The man reported that he and two other McGirth slaves had been captured by hostiles while on a mission to harvest corn. He had managed to escape, but his companions decided to remain with their captors. Similarly, another of Randon's slaves, while approaching Randon's plantation to gather corn for the fort, claimed to have seen a group of Indians ransacking the place. And yet, in spite of these incidents, none of the fort's defenders, including Cornet Larkin, the local woodsman, and his scouts, had so much as glimpsed an Indian.[70]

Beasley grew dangerously frustrated by what he increasingly saw as cries of wolf from panicked Africans—a people reputed among the whites to be prone to fear and exaggeration. Even so, the implications of Randon's and Fletcher's slaves' reports of August 29 could not be responsibly ignored. Accordingly, the major promptly dispatched a group of eight to ten mounted troops under the command of Captain Middleton, accompanied by the two slaves, to investigate. If the slaves' tale proved true, Beasley planned to order a larger force to the relief of Peirce's Mill. All this may have been a ploy by the Indians to lure such a force from the fort into an ambush in the woods where the Indians' tactics were best employed. For Fort Peirce was never attacked, nor is it likely that if the Indians had intended to attack it they would have given the defenders such advance notice. Whatever the slaves witnessed left no trace that the whites could detect. After scouting the woods for some hours, an irritated Middleton and his command returned to Fort Mims around sundown with the report that they had found no signs of Indians.

At this news, Beasley fell into a savage rage, perhaps fueled by the samples from the recently arrived barrel of whiskey, and ordered the two slaves punished for spreading false rumors, an order he conveniently omitted from his report the next morning to General Claiborne. Randon obediently turned his man over to the red-faced Beasley, who had the slave tied up in front of the whole fort and lashed repeatedly. Fletcher was made of sterner stuff, and when it came time for his slave to be punished, he refused to hand the man over to Beasley, angrily exclaiming that he believed his slave's story over Middleton's report. Doubly enraged now, and backed by the insulted and humiliated Middleton, who had a personal slave at the fort, Beasley ordered the entire Fletcher family to leave the fort by ten the next morning, August 30. Would that they had.[71]

That night, Fletcher's many friends among the fort's inhabitants descended en masse on Beasley' cabin near the still-open east gate and begged him to rescind his order. The cooled-off Beasley agreed—on the condition that Fletcher relent and allow his slave to be tied up that morning and given one hundred lashes (a number that sounds greatly inflated, given that Randon's slave who had received a similar brutal punishment that evening was up and about the next morning). Fletcher's friends then turned their entreaties from Beasley to Fletcher, who, no doubt also assailed by his terrified family, reluctantly acceded to Beasley's horrific demand. Satisfied that his and Middleton's honor was preserved, Beasley ordered the sentence carried out at 10:00 A.M. the next day, shortly before the newly arrived drum would beat for lunch.[72]

At this point, Beasley appeared to descend into a kind of blind madness. The mystery is why the courageous, level-headed Dixon Bailey, with an independent company of proven fighters under his command, did not oppose Beasley's ruinous behavior. Bailey and his men, Indian and mixed-blood alike, had lived in this region for years; they had hunted, trapped, and fished its woods and swamps and rivers, and they knew the region better than the approaching hostiles themselves. Perhaps the month of quiet in that steamy, fetid, and diseased place had drained their energies and eased them into the same innervated lassitude that seemed to have infected Beasley and his men. Bailey's good advice to Colonel Caller during the Battle of Burnt Corn Creek had been fatally rejected by the colonel, and perhaps Bailey felt it would be futile to approach the equally arrogant and peevish Major Beasley. But even without Beasley's permission, Bailey could easily have slipped out of the loosely guarded fort with several men and scouted in-depth the fort's perimeter. It could not have been difficult for these experienced woodsmen to detect the signs of the hundreds of Indians and their horses who now lay hidden in the woods three quarters of a mile away.

Whatever Bailey's reasons for failing to send out his own scouting parties, it is ironic that while Beasley enters history's inconstant ranks as an arrogant, almost cartoonish, bumbler, Bailey is lionized by posterity as the martyred hero of the disaster he had such a hand in making.

On the morning of August 30, 1813, Ensign Chambliss handed the dispatch rider a report to General Claiborne detailing the strength of the garrison at Fort Mims. That report listed as available for duty 1 major, 3 captains, 5 ensigns, 11 sergeants, 6 corporals, 5 musicians, and 75 privates—a total of 106 men. But six fortunate individuals of this number were on leave in Mobile. Chambliss also noted that some of the men were "a little indisposed," although at least one man appears to have been seriously ill, because in his letter to Claiborne that morning, Beasley asks, on behalf of Dr. Osborne, for a few bottles of wine needed to save one patient's life. In addition to the Mississippi territorial volunteers, Beasley also had Captain Bailey's company of forty-one mixed-blood and Indian militiamen. There were also twenty-four families sheltering in the fort, six of whom were of mixed-blood, and seven of whom were of Indian blood—about 160 free individuals, as well as one hundred or so slaves. In all, the best estimate to date of the individuals present in the fort that morning is approximately four hundred.[73]

The Indian forces gathered around the fort numbered around 700 to 750 warriors. Thirteen towns had been assigned to furnish warriors for the attack, while several other hostile towns along the lower Tallapoosa had been assigned the task of screening the expedition to the forks from the friendly Creek towns along the Chattahoochee. The war party was led principally by William Weatherford, Peter McQueen, Hopie Tastanagi (or in English the intriguing sobriquet of the Far-Off Warrior), High Head Jim, and the prophets Paddy Walsh and Seekaboo, the latter two functioning as religious commissars. Toward the end of August, the Red Club leaders had marshaled their forces at Flat Creek, near the point where it flows into the Alabama River, in present-day Monroe County.[74] Amazingly, and perhaps because of the depopulation of the countryside, the Red Clubs had managed to travel the several hundred miles from their settlements on the Coosa and Tallapoosa rivers to Flat Creek undetected. At that point, they were a mere forty-four miles or so northeast of Fort Mims.

The Red Club army proceeded to cover that distance over a leisurely four days. The slow pace was probably dictated by a desire to approach the fort undetected and to obtain through scouting parties a complete picture of the defenses of the fort and the size of its garrison. At least one scouting party made an important discovery about the fort. As we have seen, on August 18, three of Zachariah McGirth's slaves had been captured by a band of Indians.[75] Although one of the slaves managed to escape, the other two remained with the Creeks. One of these, "an intelligent fellow, named Joe" who may have been inspired by the timing of the Americans' attack on the lunching Creeks at Burnt Corn Creek, cleverly advised the Indians that the best way to take the fort was to conceal themselves in the surrounding woods and then wait for the fort's drummer to summon the soldiers and the citizens of the fort to lunch. Then, while the inhabitants were occupied in enjoying their meal, the Indians should rush the post. Joe's suggestion apparently intrigued the Creek leaders.[76]

The day after Joe's capture, Sunday, August 29, the Red Club war party paused six miles from Fort Mims to rest. They had apparently learned their lesson at Burnt Corn Creek, because they had scouts well out from their camp. Some of the scouts spied two Americans on horseback, traveling down a road about three hundred yards from the main body of hostiles, perhaps part of Captain Middleton's troop. The two Americans had their horses at a walk and were deep in conversation, blissfully unaware that hundreds of the very hostiles they were assigned to scout for were camped nearby. When the Indian scouts reported this sighting to their leaders, there was a brisk debate whether to kill the scouts or let them go on to the fort. A number of the warriors wanted to kill them. Wiser heads argued that if the Americans returned to the fort and reported they had seen no sign of Indians, the Americans would remain off guard and easier to surprise. This argument prevailed, and the two scouts were permitted to return unmolested to the fort, where they reported that there were no Indians about. Keeping a discrete distance behind the Americans, the Indians simply followed them back to Fort Mims.[77]

That evening the main body of hostiles moved its camp to about three-quarters of a mile from the fort. After dark, probably late at night when the fort's inhabitants were asleep, William Weatherford and two companions scouted the fort up to its very portholes. Peering inside the stockade they could learn very little, for the area was only fitfully lit and the moon was a waxing crescent providing minimal illumination.[78] They did learn, however, that it would be relatively easy for an attacker to seize the low-placed portholes and how carelessly the soldiers guarded the fort. What must have amazed them most of all, however, was the fact that the eastern gate of the fort had not been shut for the night. This information argued for a predawn attack, with an advance party seizing the gates and key portholes in the dark, and the main body rushing the place as the eastern sky lightened.

The Creek leaders, however, adopted a different plan, the one reputedly suggested by McGirth's captured slave Joe: an attack on the fort while its defenders enjoyed their midday meal. This plan had the crucial element of surprise but also the added risk of discovery through delay. But the delicious irony of avenging the Americans' surprise luncheon attack on the Creeks at Burnt Corn Creek with a similar attack of their own at Fort Mims apparently proved irresistible. Thus it was that early on the morning of August 30, 1813, the hostiles advanced from their encampments, took up positions around the fort, and waited patiently for its drummer to sound for the midday meal.

They had prepared for the coming battle by earlier ingesting a powerful emetic. In this way they would reduce the risk of infection from an abdominal wound. They further guarded themselves from infection from bits of fabric driven into the flesh by ball or blade by stripping to a loincloth, although the Shawnee prophets with them were said to have been dressed in deer-hide clothing. In place of clothing they painted their bodies scarlet and blackened their faces into horrid grimaces. Many wore elaborate feathered headgear. All carried a mixture of weapons: guns, war clubs, tomahawks, shot pouches slung from a shoulder, and bows and arrows, as well as the ubiquitous scalping knife. These sinister and fantastical trappings were designed to freeze their enemies with terror.[79]

The estimates of Red Clubs quietly positioning themselves about the fort that hot August morning vary from five hundred to one thousand warriors; most likely there were around 750.[80] Their scouts had located a particular feature in the terrain around the fort that they quickly recognized would facilitate the assault: a brush-filled ravine about four hundred yards from the open eastern gates large enough to conceal several hundred warriors. Soon the ravine was filled with them, stretched out flat against the rough ground, stolidly enduring the intense heat of the late morning sun and the sting of insects on their flesh. Hundreds of their companions lay concealed in the woods opposite the also-open western gate and along the southern flank of the fort, patiently waiting for the signal to attack.

While the Red Clubs waited long into the morning, the garrison began gradually to unfold itself after a night of frolicking. Among the first to rise was a young hostler named Nehemiah Page. Awakened by the hot glare of dawn, he arose from wherever in the noisome fort he had managed to collapse the night before, with a ferocious hangover that would save his life. Page's cottony mouth held a terrible thirst and his throbbing skull an even more terrible headache, neither of which was improved by the morning sun. After slaking his thirst at one of the fort's wells, he made his way through the outer east gate and staggered across the open ground to the familiar stables where he worked. Entering the cool, quiet dark, with some of the horses nickering at the familiar smell of their keeper, he pulled himself up into a hay loft and passed out on the fodder.[81] It would take a legion from hell to awaken him. It was not long in coming.

The rest of the fort's inhabitants struggled to their feet from wherever the previous night's frolic had left them and began yet another long, hot, and tiresome day. Those who had the taste for it could look forward to the sorry entertainment of a slave whipping in the forenoon or a trip to the lake. Others had more pressing concerns. McGirth decided to return to his farm and gather food. Leaving his wife and eight children to the safety of the fort, he took two of his slaves and poled a flatboat up the lake to his farm several miles away. Later that morning two teenagers, Peter Durant

and Viney Randon, strolled out of the fort toward the Alabama River, purportedly to search for wild grapes, but the two may well have been more
interested in the charms of each other than the sour/sweet charms of the
muscadine grape. Meanwhile, Peggy Bailey, who was one of Dixon Bailey's
sisters, and some other women carried their laundry over to the lake for
washing. Peggy Bailey was "a stout, heavy built woman who could ride and
shoot equal to a man."[82]

Beasley, who, like young private Nehemiah Page and many others in the
fort, had enjoyed a "long night of dissipation,"[83] jump-started his day with
an eye-opener of whiskey. Refreshed, the major began composing a letter
to General Claiborne for the morning dispatch rider. In his report, Beasley
complained that the dispatch of troops from his command to protect
Peirce's place and Hanson's mill had so weakened the garrison at Fort
Mims that he could not mount an offensive against the Indians should the
opportunity arise, particularly given the poor quality of the "volunteer
militia" under Captain Bailey's command. Beasley also complained about
the previous day's false alarm that the "two negro boys" had raised, leaving
out any mention of their punishment. But Beasley proudly reported to the
general his pleasure at the reaction of his men to the slaves' report. "When
it was expected every moment that the Indians would appear in sight, the
soldiers very generally appeared anxious to see them."[84]

Beasley was given one last chance to save himself and the people in the
fort for whom he was responsible. In mid-morning of that day, Jim
Cornells, the wealthy metis planter whose farm had been burned by Peter
McQueen on his way to Pensacola, rode his horse up to the open gate and
asked for the good major. Cornells suffered from tertiary yaws, a disfiguring skin condition common to the tropics, which had pulled his mouth
into a grotesque pucker and made it difficult for him to form words. The
lone horseman must have resembled a figure out of the Apocalypse as he
leaned down from his horse toward Beasley and, in an unearthly voice
coming from his ruined face, informed him that he had seen Indians in the
woods and believed that the fort would be attacked at any time. According
to Cornells, Beasley was drunk and yelled at Cornells "that he had only
seen a gang of red cattle." Those red cattle, Cornell saucily replied, "would
give him one hell of a kick before night." Enraged at the man's imperti-
nence, Beasley attempted to have Cornells arrested, but Cornells quickly
spurred his horse and sped off toward Fort Peirce before Beasley's men
could seize him.[85]

It was now after 10:00 A.M. The dispatch rider had been delayed, and
Beasley took the opportunity to write a last, short note to Claiborne. In it
he assured the general that he could defend the fort against "any number
of Indians." That task completed, and the lucky dispatch rider off to
Claiborne, Beasley turned his attention to the punishment of Fletcher's

young, alarmist slave. The poor fellow's companion on the previous day's expedition, his back shredded from the evening's whipping, had already been sent by his master to gather crops. Randon's slave's time under the lash had taught the young man well. This time, when he spotted a troop of Indians on his journey to Randon's plantation, he fled to Fort Peirce and left Beasley, his master, and the people of Fort Mims to their fate.[86]

It was not long in coming. Hidden in the ravine, William Weatherford and his unmoving warriors patiently observed all the comings and goings at the fort; the hurried exchange between Cornells and Beasley must have caught up Weatherford's breath until, unbelievably, Cornells suddenly turned his horse's head and galloped away from the major and the fort. As the incredulous Indians looked on, Beasley left the eastern gate still agape and strode off to supervise the punishment of Fletcher's slave.

Within the fort, a group of soldiers played cards near the main gate. The sentry posted there looked over the players' shoulders at the action. Two circles of soldiers lounged on the ground of the fort's yard—the guns of many unloaded or misplaced—yammering idly about what they would do to the Indians if the savages were so foolish as to attack the fort. Dozens of children were at play, their mothers engaged in the daily drudgery of chores. Smoke from cooking fires lazed bluely through the hot morning air. The spritely sound of fiddling lent the scene a festive air.[87] Then amid this pleasant slice of fort life, Fletcher's terrified slave, stripped to his trousers, was led out of his pen by the punishment detail and tied to the whipping post.[88]

The time for Beasley's lesson for alarmist slaves was at hand. A group of spectators gathered round the whipping post; mothers shooed away any children who tried to look. Beasley gave the order, his veteran drummer raised his sticks, and the urgent roll of the drum sounded. At what hour of the morning is in dispute; one eyewitness reported the time around 10:00 A.M. Lieutenant Andrew Montgomery, the officer in command of nearby Fort Peirce, said he heard the roar of firing coming from Fort Mims around 11:00 A.M.; Judge Toulmin, who interviewed a number of survivors just after the battle. agreed. Dr. Holmes, who was there, told Albert J. Pickett that the drum sounded at the noon lunch hour.[89] More likely, the drum heard was heralding the punishment of Fletcher's errant slave and sounded earlier than noon.

Whatever the exact time, at the sound of the drum, two hundred warriors, led by Weatherford, poured out of the ravine and raced up a slight slope of open ground toward the eastern gate of the fort. They moved at incredible speed over a few hundred yards of intervening ground but, eerily, without voicing their usual terrible cries.[90] At the same time, two other groups of warriors sped out of the woods toward the south and west sides of the fort to seize the portholes.

The slap of hundreds of moccasins on the ground outside the stables snatched young Nehemiah Page painfully from his hungover slumbers. When he peered out of a chink between the logs of the dusty loft, he saw the terrifying sight of hundreds of heavily armed Indians, naked and painted red like so many devils, running for the fort. His first thought was to hide, but when he saw the Indians rush past the stables, he decided to abandon the stables and run for the nearby river. Watching until the last of the fantastic horde of warriors had their backs to the stables, Page eased down from his perch and sped out the door and across the broad fields to the woods beyond, a rising crescendo of gunfire sounding behind him. Yet, for all the care he had taken, he had a pursuer.[91]

The Indians Page saw covered the open ground to the fort quickly and were only thirty yards from the wide-open eastern gate before the sentry finally spotted them and cried, "Indians!" He punctuated this alarm by firing his gun into the air and then fled deep inside the fort, making no attempt to shut the gate. Finally discovered, the racing Indians let out their war cry as the startled soldiers overcame their initial hesitation of surprise and rushed for their weapons. As the howling Indians, in their red and black war paint, poured out of the ravine, it must have appeared to the astonished settlers as if hell itself had cracked open and loosed its worst denizens.[92]

It was a race for the gate, and the Indians won. The narrowness of the opening, however, limited the number of warriors who could funnel through at one time. Even when they pushed their way inside, they found themselves penned with dozens of Beasley's troops in the fifty-foot-wide rectangle of pickets that had been tacked onto the original east wall of the fort. This confined space, where Beasley's cabin stood and where the men of Jack's and Middleton's companies were stationed, quickly became a killing pen.[93]

It was reported that here Lieutenant Osborne, the first officer to garrison Fort Mims, was badly wounded twice and that two brave women dragged him to momentary safety inside a house that stood near the interior eastern gate. Once there, however, Osborne begged the reluctant ladies to carry him back outside so he could see the fight. The women finally relented, and once again, braving arrow and gunfire, helped him outside and placed him beside a dead soldier. There he lay, bravely watching his comrades fight the Red Clubs, until shot dead. Another young officer, Captain Jack, who had recently completed primary school, was equally courageous. Although his right arm was "shattered by a ball," leaving him unable to use his gun, with his good left hand he pulled from his belt the meat cleaver he favored instead of a sword and hacked at the Indians about him until killed. Captain Middleton also died heroically, fighting hand to hand, even with numerous wounds, until he fell.[94]

As for Major Beasley, however hot-tempered, arrogant, and terminally incompetent a soldier he may have been, he was also undeniably brave. While the panicked sentinel fled into the fort, most surviving accounts of the fight depict Beasley, sword in hand, courageously rushing toward the heavy outer gate that was stuck fast in the rain-softened soil in a vain attempt to push it shut. There he fell, either shot through the body or clubbed to the earth, as the Indians raced past him to seize the also-open inner gate. It was through this portal that the remaining soldiers in the outer defenses began to retreat.[95]

Although it was early in the struggle for the fort, the Indians had already seized a key position in the place, destroying several companies of the Mississippi volunteers in the process.

At about this point in the fight, a number of the terrified women convinced young Cornet Rankin, the inept scout whom General Claiborne had detailed to Fort Mims, to attempt to negotiate a surrender with the Red Clubs. The ladies furnished Rankin with a white flag, probably a bed sheet, and sent him, waving the makeshift flag, toward the mass of Indians who were shoving their way through the gate. The maddened warriors ignored the flag, shot Rankin, and kept coming.[96]

Nonetheless, the desperate garrison somehow was able to stop the warriors' charge at the inner east gate and began to rally. Captain Bailey's mixed-blood militia, so disparaged by Major Beasley, was still largely intact, and with these men, Bailey began to organize a defense. As the Americans collected themselves, the Red Clubs' attack stalled, and a long, hard fight commenced as the Indians tried to force their way through the inner east gate and the fort's defenders attempted to drive them back. The firing on both sides became so intense that the lovely persimmon tree just outside the fort was shot to pieces.[97]

While the battle for the eastern gates raged, other contingents of Red Clubs raced out of the woods across the field leading to the fort's south wall. They were led by a chief of the Wewocau town, home of the Little Warrior, who would have been gratified at what was now transpiring. Shaking off the tremendous fire coming from the fort, a group of Red Clubs quickly reached the south wall. The struggle along this section of the fort was for command of the portholes and the uncompleted blockhouse at the southwestern corner. With little cover in the broad, flat fields surrounding the fort, control of the portholes was critical for an Indian victory. Now it was the Indians' turn to suffer, as the fire of the fort's defenders proved deadly, and the potato patch outside the south walls began to fill with Indian dead. The Wewocau chief said that when he reached the portholes, he ducked beneath them, turned to look behind him, and saw that a great many Indians had been "shot down."[98] The battle for dominion of the portholes now surged back and forth. During this struggle, the fort's defenders and attackers even found themselves on opposite sides of the same portholes, each thrusting his gun from his side of the pickets and firing, sometimes simultaneously, at each other.[99]

A fight also roared around the sole but still uncompleted of the three blockhouses General Claiborne recommended Beasley build. A soldier from Jack's company reportedly clambered up into the upper story of the structure with a Jaeger rifle (a German-made weapon with an effective range of three hundred yards). From that perch, he reportedly wreaked improbable havoc on the Indians outside the pickets, laying out twenty-three Red Clubs on their backs in the field outside the fort. Finally, one of the attackers shot the sharpshooter in the head while he was ramming another cartridge down the barrel of the Jaeger.[100]

As the morning wore on, the Red Clubs' expectations of a quick and virtually bloodless (for the Indians) victory that the prophets had promised evaporated. Much blood had been let from their warriors already, and victory was still uncertain. Although the accounts vary, early in the battle, in the attacks on the portholes and the eastern gate, the Shawnee and Creek prophets entered the growing fray. They had promised their followers that they could render the American gunfire useless by splitting the musket balls, or by sending the enchanted balls straight up into the sky, or by commanding them to drop harmlessly to the ground.[101]

Now, with the prophets' followers, not the American bullets, dropping around them from these very missiles, they were forced to put their magic to the proof. One of the chief Creek prophets and military leaders, Paddy Walsh (whose ancient father-in-law, a former Tory named James Walsh, fought with him), attempted to work his magic by running three times around the fort, promising his followers that when his run was complete, the Americans' fire would turn harmless. Remarkably, although shot three times in the body, Walsh managed to complete the promised triple circuit of the fort. Unfortunately for his followers, the tiny prophets' feat had no effect on the American bullets, which continued to drop the Indians as effectively as before. Nonetheless, the badly wounded and badly crazed Walsh urged the Indians to drop their rifles and attack the fort with their red-dyed war clubs and scalping knives. Hearing his exhortations, the Americans inside the fort urged the Indians to follow Walsh's commands. Sensibly, the warriors ignored their prophet and fought on as before.[102]

At the eastern entrance to the fort, a similar deluded charade was being played out. A group of five prophets, some of them Shawnee, also decided to demonstrate to their followers the efficacy of their magic on American bullets. Showing the courage of their convictions, the prophets gathered at the open gate. Most of them were garishly painted in red and black, and from their waists hung red-dyed cowtails. For a moment they pranced about the opening in the fort, cowtails flapping about them, as they called

DRAWING OF FORT MIMS,

Found among Gen. Claiborne's manuscript papers.

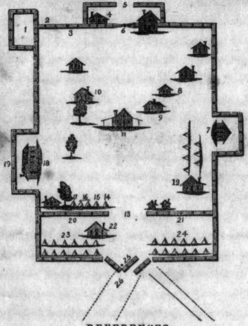

REFERENCES.

1 Block House.

2 Pickets cut away by the Indians.

3 Guard's Station.

4 Guard House.

5 Western Gate, but not up.

6 This Gate was shut, but a hole was cut through by the Indians.

7 Captain Bailey's Station.

8 Steadham's House.

9 Mrs. Dyer's House.

10 Kitchen.

11 Mims' House.

12 Randon's House.

13 Old Gate-way—open.

14 Ensign Chambliss' Tent.

15 Ensign Gibbs'.

16 Randon's.

17 Captain Middleton's.

18 Captain Jack's Station.

19 Port-holes taken by Indians.

20 21 Port-holes taken by Indians.

22 Major Beasley's Cabin.

23 Captain Jack's Company.

24 Captain Middleton's Company.

25 Where Major Beasley fell.

26 Eastern Gate, where the Indians entered.

down imprecations upon the defenders. All at once, voicing horrific screams, they rushed forward into the interior of the fort.[103] There they halted and, before the eyes of the astonished defenders, broke into a war dance, all the while daring the defenders to shoot.

Once the defenders overcame their initial shock at the prophets' antics, they were only too happy to take up the dare. Dixon Bailey is said to have raced to within several yards of the head Shawnee prophet, who was incongruously clad in buckskins, and blasted the fanatic into the spirit world. The other prophets were shot or sabered to death—all but one, that is. He ran from the unobliging bullets of the Americans to the safety of the woods. For this impressive but dubious feat, he was afterward honored with the name Na-ho-mah-tee-O-thle-ho-bo-yer—"the foremost man in danger, in the time of battle."[104]

Many of the true believers among the Indians were dismayed and disheartened by the deaths of the prophets and angered by this deadly exposure of their false powers (after the battle, Walsh's kin had to spirit him upriver to keep him from the hands of his enraged disciples).[105] The renewed ferocity of the Red Club attack faltered with the prophets' abysmal failure. Before long, however, the attack resumed under the leadership of the war chiefs, fueled by a secular desire to revenge the severe losses inflicted on them by the Americans, particularly the hated and hardfighting mixed-bloods and their families.

By early afternoon, the Indians had gained command of the portholes in the line of pickets forming the inner eastern wall. From these positions, the determined warriors kept up a ragged fire on the defenders, who had begun to seek shelter in the various buildings in the fort's interior. Two of the Bailey clan—fifteen-year-old Daniel and his twenty-seven-year-old brother, James—and several other men fighting from Samuel Mims's cottage, climbed up into the loft and knocked out some roofing shingles with the butts of their guns. From these elevated but sheltered positions they could shoot at any Indians crossing the yard below them or attacking the outside walls beyond.[106]

At the western end of the fort, a third group of warriors had initially obtained possession of the outer gate in the western wall, which the obliging Major Beasley had left open as well. From this position, the Red Clubs now sought to obtain control of the inner bastion, its guardhouse, and its inner gate, which by now was closed.[107] The settlers carelessly had left several heavy-bladed axes lying about the area. The Indians used them to hack through the frail pickets of the inner gate. Foremost in this operation was a black slave of Sam Moniac's named Siras who had joined the Indians after his capture at Moniac's plantation in July by Peter McQueen's warriors. When the former slave reached the western wall, he picked up one of the settlers' axes and cut through the pickets, allowing the Indians into the fort's western interior.[108]

A fourth fight was raging around the north side of the fort at Bailey's station. The fort's defenders had raised pickets around a large structure known as Patrick's loom house. From this position, Bailey had quickly organized a spirited defense. Not only were his men supplied with rifles, but many had also brought along their shotguns, almost all of which were double-barrelled. In fact, given the close quarters at which the fighting occurred at the fort, this horrific weapon appeared to have been the weapon of choice among many of the defenders. At the loom house, the defenders organized a system to accelerate their rate of fire. After a man discharged his gun at the Indians, he would hand it back to the woman behind him, like Mrs. James Bailey, for reloading. The loader would hand the weapon back to the shooter to fire. The shotguns were particularly effective, delivering a massive beehive of lead that would kill or badly maim any Indian within fifty yards. The effect was an almost continuous sheet of fire flowing from this impromptu fortress. All the while, Captain Bailey was moving about the house encouraging his people, rightly reminding them that Indians did not like protracted battles and would eventually move away.[109]

As an eternity of seconds, minutes, and hours passed, the Indians gradually began to gain possession of the fort. They hit on the idea of jamming fence rails into the portholes, which cut off much of the Americans' fire beyond the walls.[110] Around mid-afternoon, on the south side bastion, they managed to set fire to Captain Jack's station and to cut through the pickets. By now the Indians had also breached the western defenses and were racing everywhere about the fort as if possessed by demons.[111]

At this juncture in the battle, the defenders were forced to fall back into the remaining buildings in the fort. Fire now played a critical role in the battle. Finally discovering a way to be of use, some of the prophets reportedly advised the Red Clubs to set fire to the fort by wrapping cotton fiber around their arrow tips, lighting the twists of cotton, and shooting the flaming arrows toward the fort's wooden structures.[112] This ploy, or another one involving fire, worked all too well. The fort's buildings, which were constructed of resin-veined pine, virtually exploded into flame once the fiery arrows struck wood. Temperatures of one thousand five hundred degrees were reached, melting even the iron cook stoves inside the buildings.[113]

The Indians soon managed to set fire to the kitchen and smokehouse just behind Mims's home. Ironically, these very structures, which were constructed apart from the house for fear of fire, supplied the tinder that set ablaze the Mims home, with its crush of defenders. For as the outer buildings burned, a wind sprang up and blew the flames skyward from those structures and onto the wood-shingled roof of the Mims house. Attempts to extinguish the fire failed, and within a short time the entire structure was ablaze. Fighting from the second story of Mims's cottage, James and Daniel Bailey were among those who perished when the structure collapsed around them. Those defenders who were not immolated by the flames were forced to flee to the few remaining intact structures, primarily Captain Bailey's station.

One of these was Samuel Mims's brother David. Long white locks flying, the desparate man led his family out of his absent brother's burning home and across the length of ground between the home and the bastion. Before he could reach safety, he was shot in the jugular vein by an Indian who had gotten into the yard of the inner fort. Mims fell face first in the yard and was heard to call out, "Oh God I am a dead man." By the time someone managed to pull Mims into the loom house he was gone; the amount of blood flowing from his wound and onto the floor of the bastion reminded one observer of a hog whose throat has been cut. Around this time, 2:00 P.M., Lieutenant Osborne, who according to some reports was killed near the east gate, was said by an eyewitness to have been "shot through the body" outside Patrick's loom house. Some of his comrades carried him into that house, where he lay in agony until he died. Whatever the time or manner of his death, the ambitious young man had been granted his desire to experience combat.[114]

By now, several hours into the fight, the remaining buildings were crammed with terrified men, women, and children. At Patrick's loom house, where Dr. Holmes found himself, many of the defenders were wounded, included Bailey; all were hot, exhausted, sweat-soaked, and ravaged with thirst. Blood pooled "shoe-deep" on the floor, and its sickly sweet smell mingled with the acrid powder smoke from the guns and the sweeter smoke from the burning pine of several buildings.[115] Outside Patrick's, the fort was a flaming ruin. Bodies of attacked and attacker lay everywhere. Seven Spanish soldiers lay dead beside a well. They were deserters from the garrison at Pensacola and had sought refuge at Fort Mims. Bailey had taken them in. The Creeks had slaughtered the seven as they kneeled in prayer for deliverance beside the wooden box of the well.[116] In the yard, about the flaming ruins of Samuel Mims's home, a number of warriors pranced and hollered in delight. Their more focused comrades continued their attacks but could not take the loom house or the several remaining houses nearby. Meanwhile, the number of dead warriors in the fort continued to rise. At this point, Bailey's prediction that the hostiles would eventually abandon the fight appeared to come true. Sometime between 3:00 and 4:00 P.M., the exhausted attackers withdrew from what was left of the fort. While their followers turned to looting the properties outside its wall, their leaders retired to Mrs. O'Neal's house about four hundred yards northwest of the fort to discuss their next course of action.[117] During the lull in the madness, Dr. Holmes prudently took the opportunity to grab an ax and cut a small hole through two of the pickets at the back of the loom house, then push the pieces back into place to conceal the hole from the Indians.[118]

There are several conflicting accounts of what happened during the Creek war council. George Stiggins claims that a group of recently escaped slaves who had joined the Indians repeatedly urged the Creeks to continue the fight and eventually shamed them into doing so.[119] But it is unlikely that the haughty Creek *miccos* would permit mere slaves to attend a council of their leaders, or that a slave would be bold enough, or foolish enough, to even suggest to the Creeks that they were acting cowardly.

More controversial, among both contemporaries and historians, was William Weatherford's role during the council. Dr. Holmes claims that Weatherford rode up to O'Neal's on a black horse and convinced them to return to the fight.[120] Thomas Woodward, the best man at Weatherford's third marriage, wrote that Weatherford advised his comrades "to draw off entirely" from the fight because the Creeks had already achieved their objective. According to Woodward, however, the other Creek leaders rejected Weatherford's counsel, and he rode off in a huff to his half-brother David Tate's plantation to look after Tate's slaves.[121] Another nineteenth-century historian, Cary Eggleston, gives a more high-minded explanation for Weatherford's departure from the council. He asserts that Weatherford wanted to stop the fight to prevent the slaughter of the remaining women and children in the fort. But when his comrades threatened to kill him if he persisted in his attempt to stop the fight, Eggleston writes, Weatherford left for Tate's plantation to save his brother's slaves from the Indians. If so, he failed. For when Tate finally returned to his plantation, he found that the Creeks had made off with at least sixty-one of this slaves, only eight of whom he eventually recovered in Pensacola.[122]

Whatever the reason, Weatherford almost certainly rode from Fort Mims at this point and left it to others to conclude the affair he was so instrumental in bringing about. The prophets were discredited; the Indians' "general," the Far Off Warrior, was dead, and William Weatherford, their best commander, had retired. Among the remaining Red Club commanders, the obvious candidates for animating the Creeks to resume the attack were the respected but fanatical leaders Peter McQueen and High Head Jim. As Weatherford appeared to believe, the tactical advantage of the attack had been achieved, the fort essentially destroyed, along with Major Beasley and most of his soldiers. However, the strategic aim of instilling a level of terror in the American frontier community that would drive them from the Forks altogether remained to be fully realized. Nor had the Red Clubs achieved an objective that was the driving impetus for the attack on Fort Mims: the complete destruction of the traitorous Dixon Bailey and his mixed-blood friends and relations.

There were also the many Red Club dead to be avenged. After debating the merits of resuming the attack on the fort, the Red Clubs decided to finish what they had started.

The timing of the Indians' renewed attack is uncertain. Agreement seems general that the Indians broke off their attack around 3:00 P.M., resumed it no later than 4:00 P.M., and ended it around 5:00 P.M.[123] The Indians broke off their assault with several key structures in the fort still manned. If the second stage of the battle ran from approximately 4:00 to 5:00 P.M. that gave them only an hour to finish what they had been unable to finish after three to four hours of heavy fighting. It appears more likely, as one participant in the battle, William Jones, indicated, that the Red Clubs waited until most of the fort had been seized, and the burning buildings were consumed by fire, before renewing the battle.[124] The lull gave them time, while the fires did their work, to refresh themselves and reorganize their battered forces before they tackled the remaining intact buildings, particularly Bailey's well-defended loom-house bastion. With the fort's defenders surrounded, the Indians had time on their side.

When at last the Red Clubs surged out of the smoke, howling, blood-streaked, and grimed with battle, the defenders' terror must have entered a new and unfathomable dimension. Narratives of subsequent events have an Alamo-like ring to them. The defenders' resistance reached the heights of bravery; the Baileys, men and women, passed through the ordeal into the stuff of legend. Others, all but forgotten, should have as well, among them an unnamed "large and powerful Negro man." Wielding a heavy ax like the cinematic David Crockett swinging his empty rifle by the barrel at Santa Anna's soldiers, this man reputedly killed more Indians than anyone in the fort, ironically mirroring on the American side the ax-wielding exploits of the runaway slave Siras fighting on the side of the Red Club attackers. Another defender to be remembered was a friendly Indian named Jahomobtee, who shot three Red Clubs who were "in the act of tomahawking white women."[125] Given the time it takes to fire and reload a rifle or musket, Jahomobtee probably did his work at close range with a doubled-barrelled shotgun.

Not all the defenders were heroes. A "sergeant Matthews," terrified beyond care for the opinion of his comrades, lay huddled in a corner of the bastion bleating like a sheep. One enraged woman, in an effort to get the sergeant to do his duty, stabbed him repeatedly in the backside with a bayonet. To no avail, Matthew remained curled on the floor, insensible to all but his own terror.[126]

Eventually the settlers' situation became so desperate that even the bravest of the brave, Captain Dixon Bailey, displayed a human side to his legend and, in fear for his family, cried out that all was lost. Already badly wounded, Bailey gathered up his remaining family and prepared to flee the fort through the hole in the pickets his friend Dr. Holmes had chopped during the lull in the fighting for just such an event. He entrusted his favorite son, a boy of fourteen years, who was sick, to the care of his slave Tom. Bailey guided the two through the hole in the pickets, placed the ailing boy on Tom's back, and instructed the man to run to the river. Bailey took charge of his youngest son and pushed him through the hole into the field of Indians outside. Throwing the little boy over his shoulder and with his friend Holmes at his side, he headed for the woods over a hundred yards away. Bailey carried his favorite gun, which he had specially loaded with balls boiled in oil and wrapped in hide to make them load more smoothly. Holmes carried a double-barrelled shotgun. A group of Indians spotted the three and ran off in pursuit. Shots from Holmes's and Bailey's guns felled some of the Indians and checked their companions' pursuit just enough for the pursued to reach the woods. There Bailey and Holmes somehow became separated as they made for the river.

Bailey's other son never made it to safety. Tom the slave had almost carried the boy into the safety of the deep woods when, inexplicably, he stopped, turned around, perhaps to redeem the Indians' dubious promises of freedom to slaves, and walked back with the boy to a group of hostiles. Handing the child over to the Indians, Tom watched aghast while the Indians clubbed and scalped the boy as he cried out for his father. Tom was not harmed, but only marched by his captors over to the growing herd of slaves various Indians had rounded up like cattle.[127]

Ensign Chambliss, the lone surviving officer from Beasley's command, had also retreated to the loom house. Bleeding from two wounds, he managed to make his way through Dr. Holmes's hole out into the field of Indians and fled for the woods. Before he could reach the trees, however, the Indians shot two metal-tipped arrows into him. Somehow he found the strength to stumble forward into the piney woods, where he crawled beneath the heavy brush the soldiers had piled up while extending the clearing around the fort. As he entered this sanctuary, several hogs that had bedded there burst out of their lair and thundered through the undergrowth of the woods. In addition to scaring Chambliss out of what remained of his wits, the hogs' retreat also had the fortuitous effect of steering the Indians away from Chambliss's hiding place.[128]

For some time he lay there quietly in the screaming dusk as the Indians murdered the fort's remaining inhabitants. Having gathered a small parcel of strength, although in terrific pain from his wounds, Chambliss somehow mustered the fortitude to break off the shafts of the arrows in his back. He then lost consciousness, while his wounds stiffened with congealed blood. After midnight he awoke and, as quietly as possible, groped his way to the Alabama River and safety.[129]

By the time Chambliss found his refuge, the last of the men defending the fort had been killed or disabled. The Indians then turned their attention to the remaining old men, women, and children. Those who had found a hiding place were dragged from concealment by the Red Clubs. The Indians, all skilled butchers and skinners of game from childhood, now went to work in earnest with hatchets, war clubs, and knives on their captives. With the hair of each victim clutched and pulled up and back with one hand, and a deft swipe of a blade across the crown of the head by the other, the warriors removed the living scalps from many. The youngest children were scalped, grabbed by a leg, and swung headfirst into the nearest hard object. The older children and men were clubbed to death after their scalps had been secured. Some of the wounded were thrown, scalped and still alive, into the piles of burning buildings.[130] It is even said that under the influence of the Shawnees among them, and contrary to their traditions, some of the Creeks severed the limbs of the dead, then strutted about the grounds of the burning fort waving the grisly trophies above their heads.[131]

A special fate was reserved for the women. The Indians stripped them naked, scalped both head and nether parts, then raped some with fence rails and clubbed all to death like small game. Those unfortunate enough to be pregnant had their bellies slit open. Then the glistening fetus was snatched out, cord still attached, and laid, still living, carefully by the mother's side in a horrible tableaux—in the case of Mrs. Sarah Summerlin's twins, on both sides of her. The indomitable Nancy Bailey met a similar end. When approached by an Indian who asked who her family was, she reportedly pointed to a body sprawled nearby and boldly exclaimed, "I am the sister to that great man you have murdered there." At which the enraged Indians clubbed her to the ground, slit open her belly, yanked out her intestines, and threw them onto the ground around her.[132]

Amid the massacre of the innocents at Fort Mims, there were tiny islands of mercy. Among the many families in the bastion facing destruction were the wife and six children of Zachariah McGirth. The father thought he had left them in safety that morning when he took two of his slaves to gather corn and pumpkins at his farm two miles up Lake Tensaw. With Patrick's loom house burning around her, Mrs. Vicey McGirth led her children outside, where the Indians were hard at work dispatching the settlers. The terrified mother and her equally terrified children, who were clutching at her skirts and at each other, waited their turn to be butchered as an athletic Indian, blood-painted tomahawk in hand, advanced toward them. Even though he was battle-stained and his features were contorted with war paint and battle lust, Vicey McGirth recognized him at once as her adopted child Santo.[133]

Many years earlier, a starving Indian boy had come to her home seeking food and shelter. For some reason, he had been abandoned by his clan. Vicey McGirth took him in, and eventually she and her husband adopted him as their son. He grew to manhood among the family but, for some reason, left and joined the hostiles. Now he was about to murder his own mother and siblings. However, as he closed on the family, he recognized them as well and stopped. There was no time for a reunion. Some of his companions were advancing on the family, eager to assist him in harvesting their precious scalps. Before they could strike his adopted family, Santo stepped in front of the McGirths and backed the oncoming Indians away, informing them that the family were now his slaves. His stature among the Indians was apparently such that he was able take them out of the fort to a camp in the woods. The next morning he placed them on horses and led them back into the nation.[134]

Dr. Holmes, who had fled the fort with his friend Bailey, showed up at Mount Vernon battered and half-starved. He and Bailey had become separated during their flight. After several days of wandering through swamp and forest, Holmes was rescued by a farmer whose home he had stumbled on. As for Bailey, whose fighting skills, courage, and leadership had come close to saving the fort, he was never seen alive again. Sometime after the war, however, the skeletons of a man and a child were discovered lying near a stream running into the Alabama River, not too far from the fort. A rifle had been thrust barrel down into the earth next to them. The metal plate on the butt of the gun bore the name "Dixon Bailey." It appears that the former Quaker student had died of his wounds and that his little boy had expired beside his father of hunger and exposure. Fittingly, the brave Dixon Bailey, even in death, had thwarted the Red Clubs' hunt for his scalp.[135]

Bailey's sister Peggy was more fortunate than her brother. When she and her companions at the lakeside heard the sudden roar of battle and realized that the fort was under general attack by the Indians, they headed toward the Alabama River. When the terrified party arrived at its bank, they realized they had no way to cross its broad waters except by swimming. But this was no simple matter, even if all the women had been good swimmers. In this warm month of August, the low river waters were alive with enormous alligators, some approaching twenty feet in length, weighing over one thousand pounds, and fully capable of devouring a human being. Almost equally fearsome were the ubiquitous water moccasins. The adult males were thick as a man's arm and extremely aggressive if disturbed. Fortunately, the women spied a flatboat moored to the riverbank. Unfortunately, it was moored to the opposite shore. Nonetheless, Peggy Bailey dove into the river, made the long and hazardous swim to the other shore, and brought the boat back to her companions. The party was then able to float to safety. Several years after the war, in recognition of her bravery, a grateful Congress awarded Peggy Bailey a substantial grant of land overlooking the Alabama River that became known as Peggy Bailey's Bluff.[136]

Over the next several days, other survivors of the Fort Mims battle staggered into various forts in the region, including the craven Sergeant Matthews, who shamelessly posed at Mount Vernon as a hero until unmasked by Dr. Holmes.[137] The best estimate currently available is that of the approximately four hundred people in the fort, only twenty-eight escaped.[138] The remainder were either killed or captured. Most of the captured were slaves, but among the captured were at least two Métis families: Mrs. McGirth and her children (saved by Santo) and Polly Jones and her two sons and a daughter. The high survival rate of the slaves has been ascribed to an injunction from God. As one captured slave reported, he was told by one of the Red Club warriors during the battle that the Indians had been instructed by the Master of Breath only to kill the "white people and half breeds."[139] That injunction, however, was not always followed, as a number of African Americans lost their lives in the assault on the fort and the hostiles put captive African Americans to death after the battle.[140] A more secular explanation for the slaves' survival is that far and away they were the most valuable property in the fort.

The first reputed American visitor to the fort after the Indians departed was Zachariah McGirth. The morning of the battle, he had taken his two slaves to his plantation several miles up Lake Tensaw to gather crops. Around noon, as he and his slaves loaded their boat with ears of corn and fat pumpkins they had harvested, the men were startled out of their work by the sudden roar of guns that signaled the attack on the fort.[141] McGirth had left his wife, five daughters, and one son there just that morning, but there was nothing he could do for them now but wait anxiously with his slaves for several long hours until the intermingled cacophony of firing and fainter sounds of howls and screams stopped.[142]

Shortly after 5 P.M., as the eerie silence continued, McGirth and his two slaves, or at least their distraught master, felt it safe enough to pole the boat up the lake toward the fort.[143] Before they reached the boatyard near the fort, however, the firing started up again, even louder. At this the men shoved the boat into a cane thicket along the shore and waited. Around dusk, the firing fell off, then a single gunshot, then nothing. The sun went down, and McGirth and his slaves could see heavy smoke, alive with flames, boiling up from their former refuge. Leaving his men with the boat, McGirth crept across the open fields toward the burning ruins of the fort, outlying homes, and the Peirce brothers' cotton gin. When he reached the fort he could see that much of it had been reduced to smoldering ash. Dozens of dogs were running about, aimless and crazed but eerily making no sound. The dead were everywhere, singly and in heaps. Everywhere along the ground were scattered dozens of the Creeks' red-dyed war clubs, and the potato field just outside the wreck of the south wall was littered with their dead. The hostiles had departed to their camp. McGirth could distinctly hear the Red Clubs' celebratory cries and see the dancing sprites of their campfires among the woods to the east.

As he looked upon the desolation of Fort Mims, McGirth was certain that his entire family had been destroyed, murdered in ways he did not then or ever want to contemplate. But he could not leave without at least finding and burying them, if indeed they could be found; he could see the charred remains of many people amid the softly glowing ruins of the fort's houses. As fast and as quietly as he could, he returned to the boat and ordered his two slaves to accompany him back to the fort to search for what remained of his family. For some hours the frantic McGirth and his men stealthily shifted through the human wreckage that was beginning to stiffen with rigor mortis. They found the bodies of women and children of his family's ages, but the men could identify none. Finally, in danger at every moment of detection by the Indians, they headed back to their boat and on to Fort Stoddert. Soon thereafter, McGirth enlisted his services in perhaps the most dangerous occupation of the war: an express rider carrying military dispatches the many hundreds of miles between Fort Stoddert on the Mobile River and the American forts in Georgia.[144]

General Claiborne first learned of the Fort Mims disaster during his seventy-mile trip back to Fort Stoddert from Fort Easley when a breathless rider pulled his horse up sharply before him and cried out the news. The initial report of the disaster to the outside world came from the wounded slave Hester. She was the first survivor of the battle to reach Fort Stoddert. Dr. Holmes had helped her out of the fort through the hole he had cut in the pickets. As Hester headed for the trees, she stole a quick glance at the chaos behind her. In that foolish moment, her eyes filled with a thin slice of hell as her master stumbled about the yard of the fort in great agony, holding both hands to his face where he had been shot through the jaw. Shortly thereafter, as Hester fled for the woods, a Red Club shot her in the arm. Nevertheless, this tough lady managed to swim both the Alabama and Mobile rivers and reach Fort Stoddert at eight the next morning with a report of the battle.[145] It was this report that met General Claiborne on his way back from Fort Easley and sent him racing to cantonment Mount Vernon to manage the crisis.

For the Red Clubs, their triumph was bittersweet. They had many times over obtained their revenge for the surprise attack on them at Burnt Corn Creek by the Americans and the Red Clubs' mixed-blood kin. They had harvested great plunder of all sorts from the fort and from the surrounding plantations, but it was mostly slaves and livestock, and some silver coins in the unburned buildings. But critically, they captured little in the way of guns and munitions from Fort Mims. Indeed, some very brave defenders, in the midst of the conflagration consuming Mims's cottage, tossed their empty firearms into the flames to keep them from the hostiles. Shortly after the battle, the Red Clubs complained to the Spanish of their want of guns.[146]

The Red Clubs' victory was also a costly one. In taking Fort Mims, they had lost much precious ammunition, arms, and irreplaceable manpower—between 100 and 150 warriors killed and perhaps several times that wounded. After the fall of Fort Mims, Paddy Walsh's father James, on behalf of the prophet Josiah Francis, wrote to the Spanish governor, Manrique. In that letter, Francis reported the Red Clubs' great victory and claimed that only thirty of their warriors had been killed during the assault and of that number seven had been executed by their own comrades for "bad conduck."[147] There was no mention in the letter of the number of their wounded. This letter clearly understated the actual losses of the Red Clubs and was designed to impress the Spanish with the magnitude of the victory. The chief of the Wewocau towns, who had bravely led the initial charge on the fort's portholes, reported that fifteen of his men had been killed and "many wounded" just to reach the fort's wall.[148] And his attack was only one of many on the fort. In the event, the exact number of Red Club casualties will never be known, but unquestionably they were substantial. Tactically, in terms of lost men and material, the hostiles Creeks' victory at Fort Mims was Pyrrhic.

In terms of strategic value, the attack was a colossal blunder. In relation to the whole of the American forces on the frontier, relatively few soldiers had been killed, and the ones killed—poorly trained and disciplined militia—were not the equals of the better trained US Army regulars. Critically, little in the way of essential arms and ammunition were obtained in the attack: the fort's defenders had expended virtually all of their powder and shot in the battle, and many of their guns were destroyed in the flames. Moreover, although the Red Club attack virtually rid the entire region of its remaining settlers, it also provided the excuse the Americans had been waiting for to send their massing armies into the nation to dispossess the Muskogee people, friend as well as foe, of their enviable lands.

The next morning, after scouring the area for additional plunder and half-heartedly disposing of their dead, the victorious hostiles left their campsite and headed east for their respective homes in the central part of the nation. Those seriously wounded were sent by boat up the Alabama River; among them was the prophet Paddy Walsh, wounded three times and fleeing for his life from his own people who did not appreciate the deadly outcome of his magic. It took the majority of the Red Clubs eight days to reach their homes, encumbered as they were by their wounded and considerable booty, but to Benjamin Hawkins's amazement, they managed to make the trip unmolested and even undetected by the Americans.[149] Behind them in the Tensaw country they left a number of sizable war parties to scourge the region of people and property, in particular a party of some one hundred warriors under the prophet Josiah Francis who were seeking another settler fort to destroy. The Red Clubs even had their eye on an attack on Mobile in conjunction with the Spanish in Pensacola.[150]

Whatever the Red Clubs' long-term ambitions, for the immediate future the main body of their army would need time at home to recuperate from its wounds, mourn its dead, and savor the hard-won fruits and laurels of an astonishing victory. The rebel Creeks had done the unheard of—destroyed a major American fort and its defenders. This was an achievement to celebrate. There was still time to ponder their next move against the American armies massing on the nation's northern and eastern borders. Moreover, although the conquerors of Fort Mims had sustained some serious losses, the majority of the nation's warriors, among them some of its most skillful and ferocious fighters, had not been engaged in that attack. These warriors would demand to be part of any debate concerning the future conduct of the war.

The Day of the Dogs: The Attack on Fort Sinquefield

WITH the fall of Fort Mims, the Indians were still not finished with their original plan of attack on the inhabitants of the Tensaw region. Shortly before Fort Mims fell, a group of one hundred warriors under the spiritual leadership of Josiah Francis and the military leadership of the Dog Warrior stole into the neighborhood of a fortlet of settlers with the grand title of Fort Sinquefield.[151] The fort lay in the wild northern borderlands between the Choctaw and the Creek nations. The countryside about was rolling, heavily forested hills that stretched to the horizon in unbroken green waves. The fort had been erected on the fairly level top of a red clay ridge, where it stood like a tiny island in a sea of green. The land on the south side of the fort fell off abruptly toward a spring that seeped up from the base of a ravine several hundred yards below the fort. Like the other fortifications in the region, it had been named after a prominent local landowner. Unlike Fort Mims, however, Fort Sinquefield had been built outside, not around, the landowner's house, which stood near the little fort. Like Fort Mims, it contained a single blockhouse and portholes cut at intervals in the pickets.

About fifteen men of fighting age and their families, who had farms along nearby Bassett Creek, had gathered there for protection. The place was a miniature version of Fort Mims, an isolated, hot, and noisome pesthole, but at least it possessed a completed blockhouse. Toward the end of

August, after weeks of great discomfort and no Indians, two of the wealthiest families in the area—the Kimballs and the Jameses—decided they had had enough of fort life and decamped for the Kimballs's nearby spacious plantation home. The house was built along a small stream in the midst of the cooler woods a mile or so north of Fort Sinquefield. Some twenty-one people, mostly women and children, were now living there, going about the business of plantation life and happy to be away from the unpleasant conditions at the fort.[152]

This relatively idyllic sojourn was soon disturbed in a subtle but unsettling fashion. Late in the night of August 31, the day after the attack on Fort Mims, the family dogs began furiously barking outside the house. As the inhabitants listened they could detect among the uproar of the hounds the more disquieting sounds of running footsteps on the packed earth of the yard. Then the sound of the footsteps disappeared, the dogs stopped barking, and all that could be heard was the constant whirr of the night insects. Apparently no one dared venture outside the house to investigate the disturbance.[153]

After a restless night, the Kimball-James party emerged from the house to a quiet dawn. Surprisingly, they failed to return to the nearby fort, which, given the previous night's alarm, provides a good indication of the intolerable conditions at that post. Instead, despite the risk, they remained at the Kimball home going about their business. As early morning passed without incident into mid-afternoon, the Kimball-James party must have felt the decision to remain on the farm had been a wise one.

It was not. At around 3:00 P.M., a party of warriors swept out of the woods, and before any effective defense could be organized, fourteen murdered men, women, and children lay sprawled across the yard and about the interior of the house. After securing the scalps of their victims, pillaging the house, and killing the livestock, the Indians disappeared into the surrounding woods. Amazingly, five of the settlers, who were outside the house when the attack began, managed to escape and make their way to Fort Sinquefield; a sixth, a little Kimball boy, got separated from his teenage brother, Isham, in the brothers' flight through the woods to the fort and was never seen again.[154]

That night, while the inhabitants of Fort Sinquefield prepared to defend the post, a light rain fell on the land and on the bodies lying about the yard of the Kimball plantation—fell softly as one of the scalped figures rose to her knees and began searching in the dark among the bodies around her for her child. This woman was Sarah Merrill, a daughter of Abner James, a local settler. Her husband was off to the south with General Claiborne's troops. In the assault on the plantation, an Indian had clubbed her to the earth, cut four scalps from her skull, and left her for dead. Nearby where she lay on the ground was her year-old son. An Indian had seized the child by a leg and dashed him against the house. The warrior then made an attempt to remove the infant's scalp by making an incision with his knife around the skull right to the bone, but the boy's short hair defeated the warrior's efforts to remove the scalp. Frustrated, the warrior left the child for dead.[155]

Feeling about her, Merrill was able to locate her baby in the dark by the way its clothing had been fastened, and to her delight, she found that the child still drew breath. As she fed her child from her breast, he recovered from his ordeal sufficiently for her to risk an attempt to reach Fort Sinquefield. The next morning, the fort's garrison was treated to the horrible sight of a scalped and beaten woman dragging herself along to the gate in the steaming dawn. So weak was she from her ordeal that she had been forced to stash her baby in a hollow log along the way and employ the last of her strength to struggle to the fort. Soldiers were dispatched to retrieve the baby, still miraculously alive. Against great odds, she and her son survived, but she had yet further terrors to endure before the week was out.[156]

On the morning of September 2, following news of the Kimball-James massacre, Colonel Joseph Carson, commanding at nearby Fort Madison, dispatched Lieutenant James Bailey (no relation to Dixon Bailey) and seven dragoons from the fort, accompanied by three spies, to the Kimball plantation. Included in this party were two men who were destined to become Alabama legends: Isaac Hayden and James Smith. While the spies searched the surrounding woods for hostiles, fruitlessly as usual, Bailey and his men began the nauseating task of loading the mutilated bodies of the twelve settlers on an ox cart. With no sign of lurking hostiles about, the party escorted the remains of their neighbors and friends to Fort Sinquefield without incident. There Bailey and his men tied up their horses outside the fort and, with the assistance of the garrison, began the unenviable task of unloading the twelve stiff and rapidly ripening corpses from the cart.

Some fifty yards from the fort's western gate, a detail of men excavated a large pit for the burial of the massacred settlers. Late on the morning of September 2, most of the fort's inhabitants gathered around the pit for funeral services, but not all. Some 275 steep yards downhill from the funeral, a group of women stooped over a spring washing laundry. It was a lovely spot. The spring's clear waters, cool even in summer, seeped up from the head of a ravine treed with hardwoods and quickly formed a little creek that spilled to the south. To reach the spring the women had to ease themselves some fifty feet down the steep right bank of the ravine. It was a delightful retreat from the stifling confines of the fort. The air was cooler here, and fallen leaves from past autumns had left a soft carpet on the slopes around the spring and the little creek that bubbled forth cheerfully from it. As they took their turns drawing water, concealed from the surrounding countryside in the quiet of the little glade, they chatted idly, for the moment happily insensible of the danger around them. These ladies were soon joined by several more women carrying wooden buckets. These newcomers had strolled down from the fort to fetch water, no doubt also glad to have an excuse to leave the fort and the gruesome interment taking place outside the western gate. Among the newcomers willing to endure the rigors of the down and up of the hill was the very pregnant Sarah Phillips, whose husband, Charles, was at the funeral.

Several men had been sent to guard the women, but halfway down the path to the spring they came upon a narrow shelf of land across which an inviting log had fallen. This place afforded an ideal location to sit and have a conversation, which they immediately proceeded to do. While the guards talked among themselves, the women went about their chores. Outside the fort above them, the funeral oration was being given above the pitful of bodies. Meanwhile, the Dog Warrior, the prophets, and about one hundred of their warriors, just as their scouts had advised, stole toward the fort at a crouch through the western woods. Luck again was on the Indians' side; it was Fort Mims all over again, but even better. Not only was the western gate wide open, but the majority of the fort's inhabitants were well outside its walls, seemingly unaware that death was only moments away.

As the Indians neared the edge of the clearing around the fort, Charles Philips's father, also named Charles, was lounging outside the open gate talking with Isham Kimball about the teenager's narrow escape from the previous day's Kimball/James massacre. Looking up toward the western woods, Phillips spied what his old eyes told him was a large flock of turkeys moving toward the fort. Delighted, he pointed the birds out to his companion, whose young eyes saw instantly that these creatures were not turkeys but Indians wearing crowns of turkey feathers on their heads. Immediately, the boy cried out, "Indians!" and was joined in the same cry by Phillips. The crouching Indians stood up from concealment, howling and flapping their red-dyed cowtails about them, and the stampede for the western gate was on. The funeral party made it first. Next were the two men assigned to guard the women at the spring. Roused abruptly from their conversation by the cries above them and wasting no time in abandoning their now dangerous assignment and the women, they sprang up from their comfortable log and scrambled up the steep half of the hill for the fort. The terrified women were now alone, facing the half-again longer uphill run to safety from the fast approaching Indians. After the women made the hard scramble out of the steep-sided ravine, the slope of the hill eased and the climb gentled. But when the women reached the shelf of ground that their would-be protectors had so recently abandoned, the hill steepened again. By the time the ladies finally crested the top of the hill, the heat and the weight of their long dresses began to take their toll. Breathless now, their sweating pace slowed, they strung out in a ragged line as they made their way across the clearing toward the fort.

Frustrated by the escape of their main target, the funeral party, the Indians now turned their attention to the approaching women. A black woman with a metal pot balanced precariously on her head led the way, with the heavily pregnant Sarah Phillips bringing up the rear.[157]

There was little or no chance the women could reach the gate before the Indians were on them. Fortunately, among the burial party was a half-educated farmer and rumored horse thief named Isaac Hayden. He was a slender six-footer, about forty years old, and had immigrated to the Forks from Georgia in 1811. Hayden was one of the men who had accompanied Lieutenant Bailey's party to retrieve the bodies at the Kimball plantation the previous day. He had a great passion for hunting and a large and ferocious pack of animals at hand that delighted in assisting him in indulging that passion. Immediately, Hayden seized on a novel plan to save the women running up from the spring. Gathering his pack of hounds about him, he mounted his horse, pulled his long cowhide whip from its loop on his saddle, and with several loud cracks of that instrument drove his dogs at the oncoming Indians. These stout creatures, whose chief mission in life was running to earth deer, panther, and bear, set on this new type of prey with enthusiastic and unbridled ferocity. They were joined in their sport by other dogs from the fort. While the astonished Indians, wielding their war clubs, fought for their lives amid the snarling animals, the women ran toward the fort.[158]

The gate had been shut against the Indians, but the fort's defenders opened it slightly to admit the women. First to reach the slight opening in the gate was the African American woman, the heavy wash pot still perched on her head. Behind her one by one, the other women staggered through the gate. Just before she reached the entrance, one of them, Winnie Odom, fell exhausted to the ground. Fortunately a soldier, gun in hand, had the presence of mind amid the terror of the moment to spring through the gate to her side. With one hand clutching his gun, he used the other hand to unceremoniously grab Miss Odom by the hair and drag her into the fort. Not so fortunate was the pregnant Sarah Phillips. Abandoned by her terrified companions, she alone remained outside the fort. As she heaved herself across the clearing toward the beckoning opening in the fort's walls, she suddenly stumbled to the ground just short of the gate. While a dancing prophet waved a cowtail banner before the gate and exhorted his warriors to destroy the fort, Hayden, still on his horse outside the fort, rode into the midst of the pursuing warriors. Hayden shot one of them with his pistol. But before he or any of the riflemen in the fort could save Sarah Phillips, another Indian clubbed the life from her and took her scalp. At this, a defender edged his rifle out the narrow opening of the all-but-shut gate. His field of vision was so restricted that he could not see the warrior who had killed Sarah Phillips. But he could see the dancing prophet and shot him instead.

Hayden now found himself shut out of the fort, his dogs dead, wounded, or in retreat, and a number of Indian guns aimed in his direction. For some reason, perhaps unknown even to Hayden, rather than head for the woods he began to race his horse around the fort, waiting for the gate to open. Lead balls from Indian guns snatched at his coat as he rode. At last the fort's terrified defenders opened the gate just wide enough for Hayden and his mount to enter. Hayden saw his chance, turned his horse sharply in the direction of the fort, and galloped the animal toward the beckoning opening. The two were almost into the fort when a ball struck Hayden's horse to the earth. In obedience to the first law of physics, the animal's momentum carried them through the gate, where the two crashed to the ground. When Hayden picked himself up and patted himself down for wounds, he found he had five bullet holes in his coat but was otherwise untouched. Amazingly, an hour later, the horse, which appeared to be dead, enjoyed a miraculous recovery and staggered to its feet.

While Hayden was frantically galloping around the fort, the battle swirled uproarious and unabated about the little sanctuary. The Americans had placed their best marksmen in the blockhouse and their women and children in the story below, including the mutilated but still living Merrill. As she huddled there among the others with her battered infant, even beneath the layer of constant pain, she must have been crazed with terror at the explosion of the guns, the shrieks of her companions, and everywhere the howls of the Indians.

Midway through the attack, the best sharpshooter in the blockhouse, Stephen Lacey, was struck in the neck by an Indian bullet. He was firing at several Creeks hiding behind a large pine tree about seventy-five yards away. At last he hit one of the attackers and excitedly yelled out the news. His celebration was all too premature. His wife had come up behind him as he poked his gun out of the porthole for another shot. At that moment, a Creek marksman who had been patiently waiting until the snout of Lacey's gun reemerged from the porthole shot him in the neck. Lacy toppled backward to the floor at his horrified wife's feet; others in the blockhouse had to restrain her from screaming lest the Indians learn of their kill.

Aside from the murder of Sarah Phillips, the shooting of Stephen Lacey, and the wounding of a child sheltering within the fort, the Indians made little progress in their attack. Some of them took up positions in the nearby Sinquefield home and fired on the fort from there. Others adopted the tactic of dropping to the ground after firing their guns, rolling away from the garrison's fire, reloading, and firing again. Nothing worked. After over two hours of hard combat and the loss of five killed and many more wounded, it became clear to the Indian leaders that they could not take the fort with their current force. Gathering the horses left outside the fort by the settlers and Bailey's dragoons, and rigging litters for their seriously wounded, the Indians retreated through the woods, headed for the Burnt Corn Springs campground and from there to their distant homes.[159] Josiah Francis's foray onto the field of Mars had come to an inglorious end.[160]

A Deadly Silence in the Forks

A WILDERNESS quiet fell upon the Forks. The attacks on Fort Mims, Fort Sinquefield, and the Kimball plantation, as well as the many Red Club depredations on the isolated farms throughout the region, effectively emptied the Forks of most of the remaining settlers. Those foolish enough to stay or to embark on perilous forays to their farms to harvest crops died, usually horribly.

At nearby Fort Peirce, forty soldiers under Lieutenant Montgomery and over 160 settlers (including William Weatherford's half-brother, David Tate) spent the afternoon of the attack on Fort Mims listening for hours in terror at the sounds of the cataclysm coming from the beleaguered post.[161] When darkness fell, the horrifying noises fell with it, only to be replaced by the hellish glow of the burning fort and its outbuildings. Expecting to be attacked at any moment, the people at Fort Peirce spent a sleepless but uneventful night. The following day, around noon, Montgomery felt sufficiently confident to dispatch an officer and three soldiers on horseback to scout the mile or so of country between that fort and Fort Mims. They rode close enough to the battlefield to report, on their return to Fort Peirce, that what was left of Fort Mims was in the hands of the hostiles.[162]

Montgomery decided to abandon Fort Peirce and escape with the settlers and soldiers by boat down the Alabama River. Prudently, however, he first ordered out a detail of men to scout the way between the fort and the river. On their return, they reported the way was blocked by hostile Creeks, whereupon a desperate Montgomery decided to make the perilous retreat to Mobile by land.[163] From the well- to ill-bodied, young to old, men and women, the fort's inhabitants packed as best they could for the journey. By dark the motley party was ready, and its members stole as quietly as they could from their threatened refuge toward the distant sanctuary of Mobile. After traveling all night and all the next day, and for two succeeding days, early on the morning of September 4, 1813, the exhausted party straggled into Mobile.[164] Not long after they had abandoned Fort Peirce, the place was in flames.

The tiny garrison at Hinson's Mills, farther down the Alabama River, also had learned of the attack on Fort Mims when Peggy Bailey and her companions arrived by flatboat that afternoon. Not long thereafter, its commander, Ensign Isaac Davis, decided to abandon that exposed outpost. He loaded its garrison on a schooner and sailed to Mobile.[165] Soon after their departure, the Creeks put the millworks to the torch.

Judge Toulmin was at Mount Vernon when the attack on Fort Mims commenced. That afternoon he learned of it from people who had been outside the fort when the assault began and were able to escape the holocaust to safety. As Toulmin wrote to General Flournoy that day, he had yet to learn the outcome of the affair, but from the banks of the Mobile River below Fort Stoddert, smoke from burning buildings could be seen. It was not until 10:00 P.M. the next day that survivors from the doomed fort reached Mount Vernon with firsthand news of the disaster.[166]

The cantonment there had anxiously been waiting for news from the fort for over a day. Because Mount Vernon was only lightly manned, largely by invalid soldiers, the citizens huddled there debated during the wait whether to abandon it for Mobile. But with the news from Fort Mims, people fled that very night by land and water to Mobile, with Toulmin, his pregnant wife, and the rest of his family among them. By midnight the flat waters of the Mobile River were decorated with a ragged string of vessels of all sizes and descriptions rowed or paddled furiously downriver. Those less-fortunate refugees without marine transportation struggled through the dark by horse and foot over the land route leading to Mobile.[167]

Panic fueled by rumor spread as fast as the express could ride from Mount Vernon to Natchez. There, on hearing the news of Fort Mims, the local captain of dragoons became so frightened that he fled with his family across the Mississippi River. Later he was forced to resign his commission in disgrace. For the planters, even more frightening than an Indian uprising was the prospect that their slaves would unite with the Indians and bring a holocaust of blood and fire down on the whites in the Mississippi Territory. But it wasn't just the ordinary citizens who had given dominion to this fear. The usually unflappable General Claiborne expressed concern that the slaves would unite with the hostiles and, in a letter to Flournoy, warned the general that as a result of their attack on the settlements, the Creeks had obtained possession of one hundred of these people.[168] Flournoy responded to this news by instructing Claiborne to "exterminate" any slaves found with the Red Clubs.[169]

The specter of a slave revolt ran like an endless nightmare through the psyche of the white inhabitants of the Mississippi Territory. The conflagration in the French colony of Haiti had begun with a slave uprising on the plantation of an impossibly sadistic master and leaped from plantation to plantation until the rich northern plains of Haiti were in flames. The fact that the only successful slave revolt in history ended in state-sponsored genocide of the remaining whites in the new nation only ratcheted up the fear running through the Mississippi Territory. Nor was this fear entirely unfounded. In 1811, in the plantation country along the east bank of the Mississippi River just north of New Orleans, hundreds of slaves led by a Creole (mixed-blood) slave named Charles Deslondes formed an ad hoc army and began looting, burning, and murdering their way toward New Orleans. Fortunately for the virtually defenseless city, General Wade Hampton had arrived days before with a small command of US regular army soldiers. He ordered a company of cavalry commanded by Major Homer Milton to approach the west side of the rebel forces while he moved upriver with his camp toward them. Hampton was joined in his attack by a group of planters from the west bank who had raised a force of their own. Surrounded by the whites, the rebels were destroyed in the cruelest fashion.[170]

Indeed, the perpetually alarmed Harry Toulmin believed that fear of a slave revolt infected the very government of the Mississippi Territory, to the detriment of the defense of the frontier against the hostile Creeks. As he informed President Madison just after the Fort Mims massacre, the beleaguered citizens of the frontier had heard nothing from "our excellent governor," as the judge sarcastically referred to Governor Holmes, and he went on to suggest to the president that Holmes's inattention to the crisis in the Tensaw region was the result of political pressure from the western part of the territory "on account of the apprehensions they are under from an expected insurrection of their own domestics."[171] Toulmin's concerns had merit. Holmes had written to General Wilkinson over a year earlier that while he was not overly worried about the territory's ability to handle an Indian uprising, a slave revolt was another matter:

> Of the slaves, who compose so large a portion of our population I entertain much stronger apprehensions. Scarcely a day passes without some information relative to the designs of those people to insurrect. It is true that no clear or positive evidence of their intentions has been communicated; but certain facts and expressions of their views have justly excited considerable alarm amongst the citizens. For my own part I am impressed with the belief that real danger exists, and it is my duty to lose no time in procuring arms for the defense of the Country.[172]

In their ignorance of Indian culture, and slave culture as well, the whites did not appreciate the absurdity of this notion. Many Red Club leaders themselves were prominent slaveholders, and many shared the settlers' disdain for the blacks. The Choctaws, in particular, were so ill-disposed toward African Americans that they even refused to carry away the "wooly scalps" sliced from black skulls, deeming them unworthy trophies of a warrior and tossing them aside like so much trash.[173] Even if the slaves had wanted to join the Red Clubs in a general rebellion against the whites, and certainly a number of them did, the bondsmen were isolated on distant plantations, weaponless, and without charismatic leaders who could persuade significant numbers of them to take the risk to join the Indians. In the coming decades, the slave population in the Deep South would far exceed its Indian neighbors and in many places the white populations. But no serious revolt ever arose among them.

Astonished by the fall of a post he believed well defended and forewarned of attack, General Claiborne had two primary concerns as he hurried to Mount Vernon: how to defend the rest of the region and his shattered military reputation. He immediately addressed the latter concern by blaming the distant Benjamin Hawkins in the press for lulling him and other of the territory's notables into complacency about the Creeks' intentions. To his shame, Judge Toulmin joined the general in this preposterous attack on the agent.[174] Indeed, the governor of the Mississippi Territory, David Holmes, informed Secretary of War Armstrong that Hawkins's reports on affairs in the Creek Nation did not prevent the governor from sending more troops to the eastern frontier; that to the contrary, General Flournoy had assured him that the current force was adequate.[175]

On September 3, 1813, the day after he had arrived at Mount Vernon, Claiborne sent an express to General Flournoy and Governor Holmes informing them of the disaster at Fort Mims.[176] In response, Flournoy ordered the 3rd US Infantry Regiment to Fort Stoddert, and Holmes dispatched two hundred Mississippi cavalrymen to the same post. Claiborne held a memorial service for the dead and squabbled with Flournoy over strategy, but he took no military action against the Creeks. Indeed, it was not until September 8 that Claiborne even felt confident enough to send a small party of eight soldiers, commanded by his friend Captain Joseph Kennedy, a sometime crony of the Caller brothers, the short distance to inspect what was left of Fort Mims. This small party arrived at the boatyard landing and marched nervously up to the site of the former fort, arms primed and at the ready, heads swiveling this way and that at the woods around them. As the men approached, they saw spread out before them among the ruins of the fort and on the surrounding fields a scene from the deeper circles of hell.[177]

The soldiers reached the east gate first. There, stomachs heaving, they decried naked bodies of all races, ages, and sexes heaped up in horrible piles of decaying flesh. Among them was Major Beasley, sprawled in death behind the still-open gate he had futilely attempted to close. Another heap of forty-five naked and horribly mangled bodies was found inside the fort to the left of the east entrance. Samuel Mims's house was a mound of ashes festooned whitely with the bones of those who had been burned within its walls. Outside of what remained of the fort—the blockhouse and fragments of its adjacent walls—bodies lay singly or in clumps about the fields and into the woods. The soldiers tallied among the dead forty children, including ten infants; seventy-one men; twenty-nine women; and nine "Negroes," segregated even in a death count. They also found what they deemed two chiefs and twenty-two other Indians about the fort. Scores of the red clubs that had been brandished by the Creeks dotted the landscape. The stables where Nehemiah Page had hidden stood intact.[178]

Left unsaid in the party's report was the undoubted fact that in great profusion, the carnivores of the forest, the scavengers of the skies, and the dogs of the dead had feasted on the bodies. In fact, it is open to question whether Kennedy and his men conducted much of a survey of the battlefield at all. As Toulmin wrote President Madison, because of the numerous human and animal corpses, "it is not possible, as I was informed yesterday by a person just returned from there . . . during the present hot weather to venture with safety across the ground where the fort and dwelling of house of Mr. Mims lately stood."[179] All this combined to make an accurate account of the dead, which naturally was done quickly, problematical.

Two weeks later, on September 22, Claiborne ordered the newly promoted Major Kennedy and some three hundred unlucky troops from the 1st Mississippi Territorial Volunteers to Fort Mims to bury the dead. Accompanying them was Zachariah McGirth, still in search of his family, and a slave named Dick Embree, said to have "familiarity with firearms."[180] At the beginnings of the troubles with the Creeks, Embree had accompanied his master, also named Embree, and his master's family to Fort Madison. Once there, the master volunteered his slave as a "substitute" soldier, probably in place of his master.

The intervening weeks had not improved the safety of the countryside. Indicative of the still dangerous situation, Claiborne cautioned Kennedy to be prepared for a Creek attack on the major's burial detail. When the apprehensive soldiers reached Samuel Mims's ruined plantation at around nine in the morning, Embree was struck by the stench hanging like a rancid fog over the place. The smell that rose from the unburied bodies was described as resembling a field of rotting eggs, and it induced "the most violent vomiting" among many of the soldiers. The site was covered with dogs and scavenger birds. As the soldiers approached, the birds, mostly vultures but also, eerily, ravens, "never seen before & . . . not . . . seen since," boiled up heavily in an agitated cloud into the sky and flew to the nearest trees, where they perched, waiting.[181]

With some lucky soldiers posted as sentinels about the area, their mates dug two twenty-foot-square vaults. The soldiers were said to have simply rolled the bodies into the vaults and filled the excavations with earth, including what McGirth believed to be his wife and children.[182] But the task can hardly have been so simple given that the bodies were unburied for three weeks and subject to all sorts of efficient outrages that an implacable and indifferent nature can inflict on flesh and bone.

In any event, the accuracy of the reports on the two visits to the battlefield regarding the state of the human remains found there is seriously open to question. The first visit to Fort Mims by Kennedy's party occurred nine days after the battle. The subsequent visit by Kennedy and his much larger command occurred twenty-three days after the battle. The authors of the known reports of these visits all insist that the unburned bodies were recognizable, even as to race, and that even after more than three weeks' exposure to the elements they were sufficiently intact to be able to be "rooled" (Holmes) or "dragged" (Halbert) from one part of the fort to another for burial.[183] Although the science of the decomposition rates of human bodies is a complex subject, with many variables, what we know of the conditions present at Fort Mims undercuts the postmortem reports.

The rate of decomposition of a human corpse is the product of a number of factors. Aside from external factors, such as feasting birds, mammals, and insects, at the moment of death, enzymes in human beings start devouring their host. The activity of microorganisms within the digestive tract quickly produces gases that cause grotesque bloating of the corpse and turn the skin of whites green and eventually black. (Ironically, the same process destroys the pigments in African American skin and turns it white.) Temperature and humidity are perhaps the most significant factors in rate of decay. The higher the temperature and humidity, the greater the rate of decay. This is because high temperature and humidity increase insect feeding activity on decaying flesh.[184] These conditions were present for weeks after the destruction of Fort Mims.

All the most significant factors causing rapid decomposition of a human being converged at Fort Mims. By Kennedy's first visit to the fort, many of the bodies would have been largely reduced to disarticulated skeletons, and those still intact would have been unrecognizable by name and probably even by race. When Kennedy returned to the site two weeks later with a burial detail, he was probably greeted with a field of largely sun-bleached bones, some perhaps still held together with the tough connective fibers of ligaments and tendons, the skulls retaining a few last hanks of hair, and the bones raggedly covered with shreds of flesh. Nonetheless, Kennedy reported that his soldiers buried 247 "men women and children." In contrast to the twenty-four Indians that Kennedy's first party found at the fort, this second party discovered "at least" another one hundred Indians hastily interred under fence rails and brush in the surrounding forest. The soldiers were able to identify the bodies as Indians by "their war dress and implements." But again, after three weeks in the forest, one wonders how one hundred Indian corpses, war dress and all, could have remained reasonably intact.[185]

Meanwhile, virtually all of the country north of Mobile outside a few scattered forts remained in the control of the hostile Creeks. The area was now filled with war parties that were energetically plundering the rich plantations in the surrounding countryside of their crops and livestock and carrying off or destroying the settlers' abandoned property. As Kennedy observed in his September 9 letter to Claiborne describing his September 8 excursion to Fort Mims, "the whole of the rich Tensaw settlement was a perfect desert."[186]

From time to time the more intrepid or foolish of the settlers, in search of food, left the dubious safety of their stockades and wandered tentatively into the no-man's-land that the area of their former homes had become. On September 6, Josiah Fisher, who was married to a Creek woman, left Fort Madison with their three sons to gather food at their farm on the Alabama River. Trouble began quickly. One son, Ben, hard at his task of harvesting food, was shot in the back but somehow managed to flee to the woods. When his father ran up at the sound of the shot, another Red Club fired a ball that went through his breast and out his back. Amazingly, the father, too, was able to run for the woods. The other two Fisher boys in the foraging party made it safely back to Fort Madison. The badly wounded Ben Fisher made it back to the fort as well. Even more remarkably, his father, some hours later, materialized at the stockade gate. He had walked the whole way hunched over to stanch the flow of blood from his wounds; to the surprise of many, perhaps even himself, he survived.

Other settlers could not seem to learn from the misfortunes of their fellows. Sixteen-year-old Ben Arundel, against the advice of his elders and with the imagined invulnerability of the young, left the fort to dig potatoes. He was later found lying in a field, scalped and with the bayonet from his musket stuck through his throat. A soldier named Beard stationed at Fort Madison, who had tired of eating ham without collard greens, rode a half-mile from the fort to a farm where a collard patch lay. While he was hard at work picking the tasty greens, he was ambushed by several Creek warriors. One of these dispatched the hungry youngster with a blow to the head with his war club. The Creeks exhibited more leniency toward slaves. Moses Saval's slave Phil was captured by the Indians while gathering corn at Saval's Mill on Bassett's Creek. He stayed with the war party for five days and supposedly was well treated the entire time. Nonetheless, after five days in relatively comfortable captivity, he unaccountably decided to escape the Indians. He returned to Fort Madison—and American bondage.[187]

Sometimes, however, the marauders picked on the wrong American. One such man was James Smith, who was part of the Kimball-James burial party and who had fought at Fort Sinquefield. He later became a principal actor in one of the most celebrated fights between red men and whites during the war. But for now, like so many others, he was cooped up in Fort Madison, bored and restless and anxious about his farm some eight miles away. Finally, he decided to leave the fort and travel to his farm to check on its condition. When he arrived at his homestead he was relieved to see that his house was intact. Nonetheless, he crept up on it carefully, gun at the ready. As he approached the place, he heard the clang of metal coming from the open door. Sidling up to the entrance, he peeped inside and saw two Indians busily gathering up his tools and other moveable possessions. Leveling his gun at the startled thieves, he eased them carefully out of his house into the yard. Gun at their backs, Smith then forced them to march in front of him toward the fort. When the three reached heavy cover, the Indians bolted in opposite directions. Smith shot and killed one, then pursued the other into the forest. Catching up to the fugitive, Smith snatched up a pine knot from the forest floor, knocked the Indian over with the ad hoc weapon, and used it to crush the warrior's skull.[188]

There were other isolated, vicious clashes of small parties of Creeks and settlers, but the area was free from any large-scale violence, and the Indians made no further attempts to attack any of the remaining forts. There was no crying military need for the hostiles to do so. Employing only a few hundred warriors, they had virtually bottled up in various stockaded pestholes the entire population of white settlers on the nation's western frontier. In the Forks region, the Creeks, therefore, wisely contented themselves with ransacking the rich farms throughout the area and destroying their owners' homes, outbuildings, and possessions while the territory's military and civilian bureaucrats debated strategy and their soldiers otherwise chased their tails. The nation's attention was now primarily focused on Tennessee to the north and Georgia to the east, where more immediate threats from the Americans lay.

The massacre at Fort Mims, August 30, 1813. (*Tennessee State Library and Archives*)

Andrew Jackson, c. 1819: The novice general's journey to the White House began on a wilderness road cobbled with Creek bodies. (*Yale University Art Gallery*)

John Coffee: Andrew Jackson's business partner, best general, and closest friend. (*Hermitage Association*)

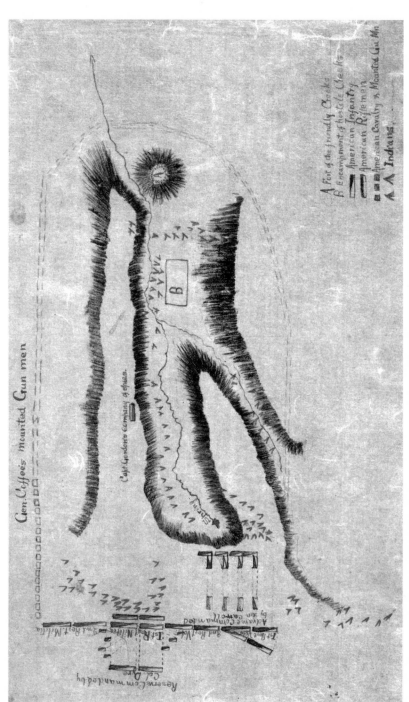

Contemporary hand-drwan map of the Battle of Talladega. (Alabama Department of Archives and History)

The Battle of Talladega, November 9, 1813. (*Tennessee State Library and Archives*)

John Floyd: Hard fighting commander of the Georgia militia army whose expeditions against the Creeks were bedeviled by supply problems. (*University of Georgia Library*)

Jeremiah Austill: As a teenaged soldier was the hero of the Canoe Fight. (*Alabama Department of Archives and History*)

"The Georgia Militia under General Floyd, attacking the Creek Indians at Autossee on November 29th, 1813." Painted by J. W. B., c. 1820. (*Hargrett Rare Book & Manuscript Library, University of Georgia*)

5. THE LION UPON THE FOLD

Andrew Jackson and the Invasion of the Tennesseans

T HE valley of the Tennessee River begins where the river emerges from the Appalachian Mountains near what is now Chattanooga, Tennessee, and loops like a rough cord down through the hills of northern Alabama and turns, unusually, back north[1] as it approaches the state of Mississippi near Memphis, Tennessee, on its way to the Mississippi River. This lovely valley is one of the most beautiful and fertile lands on Earth. Although little more than one hundred miles from the plains of western Georgia and 250 miles from the swamplands of the Tensaw Delta to the south, for all of its distinctiveness it might as well be one thousand miles away. The lands of the Cherokee Nation occupied the mountainous eastern end of the valley, and the lands of the Chickasaw, the rolling hills of the river's western end. In the land south of the river the Muskogee Nation held sway; its favorite hunting grounds were here. To the north, the Americans had established a foothold on lands bought from the Cherokees in 1805 at what is now Huntsville, Alabama.

This little town beneath the hill country to the north and rugged, heavily forested mountains to the northeast was started by John Hunt, a Revolutionary War veteran. Hunt built a cabin in 1805 at a likely spot on a rocky bluff overlooking a large, spring-fed pond. Hunt's choice for a home was an unfortunate one, however, because the bluff was already the tenement of thousands of rattlesnakes. A battle royal ensued between the stubborn Hunt and the venomous snakes, which Hunt attempted to blast from their rocky dwellings with gunpowder. At some point the serpents were defeated; "vast" numbers of their skeletons were found several years later when a vault for the town bank was cut into the bluff. But although the town retained Hunt's name, a land speculator named LeRoy Pope (a reputed descendant of the great English poet Alexander Pope) and his cronies gained control of the area. Under their patronage, a town formed around the formerly snake-infested bluff and nearby pond. In the countryside outside the town, the fertile lands of what was called Madison County were transformed into prosperous farms. On the eve of the Creek War, the town boasted a school, a library, a Presbyterian church, a newspaper, and the bank planted on the rattlesnakes' former rocky tenements.[2]

Perched on the edge of an immense forest, troubled by sharp hills, and cut by quick streams, Huntsville was poised to be the jumping off point of an army of west Tennesseans against the Creek Nation to the south. This army of amateur soldiers was led by an amateur general named Andrew Jackson. Jackson was a tall, slender man with thick, reddish-blond hair arranged by nature into a widow's peak, striking blue eyes, the face of an ill-fed bird of prey—and a disposition to match. He was a man of many talents and occupations: planter, politician, lawyer, jurist, merchant, land speculator, and all-around entrepreneur. What he was not, unlike Ferdinand Claiborne, was a professional soldier. Now at long last the opportunity to put his nascent military command skills to the test had arrived with the news of the Fort Mims massacre. It could not have come at a worse time. Because of an almost pathological sense of honor (even for that thin-skinned age) that guided him in all human relations, Jackson nearly forfeited that life-altering opportunity. Indeed, when the news of Fort Mims reached Nashville, he was lucky to be alive.

All of that murderous summer of 1813, while the Creek Nation descended into civil war and the settlers of the Mississippi Territory prepared for an Indian war, Andrew Jackson and a future US senator, Thomas Hart Benton, pursued an increasingly nasty personal feud, one that began on paper and ended in blood. At the time, Benton was a Jackson protégé and a member of his military staff. In July 1813, while Benton was in Washington City on military business for Jackson, the middle-aged Jackson foolishly inserted himself in a duel between Benton's brother, Jessie, and another Jackson protégé, Captain William Carroll, by agreeing to serve as Carroll's second. During the duel, Jessie Benton, who fired first, merely nicking Carroll in the thumb, disgraced himself. Protocol strictly dictated that Benton stand still and receive Carroll's shot. Instead, as Carroll went to fire, Benton squatted on this haunches to avoid the shot. This maneuver was only partially successful, as Carroll's shot plowed a deep furrow across Benton's ample buttocks, making Benton the laughing-stock of west Tennessee.

Jessie Benton blamed Jackson for his disgrace and ridiculously accused him of rigging the duel in Carroll's favor. Thomas Benton supported his brother. Letters were exchanged between the two friends like pistol shots, with Benton eventually charging that Jackson had managed the duel in a "'savage, unequal, unfair and base manner.'"[3] Reports also reached Jackson that Benton was impugning the general's character in public places.[4] His precious honor pierced to its core, Jackson vowed to horsewhip Benton (a mortal insult among gentlemen) when next he saw him.[5]

Accompanied by several of his friends, Jackson traveled to Nashville on September 3, 1813, where the Bentons were staying in a hotel on the town square. The next morning, after visiting the post office and the bank,

Jackson, accompanied by his best friend, Colonel John Coffee, confronted Thomas Benton in the lobby of the hotel. As Jackson pulled a pistol from his pocket, Jessie Benton walked into the room, pulled his own pistol, and shot Jackson. Having anticipated trouble with the Jackson crowd, Jessie Benton had loaded his gun with a slug and two balls. The slug shattered Jackson's left shoulder, and one of the balls broke his left arm. Somehow Jackson got off a shot against Thomas Benton, who returned fire. Both men missed. Coffee, promptly followed by Jackson's other companions, entered the hotel, and both sides ineffectually tried to kill the other until bystanders separated them. A grievously wounded Jackson was taken back to his hotel, where it took two mattresses to stanch the bleeding from Jackson's wounds.[6]

A week passed while Jackson struggled for his life. Then, on September 12, a message arrived for Jackson that irrevocably changed the course of his life. That night, a Sunday, an exhausted nineteen-year-old, Samuel Edmondson, rode an equally exhausted horse into Nashville with news of the Fort Mims massacre.[7] Late on the night of August 31, 1813, the enterprising George Gaines, factor of the Choctaw trading post at Saint Stephens, had recruited the young man to carry letters to Jackson and Tennessee governor Willie Blount advising them of the massacre at Fort Mims and pleading for their help against the hostiles. Gaines provided the teenager with the appropriate credentials and letters of credit to gain safe passage through four hundred miles of Choctaw and Chickasaw territory and to obtain relays of fresh horses for the long and wearing journey to Nashville.[8]

At the time Edmondson reached Nashville, Jackson was still bedridden with the serious wounds he had received from Jessie Benton a week earlier. Nonetheless, as if invigorated by the news, two days later the general was sufficiently recovered to at least dictate an exhortation published in the September 14, 1813, edition of the *Nashville Whig*. Addressed to his "Fellow Soldiers," Jackson urged them to set out as once for Fort Saint Stephens to strike at the Creek "hell-hounds" who had destroyed Fort Mims. His regret, he wrote, was "that indisposition which from present appearance is not likely to continue long, may prevent me from leading the van."[9] Acting quickly, as if the Creek lands would vanish before he could get his paws on them, Governor Blount summoned members of the Tennessee legislature into emergency session to come up with a plan to purportedly save the people of the Mississippi Territory from the Creeks until aid could arrive from the despised federal government. When one of the legislators, Jackson's good friend Enoch Parsons, arrived in Nashville on Saturday, September 18, he found a large number of agitated townspeople assembled in the public square. The excited crowd was being harangued with great eloquence by various politicians on the subject of the Fort Mims massacre. Looking at the scene, Parsons wryly observed that "the talking part of a war was never better performed."[10]

Like so many of the movers and shakers in the southern states, forty-four-year-old Willie Blount was well educated, having attended Princeton and Columbia colleges. He had followed his half-brother, the former politician and disgraced land speculator William Blount, to Tennessee, where he served for a time as his secretary. He then embarked on the well-blazed path to political prominence in the Old Southwest, serving as a state judge and state legislator before being elected governor in 1809. Youthful looking, round-faced, with a hooked nose, long sideburns, and close-cropped brown hair, Willie Blount was a tiresomely prolix letter writer and political acrobat who deftly walked a high and thin wire between pro- and anti-Jackson factions in Tennessee. He was no friend of the Indians, whom he saw as simply another, albeit enormous, pocket to pick. Thus, when the news of the Fort Mims disaster arrived in Nashville, Governor Blount was quick to lead Tennessee officials in raising the necessary money and men to prosecute a war against the Creeks.

The state legislature went into session on Monday, September 20, 1813. A bill was drafted by Enoch Parsons that very day for financing the war and was approved by the legislature the following Wednesday.[11] Other officials began calling up men for military service. Jackson's brigade of Tennessee volunteers, whom he had marched from Nashville to Natchez and back on an abortive mission to protect New Orleans from the British, was given only a couple of days to pack its gear and gather at the designated assembly point. The volunteers had been accepted into the service of the United States on December 10, 1812, for a term of enlistment under US law of one year. Jackson had discharged them from duty on April 20, 1813, after their return from the Mississippi Territory to Tennessee. Having already been in service and purportedly discharged, the men understandably wanted to know when their present term of service in the campaign against the Creeks would expire. Their officers assured them that their period of enlistment would end on December 10, 1813, one year from the date of their prior enlistment. Accordingly, the men prepared only for a fall campaign and brought with them clothing appropriate to that clement season. If Jackson had another view about their term of service at that time, he did not make it known. Perhaps he believed he could finish off the Creeks before winter set in and before the men's term of service, as they understood it, expired. That appears to have been the case.[12]

Jackson's failures to prepare his army for a winter campaign and to make clear to his soldiers the length of their term of service had disastrous consequences for the expedition against the Creeks. A good part of the problem was in the nature of the militia, and in various ways and degrees, the problems Jackson experienced with his troops were mirrored by the experience the Georgia and Mississippi commanders had with theirs. Militiamen were raised by each state and were under the control of the governors of each state. They were not professional soldiers, and the organization was highly politicized. The men elected their own company-grade officers—lieutenants and captains—while the higher grades of officers were either appointed by state officials or chosen by the elected lower-grade officers. Political cronyism was rife, and for men who had yet to see combat, an officer's popularity stood him in greater stead than his skill in arms.[13]

The training in the military arts given a soldier in the militia was rudimentary, and the men were expected to provide their own clothing and equipment. Some of the militia units were composed of a better trained set of men known as volunteers. These were men who, rather than being compelled by state authorities to serve, had an interest in soldiering. Under the leadership of some prominent local citizen, the locals organized themselves into company-sized or larger units and in their free time voluntarily trained for the role of soldiers. The volunteer militia organizations also served as a springboard for social and political success, and thus their ranks were heavy with ambitious young men.

The militias' lack of professionalism did not mean that the men who served in their ranks did not have the capacity for soldiering. To the contrary, as raw material for soldiers they were more gold than dross. As the experienced Indian fighter, general, and later US president William Henry Harrison described them, "The American backwoodsmen ride better in the woods than any other people. A musket or rifle is no impediment to them, being accustomed to carry them on horseback from their earliest youth."[14]

As Willie Blount set the political machinery into motion for authorizing and paying for the campaign against the Creeks, Jackson began the task of raising several thousand troops. In the meantime, they were peppered with cries for help from every corner of the threatened frontier. In Madison County, just north of the Tennessee River, a third of the inhabitants were said to have fled to Tennessee by every conveyance possible, abandoning a rich harvest of crops to the "savages." Not altogether fantastic rumors of Creek plans of attack spread from settlement to settlement: the Creeks were going to attack the town of Huntsville in Madison County; another party of six hundred warriors was going to attack Mobile; another army of one thousand two hundred warriors were going to attack the Georgia settlements. One absurd but widespread fantasy was that the entire Creek Nation—men, women, and children—was in the process of packing up its belongings and leaving its beloved land to join the northern Indians or to settle in new homes across the Mississippi—exactly the place the Americans wanted the Creeks to move and exactly an outcome that the nation was willing to die to prevent.[15] Of more immediate concern to Jackson was the real threat of the Choctaws and the Chickasaws defecting en masse to the hostiles. As former Choctaw agent John McKee wrote to John Pitchlynn, the US Choctaw interpreter, on September 14, 1813, reporting a situation among the Choctaws reminiscent of the situation among the Creeks eight months prior, "The young men fond of distinction will go to war however well the chiefs may be disposed to prevent it."[16] Indeed, a number of young Choctaw warriors were already fighting with the Creeks.

Along with the Choctaw issue, Jackson faced the question of where his army should strike first. Initially, the best intelligence the Americans possessed suggested that the Creeks planned to attack Saint Stephens or more likely Mobile, which their Spanish arms suppliers were eager to recover from the Americans.[17] Eventually, toward the end of September, the Tennessee leaders decided on a two-pronged attack against the hostiles. Jackson's army would move south toward Saint Stephens to break up any attack on that town or on Mobile. General Claiborne's smaller force would hold its ground in the Forks and send supplies up the Alabama River. Major General John Cocke's east Tennesseans would move south down the valley of the Coosa River and cooperate with the Georgians driving directly west along the Federal Road from their base at the friendly towns of the Lower Creek Nation. The east Tennesseans and the Georgians were to meet at the juncture of the Coosa and Tallapoosa rivers in the center of the Red Clubs' power base.

On September 24, Jackson published in Nashville a stirring address to his troops, composed as usual in his best Napoleonic style (referring to himself as "your General") but without the emperor's underlying cynicism: Jackson truly cared for his men, even as he used them to realize his personal ambitions. The mission of the troops, Jackson told them, was to stop the savages, who even now were advancing on Tennessee with "their scalping knives unsheathed, to butcher your wives, your children, and your helpless babes." And he would lead them against the savage foe. "The health of your General is restored," Jackson declared, "he will command in person."[18]

That same day Governor Blount ordered Jackson to march "2000 of the militia and volunteers of your division" as soon as possible to Fayetteville, Tennessee, seventy-one miles south of Nashville near the present border with Alabama. Blount had just received information that the Creeks were about to attack Huntsville and move north from there into Tennessee. Jackson must assemble his army and move to meet them: "Delay is inadmissible," the governor admonished.[19]

The information Blount received of the impending attack on his state was quickly determined to be mere rumor. By September 29, Jackson was mending at the more congenial surroundings of his home known as the

Hermitage. Sorting through the various reports concerning the hostile Creeks, he logically considered Mobile to be the Creeks' next target, unaware that Governor Manrique of Pensacola had dissuaded the Creeks from attacking that town. Jackson, therefore, decided that he should have Colonel Coffee assemble an advance party of mounted riflemen at Huntsville and from there move south down the valley of the Black Warrior River to its juncture with the Tombigbee and on to Saint Stephens. Forty-one-year-old Coffee was a large, powerful, fearless, but taciturn man over six feet tall and two hundred pounds, with black hair and blue eyes.[20] He was married to Jackson's wife's sister, Mary Donaldson. Colonel Coffee would prove a fortunate choice as Jackson's second in command.

Jackson himself planned to assemble his infantry at Fayetteville and march to Huntsville, thirty miles south. There Jackson would wait to hear from Coffee whether Jackson should join him in defense of Mobile. If not needed there, Jackson contemplated launching an attack on the Muskogee Nation from Ditto's landing on the Tennessee River, ten miles directly south of Huntsville. From that assembly point, Jackson intended to move his forces several hundred miles southeast down the valley of the Coosa River to the river's juncture with the Tallapoosa River—the heart of the Creek Nation.[21]

On September 26, Coffee's regiment of five hundred horsemen departed for Huntsville. By the time Coffee arrived there on October 4, 1813, additional reinforcements had swollen his command to one thousand two hundred men. In fact, so contagious was the war fever among the populace that the colonel had to turn away several hundred would-be soldiers because he did not have sufficient provisions to feed them.[22]

The day after Coffee arrived at Huntsville, General William Henry Harrison, a thousand miles away in southern Canada near Detroit, penned a brief note to Secretary of War Armstrong, informing him of a victory over British general Henry Proctor and his Indian allies at the Battle of the Thames River in Canada. What Harrison did not say in his note was that among the slain in that battle was the man whose visit to Alabama two years before had set the Creek war in motion. Tecumseh was shot while bravely leading his men against the American lines while his British allies fled. Tecumseh's Shawnee comrades later returned to the abandoned battlefield and spirited away the chief's body for burial. Tecumseh's burial place has never been found, although its location is said to have been passed down from generation to generation among a select group of Native Americans.[23]

Not long after Coffee had departed for Huntsville, Jackson rose from his sickbed at his beloved Hermitage, mounted his horse, and followed Coffee's line of march south. His arm was still in a sling, and his shoulder in particular caused him great pain as he jogged the seventy-plus miles along on his horse.[24] An ambitious young lieutenant in the volunteers and future governor of Florida, Richard Keith Call, who within weeks became one of Jackson's most ardent disciples, left a marvelous, if overworshipful, description of Old Hickory on the march, one that deftly encapsulates why so many brilliant men were willing to suffer extreme personal discomforts and to risk their lives for the general:

> He was still suffering pain and was looking pale and emaciated from the wound received in the famous duel with Benton. He was mounted on Duke, the brave old war horse that afterwards bore his gallant master so proudly on many glorious battlefields. His graceful, manly form, usually erect, was now bent with pain, while he still carried his arm in a sling. The expression of his countenance was grave and thoughtful, and his pallid cheek gave evidence of suffering, yet there was something in the lineaments of his face, a slumbering fire in his pale, blue eye . . . that made me and every one, recognize the presence of a great man.[25]

On the evening of October 7, 1813, Jackson arrived at Camp Blount near Fayetteville, only thirty-two miles from Huntsville. All was not as he had hoped. A good number of the men and equipment he expected to find there had not yet arrived.[26] Jackson promptly sought to remedy that situation. By October 11, Jackson felt his command was in good enough shape to make a march to Huntsville. General William Hall led the volunteers. General Isaac Roberts led the militia. Amazingly, the troops were said to have made the trip in just under six hours; unless someone told the troops that there were buckets of free whiskey at the end of the journey, it probably took longer. The march had been prompted by a message from Coffee that arrived by express rider around 1:00 P.M. In that message, which was based on information Coffee had received from his scout David Crockett, the anxious colonel advised Jackson that the hostile Creeks were approaching Coffee's camp in force.

At this point in the campaign, Coffee had led his seven-hundred-man force ten miles south of Huntsville, crossed the Tennessee River, and encamped on a bluff that commanded the south bank of the river two miles upstream from Ditto's landing. When he reached the landing, Coffee dispatched a scouting party to the wild Coosa River country south of his camp. Among the scouts was the young, lanky, independent-minded frontiersman David Crockett. When the call went out for volunteers for Jackson's campaign against the Creeks, Crockett had left his protesting wife and his bewildered children alone on their Tennessee farm and joined up. He was off to do his duty, he told her, but, as the restless Crockett later confessed, "my dander was up, and nothing but war could bring it right."

In part his decision may have been influenced by the fact that his grand-parents had been killed by the Creeks.[27]

Crockett was a popular man with his fellow soldiers, full of fun and funny stories, and generous to a fault. Like most of his comrades, the young scout was acutely allergic to authority. He had been recommended for the job by his company captain because of his reputation as a skilled and savvy woodsman. As a member of the scouting party ordered south by Coffee, Crockett soon had an opportunity to put his talents to use.

Crockett's scouting party left camp before Jackson had begun his march south. It was composed of Crockett and twelve other mounted men. The party was led by a Major John H. Gibson, but the first day out he decided to divide the command so as to cover more ground. Gibson took seven of the men and Crockett four, including his young friend George Russell. On the night of the second day, while staying at a camp of friendly Creeks, Crockett learned from a black man there, who had heard from a Creek outside the camp, that a large Creek war party had spent the entire day crossing the ford at a place called Ten Islands on the Coosa not far away and was now heading north to attack the American forces. Crockett and his party immediately saddled their horses and rode sixty-five miles through the night and early morning to warn of the advancing hostiles.[28]

When Crockett reported his findings to Coffee, it appeared to Crockett that the colonel was skeptical of the scout's report. The touchy Crockett immediately assumed that Coffee did not trust his report because Crockett was a mere enlisted man. However, Gibson and his command had not returned to camp, and it was believed that they had been killed by the Creeks. Thus, whatever Coffee thought of the reliability of Crockett's alarming report, the colonel immediately sent an express courier to summon Jackson from Camp Blount. Jackson at once put his army on a quick march south for Coffee's camp. Speed became more imperative when a second messenger, who reached Jackson on the march, reported that the Creeks had killed Gibson. That report was false. The day after Crockett's return to camp, Gibson and his men appeared.[29]

Gibson, however, delivered a report that was even more alarming than Crockett's. The upshot of the Gibson/Crockett reports was that, as Coffee told his wife, Mary, they expected that "the whole Creek Nation was moving on this way in one body" to attack their camp. Throwing up fortifications as fast as they could, Coffee and his men waited for an anxious two days and nights for the Red Clubs to attack. That trying time for Coffee and his command ended when Jackson and his army arrived on October 12, although by then Coffee had determined that the anticipated Red Club attack was a mere rumor.[30]

By the time Jackson's exhausted army filed into the little town of Huntsville around eight o'clock the night of October 11, Coffee had already sent a message to the general that the scouts' report of a large-scale Creek attack on the settlements was unfounded. Jackson's army got a nice sound sleep in camp outside the town, and in the morning, footsore but somewhat rested, it headed south for Coffee's position. Compared to the previous day's outing, the march was a treat for Jackson's soldiers. They moved at a comfortable pace over dry, even ground through the autumn countryside. The air was clear and temperate, and the leaves of the thick forest climbing the near hills to the south were beginning to color. Ten miles on, the soldiers reached a ferry at Ditto's Landing on the Tennessee River. They took the ferry to the south shore and were soon laying out their quarters at Camp Coffee. As a reward for their hard march south from Camp Blount, Jackson excused them from guard duty.[31]

As it turned out, the Red Clubs never did mount an attack on the frontier settlements and probably never intended to. Their apparent strategy was to wait for the Tennesseans to come to them on a battlefield of the hostiles' own choosing.

Colonel Coffee's Expedition to the Black Warrior Country

O N arriving at Camp Coffee on October 12, Jackson wasted no time setting in motion his campaign against the hostile Creeks. On October 13, he wrote an order directing Colonel Coffee to take a detachment of his mounted riflemen and ride to the Creek town at the falls of the Black Warrior River, where the unfortunate Martha Crawley had been held captive. Coffee was to destroy that town and any other Creek habitations in the vicinity.[32] This expedition was essentially a reconnaissance in force with a punitive component. Jackson was primarily interested in learning whether the Creeks had gathered in any significant force in the region to the southwest of his present position. That intelligence would allow him to decide in which direction the main body of his army should invade the nation.

The following morning, Coffee assembled seven hundred soldiers, including his wife's brother, Jack, and the disgruntled Crockett. With this sizable force, he crossed over to the north bank of the Tennessee at Ditto's Landing and rode a pleasant forty miles northwest through the valley of the Tennessee to Fort Hampton at the juncture of the Elk and Tennessee rivers. Just below the fort, the Tennessee River explodes into several miles of leviathan rapids that race like a beast on fire through heavy forests and around slender islands. Coffee's detachment crossed at the upper end of the rapids at a place called Melton's Bluff.[33] Several years after the war, a traveler struck with its beauty wrote: "You cannot imagine a site so beautiful as this country exhibits to this place. But the sight of the Bluff at a mile's distance fairly entranced me. It is an even high plain and resembles a hanging garden. The sun favored us with his rays as we drew in sight and shed a beautiful lustre on the Bluff. This land is so clear of undergrowth that you may drive a wagon anywhere through the woods; and this body I am told extends twenty miles in width."[34]

The land was well into autumn when Coffee passed through, and the river was low but full of sharp-angled rocks. Some of the horses caught their hoofs between submerged stones and tragically had to be abandoned.[35] As the later traveler found, the countryside around the violence and danger of the river was of great beauty. But the current residents of that area were not so attractive. One of the most prominent was the Irishman John Melton, for whom the enchanting bluff where his plantation home stood was named. Here he lived in feudal splendor with his Cherokee wife and their several sons.

The original Melton family business was river pirating, by which Melton had become wealthy. Despite what he might have heard about Melton's unsavory reputation, Coffee put any scruples aside and met with the old reprobate in hope of finding a guide to the Black Warrior town. The best Melton could come up with was one of his sons, who confessed to Coffee that he did not know the way but could show him a path that he had heard would take Coffee to the Creek towns.

Having no other choice, Coffee took the path pointed out by young Melton. The trail wound through thickly forested hill country and over rocky, quick streams flowing to the south. On the third day, at the eightieth mile down the path, Coffee met a scout named Russell whom Jackson had sent some weeks earlier to investigate the Creek presence in the region. The intrepid Russell informed Coffee that he indeed was on the right path to the Black Warrior town. In verification of Russell's information, they soon came to a small Indian village beside a little river. About fifteen miles farther on they came upon a second village. They burned both villages, which were deserted, and harvested the corn in the nearby fields. As they moved south, the hills fell away and the river they had been following widened. Eight more miles on they found the Black Warrior town. It consisted of fifty houses arranged around the typical Creek public square and was set dramatically on a bluff overlooking the magnificent falls of the Black Warrior River. Fields of ripe corn and beans stretched away from the town. The place was deserted. As Jackson had ordered, Coffee's men burned the town and everything in it to ashes, but they prudently collected the corn and beans for their own use.[36]

At this point in his campaign, Coffee ran out of Creek settlements to plunder and burn, and his army was fast running out of food. The colonel decided to return to Jackson's army. He ordered the scout Russell to guide the expedition to an encampment called Fort Deposit, which Jackson had established October 12. Fort Deposit was twenty-four miles upriver from Camp Coffee at the point where Thompson's Creek entered the Tennessee River and sixty mountainous miles[37] from the nearest Creek encampment in the Coosa River valley to the south. Jackson had established the fort there to be closer to his projected main source of supplies in east Tennessee.

Once Coffee had reached Fort Deposit with his report that the country to the southwest was clear of Creeks, Jackson felt free to pursue the strategy that from the first he believed would put a quick end to the war: a strike down the Coosa River valley to the very heart of the Muskogee Nation where the Coosa and Tallapoosa rivers joined to form the larger Alabama River. A few days earlier, on October 22, Jackson had received a letter that determined his decision to now implement that strategy. The Cherokee chieftain Path Killer was writing from his home at Turkey Town, a large settlement strung out for miles along the west bank of the Coosa River.[38] From there the chief had been organizing war parties of his people to join the Tennesseans. The previous day two hostile Creeks had entered Turkey Town with a message for Path Killer, probably from Peter McQueen. The message advised Path Killer that the Creeks had dispatched two armies: one against the Lower Creeks, forted up at Coweta, and the second against a friendly Creek chief named Old Chenibee, of the Natchez tribe, who was head of a town in the upper Coosa Valley called Talladega.[39]

Old Chenibee had traveled with Alexander McGillivray to New York in summer 1790 for treaty negotiations with the Americans and was a signatory to the treaty named for that city. Chenibee's land was home to the Natchez people. They had fled to this area from Louisiana in the early 1700s—driven out by the French in an ethnic cleansing—and had joined the Creek Confederation. Like many of the Creeks living on the borders of Georgia and Tennessee, Chenibee and his people had not joined the prophets' party. Illustrative of the complex relations among the Creeks involved in the war, Chenibee's sister had a daughter who would become William Weatherford's third wife, and a son, George Stiggins, the Creek historian. Further complicating the situation in the Natchez lands was the fact that the Natchez were living among a people known as the Abekas. An older people in the region, it was they who, over a hundred years earlier, had welcomed among them the Natchez tribe fleeing from the exterminating French to the south.[40] Now the Abekas had joined the prophets' party, and Chenibee's defection to the Americans placed these old neighbors at odds.

When he was informed by Path Killer of the impending attack on Talladega, Jackson, with his usual dispatch, determined to march south to meet the Creek force. He assembled the army on October 24 and gave a rousing speech to prepare the men to face the "inhuman Creeks." In his speech, Jackson advised his army how to behave in the face of the enemy and cautioned them against the dangers of retreat. Why, he would rather "rush into the thickest of the enemy, and submit himself to their scalping knives," Jackson exclaimed, than endure the sorry spectacle of his army in retreat. Of course, Jackson concluded, he had no fear that his brave soldiers, disciplined as they were, would ever commit such a crime. Instead, he was certain that their general would lead "his soldiers" to a glorious victory.[41]

Jackson's army departed from camp on October 24, 1813. That day, his military secretary and aide-de-camp, thirty-one-year-old Major John Reid, who had been recommended to Jackson by Jackson's enemy, Thomas Hart Benton, learned that his wife, Betsy, had given birth to their son.[42] By October 26, the Tennesseans were camped on the west bank of Willis Creek, a tributary of the Coosa River. They were now just inside the Creek Nation. The next day, Jackson sent two hundred cavalry under the command of Lieutenant Colonel Robert Dyer to attack the Creek village of Littafutchee twenty miles east on Canoe Creek, another Coosa tributary. Littafutchee was the Creek equivalent of an industrial town. The plentiful supply of flint there made it a center of arrowhead production, supporting upwards of one hundred people. The village was ruled by a chief known as Robert Catula. Dyer quickly captured the place, apparently without a fight, and burned it. Then with twenty-eight prisoners—men, women, and children—in tow, the Tennesseans traveled all night in a cold and steady rain, reaching Jackson's camp at four the next morning.[43] Catula managed to avoid Dyer's raiders but was captured three days later by another of Jackson's raiding parties.[44]

When Dyer arrived with his prisoners, Reid was particularly disturbed by the cries of the naked, cold, and hungry children among them, which he could hear as he wrote his wife. "I have never been more affected in my life," he told her. Contrary to his fellow officers, he was also upset with the rough treatment accorded the male prisoners and complained so emphatically to Jackson that he was concerned that his pleas for mercy might irritate his beloved commander. In fact, Reid was so disturbed by the lot of the prisoners that the young soldier wrote his wife that he was not born to be a warrior. The prisoners were soon sent north to the jail in Huntsville.[45]

For some unexplained reason, given the state of the army's supply situation, Dyer had failed to secure the food he found at the village. As Jackson wistfully noted in a letter to Governor Blount, "they found in the fields near the Village, a considerable quantity of corn & in the Country roundabout many beeves; but they brought in none."[46] Particularly given that the army was now without corn, Jackson probably had some choice words for Dyer. Immediately, the general sent another detachment back to the village to harvest what he was told was one thousand bushels of corn.[47]

By November 2, 1813, the American army was encamped four miles farther on at Ten Islands, about twenty-five miles down the Coosa River from
Turkey Town. Ten Islands was a famous landmark in the region. As the
name indicates, it was a string of ten islands in the river. It had a good ford
at their northern end. The islands lay near the boundary of the Creek and
Cherokee nations. De Soto was thought to have crossed the Coosa here
during his devastating *entrada* through the southeastern United States
almost three hundred years earlier. For centuries the islands had been
home to various groups of Native Americans.[48] Now it was to be Jackson's
entryway into the Creek Nation.

The Battle of Tallushatchee

WHILE Jackson was settling his army down at Ten Islands, his scouts
informed him that a large party of Creek warriors was encamped at
the town of Tallushatchee, thirteen miles east on a creek of that name. On
October 30, Jackson promoted Coffee to brigadier general. On November
2, he ordered him to assemble one thousand men from his brigade and
attack Tallushatchee. In his order, Jackson spelled out exactly how he
wished his friend to proceed. Coffee was, "with all practicable dispatch," to
cross the Coosa at a place upstream from the Ten Islands known as Fish
Dam Ford. There he was to divide his force. Coffee, with five hundred
men, was to attack Tallushatchee and in Jackson's words "destroy it." The
other half of Coffee's command was to move downstream and "scour" the
country in the vicinity of the Ten Islands; at the same time, this wing of the
American forces would act as a covering force for Coffee's troops.[49]

Coffee's army did not complete the crossing of the Coosa until just
before dark. As he wrote Jackson that evening, the way to the crossing and
the crossing itself were "much more difficult than represented." Consulting
with his Indian allies, Coffee learned that it would take a two-hour march
in the dark to reach their objective. They also advised him that they did not
believe there were any Indians to "scour" in the Ten Islands area, something the scouts apparently had neglected to inform Coffee of before he
left camp. Given this information, Coffee decided to alter Jackson's plan—
informing Jackson of this fact by express rider—and to attack
Tallushatchee at sunrise with his entire force: about nine hundred soldiers
plus, reportedly, a mixed company of two hundred Cherokees and
Creeks.[50]

Incredibly, even though the Red Clubs had been "fully informed" by late
October of the movements of Jackson's army, Coffee's command rode
undetected by the Creeks across twelve miles of countryside in the dark to
within one and one-half miles of Tallushatchee.[51] There, on November 3,

Coffee halted and arranged his command for the attack. His plan was simple but if carried out properly would be devastating. One-half of his force, the 2nd Regiment of Volunteer Cavalry commanded by Colonel John Alcorn, would cross an intervening creek and swing around the right side of the town. The other half, the 2nd Regiment of Volunteer Mounted Riflemen, commanded by Colonel Newton Cannon, whom Coffee would accompany, would swing around the opposite side of the town. When the two wings of the army met, the place would be ringed with mounted riflemen.[52] This plan assumed that the Creeks would not first detect the approach of Coffee's sizable command as it moved through the forest and break up his formations among the trees before they could maneuver into place. Surely the Red Clubs had ample warning of Jackson's army as it lumbered down from Huntsville, particularly after the attack on nearby Littafutchee, and would have scouts in the field monitoring its every movement. Incredibly, as things turned out, they had not even taken this elemental precaution against surprise. Instead the heedless town slept while its destruction stole upon it.

Near dawn, Coffee's army embarked from its staging ground for Tallushatchee. The land was flat and open-wooded, and the going was smooth. The town was built among huge pines in a parklike setting. The houses were large and constructed with heavy logs. The soldiers were within one and a half miles of the town before the Indians finally detected them. At once the Red Clubs began sounding drums and uttering their war cries as they prepared for battle.[53] The sun had been up about an hour when the army began maneuvering into position. The hostiles allowed them to do so unmolested, and the town was now encircled by mounted riflemen. Coffee then ordered Captain Eli Hammond and his company of rangers to ride out of the woods toward the town. They were bait "to bring on the affray," as Crockett later wrote.[54]

All went as Coffee planned. Hammond and his men trotted out in front of the town and fired off some shots at the hostiles. Apparently unaware of the ring of horsemen around them, a large body of Indians charged Hammond's company, which fell back as planned onto the main body of troops. The soldiers fired their guns effectively from long range at the oncoming Indians, who began to drop. The Indians' return fire was ineffective, but after firing once they shouldered their rifles and smoothly transitioned to the bow, drawing arrows from quivers that held fifty of the missiles, which John Reid reported to his father were "a much more fatal weapon" than he had supposed. Nonetheless, the ring of horsemen steadily constricted its grip on the town. A number of Indians quickly realized they were trapped, and some tried to surrender. The women in particular ran pleading up to the soldiers and even grabbed onto their legs or the long tails of the hunting shirts many soldiers wore. One soldier had seven

Indian women holding onto him for dear life.[55] Most of the men, and some of the women and children, however, retreated into the cabins and fought with unparalleled courage from there.

In the midst of the battle, a Red Club prophet, fantastically painted and feathered like some demented rooster, mounted the crest of a cabin and, looking over the battle below, began haranguing the warriors to drive back the onrushing horsemen. He had filled the air with spirits, he shouted: these invisible creatures would catch the American bullets before they could reach their mark. As proof, he pointed to himself, standing in plain view of the Americans and yet unharmed. Soon after this boast, a shot from an American rifle toppled the prophet from his perch, and the Americans continued to press the Creeks back into their houses.[56] The soldiers now embarked on a bacchanalia of death and destruction. They relentlessly killed every warrior in the cabins and a number of women and children as well. In his after-action report, Coffee sanctimoniously wrote that the deaths of these noncombatants was an unavoidable tragedy that "every officer and soldier of the detachment" regretted.[57]

The irrepressible Crockett, however, had another story to tell. While some of his fellow soldiers made prisoners of the women clutching at the men for dear life (and presumably their children), Crockett counted off forty-six warriors running into one of the large cabins. Some of the soldiers secured the prisoners while Crockett and other men made for the cabin where the warriors had gathered for defense. As they neared the building, however, they were brought up short by a curious sight. Just outside its entrance, amid the roar of battle, a solitary "squaw" sat on the hard-packed ground loading a bow. Frozen in place, as if by a prophet's spell, the Americans watched as the woman placed her feet against the curve of the stout bow, notched an arrow in the rawhide string, drew back the bow, and, raising both feet, shot the arrow into one of the spectators, a Lieutenant Moore. The astonished soldiers' reaction was immediate and terrible. They shot the woman to pieces—"at least twenty balls blown through her" —and rushed the house where the warriors had fled. Crockett and his comrades "shot them like dogs," then set the house on fire and burned it up with the forty-six warriors in it.

Just outside the house was one of Coffee's unavoidable casualties of the fight: a young boy shot in the arm and thigh, both bones broken, pulling himself along the ground from the burning house. His body fat "was stewing out of him. In this situation he was still trying to crawl along; but not a murmur escaped him, though he was only about twelve years old. So sullen is the Indian, when his dander is up, that he had sooner die than make a noise, or ask for quarter."[58]

Crockett does not say what they did with the boy, but they probably shot and scalped him. As for the forty-six warriors Crockett claimed had per-

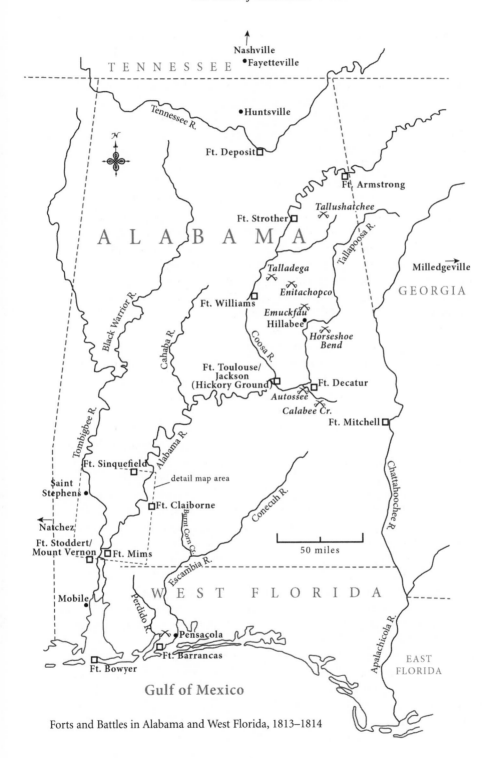

Forts and Battles in Alabama and West Florida, 1813–1814

ished in the house, that figure was probably derived from the scalps the soldiers took before leaving the bodies to the flames. As Crockett had bragged to a "Negro" during a scouting mission some weeks back, if Crockett came across an Indian, he hoped to "carry the skin of his head home to make me a mockasin."[59] He could now make several pairs.[60]

The fight was soon over, the village burned to ashes, and the prisoners herded together. General Coffee's official battle toll of the hostiles was 186 warriors killed, an unknown number of probable dead in the woods, and 84 women and children taken prisoners. There is also evidence that a number of Creeks fled to the Coosa River and were killed attempting to cross it. The Americans lost five killed and forty-one wounded; five of the wounded were from Captain Hammond's company. A large number of the Americans' casualties were inflicted by arrows, indicating that the Indians were poorly equipped with firearms.[61] Coffee characterized the affair in a letter to his wife, Mary, as a "small skirmish with the Indians" and confidently predicted that after this battle, he did not "expect the enemy will ever meet us, they have no kind of chance."[62] The Red Clubs would make the newly minted general eat those words before the war was done.

The captured Creeks were transported to Huntsville and from there to Nashville, where they were jailed, the jailer sarcastically referring to the prisoners as his "pets."[63] The prisoners were sent to Nashville in large part for their safety. On November 1, 1813, twelve miles outside of Huntsville, five members of a family had been massacred by Creeks. Now the remaining relatives of the family and their outraged neighbors were threatening to storm the jail and massacre the Creek prisoners.[64] One of these Tallushatchee captives, a baby just short of a year old, would never see the inside of a jail. Incredibly, he became a brother to Jackson's adopted son Andrew. This was Lyncoya, named by the doyen of what passed for Huntsville society, Judith Sale Pope, wife of LeRoy Pope. Coffee's men had found the little fellow toddling about the Tallushatchee battlefield terrified out of his mind. Lyncoya's entire family was slaughtered during the battle, courtesy of another of Coffee's troops' "mistakes," and he was now its sole survivor. The Indian women whom the soldiers asked to care for the boy refused, purportedly because of the extinction of his entire family, and recommended that the soldiers kill him. One of Jackson's interpreters, an Indian trader named James Quarles, intervened and, placing the child on his back, rode with him all the way back to Fort Strother, where Quarles presented the boy to Jackson.[65]

When Jackson learned the boy was an orphan, his own sad childhood miseries apparently came rushing back, and he decided to adopt the child. On November 4, 1813, he wrote to his wife, Rachel, "I sent on a little Indian boy for Andrew to Huntsville with a request to Colonel Pope to take care of him until he is sent on." Some historians have cited this act as evidence of Jackson's humanity. A cynic might say Jackson's act was more like that of a father away from home on a business trip acquiring a souvenir for his child, particularly because he referred to such presents as "pets."[66] In fairness to the childless Jackson, however, he was apparently smitten with at least the idea of the little orphan as a son, writing his wife that he intended to adopt him "as one of our family." And throughout the remainder of the war, almost every letter Jackson wrote his Rachel contained an inquiry as to whether Lyncoya had yet reached the Hermitage. For some reason that happy event was delayed almost six months, and Lyncoya remained at Colonel and Judith Pope's Huntsville mansion until late April 1814, when Jackson arrived to take him home.[67]

The little Indian boy grew up in the Jackson household and became a strapping young man. But perhaps encouraged by the Creek *miccos* who visited the Hermitage from time to time, Lyncoya displayed a fondness for Indian dress and sudden ambushes of visiting children; at times he even expressed a longing to return to the unremembered place of his birth.[68] Sadly, at seventeen, the young man contracted tuberculosis and died at the Hermitage, greatly mourned by Andrew Jackson.

A Wasted Opportunity: The Battle of Talladega

COFFEE and his victorious command rejoined Jackson at Ten Islands. There Jackson's men were already hard at work constructing a fortification named Fort Strother after Jackson's topographer. Jackson did not know it then but this fort was to be his principal headquarters for most of the war for the very reason that was already tormenting him in this campaign: lack of food and other supplies. Indeed, Coffee and his men had barely settled into the Ten Islands encampment before Jackson ordered two hundred of them to bring in all the cattle they could find in the surrounding countryside. The following day, November 6, Jackson sent five hundred of Coffee's men, under Colonel Alcorn, back to Tallushatchee to collect all the corn and cattle they could find.[69]

They were also to investigate a trail leading from that town that a cavalry patrol had discovered the preceding day. Crockett was with them, and his scrounging activities took him back to the house where his company had killed the forty-six Indians and burned the house to the ground around them. Partially burned Indian bodies littered the area by the fire, sculpted into blackened and grotesque figures. While poking through the ruins of the house, Crockett and his companions found beneath the ashes a cellar intact and full of potatoes. The soldiers had been on half rations for several days, and to them this find presented a feast. As they gathered up the potatoes they noticed something strange about them; they appeared to have "been stewed in fat meat." Then it dawned on the men that oil from the heated fat of the roasted Indians on the floor of the burning house above the cellar had dripped through the boards and onto the potatoes. Crockett and his men were so hungry they ate the potatoes anyway.[70]

In contrast to Crockett, when Lieutenant Richard Call's unit passed through Tallushatchee a few days after the battle, the sight he witnessed (ironically much like the scene Captain Kennedy witnessed at Fort Mims) spoiled Call's appetite: "We found as many as eight or ten dead bodies in a single cabin. Sometimes the dead mother clasped the dead child to her breast, and to add another appalling horror to the bloody catalogue— some of the cabins had taken fire, and half consumed human bodies were seen amidst the smoking ruins. In other instances dogs had torn and feasted on the mangled bodies of their masters. Heart sick I turned from the revolting scene."[71]

Young John Reid, who like Call had never witnessed the aftermath of a battle, reported to his wife that as he rode across the field of battle, his horse stepping delicately to avoid the dead, "[n]ever did I witness so horrid a spectacle as the field of battle exhibited after all was over."[72] These two talented young men would witness the aftermath of far larger battles, but none worse.

The desolated town also had some Indian visitors shortly after its destruction. A party of four hundred Cherokee warriors under the command of Major John Lowrey reached Tallushatchee and found that Jackson's army had preceded them. Surveying the ruins they discovered additional victims of Coffee's attack: twenty women and children who were accidentally wounded, many of them badly. They also found two of the Tennesseans' horses and saddles.[73] The Cherokees wished to keep the prisoners and the horses and saddles, but Jackson informed them that they must send the prisoners to the Huntsville jail to join their imprisoned countrymen from Littefutchee and turn the horses and saddles over to the American army.[74]

Jackson would have been far happier if the Cherokee war party had provided him with food. The Coffee and Alcorn foraging expeditions were stopgap measures. Jackson's hope for a primary source of supplies lay in the troops from east Tennessee commanded by General Cocke stationed twenty-five miles upriver at the Cherokee settlement Turkey Town. He had ordered Cocke's second in command, Brigadier General James White, to deliver supplies for Jackson's army at Fort Strother as well as men to garrison the fort in Jackson's absence. Once White arrived, Jackson planned to march his entire army south into the Creek Nation, destroying in its path everyone and everything.

General White had assured Jackson he was on his way to meet him and had, in fact, started his march to Ten Islands from Turkey Town. On

November 7, however, as his brigade marched to join Jackson, White received an order dated November 6, 1813, from his direct superior, General Cocke. Cocke ordered White to about-face and march his command upstream and join Cocke on the Chatuga River, where Cocke was deeply engaged in building a fort named in honor of Secretary of War Armstrong.[75] Cocke's order appears to have been issued for the pettiest of reasons: he was jealous of Jackson and wanted to harvest from the Creeks his own measure of glory. Unbeknownst to Jackson, in his order to White, Cocke imprudently included a passage that would have grave consequences for Cocke in the coming months: "If we follow General Jackson and his army, we must suffer for supplies; nor can we expect to gain a victory. Let us then take a direction, in which we can share some of the dangers and glories of the field. You will employ pilots and advise me which side of the river you should move up."[76]

White obeyed his superior's order and started his army on a return march twenty-five miles north to Cocke's encampment. Not yet aware that White was not coming, Jackson's young aide, John Reid, wrote a letter to his wife, Betsy, at 9:00 P.M. on November 7, 1813, that reflected Jackson's frustration with the apparently dilatory White: "Gen'l White has not yet joined us, nor do I believe he will until the work is finished. I am astonished at his tardiness."[77]

Unlike her husband, Betsy Reid was an indifferent correspondent, and in his letters to her he constantly complained about her lack of letters to him. Reid had just finished his letter to his wife when a friendly Creek messenger from Lashley's fort at Talladega, where the friendly Creeks had taken refuge, rushed in to Jackson's camp with the news that the fort was under attack by a horde of Red Clubs and that Jackson should come quickly or all would be lost. The messenger was said to be the prominent warrior Selocta, the son of Old Chenibee. According to a popular story, the young man had disguised himself in a hog skin and crawled unnoticed through the Red Club lines around the fort. Thomas Woodward, a teenaged enlisted man in General John Floyd's army of Georgia militia and in his later years a chronicler of the Creek War and debunker of good tales, claimed the story was sheer fantasy. But the apparent crisis at the fort related by the messenger was no fantasy and gave birth to a vicious battle.

John Lashley was a mixed-blood trader who had built a home and trading post in the Talladega Valley. In the manner of Fort Mims, the friendly Creeks of Chenibee's town had constructed pickets around Lashley's trading house to create a fort for protection against the prophets' party. The small bastion held 180 Creek warriors and their families.[78] They gathered there to escape the depredations of the prophets' men on friendly Creek towns along the Coosa River valley to the south. Now one thousand Creek warriors from the hostile towns in the Tallapoosa River valley had poured into the Talladega Valley and besieged the fort. Strangely, they did not attack or do anything more than try to convince their fellow Creeks to join them in the war against the Americans. Nonetheless, according to the messenger, the fort's inhabitants were almost without water and down to a handful of corn. If Jackson did not come at once, the friendly Creeks would be destroyed; or so Jackson was told.

Ever decisive, and realizing the bad effect his failure to rescue the Americans' Creek allies besieged virtually on his doorstep would have on other friendly Creeks, Jackson ordered his army to march the thirty miles southeast to Talladega to rescue the Creeks penned up in Lashley's fort. Furious that White had not arrived with the critical rations and men to protect the sick and wounded at Fort Strother, Jackson was forced to leave part of his command to do so. For his planned attack on the hostiles besieging Lashley's fort, Jackson assembled eight hundred horsemen, one thousand two hundred infantry, and a party of two hundred Cherokee warriors led by Colonel Richard Brown, a prominent mixed-blood tribesman. The men were issued a half day's ration of beef and marched off into the midnight dark. When they reached the Coosa, the infantry forded the one-half mile of iron-cold river by holding onto the tails of the horses.[79]

That evening the army encamped about six miles from Talladega. Around 11:00 P.M., Jackson sent his interpreter George Mayfield and two friendly Indians into the night to reconnoiter the hostiles' position. They soon returned because the Creek encampment was too well screened by sentinels for the scouts to approach closely. They did, however, bring the intelligence that the main hostile force was camped about a quarter of a mile north of the fort.[80] Shortly thereafter, Jackson received news that would affect his whole campaign and destroy his relationship with General Cocke.

Old Chenibee entered the camp and handed Jackson a note from White advising him that the general would not be joining him. The astonishing news (Jackson had given the man a direct order) was doubly disturbing because Jackson had counted not only on the supplies White was bringing but on his men protecting the sick and wounded soldiers at Fort Strother. Jackson had left behind only a small guard to protect those men and quickly decided that the best way to protect them and to save the friendly Creeks was to launch an immediate attack on the Creeks besieging Lashley's. By 4:00 A.M. November 9, Jackson had his soldiers on the march toward the besieged fort.[81]

The army marched in three columns, with parties of men on its flanks and at its head to prevent ambush. By 7:00 A.M. they were within a mile of the fort, which they could now see in the dawning distance, but no hostiles were in sight. There in the morning cool, Jackson arranged his troops for the assault. Each regiment was placed in three lines. Colonel Edward

Bradley's 1st Regiment of volunteer infantry made up Jackson's right wing. Jackson placed Colonel William Pillow's 2nd Regiment of around four hundred volunteer infantry on Bradley's left. Next to Pillow's regiment was Colonel John Wynne's 1st Regiment of 417 west Tennessee militia, and to Wynn's left was Colonel Thomas McCoury's 2nd Regiment of west Tennessee militia. This smaller regiment anchored the far left of Jackson's line. Colonel Robert Dyer's cavalry and mounted riflemen—250 strong— were positioned behind the center of the line as a reserve. Finally, employing Coffee's maneuver at Tallushatchee, Jackson ordered his friend's mounted riflemen and cavalry to curve around either side of the hostiles until they had encircled them. Jackson cautioned his commanders to tie the near ends of the lines of horsemen into the advancing infantry regiments so as to close any avenues of escape between these two disparate elements of his command.[82]

Four hundred yards in advance of his main force Jackson placed Colonel William Carroll's command and Captain John Gordon's company of spies. Jackson's plan, which ironically employed a standard Indian battle tactic, was to use these troops as bait to draw the hostile Creeks out of concealment. When the Creeks attacked, Carroll's men would retreat back up the valley, drawing the hostiles after them like iron filings to a magnet and onto the anvil of Jackson's main force. With the northern end of the valley plugged by the core of his army, Coffee's brigade would seal off its eastern and western sides and come together behind Lashley's fort to the south. Jackson's main force would then advance by companies against the oncoming Red Clubs. If Jackson's plan was successful, it would be Tallushatchee all over again but on a much larger and bloodier scale.

Talladega was in the heart of the prime hunting country of the Creek Nation in a valley of astonishing and heartbreaking beauty. To the west the valley fell away in low wooded hills toward the Coosa. To the east rose the tallest mountains in Alabama, seemingly taller because the valley lay so low. The tallest of these mountains was named Cheha after a legendary Indian chief. It was 2,413 feet high, heavily forested at its base, and studded with spurs of gray-lichened rock along its upper course. Quick streams laced its lower slopes. Atmospherics in the region turned the mountain blue toward late afternoon. The trees on its slopes were past their prime of autumnal colors. These mountains were the home of all manner of game, particularly wolves, which could be found there until the 1830s, when the settlers finally hunted the last of them out. Even as the fear and excitement of battle rose in Jackson's men and focused their attention on their hunt for Indians, some remarked on the beauty of the place, and at least one later returned to live here.[83]

So, too, a number of the waiting Creeks must have given a fond, and for many a last, look at one of the nation's favorite places. Just over one thousand of them from nine upper Tallapoosa River towns were encamped on the north side of Lashley's fort about a quarter mile away. Unlike at Tallushatchee, they knew Jackson was coming, and coming with over twice the force they could muster.[84] They wanted him to march here onto a battleground of their choosing, with Lashley's fort as bait. That is probably why the little fort still lay unmolested. That is why they let the messenger from the fort go through their lines and on to Jackson's camp. That is why their scouts had screened the ground from Jackson's spies. The Red Club leaders hoped to make this lovely blue valley of tall grass a killing ground for the Americans.

It is unknown what leaders of the Red Clubs were at Lashley's fort except for one. Contrary to some accounts, William Weatherford was not among them. He was in the Tensaw region watching the initial moves of General Claiborne's army up the Alabama River valley and conducting a guerrilla-style bush campaign against the Americans. The only Creek commander who is named in the written records is a Hillabee known as Billy Scott.[85]

The American attack jumped off at eight Tuesday morning, November 9, 1813. Colonel Carroll's command, as planned, had been stationed several hundred yards in advance of the right wing of Jackson's main force. Under him Carroll had three companies, led by Captains David Dederick, George Caperton, and Abraham Bledsoe, as well as John Gordon's company of spies. Dederick's company was something of a novelty in that it was actually an artillery command, now armed with muskets. These men had temporarily changed branches of the service because Jackson had determined that it would take too long to transport their cannon to Talladega to arrive in time for battle. Dederick was outfitted in particularly novel fashion, and he must have been something of a deranged romantic because he went into battle wrapped in a flag of cream-colored silk bordered by roses within which an eagle spread its wings below thirteen stars and above the motto "God Armeth The Patriot." The flag had been stitched by a group of west Tennessee ladies and presented to the troops.[86]

As Carroll's troops advanced, with Carroll leading them from horseback, they could see Lashley's fort atop a knoll in the near distance to their front. The land before them rose in a large grassy tongue toward the fort. They passed a spring from which a stream pleasantly bubbled. The margins of the stream were swampy and thick with undergrowth. Here hundreds of Creek warriors lay concealed in "good order" in ambush.[87] As the Americans moved nearer to the fort, they could see its defenders lining the ramparts. They were waving their arms and yelling in an attempt to warn the Americans of the pending ambush. The warnings came too late. The hostiles emerged from concealment and attacked the American vanguard. They were painted scarlet from head to toe and howling at the limits of breath.[88] At least one was carrying a pole from whose top waved a flag embroidered with the Spanish cross.[89] As the Creeks raced toward the Americans they paused long enough to fire two heavy volleys but, true to their usual execrable marksmanship, hit nothing.[90]

Eventually the Indians' marksmanship improved, and Carroll described this initial clash with the Red Clubs, which lasted all of fifteen minutes, as the hardest of the entire battle. His horse was shot from under him by an arrow, and his brother-in-law, Larkin Bradford, was killed.[91] In return, Carroll's men fired several "galling rounds" into the charging Indian formations. After a sharp skirmish, Carroll determined that the entire Creek force had at last emerged from concealment and was now fully engaged. The vanguard managed to turn the main Indian force toward that portion of Jackson's line where the militia was stationed, waiting for Jackson's order to charge.

His task accomplished, Carroll, as planned, ordered a retreat toward the center of the main body of American forces sealing off the mouth of the valley. Sensing victory, the Creeks foolishly took the Americans' bait and raced into the jaws of Jackson's waiting infantry and Coffee's encircling cavalry. About half a mile from the point where Carroll's command had retreated, a mass of scarlet-and-feathered demons of gigantic size brandishing red-painted war clubs with vicious metal blades in their ends and uttering terrifying cries hit the lines of waiting militia hard. Young John Reid, who was at Jackson's side as the Red Clubs charged, opined that no whites would be brave enough to make such a charge.[92]

Virtually none of the American infantry, waiting to meet the Indians' charge with a charge of their own, had ever seen such a sight. Among these men, staring in astonishment and terror at the onrushing Indian legions, was seventeen-year-old Washington Perry Ewing. He was the grandson of General William Lee Davidson, the Revolutionary War hero and Jackson's personal hero, for whom North Carolina's Davidson College is named. In response to Jackson's call that autumn for volunteers to fight the Creeks, the impetuous Ewing, without his parents' knowledge, left school and joined the army as a member of Captain David Smith's company, Colonel Dyer's regiment of Coffee's mounted volunteers.[93] Now he was in for the experience of his life. As the mob of Red Clubs moved within range of the American infantry, three companies of General Roberts's brigade of militia were overcome with terror. Rather than charging the enemy as ordered, they wildly fired their guns at the mass of attacking Indians, then turned and fled to the rear. Other American troops who, against all reason, had held their ground now began to topple from the Indian balls and arrows. For a short time the firing at this point in the American lines was "tremendous."[94] Colonel Pillows, commander of the 1st Regiment of west Tennessee militia, however, refused to retreat and abandon his wounded to the Red Club scalping knives. He stayed with his men, but his brave fidelity was rewarded with an Indian musket ball through his body.[95]

Jackson, too, along with his staff, found himself in the middle of the fiercest fighting, but he refused to be panicked. From his perch on his horse Duke, the general dispatched his aides—John Reid, Robert Searcy, Stokely Hays, and James Sittler—about the battlefield with his orders for his troop commanders. On Jackson's front at this point, the Red Clubs outnumbered the Americans three to one.[96] Jackson sent one of his aides through the melee to Colonel Bradley with an order to bring up his regiment of volunteers to plug the gap in the American lines made by the fleeing militia. Bradley, however, refused to move his men from the "eminence" upon which his regiment was stationed, declaring he would remain where he was and let the Creeks attack him.[97] Jackson was, therefore, forced to order the reserve under Colonel Dyer to dismount their horses and rush up to fill the gap left by the panicked militia.

Dyer's counterattack struck the advancing Indians within eight yards of where Jackson was standing with his aides. Fire from the reserves' rifles killed twenty-seven of the enemy and stopped their charge. Shamed by the brave conduct of Dyer's men, among them the truant student Ewing, the fleeing militia returned to the fight. As at Tallushatchee, the surrounding cavalry began constricting its lines around the Red Club force. Another slaughter began as the Creeks found themselves caught between firing from the head of Jackson's army and its two wings. Fortunately for the hostiles, and contrary to Jackson's orders, the far right flank of Bradley's regiment of volunteer infantry and the 2nd Regiment of Volunteer Mounted Riflemen under Alcorn had not tied in, leaving a large gap between the lines through which the defeated Creeks quickly poured and then fled, pell-mell, to the safety of the mountains several miles away.[98]

To the delight of the formerly besieged friendly Creeks in the fort, a chase began as the mounted soldiers shot and sabered the racing Indians through the tall grass for three miles toward the mountains until the heat of the day and fatigue put an end to the Americans' sport.[99] According to Jackson's account of the battle, the Indians left 290 warriors on the field (Reid says 299), and blood trails from uncounted wounded ran through the tall grass of the plateau leading toward the mountains. But this chase, as published accounts suggest, was not altogether a game, so favored in the Deep South, of beagle hounds after rabbits. These rabbits could and did bite. Among the officers, infantry colonel William Pillow, cavalry colonel William Lauderdale, Major R. Boyd of the mounted infantry, and Lieutenant Sarquel Barton of the cavalry were wounded in the pursuit; Barton later died.

Overall in the battle, Jackson's army lost only seventeen killed and eighty-five wounded, several of whom later died at Fort Strother. General Coffee's brigade, which was attached to the vanguard commanded by

Colonel Carroll, suffered the worst by far, with ten men killed and fifty-one wounded. Apparently the losses of Jackson's Creek and Cherokee allies in this battle were not officially reported, but we do know that a Cherokee named the Whooping Boy suffered serious wounds during the fight. Sadly, while Whooping Boy was recuperating from his wounds, some of General White's men on their return to Tennessee stole eight of his horses.[100] The truant student, young Washington Perry Ewing, survived the fight unscathed and acquitted himself bravely. Jackson apparently sent him back to his anxious parents none the worse for his adventure except for the hard memories of what he had witnessed.

Although he had won a significant victory and handled his first battle with coolness and his usual bravery, Jackson was not satisfied. Even though only half of his army was engaged, and even though several companies of the militia had bolted from his lines, if colonels Alcorn and Bradley had executed his order to tie the lines of their respective cavalry and infantry together, Jackson believed he could have destroyed every hostile; or, alternatively, if Jackson had not had to dismount Lieutenant Dyer's infantry to plug the gap in his lines created by the panicked militia, he would have had the mounted force he needed to run every last one of the fleeing Creeks to earth. Nonetheless, Jackson was pleased at the immense slaughter his tactics and the Red Clubs' foolish charge had produced.

So proud was Jackson of his bloody achievement that the gallant general dispatched Captain Thomas H. Fletcher all the way to Nashville with not only news of Jackson's great victory but also with a special trophy for some special ladies. One of Jackson's soldiers, Lemuel Hall, had captured a battle flag carried by a Red Club warrior he had slain.[101] The flag was emblazoned with a Spanish cross, reinforcing the frontier conviction that foreign powers were behind the prophets' movement. Jackson had Fletcher deliver that flag to the Nashville ladies who had sewn battle flags for Jackson's army that flew from the Americans' standards at Talladega.[102] The needlework on the Spanish flag, as Jackson smoothly informed the ladies in his accompanying message, was not nearly so grand as their own handiwork.[103] While in Nashville, Fletcher was treated to the sight of an illumination of the town and the joyous sounds of ringing church and town bells in celebration of Jackson's triumph by the jubilant Nashvillians. Some of the same bells pealed in recognition of the dark side of the victory: seventeen rings for the seventeen men killed in the battle.[104]

Jackson's troops and his Indian allies left the dead hostiles where they fell after stripping every one of them of their scalps and personal possessions. Jackson buried his dead in a pit on the battlefield. Those of his wounded who were too seriously hurt to walk or ride were placed in litters and transported with the rest of the army to Fort Strother. Along the rough way to the fort, two of these men died.[105]

It was November 12. All of Jackson's men were practically starving, having eaten virtually nothing for three days, and they looked forward with great relish to devouring a good meal on their return to the fort. When the troops were almost in sight of their camp, which would become Fort Strother, and were about to realize their dream of ample rations and warm fires, they were faced with a final cruel obstacle in their path. Five hundred yards of icy Coosa River water lay between them and the eastern shore where their camp lay. When they reached the ford across the river, the night was bitterly cold, and frost was on the ground. The river was running quick and cold, and the footing on the rocky bottom was treacherous. Nonetheless, driven by their dream of food and warmth, they managed to cross the seemingly endless yards of river running as high as their midsections. Shaking off the cold and damp as best they could and arraying themselves in rough formation, the troops trudged the final distance into camp, picking up the pace when their goal came in sight. But they were terribly disappointed, for when they at long last arrived at the camp, they found the eagerly anticipated food supplies were not there.[106] The day Jackson's victorious but shivering and starving army reached Fort Strother proved to be the beginning of the most serious test of Jackson's generalship since the campaign began, altering his relationship with his men and transforming him as a commander of men altogether.

As for the Creeks, the disaster that was Talladega was substantially of their own making. Their amazing and unquestioned bravery was no substitute for proper tactics. For some reason, at Talladega, the Creeks abandoned the Indian mode of fighting that over the long years had produced astonishing successes, from King Philip's War in New England in the late 1600s to British general Edward's Braddock's defeat in 1763 near Fort Pitt during the French and Indian War and more recently the crushing defeats of Generals Josiah Harmar and Arthur St. Clair in the Ohio Valley in the 1790s during President Washington's administration.

These successes and others were first and foremost due to the Native Americans' superior knowledge of the terrain through which the white armies were moving and the ability to select from that terrain the place most advantageous to their mode of fighting from ambush, as well as terrain that provided them with a line of retreat should their attack fail. They were not trained to attack lines of massed soldiers, supported by cavalry, who outnumbered and outgunned them. And although the Red Club leaders chose the battleground at Talladega, their choice was inexplicably catastrophic. The land was flat and largely treeless, and their nearest sanctuary in case of defeat, Mount Cheha, was three miles away across open country.

These northern Creeks would not make the same mistake in their next clash with Jackson's army, but so chastened were they by the Battle of

Talladega that a principal part of their army, composed of warriors from the Hillabee towns, was now ready to sue for peace and sent word to General Jackson to that effect. Tragically, however, General White, who was supposed to have conveyed the critical supplies to Fort Strother, put a quick end to the Hillabee peace overture. Disobeying Jackson's orders because of orders from his direct superior General Cocke, he had reversed his march to Fort Strother and returned north to Fort Armstrong. From there he soon launched a misbegotten and murderous expedition against the Hillabees that immediately ended Jackson's peace negotiations with that tribe. Sadly, Cocke's and White's blunders would prolong the war for months and result in the deaths of more of Jackson's men and the general destruction of Creek settlements across the Muskogee Nation.

A Fatal Triumph: The Hillabee Massacre

S HORTLY after the Battle of Talladega, the aged Robert Grierson received the first good news he had had in five months. Grierson, a native of Scotland, was a licensed trader who had lived comfortably with his large family for many years on a farm several miles outside Hillabee town. The Hillabees were members of the Abeka tribe and had been living in the area since 1718.[107]

Grierson had lived among the Hillabees since the 1790s. He had come to the nation to trade and, like so many in that occupation, ended up staying there. He had an Indian wife and six children and had become a prosperous farmer. But the rise of the prophets cost the old man dearly. They murdered his son David and David's family on April 21, 1813. On July 13, his Hillabee neighbors killed Grierson's grandson Pinckney Hawkins and his family. They also exiled other of the old man's family and friends from the Hillabee lands. Finally, shortly before the Battle of Tallushatchee, the Red Clubs took his house, his slaves, his livestock, and everything else he owned. On top of all these troubles, Grierson suffered from "the palsey."

Thus it was with no little satisfaction that the old Scotsman listened while a delegation of his now profoundly humbled neighbors—fresh from the slaughter at Talladega—implored him to save them from the terrible Jackson. On November 13, Grierson penned a letter to the general, advising him that the Hillabees were prepared to cease fighting the Americans and to accept such other terms as Jackson saw fit to impose upon them. The hostiles were "panic struck" with their defeat at Talladega, Grierson advised Jackson, and had "no ammunition nor resources of any kind." If Jackson attacked them now, he could "conquer them in two weeks." On his own account, Grierson also begged Jackson to extract restitution from the hostiles for the harm they had caused him and his family. Not quite destitute, of slaves at least, Grierson handed the letter to Jackson to his "negro man (Pompey)," provided Pompey with an Indian guide and a flag of truce, and sent him on to deliver the letter to Jackson at Fort Strother.[108]

When the two reached Talladega, Pompey's terrified Hillabee guide refused to go any farther. The resourceful Pompey completed the final thirty miles to Jackson's camp, found the general, and delivered Grierson's letter to him.[109] Grierson followed this letter up with a short note to Jackson dated November 15, advising him that the entry of an army of Georgians into the nation had sent the war parties fleeing in all directions and urging Jackson to march south and complete the hostiles' rout, not knowing that Jackson, in a desperate attempt to retain command of this army, was moving with most of his men in the opposite direction.[110]

On November 17, Jackson sent Pompey back to Grierson with a letter in which he outlined terms for the Hillabee surrender. Jackson required the Hillabees to give up all prisoners and plunder they had taken from the whites and friendly Creeks, to turn over to Jackson the "Instigators of the present war," to provide Jackson's army with provisions when it arrived at Hillabee, and to join Jackson in his fight against the remaining hostiles.[111] A copy of this peace proposal went by express to Governor Blount, who, predictably, had conditions of his own to add. These conditions, not surprisingly, were intended to facilitate the exploitation of the Creek country by the Tennesseans. Blount wrote Jackson that he wanted the Creeks to agree to open their rivers to navigation, to permit improvements in the waterways to facilitate navigation, and to allow the construction of roads and military posts in Creek territory. On November 18, Jackson sent a letter to General Cocke at Fort Armstrong apprising him of the Hillabees' offer of surrender and the terms of Jackson's response.[112]

What Jackson did not know when he penned that letter to Cocke was that on November 11, Cocke had sent General White on an expedition to the Hillabee towns one hundred miles south. Cocke had learned that the "famous" Indian leader at Talladega, Billy Scott, lay wounded in the Hillabee settlements. The ambitious Cocke decided to grab a share of glory for himself and his east Tennessee troops by attacking the Hillabee settlements and seizing Scott. Cocke, therefore, ordered White to conduct a quick strike deep into Creek country where the Indians believed themselves beyond the reach of the Americans and thus susceptible to surprise. Accordingly, for what he saw as a brief operation, Cocke allotted White and his raiders only four days' rations.

White departed from Fort Armstrong on the Coosa River seventy miles northeast of Fort Strother. His command consisted of cavalry, mounted infantry, and a company of Cherokees under Colonel Gideon Morgan. Their line of march took them through rugged, heavily forested hill country largely devoid of Indian settlements toward the upper reaches of the west side of the Tallapoosa River. The first town they arrived at was Little Okfuskee, a village of thirty houses on a tributary of the Tallapoosa. It was deserted except for five warriors lurking in the area whom the Americans took for spies and captured. White burned the town and rode on to a more substantial settlement of ninety houses called Genalgo. He burned that town as well, which was also deserted, and rode on to a third settlement called Nitty Chopta. White prudently decided to spare this village of twenty-five houses in the event he needed a place to retreat to should his enterprise against the Hillabees go awry.[113]

By the evening of November 17, White was six to eight miles from Hillabee town, where he had been informed a large group of hostiles were gathered. Pausing his march to camp for the night, White considered his next move and decided on a daybreak assault on the town, which was at the fork of two pretty little creeks. To effect this plan, he sent Colonel Morgan's Cherokees ahead of a group of dismounted soldiers commanded by a Colonel Burch. Once they reached Hillabee, the Americans and their Indian allies were to employ the whites' usual tactics and surround the town. However, the white soldiers in the attacking force had trouble finding their way in the dark through the unobliging country to their objective, and the sun had already risen before the assault party was in place.[114] The delay did not affect White's plan, however, because the unsuspecting Hillabees believed a truce was in place with the Americans while they negotiated surrender terms with General Jackson.

Thus, when White's initial assault party of Cherokees, led by the redoubtable Gideon Morgan, burst upon Hillabee town out of the surrounding forest, the Hillabee warriors were unprepared to meet the attack. By the time White's main force stumbled on the scene to join the attack, the battle was over. Within minutes, some sixty warriors had been killed "on the spot" and 256 men, women, and children taken prisoner, along with "about eighty negroes." Most if not all of the slaves belonged to the chronically unfortunate Grierson.[115] "We lost not one drop of blood in accomplishing this enterprise," White proudly reported to Cocke, an assertion echoed by Morgan to the Cherokee agent, Colonel Return Meigs.[116] This assertion is not surprising given that it was reported that the clueless Hillabees fired only one gun at their attackers.[117]

In his letter to Meigs, Morgan recounted what occurred in the battle. During the approach to the town, the Cherokees moved so quickly through the forest dark that they left the American soldiers well in their wake. Seeing that the Hillabees were unprepared for an attack, or even aware that their enemies were upon them, the Cherokees decided to take advantage of the element of surprise and launch an immediate assault. Leaving a group of warriors under Major John Walker on a piece of high ground to prevent any Hillabees from escaping, the remaining Cherokees, under Colonel Morgan, rushed out of the dark forest on the unsuspecting hostiles. The slaughter of the astonished and defenseless inhabitants was quick. During the attack, one of the Cherokees, Major Lowrey, is said to have slain six Hillabees with his sword, a sad indication of the strength of the resistance the astonished Hillabees were able to muster.[118] Finally, one of the Hillabees had the presence of mind to raise a white flag. Seeing this, Morgan ordered his men to stop the attack.[119] The "battle" was over so quickly that poor Walker and his men had no opportunity to participate. Not one Hillabee escaped the attack.

Deprived of the chance to distinguish himself, Walker recruited a Captain Saunders and a Lieutenant Ridge, along with some other Cherokee warriors, to accompany him on an expedition to another Hillabee town six miles away. During their ride to the town through the early morning woods, they encountered three Creeks, whom they promptly killed. On arriving at the unsuspecting settlement, they spotted a gathering of forty women and children, whom they quickly rounded up and made prisoner. Then Walker's war party dispersed among the Hillabee cabins for the usual bout of plundering the inhabitants' possessions before burning the town.[120]

Before Walker could join in the sport, he was surprised by eighteen armed Hillabee warriors, their guns leveled at him. Flight was futile, fight was impossible, so Major Walker turned to "stratagem" to save himself. He strode boldly toward the Creeks and demanded their immediate surrender; if they did not, he told them, they would be executed. The startled Creeks, fooled by the ruse, lay down their weapons and capitulated to Walker. He then herded his catch of Hillabees into the collection pen of other prisoners. There they remained until the Cherokees finished despoiling their town, after which the triumphant major, prisoners in tow, marched in search of General White's army, which at that time was already returning to Fort Armstrong. Along the way some of Walker's men left the war party to hunt for other Creeks. By the time he reached White, Walker had only four or five of the captured warriors left with him, about ten Creek warriors having managed to escape along the march. Walker also brought with him about fifty captive women and children, as well as around eighty blacks.[121] Shortly after this reunion with White's army, the heavy, cold rains, the rough country, and the lack of provisions turned the army's return march of heroes to Fort Armstrong into a hellish journey.

On a rainy Tuesday, November 23, General White's rain-soaked and bedraggled army and its even wetter and more bedraggled prisoners arrived at Fort Armstrong. Twenty-seven warriors were among the prisoners, some of whom were wounded. When the prisoners were examined, it was learned that among the wounded warriors was a Creek identified as Billy Scott.[122] As Grierson had advised Jackson, Scott had been one of the

Red Club leaders at the Battle of Talladega and had been recovering from wounds received at that battle when captured during White's attack on the Hillabee settlements.

After the Hillabee affair, Major Morgan proudly reported to agent Meigs that, with the exception of one Hillabee killed by a white soldier, the Cherokees had killed the rest of the dead counted and had taken all the prisoners. With this one exception, Morgan proudly wrote, the "achievement" at the Hillabee towns "belongs entirely to the Cherokees." However, Morgan's report also contained a somber counterpart to his cheerleading: a plea for justice for the Cherokees from the whites: "Will not shame redden the face & silence mute the tongue of those who have pretended to doubt the attachment of the Cherokees to our Country. They must now if they continue to murmur advance their real views, a thirst for their property and their lives."[123]

Could Major Morgan really have believed that his gift to General White of Hillabee blood and captives would quench the whites' thirst for Cherokee land and blood rather than bringing that objective closer to fruition? If so, Morgan was either delusional or unaware of the proverb "He who would sup with the devil had best bring a long spoon." He need only have read White's report of the battle, which White touted as a triumph of American arms (with some help from the Cherokees), to realize how little the Cherokees' aid was valued by the Americans.

Public opinion of White's campaign against the Hillabees fell into two camps. The *Nashville Clarion* voiced the opinion that the Hillabees got what they deserved as the result of the atrocities (in which they were not involved) committed by the Red Clubs on the settlers on the Duck River and at Fort Mims. Citing, of all things, the murderous conduct of the Spanish against the Native Americans who fell under their rule, the *Clarion* made the further astonishing argument that it was wise and in fact a "humane" policy to make a "dreadful example" of any Indian people who opposed the Americans. Through cruelty to these people, the war would be shortened, future warfare would be prevented, and hostile conduct by the "friendly tribes" would be discouraged. "The history of Spanish America proves to us," the *Clarion* opined, "that this is the wisest policy to pursue with the Aborigines; they were sure to make examples of those tribes that were unfaithful, and have in consequence, with a weak population had fewer wars with them than any other European power in proportion to the extent of country they had in possession."[124] The *Nashville Whig*, on the other hand, took a dimmer view of White's attack on the Hillabees. It described the "battle" as "butchery" and opined that the prior atrocities of the Red Clubs on the settlers did not excuse such conduct by American armies.[125]

The ultimate price of White's "triumph," however, was the undying and unrelenting enmity toward the Americans of the Hillabee people. From this day until the end of the war, they were among the fiercest and most uncompromising of the Creek warriors Jackson had to face. More importantly, the Hillabee massacre undoubtedly prolonged the war. Had the powerful Hillabee tribe surrendered to Jackson, as it clearly was prepared to do, that likely would have pulled in its wake the surrender of other tribes, particularly the Hillabees' Okfuskee neighbors led by Menawa. The loss of these two Upper Creek powers would have gutted the Red Club confederacy. Instead both tribes became perhaps the Americans' fiercest and most implacable enemies.

What Jackson thought of the Hillabee massacre is unclear. Contrary to one of his first biographers, who wrote that Jackson was outraged at White's perceived perfidy, no direct evidence exists that Jackson gave the matter much thought. Given that Jackson often referred to the Creeks in such terms as a "Satanic Savage foe" and the "fiends of the Tallapoosa," and frequently used words like "exterminate" and "extirpation" in describing his intentions toward them, and had warned Grierson that when he was finished with the Creeks they would long "remember Ft. Mims in bitterness & tears," it is unlikely Jackson was overly troubled by White's attack on the Hillabees.[126] Indeed, he may have welcomed the outcome of White's murderous expedition. For by destroying negotiations with the Hillabees and killing many of their people, White gave the ambitious Jackson the opportunity to more easily burnish his military reputation in future battles against a diminished foe. If such was Jackson's thinking, he, like Major Beasley, grievously underestimated his enemy.

With the conclusion of White's raid, no further battles took place between the Tennesseans and the Creeks in the waning months of 1813. Nor were Generals White and Cocke ever again a factor in the conflict. As for Jackson, the next several months were among the hardest of a hard life. Just to maintain his army in the field required all his political skills, his enormous capacity for physical suffering, and his undoubted personal courage. The war now moved to other theaters in the nation. Jackson's supply problems, a mutinous army, and, in Jackson's strongly held view, Cocke's failure to cooperate with Jackson had ended an opportunity to bring the Creek War to an early conclusion. Amid all the hardships to come, a vengeful Jackson, apparently thoroughly steeped in the Old Testament, neither forgot nor forgave Cocke's recall of White on the eve of the Battle of Talladega.

6. Upon the Silver Plain

The Georgians' First Campaign

GEORGIA had been preparing to invade the Creek Nation since the end of July 1813. On July 30, the commander in chief of the Georgia militia, by order of the US secretary of war, issued a general order to the commanders of the various state militia companies to ready their men to rendezvous at a place to be determined in the near future. A force of two thousand five hundred volunteers and draftees was to be raised, although the draftees could hire acceptable substitutes. The men were advised to provide themselves with "knapsacks and haversacks, and suitable clothing for camp or field duty." The prospective soldiers would be issued arms and ammunition when they arrived at camp.[1] As they left for the front, some of the men placed notices in their local paper advising the public of the identity of the individual who would represent their commercial interests while they were at war. They need not have placed these notices so promptly. It would take three months before the army was ready to march.

Of the three directions from which the Americans planned to invade the nation, the path from Georgia was the shortest and most direct and presented the fewest natural obstacles. Indeed, the Federal Road led straight from the Georgia settlements into the nation's population center around the juncture of the Coosa and Tallapoosa rivers. Although considered by some even decades after the war as the "very worst" road in America, it could still accommodate wagons and the Georgians' cannon.[2] Benjamin Hawkins, however, called it a "fine road, bridges, and flats [ferries] to the heart of the nation."[3] As the embattled Big Warrior crossly observed to Hawkins, the Americans at last had the wagon road through the nation they had wanted, and now was the perfect time to use it.

Also of great advantage to any army invading the nation from Georgia was an excellent jumping-off point at the friendly Lower Creek town of Coweta. That town was on the west bank of the Chattahoochee River just sixty miles or so from Tuckabatchee along the Federal Road. There, following the hostiles' siege of Tuckabatchee, hundreds of Creek warriors from four of the friendly Lower Creek towns, as well as the Big Warrior's Upper Creeks, had gathered. They had fortified the town, and now, at Hawkins's urging, were happily sending raiding parties against the Upper Creek towns.[4] Hawkins's plan was to use these raiding parties from Coweta to keep the Red Clubs off balance and delay an attack on that town until the Georgia militia arrived. Toward the end of August, one of these raiding parties of 375 Lower Creeks, led by William McIntosh, destroyed Peter McQueen's town at Chattacchufaulee.[5] Toward the end of September, another party of raiders had even penetrated into the remote Hillabee country, where they "took" some horses. As the exasperated Hawkins observed, however, his Indian army was more interested in plunder than war.[6]

These raids had also gotten the Red Clubs' attention. Since the attack on Fort Mims, to which they had diverted their forces from their original objective of Coweta, they had been largely inactive in the Georgia theater. This inactivity likely was the result of the Fort Mims battle itself. A number of their warriors had been wounded in that hard fight, and they needed to recuperate; also, the Red Club forces needed to regroup.[7] Toward the end of September, they were ready to refocus their attention on the critical tasks of weaning the Lower Creeks from Hawkins's and the friendly chiefs' influence and unifying the nation for the coming struggle with the Americans.

Initially the hostiles employed a carrot-and-stick approach toward the Creeks to the east. Their victory at Fort Mims hard on the heels of their "victory" at Burnt Corn Creek was paraded before the populace as proof of the prophets' power. The Red Club leaders' promise of far greater plunder and honor once the nation was united against the Americans was directed at the Lower Creeks' cupidity. The promise of British aid in the form of supplies and even troops was directed at their fear of American power. And for those still unconvinced souls, the Red Clubs promised that all manner of retribution, natural and supernatural, would fall on those Lower Creeks who failed to join them.[8] To their brothers fortified at Coweta they sent a message that if they gave up the Big Warrior, McIntosh, Little Prince, and other of the friendly chiefs and joined the hostile party, their past defiance would be forgotten. Although the prophets had some success with the Uchee tribe, who left their towns and joined the hostile party, the majority of the Lower Creeks decided either to hedge their bets and remain out of the conflict or to join forces with the friendly chiefs at Coweta.[9] Thwarted in their attempt to resolve the situation peacefully, the Red Club leaders prepared to besiege Coweta.

Through his spies, Hawkins was well aware of the prophets' attempts to bring the friendly towns over to their side and to eliminate the pro-American chiefs at Coweta. From late September into October, Hawkins pleaded with the civil and military authorities of Georgia to send troops to Coweta and from there to invade the nation. Governor Mitchell of Georgia had called up the militia in August, but the usual supply and organizational problems delayed its entry into the conflict. A contemporaneous account from Fort Hawkins by one of the militiamen, Private James Tait, described the army's situation in early September: "When we shall march against the Indians is not known, probably in 5 or 6 weeks. Matters are not yet well organized. Officers in the contracting or victualing department must give better proofs of their activity and management, or perhaps we should not in 3 months, move to the object of the expedition."[10]

The militia was commanded by yet another planter-politician, forty-four-year-old brigadier general John Floyd. Floyd's father, Charles, was a hero of the Revolutionary War. That conflict, particularly the internecine fights with the Tories, had destroyed the Floyd family fortunes. To afford his son a start in life, the best the father could do was to find him an apprenticeship to a carpenter. In 1795, the Floyd family moved from South Carolina to McIntosh County, Georgia, where they took up farming. The son rose fast in this frontier community and in 1806 was appointed a brigadier of militia by the governor.[11]

Private Tait described Floyd as the general reviewed the troops: he was "dressed in a blue frock coat, with very splendid epaulets and rich gold lace. He is a man of stature, about the middle size, of a dark complexion and formed for strength, appearing to possess the capacity, so necessary for a commander, of enduring much fatigue." Tait also expressed great confidence in the general's leadership and military abilities: " I expect that he is the most able, or skillful, commander in the southern country; very nimble in the field, possessing great presence of mind, and delivering his orders with great precision, accuracy, and distinctiveness."[12] Likewise, when Hawkins first met Floyd at Fort Hawkins around September 21, 1813, he reported that the general impressed him as "a brave active intelligent officer."[13] During the ensuing months, Hawkins's initial opinion of Floyd would change radically.

On September 29, elements of Floyd's army left Fort Hawkins and marched west to the Creek Indian agency on the east bank of the Flint River thirty miles away. They arrived there on October 1, and the morning of the following day the raw recruits waded the river "like a soldier" and encamped before Fort Lawrence. The first frosts had already arrived, and by the time they reached Fort Lawrence, men had already begun to sicken and die of the usual illnesses, particularly dysentery, which afflicted the armies of that era.[14] There they remained for just over six weeks while sickness among the troops mounted.

Meanwhile, Hawkins was doing all that he could to get Floyd moving against the hostile Creeks. When they had met at Fort Hawkins in September to discuss the situation, Floyd explained to Hawkins that Governor Mitchell had yet to give him the necessary orders to march. Several days later, Hawkins, now at the Creek agency, informed Floyd at

Fort Hawkins that he had learned from his sources that the prophets were proselytizing the friendly Creeks to join their party and that if the Georgians did not send troops promptly, there was a danger that, if only from fear, many of the friendly Creeks "will be compelled to join the Red Clubs."[15]

On September 30, Hawkins again wrote Floyd, informing him that an attack by the hostiles on Coweta was imminent and that the prophets had threatened to "put to death every red man who does not join them." The prophets were boasting to the Lower Creeks that "[t]he Master of Breath has permitted a conquering spirit to arise among them like a storm, and it shall ravage like a storm." This sort of talk, coupled with the victory at Fort Mims and the inaction of the Georgians had already caused the Uchees to join the Red Clubs and terrified many of the other friendly Creeks, "which nothing but the presence of our army will remove."[16] Hawkins urged Floyd to pass this information on to the governor.

Floyd had already asked Mitchell for orders and by the end of September had sent elements of his two-thousand-five-hundred-man army across the Flint River to Fort Lawrence. But supply problems made it impossible for him to follow promptly with his main force. Indeed, on October 8, Floyd's quartermaster general, Abram Fannin, placed a notice in the *Georgia Journal* seeking wagons and teams to haul supplies for the army on its expedition against the Creeks. They were not to report to the army, however, until October 20. Although as of October 23, Floyd had still not marched his army to Coweta, Hawkins was sounding less desperate and even optimistic. On that date he wrote Judge Toulmin at Mobile that "[our] movement from this quarter, combined with that of Tennessee and Mississippi territory, will render the campaign decisive in our favor."[17]

By October 25, Floyd's army still had not moved, because the general was waiting for sufficient cattle to arrive to feed the army on its march. Soon thereafter, the Big Warrior and the Little Prince, along with an interpreter, left Coweta to meet with Hawkins at the agency. During that meeting, the Big Warrior later claimed, he and the Little Prince discussed with Hawkins the political landscape after the Red Clubs' defeat. According to the Big Warrior, Hawkins informed the two chiefs that after the war, the government would send representatives to negotiate terms with the chiefs. The Big Warrior had already generously offered to pay the costs incurred by the Americans in defeating the Red Clubs out of Red Club land south of the Alabama River, and he and the Little Prince understood that this offer would be the basis of any settlement with the United States after the war.[18]

The Big Warrior claimed that after this meeting with Hawkins, he and the Little Prince, accompanied by Hawkins, met with Floyd at the general's headquarters, where he restated Hawkins's purported assurances about the basis of settlement discussions following the conclusion of the war.[19] At this conference, the friendly Creek leaders and the Georgians also discussed coordination of their respective forces. The Indians provided the Georgians with intelligence about the numbers and dispositions of the hostile forces as well as about the topography of the country on the army's route of march. Unfortunately, however, at this meeting or soon thereafter, Floyd and Hawkins had a falling out that affected the general's campaign against the hostiles. This contretemps appeared to have its source in Colonel Hawkins's resentment at Governor Mitchell's efforts to direct the campaign. Although few, if any, Americans had better knowledge than Hawkins of the hostile forces Floyd was about to attack or the country that lay between the Georgians and their objective—the lower Tallapoosa River towns—Floyd declined Hawkins's offer of "guides, interpreters, and a map of the country."[20] Instead, Floyd chose to accept the map, guide, and interpreter provided by Mitchell.

The man selected as guide may have been someone Hawkins once described as a "Jew of bad character," Abraham Mordecai, who claimed to have been on the expedition. If so, the choice would have seemingly been a wise one. Mordecai had lived for many years near the Cluwallee tribe, who lay at the heart of Floyd's objective. Their main town called Cluwallee, or Hoithlewaulee, was on the north bank of the lower Tallapoosa River along Line Creek, about ten miles downstream of Tuckabatchee. Two miles away from Hoithlewaulee, on Line Creek Road, Mordecai had established a trading post, built "in the Spanish style" by a group of Spanish deserters.[21] This establishment was destroyed by the Red Clubs in 1812, leaving an embittered Mordecai free to join Floyd's army.

Floyd's choice of guide or interpreter, however, probably turned more on politics than merit. Given that Mitchell was his commander, Floyd may have felt politically constrained to follow his recommendation. He may also have been offended by Hawkins's overbearing manner. Ever jealous of his prerogatives, Hawkins considered Floyd an "officer of the United States" and under no constraints to obey Mitchell.[22] In any event, Floyd's decision to follow the governor's recommendation had a significant impact on the campaign.

General Thomas Pinckney Takes Command

In mid-October 1813, President Madison made a fateful decision that had important consequences for the prosecution of the Creek War. The titular commander of the war against the Creeks, David B. Mitchell, resigned as Georgia governor. The resignation gave Madison the excuse to remove Mitchell from charge of the campaign and replace him with a real military man. Luckily, just such a man was at hand: Major General Thomas Pinckney, commander of the 6th Military District, which was headquartered in Pinckney's home town of Charleston, South Carolina.[23]

Pinckney was born in 1750 into an old, rich, and distinguished Charleston family. His father was chief justice of South Carolina's highest court during colonial rule. Young Pinckney was educated at the finest schools in England: Westminster public school (the equivalent of an American private school) and Christ Church College of Oxford University. Following his matriculation at Oxford, Pinckney spent a year at the famous French military college at Caen. From Caen, the multitalented Pinckney returned to England, where he spent a year studying law at London's famous Inner Temple. He returned to South Carolina in 1773 and was admitted to the bar in 1774. Despite his English education, and perhaps because of his experience while abroad as a mere colonial among his aristocratic classmates, on his return, Pinckney quickly became embroiled in revolutionary politics on the side of the colonials.

Pinckney served with great distinction in the War for Independence. In 1775, he was commissioned in the US Army as a captain in a South Carolina regiment. In that position, Pinckney saw considerable action against the British. In 1780, he was wounded and taken prisoner by the British at the Battle of Camden. Later released, he fought under General Lafayette in General Washington's Virginia campaign. After the war he entered politics. He was governor of South Carolina from 1787 to 1789, and a member of Congress from 1797 to 1801. He ran unsuccessfully on the Federalist ticket as a candidate for vice president and enjoyed a distinguished career as a diplomat, returning to the land of his schooling as ambassador to Great Britain in 1792.

Several years later, George Washington appointed Pinckney "Envoy extraordinary" to the court of Spain. In that capacity he negotiated an important treaty with the Spanish government known as the Treaty of San Lorenzo, or Pinckney's Treaty. This treaty, executed in 1795, was of critical importance to the United States' future in the Old Southwest. It established the boundary between Spanish and American possessions from the Mississippi River and the Atlantic Ocean along 31 degrees of latitude; it gave the United States free navigation from the source of the Mississippi to its mouth; it allowed US merchants to deliver their goods duty free to the Spanish port of New Orleans; and, significantly for the southern Indian tribes, it required the United States and Spain to refrain from supporting those tribes living in Spanish or American territory in attacks on the territory of the other nation.

In sum, Pinckney was everything that Jackson was not and everything even the aristocratic Claiborne and Floyd strived to be. And beneath his seductive wealth and glittering personal accomplishments, Pinckney was a decent, fair-minded man without hatred of the Indians or any desire to enhance his career over the bodies of those people. Moreover, as he was soon to demonstrate, Pinckney possessed a degree of military acumen and organizational skills that the younger men lacked.

Following his appointment as commander of the Creek War, Pinckney quickly and correctly sized up the military situation. On November 16, 1813, he issued a general order to his commanders from his home in Charleston. In that order, he urged his commanders to seize and hold Creek territory rather than make temporary incursions into the nation against Creek settlements, which left towns destroyed and people killed but the Red Clubs still in control of the land. Instead, for the duration of the war, his generals were to establish strong forts in the "heart of the country." From these positions the Americans would send out detachments of troops to subdue the hostiles. In order to achieve this objective, Pinckney recognized that the problem of adequate supplies for the armies would have to be addressed first. To this end he directed that his generals establish a series of supply depots along each army's line of march. He also recognized that in a land without roads, overland transportation of supplies was too slow and expensive to be practicable. Instead, he directed that wherever possible, transport should be by water; the army could buy or build boats for this purpose.[24]

From the outset of his appointment, Pinckney had decided that the Americans' primary military objective was to establish a strong post at the fork of the Coosa and Tallapoosa rivers. To that end he planned for General Floyd, who was already on the march from Georgia, to take the Federal Road to the fork of the two rivers. General Jackson would descend the Coosa River, and General Claiborne would come up the Alabama and join their commands with Floyd's. It was essential to the success of this plan, Pinckney said, that the separate armies use every means to regularly communicate their positions and plans. Pinckney also warned in his order that his commanders must resist the temptation to hold the Creeks in contempt. They should employ companies of spies and friendly Indians to obtain information about their enemies: what their strength was and the nature of the ground over which the army would have to travel. In furtherance of their security, the armies should march with an advance guard, a rear guard, and flankers. When camped, the officers should select "advantageous ground" and post strong pickets and a chain of sentinels about the camp. Lastly, each camp should maintain a strong reserve of soldiers who were free to move to the point of greatest danger should the Indians attack.

Although it was prudent for Pinckney to issue these latter instructions for securing the army's line of march and encampment, it was not strictly necessary. Claiborne, Floyd, and Jackson were all well aware of these methods for securing their troops from the surprise attacks at which the Indians were so adept. It was another matter altogether to get their soldiers to obey their instructions.

As for Pinckney's strictures to his commanders against underestimating their enemy, his subordinates would have to learn that lesson the hard way. All three men were confident that if given reasonably sufficient resources, theirs would be the decisive blow against the hostiles. Claiborne had his dated experience at Fallen Timbers on which to base his poor opinion of Indian powers of resistance. Even William Weatherford's deft and frustrating guerrilla tactics in the Forks region the preceding two months had not materially changed his views. Jackson's already low opinion of his Creek opponents at the start of his campaign had been dangerously reinforced by his easy victory at Talladega and Coffee's at Tallushatchee. Floyd's experience at fighting Indians was nil. His confidence that he could achieve a quick victory over the hostiles was grounded largely in a frontier aristocrat's general contempt for Indian abilities. Whether the three generals ever admitted it or not, all of them would soon modify their dismissive attitudes toward their opponents.

At the end of the day, however, the most crucial item in Pinckney's order was logistics. If the Americans could not get to the Creeks, they obviously could not defeat them. Pinckney had correctly discerned the three best invasion routes into the nation: the Alabama and Coosa rivers and the Federal Road. It remained to be seen, however, whether the Americans could organize the necessary supplies and their transportation to sustain an extended campaign into the nation by even one of these routes.

Less than two weeks after laying out his instructions for conducting the war, Pinckney turned to managing its immediate conduct on the ground. By this time he had established his headquarters at the Georgia state capital in Milledgeville. In the intervening days since his departure from Charleston, Pinckney had not altered his initial assessment of how the war against the Creeks should be fought. In a letter to Jackson dated November 29, 1813, Pinckney restated the need to establish supply lines down the major rivers leading to the fork of the Coosa and Tallapoosa rivers. There Pinckney wanted a substantial fortification to be built to store supplies and to house the soldiers who would sally forth from that place to scourge the nation. To this end, Pinckney dispatched his aide-de-camp, a Lieutenant Morris, to the main Cherokee town of Hiwassee on the river of that name. There Morris was to rendezvous with the federal Indian agent for the Cherokees, Colonel Return Meigs, and seek his advice on whether the rivers leading into the nation were sufficiently navigable to transport military supplies. From Hiwassee, Morris was to travel to Fort Strother with dispatches from Pinckney to Jackson and to apprise the general of the results of his meeting with Meigs.[25]

While Pinckney made his plans and Floyd attempted to resolve his food-supply problems, the Red Clubs were moving their warriors toward

Coweta. During the first week of November, Hawkins noted that clashes on the outskirts of the town between his scouting parties and the Red Club scouts had become more frequent and more violent. Already, fourteen warriors on each side had been killed in these skirmishes.[26] The Big Warrior, if possible, now became even more frightened of an impending Red Club attack. Day after day he and the other friendly chiefs sent runner after runner to Fort Lawrence, urging Floyd to come to their aid. By November 14, the Red Clubs' main force had moved to within half a mile of the Coweta fortifications. Other hostile parties were busily burning Lower Creek towns and destroying crops and livestock in the surrounding countryside.[27]

The friendly forces were afraid to leave their fortifications and engage the hostiles because "[t]hey are more than double our number," and because if defeated, their families in the fort would be left defenseless. The fort's leaders sent one, then another runner to Floyd apprising him of their desperate situation but received no answer. Finally, on November 18, the assistant Creek agent and Tuckabatchee chief, Alex Cornells, composed a letter to Floyd signed by the Big Warrior, William McIntosh, and the Little Prince. In the letter the friendly chiefs begged Floyd to come at once, advising that the hostiles were camped in an "open pine woods" where Floyd's army could easily attack them. The chiefs also chastised him for his delay so far—"[y]ou have had full time to come"—and, in addition to the letter, even sent Floyd a guide. But by then Floyd was finally on the move.[28]

The Battle of Autossee

ON November 18, 1813, General John Floyd and his army, leaving behind "250 sick men" and a garrison of two companies at Fort Lawrence, began the sixty-mile march over easy ground to Coweta. As the Georgians approached, the hostile Creeks lifted their siege and retreated deeper into the nation. On arrival at Coweta, the army began construction of a fort that Floyd named, probably to Hawkins's chagrin, Fort Mitchell. There they learned that the hostiles under Peter McQueen had gathered at Autossee town on the lower Tallapoosa River some sixty miles northwest.[29]

Hawkins sent Floyd an interpreter who had been raised to manhood at Autossee to guide the expedition, probably Sam Moniac's friend John Ward. To Hawkins's disgust, however, Floyd rejected the agent's choice and selected Abraham Mordecai instead. Accompanying the general was his personal body servant, an African American named Anselm, to whom, after the war, Floyd would leave a bequest in his will of one "suit of cheap broadcloth, a hat and a pair of shoes, $10 per annum and his provisions so long as he lives," for his "faithful service & fidelity" to Floyd in the war.[30]

Incredibly, suggesting his dismissive opinion of the Red Club army, Floyd also took his sixteen-year-old son, Charles, a high-spirited young gentleman of a mischievous disposition—the epitome of a wealthy planter's son. Charles had no military training, but he was to see plenty of action at Autossee, an experience that seemed to whet his appetite for the military career he later pursued.

On November 25, with the fortifications at Fort Mitchell substantially completed, Floyd began the sixty-mile march along the Federal Road to the Creek towns on the lower Tallapoosa River. With him were 950 militia, composed of infantry, cavalry, and an artillery company wielding several English-made brass cannons captured at the Battle of Saratoga during the Revolutionary War. In addition, the army included several hundred friendly Cowetas, under William McIntosh, and a group of Tuckabatchees under the Mad Dog's son.[31] The march was unavoidably slowed by a train of eighty wagons carrying five days of provisions for the army. Like General Jackson, Floyd's foremost concern on the campaign was how to feed his army.

The journey to the Tallapoosa towns took three days in bitterly cold weather. On the twenty-eighth, the army made camp within ten miles of the important town of Autossee. Shortly before 1:00 A.M. on the twenty-ninth, Floyd's army broke camp and marched through a region of small forested hills toward that objective. By 6:30 A.M., it had emerged from the forest and onto the broad plain before the town, a mile away.[32]

Autossee, as it was called by the whites (the Creeks called it Atasi), was one of the towns the Muskogee Nation had assigned the honor to declare war on the nation's behalf. It was also the boyhood home of Dixon Bailey, whose family had a farm on the great loop in the river several hundred yards west of the town. During the Creek civil war, the people of Autossee had joined the prophets' party. As a consequence, the town was now considered sacred ground. The town contained several hundred houses and began just downstream of the mouth of Calebee Creek. From there it ran west for over a mile, hugging the high and wooded banks of the Tallapoosa River. Between the long line of the town and a parallel line of low hills shadowing the eastern horizon was a mile of table flat plain where the Autosseeans raised their crops. This plain continued down river and over the horizon where, unseen by the Georgians, six other large Creek towns lay. The Red Clubs were gathered at Autossee in strength and could draw on sizable reinforcement from the downstream towns if necessary.

Autossee was a very old place. Its history stretched back at least five hundred years to the mound-building culture of the Mississippian people. At the time General Floyd first saw it, in addition to about four hundred houses, it contained the usual town square and a massive and conical rotunda off the square. The walls of the principal buildings were daubed with clay that had been smoothed and then painted over with hieroglyphics and fantastic murals depicting human heads on animal bodies and animal heads on human bodies. Other murals were of an erotic nature. The wooden poles supporting the porticos of these building were carved into serpents—the principal clan of Autossee. In the center of the square, elevated on an artificial mound whose creation was a mystery to the present Autosseeans, stood a forty-foot pine pole.[33] Fifteen years earlier, in his travels through the nation, the critical Hawkins had described the place as a "poor, miserable looking place." Either Hawkins was mistaken, or the town must have undergone substantial improvements since his visit. For when Floyd entered the town he described it as containing several hundred houses "some of a superior order for the dwellings of savages, and filled with valuable articles."[34]

Just behind the town, the riverbank dropped abruptly about six feet, forming a narrow shelf, like a firing step in a fort. Beyond the first bank, a second bank fell steeply to the water for thirty more feet. Both the upper and lower banks were tree lined and thickly covered with reeds and brush that continued most of the way to the water. Beneath the vegetation, four feet from the water's edge, a band of clay, slick as wet rock and plastic to the touch, ran along the twisting course of the river. The inhabitants, for their protection against the Americans, had carved out cleverly concealed bunkers in the riverbank.[35]

Floyd's original plan of battle was to use his militia to pin the hostiles against the Tallapoosa River and Calebee Creek by sending his right wing between the town and the creek and his left wing to the bank of the river on the opposite side of the town. The friendly Creeks under his command, as decided the day before, would cross the Tallapoosa above the town, cutting off any escape by water. With the hostiles bottled up that way, he could destroy them at his leisure, particularly with his canon. If executed successfully, Floyd's plan could go far toward ending the war.[36]

It is said that when a battle starts, even the best plan has to be discarded. Echoing this maxim, Floyd's plan went wrong from the very first. As he arranged his troops on the broad plain before Autossee and the sun came up behind him, he was startled to see that another large town, of recent construction, stood five hundred yards downstream from the original town.[37] This town spilled onto the flats of a sixty-acre loop in the river. On the west side of the loop stood the ruins of Richard Bailey's abandoned farm, where its adjacent grove of skeletal peach trees stood like a talisman of failure. Incredibly, neither Floyd's guide nor any of the hundreds of Creek Indian auxiliaries with him had mentioned the existence of this second town, although most of them must have known of it and some had probably seen it, if only from a distance. Indeed it lay only several miles downriver from Tuckabatchee, where many of Floyd's Indian allies were from. The second town had most likely been constructed to house refugees from the war or to concentrate the Creek warriors in the center of the nation. Nonetheless, both hostile and friendly Indians moved so freely about the nation that it is surprising that the existence of this town had not come to the friendly Indians' attention.

The new town's location was certainly not happenstance, and its existence confirmed a report that Major George Colbert, a Chickasaw leader, had provided Andrew Jackson's emissary to the Choctaws, Colonel John McKee. That report, which Colbert received from some Red Club messengers in the course of delivering a communication to the Chickasaws from a Creek chief, John O'Kelly, provides a rare insight into the hostiles' strategy for defending their homeland from the Americans. The messengers informed Colbert that the prophets had ordered those Creeks who supported the war party to leave their towns and villages and to concentrate in selected locations about the nation. There they were to form separate encampments peopled by the inhabitants of their original homes. Because a number of Creek families were split between the war party and the peace party, the prophets reportedly believed that the war could be better "prosecuted" if the two groups could be isolated from each other. But most likely the predominant reason for putting the nation on this manner of war footing was correctly intuited by Colonel McKee: "to have them in a state of preparation to unite in one body to meet an invading army."[38] Unknown to General Floyd, one of these war camps had been built just downstream of Autossee.

While Floyd and his senior officers debated how to meet this unexpected challenge, the general received further unsettling news. His Indian allies by now were supposed to be in position on the opposite bank of the Tallapoosa River across from Autossee in order to cut off any escape by the hostiles in that direction and to intercept any hostile reinforcements coming from the towns on that side of the river. Now the friendly Creeks informed Floyd that the Tallapoosa was running too high to ford and was too cold to swim even if they could somehow manage to keep their powder dry during the crossing.[39] Floyd had to change his entire plan of attack on the fly and in full view of the quickly assembling enemy.

In expectation that Autossee was a single town near the mouth of Calebee Creek, Floyd had aligned his troops on the plain a half mile from the upper town. Calmly and quickly taking account of these surprising developments, and contrary to the military dictum that one does not divide one's force in the sight of the enemy, Floyd decided to send three infantry companies, a rifle company, and two units of light dragoons from his left wing to attack the lower town. The remainder of his militia forces, including the artillery, was to attack Autossee itself. His Indian allies were directed to cross Calebee Creek and prevent any escape in that direction.[40]

Floyd was spreading himself thin, and an escape route for the hostiles across the river remained open, but it was the best the beleaguered general could do under the circumstances.

Despite Private Tait's assertion that the Red Clubs were "surprised and astonished" at the Georgians' arrival, they had plainly been preparing to engage them since the morning Floyd had marched out of Fort Mitchell. As the Georgians lumbered along the Federal Road, their every movement was reported by Red Club scouts. Thus, by the time the Georgians reached Autossee, the Red Clubs had purportedly assembled an estimated one thousand five hundred to two thousand warriors from eight towns to meet them, a number that seems high.[41] As Floyd speculated, what perhaps did surprise the hostile Creeks was his night march through the woods, which put his army outside of Autossee at dawn. But even that surprise was not total. An Indian with Floyd's army had deserted in the night to the Red Clubs and informed their leaders that the general and his army were on the way.[42]

Coosa Micco, the head of the Autossees, was the overall commander of the hostile forces. However, he relied heavily on his friend, an important prophet called Tewasubbukle, from Hoithlewaulee, on the northern bank of the Tallapoosa several miles downriver, for advice as to how best to confront the Georgians. The two men were in conference late that night when a runner arrived at the town with a report that the Georgians were on the march several hours away.

On the prophet's advice, Coosa Micco took command of the Autossees of the upper town, where he was reinforced by the Tallassees from just upriver under Peter McQueen. The prophet himself took command of the hostile forces at the lower town. Their plan was to receive the charge of the Georgia militia several hundred yards out from the two towns. Because the Georgians' forces were split, with several hundred yards between each wing, the Indians also hoped their cavalry would be able to flank the ends of the American lines and rout their opponents.

As the two armies arrayed themselves before each other, the Red Clubs were confident. Although General Floyd was unable to learn the exact strength of the Red Clubs, several friendly chiefs informed him that it represented warriors from eight towns as well as a contingent of fighters from the Okfuskee towns.[43] If reinforcements were needed, they could call on the additional assistance of the gnomish prophet Paddy Walsh and his five hundred warriors assembled six miles downriver from Autossee at Hoithlewaulee. Moreover, the prophets had assured their followers that the Americans would be destroyed as they approached the sacred ground of Autossee. Nonetheless, just in case the prophets' words proved as false as they had at Fort Mims, the hostiles had also hollowed out large caves in the high bank of the Tallapoosa as places of refuge should the American soldiers not drop dead at their feet. The Creeks also planned to send their women, children, infirm old men, and slaves to Hoithlewaulee.[44]

The battle commenced just after sunrise, November 29, 1813, shortly after General Floyd had repositioned his men. The sky was clear and the morning air was windless but very cold—so cold that with the sun's rays shining over it, the thick frost on the fields between the two armies looked like silvered snow.[45] Beyond the dazzling white fields, Floyd could see the low clusters of Indian dwellings with their faint twists of early morning smoke rising from their chimneys. Near the right end of the town, where the Autosseeans had erected their main ceremonial center, Floyd spied a large and curious mound perched near the water's edge. The side that faced him was circular and sloped gradually upward for ten feet to a fifty-foot square plateau. The mound itself ran 100 feet north and south and 150 feet east to west. It appeared to be of ancient construction, but whatever purpose it had long ago served, the mound was currently abandoned and covered with tangled brush and smallish trees—a potential Indian stronghold that might have to be taken.[46]

In the cold distance, as Floyd and his army looked on, the Red Clubs emerged from their cabins and massed in good order on the silver plain before each town. Despite the biting cold, the Indians had stripped naked and painted their bodies red. Small, intermittent clouds of breath hung from the faces of the men and animals staring across the battle lines. Drums beat loudly behind the lines of Creeks and Georgians, ratcheting up the men's excitement and damping down their fear. Cheering broke out on both sides as commanders saluted their men and were saluted in return. Amid the noise, the Indian leaders attempted to steady their men to receive the Georgians' coming charge, cautioning them to aim carefully before they fired and to conserve ammunition until they had a clean shot.[47]

Calmly, Floyd gave his aides the order to advance. As his order rippled quickly outward from his command post, a roar went up from the Georgians, and they began advancing toward the waiting Creeks.

The battle began along a broad front of soldiers over a thousand yards long, with a gap of several hundred yards in its center where the soldiers veered off toward Autossee or toward the lower town. With elaborately embroidered battle flags hanging incongruously limply in the still and frigid air, the infantry and mounted soldiers quickstepped to within one hundred yards of the loud and tumultuous Creek lines.[48]

At that point the feared cannons began playing grapeshot along the Creek front, and the soldiers upped their steady pace to a charge with fixed bayonets against the Red Club lines. Even though this charge was supported by cannon fire from the artillery behind and cavalry charges on their flanks, Autossee was to be no Tallushatchee or Talladega. The Indian ranks not only held, but the jubilant Red Clubs drove the astonished Georgians back in disarray to the Americans' starting positions. To add to the confusion in the Georgian lines, soon after the battle began, the Georgians' Indian allies left their posts along Calebee Creek. They were now milling about in the rear of the militia in their disorderly hundreds, looking for direction. Quickly, William McIntosh restored some semblance of order among his Cowetas, and the Mad Dog's son was able to do the same with his Tuckabatchees. Floyd was then able to funnel the excited warriors along the army's flanks, where they fought bravely.[49]

The fight was a hard one. It had now been going on an hour, and casualties among the militia were mounting. Already, several of the officers' horses had been shot out from beneath them. Floyd's son, the impetuous but imperturbable Charles, later wrote that he "narrowly escaped death," that "a rifle ball grazed my forehead, one passed through my coat sleeve and several persons were killed and wounded in my presence."[50] Writing immediately after the battle, his father proudly informed Charles's sister, Mary Hazzard, that her brother "appeared not the least concerned."[51] In memory of his part in the battle, Charles later named one of his daughters Autossee.[52]

His father, the general, was not as fortunate. While directing his soldiers from horseback, resplendent in his blue coat with gold epaulets, Floyd was a prime target for the Creeks, who pursued him with bullets "thick as hail." Eventually a ball from a Red Club musket struck Floyd in the left knee. It shattered the the kneecap and came to rest in the flesh behind, where it remained to torment Floyd for the remainder of his life. In horrible pain, he nevertheless kept his seat and continued to direct his men from horseback as he rode his mount up and down the Georgians' firing line, still a prominent target for another Red Club marksman.[53]

Illustrative of the vicious hand-to-hand nature of the fight was Quartermaster William Tennille's adventure. During the initial cavalry charge toward the Creek lines, Tennille's horse was shot and fell to the ground, trapping Tennille beneath it. When he pulled himself from under the animal and scrambled to his feet, one of several Indians rushing toward him shot Tennille in the upper right arm, splintering the bone. Another hostile shot him in the fleshy part of the thigh. Closing in for the kill, they brandished their blood-red war clubs, hot to crush his skull and lift his scalp. His right arm dangling useless at his side, Tennille managed to pull his pistol from his belt with his left hand, cock it, raise it, and aim it toward the onrushing Indians. The sight of the pistol brought Tennille's assailants up short, and they backed away a step. Tennille aimed it at the nearest Indian, pulled the trigger, and—the gun misfired. The gleeful Indians now sprang forward to get their scalp. In terrific pain, Tennille pulled his sword from his scabbard and, using his left arm, slashed awkwardly at his attackers. Before they could finish him, Tennille's comrades made a second cavalry charge, during which a trooper cut down the Indians menacing Tennille. He was helped to the aid station, probably by now in shock, where the surgeons stabilized his condition. Later, back at Fort Mitchell, the hospital surgeon, Dr. Charles Williamson, took off his arm at the shoulder. Remarkably, unlike Captain William Bradberry of Burnt Corn Creek fame following a similar operation, Tennille not only survived the operation but recovered.[54]

In the rear of the right wing of the army, opposite Autossee, Lieutenant Colonel Walton Harris, under fire, reformed the disordered militia into line. Once the men were in proper formation, he ordered another charge, directing his adjutant, Captain Robert Brodnax, to press the men to carry the charge through the town and up to the river. The wounded were now piling up at the Georgians' field hospital. The position was exposed to Indian attack, and at the request of the surgeon, Dr. Williamson, Harris sent a detachment of men from Brodnax's command to guard it. At the lower town, the first charge of the militia had also been rebuffed. The commander there also reorganized a second charge against the place. It was this renewed charge that saved Quartermaster Tennille.[55]

The hostiles defending the lower town broke first. At the upper town, Coosa Micco was directing the Red Clubs' defense against the Georgians' second charge when a messenger reached him with the bad news. Turning his command over to a subordinate, Coosa Micco galloped his horse to the other fight, hoping to stem a rout. It was too late. The militia had killed his friend the prophet, and his disheartened warriors were retreating toward the town. Coosa Micco tried to throw groups of his warriors on the militia's flanks, but at each attempt, the soldiers skillfully maneuvered their ranks to present a solid hedge of glistening bayonets. Shot twice, and sabered across the cheek, the aged chief turned his also-wounded horse toward the upper town to see if he could do anything with the defense there.[56]

The Indians defending the upper town had also begun to give way. As the Georgians renewed their assault, a number of Indians began retreating to their homes. Some of the Red Clubs fought from the warren of cabins in the town, shooting at the pursuing soldiers from loopholes cut in the walls. Others more wisely headed toward the thick undergrowth lining the bank of the Tallapoosa River or the swampland flanking Calebee Creek, which the friendly Creeks had failed to seal off before the battle began. One elderly chief, supposedly the Tallassee King, mounted on horseback desperately waved his war club above his head in a futile attempt to direct his warriors back into effective fighting formations. When the situation permitted, the courageous old fellow fired his rifle at the soldiers racing toward him.[57]

The militia was spared the deadly task of house-to-house fighting. The cannons under Captain Jett Thomas, a self-taught artillerist, were brought up, trained on the houses, and fired volley after volley of shot, blasting the Indians' homes to pieces. After the initial volleys, the residents were said to have scampered like so many ants for the river and swamp. One of the victims of Thomas's artillery was the elderly chief on horseback, an irresistible target. The artillerymen charged a canon with grapeshot, aimed at the chief, and fired. One of the balls slammed into his neck, and he fell dead to the ground.[58]

Fate, however, was kinder to another old warrior. When Coosa Micco reached the upper town, dizzy from loss of blood, the chief quickly saw that there was nothing he could do; his people had been routed. He slid off of his poor horse and made his painful way toward a thick stand of reeds along the river. He stepped into the cover and, in a blink of an eye, disappeared like a spirit.[59]

By the time General Floyd had made the agonizing ride up from the lower town, Autossee was in flames. As he surveyed the battlefield, amid the shouts of men, the eerie cries of wounded horses, and the noise of the guns, he was struck in particular by the way the "rolling pillars of smoke" from the burning Indian houses, the thick columns of smoke from the Georgians' cannons, and the "lighter sheets" of smoke from the small arms created "various figures fantastically floating in air."[60] Satisfied that the battle was going well in that sector, he turned his horse back toward the fight at the lower town, where the Red Clubs were in full retreat toward the river.

The soldiers moved through the blazing towns like little soiled and shrieking gods, shooting or sabering every Indian of every sex and age they came upon, and snatching up any object that struck their fancy. They even found time to enter the public buildings flanking the town square and the nearby rotunda itself. This souvenir hunting yielded a haul of "relics and scalps" and a host of "valuable objects." Floyd speculated that some of this loot, particularly the scalps, had come from Fort Mims. Some of the Georgians who paused in their sack of the town noticed an eerie phenomenon. Indians, some of them warriors, squatted or stood silent and motionless in the cabins as if under a spell. When the frenzied Georgians clubbed a musket, swung a saber, or pulled a trigger at them, they let death come unmoving, making no resistance as they were slain. Not that it mattered. According to Tait, for those misguided Indians who begged the Georgians for quarter, none was shown.[61]

While the Georgians and their Indian allies romped through the towns with blood and fire and larcenous fingers, the main struggle moved to the banks of the Tallapoosa. Here the Georgians' fun and games came to an abrupt end as the Red Clubs made a last, tenacious defense on terrain

Floyd described as intended by nature "for their protection." The forces of erosion undermining the earthen riverbank had dropped several yards of upper riverbank "six or seven feet" onto a level shelf of land covered thickly with brush and reeds interspersed with isolated trees. That shelf of land extended several more yards to a second bluff that dropped sharply away to the river. The arrangement of this terrain afforded the Red Clubs an excellent defensive position. Here, protected by the lip of the first bluff, and concealed by the vegetation, they could fire almost unseen into the lines of approaching Georgians.

As Floyd described the fight for this ground, "the fire on both sides was tremendous; many were killed." The hostiles shot at the Georgians along a line running along the brush and reeds fringing the top of the riverbank. Those slain were rolled by their companions to the edge of the river, where they soon gathered in heaps, turning the waters lapping the shore red. While their comrades above bought time, the majority of the hostiles made their escape along the shore or across the icy cold waters of the river. Others hid in cleverly concealed caverns the Red Clubs had dug into the riverbank for just such an eventuality.

As this phase of the battle continued, Floyd grew concerned for the safety of his army. In his mind, it had fully accomplished its objective of marching into the heart of the Creek Nation, defeating its army, and destroying one of its principal towns. Now he was feeling exposed. The army had only two days' rations left, and any food it could have seized from the hostiles, including their dogs and cats, had been consumed in the conflagrations that were once towns. The army had many wounded, including Floyd, to be cared for and a number of dead to be buried. But what appeared to concern Floyd most was the sense that the army, which had endured a severe fight at the end of a long march, was isolated, far from any possible rescue, and outnumbered in a place where it could be quickly surrounded by its enemies "under cover of rivers, creeks, swamps, etc." Even had they won the fight along the river, Floyd was at a loss about what to do with the women and children who thronged "thick below the [river] bank as fiddlers, of all sizes, perfectly naked, scampering, and screeching, in every direction." Floyd had no means to feed them, and his other alternative was out of the question for a man like Floyd: "I had placed restraints on the friendly Indians from destroying them." Given all of these considerations, Floyd decided to break off the battle along the Tallapoosa and turn his army toward home. It was a wise decision. While he prepared his men for withdrawal from the field, a large body of Indians under Paddy Walsh moved rapidly toward him through the fields of the lower towns.

Gathering up his dead and wounded—one of whom, a Floyd family friend named Holkirk, had been injured by, of all things, an Indian blowgun—the general moved his army to a place about a mile or two east of Autossee. There he established a defensible camp where his wounded could be treated and his dead buried. It was now around 9:00 A.M., and men had been dying and torn open for almost three hours. But the killing and maiming was not over yet. While the general saw to the security of his army, his Indian allies remained behind to pillage what remained of the hostile towns. As if to confirm the wisdom of Floyd's decision to leave the battlefield when he did, Walsh suddenly appeared on the scene from Hoithlewaulee with hundreds of warriors and threw his force against the preoccupied looters. In a short time, several of the friendly Creeks lay dead, including two of their leaders, the Long Lieutenant and, a particular favorite of Floyd's with the honorific title of the Far Off Warrior, the Mad Dog's son, a man he later described as "shrewd," "well-disposed," and "enterprising."[62]

Before long, Walsh's men had cut off any retreat by their fellow Muskogees and were relishing the prospect of a harvest of scalps. Fortunately for the friendly Indians, Floyd's rear guard, comprising cavalry and riflemen, had heard the commotion behind them and came up quickly on the fight, which took place on a small rise known as Heydon's Hill. After losing four or five warriors killed in the ensuing skirmish, the hostiles retreated from the field, to the great relief of the Georgians' Indian allies. The Battle of Autossee was over. Behind Floyd and his bloodied army, following the curve of the Tallapoosa for a mile, stood a rippling canvas of flame from the burning Indian cabins and public buildings.[63]

The Americans numbered the Indian dead at around two hundred, with hundreds more wounded. The Red Clubs, on the other hand, calculated their losses at eighty dead and just over one hundred wounded.[64] Among the Red Club dead reported by the Georgians were the Autossee and Tallassee Kings. Indeed, the friendly Indians proudly presented General Floyd with a famous stone pipe said to have been owned by the Tallassee King, old Hoboleithle; the politic Floyd later presented the object to the governor of Georgia.[65] In truth, however, reports of the Tallassee King's death had been greatly exaggerated. To the Georgians' astonishment, the old man would reappear during the war very much alive.

The losses reported by the Georgians and their allies just after the battle were not as great as their opponents', reflecting their superior firepower, particularly the death-dealing cannons. The whites suffered eleven killed and fifty-four wounded, among them Floyd; their Creek allies had several warriors killed or wounded—the exact number unknown to Floyd. With great stoicism and even greater virtue, which even the ancient Romans would have admired, Floyd refused to have his painful wound dressed until all of his wounded soldiers had been treated.[66]

Within days, Floyd and his exhausted men were back at Fort Mitchell. There he improved the works by erecting a strong stockade defended by a blockhouse. He also sent spies out into the nation. They informed him that the hostiles under McQueen and Francis were concentrating their forces on the several-mile stretch of land along the Tallapoosa between the now destroyed town of Autossee and the downstream town of Hoithlewaulee. The two hostile leaders already had assembled about a thousand warriors in that area, and more were coming from other Alabama towns for security. Floyd's resourceful spies also informed him that the Spanish governor at Pensacola had offered the Red Clubs badly needed ammunition and offered them refuge there if the Americans "prove too strong" for them.[67]

Although the Americans trumpeted Autossee as a great victory, with every other man a hero, the battle was not nearly of that magnitude. Benjamin Hawkins, whose advice General Floyd had ignored, wrote a letter to Secretary of War John Armstrong shortly before the end of the war in which he peevishly called Autossee a "defeat."[68] It was hardly that either. Floyd was the first American commander to lead an army into the very center of the nation, defeat a large force of hostiles, and burn a principal town. The battle had also convinced a number of the wavering "friendly" Creek towns to join the Americans.[69] However, there was no escaping the fact that at the conclusion of the battle, the Red Clubs retained possession of the field of conflict and the Georgians had retreated fifty or so miles back to the Chattahoochee River.

Moreover, at Autossee, the hostile Creeks had gone toe to toe with the Americans in an open field, received a charge from them, and defeated it. The Americans' overwhelming advantage in arms and ammunition (some Creeks had been reduced to using blowguns), particularly the cannons, ultimately had been the deciding factor in the battle, and the effectiveness of the cannons and massed small-arms fire of the Georgians made clear to all but the Red Club fanatics that so long as the Americans retained that advantage, it was foolhardy to meet them in combat in open field. Instead, the best chance the Red Clubs had for victory was to attack the Americans with concentrated forces on a battleground of their own choosing at a place deep enough in the nation to diminish the Americans' critical supplies and time to allow the numerous diseases that afflicted every white army to kill or sicken their soldiers. This strategy, or something like it, was one that those hostile leaders not completely deluded by the prophets had begun to adopt. As General Jackson remained stalled in endless squabbles with his troops and supply contractors, and General Floyd and his troops recuperated at Fort Mitchell, General Pinckney sent another army of Georgians against the hostile towns strung out along the rugged northern reaches of the Tallapoosa River.

General Adams's Campaign

PINCKNEY's planned strike into the northern reaches of the nation was led by thirty-seven-year-old brigadier general David Adams. Uncharacteristically, Pinckney seems to have dispatched, in accordance with that dubious military principal "Let's do something," the very reconnaissance in force that he typically disdained. General Adams's force was only approximately 530 mounted soldiers, which, given its size, could only plunder and burn Creek settlements; it could not take and hold territory, but it was small enough to get into serious trouble. Adams assembled his unit near the recently incorporated town of Monticello, apparently named by the Virginians who founded the town in honor of Thomas Jefferson's stately home. The army called its encampment there Camp Patriot. It left that camp heading west for the Creek Nation on December 9. From the start, the army's journey along the red clay roads of Georgia was plagued with constant chilling rains that turned the road into a red beast that sucked at and clung heavily to the soldiers' feet. The army also soon found itself marching through rough hill country where numerous narrow passes required the packhorses to be led single file. By Sunday, December 12, when the army crossed the Okmulgee River, it had traveled only ten miles from its base.

By this time General Floyd, who was recuperating at Fort Mitchell, was in communication with General Pinckney, who had informed him of General Adams's plans. At Pinckney's direction but unknown to Adams, Floyd had detached from his command a company of light dragoons under Captain Duke Hamilton and a contingent of friendly Creeks under William McIntosh with orders to join Adams at the Chattahoochee River crossing.[70] Because of his wound, Floyd could not go to Adams's assistance nor, given the supply situation, could more of Floyd's soldiers. Moreover, Pinckney had Floyd occupied in overseeing a series of fortifications to serve as staging grounds and supply depots for the Georgians' next expedition into the nation. In any event, Floyd believed that the enemy forces opposing Adams would be "completely routed" because according to his spies, those forces totaled only around three hundred warriors.[71]

After its slow start, Adams's army picked up its pace and covered the remaining fifty miles from the Okmulgee River to the east bank of Chattahoochee River in three days. It arrived there on December 15, and at noon that rainy day crossed the river at a place known as "the War Ford."[72] They were now only thirty miles from the nearest Okfuskee town. Unfortunately, however, Hamilton's troops and their Indian allies coming upstream from Fort Mitchell failed to arrive at the Chattahoochee River crossing in time to join Adams's army, although the rendezvous point on the Chattahoochee was only a day's ride from the fort. When they finally arrived, Adams was well gone. Hamilton was for pressing after him but eventually decided that Adams was too far ahead to overtake him.[73] Hamilton also may have been influenced in his decision not to attempt to catch up with Adams by an alarming report the friendly Creeks had just received that the Indians assembled at the Okfuskee towns numbered not three hundred men, as Floyd thought, but some two thousand warriors. When they learned of this report, the friendly Indians refused to proceed farther. Adams was on his own. It is unclear if Hamilton dispatched a messenger to deliver this critical intelligence to the general, but if so he never reached Adams. [74]

Adams, ignorant for the time being of these developments, was concerned about how best to proceed against the hostile towns after making the river crossing. Convening a meeting on the banks of the Chattahoochee with his officers and guides, he decided to attempt a surprise attack. To achieve the advantage of surprise, Adams determined that the army would have to march all the rest of that day and that night. The army's primary objective was the sizable town of New-yaucau, thirty miles to the east.

New-yaucau lay on the east bank of the Tallapoosa River about thirty miles southeast of the Hillabee towns General White's expedition had destroyed the previous month. The town was founded in 1777, but was subsequently named for the important treaty Alexander McGillivray had negotiated with the Americans in 1790 in New York City.[75] New-yaucau was one of seven towns along the upper Tallapoosa River and was subordinate to the large town of Okfuskee twenty miles downstream. New-yaucau consisted of about eighty-five houses and, like the typical Creek town, was most likely arranged around a central square flanked by the public buildings.[76] The town was above the floodplain of the river on a flat terrace of land that continued in a narrow band north and south of the town. East of the town, the land rose quickly in rocky hills forested in hardwoods and pine. At this point in its course, the Tallapoosa River is about 120 yards wide with a "fine ford" across the river just north of the town.[77]

Adams did not know it, but his army was in great danger. Several hundred yards below New yaucau, the Red Clubs were constructing a fortified refugee town on a curious loop of the river. Because of its shape, this prominent feature was known to the whites as Horseshoe Bend and to the Indians as Tohopeka. Two miles downstream lay the town of Emuckfau, on a large creek by that name. Just as the friendly Creeks had reported to Captain Hamilton, the entire area was crawling with hostiles. Horseshoe Bend was a place where the Georgians should never have hoped to arrive.

But Adams and his troopers rode toward New-yaucau. The weather along the way was not kind; the downpour continued, and the night was so black the army had to use torches to light its way through the forests. After ten miles of suffering from the chill rains and the rough ground, and from the wet and springy branches of trees that seemed to strike out malevolently at the faces of the men and their horses, Adams finally called a halt. The sodden army and animals spent the night hunkered down in deep misery against a chilly rain that lasted until morning.

When the army stirred at first light, it found itself eighteen to twenty miles from its destination and unready to fight. Not only were a number of the men and most of their baggage soaked through, but their muskets and rifles were so wet as to be useless. It took them several hours to dry and oil their guns, and it was not until midmorning that they resumed the march. As they soon found out, whatever element of surprise they had enjoyed had vanished.[78]

The army had gone only several miles when it stumbled on a small settlement in the woods known as Mad Warrior's village. The place contained only eleven houses, and its inhabitants had recently fled. Adams sent out detachments of horsemen to scour the surrounding forests for Indians, but they did not see a soul. Disappointed, and aware that it had lost the element of surprise, the army consoled itself with stealing the Indians' corn and such meager possessions as had been left behind. The soldiers then followed the standard procedure of burning the village and went on their way, although with a now more heightened sense of unseen danger as they passed along through the trees and rugged defiles between the hills.[79]

When his scouts informed Adams that the army was only three miles from New-yaucau, he called a halt and the army went into bivouac. For some reason, Adams apparently entertained the illusion that he could still surprise the Creeks, and to the great discomfort of his men he ordered that no fires should be built to warm his troopers and dry out their clothes. Of course, by now, no one in the army could have had even the slightest doubt that the hostiles were well aware of the army's presence.

Early the next morning of Friday, December 17, after yet another miserable night spent in the cold and damp, Adams assembled his soldiers. In accordance with the American tactics of the day, he organized them into three columns for the attack on the hostile town. In this manner, the army traveled three miles through narrow passes and over forested and hilly ground. About a half-mile from New-yaucau, the guides led them to a rock-strewn, sparsely vegetated hill overlooking their objective. At this vantage point, Adams ordered everyone to dismount except the cavalry under a Captain Martin and eighty-five riflemen under a Captain Cocke. Much like Coffee at Tallushatchee and Jackson at Talladega, Adams planned to strike the town with his center column while his right and left columns swung around the upper and lower sides of the town cutting off the escape of any hostiles in those directions. Meanwhile, the cavalry and mounted riflemen would form along the riverbank, cutting off any retreat by the townspeople across the river. It was the same plan General Claiborne would adopt a week later against the hostile Creek stronghold called the Holy Ground far to the south.[80]

Leaving forty men to guard the horses and pack animals, Adams and his soldiers descended to the town. When they emerged out of the woods onto a small hill overlooking New-yaucau, they realized for the first time to their "mortification" that the hostiles had already abandoned the town. But the Red Clubs were not far away. From across the swollen river they could hear the yells of the hostile Creeks, obviously taunting them. In frustration, Adams ordered his men back to the hill, where they had left their horses, intending to return with the animals to New Yaucau to feed on the town's corn supplies and then carry away the remainder. As they neared the depot, they suddenly heard the eerie cries of other hostiles among the trees. At these alarming sounds, Adams sent his men scurrying off to their baggage depot to rescue their vital mounts and supplies from the Indians. Once the army arrived there, to the great relief of the forty soldiers guarding the horses and baggage, Adams ordered out two detachments of horsemen to scour the forests for Indians. Concealed by the forests and the folds of land in the hilly terrain, not a single hostile was found.[81]

Adams and his men now returned to New-yaucau and he set them at the delightful task of looting (mostly a "considerable quantity of corn") and burning the place. The Americans also inspected what Benjamin Hawkins described during his travels through the nation in 1797–98, as a "fine ford" just upstream of the town to determine whether they could cross the river there and attack the downstream Creek towns on the other side.[82] Here the river is about 120 yards wide and falls for 1.8 miles over a series of eight shoals, now known as Griffin Shoals, none of them more than an eighteen-inch drop. The shoals themselves are usually about two feet deep in most seasons and can be easily crossed.[83] When the Georgians got there, however, they found that the fall rains had swollen the Tallapoosa and submerged the shallow shoals beneath high and fast water, which Adams's Indian guides advised him would be impossible to cross. In addition to the risen river waters, the difficulty of the crossing was compounded by the presence of a Red Club force spread among the wooded brow of a "small hill" commanding the ford.[84]

Given the situation, Adams decided not to attempt the ford, but it is questionable how eager he was to do so in any event. Almost certainly the water in this upper region of the river, flowing over what were tame shoals, could be safely crossed even at high water by determined men. As for the hostiles gathered on the far shore, the length of the shoals was such that they would have a difficult task covering almost two miles of fordable water. It may well be that Adams's Indian guides saw no profit and much danger in a further excursion into this wild country and had exaggerated the dangers of the crossing. That conclusion is supported by a report from a friendly Creek "spy" dispatched by the Little Prince from Coweta on an incredible thirteen-day mission that took the man through the Upper Creek Nation all the way to New-yaucau and the corpse-strewn and burned towns of the Hillabees.[85] This man apparently joined Adams's expedition just as it entered New-yaucau and observed the desultory firing among the Georgians and Red Clubs and the burning of the town. Significantly, echoing Hawkins's observations years ago, he reported there was a very good ford right above New Yaucau where Adams might have crossed the river without difficulty.

If so, why would Adams not attempt the crossing? Certainly it is difficult to imagine a Claiborne or Floyd, much less a Jackson, being defeated by such an obstacle without even making an attempt to surmount it. Adams, however, does not appear to have been so driven a man. He and his army had endured much, accomplished at least something with the burning of two hostile settlements, and were now given a ready excuse to abandon the enterprise. But there was some excitement yet to be had before the army turned homeward.

While it was occupied in destroying New-yaucau, several of the more adventurous and less disciplined soldiers decided, in disobedience of Adams's direct orders, to investigate the neighborhood. Three or four soldiers stole their way to the bank of the Tallapoosa, where one hid behind an Indian hut and the others concealed themselves in the brush that had grown up in an abandoned cornfield. From their hiding places, the men began taking shots at the Indians they saw on the opposite bank of the river. At the same time, Adams's adjutant, Thomas Berrien, was nearby, scanning the far bank of the river through his spyglass for hostiles, when he heard shooting from the near shore. Turning his glass in the direction of the firing, he saw a Red Club crumple to the far ground following the fire from the weapons of two of the frolicking soldiers along the near shore.[86]

While the fallen hostile was dragged out of sight by some of his comrades, the others attempted to extract their revenge. One of the American shooters, Jon Patrick, who along with his companion, Zachariah Simms, appeared to Berrien to have shot the fallen Indian, now turned his attention to a group of Indians among the trees. As he stooped low to aim his rifle at one of the warriors, another Red Club shot him in the left shoulder. The hunters now became the proverbial hunted, as the more numerous Creeks began to increase their fire. Badly wounded and in agony, Patrick lay on the soggy ground while his friends attempted to extricate the wounded man and themselves from the field. Scrambling low to the ground, the men were able to get Patrick to his feet and make their way out of range of the lead balls singing out around them.[87] Perhaps Adams thought Patrick's wounding and the near escape of them all from death served as sufficient punishment for the soldiers' disobedience of his orders, because there is no record of a court-martial being convened to try the soldiers.

Following this brief skirmish and the looting and destruction of New-yaucau, Adams, like Jackson and Floyd the month before, decided to retire to his base. His stated reasons for this retrograde movement were similar. His men were low on provisions, many of which had been spoiled by the continual rains, and without further supply he could not move deeper into the nation. In addition, Adams believed that the risen waters of the Tallapoosa prevented him from reaching his objectives: the Creek towns of Tuckabatchee, Tallahassee, and Emuckfau on the opposite shore. This reason for Adams's retreat ignored, or perhaps his guides didn't inform him of, the presence of several nearby Creek settlements, both upstream and downstream of New-yaucau, that he easily could have destroyed.[88] All in all, it appears that Adams had had enough of miserable weather, rough country, and an elusive foe to suit his taste for military adventure.

That afternoon, Adams prudently marched his men two and a half miles from the burning town and the surrounding hills before they made camp. There the army needlessly endured yet another long and "very cold night" without fire. As the men lay with their arms at the ready, prepared to repulse a Red Club attack, their repose was continually interrupted throughout the night by the yells of the hostiles from the trees. Adams "generally supposed" that these sounds came from the "opposite side of the river."[89] But given that some Creeks had earlier that morning been spotted scouting the little hill where Adams had left his horses, it is more likely that Adams's supposition was in the nature of whistling past the graveyard, and that the Red Clubs were all around his encampment, although not in sufficient force to mount an assault.

And if it is a mystery why Adams did not cross the Tallapoosa River at the ford above New-yaucau and engage the warriors taunting him from its far shore, the bigger question also hangs why the Red Clubs, after having failed to lure him across the river, did not pounce on his small and exhausted force while it was strung out in the heavy forests and rough hill country on its march home. As Jackson would learn in the same region a month later, it was not for lack of determination, military skill, or courage that the Creeks let Adams and his army escape the deep woods of their homeland unmolested. Rather, one need look no further than to the three engagements these Creeks had fought the past November against Jackson's, Coffee's, and White's troops. Those fights had cost the Creeks hundreds in killed and wounded, and one of their principal leaders, Billy Scott, had been captured in the Hillabee massacre. The defeated warriors needed to heal their wounds, replenish their supplies, obtain reinforcements, and fashion a strategy to meet the next certain-to-come white incursion. The Adams expedition presented an attractive target, but at the time, the Red Clubs lacked the capacity to seize the opportunity.

Thus it was that the next morning, Adams started his soldiers in the happy direction of Georgia. When they finally crossed the Chattahoochee to safety, the relieved and tolerant general let the men off their leashes to proceed on the rest of the journey home "in the order they chose."[90] This decision "very much facilitated the march," and the men were soon back at their base outside Monticello in time for Christmas.[91] Among them was their only casualty, the reckless Jon Patrick. The surgeon had been unable to remove the Indian ball from Patrick's shoulder, but he at least survived the painful journey home and was "on the mend" with a good prognosis for recovery.[92] This army would not return to battle the Red Clubs. With Floyd badly injured and Jackson fighting to keep his army together, the focus of the relentless war now moved to the southwest, in the region of the Forks.

Cat and Mouse in the Forks

AFTER the war, in August 1814, Major Howell Tatum, Andrew Jackson's topographical engineer, accompanied the general on a journey by boat down the length of the Alabama River starting at its source near old Fort Toulouse. Tatum's assignment was to survey the lands and waters along the way. The result of his efforts was a detailed description of the countryside of the Alabama River valley. Tatum wrote, "[t]he rich lands on the river sides are far superior to any I ever saw." Although the trip offered him no opportunity to travel up the Cahaba River, whose mouth he floated past, Tatum could not refrain from remarking that many of the officers who had scoured the Creek settlements on that stream during the war considered it "the Acadia of America."[93] His commander on the boat echoed the engineer's opinion of the landscape through which they traveled. As Jackson wrote to his wife, Rachel, after reaching Mobile, the expedition has passed "down a beautiful river, washing a meandering and fertile bank upwards of three hundred miles, with abundant fine springs, and some of the most beautiful bluffs fronting extensive and rich bottoms that the eye [e]ver beheld." Hawkins called it the "granary" of the upper towns of the Creek Nation. Jackson, ever the real estate promoter, predicted—accurately as it happens—that "in a few years, the Banks of the allabama will present a beutifull view of elegant mansions, and extensive rich & productive farms and will add greatly to the wealth as well as the security of our Southern frontier."[94] Left unsaid from Jackson's testimonial was the fact that in order for his vision to be realized, thousands upon thousands of enslaved Africans would have to twist their spines in unremitting and unrequited toil on this rich and beautiful land. This, then, is the country over which the Creeks and the American soldiers, stationed in the Forks, fought in fall and early winter 1813.

In September 1813, after the fall of Fort Mims and while Jackson and Coffee rampaged through the Creek country to the north, in the southwestern part of the nation, General Claiborne was having trouble locating even one hostile Indian to kill. Following the attacks on Fort Mims and Fort Sinquefield, General Flournoy had ordered the small stockades abandoned and concentrated his soldiers and the settlers at Saint Stephens, Mount Vernon/Fort Stoddert, and Mobile. Not all the settlers obeyed. At Fort Madison, Evan Austill and Sam Dale refused to follow the fort's commander, Colonel Joseph Carson, and his troops to Mount Vernon. Instead, they convinced some fifty-five men and their families to remain. By various stratagems, such as dressing women in men's clothing and parading them about the fort by day, and at night suspending lanterns from one-hundred-foot poles angled out toward the forest darkness along the fort's perimeter, the defenders believed they had dissuaded the lurking Creek bands under William Weatherford from attacking.[95]

They were wrong. Weatherford not only reconnoitered the post with several of his warriors from the surrounding forest, he personally and alone visited its interior disguised as a local settler. Following a thorough inspection, Weatherford concluded that the fort was too strong for his men to take. As he left to rejoin his scouting party, he helped himself to two horses and a saddle.[96]

General Flournoy assigned General Claiborne the role of protecting the remaining forts in the Forks and chasing the many hostiles who now roamed freely through the region burning farms and killing or driving off the livestock.[97] On October 12, Flournoy issued more definitive orders from Saint Stephens to Claiborne. Claiborne was to take command of the Mississippi volunteers and the local militia and proceed to the Forks. The first objective was to drive the Indians from the immediate area so the citizens could harvest their crops. In the course of this sweep through the countryside, Claiborne was also to seize all Indian boats and canoes the army discovered. Those it did not require for its immediate use were to be sent to the landing at Cedar Creek near Mount Vernon for use by the American forces. Once that objective was achieved, Claiborne was to establish a post in the Forks with ample provisions for the men and forage for the horses. From there he was to attack the Indian towns on the Alabama and Tombigbee rivers and to "literally burn, kill and destroy." [98] Flournoy explained that he regretted resorting to this uncivilized mode of warfare but that the British had given him no choice but to fight fire with fire. They had unleashed the savage Creeks on the frontier knowing full well the savages' mode of warfare. Now the Americans would repay the Indians in kind.[99] From his initial appearance on the frontier back in early August, Claiborne had been counseling an attack on the Indian towns as the surest and fastest way to end the conflict. At last, or so he thought, Flournoy had given him the go ahead.

Before he could move east against the Creeks, however, Claiborne had to secure his rear from an attack by the restless Choctaw Nation. Writing in the *Mississippi Republican*, Claiborne claimed he immediately recognized the danger the Choctaws presented to the Tensaw settlers. Already fifty or so Choctaw warriors on the Choctaws' eastern border had joined the Red Clubs, and much of that powerful nation, according to Claiborne, was "wavering" as to whether to follow their fellow tribesmen. To eliminate this danger, Claiborne said, he "opened" negotiations with Tecumseh's old adversary, Pushmataha. These negotiations, which Claiborne claimed were supported by Flournoy, led to an alliance with the some of the Choctaws against the renegade Creeks.[100]

But George Gaines, the young American who ran the Choctaw trading post in Saint Stephens, told a different story. According to Gaines, thanks to the rigid Flournoy, an American alliance with the Choctaws almost did not come about. As soon as he heard about Fort Mims, Pushmataha, one of the Great Medal Chiefs of the Choctaw Nation, traveled to Saint Stephens to offer to provide military assistance to the Americans. There he met with Gaines, the man who had helped in the rescue of Mrs. Sarah Crawley and who had arranged for the young express rider Samuel Edmondson to deliver the first news of Fort Mims to Andrew Jackson. Pushmataha expressed great sadness to Gaines over the massacre: "You know the Tensaw people, they were our friends. We have played ball with them & whenever we journeyed to Pensacola we stopped at their houses and they fed us."[101] For his part, Gaines was delighted at Pushmataha's offer of assistance; it was what he had been working to achieve for some months. However, he had to inform the chief that as a civilian he was not authorized to accept the service of military forces but would ride with the chief to Mobile where General Flournoy had his headquarters. Gaines assured the chief that Flournoy would be very pleased to accept Pushmataha's Choctaws into the American army.[102] Gaines obviously did not know the general very well, but he apparently believed that the notables of Mobile had paved the way for a favorable reception.

Flournoy had arrived at Mobile on September 28, 1813, and had previously been advised of the reason for Gaines's visit. On Flournoy's arrival, he was presented with a letter signed by the ubiquitous Judge Toulmin, George Gaines, and two other leading citizens of the town, Josiah Blakely and John Hinson.[103] In that letter the authors urged the general to avail himself of the military services of the Choctaws who had offered to assist the Americans in defending their settlements against the hostile Creeks. They warned Flournoy that some Choctaw leaders were sympathetic to the British, who were even now attempting to bring the Choctaws to their side, and that any delay in enlisting the friendly Choctaws on the American side could be fatal to the American presence in the Mississippi Territory. Anticipating the cautious Flournoy's response, the authors explained to him that he did not need to obtain permission from his superiors in Washington to enlist the Choctaws: by the time he received a response, which would clearly be favorable, it would be too late.[104]

On September 29, Gaines and Pushmataha found Flournoy at his headquarters in the old Spanish fort on Mobile Bay and were ushered into his presence.[105] Through an interpreter, Pushmataha laid his offer before the general, no doubt expecting he would immediately accept it with gracious enthusiasm. After all, the powerful Choctaw Nation was at the back of the American settlements along the Tombigbee River, and already a number of its young warriors had joined the hostile Creeks. If the two Indian nations were to combine, and perhaps convince the Chickasaws to join them, the American settlements in the Forks, the town of Mobile, and perhaps even the settlements in western Mississippi would almost certainly fall. But instead of agreeing to Pushmataha's plan and offering profuse thanks, Flournoy, to the astonishment of the chief and Gaines, brusquely informed them that he had no authority to accept Pushmataha's offer.

This response was too much for the courtly Gaines, and he made what Flournoy considered an impertinent attempt to salvage the situation. Flournoy's lack of authority was not an issue, Gaines said. It was Flournoy's job to protect the settlements, and the president would certainly approve, after the fact, of the enlistment of Pushmataha's Choctaws into the American forces. Flournoy was not pleased to hear some pup of a civilian lecture him about the scope of his duties. Curtly brushing aside the young man's arguments, he informed Gaines in a tone of dismissal that if he ever desired Gaines's advice, he would let Gaines know.[106] And so it was, according to Gaines, that Flournoy, the pettifogging former lawyer turned general, placed the entire southwestern frontier at yet greater risk.

It was a distraught and angry Gaines, and a puzzled Pushmataha, who made the long ride back to Saint Stephens to give its citizens the bad news. If Flournoy was one of the Americans' top generals, why was he of such "very small calabre," the chieftain asked along the journey. The quick-thinking Gaines had an ace in the hole. He replied that he had sent an express to General Jackson of Tennessee, who was a far greater warrior than Flournoy. Jackson would be here soon with a large army and would happily accept Pushmataha's warriors into his command. This news "appeared to relieve the old warrior considerably," although Gaines had no way of knowing whether his assertion about Jackson's arrival was true.[107]

It was near dusk when Gaines and Pushmataha reached Saint Stephens high on its limestone bluff beetling whitely over the Tombigbee. On their arrival, the anxious townspeople rushed out of their little fort to hear the outcome of the meeting with Flournoy. A hundred men, women, and children quickly surrounded Gaines and Pushmataha before either could dismount from his horse. As Gaines spun out the tale of his meeting with the general, the crowd's anger grew at Flournoy's outright stupidity and insensitivity to the tiny settlement's plight. Choice comments about him began to rise from the crowd, when all at once an express rider rode up on his lathered horse shouting that he had a dispatch for Gaines. The crowd that had gathered around the factor and the chief parted to allow the rider to deliver the dispatch. Surprisingly, it was from Flournoy. It seems that on further reflection, probably at the insistence of his officers and the town fathers, he had changed his mind. He would accept Pushmataha's offer of assistance and directed Gaines to accompany the chief to the Choctaw Nation to raise a contingent of Choctaw warriors.

Gaines, after spending the night with his now-pregnant young wife, and the chief left early the next morning for the Choctaw Nation, accompanied by a townsman with the unusual name of Flood McGrew. After a day's journey north along the western bank of the Tombigbee, Pushmataha left the two Americans for his home twenty miles west. A date was set when he would hold a council with his people to discuss military aid to the Americans. Gaines and McGrew then rode to the US interpreter John Pitchlynn's plantation two days farther north, at the border of the Choctaw and Chickasaw nations, to await the council. While there, they encountered Colonel John McKee of Tennessee, who informed them that Jackson had charged him with raising a Choctaw and Chickasaw army to attack the Creek towns in the Black Warrior River country. McKee and Gaines agreed to split this endeavor; McKee would work with the Chickasaws and northern Choctaws while Gaines would work with Pushmataha and his southern Choctaws.[108]

The council called for by Pushmataha assembled near present-day Quitman, Mississippi. When Gaines arrived there, he found several thousand Choctaws assembled, waiting excitedly for Pushmataha to address them. The council took place around a large oak tree. Pushmataha spread a bearskin beneath its enormous branches and seated himself, where he remained silent for some fifteen minutes, letting the suspense build. When he finally rose to address his people, he spoke of his visit years ago to Philadelphia and the kindness shown him and his fellow Choctaw emissaries by George Washington. He stressed that Washington urged that the various Indian tribes should not make war on each other. However, Pushmataha proclaimed, despite the president's wise advice, he found it intolerable to stand by and watch the British-inspired Creeks slaughter the

Choctaw's American neighbors. I am a man and a warrior, the chief declared, drawing his sword and flourishing it for emphasis. Follow me against the Red Clubs, he exclaimed, and reap victory and glory. The warriors in the crowd—most of them anyway—sprang to their feet and hollered out that they would follow Pushmataha. At Pushmataha's invitation, Gaines then spoke to the crowd. He was brief, but his talk was well received. Wisely, he promised to arm every warrior who joined Pushmataha and to arrange to pay them at the same rate as their white counterparts.[109]

In addition to wooing the Choctaws, the United States also sent reinforcements to the beleaguered settlements. In September, a company of regular army soldiers commanded by Captain Uriah Blue of the US 7th Infantry Regiment arrived at Mount Vernon. Blue and his men had been stationed in Mobile, but, desiring to get closer to the action, the ambitious captain volunteered his company as reinforcements to General Claiborne. Ultimately, Blue came under the command of General Flournoy. Not long after Blue's arrival at Mount Vernon, Flourney ordered him to assemble 140 men and retake the eastern side of the Alabama from Weatherford's hostiles. For his base of operations, Blue was ordered to rebuild Fort Peirce, which had been burnt by the Red Clubs following the destruction of Fort Mims. From this newly built bastion, Blue was to send out parties to drive the hostiles from the region.[110]

On October 9, 1813, Blue dutifully traveled fourteen miles to the charred ruin of Fort Peirce. Near the old fort he constructed one of the finest timber forts in the region. Ridding the countryside of the hostiles was quite another matter. A month later, on November 10, Flournoy ordered Blue and his men to abandon the fort and rejoin their regiment, now bound with Flournoy for New Orleans. In the intervening month, the captain and his men had done little more than engage William Weatherford in a game of cat and mouse about the countryside. For the clueless Blue, however, the mission had been a success. As Flournoy explained to Claiborne, he had ordered Blue to abandon Fort Peirce because, according to Blue, the Indians had disappeared from that neighborhood.[111] Incredibly, Flournoy complained that the "Citizens have not availed themselves of the opportunity afforded them [by Blue's efforts] of gathering their crops which is to be regretted."[112] But any citizens who had availed themselves of the "opportunity" afforded by Blue would have been dead in minutes. Just because Blue could not find Weatherford did not mean he was not there. In fact, at the time Flournoy wrote this, Weatherford and dozens of his warriors were just up the Alabama River from Fort Peirce raiding the former plantations of Dixon Bailey and his neighbors. As Claiborne was currently finding out, it was one thing to chase Weatherford; it was quite another thing to bring him to ground.

While Blue built his fort and ordered fruitless searches for hostile Indians, Claiborne was assembling a force with which he could take the fight to the Indians. On October 17, he received welcome reinforcements of a contingent of Mississippi horsemen led by his friend and relative by marriage, Major Thomas Hinds.[113] Sam Dale described Hinds as "a small, square-built, swarthy-complexioned, black-eyed man, moving rapidly, speaking imperatively, beloved by his troops, and one of the most intrepid men that ever lived."[114] Hinds and Claiborne's other planter friends had raised a group of young gallants who were eager to leave their comfortable but mundane lives along the Mississippi River for a chance at adventure and easy glory in the wilds of Alabama. One early historian of the war described this company as "[m]ade up of the sons of the first families of the Mississippi Territory" and said "the troopers bore themselves a trifle arrogantly but cheerful and almost lightly amidst every privation and hardship."[115]

In order to ameliorate these young gallants' "privation and hardship" in the forest and swamplands of the Tensaw Delta, they brought along on their adventure their black body servants as well as a contingent of cooks.[116] The official muster rolls for Hinds's battalion of cavalry lists nineteen servants, three of whom, for some reason, are identified with the word "nigger" in parentheses after their Christian and only name, an epithet not found in the muster rolls for any other unit of soldiers and rarely found in the many thousands of references to African Americans in contemporary documents in the region.[117] In addition to the servants listed in the muster rolls, it may well be that Hinds and some of his officers brought their personal servants. Nonetheless, despite their servants' best efforts, instead of easily won martial glory, the young aristocrats got hard, uncomfortable, and dangerous duty in the forests, swamps, and canebrakes of the Tensaw Delta pursuing an elusive and deadly enemy.

Typical of their experience was Claiborne's expedition in mid-October from Saint Stephens to Early's Fort on the northwestern border of the nation. On October 12, Flournoy issued an order giving Claiborne the command of Hinds's dragoons, the twelve-month volunteers, and the local militia commanded by Benjamin Smoot of Burnt Corn Creek fame, who was now a major. Flournoy ordered Claiborne to use this force to "scour" the Forks of Red Clubs.[118]

Already one such scouring expedition had come to grief. In early October, Colonel William McGrew, one of the participants in the Burnt Corn Creek debacle, and twenty-five militiamen left Saint Stephens and headed north through wild country toward Fort Easley. McGrew had received reports of a band of hostiles ransacking the area and determined to engage them. Along Tallahatta Creek, near Fort Easley, the Americans rode into a classic Creek ambush. The Indians were concealed in the heavy undergrowth and thick trunks of fallen trees. An Indian leader raised the fanlike tail of a turkey above a log to signal the attack, and a brisk fight ensued. McGrew's company got the worst of the engagement. He and three of his men were killed, and the remainder of his company fled, leaving their dead comrades on the field of battle.[119]

Soon after this, Claiborne, pursuant to Flournoy's orders, started his own Indian-scouring expedition toward the Fort Easley area. This expedition consisted of Major Hinds's Mississippi dragoons, some militia companies, and a part of Colonel Carson's volunteers. The Americans, watched closely by Creek scouts, crossed the Tombigbee River and headed north, choosing an "indirect" line of march. From the start, Claiborne's campaign did not go well. On October 16, in advance of his main body of soldiers, Claiborne had sent fifty infantrymen, fifty mounted riflemen, and a cohort of cavalry under Hinds's command to locate McGrew's battlefield.[120] The first frosts had come, heralding the severe winter ahead but at least providing the welcome benefit of diminishing the kingdom of insects swarming about them.

The country through which they marched was heavy forest cut with ravines and dark swamps. An ambush by the party of Indians shadowing the advance was not long in coming. Fifteen warriors suddenly materialized out of the trees and began shooting. Three of Hinds's men were wounded before the vastly outnumbered Indians vanished down a ravine and into the swamps, leaving the pursuing soldiers in their wake. As if to punctuate the dangers this warfare among the shadows presented, Claiborne's army that evening happened on the bodies of McGrew and several other "respectable" citizens. The discovery was no surprise. McGrew's horse had appeared at Saint Stephens with blood on its saddle and a pistol missing from its holster. Claiborne halted his command nearby for the night. In the morning they buried the bodies before leaving for Fort Early.

Claiborne spent two days at his former post sending out scouting parties for Indians and setting ambushes. For all of their efforts, his soldiers did not so much as see an Indian, much less ambush any. Claiborne summarized this frustrating situation in an October 22 letter to Flournoy, "My present impression is that there is no body of the enemy in the Fork that is strong enough to contend with the force under my orders but that there are many small parties lurking about the different settlements and doing much mischief I am well convinced of, but to catch them is very difficult."[121]

The soldiers who participated in Claiborne's campaign had a more colorful term for the abortive affair. They dubbed it the Potato Expedition, because that tuber was almost the only thing they had to eat and the only thing they captured while chasing their will-o'-the-wisp opponents.[122]

Claiborne's soldiers, particularly the frontier aristocrats under Major Hinds, were even more frustrated. As Claiborne's son wrote many years after the war, "They came for battle and glory and could see neither in the lonely scout, over swamp and canebrakes, and the weary watch over isolated corn-fields and log cabins."[123] Or as a nineteen-year-old local militiaman, Jeremiah Austill, laconically and concisely put it, "The result of [Claiborne's expedition] was the getting of Some of his men killed . . . not an Indian was seen upon the expedition That I was apprised of."[124]

For the Creeks under Weatherford, their hit-and-run guerrilla tactics were working beautifully. With a limited number of warriors they had corralled the American settlers on the nation's western boundary in a string of small forts. They had also tied up the American military forces in the area in defending those forts or in chasing their own tails in fruitless efforts to bring small parties of warriors to bay. The leading Red Club prophet, the timid Josiah Francis, to gratify his envious followers, even joined in the fun. In addition to looting the settlers' homes and carrying off their livestock, Francis and his raiders hit on the idea of using captured slaves to point out where the Americans had buried their family treasures.[125] As one of Claiborne's officers complained, "[t]he savages are continually hovering around our camp"; but the soldiers were unable to engage them.[126] In harassing the Americans in this fashion, Weatherford freed up hundreds of warriors to face the more immediate threat posed by generals Jackson and Floyd.

After a month of flailing about the countryside with his semiprofessional army in search of Indians, Claiborne decided, or was ordered by Flournoy, to camp at a place known as Pine Level on the east bank of the Tombigbee River ten miles from Saint Stephens. There he was not yet in the nation proper, but his men were exhausted from their wanderings through the difficult country of the region, and Claiborne decided to let them recuperate at Pine Level. Before the general reached that place, however, five more of his men were severely wounded by Creek ambushes. One of these was a lawyer turned soldier, Captain Bradberry, who was among the handful of Americans who had possessed the courage and presence of mind to hold off the Creek pursuit at Burnt Corn Creek. His advance guard was fired on by hostiles from ambush, and he was hit in the arm by a Creek ball. He survived the excruciating trip back to Saint Stephens, where a doctor amputated his arm at the shoulder. After lingering in agony for five days, he died of his wound.[127]

Bradberry was not the only notable soldier to suffer injury during Claiborne's expedition. The brave and inventive Isaac Hayden, of Fort Sinquefield fame, received a disfiguring wound while going to a creek for water one night. On the way, an Indian shot him from ambush through the face. The ball almost severed his tongue and blew out teeth on both sides of his jaws as it entered and exited his flesh.[128]

Claiborne remained at Pine Level for almost two weeks. During that time, his martial skills were largely confined to pen and ink as he jousted in writing with Flournoy over the future of his stalled expedition. From his experience under General Wayne in Ohio, Claiborne rightly saw that the best way to quickly defeat the hostile Creeks was to strike them in their population centers. Flournoy, with his wider responsibilities, was more concerned with meeting an attack by the British on the Gulf Coast than with chasing savages through the wilderness. Indeed, on November 7, Flournoy wrote Claiborne from Mount Vernon that he and the 7th Infantry Regiment had been ordered to New Orleans and that he was leaving at once. He feared that the British might attack New Orleans in his absence and that he would be blamed for its fall. Flournoy then spelled out his strategy for the conduct of the Creek War in the West.[129]

Flournoy explained that although the newly arrived US 3rd Infantry Regiment under Colonel Gilbert Russell was not subject to Flournoy's orders, because Russell had been ordered by the secretary of war to cooperate with the Georgians several hundred miles east, Flournoy had recommended to Russell that he march to Weatherford's Bluff and establish a fort there. Claiborne was also to take his command there, and Flournoy had advised Russell to "cooperate" with Claiborne. Flournoy expected that very soon General Jackson would have penetrated the nation to its population centers around the juncture of the Coosa and Tallapoosa rivers and that the Creek warriors and their families would be fleeing from Jackson's army down the Alabama River valley. Claiborne and Russell were to cut off their escape and to also guard the provisions to be sent to the fort for Jackson's army.

The cautious Flournoy was also intent on curbing Claiborne's aggressive instincts. He instructed Claiborne that he was "decidedly of the opinion" that Claiborne should act defensively until Jackson arrived. Flournoy had recently consulted with Jackson's emissary to the Choctaws, Colonel McKee, whom Flournoy was convinced had great knowledge of the Indians, on the proper strategy for conducting the war in the west. McKee had told Flournoy what Flournoy undoubtedly wanted to hear: that Flournoy did not have sufficient forces to invade the nation. Flournoy had already attempted to soften up Claiborne on this subject. On November 7, as a further hedge against Claiborne's acting rashly, Flournoy warned him that if he fought a battle with the Creeks, Claiborne would probably be defeated. If so, Flournoy wrote, Claiborne would be responsible for the destruction of the whole of the western settlements—a cruel dig at Claiborne's failure to prevent the Fort Mims disaster and a canny exploitation of Claiborne's fear of the loss of his military reputation.[130]

Claiborne did not willingly accept Flournoy's decision. In a letter dated November 8, 1813, the proud Claiborne all but begged Flournoy to allow him to attack the Creeks. His small force had been reinforced by a contingent of fifty-one Choctaws under the famous Pushmataha, a disappointingly small turnout given the ardor for combat the chief's warriors had expressed at the recent council but sufficient for Claiborne's purposes. With some additional firearms, and $300 to pay his soldiers, Claiborne told Flournoy he would be ready to meet the Creeks. His men, he advised, were disgusted "garrisoning stockades and securing crops."[131]

This latter sentiment was the offshoot of the growing unhappiness of Claiborne's fellow Mississippians under Major Hinds with the course of their service to date. Since the ill-fated Potato Expedition, they had been lobbying Claiborne to go on the offensive against the Creeks. Hinds even convinced Claiborne to act as a conduit of a letter dated October 26, 1813, that Hinds had written to Flournoy on behalf of the officers in his cavalry squadron. In that unorthodox communication, ill-advisedly delivered by Claiborne to Flournoy, the arrogant Hinds set before Flournoy the same complaints Hinds had made to Claiborne about his commands' passive role in military operations, as well as their harsh living conditions. Flournoy's response to this "injudicious and unmilitary conduct" was immediate and unequivocal. As Flournoy informed Claiborne, he had "returned them [Hinds and his fellow officers] to Governor Holmes, to be disposed of as he may think proper." Claiborne, Flournoy instructed, was to have nothing further to do with them.[132] At the Battle of New Orleans fifteen months later, Andrew Jackson was most appreciative of Hinds and his dragoons' contribution to that improbable victory. These men were obnoxious but could fight, yet the hidebound, legalistic-minded Flournoy could see nothing beyond rules and regulations.

On the same day Flournoy wrote this letter to Claiborne, Claiborne's other master, Mississippi territorial governor David Holmes, also wrote Claiborne a letter of complaint regarding Flournoy's recent behavior. It seems that on November 9, 1813, Holmes had arrived at Mount Vernon on a fact-finding tour expecting to find Flournoy and his troops there protecting Holmes's constituents. To Holmes's astonishment and anger, he was informed that without so much as a "by your leave," Flournoy had set off for New Orleans. To worsen matters, Holmes also learned that Captain Blue and his garrison had gone with the general, thus abandoning the newly built Fort Peirce, as well as the countryside, to the Red Clubs.[133]

From his camp at Pine Level, Claiborne immediately responded with a letter of his own to the threat to his plans that Holmes's letter presented. Claiborne was now rid of the overcautious and overbearing Flournoy and had at last obtained welcome orders to march deep into the nation. He could see plainly from Holmes's letter that he wanted Claiborne to detach a substantial portion of Claiborne's command and send it back to garrison duty at Fort Peirce. Claiborne was having none of it, however. He regretted that Flournoy had abandoned Fort Peirce, he told the governor, but he had been ordered to a point on the Alabama River to establish a critical supply depot for use by Jackson in an attack on Pensacola. As much as he wanted to assist the governor, he wrote, it was simply not in his power to garrison Fort Peirce. Orders were orders. Beside, Claiborne said, Blue had reported that there were no more hostiles in the area—something Claiborne must have known was untrue given that William Weatherford had been dishing out constant punishment in the form of skillful ambushes on Claiborne's men.[134] But Claiborne at last had the chance for which he had been waiting months; he was not about to let an abandoned fort stand in his way.

Meanwhile, Claiborne, who needed every man available for defense of the frontier, was also attempting to smooth over the friction between Hinds and the irascible Flournoy. By this time, Flournoy was already in Mobile, waiting to depart by ship to New Orleans. But distance, and the prospect of a far better posting, did not improve the peevish Flournoy's temper. By letter dated November 10, Flournoy, in no uncertain terms, informed Claiborne that his decision regarding Hinds was final and admonished Claiborne that in passing Hinds's letter along to him, Claiborne had "acted not only without, but against orders."[135] By this time, however, the temperamental Hinds was long gone back to Mississippi. But before his return to Natchez, as if thumbing his nose at Flournoy, Hinds committed an act that revealed a dark side to his character.

In late October, on their way home, Hinds and his fellow gentlemen attacked a party of hostiles, killing ten Creeks and several "disenchanted" Choctaws. Hinds's small triumph was actually a massacre. It occurred in the morning along the Alabama River, near Lower Peachtree Landing, when Hinds and a squad of his mounted dragoons surprised several Creek families and some slaves shelling corn in an abandoned field. The soldiers drove their horses on the startled Creeks and shot or cut most of them down. Hinds killed one Indian who had managed to escape to the river. As the man swam toward the opposite shore, Hinds shot him. On his return to Natchez, he and his fellow killers were celebrated as heroes by its deluded citizens.[136] By this time, however, Flournoy was in the Crescent City, and a reinvigorated Claiborne was leading an invasion of the Creek Nation—both men far from the slings and arrows of a backwoods scold.

Part Three

7. INVASION

General Claiborne's Alabama River Campaign

GENERAL Flournoy's orders to General Claiborne were modest as usual. Claiborne was to march to a well-known landmark on the Alabama River called Weatherford's Bluff named for William Weatherford's brother John, who operated a ferry just downstream. There Claiborne was to build a fort and wait for supplies, which would be stockpiled for General Jackson's army. Flournoy expected that Jackson's army would soon reach the confluence of the Tallapoosa and Coosa rivers. From that strategic position where the Alabama River is formed, Jackson would move downriver to attack Pensacola. But Jackson would need to be resupplied along the way there. A substantial part of those supplies was to come up the Alabama River from Mobile to the new fort at Weatherford's Bluff. Claiborne was to guard those supplies until Jackson's arrival. Moreover, in addition to serving as a supply depot for Jackson's army, the fort and its garrison were also tasked with disrupting, if not severing, the Creeks' supply line to Pensacola.[1]

Claiborne broke camp at Pine Level on November 16, 1813. The main column was screened by flankers under the command of Captain Joseph Kennedy, a Captain Bates, and by Lieutenant Adlai Osborne, the brother of Spruce Osborne killed at Fort Mims; Pushmataha's Choctaws scouted ahead. On November 17, Claiborne and his main force of 550 men reached Weatherford's Bluff, which had been secured some days earlier by an advance party from his command. At mid-morning of the seventeenth, the main army crossed the Alabama River on rafts. The crossing was uncontested by the Creeks.[2] Claiborne and his men now found themselves eighty-five miles inside hostile territory with no supporting forces nearby. Despite the danger, soldiers were struck by the beauty of the Creek country and its potential for riches to be gained by the "enterprising and industrious." As one soldier lovingly described it: "Fertile high lands, extensive rich low grounds, and high healthy situations finely watered, and the deep, broad, limpid Alabama, providing an extensive navigation from the mountains to the ocean."[3]

Weatherford's Bluff was ideal for Claiborne's purposes. It was formed of weathered limestone and reared up 150 feet from the east bank of the river, its white face gleaming in the sun like a beacon above the bottomlands to the west. The top of the bluff was relatively flat tableland covered with pine. A fine spring lay near the edge of the bluff. The countryside around contained vast fields of corn and pumpkins as well as some cattle and hogs.[4] To the east the land rolled gently in wave upon wave of immense forests. It was east that the army was going.

Claiborne was delighted with the prospect before him, and on arriving he immediately ordered the construction of fortifications on the bluff. The fort was laid out in a two-hundred-foot square quadrangle with three blockhouses. On the river side of the fort, a half-moon battery of cannon was constructed that commanded the river below. By November 29, the works were almost complete and were given the name Fort Claiborne.[5]

The cannon emplaced in the battery came courtesy of Lieutenant Colonel Gilbert Russell and his 3rd US Infantry Regiment, who had arrived at the bluff November 28, along with some swivel guns. The thirty-one-year-old, Virginia-born Russell was a regular officer in the US Army and one of its rising stars. He had black hair and thick black sideburns framing an angular face and was described as a "large and handsome man."[6]

In 1809, while commandant at Fort Pickering, the US military post on the site of present-day Memphis, Tennessee, Russell became friends with explorer Meriwether Lewis, who had stopped there on his way to Washington City. Lewis was drinking heavily against the pain of an unknown malady, probably malaria, and for two weeks Russell did his best to relieve the explorer's suffering. Russell was determined to accompany Lewis on his journey to Washington but was unable to obtain permission from his superiors before an insistent Lewis departed. Several days later, on October 11, 1809, Lewis killed himself in a seedy tavern along the Natchez Trace where he had taken a room for the night.[7]

At some point in his promising military career, Colonel Russell, like his friend Meriwether Lewis, appears to have soured on life. He left the military, married into a prominent Tensaw Delta family, and moved to Mobile. The historian Albert J. Pickett described Russell in his later years as an intemperate man with malevolent feelings and the strictest imaginable prejudices who began his conversations with the "abuse of all of his contemporaries."[8] Unfortunately for Claiborne, by the time in Russell's career when he joined the general's army, the traits Pickett had observed in the older man had already begun to emerge in the colonel's younger self.

With the addition of Russell's regiment to his command, Claiborne could now plan a more ambitious and active enterprise for his army than guarding supplies. In the meantime, in compliance with his orders, Claiborne kept his men busy on expeditions into the countryside with the main objective of interdicting the hostiles' supply line to Pensacola. To that end, Claiborne sent Lieutenant D. M. Callihan and a party of Choctaws to the Pensacola Road and another band of militiamen in the opposite direction. However, they failed to interdict a Creek supply train of packhorses from Pensacola that was carrying one thousand "weight of powder and a proportionate quantity of lead" and was guarded by two hundred warriors, probably under William Weatherford and Peter McQueen.[9]

But for now, with the addition of Russell's regulars, things were looking up for Claiborne. He was in command of substantial forces, in control of the immediate surrounding countryside, lodged in one of the most fruitful parts of the nation, and astride the Red Clubs' favorite route to Pensacola. Although his attempt to intercept the latest Creek powder train had failed, another body of soldiers under his command had achieved a signal victory over Weatherford's forces ten miles down the Alabama River. Sam Dale, at Fort Madison, had recovered from the fearsome chest wound he had received at Burnt Corn Creek and was about to embark on an expedition into Creek country that would cement his legend.

The Great Canoe Fight

THE famous Canoe Fight between the hostile Creeks and the American frontiersmen took place November 12, 1813, just as Claiborne was shifting his base of operations to Weatherford's Bluff. Colonel Joseph Carson, who had by this time returned to Fort Madison, ordered a sizable detachment of his soldiers on a reconnaissance in force up the Alabama River valley. They were to sweep the area of the hostiles who had been rumored to be gathered in large numbers collecting supplies from the deserted plantations along the river.[10]

The Red Clubs, led by Weatherford, were wreaking havoc about a large swatch of country in the lower valley of the Alabama River. A party of warriors had recently ambushed a party of Claiborne's scouts let by Sarah Crawley's rescuer, former blacksmith Tandy Walker. Claiborne had assigned Walker to scout along the Alabama River for hostiles.[11] With him were two other experienced woodsmen, a quadroon named Evans and a renowned hunter named George Foster. The three rode out from Fort Madison around November 3 heading toward James Cornell's burned out plantation. When they reached it, the little party discovered a lone Indian digging for sweet potatoes in the abandoned fields. Led by Evans, the scouts dismounted and sneaked through the brush until they were well within shooting range. Evans immediately shot the unsuspecting Indian, carefully approached the corpse, and scalped it.[12]

The scouts then spread out to search for signs of other Indians in the area. They soon found the camp of a large number of hostiles and their abandoned equipment. Apparently the more numerous hostiles had fled at the sound of Evans's gun. Realizing the all-too-real danger, the Walker party gathered up its booty and rode briskly for the nearby Alabama River. When they reached the abandoned Sizemore plantation, where the owner formerly operated a lucrative ferry business, they decided to stop for the night in a field of unpicked corn. Here they could feed their hungry mounts and rest for the night before crossing the river on the journey to Fort Madison the next morning. It was a fatal mistake, compounded when the men built a small fire to warm themselves against the cold of night and concomitantly disclosed their exact position. But perhaps in the end the fire made no difference. The vengeful Red Clubs had tracked them to their camp and even now were silently stealing into position to destroy the scouts at first light.

That night of November 4, as the Americans slept in the midst of death, Foster was awakened by a nightmare of a Red Club assault on them. He roused his comrades and explained the danger, but they just laughed at him and slid back into sleep. The more superstitious—or prescient—Foster stole away from the fire and concealed himself in the tall grass at the edge of the field near a thick canebrake where he went back to sleep. The explosion of a gun drove him from a fitful rest, and he fled into the canebrake and swam across the chill November waters of the Alabama River to safety. His incredulous companions were not so lucky. The Indians fired from concealment, and the first volley from their guns killed the scalp lifter Evans and hit the blacksmith Walker in his side and arm. The balls from several guns broke Walker's arm in two places, but fortunately the ball he received in his side hit his hunting knife and only badly bruised him. Supercharged with adrenalin by the prospect of death quickly closing in on him, Walker somehow managed to elude his pursuers and after two days make his way back to Fort Madison, where Foster had already reported his death. [13]

It was to eliminate the constant Indian threat to the settlers' lives in the region that Captain John Jones of the Mississippi Rifles and the former smuggler Captain Sam Dale, one of the few American heroes of the Burnt Corn Creek debacle, organized an expedition from Fort Madison to drive the Indians from the nearby lands. It consisted of two commands: forty-five men under Captain Dale and Lieutenant G. W. Creagh, another untainted veteran of Burnt Corn Creek, and a squadron of forty men under Captain Jones and Lieutenant Andrew Montgomery of the Mississippi Rifles. Dale was in his usual attire: hunting shirt, homespun pants cinched by a panther-skin belt, buckskin leggings, moccasins, and a cap made of bearskin. He was armed with a hunting knife, rifle, and shot pouch.[14] His men were dressed in similar informal fashion.

The party left Fort Madison on a cold November 11 and marched eleven miles southeast to French's Landing on the Alabama River. There they crossed the river using two canoes secreted along the bank by a free black man known as Caesar who accompanied the expedition in an unspecified capacity. There, in the midst of a heavy frost, the thinly clad soldiers spent an uncomfortable night without fires in a canebrake. Rising early the following morning, they marched several miles upstream to Dixon Bailey's abandoned farm. Young Jeremiah Austill and several other men travelled upriver in the canoes parallel to the line of the soldiers' march.[15]

Bailey's former residence was on the east bank of the river and his fields were on the west. When Dale's company and Austill's canoeists joined up at the ruined Bailey home, Dale had Austill paddled him across the river to inspect Bailey's fields on the west bank for signs of Indians. They found plenty of fresh evidence on the soft earth of a large party of Indians but saw none. When they recrossed the river to the east bank, however, they saw a large canoe made of a hollowed out cypress tree filled with eight Indians paddling downstream toward them. Dale ordered Austill and his tiny flotilla to head for the Indian canoe. Meanwhile Dale and the main force proceeded by land for several miles upriver to the plantation home of another victim of Fort Mims, John Randon.[16]

Upon seeing Austill's two canoes paddling toward them, the Indians turned their canoe about and fled upstream. By the time Austill rounded a bend in the river near the mouth of Randon's Creek, the Indian canoe had disappeared. Looking about him, Austill concluded that the Indians had paddled their canoe up the creek and were now waiting, concealed in the thick stands of cane lining its banks, for Austill and his companions to appear. Austill prudently decided to break off his pursuit and continue upriver to Randon's home. About that time, Austill heard heavy gunfire coming from up the creek.

Dale and the main body of troops were laboring up a narrow, briar-choked path lined with swamps and canebrakes that led from Dixon Bailey's residence to Randon's. Dale, as usual, and in violation of normal military procedure for the senior commander on the ground, was some one hundred yards in front of the main force, accompanied by only a single man, George Foster, the uninjured survivor of the recent Tandy Walker foray. As they emerged from a turn in the path, the two Americans ran headlong into a party of five mounted warriors. Dale quickly threw his rifle up to his shoulder and shot the leader of the war party, only in that instant recognizing to his dismay that the man whom he had just killed was his good friend Will Milfort. Foster shot and wounded another warrior, and the remainder fled into the cane.[17]

Dale was heartsick at what he had done. Mitford was the son of the French-born war leader of the Creeks, LeClerc Milfort, and Alexander McGillivray's sister Jennet. Young Milford and Dale had been close friends for many years, but under the influence of William Weatherford, Milford had joined the hostiles. The big-hearted Dale later returned to bury Milfort's "fleshless bones" on the spot where he had killed him and claimed that when he was alone in the woods at night, he could hear his friend's plaintive voice in the trees. But for now he pressed on to Randon's plantation.[18]

Some twenty minutes later, Dale and Austill were reunited at Randon's home on the east bank of the river. Like Bailey's plantation, Randon's fields were on the west bank. No Indians were in sight, and the commanders decided to move farther upstream to Jim Cornell's plantation. From their scouts, Dale and Captain Jones learned that the route up the river's east bank would force them too far from the river, so they decided to move their men up the west bank. The two canoes were pressed into service and began the slow task of ferrying the soldiers from the landing below Randon's plantation to the west bank of the river. Jones's men went first. Caesar paddled one of the canoes.

Dale and eleven of his men, including Lieutenant Creagh, James Smith, and Austill, decided to have lunch while they waited to cross the river. They spread themselves out in a field of several acres between the river and the bluff on which Randon's plantation houses stood and built a fire to roast the beef and potatoes they had recently found abandoned in a field by the Creeks. Just as they began their meal, they heard Captain Jones frantically screaming at them. So engrossed were the men in their meal they had failed to notice that dozens of Indians were scrambling down the bluff above them, pinning them against the river. The lunch party leaped to their feet and raced for the riverbank, leaving their repast to the Indians. The steep bank afforded them temporary protection from the Indian guns while they waited for the canoes to return from the west bank.[19]

The small canoe, with Caesar paddling, launched first. As the luncheon party anxiously watched his progress, they spied a huge canoe, thirty feet long, three feet wide, and four feet deep, coming down the river. The vessel had been hacked from an enormous cypress tree and was used by the Indians to haul corn. The vessel now doubled as a troop carrier and stable fighting platform. In that reincarnation it was now hauling eleven heavily armed Indians. They were dressed in breechcloths and painted red. A chief with a panther's skin draped down his back commanded them. The Americans on both banks of the river formed up and waited for the boat to come within range. When the craft hove into the kill zone, however, the men on the west bank were overcome by excitement and fired prematurely, before the vessel came within range. Dale's men on the east bank were within range of the canoe when they fired but failed to hit any of the Indians. The occupants of the canoe returned fire but also hit no one. However, two of the Indians in the canoe jumped overboard and headed for the eastern shore about sixty to eighty yards above Dale and his party.

James Smith yelled to Austill, "Let's kill them!" And the two young men took off along the slick slope of the muddy riverbank after the warriors. Creagh followed.[20]

The two Indians waded to the shore carrying their guns above their heads. Austill and Smith crossed a little stream deep with water and mud. As they trudged through the mucky bottom, Austill's leggings filled with water. The two Indians had just reached the river's shore. As the young men scrambled along the riverbank toward the Indians, Austill's water-logged leggings caused him to slip and fall to the riverbank. Like a sled on ice, he flew some twenty feet down the riverbank and into the water almost at the feet of the two Indians. Smith shot one in the head. Austill pulled himself to his feet and took off after the other. As Austill pursued the Indian, a shot from a gun passed over his head. Austill stopped, thinking another Indian had gotten behind him, but it turned out that the shot came from Creagh. The lieutenant had followed Austill after the Indian and, mistaking Austill for an Indian, had discharged his weapon. Fortunately Creagh realized his mistake in time to raise the gun barrel barely enough to send the ball over Austill's head. By this point in the pursuit Austill's Indian had escaped, so the three men rejoined their companions downstream.

Dale and his men were in a tight spot. They were surrounded by Indians on the land side and cut off from the main body of soldiers on the opposite bank by the Indians in the large canoe. Austill told one of his comrades, a Private Bradley, who was a shoemaker in civilian life, to climb the river bank and determine the location of the Indians approaching from the landward side. When Bradley reached the top of the bank, a volley of shots rang out and the shoemaker suddenly flew twenty-five feet down the riverbank toward his friends. When he got to his feet, they found his clothes were riddled with bullet holes and the breech of his musket was shot off, but miraculously, he himself was unharmed.[21]

The Indians who shot at Bradley were led by William Weatherford and could have destroyed Dale's party at any time. Fortunately for Dale, Weatherford was under the misimpression that Dale commanded a much larger body of soldiers concealed below the riverbank and that it would be suicide for the Indians to charge them across the open field that lay between the two parties. Weatherford had planned to ambush the Americans as they moved up the east bank of the river from Randon's plantation, but his plan was spoiled when the Americans decided to cross over to the other shore.[22] Now, although Weatherford had Dale pinned down, he was not sure what to do with him.

Dale, however, was not at all uncertain what to do. By now Caesar had reached Dale's party with the canoe. Dale immediately yelled over to Jones on the opposite shore to use the Americans' large canoe to attack the

Indian canoe. At Jones's command, the Americans filled the vessel with eight soldiers and paddled toward the Indians. As the Americans drew near the enormous Indian vessel filled stem to stern with ferocious-looking warriors, the soldier in the bow panicked and yelled out to the sternsman to back paddle away. This man was all too happy to comply with his companion's request, and to Dale's disgust, the Americans in the large canoe returned to the western shore.[23]

Dale's response to the American retreat was to call out to his men for volunteers to board the little flat-bottomed dugout paddled over by Caesar and attack the much larger Indian canoe. The young crazies—Austill and Smith—at once volunteered and along with Dale leaped ten feet from the riverbank to the landing below. Although Caesar's canoe had room for one more person, none of the other soldiers were brave enough or foolish enough to take up Dale's challenge; Dale apparently "volunteered" Caesar as the fourth passenger.[24]

The two young men who followed Dale were as tough and powerful as they were reckless. Nineteen-year-old Austill was a shade over six feet two inches tall and weighed around 175 pounds. Twenty-five-year-old Smith, at five feet eight inches, was much shorter than Austill but at 165 pounds more compact. Both men had spent much of their lives on the frontier and were no strangers to hardship and danger. Like Dale, the two wore dress coats cut from Lindsey cloth and the usual frontier accouterments, such as hunting shirt, leggings, and boots. Then there was Caesar. He was a dark-skinned freedman of middle age who lived among the friendly Creeks. Caesar was about the burly Smith's size and, like Smith, powerfully built. Years ago Caesar's father, Bob, had been implicated in a notorious murder of the Kirkland family along a creek that later became known as Murder Creek for the horrific incident.[25] But that savage act does not appear to have been held against the son.

Dale clambered into the canoe first, followed by Smith and Austill. Caesar entered last, pushing the boat off and then settling himself in the stern to paddle. When the Americans got within twenty yards of the Indian canoe, Dale, Austill, and Smith rose to their feet in the unsteady craft and attempted to launch a broadside from their rifles at the Indians. Dale's and Austill's guns failed to fire because they had wet the priming of the weapons when they climbed into the boat, and the rocking of the vessel caused Smith to miss his target. Dale then commanded Caesar to paddle the boat alongside the Indian canoe while his shipmates crouched low. As Caesar paddled, one of the Indians fired his gun at the oncoming Americans but missed. Another warrior snapped a knife at Dale that grazed his thigh and passed through the side of the canoe. Dale's canoe was now within ten feet of the Indians. The first three Americans in the boat rose to their feet. The chief in the Indian boat also rose up and, recognizing Dale, hollered out, "Now for it big Sam!" The canoes drew together, and the fight began in bloody earnest.[26]

Amid a terrific din raised by dozens of their cheerleading companions onshore, the Americans and the eight Indians began flailing at one another with war clubs and empty guns held by their cold metal barrels. The resulting melee was quick, confused, and unimaginably brutal. Austill swung a paddle at an Indian in the boat across from him who was about to shoot the young soldier. The Creek dodged Austill's paddle and in turn brought his clubbed gun down on Austill's hand, deadening the boy's arm to the shoulder. The boats had drifted close now, and Austill grabbed the end of his opponent's gun barrel and attempted to pull it from the man. Austill's tug on the warrior's gun brought the boats within the reach of Dale's and Smith's guns. Dale had already used his empty rifle to club one Indian down, and now he and Smith swung their guns into the skull of Austill's tormentor, bringing him down.[27]

The reckless Dale and Smith hopped neatly into the Indians' canoe and began beating the warriors about the head and shoulders with their guns. One of the warriors knocked Austill in the head with a war club, sending him sprawling across the Indian boat. Somehow the young man had caught hold of one end of the club, and when he struggled to his feet, one foot in each canoe, he was able to wrest it from his opponent. Before the Indian could find another weapon, Austill used the club to sweep the warrior overboard. When the Indian surfaced, Austill smashed him in the head with the man's own club, and the Indian went under the frigid waters.[28]

Meanwhile, Dale and Smith were both now in the Indian boat, with the remaining Indians trapped between them and unable to use their superior numbers against the Americans. Fighting from the bow of the Creek canoe, Dale had broken his gun over the head of one warrior and now found himself weaponless and face to face with a particularly powerful warrior, a noted wrestler named Tarhee, who growled at Dale to "come on!" However, instead of waiting for Dale to come at him, Tarhee stepped forward and swung his gun by its barrel at Dale's head.[29] Dale dodged the blow, which fell on his left shoulder, driving the ball of his arm from its socket. Ignoring the pain, Dale grabbed the musket Caesar passed across to him and used it to twice bayonet Tarhee. With Tarhee dead in the bottom of the canoe, Dale turned his attention to a wounded warrior in the boat who had futilely been attempting to fire his gun at Dale. Dale thrust Caesar's musket at the man and pinned him to the bottom of the canoe with its bayonet. By now Smith had dispatched the warriors at his end of the boat and the fight was over. The canoe was shoe deep in a slush of blood and brain tissue in which dead Creeks lay like animals on a slaughterhouse floor.[30] But the victorious Americans were not yet out of danger.

On the return trip to shore, Smith held the two boats together and Caesar did the paddling. Dale and a battered Austill stood in the Indian boat, tossing their victims overboard. As the four Americans floated toward their companions huddled beneath the bank of the eastern shore, three Indian marksmen on the top of the bank began firing at Dale and his men. Austill watched, apparently for the first time that day experiencing real fear, as an Indian rested his large-bore gun on a stump and sighted it at him. Turning sideways and sucking in his breath, Austill froze as the ball from the Indian gun passed an inch from his belly.[31]

The Indians on the riverbank then retired, and Caesar beached the two boats at the landing. After receiving congratulations from their relieved companions stranded on the eastern shore, everyone ferried over to the main body of troops on the western shore. From there they marched without incident to Cornell's ferry. Seeing no Indians about and without provisions, the soldiers trudged back to Fort Madison. Austill was the only real casualty among the four Americans. He sustained a severe head wound and for several days lost the use of his left arm from warding off blows from the Indian clubs and rifles.[32]

Thus ended the famous Canoe Fight, about which all Alabama schoolchildren learn, if they learn nothing else of Alabama history. But aside from being a great tale, this colorful affair had real significance to the frontier people of the Forks. After several terrifying months of being on the defensive, and months of being frustrated by Weatherford's tactics, the Americans had finally scored, however meager, a morale-boosting victory against that seemingly unbeatable Indian leader. On the same day the Canoe Fight took place, General Claiborne prepared to move his command up the Alabama River valley deep into the nation. Weatherford and his warriors would now be the ones on the defensive during the closing months of autumn.[33]

The Battle of the Holy Ground

O N December 6, Claiborne wrote Jackson that he planned to march to what he mistakenly called "Weatherford's town" on the "Cahaba in a few days," but he did not embark on his expedition until December 13. The objective of his expedition, however, was not on the Cahaba River but on the Alabama River, and it was not Weatherford's town but a large and mysterious religious settlement established by Josiah Francis called Eccanachaca by the Creeks and the Holy Ground by the whites. Claiborne's stated objective for his expedition was modest, circumscribed as he was by his supply problems.[34] He would march his army one hundred miles to a hostile town that none of the whites had ever seen. There his army would destroy the town and any other hostile settlements within striking distance, then return to Fort Claiborne. Joining him on this expedition was Colonel Russell's 3rd Infantry Regiment. Russell claimed that the expedition was his idea and that he only involved Claiborne because he believed he needed additional troops. So although Russell was technically under the command of the governor of Georgia, the colonel agreed to combine his regiment with Claiborne's army under Claiborne's overall command, a decision Russell later regretted.[35]

From the first, it appears that Claiborne's primary objective in invading the nation was not to sit idle on the outskirts of Creek country at Fort Claiborne guarding supplies designated for Jackson, but to redeem a military reputation battered by the attacks on Fort Mims and Sinquefield and by the unchecked Red Club depredations in the Forks over the last several months. With the addition of the US 3rd Infantry Regiment and Pushmataha's small war party to his command, Claiborne now had the instrument with which to regain his reputation. He also now had the right target against which to employ that instrument.

From the time of Tecumseh's visit to the nation, the Alabama towns had made up the heart of the prophets' movement. Some months before the war began, the prophets determined to build a sanctuary and stronghold among the Alabama people at a remote location they called Eccanachaca. The site selected was on the west bank of what is now known as House Creek, one-half mile upstream of the bluffs along the south bank of the Alabama River, miles downstream of present-day Montgomery. The bluff ran about 40 chains (880 yards) along the river and was covered with hickory, oak, and pine trees. The river was about two hundred yards wide here, and the land beyond the town was troubled by extensive swamps and deep ravines choked with vegetation. The town also lay between two sizable creeks. Downstream from the Holy Ground, a watercourse known as Double Swamp Creek poured into the Alabama River. Several miles upstream, the smoothly coiled waters of Pintlala Creek did the same.[36] Amid this remote and natural fortress, the prophets, under the leadership of Josiah Francis, had established a town of some two hundred houses. Employing spells and incantations, they further fortified the place by running a magic line around its perimeter. Any enemy who attempted to cross this line would fall instantly dead. William Weatherford and his former brother-in-law Sam Moniac had homes nearby, although Moniac's home was now in the hostiles' hands.

Doubtless it was Moniac who brought the Holy Ground to Claiborne's attention, for it was Moniac, along with one of Alexander McGillivray's former slaves, who guided Claiborne's army there.[37] When the campaign began, Claiborne had formed a vague notion of striking the hostile towns on the Cahaba, a lesser but pretty river that joins the Alabama on its northern side miles below the Holy Ground. When he left Fort Claiborne with the army, however, Claiborne bypassed those towns and went on toward the Holy Ground. But as with every military venture Claiborne intended, this latest one faced difficulties from the outset.

Aside from the undercurrent of jealousy that had begun to run between the militia and the US regulars, there was the weather. The frosts that Jeremiah Austill had complained of back in early October had proved the harbingers of a hard winter. The biting cold of early December was accompanied by frequent, soaking rains, and the army had no clothing for a winter campaign. Of particular concern in this rough country, many of the men were without shoes, many were unpaid, and many others' terms of enlistments were about to expire. As if these troubles were not enough, when the men looked out from Fort Claiborne beyond the fallow fields to the west, all they could see was an ocean of trees, the bare spires of the hardwoods intermixed with the green bristles of the immensely tall and stately longleaf pines, waiting to ingest their little force.

The prospect of striking off ill-supplied into those forests in this weather, when their next step might bring an arrow or a ball unbidden into their flesh, traveling in the long dark of a quickly approaching winter solstice was daunting—so daunting that before the expedition left Fort Claiborne, nine captains, eight lieutenants, and seven ensigns presented a written petition to Claiborne virtually begging him to call off the expedition but reluctantly agreeing to follow whatever orders the general issued. The hard-nosed Sam Dale, who was present when the petition was read, caustically observed, "Most of those volunteers were young men, accustomed to the comforts, many of them to the luxuries of life," a charge that could never be leveled against Dale.[38]

Claiborne listened patiently to their petition. He knew his audience well. They were the sons of his friends and acquaintances, members of his own class of frontier aristocrats. A number of them later became senators, judges, and governors of Mississippi. Straightaway, he appealed to their sense of honor and cleverly reminded them what was in store for them back home if they abandoned him: "the taunts of their traducers on the banks of the Mississippi." Immediately they shouted that they would follow wherever he led. With that Claiborne and his men reconciled. Soon thereafter, on December 13, the army marched out of Fort Claiborne and into the forests with their bands appropriately playing "Over the Hills and Far Away."[39]

Claiborne's command was around one-thousand-men strong, an odd assortment of professional soldiers, frontiersmen, Mississippi planters, local militia, and fifty-one Choctaws. Colonel Russell commanded the 700 men of the 3rd Infantry, and General Claiborne had roughly 250 men in his command. Colonel Carson led the twelve-month Mississippi volunteers. The local militia was commanded by a Burnt Corn Creek veteran, Major Benjamin Smoot, with his fellow Burnt Corn veterans Patrick May as adjutant and Sam Dale as captain. The cavalry, or battalion of mounted riflemen, as it was officially called, was commanded by Major Henry Cassels. Pushmataha led the Choctaws. Among Claiborne's force were the tough frontiersmen Jeremiah Austill and James Smith of Canoe Fight fame.[40]

From almost the outset of the march, the latent friction between the 3rd Infantry Regiment and the soldiers in Claiborne's original command began to manifest itself. The impression took hold among at least some of the officers and men of the 3rd Infantry that Claiborne's soldiers were destroying and wasting its supplies and retarding the army's progress toward defeating the Indians. There was also a feeling among some in that regiment that Claiborne had been tardy, even reluctant, to invade the Creek Nation—an unwarranted accusation.[41] From Claiborne's first appearance in the Forks, he had actively urged this course of action. For now the discord between the regulars and the militia was minor. It remained to be seen how it would play out as the expedition matured.

On the hostile Indians' side, Weatherford had watched with alarm as Claiborne built his fort on Weatherford's brother's land and assembled an army there. His spies told him Moniac was among them, as well as Sam Dale. When the Americans marched off into the forests with Moniac as their guide, there can have been little doubt in Weatherford's mind where the army was heading. The question now was how to stop it.

Most of the warriors in the nation were occupied facing Jackson to the north and Floyd to the east. Contrary to Claiborne's assertion that a "considerable" number of Creek warriors were forted up at the Holy Ground, Weatherford had no more than fifty warriors and around thirty "Negroes" under his command, and Josiah Francis had two hundred warriors under his dubious command.[42]

Weatherford had also recently received a significant setback in his attempt to arm his men. Some weeks earlier, the Indians had written Governor Manrique in Pensacola seeking supplies, particularly arms and ammunition. While Claiborne was organizing his campaign against them, the Indians received a reply from Manrique dated November 15, 1813. It was the usual smarmy, evasive, and condescending claptrap that the Creeks had come to expect from the Spanish. Their great friend the governor wrote that he knew how poor and destitute the Indians were, but the matter of the supplies was out of his hands: he had none for them, so as a "brother" he advised them not to waste their time traveling to Pensacola in expectation of receiving any. However, he had written their "firm friend," the captain general of Havana, about their desperate situation and asked him "to send me some goods for you." Manrique was sure the captain general would comply with Manrique's request, and as soon as the supplies arrived from Havana, the governor would inform the Creeks by express.[43]

Weatherford probably considered striking Claiborne's army as it was strung out on its line of march but was deterred from doing so by the precautions Claiborne had taken against such an event. Several hundred yards ahead of his main force rode a substantial troop of dragoons and ahead of them spies. On both sides of his main columns and behind his rear guard he rode flankers whose task was to give the alarm of approaching hostiles. Scouting parties, particularly Pushmataha's Choctaws and Dale's woodsmen, ranged daily about the countryside seeking to engage any hostiles following the army. So effective was Claiborne's screen of horsemen that Weatherford's men were reduced to irritating but inconsequential attacks on the troops along the march.[44]

Weatherford did have to his advantage the hard distance to the Holy Ground. He could see that Claiborne's men were not well supplied and were ill clothed for the weather. Thus, with little in men and arms to assist him, Weatherford would enlist cold and hunger, sickness and exhaustion as his allies to wear down Claiborne's army. Expecting that the Americans would continue traveling up the Federal Road, he decided to ambush them at a point fifteen miles from the Holy Ground.[45] By then they would be debilitated from the journey and vulnerable to attack but still a day's march from the town. If that attack failed, he had to hope he could persuade the prophets to permit him to move the women and children, among whom was his new wife, Suplamy, from the Holy Ground before Claiborne's army arrived.

By December 21, the army had marched eighty long and difficult miles through mud, heavy rains, and bitter cold to Double Swamp Creek. There Claiborne did the unexpected: he paused long enough to throw up a hasty stockade named Fort Deposit to protect the army's wagons, cannon, and sick men, and posted one hundred soldiers to guard the place, then the next morning the army turned left off of the Federal Road and into the trackless forests and swampland leading to the Alabama River. All that day and into the night it struggled through that hellish terrain while Weatherford and his warriors waited along the Federal Road to ambush an army that never appeared. Although it was bitterly cold, when the Americans finally camped for the night, Claiborne forbade them to light fires to warm themselves or cook their meager provisions. However, as luck would have it, that night some roving Creeks who were hunting deer by torchlight stumbled on Claiborne's encampment and escaped back to town to warn their astonished comrades.[46]

On the morning of December 23, the army resumed its journey toward the Holy Ground. Later that morning, Claiborne ordered a halt near what is now the little town of Whitehall. Since the morning of the twenty-second they had marched some twenty-five miserable miles but were at last only a few miles from the town. On this higher and firmer ground, Claiborne arrayed his troops for an attack on Francis's sacred settlement along the bluffs of the Alabama River. The soldiers had some idea of the layout of the town they would be assaulting because William Colbert, the Chickasaw chief who had accompanied his good friend Colonel Russell on the expedition, had captured an Indian woman that day from whom they extracted this information. That this is so is evidenced by the manner in which Claiborne organized his attack so as to encircle the unknown town.

The general ordered his command to advance in three columns, but there is some evidence the plan of battle was actually devised by Russell.[47] The center column, which Russell commanded, consisted of his 3rd Infantry and the dragoons of the militia. The right column was made up of the Mississippi volunteers under the command of Colonel Carson. The left column, commanded by Major Smoot, consisted of the remaining militia and Pushmataha and his Choctaws. Major Cassels and his cavalry made up a fourth element of attackers. Guided by Sam Moniac, this unit was supposed to swing around the upriver side of the town through the woods and cut off the Indians' retreat across or along the Alabama River. Captain Archeleus Wells's dragoons and Captain Josiah Lister's guards made up Claiborne's reserve.[48]

When the army was several miles from the Holy Ground, it encountered a troop of "well mounted" warriors led by Weatherford but did not engage them.[49] While Weatherford's troop rode off to alert the town to ready for an attack, Claiborne's army toiled forward through the rough country. Even when the men got within a few miles of the Holy Ground, their ordeal in the woods was not yet over. Between them and the town lay more dense swamps and flooded woodland cut with deep ravines. To compound their troubles, the swamp and flooded pineland were frozen over with an inch of ice. When the men broke through the ice on their way forward, they were greeted with frigid water and muck that in places came up to their knees. While Francis and the other prophets prepared to destroy the Americans with their magic, Weatherford had the women and children ferried over to the other shore in canoes. From there they were escorted to a place downstream known as Durant's Bend.[50]

When the Americans finally emerged from the woods onto firm ground near the Creek positions, Claiborne paused to organize for the attack. They probably did this at what is now known as Crawley's Hill, a small eminence of reddish earth overlooking Holy Ground Creek and the town beyond. It was now about noon. The town of some two hundred houses sprawling for fifty acres along a U-shaped plateau above the river was now in sight.[51] Surprisingly, given the nativistic creed of the prophets, the Indian cabins were not built in the traditional Creek style. Instead they were constructed of notched logs laid horizontally in the fashion of the whites.[52] Across the neck of the plateau the Indians had piled a two-foot barrier of resin-veined splits of pine. Highly flammable, this lightwood, as it was called, was commonly used on the frontier for starting cooking fires. This barrier was part of the system of magic fortifications devised by the prophets to protect the town. Once lit, no enemy could approach the barrier without dropping dead.[53]

Beyond this magic barrier the more practical Indians had erected a line of pickets across the neck of the peninsula on which the town stood. But before the army crossed the two hundred yards to the fortifications protecting the town, it had to ford Holy Ground Creek, which ran into a deep ravine full of brush and downed trees.[54] This ravine was the centerpiece of the battle and afterward a source of much contention in the local papers as to which unit of soldiers crossed it first. Here, in this natural fortification, Weatherford had concealed a number of his men, hoping to delay the Americans while his people escaped the prophets' deathtrap of a town. He stationed other warriors behind a huge fallen log that also lay athwart Carson's route.

A cacophony of Indian drums and screams of the prophets greeted the Americans advancing through the trees. One of the Shawnee prophets, painted and bedecked with cowtails, danced about among a group of Indian bowmen near the town, screaming imprecations at the soldiers. To the utter astonishment and outrage of the Americans, they also saw a number of armed African Americans among the Indians.

According to Claiborne's version of the battle, Carson's Mississippi volunteers led the advance against Weatherford's position. As these soldiers came closer to Weatherford's defenses, Weatherford's warriors fired on them. Their firing was heavy, and it appears that Carson's attack stalled; but as usual, the Indians' marksmanship was execrable. Dodging behind trees and firing as they moved, the Americans advanced raggedly but relentlessly into the steep-sided, ankle-turning ravine. A group of Indian bowmen who had gotten around the soldiers' flank loosed volleys of arrows, but most failed to hit their mark. The Americans' center and left columns had not yet come up, impeded by the rough terrain, but Claiborne had sent his reserve, commanded by Wells and Lister, to support Carson's attack. However, by the time the reserve arrived, Carson's troops were already crossing the ravine. Smoot's command followed. Carson attempted to restrain the pace of the advance of his men until the other columns and the cavalry were in position, sealing off any Creek retreat.[55]

In the open ground before the town, with red-dyed cowtails flapping from each arm and about his waist, a particularly notable Shawnee prophet performed a highly manic dance, periodically darting behind and out from Indian cabins. Finally, one of Carson's soldiers named Gatlin steadied his gun against a tree and fired a ball that ended the performance. A group of other soldiers fired a volley that cut down a number of warriors. At this, the Creeks commanded by Francis broke and fled toward the river, with Francis foremost among them. Sensing that he could no longer restrain his men, Carson ordered them to charge. They responded eagerly, crossing the magic circles unharmed and leaping the curious lightwood barrier, for some reason never lit, in pursuit of the broken Indian force. The rout was on. In sheer panic, a number of the warriors tossed aside their precious guns in their flight to the river or down its banks.[56]

There is another version of the fight authored under the nom de plume "TRUTH," which was probably the work of one of Colonel Russell's officers, as well as a version by Russell himself. These accounts give an entirely different version of the American attack on the Red Club sanctuary. According to their version of the battle, Major Cassels's cavalry was supposed to swing around the right flank of Colonel Carson's troops and get behind the town, cutting off the Creeks' escape to the Alabama River. Instead, out of "stupidity and cowardice," Cassels halted his men about a half mile from the town.[57] Shortly thereafter, Cassels's troops encountered Carson's men, whose guide had led them to the wrong position. When Carson's men finally arrived at the ravine separating them and the town, they stopped, content to exchange fire with the Creeks on the other side rather than enter the ravine where the Creeks would be able to shoot down on them. At this point, Russell's 3rd Infantry came up and promptly plunged down into the ravine and clambered up the other side, driving the Red Clubs before them. This gallant charge was assisted by two companies of mounted riflemen who had found their way into the town. Caught between the two forces, the Red Clubs abandoned their positions and fled across the river. The soldiers of the 3rd Infantry were already in the town before Carson's men, with a few exceptions, finally got the nerve to cross the ravine.[58] The Mississippi volunteers did not take these aspersions on their warriorhood lightly. Months after the battle, the fight roared on in print, with Carson, Smoot, and Lister all publically disputing TRUTH's version of the battle. Indeed, these officers asserted that the 3rd Infantry was the last unit to cross the ravine.[59]

In any event, no one disputes that the Americans broke through the Indian's defenses and swarmed about the town and through the woods in search of Indians to kill. Weatherford attempted a rearguard action, but the other two American columns had appeared before the town and began rapidly advancing. In short order, the Holy Ground was almost surrounded by the Americans, but as happened with Jackson at Talladega, there was a gap in the American lines. Depending on whom one believes, because of an impenetrable swamp, an inept or deceitful guide, cowardice, or sheer incompetence, Cassels and his cavalry had failed to reach their assigned blocking position between the town and the river and had in fact run into the head of Carson's off-track infantry.[60] In the absence of Cassels's cavalry, the Creek warriors were now running through this gap toward the river and safety. When Cassels finally reached his assigned position, most of them had escaped in canoes, by swimming to the other shore, or by fleeing through the swamps and thick canebrakes lining the river. One of Cassels's troopers managed to shoot a Red Club just as he reached a bluff overlooking the river, but most of his men were reduced to firing futile shots at the survivors who had reached the other shore.[61]

But the greatest prize remained within the Americans' grasp. Weatherford and several of his warriors were still on the battlefield after fighting a courageous rearguard action that enabled many of their countrymen to escape. Having done his utmost to delay the American pursuit, Weatherford had mounted a splendid looking and very powerful horse and was anxiously searching for a way out of the trap the Americans had belatedly laid around the Holy Ground. In an attempt to escape the Americans, Weatherford and his mixed-blood uncle, Malcolm McPherson, who was also mounted, guided their horses upriver toward the juncture of the Alabama and a creek running through the Holy Ground. There they were stopped by a steep bluff overhanging the river. Its height is variously reported as ten to sixty feet, but was probably no more than fifteen—considerable nonetheless. Quickly assessing the drop and the mettle of his horse, Weatherford rode thirty yards away from the river and turned the animal about. His rifle in one hand, the reins in the other, Weatherford put his spurs to his horse. As the astonished McPherson looked on, Weatherford's horse raced forward toward the river and without hesitation leaped from the bluff into a leaden sky. Horse and rider sailed out and away from the bluff and, traveling in a spectacular parabola, landed well out into the icy water.

Gaining control of his horse, rifle still in hand, Weatherford glanced back at the river bluff and saw, with delight and amusement, McPherson and his horse falling from the sky like a "cormorant or fish eagle" after prey into the river not far from him. While American bullets danced in the waters around them, the two men swam their horses at an angle to the strong current until they reached the far shore. Leading the animals up the muddy bank to dry land, they stopped, settled their horses down, checked their gear, and, with studied nonchalance, calmly dried themselves off as best they could. The fuming American soldiers on the other shore continued to fire away, but the two were well out of range. Another Alabama legend was born: Weatherford's spectacular, last-second leap at the Holy Ground.[62]

Little more than thirty minutes had passed since the Creek line broke and the Indians had fled. The Americans attempted to pursue the defeated warriors, but their pursuit was ineffectual. Many of the hostiles escaped in canoes or by swimming the river, and the pursuit of the others fleeing along its banks was impeded by the ravines and swamplands about the town. Dr. Neal Smith, a surgeon with the militia, writing to a friend shortly after the fight, described it as a "small Battle." According to Smith, the Americans killed "about twenty Indians and Negroes" at a loss of one dead and five wounded. A slave captured by the Red Clubs at Fort Mims and recaptured by the Americans at Holy Ground reported that the Americans killed seven Indians and eighteen "Negroes." Claiborne put the Indian loss at thirty dead and many more wounded. But it appears that he exaggerated these numbers. TRUTH wrote in the *Washington Republic* that only twelve Indians and seven "negroes" were found on the battlefield, which is essentially what Dr. Smith, who had no military axe to grind, wrote.[63]

Claiborne put his own losses at two dead, an ensign and a corporal, and five wounded, two sergeants, one corporal, and two privates. The dead ensign was the very unlucky James Luckett, one of the officers who had signed the petition some two weeks earlier urging Claiborne to abandon the expedition to the Holy Ground. The Choctaws, under Smoot's command, who had entered the battle late, suffered five dead and several wounded.[64] For some reason they did not deserve mention in Claiborne's report to Secretary of War John Armstrong and were said by Russell to have behaved cowardly, a claim that does not square with their losses. [65]

The battle over, the victorious army entered the abandoned town. Claiborne had forbidden his men to plunder the place, awarding that task to Pushmataha and his Choctaws. Surprisingly, this ordinarily happy task was not entirely to their liking. They kept the Creek scalps but, like offal, left the scalps of the slaves to rot on the ground, refusing to keep trophies taken from a people for whom they had great disdain.[66]

When the soldiers entered the town square, they were immediately greeted with a horrific sight. From a long pole of pine set in the ground at a steep angle fluttered hundreds of scalps, from the short hair of infants to the grey hair of the aged—trophies taken at Fort Mims. As the soldiers looked on under Claiborne's sanctimonious eye, the Choctaws looted the town, hauling off livestock, blankets, clothes, and a profusion of silver ornaments the fleeing Creeks had left behind. The soldiers then fired the houses and administrative buildings. One Indian woman who had somehow escaped the attention of the rampaging Choctaws was found by a soldier and taken to Claiborne for disposition. The general instructed that she be fed and, when circumstances permitted, returned to her people. Another resident of the town was not so fortunate. A large mulatto slave who apparently preferred life as an Indian to life as a slave had also managed to hide in one of the houses. As the building began to burn around him, he was forced to flee outside into the midst of the soldiers and Choctaws. They shot him to pieces.[67]

Why Claiborne ordered the town fired and many of the supplies found there destroyed that afternoon is not explained. The day was bitterly cold and wet, and his men were ill clad and exhausted from the prior day's march and the recent battle. The Indian houses would have provided welcome shelter from the weather. Equally puzzling was Claiborne's complaint to the secretary of war shortly after the battle that his men were all but destitute of food. The town, however, was said to be filled with all manner of loot, from food to silver ornaments, as well as blankets and clothing plundered from Fort Mims. Indeed, the Choctaws were said to have seized all sorts of livestock as well as blankets. Surely Claiborne did not let the Choctaws hoard these supplies while his troops went cold and hungry. Be that as it may, Claiborne's men had to spend a long and miserable night on the battleground.[68]

The following day, December 24, was devoted to destroying all the Creek settlements and property in the surrounding countryside. The hostiles across the river started the day by firing on the troops. The riverbank below them was lined with a number of canoes. Colonel Russell offered fifty dollars, a large sum in those days, to any man who would swim across the river and bring back a canoe. This offer was not an idle gesture. Russell wanted to procure the vessels for an expedition to attack a reported concentration of fifty to sixty warriors as well as women and children at a nearby town downstream, perhaps at Moniac's Island, where the Holy Ground inhabitants had taken refuge.

A soldier volunteered for the dangerous assignment and somehow managed to swim across two hundred yards of strongly flowing and icy waters under the guns of the hostile Indians, seize a large canoe, and paddle it back to the other side. When the exhausted man shoved it up the bank, Jeremiah Austill, Pushmataha, and five of his warriors jumped in and paddled to the other side. Then, while Pushmataha and his men lay under the cover of the riverbank, Austill paddled the boat back across the river, picked up six soldiers, and returned to the far side.[69]

The hostiles were concealed in a nearby canebrake. The American force scrambled up and over the slippery riverbank and charged into the canebrake. The hostiles fled and the victors were rewarded with a cache of booty; Austill himself grabbed a pair of beaded gaiters. The little band then loaded their plunder into the hostiles' canoes and paddled back over to join their envious companions. Russell's expedition never materialized, however, as a council of officers, the majority including Claiborne, vetoed it.[70]

Later that morning, a large detachment of mounted soldiers whom Russell had dispatched the previous evening under one of his subordinates, Major Matthew Arbuckle, accompanied by Russell's friend, the elderly Chickasaw warrior General Colbert, began the work of ravishing the countryside upriver from the Holy Ground.[71] Eight miles upstream, at the mouth of Pintlala Creek, they discovered a town of sixty houses called Chooksaputka, which Claiborne says they fired.[72]

Also in the neighborhood were a number of plantations, including Weatherford's, Ward's, and Moniac's. The Americans burned them all. According to TRUTH, at Ward's house, a detachment of soldiers surprised three important Shawnee prophets.[73] The Indians fled into a canebrake, which the soldiers promptly surrounded. Through an interpreter, the Americans called out to the Shawnees to surrender.[74] The Indians answered from the dense cane with gunfire, and a brisk fight ensued. The Shawnees' gunfire hit no one. The Americans' more numerous guns eventually killed all three hostiles, one of whom was shot by Colbert.[75]

But Claiborne's men made a far more important catch than the three Shawnees that day. In the course of ransacking Weatherford's home, a soldier discovered letters from the Spanish governor at Pensacola to the Indian leaders. Claiborne must have issued strict orders that any papers from Weatherford's home be delivered to him intact, otherwise they would have likely ended up being used as toilet paper by some illiterate soldier. Fortunately his order was obeyed, and Claiborne now had a prize in hand that verified Spanish involvement in the Creek uprising. These were the letters from Governor Manrique dated September 29, 1813, and November 15, 1813, in which he congratulated the Creeks on their victory at Fort Mims and promised them Spanish aid, although he delivered little or none. Claiborne was so delighted with this discovery that he did not bother to send the letters to his direct superior, the absent General Flourney. Instead, on New Year's Day, after arriving back at Fort Claiborne, he immediately dispatched the originals of Manrique's letters to Secretary of War Armstrong along with a brief description of the expedition to the Holy Ground.[76]

After a long day wreaking all manner of havoc on the Creeks, the exhausted army spent a forlorn Christmas Eve in one of Weatherford's fields. Officers and men alike dined unhappily on parched corn and boiled acorns under a torrential downpour. That evening, in consultation with Russell, Carson, and other senior officers, Claiborne must have made the decision to return home. Claiborne had hoped to destroy the towns on the lower Tallapoosa forty-five miles northeast "where [Peter] McQueen was reported to be." But the condition of Claiborne's Mississippi volunteers was particularly acute—most were without shoes or blankets—and the army as a whole lacked sufficient provisions.[77]

Thus, on Christmas morning, the bedraggled army began its march back to Fort Claiborne. The 110-mile return journey became another endurance test for the men, who by then had been subsisting on parched corn for some nine days.[78] After stopping at Fort Deposit to pick up the men, cannon, and baggage left there, the army struggled onward to Fort Claiborne, where it arrived shortly before the New Year.

At the fort, the exhausted men were issued rations. These included a generous allotment of whiskey, which most men immediately began drinking. As Austill remembered, "before anything could be cooked, three-fourths of the army was drunk, and all of the Indians but one were stretched out on the ground."[79] When Lieutenant Robert Burton reached Saint Stephens late at night on December 30 with the news of Claiborne's victory at the Holy Ground, it touched off a huge and no doubt very liquid celebration in which the citizens illuminated the whole town. A band played and the people sang Claiborne's praises. The militia's surgeon during the Holy Ground campaign, Dr. Smith, writing from Saint Stephens shortly after his return, probably spoke for many of the "now idle" troops when he informed his correspondent that he was leaving the army and "preparing to settle again at the Pine Level and return to my private practice which is much more agreeable than taking campaigns through the Indian Nation and warfaring."[80]

Claiborne spent New Year's Day writing letters to his superiors in which he attempted to cast his expedition in the best light. Admittedly only a small number of the enemy had been killed, but that was because, upon being attacked, they had quickly fled into the countryside through which pursuit was not possible. However, Claiborne wrote Armstrong, his starving and half-clad army had not only burned about two hundred houses at Holy Ground but had also destroyed "a large quantity of provisions and immense property of various kinds." Someone must have brought the incongruity of the starving army and the burning of the "large quantity of provisions" to Claiborne's attention, because on January 24, 1814, he wrote Armstrong a second letter in which he amended this assertion.[81]

He had been "filing away" his papers, Claiborne wrote, when he decided to reread his letter of January 1. During that rereading he was dismayed to discover that someone had wrongly stated that the army had destroyed at the Holy Ground "a large quantity of provisions." Eerily echoing modern politicians caught in an embarrassing inconsistency, Claiborne explained that where the letter said "a large quantity of provisions" he had intended to say "a large quantity of corn." Actually, Claiborne said, he was even unsure if his original letter had contained this "mistake." However, "to guard against even a possibility" that this mistake was in the original letter, he begged "leave to state that if the word 'provisions' was used it was improperly substituted for 'corn' as that was almost the only article of provisions we found in the town." Claiborne then went on to explain to Armstrong that in addition to the other reasons given in his original letter for aborting his expedition, he wanted to add the "want of flour and meat."

As if concerned that this emendation to his January 1 letter was not convincing enough, Claiborne further ascribed the abortion of his mission for want of food to the unrealized "expectation of finding beef in the course of our march and the great scarcity of transportation."[82]

What this second letter to Armstrong does not explain is why, if aside from the issue of provisions, "immense property of various kinds" had been found at the Holy Ground, his men lacked blankets and clothing. The late-nineteenth-century historian Henry Halbert says there were many blankets at the Holy Ground and he had his information from the son of an eyewitness. It may well be that after December 24, the men would go no farther, particularly those who had protested the expedition in the first place. Claiborne's complaint about clothing appears to be limited to the volunteers. They had been against the expedition from the first, and even before it began had complained of want of food and clothes, especially shoes.

Thus it may well have been that when the army camped in Weatherford's field that dismal Christmas Eve, the officers of the Mississippi volunteers, whose men had suffered the majority of the casualties at the Holy Ground, met privately with Claiborne to plead with him to call off the campaign. Claiborne, by this time, was physically worn out from the numerous hardships of the expedition. He had an imperfect victory in hand, although a victory nevertheless, and he must have realized it was time to go home. Although there was friction between Claiborne's men and the men of the 3rd Infantry, those regular soldiers also seemed to have had enough of the campaign. They, too, were unhappy with the lack of provisions, complaining that they had subsisted on "corn and bread alone" from December 22 until they returned to Fort Claiborne on December 31.[83] In fact, shortly after arriving back at the fort, a group of them petitioned Claiborne to conduct an investigation into the failure of the contractor to the army to provide sufficient supplies. Thus, even if, as he says, Russell had wanted to continue the war deeper into the Creek Nation, he did not have much support from his men.[84] As General Jackson was currently finding out up north, in this age of citizen soldiers and frontier democracy, a general's rule was far from absolute.

Claiborne did not remain at his eponymous fort very long. Shortly after the army's arrival there, Colonel Carson's Mississippi volunteers, the Mississippi cavalry, and Pushmataha and his Choctaws were mustered out of service. By January 15, Claiborne and the Mississippi volunteers were at Mount Vernon on their way to their homes in western Mississippi.[85]

Claiborne was still beloved of his men, and deservedly so, but they were not happy with the way they had been treated by their government. For several months they had been unpaid, underfed, and underclothed. Once home, they understandably declined an offer from the federal government to serve in the regular army.[86] Only Pushmataha and his men seemed to have enjoyed their time in the service. They had plunder, many scalps, great honor, and stirring tales of valor with which to regale their envious tribesmen around the council house fire.

So what had Claiborne accomplished? One of the architects of the campaign, the irascible Colonel Russell, would have answered "nothing." In a letter from Fort Claiborne to his superiors dated January 16, 1814, he summed up the affair by saying, "[T]he project failed & after killing a few Indians, burning a few towns & committing some capital blunders, we contented ourselves with what we had done & marched back."[87] That assessment, however, seems unnecessarily harsh. Although the Battle of the Holy Ground failed to produce a great effusion of Indian blood, its consequences went beyond mere body counts. The battle effectively cleared the Forks and the lower Alabama River valley of hostiles and deprived the Red Clubs of a major source of food. It also greatly raised the spirits of the American settlers in the region while concomitantly dashing those of the Red Clubs, who found that even their most remote and sacred sanctuaries were not beyond the reach of American arms.

In the aftermath of the expedition, Major Cassels and the contractor in charge of supplying Claiborne's army were selected as the scapegoats for the debacle. Russell had courts of inquiry convened to try both men. Not surprisingly, in that patchwork and most political of armies, Cassels was acquitted on the dubious grounds that the cavalry had been led astray by the army's guide, the loyal Sam Moniac—a resident of the area who somehow was unable to find the near bank of the only river within miles.[88] The contractor did not fare as well as Cassels. His judges, Colonel Carson and 3rd Infantry officer Lieutenant Joseph Wilcox, found him responsible for the starving condition of the army and for failure to follow Claiborne's orders for the supply of sufficient provisions for the troops, but what punishment, if any, he received is not memorialized in Claiborne's papers.[89]

Russell was now in command of Fort Claiborne. With him was the 3rd Infantry and the local militia. While his men were recuperating from their ordeal on the Holy Ground expedition, he began planning a new expedition up the Alabama to the hostile towns on the Cahaba River.[90] This campaign was intended to complete the one Claiborne had abandoned several weeks earlier. To remedy the supply situation that had dogged the first expedition up the Alabama, Russell obtained a schooner armed with a small cannon on a swivel and another boat. He intended to load the vessels with provisions in Mobile and have his trusted subordinate, Captain James E. Dinkins, sail them upriver to the mouth of the Cahaba River. There the boats would rendezvous with the 3rd Infantry and the local militia, who would proceed by land up the west bank of the river. Then, newly supplied, Russell's command would be in an excellent position to ravage the Creek towns and villages his spies had told him stretched along the banks of the Cahaba.

By mid-January the proposed operation had been put into motion. As Russell wrote Claiborne on January 15, 1814, the boat "will be at Pierce's by the time this reaches you." In the meantime there was a more immediate problem for Russell to handle. Two Indians had just informed him that a party of about one hundred mounted Creek warriors under the command of Peter McQueen and William Weatherford was traveling down the Wolf Path toward Pensacola to obtain munitions.[91] Russell rightly felt it critical that this Indian party be intercepted and made plans to do so before heading into the nation. As he confidently reported to his superiors, "I shall watch his path and take away his goods as he returns."[92] To ensure success, he sent the trusted Captain Dinkins and a contingent of one hundred horsemen to set an ambush of the Red Clubs as they returned from Pensacola on the Wolf Path.[93]

Unfortunately for John Floyd's Georgians, Russell's confidence was misplaced. According to the ubiquitous Dr. Thomas Holmes, who had recently joined the 3rd Infantry as a surgeon's mate, the Creeks thwarted Dinkins's ambush by avoiding the Wolf Path and returning to the nation along a route that ran on the eastern side of Pensacola Bay.[94] Thus the munitions Russell planned to seize from the Red Club pack-train party escaped his clutches and found their way to the Calebee Creek battleground less than two weeks later.

Aftermath of Claiborne's Campaign to the Holy Ground

ALTHOUGH General Claiborne was only forty-two when his service in the Creek War ended, that service had destroyed his health and wrecked his finances. His remaining two years were spent at his beloved home, Soldier's Retreat, in Natchez. From that estate he spent considerable time attempting to fasten public blame on Benjamin Hawkins for the disaster at Fort Mims and in defending his own reputation against the attacks of local politicians over his conduct of the war. In anonymous tracts in the press, his enemies skewered him for his failure to prevent the Fort Mims massacre, for his failure to invade the Creek Nation at the beginning of the war, and for his conduct of the expedition to the Holy Ground. Ever the soldier and patriot, he spent the last of his fortune on an illumination at his Soldier's Retreat plantation celebrating Jackson's victory at New Orleans. He died shortly thereafter, on March 22, 1815, bankrupt and worn out at age forty-four. His son later wrote his father's story and attempted to refute his critics. In the end, his interdiction of Creek access to the breadbasket of the nation by the establishment of Fort Claiborne was perhaps his most valuable contribution to the American efforts in the war, adding a new and potent weapon—starvation—to the Americans' arsenal.[95]

As for the defeated Creeks, William Weatherford's immediate concern after the battle was transporting the women and children to a place of safety known as Dutch Bend, on the north bank of the Alabama River several miles downstream of the Holy Ground.[96] Once there, the refugees had to immediately begin constructing shelter from the cold and wet December weather. They also had to quickly find replacements for the one thousand five hundred barrels of corn the Americans destroyed at the Holy Ground. Once Weatherford had secured his people's safety, there was the pressing matter of how to defend them and the rest of the nation from the relentless white attacks. Securing an adequate supply of munitions was of paramount importance, and Weatherford and McQueen would attempt to address that need shortly after the New Year with another trip to Pensacola. Almost as important was determining where the whites would attack next and how best to defeat that attack.

Weatherford, despite his defeat at the Holy Ground, had to feel pleased with the outcome of the battle. At the cost of a handful of warriors, the Creeks had forced the vastly larger American army to retreat over eighty miles west to Fort Claiborne. The other defenders killed were African American slaves, who, as a race, at least, were held in low esteem by the Creeks. Indeed, a number of the more conservative Creeks were appalled that the leaders of the Creek defenders at the Holy Ground employed slaves as warriors. One such Creek was Kinnie Hadjo, a participant in the battle. He exclaimed afterward that in using slaves as warriors at the Holy Ground, his people "had compromised the dignity of their nation in stooping so low as to call to their aid the services of such a servile and degraded race as negroes to assist them in fighting the battles of their country; that this act, too, was especially exasperating to the whites and tended to increase the bitterness of their prejudices against the Creeks."[97]

Whatever his concerns about the injury to the Creeks' dignity that the use of slaves as warriors caused, Kinnie Hadjo's remarks reveal a more central and dangerous consequence of this act. In using the runaway slaves against their masters, the Creeks had confirmed in this single act the whites' worst fears of a possible Indian-supported slave insurrection. This terrible threat would now hang more concretely over the whites in the region as long as any of the Indian nations remained in the old southwest. The specter of a slave uprising that the Holy Ground Indians had loosed on the Deep South poisoned Indian-white relations for decades in the region until the Indians were finally transported to Trans-Mississippi lands.

The Fight for the Black Warrior Country

E IGHTY miles or so upriver from Saint Stephens, the Tombigbee River
meets the Black Warrior River. The latter flows steady and strong from
its sources in the northwestern hill country of present-day Alabama. Just
above what is now Tuscaloosa, Alabama, however, the land abruptly flat-
tens. Here the Black Warrior loses its velocity as it pours over an enormous
falls and onto a broad and rich plain spreading south. Several hundred
years earlier, when de Soto was abroad in the South, this land was the
home of a great Mississippian chiefdom centered at an extensive complex
of mounds along the river's eastern shore ten miles below the falls. In fall
1813, these lands formed the boundary of the Creek, Choctaw, and
Chickasaw nations. In the long years since the *entrada*, this country had
been the scene of innumerable small conflicts among these neighboring
polities—a field where warriors could prove themselves and secure the
trophies and honors that defined their lives without risking the destruction of their respective nations. After Fort Mims, everything changed. The
war that had begun as a relatively bloodless, semicomical affair at Burnt
Corn Creek had taken on a Shermanesque character of total war embrac-
ing soldier and civilian, home and farm alike. In late October 1813,
General John Coffee rampaged through the northern reaches of this country, burning and looting towns and villages and destroying crops. But even
before Andrew Jackson ordered the Coffee expedition, he had begun the
process of bringing the Choctaws and Chickasaws into the American
camp; Tennessee's official policy was to first obtain the neutrality of these
tribes in the Creek War and later to coax them to join the Americans
against the Creeks. Jackson's unofficial policy was to skip the first step and
go immediately to the second.

Jackson chose a fellow Tennessean and acquaintance, Colonel John
McKee, to recruit the Choctaws to the American side. In so doing he
ignored the authority of yet another Jackson enemy, the US Choctaw agent
Silas Dinsmoor. Dinsmoor had been appointed agent in 1802, replacing
McKee. Some years after his appointment, Dinsmoor relocated the agency
to a strategic position along the famous Natchez Trace, which ran from
Natchez to Nashville. Here Dinsmoor was able to monitor the comings
and goings of travelers through the Choctaw Nation. These activities
brought him into conflict with Jackson.

Several years before the Creek War, Dinsmoor made the mistake of
enforcing the US law governing the transportation of slaves through the
Choctaw Nation. That law, which was designed to prevent runaway slaves
from taking refuge among the Indians, required the owner of any slaves
passing through the Chickasaw Nation to have a passport for travel and
proof of ownership of each slave. If any traveler and his slaves appeared at

Dinsmoor's establishment without the necessary paperwork, Dinsmoor would confiscate the slaves. When Jackson learned of what he considered an assault by Dinsmoor on a citizen's freedom to travel, he characteristically determined to act immediately to correct the outrage. Jackson had a ready excuse: he was a silent partner in a slave-dealing concern operating out of New Orleans.[98]

Jackson used that position to transport several of the company's slaves, without the necessary papers, to Nashville and dare Dinsmoor to stop him. To ensure his success, Jackson obtained a rifle for himself and, remarkably, also armed several of his most trusted slaves with guns. He then marched his little troop to Dinsmoor's place, prepared for an armed confrontation with the agent. Unfortunately for Jackson, and fortunately for the agent, Dinsmoor was not home, and a potentially deadly confrontation was avoided. Nonetheless, Jackson and his slaves marched into Nashville, where he was acclaimed as a hero, at least by the planter class and its cronies. Dinsmoor, however, was undeterred by Jackson's antics and continued to apply the law regarding the transport of slaves through the Choctaw Nation. Thereafter, Jackson confined his assaults on the agent to print in articles railing about the tyrannical Dinsmoor's assaults on the rights of free men. Although Dinsmoor ignored Jackson's rants, Jackson did not forget Dinsmoor. For the agent's temerity to enforce a law Jackson disliked, Jackson would eventually destroy him.[99]

Jackson's decision to employ Colonel McKee to manage relations with the Choctaw was an excellent one. Born in Virginia, the forty-two-year-old McKee was an expert in Indian affairs and, like Benjamin Hawkins, actually liked and cared for the Indians under his charge. In 1794 he had served as temporary US agent for the Choctaw Nation, an appointment made permanent by President Washington. In addition to these qualifications, McKee also had enjoyed a long relationship with Tennessee governor Willie Blount's family, having served Blount's brother William—the Dirt King—in negotiating a border dispute with the Cherokee Nation. In 1802, with a change in administration, the federal government replaced McKee with Dinsmoor.[100]

McKee was in Nashville when an exhausted Sam Edmondson rode into town with a letter to General Jackson and Governor Blount from George Gaines, the Choctaw factor, reporting the terrible massacre at Fort Mims. Although McKee was a private citizen with no responsibilities for Indian affairs, Blount and Jackson, with the assistance of the Tennessee General Assembly, moved quickly to repair that legal deficiency. McKee went immediately to work to perform Jackson's bidding.

On September 14, McKee dispatched a letter to his old friend John Pitchlynn, the US interpreter for the Choctaws. At this time, Pitchlynn was about forty-five, a handsome man of medium stature and black hair and eyes. His father had been a British commissary who died on a visit with his son John to the Choctaws. John grew up hard among the Choctaws, at one time contracting mange from the dogs with whom he slept at night for warmth. But, like many whites among the southern Indians, he quickly adapted to his surroundings and soon began to flourish, assisted by his marriage into the prominent mixed-blood Folsom family and his appointment by President Washington as interpreter for the United States. In 1810, Pitchlynn moved his family to a beautiful and exceptionally fertile tract of land known as Plymouth Bluff along the western shore of the Tombigbee River where Oktibbeha Creek enters that stream a mile or so northeast of present-day Columbus, Mississippi. The Pitchlynn homestead was a strategic one, located where the border of the Choctaw Nation met the border of the Creek Nation to the east and the border of the Chickasaw Nation to the north. Here goods transported from the Tennessee settlements by horse were off-loaded onto boats and floated down the Tombigbee to the factory at Saint Stephens and on to Mobile. During the Creek War it became the unofficial headquarters of the American effort against the Creeks in the Black Warrior country some forty miles east.[101]

Since the rise of the Creek prophets in spring 1813, Pitchlynn had been working diligently to keep officials in the frontier settlement apprised of the movements of the hostile Creeks. Following the Fort Mims massacre, the chief of the southern district of Choctaws, Pushmataha, had persuaded his people to side with the Americans, and with about fifty or so warriors had even joined General Claiborne's army. But the more numerous northern district Choctaws, among whom Pitchlynn lived, were a different matter. Their chief was a cunning man named Moshulitubbee, and he faced a dilemma. Ambassadors from the Red Clubs had been pressing his people hard to join them in the war with the Americans and enjoyed some success in enrolling a group of young Choctaw warriors in their cause—a cause to which Moshulitubbee was sympathetic.[102] Other of the northern Choctaws wanted nothing to do with the Red Club war. This split in the tribe laid the ground for a ruinous civil war among them. In order to prevent civil war, Moshulitubbee had to decide whether to join the side of the Red Clubs or the Americans. Neutrality was not an option; the young men wanted to fight someone. Moshulitubbee needed to play for time to make the right decision. It was a political dilemma that would have challenged even the slippery Willie Blount.

In his September 14 letter to Pitchlynn, McKee could not refrain from taking an initial swipe at Jackson's old enemy, agent Dinsmoor, whom he noted was regrettably "absent" from the Choctaw Nation at this "very critical" juncture in the nation's history. It seems Dinsmoor had failed to heed McKee's unsolicited advice that the United States establish an arms depot convenient to the Choctaws for just the sort of contingency currently presented by the Creek uprising. Now, just as McKee feared, the arms were not available when needed most. Following this gratuitous dig at Dinsmoor, McKee got down to business. Immediately he dismissed the notion of taking time to secure the Choctaws' neutrality. "Indians cannot well support a state of neutrality," he declared. "The young men, fond of distinction, will go to war however well the Chiefs may be disposed to prevent it." Given that the young must fight, the chiefs must be made to understand that their national survival depended on their warriors choosing the right side from which to discharge their martial energies. Explain to the chiefs, McKee implored Pitchlynn, that the Americans, like the Indians, and unlike the British and Spanish whose homes were far across the sea, had their homes in these lands and were here to stay. Eventually, McKee said, the Europeans will return to their distant homes. Then, as McKee knew from his acquaintance with Jackson, there would come a hard reckoning, and the Choctaws must do whatever it took not to find themselves on the wrong side of that reckoning. If the Choctaws were to save their nation, they had to declare war on the Creeks now.[103]

On September 20, McKee followed up his initial letter to Pitchlynn with another. In it he informed his colleague that the Cherokees had just declared war on the Creeks and expressed the hope that "your Choctaw friends will follow a good example." McKee further pointed out that the Creeks had settled in the Black Warrior country claimed by the Choctaws, and if the Americans were the ones forced to oust the Creeks from these lands, the Americans would keep what they had conquered. McKee advised Pitchlynn that Tennessee was raising as many as five thousand soldiers for a campaign against the Creeks and, in connection with that campaign, would be sending a small advance party to Saint Stephens within a week. McKee intended to travel with this party and expected to be at Pitchlynn's home soon.[104]

On September 28, the Tennessee General Assembly passed a resolution authorizing Governor Blount to appoint "a confidential agent" to travel to the Choctaw Nation and "in concert with the U.S. Agent" obtain a promise of neutrality of the Choctaws in the Creek War. With this new authority, Blount appointed McKee to the post that evening.[105] Of course, as Blount and Jackson well knew, by then McKee had already exceeded his newly granted authority and was working hard to secure Choctaw participation in the war against the Creeks. As all three men also well knew, the language in the assembly's resolution about its "confidential agent" working with the US agent was a mere sop to the federal government in Washington. Jackson had no intention of allowing Dinsmoor the slightest involvement in Jackson's plans for the Choctaws and Chickasaws.

McKee left Nashville the following day and caught up with General Coffee's command on its way south to Camp Beaty. On October 4, McKee parted company with the colonel and, accompanied by Coffee's brother-in-law Sandy Donaldson, Captain George Smith, and a detachment of soldiers under Smith's command, traveled through the Tennessee River valley toward the Choctaw Nation. On the evening of the fifth, they arrived at Fort Hampton on the Elk River just north of Muscle Shoals. From there McKee traveled a short distance to Lewis Colbert's ford on the Tennessee River. There he learned that a Creek messenger, ostensibly from the friendly Creeks, had preceded him. McKee doubted the truth of it but was unable to learn much more. He finally arrived at Pitchlynn's on October 13 and sent runners that same day into the surrounding countryside to assemble the chiefs for a council to discuss war with the Creeks.[106]

These northeastern Choctaws had already made tentative steps in that direction. On October 4, their chiefs dispatched a group of nine Choctaw spies from Pitchlynn's plantation to scout the Creek settlements along the Black Warrior River. A dangerous journey through seventy to eighty miles of wilderness controlled by the Red Clubs and their Choctaw allies took them to the principal Creek town on the Black Warrior. While six of the scouts remained concealed in the woods, three scouts approached the stockaded town of two hundred warriors. As they stole upon the town, the Choctaws noticed that the cornfields had not been harvested, and, to their surprise, they found the place seemingly deserted. As they searched through the abandoned houses they finally discovered five women who were in the midst of preparing to take a canoe downriver to collect salt. The sudden and unexpected appearance of the Choctaw warriors at first alarmed the women, but following assurances from the warriors that they meant them no harm, the women calmed down and submitted to questioning.[107] From the women's responses to their questions, and the fact that the hostiles had removed all their stock from the area, the Choctaws concluded that the chief of the place intended to move his people to the area around the confluence of the Coosa and Tallapoosa rivers.

On October 10, the Choctaw spies returned to their nation and delivered their report to the chiefs. McKee arrived three days later. At McKee's and Pitchlynn's urging, on October 19, the principal chiefs met in council to debate the Americans' request that the Choctaws unite with them in their war against the Creeks.[108] McKee hoped to persuade the Choctaws to join him in an expedition against the hostile settlements along the Black Warrior River, then to join General Jackson and his army at the Hickory Ground.[109]

The following day, McKee was permitted to address the council. With Pitchlynn translating, McKee described his speech as "a short appeal to their prudence and good sense." It was the usual pastiche of the overwhelming strength of the Americans and the dangers of a Choctaw civil war if the Choctaws did not unite against the Creeks.[110] But it was McKee's promise to arm the Choctaws before they were asked to fight the Creeks that plainly got their attention.

Following McKee's talk, certain chiefs made their own speeches and adjourned to discuss the matter among themselves. Moshulitubbee apparently seized on McKee's promise of arms as an opportunity to obtain more time to decide which side to join in the Creek War, for to McKee's delight, after the council finished considering the issue, it informed McKee that the eastern district Choctaws determined to declare war on the Creeks once they received the promised arms and ammunition.[111] As Moshulitubbee well knew, McKee did not have the arms with him and would have to travel a good distance to obtain them.

The Choctaw arms situation presented McKee with a serious problem. He had no money and no authority to purchase the arms the Choctaws required. His immediate and best hope was the irascible and mercurial General Flournoy, currently residing at Mount Vernon. Flournoy had earlier promised the Choctaws arms and ammunition, and McKee's obvious course was to attempt to collect on that promise. Accordingly, on October 24, several days after the end of the council, McKee left Pitchlynn's for Saint Stephens to obtain the necessary munitions. Along the way, as promised by the Choctaw council, he was joined by around fifty-four "chosen" Choctaw warriors. If he could not obtain the necessary supplies at that post, McKee planned to proceed downriver to Mobile and attempt to procure them there. He left behind him Captain George Smith and a small detachment of soldiers. When McKee and his little band first arrived among the Choctaws, he had stressed to the men the importance of maintaining good relations with their hosts, and so far they had complied.[112]

Around November 3, a Creek emissary from some Red Club leaders entered Moshulitubbee's camp bearing the traditional gift of tobacco. He informed the Choctaw leaders there that his chiefs wanted to know if the Choctaws would join the Red Clubs in their war against the whites. At the very least, should it became necessary, would they permit the Creeks to retreat through Choctaw lands unmolested to the trans-Mississippi country. Moshulitubbee dutifully reported this incident to the Americans. He also told them that he had ignored the Red Club request and returned no reply, on the dubious grounds that he had joined Pushmataha in declaring war on the Red Clubs.[113]

Indeed, the Choctaws' need for military supplies before they could go to war gave the chief some breathing room. It would take McKee some weeks to journey to Saint Stephens, procure the supplies, and return with them. Who was to say that when he returned with the supplies they would be sufficient? Although Moshulitubbee was inclined to favor the powerful

Americans, and his council had promised McKee that he would support an attack on the nearby Red Club forces, the situation among his people obliged him to move cautiously in dealing with the Americans. A number of his tribe had joined the Red Club cause and were even now forted up on the Black Warrior with the hostile Creeks.[114] An attack on these Choctaws could call down on the attackers retribution from the renegades' clans. And many among the Choctaws were sympathetic to the Creeks. As a Scotsman, Adam James, living among the Choctaws wrote to the "head Chief in the Creek Nation" aside from Pushmataha and twenty of his warriors, the rest of the Choctaw Nation wished to remain at peace with the Creeks "as we are two people a like."[115]

When McKee arrived at Saint Stephens, he found little ammunition. He left there for Mount Vernon, where Flournoy was headquartered. McKee obtained an interview with the general, but it was not a pleasant one. To McKee's surprise, the mercurial Flournoy expressed "serious doubts of the fidelity of the Choctaws and the policy of arming them and supplying them with arms and ammunition." That avenue closed for now, McKee turned to the Choctaw factor George Gaines. But Gaines was having his own problems obtaining munitions from Flournoy, so he had turned to a local militia leader, Major Smoot, one of the few officers who had performed well in the Burnt Corn Creek debacle. Smoot and Gaines were able to arrange a credit for McKee in Mobile for one thousand pounds of powder and ten thousand pounds of lead. McKee immediately notified the Choctaws that he had obtained the promised munitions. He concealed from them, however, Flournoy's and his own growing suspicions of their trustworthiness, fearing that if he confronted them with his suspicions it would "excite and justify their treachery." On his way to Mobile, he met with Flournoy once more and this time was able to procure from the inconstant general authorization for an additional one thousand pounds of powder and two thousand pounds of lead with which to arm the Choctaws. McKee picked up these supplies at the US Choctaw factory in Saint Stephens and headed back to Pitchlynn's.[116]

In late November, news of Moshulitubbee's wavering loyalties reached McKee on the road. A friendly Choctaw informed him that Moshulitubbee's fellow chiefs had persuaded him to renege on his promise to McKee to attack a Creek village on the Black Warrior River where a number of Creeks and "a considerable number of Choctaws who are disaffected towards the Whites are concentrating."[117] The action of the chiefs immediately undermined Moshulitubbee's waiting strategy. It was probably prompted by recent reports that also reached McKee that a British expeditionary force of two thousand men had sailed into Pensacola Bay and were threatening to attack Mobile. These reports had already alarmed the American commander at Mobile, Colonel John Bowyer, who had repositioned the bulk of his command at the point of land guarding the entrance to Mobile Bay, leaving the city largely defenseless. Accordingly, he wrote Colonel Russell at Fort Claiborne to hurry, if at all possible, his regiment back to Mobile to defend the city.[118]

Plainly when rumors reached the Choctaws, they prudently decided to hedge their bets and await the outcome of this new development. On receiving the reports of Moshulitubbee and the other Choctaw chiefs' apparent defection, McKee hastened back to Pitchlynn's the next morning, where he arrived on November 25. From there he called a council at Moshulitubbee's town with the Choctaw leaders for November 30, where he would present them with the munitions. To McKee's annoyance, the chiefs informed him that the supplies he had so laboriously worked to obtain were insufficient. Questioned, they admitted that they dreaded war with the Creeks, particularly because their adherents in the Choctaw Nation were "increasing to an alarming degree." If the Choctaw Nation was going to war against the Creeks, it needed to be better armed. Too late McKee finally realized the trap the chiefs had sprung on him. As long as they could keep McKee running to and fro among the American arms depots at Saint Stephens, Mount Vernon, and Mobile for munitions, they could keep out of the war until it was clear which side would prevail. McKee, on the other hand, dared not reveal that he knew their game. If he chastised them for their faithlessness he might drive the whole lot of them into the Creek camp. But if he returned with more ammunition, they would have no excuse but to declare their allegiance one way or another— hopefully to the Americans.[119] McKee stifled his anger and promised to obtain the additional military supplies the Choctaws purportedly needed.

To procure these supplies, McKee left Pitchlynn's on December 3, once again bound for Mobile. Ominously, he was accompanied by only one Choctaw warrior rather than the fifty-four who previously accompanied him along the dangerous way south. While McKee traveled for munitions, the northern district Choctaws convened another council at Moshulitubbee's. The council was ostensibly convened to discuss preparations for war against the Creeks. But during the council, an important Choctaw war chief known as Little Leader turned the talk away from war with the Creeks. As his name indicated, Little Leader was a small man, but he had a reputation for bravery in war and a vicious nature. Many Choctaws were unhappy with the conduct of their rapacious white neighbors, and Little Leader's talk found a receptive audience among several members of the council. Moshulitubbee, under pressure from the Little Leader and others, began to vacillate in his professed loyalties to the Americans. After considerable debate, the council decided to renege on its promises to McKee, although there is no indication the Choctaws intended to return the armaments McKee had so laboriously obtained for them.

At this juncture of the council, several Choctaws slipped away from the meeting and rode hard to find McKee. They found him that evening on the trail to Moshulitubbee's town and reported the chiefs' decision to renege on their promises. Having also learned at about this time of the impending British attack on Mobile, an alarmed McKee, who had just armed the Choctaws who were now threatening to turn against the Americans, spent an anxious night camped on the road. Early the next morning he rode quickly for Moshulitubbee's town. Along the way he met other Choctaws who confirmed what their fellows had reported about the council decision to break McKee's talk. When he arrived at the town, he found Moshulitubbee at home and confronted him with the reports that his people had turned against the Americans. Moshulitubbee denied the accusation, attributing it to a misunderstanding. What had happened, the chief explained, was that his subordinate chiefs had simply requested that he should stay safely at home while they led the attack against the Creeks in the Black Warrior country. The Choctaws, he assured McKee, would adhere to their promise to go to war against the Creeks. Not satisfied with these assurances, the colonel insisted that he be allowed to address the other chiefs.

At this great crossroads in Choctaw history, the council was reconvened. At that meeting, McKee confronted the chiefs with the report he had received that they broke their promises to him. If true, McKee threatened, he would leave the Choctaw Nation immediately for General Jackson's headquarters and inform him of their betrayal of the Americans. By now the Choctaws had doubtlessly heard of the American victories at Tallushatchee and Talladega, and the attendant slaughter of the Creek warriors. They wanted nothing to do with the formidable Jackson. Some of the chiefs pointed out Little Leader as the "author of all the difficulty." Little Leader replied to this accusation with the lame excuse that McKee's informants were at fault. They had left the council proceedings before a final decision had been reached. After further deliberations, the council had decided to declare war against the Creeks, a decision McKee not unreasonably thought had been made at the previous council meeting. At this point in the proceedings, Talking Bird, one of the principal war chiefs, stepped forward and confirmed that the Choctaws would go to war against the Creeks. When he had left home he had vowed to kill Creeks and would not return home until he had done so. His friend the Humming Bird had taken a similar vow and would soon be joining him in the field. McKee expressed satisfaction with these assurances and promised to resume his journey south for munitions.[120]

Before he left for the south, however, McKee assigned the inconstant Moshulitubbee a special and dangerous task. The chief was to travel through that part of the nation that was most disaffected with the

Americans and persuade it to declare war against the Creeks. This trip, McKee realized, would require the usual lengthy debates around the camp-fires and buy time for Moshulitubbee to persuade his people to join the Americans.

The wisdom of McKee's decision was soon realized. Spies that Claiborne had sent to Pensacola returned to his encampment at Weatherford's Bluff the evening of December 5 with good news. The British naval ships carry-ing two thousand British regulars that Colonel Bowyer had reported at anchor in Pensacola Bay turned out to be only British privateers.[121] Although the privateers had captured some small American vessels, they were of no threat to Mobile, much less to any American land forces. Claiborne was now free to launch his expedition against the hostile towns in the upper Alabama country, and McKee could now begin his expedition against the Red Club strongholds in the Black Warrior country.

On December 20, McKee returned to Pitchlynn's with "a small supply of arms" and the welcome news that the Talking Bird and his friend the Humming Bird had done as promised. On an expedition to the Black Warrior country, not only had they killed four Creeks and several of the rebel Choctaws, but they also claimed, improbably, to have severed com-munications between the two nations, at least in the immediate region. This news, an exasperated and exhausted McKee wrote, relieved him from "the greatest anxiety."[122] Nonetheless, preparations for a major Choctaw expedition against the Black Warrior settlements continued to inch along through the remainder of December. Finally, by the advent of the New Year, preparations were essentially completed. The necessary supplies had been procured for at least a limited foray against the Red Clubs of several hundred Choctaw warriors into the Black Warrior lands.

The expedition was scheduled to depart on January 11, 1814, but it was not until the following day that the tiny Choctaw army began its march, led by McKee, Moshulitubbee, and Pitchlynn. It was joined by other Choctaw warriors along the way, and it was just over four hundred strong by the time it reached the Tombigbee River. There it waited for an addi-tional contingent of Choctaw warriors from the upper towns and a con-tingent of Chickasaws. The final impetus for this long-planned expedition seems to have been news of Claiborne's victory over the Creeks at the Holy Ground that McKee received from Gaines by express rider on the night of January 5, 1814. The impact of the news of this victory on the recalcitrant Choctaws was such that the following day, McKee was able to report with some relief to Jackson that the "Choctaws are now unequivocally at war with" the Creeks.[123]

Claiborne's victory also appeared to presage to McKee an imminent American victory over the entire Creek Nation, because in his letter to Jackson, McKee surmised that "the Creeks will soon sue for peace." This prospect plainly prompted McKee to get his Choctaws into the field as quickly as possible to gain some consideration for the Choctaw people in the coming peace negotiations. Accordingly, in his letter to Jackson, the loyal McKee importuned the general to "include the Choctaws" in any treaty with the Creeks, pointing out that "the contemplated expedition will aid in compelling them to peace by attacking them in their hiding places between the Cahaba and Black Warrior."

McKee was quick to follow up this letter to Jackson with another letter dated January 6. In this letter he proudly informed Jackson that for the coming expedition against the Black Warrior Creeks and "renegade" Choctaws, he anticipated having an army of "seven hundred Choctaws and some Chickasaws." Preliminary Choctaw sorties against the Red Clubs and their Choctaw allies had already yielded four dead Creeks and four dead renegade Choctaws. Three of the latter had made the mistake of returning to their homeland and displaying the scalp of a white man taken as a trophy. The scalp was buried and the formerly proud trophy holders were put to death.

In his second letter to Jackson, McKee also warned that unless his "poor honest Choctaws" received additional supplies and payments, he would not be able to keep them in the field for any length of time, particularly given the current rigors of winter. If he were afforded such supplies and payments for his warriors, McKee claimed he could raise six hundred to one thousand warriors to block any Red Club attempt to escape across the Mississippi or to "cooperate with you in their final destruction or subjugation."[124]

Plainly, McKee understood that the Americans' goal of the war went well beyond a straightforward military defeat of the Red Club faction of the Creek Nation, and he was striving to prevent his "poor" Choctaws from being swept up in the coming Creek tragedy. What McKee apparently did not realize when he wrote his letter to Jackson anticipating a quick and total victory over the Red Clubs was that Jackson's army had all but disintegrated and that there would be no quick and easy end to the war.

The Chickasaws were also making their excuses to Jackson for having not yet entered the war against the Red Clubs. On January 9, 1814, one of their leaders, James Allen, wrote Jackson, claiming that the War Department had instructed the Chickasaw agent, James Robertson, to keep them at home. It was only now that US officials had given them leave to enter the fight as part of the expedition to scourge the Creek settlements in the Black Warrior lands. They were now, if adequately supplied, ready to enter the fray.[125]

The following day, January 10, the important Chickasaw leaders George and James Colbert wrote Jackson in a similar vein, claiming that the War Department had instructed Robertson to keep the Chickasaws out of the war. At last, the Colberts said, the government had lifted this restraint, and accordingly they planned to depart the nation in six days with a war party and would join the Choctaws' campaign against the Creeks. They also promised during this expedition to seek out the murderers of a group of white travelers on the Natchez Trace known as the Mackey party; the Chickasaws had the war clubs with which the members of that party had been slain and would "carry them along and let the owners claim them" as "every nation has their own method of making their war weapons."[126]

Unfortunately, the Chickasaws were late to the Choctaw party. About the time the Chickasaws left their country to join the Choctaw expedition, the Choctaws were already on their way to the Black Warrior country. On January 15, tired of waiting for its tardy allies, the main Choctaw army crossed the Tombigbee. During this crossing, the incorrigible Choctaw chief, Little Leader, again attempted to foment dissent among his fellow warriors against the expedition. His scheme failed and he left camp without having recruited one man to his cause. The Choctaws celebrated Little Leader's failed coup with a "great war dance."[127]

McKee's little army remained camped along the Tombigbee for several days awaiting the arrival of the Choctaw and Chickasaw reinforcements. By January 18, when the expected allies still had not appeared, the army broke camp and marched east for the Black Warrior River, leaving men behind to meet the reinforcements and send them on after the army.

On January 20, McKee's army neared the west bank of the Black Warrior and halted. There McKee received word from his scouts that the hostiles had abandoned their fort and houses on the opposite bank. Here the army remained for several more days, waiting yet again for its allies. When the expected reinforcements still had not arrived by the afternoon of the twenty-second, McKee ordered his army to cross the river and attack the hostile settlement. This effort proved exceedingly difficult. The banks of the river were steep and walled off by what McKee described as an "almost impenetrable canebrake." These obstacles proved so difficult in fact that the Choctaws left their horses behind on the river's west bank to where they could happily feed on the troublesome cane. When the Choctaw army finally reached the hostiles' fort and settlement, it found the place deserted. It did find a number of free-ranging hogs and some bushels of corn. These it expropriated to supplement its meager provisions and camped at the fort for the night.[128]

The next morning, Pitchlynn and his son John left the encampment and crossed the chilly river waters to retrieve the horse herd. They were accompanied by fourteen Choctaw warriors. Unknown to them, their every movement was closely watched by a band of about fifty hostiles concealed in the woods along the opposite shore. As the Pitchlynn party clambered up the riverbank, the hostiles opened fire. Two mixed bloods in the Pitchlynn party, Dan McCurtain and Charles Durant, were immediately but not seriously wounded. At the sound of the firing, a group of warriors from the Choctaw encampment hurried down the eastern bank toward the fighting. As they came upon the little battle, they began firing at the hostiles. One of the Choctaw relief party was badly wounded by a ball to the thigh, but the others managed to swim the river to their embattled comrades. At the arrival of these reinforcements, the hostiles retreated, taking about twenty-eight Choctaw horses with them.[129]

The pursing Choctaws found signs that the hostiles had dragged the body of a comrade to the river and carried off another on horseback. When they located the hostile encampment, they also discovered signs that three other hostiles had been wounded in the melee. The Choctaws searched the countryside for several days for the hostiles without finding a single one. Finally they abandoned the hunt, concluding that their opponents had vanished into the wilderness, making for hiding places "beyond the reach" of the Choctaw scouts. Back at the hostile settlement the day following the skirmish, the victorious Choctaws began the task of destroying the settlement and all the provisions the Choctaws could not carry. By January 27, they had effected this task and then "burned the fort and all the houses and huts in the neighborhood on both sides of the river"—more than forty in all. That day they crossed the Black Warrior, where they finally met up with the long-awaited contingents of Choctaws and Chickasaws.[130] These new arrivals were too late. On January 28, the expedition began its journey home down the western side of the Black Warrior, all plans of marching on to the Creek stronghold on the Cahaba now abandoned for a reason with which Jackson was now all too familiar: the want of sufficient provisions and proper clothing for a winter campaign.

Although in his report to Jackson, McKee attempted to cast the Black Warrior campaign in the best light, it really was a sorry affair. The Americans had spent months of cajoling and politicking the Choctaws and Chickasaws to take up arms against the hostiles and obtaining weapons with which to arm them. The result of all that effort was little other than the usual burning and looting of some small hostile settlements and a minor skirmish in which the Creeks were arguably the victors. McKee had promised Jackson that his Black Warrior expedition would hasten the end of the war, but it fell far short of that promise. Nonetheless, McKee did not shy away from once more importuning Jackson to remember the Choctaws in any treaty with the Creeks. But there was little in the way of a Choctaw contribution for Jackson to remember, even in the unlikely event he were so inclined.

From this point, the war in the Black Warrior country devolved into the ways of time immemorial, with small bands of young warriors conducting impromptu horse-stealing raids and back-and-forth ambushes with the ultimate prize being an occasional scalp or two that the victor could wave about the campfires. The bulk of the Choctaw and Chickasaw warriors who had joined the Americans in their war with the Creeks would shortly rendezvous with Colonel Russell at Fort Claiborne for the long-delayed expedition to the Hickory Ground.

The Brink of Ruin

A FTER the Holy Ground battle, once he had seen to the safety of his people, William Weatherford turned his attention to the critical military situation facing the nation. The Georgians under General Floyd had retreated from the central Creek towns to Fort Mitchell, where they were reorganizing; General David Adams had done little harm and apparently had left the field. The Mississippians were back at Fort Claiborne, where they showed no signs of mounting another invasion up the Alabama River valley. Finally, Jackson and his Tennesseans still hovered on the nation's northern border, mysteriously inactive since their great victory at Talladega. Having turned back these serious threats, the Creeks still retained their fighting spirit. As one Red Club, John Durant, wrote his brother Sandy even before he knew of the retreat of Claiborne's and Adams's armies, "we have had two powerful armes [Jackson's and Floyd's] in our country this winter but they have had to run back faster then they came . . . all we lack is powder and led."[131] Weatherford and the other Red Club leaders knew, however, that one army, or perhaps all three in conjunction, would soon move against the nation.

Shortly after the Holy Ground battle, the Indian leaders met at Hoithlewaulee, on the lower Tallapoosa River, to determine how best to defend the nation from the American attacks they knew were coming. The town was one of the main assembly areas for a number of the many different tribes of the Muskogee Confederation, such that a veritable babble of tongues rang through the crowded settlement. From Hoithlewaulee and the large towns nearby, the Red Clubs could promptly raise close to two thousand warriors.[132]

Weatherford and William McGillivray were there, as most likely were old Hoboheilthle and Peter McQueen, as well as Creeks from the upper Tallapoosa towns.[133] In addition to these secular warriors, the prophets Paddy Walsh, who had survived the extensive wounds he suffered at Fort Mims, Josiah Francis, and High Head Jim were also present at the Red Club council. The hostiles' losses so far in the war had been severe, although perhaps not as severe as the whites liked to think. The Americans believed upwards of one thousand of the Indians' original force of four thousand warriors had been killed or "disabled."[134] The actual number was probably a few hundred shy of that figure.

Munitions, however, were the most pressing problem. The Creek leaders had recently taken an inventory of the powder and shot available to their warriors. This inventory, a sadly quick process, only served to confirm what they already knew. There was an insufficient quantity of these items to meet the Americans on anywhere near an equal footing. Back in November, Weatherford had persuaded the Spanish governor at Pensacola to furnish the Indians with these critical commodities, and he was appointed to return for more. With him went McQueen and an escort of several hundred mounted men. According to Floyd's report to Jackson, the Red Club expedition left the nation for Pensacola around the New Year.[135] The Creeks probably arrived around January 7, 1814, no doubt much to the dismay of the beleaguered Governor Manrique.

This powder expedition was clearly the one Colonel Russell had mentioned in his January 15, 1814, letter to General Claiborne, and the one that the overconfident colonel assured General Pinckney he would intercept. Given the head start the Indians had on Russell, who went after them no earlier than January 16, Russell's mission failed. For according to George Stiggins, Weatherford returned from Pensacola with a number of horse loads of the critical supplies. Stiggins says three horse loads and characterizes this amount as "plenty of powder and lead." [136] Stiggins is either wrong about the number of horse loads Weatherford obtained or that the amount obtained was sufficient. Three horse loads would hardly be enough to equip the warriors of a single town.

On the plus side, the Creeks had survived attacks from four armies—those of generals Claiborne, Jackson, Floyd, and Adams—yet the borders of the nation were largely intact, and the fighting spirit of their warriors still high. The Red Clubs had the advantage of fighting from interior lines, which allowed them to move men quickly to meet the most immediate American threat. They also had a silent partner in the countryside itself. It was as if the land intuited the devastation that was coming for it if the whites won the war and was throwing up obstacle after obstacle to the various American intrusions. Thus far the Americans had not learned to overcome the problem of supplying their armies in rough and largely roadless country sufficiently to exploit their successes in battle against the hostiles. Finally, the Creeks were the beneficiaries of the Americans' inability to overcome their own internal divisions and jealousies, particularly between Jackson and Cocke, and their inability to enlist or conscript men for a period of time sufficient to transform them into veterans and to hold any gains in land they had won. Of course, the Creeks also shared the Americans' internal divisions among their own leaders, which, as we shall see, would hinder their response to Floyd's second incursion into the nation.

As for the Georgians, the war now turned back to their theater of operations. Floyd's serious leg wound had rendered him incapacitated all through December and into January. On Christmas night, he wrote his daughter Mary "in a wilderness west of Chattahoochee" that the bullet wound in his knee had healed, "but the joint is so much affected that I have hardly any strength in that knee."[137] The new governor of Georgia, Peter Early, was understandably feeling pressure from his constituents to promptly launch another campaign against the hated Creeks. With the advice of General Pinckney, he cast about for a replacement for Floyd to command a second expedition against the hostile forces gathered in the Tallapoosa towns downstream from Tuckabatchee. On December 10, 1813, Early and Pinckney decided on a Brigadier General Williams of the state militia.[138] When Williams resigned his commission a few weeks after his appointment, the governor on January 4 appointed General David Blackshear to replace him. Meanwhile, Floyd had convinced Pinckney that he was ready to take the field. Accordingly, the day after Blackshear's appointment, Pinckney countermanded it and left Floyd in command of the army.[139]

Floyd was an able commander, cool and courageous under fire and decisive in battle. But given the poor condition of his knee that he reported to his daughter, it is doubtful that it improved significantly in the intervening two weeks. It thus appears that Floyd concealed the true condition of his injury from his superior in order to take the field and finish what he had started a month earlier. As events would show, the general's severe and painful wound may have materially affected his command capabilities in the desperate fight to come.

While Early was preparing to remove Floyd from command of the Georgia militia, Floyd called a meeting of Lower Creek leaders from five towns. Floyd's relations with the friendly Creeks were troubled to say the least. These warriors had fought bravely at Autosse and naturally felt that the whites should acknowledge their contribution to that victory. That had not been the case. The United States had, with no reason given, failed to pay the Creeks' annuity for two years, and, unlike Pushmataha's Choctaws to the west, the friendly Creeks had received no combat pay. The friendly Creek warriors also had no confidence in the Georgia militia officers and in general thought the whites moved too slowly. More fundamentally, hundreds of the refugee Tuckabatchees, and the more numerous Lower Creeks themselves, lacked clothes and food in a wet and wintery land.[140]

From Floyd's perspective, the friendly Creeks were untrustworthy: traitors to their own people seldom are viewed as reliable by their allies. In particular, the general was having trouble getting the friendly Creeks to send out scouting parties into Red Club territory, or to supply warriors to accompany a troop of mounted Georgians tasked with protecting an expedition by the army's engineer to plot the army's best course from Fort

Mitchell to Tuckabatchee.[141] This intransigence only further undermined Floyd's confidence in his allies.

To resolve at least some of these difficulties, the chiefs met on January 4 in the Broken Arrow "old fields" near Fort Mitchell. At that council meeting, the chiefs agreed to assist Floyd in his expedition into the nation, particularly as scouts and flankers "in front and rear on the right and left of your army."[142] They advised him that they could assemble their warriors for the campaign at Floyd's encampment in a matter of days.

About a week later, on January 11, this uneasy alliance was threatened by intelligence that Floyd received from a woman of "colour." This lady had a good reputation among the whites, whose cause she warmly espoused. For the same reason she was not trusted by the Indians. The woman arrived at Floyd's headquarters with the explosive news that the very Lower Creeks among whom Floyd had planted his army were conspiring with the British, who had just landed on the Gulf Coast with ships laden with arms and supplies for the Indians, to attack the Georgians. Such a coalition would put Floyd's rear, from where his supplies were forwarded to the front, in grave jeopardy once the army left Fort Mitchell for Tuckabatchee.[143] Indeed, he could find himself cut off from the provisions he needed to prosecute his campaign.

On hearing the woman's story, to which he appeared to lend material credence, Floyd arranged a meeting with the friendly chiefs at which he charged them with betraying him. These men, foremost among them the Little Prince, "with much composure" predictably denied the woman's report. Floyd, however, remained unconvinced and bided his time until the day appointed for the assembly at Fort Mitchell of the Lower Creek warriors who were scheduled to join Floyd's expedition against their Muskogee brothers.[144]

On that day, four hundred to five hundred warriors from the nearby towns of Coweta and Cusseta, as well as a contingent of Timpoochee Barnard's formidable Uchees from farther down the Chattahoochee River valley, gathered in the fields outside Fort Mitchell. The Little Prince made a talk to the assembled Creeks and the white onlookers. In that talk the old chief iterated that the majority of the Lower Creeks were loyal to the United States and again denied any involvement of the friendly chiefs with the British. On being informed by Floyd of this development, Pinckney wisely encouraged the younger man to gracefully accept this "useful ancillary force" and to make sure to supply these allies with provisions in order "to confirm them in their attachment."[145]

Floyd was now on the brink of his departure into Red Club territory. However, as if his wound, his troubles with his Indian allies, his constant scrambling for provisions and transport, and sickness among his men were not enough, an outbreak of the "mutinous disposition," of which

Andrew Jackson was all too familiar, occurred among his soldiers. The ostensible cause was, as in Jackson's army, the length of the soldiers' service. Reports began reaching Floyd that his men had decided to leave his army when their six-month terms of service expired on February 25. The injured and overworked Floyd handled this intelligence remarkably well—certainly better than Jackson would have. While passing on this news to Pinckney, Floyd assured him that trouble with the troops was unlikely so long as they gained a victory, of which Floyd was confident and, slyly adding, as long as the men were "well fed."[146]

On January 17, 1814, Floyd marched his army of about one thousand three hundred militia, made up of infantry, cavalry, and artillery units, out of its encampment at Fort Mitchell. They were eventually joined by around five hundred mostly unenthusiastic friendly Creek warriors.[147] One notable member of Floyd's army, however, was missing. On January 9, Floyd had the good luck and better sense to send his irrepressible son Charles from Fort Mitchell to deliver a message to Governor Early in Milledgeville. In light of what happened later, dispatching Charles on this errand may well have saved the boy's life.

In accordance with the strategy worked out with Pinckney and Jackson, Floyd and his men traveled the Federal Road toward Tuckabatchee. There he was supposed to unite with Jackson's army driving south. The Georgians had learned from the friendly Creeks, and a slave named Caesar, that the Red Clubs had concentrated in great strength at the town of Hoithlewaulee several miles down the Tallapoosa River from the old Autossee battlefield. Caesar had endured a remarkable odyssey through the nation over the last six months and had witnessed some remarkable events. He belonged to the wife of the mixed-blood Bernard Riley in the east of the nation, but somehow he found himself far to the west at Fort Mims during the Red Club attack. He was taken prisoner there and brought to the Holy Ground. Caesar was present at that battle, where he was captured by Colonel Russell's horsemen, and traveled for several days with General Claiborne's army on its return to Fort Claiborne. Along the journey, Caesar escaped the Americans' clutches and made his way east toward what passed for home, undoubtedly traversing the many cold miles on bare feet, in rags, without food, and with every man's hand against him.[148]

After a stopover at Coosada, home of Captain Isaacs, near the Coosa River, just above its juncture with the Tallapoosa, Caesar traveled east on the Federal Road until he reached Riley's place. Barney Riley, son of John Riley, the father-in-law of Caesar's owner, happened to be Floyd's "principal pilot." It appears that on January 16, John Riley or perhaps his son took a written statement from Caesar. That document was then given to Floyd, who had just begun his expedition into the nation. In his statement, Caesar gave a brief account of his travels and set forth recent activities of the hostile towns toward which Floyd was heading. Included in that statement was a report that a Spaniard "called short legged John," who used to live at Hoithlewaulee, had brought a letter from the Spanish at Pensacola to the Red Clubs advising them that ammunition was available there. According to Caesar, Josiah Frances and "about 100 men," including "Bill Weatherford" (whom Caesar had recently met on the Federal Road and who would have known Caesar from the Holy Ground), had gone to Pensacola to retrieve it. Caesar also reported that starvation had begun to spread among the hostiles assembled at the Hickory Ground, causing some of them to disperse to their homes.[149]

Floyd planned to march his army to the ford across the Tallapoosa River from Tuckabatchee and erect a fort nearby. Along the way, in accordance with Pinckney's instructions, Floyd also planned to construct and garrison other forts to protect his line of communications and to facilitate supply of the army. At the Tuckabatchee fort, he would store the army's baggage and provisions and ready his forces for an assault on the hostiles who Floyd's spies had reported were concentrated at Hoithlewaulee six miles downstream. Once the hostile army was defeated, Floyd planned to ravage all the hostile settlements in his reach while he waited for an expedition led by Jackson from the north to join him for a final campaign that would destroy the hostiles.[150]

On the day Floyd's army departed Fort Mitchell, the weather was miserable—cold and rainy—and the road was more mud than road. After a day's march of twelve miles, the army halted and camped for the night. There Floyd assigned a detail to build a fort. The next morning the army resumed its westward journey. As the Georgians penetrated deeper into the nation, they found the hostiles had destroyed bridges and causeways across the streams in their path and placed downed timber in such a way as to block the road. At each such obstruction, the long line of men and horses and wagons, and a moveable feast of hogs and cattle, backed up while the troops laboriously cleared the blocked passageway. Thus impeded, by January 20, Floyd's army had covered only thirty miles along the road. Here, near the juncture of Calebee and Persimmon creeks, they stopped to construct another earthwork fortification, which they named Fort Hull. The army remained there for four days, building fortifications but mainly waiting out the interminable rains and for the road to dry sufficiently to enable the wagons and artillery to move.[151]

It was an unhappy time. Rations were low and had to be doled out sparingly to the increasingly unhappy men. In response, the men became "sluggish" in constructing Fort Hull, aided in their protest by a shortage of entrenching tools. An exasperated Floyd had to restore full rations to the increasingly "clamorous" troops to head off a budding mutiny. Adding to his cares, illness had spread among the soldiers, and the names of seventy men now decorated the sick list, among them some of Floyd's best officers. On top of everything else Floyd had to contend with, his Creek allies were more disgruntled than ever. The army's supply of ammunition was low, and only minimal amounts were available for the Indians. Incomprehensibly, at least to the whites, the friendly Creeks also refused to accept the ration of corn Floyd offered them because they had no one to pound it for them; apparently they did not bring their wives on this trip.[152]

During the short stay at Fort Hull, a cavalry detachment led by Captain John P. Harvey made a bold night raid through hostile territory all the way to the Tallapoosa River. Word had reached Floyd at Fort Hull that Hawkins's chief interpreter and a principal ally of the Big Warrior's, Alexander Cornells, had double-crossed the Georgians. According to Floyd's garbled account to Pinckney, as soon as Floyd marched out of Fort Mitchell, Cornells, whose daughter was married to Peter McQueen, sent her off with two of McQueen's former slaves to recruit other slaves for the war party. Now a number of these renegades had gathered at Cornells's plantation two miles above the old Autossee battlefield. Floyd was certain that Cornells's daughter had informed the hostiles of the movements of his army—as if the painful slog of this expedition was a mystery to anyone within miles of the Federal Road.

As a result of this intelligence, on the night of January 20, Floyd ordered Harvey and his cavalry to ride twenty miles to Cornells's place on the Tallapoosa and bring in Cornells's daughter and the slaves. Dutifully, Harvey and his troopers set out in the cold and rain through the most populated region of the hostiles. For much of the way they traveled northwest along the Federal Road, then turned north off the road and proceeded several miles along the south bank of the Tallapoosa to Cornells's home. The Red Clubs plainly did not expect anyone, much less a troop of Georgia cavalry, to be out on such a night. Emerging from the wet darkness like a nightmare made manifest, the horsemen descended on Cornells's farmhouse. A sharp fight with a group of hostiles ensued, and four Red Clubs were killed. Harvey was able to collect the young lady, nine slaves, and several children and return unmolested with them to Fort Hull by eight the next morning. From there Floyd shipped them back to Fort Mitchell. While the captives were at Fort Hull, Floyd learned from the slaves that McQueen had recently returned to the nation from Pensacola, where he had been able to obtain only a small quantity of powder and lead.[153] Despite the miserable weather, things were looking up for the Georgians.

On Tuesday morning, January 25, an anxious Floyd felt that the rains had let up sufficiently to continue the journey to Tuckabatchee. As he wrote to Jackson just before departing Fort Hull, his troops' term of enlistment was scheduled to expire on February 25, and he "deemed it all important that a decisive blow should be struck."[154] Leaving a detachment of one hundred men to guard the new fort, the army resumed its laborious march along the increasingly more difficult Federal Road.[155] The constant chilling rains and high waters of the creeks in their path, not to mention the ingenious obstructions placed in their way by the hostiles, shaped the journey into a stop-and-start affair as the army halted while heavy trees with sharpened branches were chopped away, streams were bridged, and the army's many wagons were pushed and pulled from the muck. Groping their way blindly, because the Georgians' Creek allies continued to refuse to scout, the army struggled about five miles along the road before Floyd ordered a halt for the night. The army bivouacked along the road on a stretch of land facing one of the ubiquitous swamps lining the way. The ground where they encamped was so exposed that many of the soldiers feared an attack, but after an anxious night with the campfires built high, morning arrived without incident.[156]

After a meager breakfast the army continued its northwesterly march up the Calebee Valley. A short distance on, Floyd ordered the army to turn north off the Federal Road toward Calebee Creek. Apparently he had decided to march directly toward the ford across the Tallapoosa that lay just above Autossee. Perhaps he hoped to repeat his tactic before the Battle of Autossee of approaching the Red Clubs from an unexpected direction, but without proper intelligence of the country ahead he was floundering. The route he chose required the army to leave the Federal Road and cross the swampy ground leading to Calebee Creek. After several tortuous miles in this direction, as the terrain grew even swampier, the heavily laden wagons began to sink more deeply than ever into the sucking muck. It was as if the prophets' boast that they had the power to turn the ground beneath the feet of an American army into a bog and swallow the men whole was coming true. Eventually the army could go no farther as it was configured. Floyd ordered it to march back a mile to a suitable campsite on higher ground.[157]

There, at a place they called Camp Defiance, rather than retracing his steps to the more hospitable Federal Road, which would have taken him near the ford on the Tallapoosa, Floyd stubbornly reorganized the army's supplies and equipment to allow it to better traverse the intractable route he had selected toward Calebee Creek. The army's tents and cooking utensils were consolidated into one group of wagons and sent back to Fort Hull—increasing the discomfort of the already sodden troops. The ammunition and entrenching tools were loaded into the remaining five wagons in such a way as to reduce the weight the vehicles had to carry. The army's by-now-scanty rations were packed onto the cavalry horses or crammed into the soldiers' knapsacks.[158] In what turned out to be a providential decision, Floyd kept his artillery with him, even though the two cannon and their ammunition were particularly difficult to haul along the quickly deteriorating ground. While it was reconfiguring its gear, the army was joined by a troop of cavalry under Floyd's future son-in-law, Captain Duke Hamilton. They were now about seven or eight miles from the ford across the Tallapoosa and even nearer to the Autossee battleground.

The ground Floyd selected for his camp was in a piney woods slightly elevated above the bottomlands of Calebee Creek, which flowed about a mile to the west. In 1794, the Georgia militia had camped there during an expedition against the Okfuskee Creeks, and perhaps knowledge of that distant campaign influenced Floyd's choice of route and campground.[159] In neither case had the Georgians chosen well. The west and east sides of the camp were flanked by swampland and small creeks emptying into the Calebee. The soldiers hastily threw up entrenchments in the shape of a parallelogram as dictated by the terrain. The army's baggage and the cavalry horses were placed in the center of the fort. The two cannon were placed on opposite walls. Their Indian allies camped outside the walls.[160]

Not only were the fortifications built on dangerous ground to defend, but they were hastily built and poorly designed. The area enclosed by the trenches was too small to comfortably and safely accommodate the number of men intended for its occupation, and when the fort's completion was announced, the troops found themselves crammed two deep in lines facing its low earthen walls. They had no room to maneuver and were so thickly pressed together that even the dubious marksmanship of the hostiles could not fail to hit someone. Lone sentinels and a group of pickets were placed beyond the walls to provide warning of an attack. But the thick swamps around the fort made them vulnerable to the quiet knives or uproarious guns of unseen attackers. As one of the soldiers later bitterly observed, the army had ample time to build adequate fortifications; its failure to do so cost it dearly.[161]

Given what happened next, it is difficult to avoid the conclusion that the commanders of the Georgians and their numerous Indian allies had perilously overestimated their ability to easily thwart a Red Club assault on a camp fortified with cannon and also underestimated the resolve of their adversaries to attempt such a feat. During the army's long, slow creep over the cold and muddy miles to Camp Defiance, the hostiles had made no attempt to attack the drawn-out column of men and horses, even at those points along the road where they had placed obstructions. Moreover, only several days past, Captain Harvey's cavalry troop had somehow managed to ride almost to the gates of Tuckabatchee, attack a Red Club position, kill several hostiles, and come away unscathed with a dozen or so captives. Thus it was that the fatigue parties of wet and freezing soldiers had little impetus to do more than the bare minimum to create the trench and earthworks ordered by their officers. Not unreasonably as well, the hostiles' current inactivity seems to have imbued Floyd and his officers with confidence that the Indians would not dare attack them. Thus they did not push as hard as they otherwise might have on their already exhausted and discontented men in the construction of a proper fort. No doubt the belief that the Red Clubs were reluctant to engage the Georgians was underscored when the fifteen men Floyd sent to Fort Hull to obtain forage for the horses returned later that night unmolested.

Unbeknownst to the Georgians and to the friendly Creeks settling down for a winter night's rest in the dismal confines of Camp Defiance, almost one thousand three hundred Red Club warriors were assembled just across Calebee Creek a mile away. They gathered in the frigid night air around small campfires built low to the ground to conceal their presence from any American spies who might be lurking in the area. This was the largest force the Red Clubs had assembled against the Americans to date, and the warriors were waiting anxiously for the word from their leaders to attack Floyd's army. McQueen had returned from Pensacola several days earlier with a disappointingly meager load of powder and ammunition from the Spanish governor.[162] The Indians would thus have to go into battle poorly armed. This handicap became a guiding factor in the debate over their plan of attack that was going on among their leaders.

The Creek *miccos* had delegated the planning of the battle to four of their principal leaders. Unfortunately, but typically, even with the proverbial wolf at the nation's door, the four men selected were divided equally on the proper tactics for striking the Georgians. On one side were the strictly military men, William Weatherford and William McGillivray, on the other side were the prophets, but also courageous fighters, Paddy Walsh and High Head Jim.[163] As the other *miccos* looked on within earshot, the men to whom they had delegated the task of planning the attack against the Georgians sat about the fire debating tactics—a debate that became increasingly rancorous.

Weatherford and McGillivray argued that the Red Clubs should let the unsuspecting Georgians leave their entrenchments and string out their army along the narrow way through the Calebee swamp. While the Georgians struggled through the swamp, the Red Clubs could move quietly, concealed by the swampland, to surround their enemies. The signal for a general attack would be made by firing on the vanguard of the Georgians' army when it emerged from the swamp onto higher ground. Then, while the main body of the army was mired in the swamp or trying to cross the creek, the Red Clubs would attack the soldiers from all sides, with their main objects the cannon and the munitions wagons.[164]

The gnomish Walsh, his frightful features distorted even more in the dancing light of the campfire, was having none of Weatherford's plan. With the stately High Head Jim at his side, he argued for an even bolder night attack to test the strength of the white encampment under the cover of darkness. If their attack met heavy resistance or was repulsed altogether, they could retire before dawn into the safety of the swamps.[165]

Weatherford said Walsh's plan was suicidal; as they had at Autossee, the Georgians' two cannon would rule the battlefield. In contrast, Weatherford's plan took advantage of the terrain and the Indians' superior skills of fighting from ambush. On the narrow path through the boggy ground of the swamp, the Georgians' cannon would be difficult to bring into play. The swampland enveloping the troops would also allow the poorly armed Indians to get close to them on both sides of the line of march, thus reducing the Georgians' advantage in firearms and allowing the Indians to use their war clubs and tomahawks to deadly effect.[166] Employing such tactics during the French and Indian War fifty years earlier, their ancestors had virtually destroyed British general Edward Braddock's army on the road to what was now Pittsburgh. That feat, however, was not fated to be duplicated here in the swamps of middle Alabama.

The little prophet, supported by his fellow prophet High Head Jim, emphatically disagreed with Weatherford's plan, and the level of discourse soon descended to imputations involving the debaters' courage. Walsh, one of the most persuasive speakers in the nation and someone who still, against all reason, retained his prophetic aura, convinced the other still superstitiously gullible *miccos* to adopt his plan.[167] In this he was no doubt supported by the remaining Shawnee prophets among the Creeks—men who were familiar with a similar, and nearly successful, plan of attack against the Americans under General William Henry Harrison at Tippecanoe in fall 1811.

This was not Weatherford's finest hour, and it underscored a vital weakness in the Red Clubs' command structure. In high dudgeon, his authority and honor impugned by the demonic Walsh, Weatherford announced angrily that he would not follow Walsh's utterly mad plan, and with several of his Tuskegee warriors he stalked out of the conference for home. McGillivray, his sense of honor not so precious as Weatherford's, remained behind for the coming fight.[168] Ironically, while Walsh and Weatherford exchanged angry words at their Calebee camp, their respective plans of attack were being employed over a two-day period by another Red Club army against Jackson's army in the Alabama hill country one hundred miles northeast.

While Weatherford rode Achilles-like with his followers to the west, deep into the early hours of January 27, the Red Clubs led by Walsh, High Head Jim, and McGillivray moved over one thousand three hundred warriors unseen and unheard over frosted ground a mile through the cold, drizzling dark to the eastern bank of Calebee Creek. As the Indian army stole forward, the warriors could see in the distance a pocket of lights flittering in the eastern dark of trees and sky. Led by their scouts, the closer the Red Clubs approached Floyd's camp, the brighter and more animated grew the lights, until they intensely penetrated the woods ahead. As the Red Clubs moved toward the leading edge of illumination they could see the outline of the Georgians' camp lit by enormous bonfires at its center. The scouts had previously located the sentinels posted around the camp, obligingly backlit by the lights from the fort, and marked them for death. Also illuminated by the fires from the fort was the camp of the friendly Creeks. It sprawled just outside the walls of the fort and was pricked out in the darkness by its own tiny campfires. Further, the Red Clubs saw that the Georgians had placed a group of militia outside the camp to provide early warning of an attack.

Just beyond the reach of the lights from the fort, the Red Club leaders assembled their men and assigned each company its place in the line of attack. Walsh's plan was to hit the two sides of the camp facing swampland and then quickly get inside the fort among the densely packed troops. Above all, the cannon must be neutralized from the outset of the fight. By 5:00 A.M., the Red Club warriors were in place. The Georgians, wrapped in their blankets on the wet ground, lay in an exhausted, fitful sleep with, as ordered, their arms at their sides.

The crack of rifles as the Red Clubs shot the sentinels was immediately followed by a maelstrom of howls from the throats of hundreds of scarlet-painted Red Clubs moving toward the camp's earthwork. The hostile cries were soon answered by cries from the sleep-addled and now-astonished Georgians and friendly Creeks as they struggled to their feet while feeling for their weapons. Almost immediately, a storm of gunfire issued from the oncoming Creek legions toward the panicked soldiers and their allies, quickly followed by the shrieks of the wounded and dying men and horses. Camp Defiance immediately devolved into utter chaos. Panic washed over the troops, and a number of men fled the barely discernible demons running toward them out of the roaring dark. Even the officers were not immune from the terror of the Creek attack. Scared witless, one lieutenant fled to a hay bed and burrowed inside.[169]

Although startled by the attack, the unflappable Floyd retained his composure. As one aide strapped the general's sword around Floyd's waist and another readied his white horse, Floyd retained sufficient presence of mind to pull his watch from his pocket and coolly note the time of attack as precisely 5:20 A.M.[170] Then he ordered his aides to follow him and tried to assemble order from the sudden chaos. The situation was rapidly becoming more dangerous. Many soldiers had removed their shoes for the night. Now, unable to locate them amid the darkness and confusion, they succumbed to the cries of their officers to form up and went barefoot into battle over rough and frost-encrusted ground.[171] To add to the chaos, the camp was quickly filling with hundreds of friendly Creeks running for their lives into the camp with hundreds of shrieking Red Clubs at their heels. Once inside the fortifications, the panicked Indians created further chaos as they attempted to get behind the shield of the now-forming lines of militia. Moreover, in the darkness thickened with smoke from hundreds of guns, it was difficult for either side to make out the other. Thus the combatants simply fired at each other's muzzle flashes. The Americans, however, were at a disadvantage because they were backlit by the large campfires in the fort, making them better targets for the hostiles firing from the darkness.

The soldiers were falling everywhere as they scrambled amid the cries of their officers to get into fighting formation. One of Floyd's principal deputies and the commander of the 2nd Infantry Regiment, Colonel Daniel Newman, was shot three times and fell nearby.[172] One of Newman's company commanders, Captain Thomas Butts, was mortally wounded by a gunshot through the body. Just before being shot he had made himself a conspicuous target as he stood tall amid the chaos, waving his sword above his head in an attempt to rouse his men, "an imprudent course," one author wryly opined. However "imprudent" Butts's conduct may have been, it was that of a brave officer who at a critical moment for the army got his men into the fight—a fight so desperate and at such close quarters that as he lay on the ground, Butts had his two pistols placed at his side to use against the hostiles should they, as appeared likely, come within range.[173]

Within the cyclone of smoke, noise, and insanity that Camp Defiance had become, the steady Floyd formed a plan and quickly and calmly dispatched his staff officers in all directions with plain orders for his company commanders to organize a defense. Several of these officers, including Floyd's aide-de-camp, Major Joel Crawford, had their horses shot from beneath them, but within thirty minutes, Floyd had most of his men, except his Indian allies, putting up a stiff resistance.[174] His message to the troops was to hold out until sufficient daylight arrived to adequately discern the enemy formations and organize a charge. Several contemporaneous accounts quote him as exhorting his soldiers to "give them hell when daylight comes." The fighting was at such close quarters that a Red Club who overheard the general's cry—supposedly the absent William Weatherford—yelled back in English, "Damn you, we will give you hell before daylight comes."[175]

At this point, the key to the battle was possession of the precious cannon. From the outset of their assault, the Red Clubs had directed their primary efforts to killing the artillery crews and horses and capturing the guns. Accordingly, some of the fiercest fighting of the battle occurred around these weapons. As the hostiles swarmed into the fort, the artillery commander, Captain Jett Thomas, and his men frantically struggled to turn the guns on the attackers. Artillery horses were shot. Four members of one gun crew and its match man were shot down, one after the other, leaving only three men to operate the piece.[176] One of these remaining cannoneers, Ezekiel Attaway, was heard to exhort his two comrades not to abandon the piece but to "[s]eize the first weapon you can lay your hands upon and stick to your post until the last." The weapon Attaway seized was a particularly vicious one, an artillery tool known as a traversing hand-spike. It was a stout, six-foot wooden pole tipped with iron, used by the cannon crew to turn the barrel of the gun in the desired direction by inserting the handspike into an iron ring at the tail of the gun carriage and using it like a lever. Attaway now turned this wicked implement on the Red Clubs to cruel effect.[177]

Outside the fort, Captain John Brodnax and his men on picket duty found themselves isolated and cut off from the fort by the hostiles. As the Red Clubs closed in, Brodnax's detachment was in imminent danger of destruction. At the last moment, Timpoochee Barnard slammed a contingent of his Uchee warriors—who claimed, not without reason, to be the best fighters in the nation—into the fast-constricting hostile lines around the Georgians. This diversion allowed Brodnax and what remained of his men, several of whom were badly wounded, to cut their way into the fort.[178]

It was a different story with Barnard's fellow Creeks inside the fort. To Floyd's disgust, almost all three hundred of them huddled in terror behind the Georgian lines. Those lines by now were roughly organized and had considerably stiffened. Of particular note was Captain William E. Adams's company of riflemen. It had been among the first into action and had suffered severe casualties in the course of the fight: five killed, twelve dangerously or severely wounded, and one slightly wounded.[179] Adams was one of the severely wounded, as was a Baptist fighting preacher named Elisha Moseley. Sergeant Moseley was not only a rifleman in Adams's company but also a chaplain in the army. Thomas Woodward, a participant in the fight, said Adams could "pray all night and fight all day, or pray all day and fight all night, just as it came to his turn to do either." The fighting preacher was wounded several times in the course of the battle—ironically once by a gunshot to the mouth—but he survived.[180]

This expenditure of blood by Moseley and many other of Adams's men was instrumental in giving Thomas's artillery time to bring its guns into action. However, to the astonishment and consternation of the Georgians, despite the fire of the cannon, the Creeks inexplicably kept coming—coming until they were within thirty yards of the guns. One minute more and they would be on the remaining cannoneers with tomahawks, war clubs, and knives.[181]

The Georgians' inability to stop the Creek attack, even with cannon fire, was due to the darkness and the nature of the terrain onto which the cannon were firing. Camp Defiance was built on a slight slope of ground, and the cannon naturally were placed on the upper level. The Creeks were taking advantage of this feature of the landscape to crawl up the dark slope under the muzzles of the guns, which fired harmlessly above them. Finally, with most of his cannoneers dead or wounded around him, Thomas noticed in the flash of the cannon fire that his weapons were firing too high and cried out an order to his surviving men to depress the muzzles of the cannon and rake the ground with grapeshot. Despite their losses, the artillerymen managed to drop the gun muzzles level with the sloping ground. The subsequent blasts of grapeshot from the cannon threw up clods of earth about the crawling swarm of Red Clubs and tore through their flesh.[182] The attack stopped as if it had hit a wall, and the survivors ran, limped, or even crawled from the field toward the swamp.

This repulse of the hostile attack, just as the light was rising in the eastern sky to the Georgians' back, represented the turning point in the battle. At this point of the fight, those in the Georgian army who understood Muskogee, such as teenager Thomas Woodward, could hear Red Club warriors frantically crying out to each other for more powder and ammunition. Now was the time for General Floyd to unleash his counterattack. While his front-line troops held off the hostiles, Floyd organized an attacking force comprising Majors Douglas Watson and Frederick Freeman's infantry battalions on the left wing and Majors David S. Booth and Benjamin Cleveland's infantry battalions on the right. Floyd then placed Captain Hamilton's cavalry company just behind the right wing of infantry with instructions to act as circumstances dictated when it entered the battle. Captain William Ford's company stood ready just behind the cavalry.[183]

Floyd gave the order for the infantry to charge, and hundreds of soldiers, roaring at the top of their lungs, fixed bayonets glinting wickedly in the new light, rushed down on the Red Clubs, scattering them in all directions. Floyd then ordered his cavalry to sweep the field. In moments, mounted soldiers were among the fleeing Indians, sabering fifteen of those unfortunate warriors who were unable to reach the safety of the swamp. The battle had taken several harrowing hours, and the field on which it was fought was now littered with thirty-seven Indian dead and, as at Autossee, numerous war clubs and headdresses.[184]

Floyd followed up his hard-won victory by organizing a hunt for wounded hostiles, one of whom was Paddy Walsh, whose blood trails they could now make out leading into the swamp. For this coveted task he chose Ford and Captain James Meriwether's riflemen, Hamilton's cavalry, and a party of the friendly Indians. They eagerly pursued the hostiles about a mile before losing them in the swamplands. Meanwhile, most of the friendly Creeks remained behind at the camp, as they had while the militia made its sunrise charge against the Red Clubs. Now these slackers seized on the opportunity afforded by the soldiers' absence to filch the ill-clad men's blankets.[185]

Despite the best efforts of his impromptu hunting party, Floyd reported that they managed to bag only one wounded hostile, and there is good reason to doubt that he made it out of the swamp with his scalp intact. However, twenty-two-year-old Allen Brook of Ford's company claimed that on his way back to the camp, after the pursuit had ended, he encountered a Red Club with a broken leg. He stood over the wounded man and shot him in retaliation for a cousin he claimed had been killed earlier in the battle. The killer then went on his way, passing over a fallen tree whose lower side had been hollowed out by fire. Another Red Club lay hidden there, perhaps planning to aid his stricken comrade until young Brook killed him. When other militia appeared near his hiding place, the Indian panicked, rolled out from under the tree, and fled to the swamp. Shots from the guns of nearby militia cut him to pieces.[186] Days later, scouts found one grave in the swampland enveloping Calebee Creek that held seven Red Club warriors and another grave nearby that held five.[187]

As for the Georgians, Dr. Charles Williamson's after-action casualty report confirmed what they already knew: they had been in an extremely hard fight. Seventeen of the militia had been killed and 132 wounded, many very seriously. One of these, the brave but "imprudent" Captain Butts, later died after much silent suffering.[188] In contrast, their Indian allies lost six killed and fifteen wounded, indicative of their degree of participation in the battle.[189] However, given their treatment of the stiffening bodies of their now-lifeless foes scattered about the battleground, one would think they had won the victory single-handedly. With scalping knives and other sharp-edged weapons, they visited a veritable festival of blood and horror on the bodies of the Red Clubs the Georgia militia had killed.

The Georgians watched with disgust but did nothing as their Indian allies spread out in animated clusters around the fallen Red Clubs and enacted outrages on men they had not dared to face in battle. The usual scalps were swiped from enemy skulls and, with a war cry, raised skyward. The friendlies also lopped off the genitals of the dead, which they took great delight in waving about, as well as the scalped heads of their enemies; these they placed on spears and delightedly paraded about the grounds of Camp Defiance. Also among these trophies was a heart torn from the chest of one fallen warrior and carried on a stick among the exulting Indians. One group of Creek wags found great amusement setting the stiffening corpse of a Red Club warrior on a horse and, as they let go of the body, watching as it fell to the earth. "Whiskey too much," they joked, and repeated the stunt again and again.[190]

The friendly Creeks' bloody celebration on the fresh battleground of Calebee Creek, unchecked by the Georgians, was a harbinger of the coming disorders in Floyd's army. Most of the Americans' Indian allies left for home after the battle with their unearned trophies sliced from the Red Clubs and the blankets pilfered from the militia. The Georgians, however, remained at Camp Defiance under cold and rainy skies until February 1, burying the dead and caring for their many wounded. The soldiers were also put hard at work strengthening the camp's defenses, an exercise one likened to shutting the barn door after the horse has escaped. Meanwhile, hostile Creeks lurked about the place day and night threatening attack, and the Georgians became worn down by the repeated false alarms that left them sleep deprived. It was even rumored that the Red Clubs planned an attack on Fort Mitchell thirty miles to their rear, effectively cutting off Floyd's men from their base. The mere rumor of such an event was enough to send the Big Warrior and Alex Cornells scurrying for protection inside the walls of Fort Mitchell on the night of January 31.[191]

However, like every American army that had invaded the nation since the war began, lack of food was the primary cause for dissension in the ranks. The militia had been on short rations days before the battle; they had no meat, and now even their flour was gone. Several companies threatened to leave for home rather than live on the meager ration of corn they were issued and that in any event they had no means to prepare. This lack of food, coupled with the foul weather and the inadequate homespun clothing, now worn thin, in which the men were dressed, undoubtedly contributed to the fever that erupted among the soldiers such that the sick list at the camp increased "to an alarming degree." Compounding this latest blow to the army was the lack of hospital supplies with which to treat the afflicted.[192]

The men now increasingly looked away from their military duties and toward home, particularly toward the fast-approaching planting season. As Floyd fairly observed, many of his men were poor, and their families depended on their labor for support. Eventually Floyd and his commanders had to adopt Jacksonian tactics to prevent the dissolution of his entire force. When reasoning with the men failed, they called the men to parade, and Floyd threatened severe punishment on those in his army who persisted in their present course of insubordination.[193] But Floyd, unlike Jackson, did not personalize the men's disaffection and did not have his heart in making their lives even more miserable. As for himself, Floyd particularly lamented that he was in no position to assist Jackson, who he had heard had crossed the Coosa River and was marching down its east side. To that end Floyd begged General Pinckney to lend him Colonel Homer Milton's approaching regulars so Floyd could share in the termination of the war.[194]

Personally brave and cool headed amid the worst dangers, John Floyd had reached the nadir of his military career. Still awake at 2:00 A.M. on February 1, Floyd wrote Pinckney from Camp Defiance that he had received word that several companies were determined to desert for Fort Mitchell and that even the Angel Gabriel himself could not stop them. When dawn broke several hours later, and with it a heavy rain that drenched the troops and later reportedly added twenty cases to the army's sick list, Floyd marched his miserable but relieved army out of Camp Defiance and back to Fort Hull, where he intended to remain until he could transport his sick and wounded to Fort Mitchell. On the army's departure from Camp Defiance, the Red Clubs lurking about occupied the abandoned works. They destroyed part of the breastworks and expended a great deal of futile effort digging for the bodies of the eighteen Georgians their comrades had buried deep within the fort's ditch and breastworks. More alarmingly, according to Floyd's spies, the hostiles were now contemplating an attack on Fort Hull.[195]

Not long after the army reached Fort Hull, the temper of the men improved, attributable in no small measure to the seven wagonloads of supplies that had reached the fort and their escape from the miseries and dangers of the pesthole that was Camp Defiance. This development was so welcome that Floyd no longer felt his men would desert before their term of service was up, and he even held out a thin but unrealistic hope that he could persuade them to march once more against the hostiles.[196] Within the month, most of the soldiers would receive their discharge papers, and they now realized it was most unlikely that within the time remaining in their enlistments, Floyd would hazard another foray into the nation. That was finally confirmed on February 16, 1814, when the army left Fort Hull for Fort Mitchell and soon thereafter for home.[197]

Before the army departed from Fort Hull, Floyd asked for volunteers to hold the place until the scheduled arrival of a regiment of troops from North Carolina and another from South Carolina. What remained of Thomas's battered artillery company volunteered to remain, Brodnax was able to raise a company of infantry, and a Lieutenant Adarvin raised a rifle corps in which a young Thomas Woodward volunteered as his orderly with the new rank of sergeant. Just before Floyd departed from Fort Hull, these brave volunteers were reinforced by a very welcomed company of Georgians under the future celebrated general but now merely captain, David Twiggs. Not long after Twiggs arrived, the combative Woodward found himself in the stocks for beating a fellow sergeant senseless. After a short, uncomfortable stay, Woodward was released because, as he later claimed, he was a favorite of Twiggs's.[198]

General Floyd's military career would end sadly. Although he had hoped to continue to command troops against the Red Clubs, that opportunity was taken from him when his army of Georgians essentially evaporated around him. He moved on to command troops in defense of his native Savannah against the British after he and his Georgians were replaced by a new army commanded in the near term by a regular army man, Colonel Homer Milton. This new army consisted of Milton's regiment of US regulars supplemented with militia from North and South Carolina. It remained to be seen, however, whether Milton could cooperate with the irascible General Jackson and the far off Colonel Russell and seize the holy grail of the Creek campaign: the Hickory Ground.

Sadly for Floyd and his shell of an army, they could not catch a break. The long anticipated trip back to Fort Mitchell was not an easy journey for the sick, battered, and hungry men. Rations were "meager" and, although the country abounded in game, Floyd would permit no hunting, probably because of the danger the hunters would be ambushed by the hostiles. Along the way measles broke out among the troops, killing many. One worn out and disgusted soldier, purporting to speak for all, claimed that when the army reached Fort Mitchell, "every soldier" was convinced that the "campaign against the Creek Indians was a complete and total failure."[199] Their initial return to civilian life was no more rewarding. Many of them lost their service pay to con men of the type who were about to descend on the even-more-helpless Muskogee people.[200]

Floyd had a further indignity to endure. Much like General Claiborne in the western theater of the war, Floyd had barely returned home before public criticism of his performance began. A number of his fellow citizens, Benjamin Hawkins prominently among them, felt that Floyd was the general who could have and should have ended the war by now. Instead, in their view, he had accomplished little more than launching two inconclusive expeditions against the Creeks and had returned from his last expedition with a beaten, sick, and disgruntled army.

So substantial was the immediate outcry against Floyd among the public that a number of his officers felt compelled to publish a defense of his generalship in the March 16, 1814, edition of the *Georgia Journal* published in Milledgeville. Their defense was a tepid one. The familiar, and no doubt valid, excuse that a corrupt supply contractor and incompetent quartermaster general had left the army near starvation, or at least without its precious meat, was trotted out—conditions with which Generals Claiborne and Jackson were all too well acquainted. But Floyd's officers also admitted that much had been expected and little achieved by the army, other than two bloody and inconclusive incursions into the nation.[201]

Unfortunately for Floyd, and unbeknownst to his fellow Georgians, he had achieved much more than anyone at the time believed. If Calebee was a tactical success for the Red Clubs, strategically it was a disaster. Once again they had driven the Georgians from the nation, and this time they had lost fewer men in the fight (Stiggins claims that forty Red Clubs were killed, including, incorrectly, High Head Jim) and inflicted considerably more casualties on Floyd's army than at Autossee, and all without the loss of a village, much less an important town. Despite these successes, however, the Battle of Calebee Creek seemed to take the heart out of the prophets' movement and wither the fighting spirit of the Red Clubs in the southern reaches of the nation.[202] Fatally, two months later, they failed to support their brothers' upriver Coosa and Tallapoosa settlements at the most critical time in the nation's history.

The hostile Creeks remained at Camp Defiance for several days and then departed without further assaults on Floyd's demoralized army.[203] And although attacks on the settlers far to the south in the Tensaw country continued, these affairs were small and isolated events involving lonely plantations or farms. Thirty years later, too late to help Floyd's near-term reputation, the Creek author George Stiggins described the effect of the Battle of Calebee Creek on the Red Clubs: "The defeat at Calabee was fatal to the hostiles. It closed the hostile operations of the lower towns and finally broke up the unity of the hostiles and their ability to organize for hostile purposes. The defeat silenced the old and new war dance and whoop of many of their most conspicuous warriors. None of the lower-town chiefs ever entered the battlefield after the Calabee affair; they appeared to be paralyzed and inattentive to national affairs."[204]

One reason for the reluctance of these Red Clubs to continue prosecution of the war may also be found in a report by Hawkins to Pinckney dated February 16, 1814. In it Hawkins reported that his sources had informed him that the governor of Pensacola, Gonzalez Manrique, had informed a group of chiefs from twelve Seminole towns that the Spanish would no longer supply ammunition to the Red Clubs. Manrique had urged these chiefs to support the "Old Chiefs" in crushing the prophets' party, which the governor claimed had deceived the nation with lies. Manrique was also said to have advised the Creeks not to rely on the British for assistance, that the British had deceived them before and likely would do so again; that the British would never drive the Americans from the South. Although it is unlikely that Manrique had made such remarks about Spain's British allies, what was certainly true was that unless the Spanish and/or British immediately supplied the Creeks with a virtual cornucopia of ammunition and reinforced them with at least British advisers, if not troops, and British artillery, the Red Clubs had little hope of putting up effective long-term resistance against the well-armed and more numerous Americans.[205] What the Red Clubs did not know was that this sort of critical aid, destined for them, was sailing toward the Gulf Coast of Florida. In a few months it would arrive, if they could just hold out against the Americans until then.

In the event, even had Floyd been able to resoundingly defeat the Red Clubs, he would never have been able to meet up with Jackson at the source of the Alabama River and end the war. For unbeknownst to Floyd at the time, far to the north Jackson and his army were desperately fighting their way out of the Okfuskee country in retreat to their base at Fort Strother on the upper Coosa. The Red Clubs of the Tallapoosa towns may have been chastened by the battle at Calebee Creek, but their northern brothers, almost certainly under the leadership of an Okfuskee mixed-blood chief known as Menawa, had used the tactics espoused by Weatherford in council just before the Calebee fight with devastating effect on the Tennesseans.

As for Weatherford himself, he returned to the Creek refuge at Moniac's Island on the Alabama River not far downstream from the obliterated Holy Ground. When his sulk passed, he resumed the guerrilla war along the lower Alabama and the Tensaw lands that he had conducted in that region in the fall. General Claiborne had returned home from this theater of the war, and Weatherford's new opponent was the apparently more formidable (at least in his own mind) Colonel Gilbert Russell, headquartered at Fort Claiborne. Weatherford's task was to prevent Russell from moving up the Alabama with men and supplies and joining the Tennesseans and Georgians at the Hickory Ground. The tactics he employed against the Americans took him off the main stages of the war. They involved small units of men and sharp, nasty woodland fights that kept the settlers from returning to their lands and kept Russell's army penned up in the vicinity of Fort Claiborne. However, the notorious Weatherford would make one last dramatic and memorable appearance on what was destined to be the biggest stage of the war. It would not be as spectacular as his horseback leap from the bluff at the Holy Ground, or as destructive as his attack on Fort Mims, but it would win him even more renown down through the centuries in the white world.

8. JACKSON OVERREACHES

The Winter of Jackson's Discontent

B Y the end of 1813, the Red Clubs had survived assaults from the Georgians, Mississippians, and Tennesseans. For almost three months, however, their greatest threat had remained strangely inactive. General Jackson's pleasure at his triumph at Talladega evaporated almost immediately on his return to the army's encampment at Ten Islands on November 11, 1813. The provisions he had counted on had not arrived, and the men were largely subsisting on some scrawny cattle. Not only were Jackson's battle-weary soldiers surviving on subsistence rations, but they also lacked proper clothing to ward off the increasingly foul weather. Within twenty-four hours of their arrival at Fort Strother, most of the volunteers and militia were on the verge of mutiny.[1]

Jackson put up a brave front to encourage his men. He had given the wounded the personal supplies that he had purchased for himself and his staff. He and his staff even conspicuously dined on the offal remaining after the army's cattle had been slaughtered—Jackson pronouncing it delicious as well as healthy. The story was even reported that a starving enlisted man found Jackson resting under a tree chewing a mouthful of food. The man piteously begged Jackson for some food to alleviate his hunger. Smiling, Jackson said he would be pleased to share his food with a fellow soldier. Rummaging through his coat pocket, Jackson produced a handful of acorns. Take some, Jackson told the man, this is the only food I have.[2] But while this soldier was sharing the general's acorns, others were so desperate for food they were picking kernels of corn from horse dung, then parching and eating it.[3]

But Jackson's best attempts to encourage his men quickly fell short. His feigned cheerfulness was not a meal on which his army could sup. They had been without proper food for many days and saw no prospect of relief in the near future. Within a day's arrival at the encampment, the serious unrest percolating among the troops manifested itself in petitions to Jackson from the army's various brigades setting forth their "privations and sufferings." With such remonstrances coming one day after the army's return to its base, it is clear that dissatisfaction in the ranks had been simmering for some weeks and that the lack of provisions at Fort Strother was merely a flame to the tinder of the army's unrest. Jackson's secretary, John Reid, claimed that the quickly spreading discord among the troops was the work of politically motivated officers among the volunteers. According to Reid, they abused their status as men who had served longest under Jackson to goad the militia to act as a stalking horse to achieve their ambition to march out of camp toward home at the head of their grateful men.[4]

The first petition was delivered to Jackson on November 12. It came from the officers of the mounted riflemen. Their petition prudently began by reminding Jackson that his soldiers had penetrated seventy-one miles and more into the Creek Nation and routed every group of Indians they had encountered. Now, after these exertions, they were without food, the clothing necessary for a winter campaign, or horses to carry them. The riflemen respectfully asked Jackson to allow them to return home, where they could obtain these essential items. Once they had obtained the necessities for a winter campaign, the men promised to return to duty on Jackson's call.[5]

The riflemen's petition was the first salvo in two months of unrelenting and impossibly bitter internecine warfare between Jackson and his soldiers as Jackson and his few loyalists in the army struggled to hold the army together. Similar petitions from other units were presented to Jackson the following day. He was particularly grieved that one of them came from perhaps his favorite unit: the 2nd Regiment of Tennessee volunteers. These men had been with him during the terrible march from Natchez to Nashville the previous winter. Now this regiment added its voice to the clamor of unrest spreading among the soldiery. In a letter dated November 13, 1813, signed by the 2nd Regiment's officers, the officers informed Jackson that their men were starving, many were bare-footed, half-naked, and without even blankets. The officers suggested that at the very least, as a "stimulus to the men," Jackson should inform the soldiers of their discharge date.[6]

Despite the recent arrival of forty-five cattle, which Jackson had hoped would allay the men's distress, the storm of discontent among the troops finally broke that afternoon on the incredulous Jackson. The militia, who Reid believed had been aroused by the machinations of officers from the volunteers, acted first and prepared to move out of camp. Some men among the volunteers alerted Jackson of the militia's intentions. He immediately formed up the volunteers to block the road leading north from the fort. These men forced the rebellious militia back into camp. Now it was the volunteers' turn. Shortly after they had quelled the militia's revolt, the volunteers themselves decided to leave the fort for home. Jackson had little trouble enlisting the betrayed militias to block the volunteers' route home and to force them back to quarters.[7]

Thus far, the tempestuous Jackson had been remarkably restrained in the face of the "mutinous disposition" among his troops that threatened an inglorious termination to his campaign against the Creeks. The unexpected outburst among his soldiers seems to have stunned him. Even after the charade between the volunteers and the militia, Jackson moved cautiously. On November 14, he called a council of all of the field officers and captains in his army. Jackson informed them that on the best of authority, an enormous quantity of corn meal, flour, and hogs were at Fort Deposit and would be at Fort Strother in a day or so. He reminded the officers that the army had already sent its wagons to Fort Deposit for the supplies. If they left for home now, they would have no means to transport their baggage and would necessarily have to abandon it. More importantly, without the wagons, they would have to abandon to the terrible mercies of the Red Clubs the wounded and the rapidly growing list of sick men. Finally, Jackson appealed to the soldiers' patriotism and sense of honor to persuade them to continue the campaign. He then dismissed the officers with instructions that they meet among themselves, consider his words in private, and report back to him the results of their deliberations.[8] Not yet realizing how serious his army's disgruntlement had become, Jackson thought it would easily be cured by the arrival of the abundant provisions he had been told were on their way from Fort Deposit.

That evening, Jackson received answers from the three brigades. Not surprisingly, his friend General Coffee returned an answer first, then General Roberts, and finally General Hall. The answers were not promising. Coffee and Roberts advised Jackson that their men were willing to wait several days for the promised supplies to arrive. If they did not appear within that time, these generals advised Jackson that to avoid mutiny, they would have to march their men north to meet the provisions. But the 1st Brigade of Tennessee Volunteer Infantry, commanded by General Hall, was not willing to wait even another day. That evening the brigade delivered a letter to Jackson that was signed "Chairman" by a very brave Colonel William Martin, who commanded the brigade's 2nd Regiment. In Martin's letter, the brigade's officers advised Jackson that "nothing short of marching the army back to the settlements will prevent that disgrace which must attend the desertion of the Camp by the soldiery." In its petition, the brigade explained to Jackson, in respectful terms, that the soldiers' desire to return home was understandably based on the "scarcity of provisions" and the men's lack of proper clothing for a winter campaign.[9]

Colonel Martin was another of the capable officers serving under Jackson with substantial experience in Indian warfare. When the first white settlements were taking root in eastern Tennessee, Martin commanded a company of soldiers from North Carolina whose mission was to protect the settlements from Indian attack. He served in that post for two years and was said to have been cool and brave under fire. Some years after his tour of duty, Martin returned to settle in Tennessee. He entered politics and was elected a member of the state legislature. In 1804 and 1808, he served as a presidential elector, voting for Jefferson and Madison. In 1807, he was appointed one of the commissioners to settle land claims in the state. In late 1812, he joined Jackson's abortive expedition to Louisiana as a major of the 2nd Regiment of volunteers. In September 1813, he was a member of the committee in Nashville responsible for formulating a military response to the Red Club attack on Fort Mims. In that position he assisted in the raising of troops for Jackson's expedition in the Creek Nation and served in that expedition as well, fighting bravely at the Battle of Talladega. He and Jackson were on good terms, but the good relationship between the two men suddenly foundered over the issue of the term of the volunteers' enlistments.

On the heels of the 1st Infantry Brigade's letter, General Hall personally reported to Jackson that his brigade was determined to march out that day to meet the supply train. Hall further warned Jackson that after they received the supplies, his men wanted Jackson to permit them to return home with an honorable discharge. Ominously, Hall reported that if Jackson refused that request, they would return home without his permission. All the brigade commanders, he informed Jackson, vowed to remain with him whatever their men might do.[10]

Jackson was able to persuade his soldiers, except for the 1st Regiment of Hall's brigade of volunteers, to wait a few days for the provisions to arrive. He had received word that ample provisions were on their way from Fort Deposit and gambled they would arrive before it became necessary to keep his promise to his men to allow them to depart camp. Jackson's assurances did not satisfy the 1st Regiment of volunteers, however, who marched out of camp unmolested on November 15 headed for Fort Deposit, where they arrived, half-starved and sick, after marching through a cold and constant rain and over the two mountain ranges between Fort Strother and Fort Deposit.[11] Half of Coffee's men left Fort Strother that same day for Fort Deposit as well, but with Coffee's permission. Given the poor condition of his men's horses and the lack of fodder in the area, Coffee had ordered that the men travel north to the Huntsville countryside to find forage for their starving mounts.[12]

On November 17, when the promised supplies still had not arrived, Jackson reluctantly marched his remaining soldiers toward Fort Deposit. The soldiers' spirits rose as they stepped off on the road toward home. Behind him, Jackson left around 150 men under command of the steady and dependable Colonel Carroll to guard the sick and wounded and to complete the construction of the fort.[13]

About twelve miles from Fort Strother, Jackson and his disgruntled troops met the promised convoy coming toward them with 150 cattle and nine wagons of flour. The arrival of these stores gave Jackson the excuse he needed to order his men back to the fort. But the men viewed the supplies with mixed emotions. They welcomed the food, but they did not welcome returning to Fort Strother as they had promised Jackson they would do. Once fed, the soldiers simply decided to go home. One company was already well down the road before Jackson knew it. Apprised that his soldiers had begun an exodus for home, Jackson gathered a few aides, took a shortcut across a field, and soon reached a spot on the road just ahead of the unsuspecting mutineers. Coffee and a small force from his brigade were already there. Jackson arrayed his tiny command across the road and waited.

The mutineers soon appeared and pulled up short of Jackson and his men. In the face of this small but determined force and under the lash of Jackson' curses and dependable threats of violence, the company of mutineers gave way and made a quick retreat back to their encampment. There they found that the camp was quickly breaking up, as the main body of troops prepared for a return march home themselves. On receiving this report, Jackson rode alone to the encampment to ascertain the situation. When he arrived he found himself face to face with a far greater problem than he had just resolved: virtually his entire army was leaving for home.[14]

In an instant Jackson realized that his campaign against the Creeks was about to come to an ignominious and inglorious end. Jackson was nothing if not decisive. He leaned down from his horse and, with his good arm, snatched a musket from a surprised soldier. He then turned the animal into the middle of the mutineers' road home. Because his wounded arm was in a sling, he lay the borrowed musket across the withers of his horse and pointed the weapon at the men. At the top of his lungs he screamed out that he would kill the first man who attempted to pass.[15]

Not a man doubted that Jackson would shoot to kill. He had done so many times over the course of his life with much less provocation. But his reputation as a killer and a man without any known fear could not have saved him. Hundreds of angry men were all around him—to his front and to his side. It would have been an easy matter for someone concealed in the crowd —many were in pistol range—to have shot him with no immediate risk to themselves. But something stayed the hand of the coward, the assassin, and the men who had killed or wounded hundreds of Creek men, women, and children over the past month.[16] There was something unearthly, and unfathomable, something that went beyond ordinary human experience, in the apparition before them. It gave them pause, and in that pause, what probably saved Jackson, even from those wicked souls among the crowd willing to kill their own mothers for a twist of tobacco, was the realization that in the very near future they were certain to receive death at the hands of Jackson's numerous friends and admirers on the frontier. Essentially, Andrew Jackson was untouchable.[17]

Finally, the seemingly endless moment passed. Coffee and Reid rode up to Jackson's side, and though there were additional anxious moments when the two groups stared one another down like duelists on the precipice of combat, other of Jackson's officers were able to assemble two companies of men still loyal to the general and form them up behind him and his two friends.[18] The crisis passed and, with some choice words from Jackson urging them on, the putative mutineers slunk back to their camp. As one officer, a Captain Burlison, who was present at the affair exclaimed, "there is not such a man in the world—for one man with one arm to stop a whole brigade! He is the most undaunted being in creation."[19]

While his men returned to Fort Strother, Jackson continued on with General Coffee and Major Searcy to Fort Deposit. There, what he intended to be a several days visit lasted until the end of November while he badgered the sorry and slippery contractors to ensure they produced a steady stream of supplies for his men.

Nature also conspired to make Jackson's life difficult. Aside from the contractors' infuriating incompetence, general bumbling, and outright thievery—Jackson declared that the chief US contractor for Tennessee, Barclay McGhee, should be "scourged"—the lines of mountainous terrain between Forts Deposit and Strother that rose and dipped like a series of enormous waves and the rainy weather that swelled the intervening creeks greatly complicated the transportation of supplies south.[20] Meanwhile his army continued to disintegrate from sickness and desertion. It was during this period that John Reid noticed, for what he believed was the first time in the general's life, that Jackson was despondent.[21]

When Jackson's unhappy brigades reached the Ten Islands they were greeted with an almost-completed structure consisting of a stockade and blockhouses and named Fort Strother in honor of Jackson's topographer. The energetic Carroll and his men, encouraged by the threat of a Red Club assault on the place, had worked wonders in construction.

But trouble among the troops emerged once again, this time in the form of "strong symptoms of mutiny" involving the 1st Brigade of the Tennessee Volunteer Infantry, the unit Jackson thought his finest and most loyal soldiers.[22] As Carroll reported to Jackson on November 20, the men of this unit, encouraged by their officers, had gotten it into their heads that under the terms of their service they were due to be discharged by December 10.[23] They claimed that in 1812, they had enrolled in the army for a year's service. That year was up December 10, 1813, and whether Jackson liked it or not, they intended to leave for home by then.

Jackson was back at Fort Strother by the beginning of December and a few days later received formal notice of the volunteers' intent to depart on December 10. It came in the form of a hand-delivered letter from the importunate Colonel Martin of the 2nd Volunteer Regiment. Martin's letter was essentially a lawyerly and respectful discourse over the meaning of the word *discharge* in the context of his men's length of service. But the tone of the letter set off the inveterate lawyer in Jackson, who stooped to quibbling at great length over the meaning of the terms *dismissal* and *discharge*. The vituperation in the correspondence between the two men, who seemed to forget that they were in a military campaign and not in a court of law, escalated to such a degree that on December 8, Martin wrote Jackson a letter in which he essentially called him a liar.[24] And there the matter stood until the evening of December 9, when Jackson found himself faced with what John Reid described as a serious manifestation of the "ungovernable spirit of the men."[25]

Around nine o'clock that night, according to Reid, the commander of the 1st Brigade of volunteers, General Hall, burst into Jackson's tent and breathlessly informed him that a full-blown mutiny had broken out among his brigade and that the men were at that moment preparing to march for home.[26] One of the officers, a Colonel Douglas, however, tells a different story. According to Douglas, Hall maintained that he did not inform Jackson that his brigade was about to leave camp but rather that the men were insisting that their term of service ended the following day. In fact, at that moment, most of the brigade was asleep and, other than the sleepwalkers among them, were in no position or mood to leave camp that night.[27]

Perhaps spurred on by men among his personal staff such as John Reid, and not one burdened in a crisis by indecision, Jackson at once issued orders that the officers of the 1st Infantry Brigade of Volunteers assemble their men on the parade ground on the west side of the fort by 9:00 P.M., where Jackson planned to have them disarmed.[28] As the hundreds of grumbling, half-asleep veterans formed into ranks, they found that Jackson was ready for them. To their front and rear squatted cannon charged with canister. On the high ground above them Jackson had placed his unit of militia. The hard-eyed fighters of Captain John Gordon's spy company looked down at them from horseback. On horseback near them, between the mutineers and the cannon to their front, was Jackson. As fond as he was of these soldiers—whom he sadly confessed to his wife, Rachel, several days later that he "once loved like a father loves his children"—Jackson was in no mood to tolerate mutiny of any sort, even a phantom of one.[29]

For a time he rode along the brigade's lines, pausing before each company to address the men, praising their past conduct and condemning their present behavior; the men, however, apparently chose to hear only the latter.[30] Jackson informed the soldiers that he had asked Governor Blount for his opinion on their discharge date and expected a reply shortly. All he was asking was that they remain at Fort Strother until then or at least until Colonel Carroll or Major Searcy arrived with reinforcements. Jackson informed them, however, that he was "done with intreaty." Either they returned to their quarters or he would take extreme measures to force them to do so.[31]

Not a man of the mutinous brigade stirred. Frustrated, Jackson demanded a response from them. The men remained silent. Determined to break this stalemate, Jackson ordered his artillery men manning the two cannon to light their matches. With a thin hiss, fire leaped into the dark from the point of a long matchstick and illuminated the cannon muzzle behind Jackson. The general hesitated before moving to the side and giving the order to fire. The soldiers knew Jackson too well to push him any further. They began murmuring along their lines that they should do as he ordered. Shortly thereafter, a group of their officers approached Jackson and advised that they were returning their men to camp and awaiting the arrival of the new recruits under Carroll or Searcy.[32]

Although Jackson had "quelled" their mutiny for a time, he was reluctantly "for reasons of policy" forced to permit the volunteer infantry brigade to return to Nashville. He wrote Blount on December 12 about this disheartening situation and advised the governor to discharge the troops on their arrival in Nashville, as Jackson had no authority to do so. Jackson did make a last attempt to persuade the brigade to remain with him, and, true to his word, the following morning, December 13, he had the brigade's officers assemble their men on the parade ground, where curiously he had John Reid read them a passionately written appeal to stay.[33] The brigade, led by General Hall, left the following day, arriving at Fayetteville, Tennessee, on December 25. There Blount dismissed the unit pending further orders from the secretary of war.[34]

Jackson was so dismayed and astonished by the conduct of these soldiers, whose fighting abilities he genuinely admired, that after their departure he wrote Rachel that his men seemed bewitched: "The Phisic of the indian prophets must have curiously worked upon them to occasion those men, once so brave, once so patriotic to conduct so strangely and so disgracefully to themselves and country."[35]

If anyone in the affair was bewitched, it was Jackson. He had allowed what had begun as a reasonable complaint by a starving, ill-equipped but victorious army about supplies to escalate into a virtual mutiny among most of his command. Not long after the army's return from Talladega to Fort Strother, it should have been evident to Jackson that his campaign against the Creeks could not continue without an adequate system of supply and the recruitment of fresh, well-equipped troops. Jackson's response to his troops' discontent was more that of a brawler than a leader of men, with predictable consequences. His amateurish management of the crisis stands in stark contrast to that of Confederate general Robert E. Lee's management fifty years later of the same sort of men fighting against greater odds under equally trying conditions. "Lee's Miserables," they proudly called themselves, and however they might grumble, they followed their general into and through hell. But unlike Jackson, Lee had the loyalty of an army, Jackson only the loyalty of his friends.[36]

Worse was yet to come for Jackson and his steadily dwindling army. The horses of General Coffee's brigade of cavalry and mounted soldiers were so worn out that on November 22, Jackson had been forced to send the one-thousand-man brigade back to the settlements to "recruit their horses" and obtain proper clothing for a winter campaign. They were to return to Huntsville County around December 8 and from there ride on to Fort Deposit to await Jackson's orders.[37] Coffee duly assembled his brigade on the men's return to Huntsville and, pursuant to Jackson's recent order, sent them on to Fort Deposit under his senior officers. Unfortunately, the usually robust General Coffee was not a well man. He had left his home for the campaign against the Creeks with an unidentified medical condition, perhaps malaria, which became increasingly "aggravated" over the weeks until now he was unable to sit a horse.[38] On the morning of December 17, 1813, obeying what he thought was Jackson's order, Coffee ordered his mounted brigade to ride to Fort Strother, where Coffee believed Jackson wanted them to join General Cocke's East Tennesseans for a campaign against the Creeks before their term of service expired.[39]

Senior officers in Coffee's regiment of mounted men had recently advised him that the regiment believed they had enlisted for only three months, and that they, therefore, intended to return home at the expiration of that period, December 24. Likewise, officers of Coffee's other regiment—the volunteer cavalry—predicted that when their regiment encountered the volunteer infantry already on their way home from Fort Strother, the cavalry regiment would surely leave on the twenty-fourth with the regiment of mounted men.[40]

Coffee was fast losing control over his men. Around December 16, a mob of troops stationed in Huntsville rioted, harassing the local citizens they were there to protect from the Creeks. Coffee placed a number of the rioting soldiers in jail, but their fellow soldiers stormed the Huntsville jail and forced the jailer, on pain of death, to release the prisoners.[41] The seriously ill Coffee was on the mend but still physically unable to act with his usual authority and decisiveness and stop the riot.[42] In any event, so great were the soldiers' numbers and even greater their determination to see home that even a healthy Coffee would have been powerless to prevent their departure. And still Coffee's troubles with his subordinates were not yet over.

On December 20, Colonel Alcorn wrote Coffee that he would remain at Fort Deposit with his brigade until ordered forward to Fort Strother. However, he repeated to Coffee his prior warning to Jackson that the entire brigade was determined to decamp on the twenty-fourth. That same day, the other officer in command of Coffee's other regiment, Colonel Allen, also wrote Coffee, advising him that the brigade expected its discharge on the twenty-fourth and urging Coffee to persuade Jackson to grant their wish.[43]

About that time, however, Coffee, still recuperating in Huntsville, was finally able to provide Jackson with some good news. On December 20, the same day Coffee's colonels wrote him of the brigade's resolution to leave the service, Coffee informed Jackson that Colonel Carroll was on his way from his recruiting trip to Nashville with around one thousand mounted men, that General Roberts was in Huntsville with two hundred men, and that he had also received a dubious report that Colonel Nicholas Perkins had been able to raise about 250 "motley" mounted troops from Madison County. Thus, as Coffee summarized to Jackson, in Coffee's "quarter" he had 700 men at Fort Deposit, 150 soldiers from an assortment of broken companies in the Huntsville area, plus Roberts's 200 recruits and Carroll's one thousand men for a total of 2,050 effectives. As for his own brigade, an embarrassed Coffee had to confess to Jackson, "I am really ashamed to say any thing about the men of my Brigade doing any thing, ever again," particularly now that they had met up with the men of the homebound volunteer infantry brigade. Coffee further lamented to Jackson that his men had paid no attention to his orders, and he asked Jackson for advice on how to handle the situation.[44]

Finally, a reluctant Jackson acted. On the morning of the twenty-third, he transmitted to Coffee's brigade's senior officers a copy of Blount's letter of December 15 expressing the governor's opinion that the troops should be discharged. On the twenty-fifth, Jackson sent a lengthy rejoinder, written in a lawyerly fashion, to the various letters he had received from officers in Coffee's brigade in which the men set forth the reasons they believed the brigade was entitled to a discharge on the twenty-fourth.[45] Nonetheless, as Coffee's commanders had predicted, the germ of mutiny now spread among Coffee's own brigade as the volunteer infantry passed through Madison County on their way home. The cavalry arm of that brigade was part of the volunteers who had enlisted in 1812. Having learned that their fellow enlistees in the infantry were being marched home on the grounds that their one-year enlistment had expired, the cavalrymen naturally decided that their enlistment also had expired. Following the same reasoning, Coffee's regiment of mounted solders, who had enlisted on December 24, 1812, decided to leave for home when their year was up. But as the new year began, Jackson's military situation began to improve.

David Crockett: Masterful self-promoter who served several months under Andrew Jackson during the Creek War and afterwards became his political foe. (*Tennessee State Library and Archives*)

Sam Houston: His reckless bravery at the Battle of Horseshoe Bend almost cost him his life. (*Library of Congress*)

Andrew Jackson quelling mutinous volunteer troops, December 1813. (*Library of Congress*)

Battle of Enitachopco Creek, January 24, 1814. (*Tennessee State Library and Archives*)

The Battle of Horseshoe Bend, March 27, 1814. (*New York Public Libary*)

Jackson Finds an Army

O N December 12, the day before Jackson's veterans of the 1st Brigade of Tennessee Volunteer Infantry marched out of Fort Strother, the general's anxieties about his long-stalled campaign were somewhat relieved when a large number of reinforcements marched into camp. The first week of December, Jackson had sent an express to his rival General Cocke at Fort Armstrong ordering him to march his command to Fort Strother and join Jackson by December 12. Cocke's army of some 1,450 east Tennessee troops started for Fort Strother on the eighth. Their march was slowed by the numerous high-running streams in their path. On the eleventh, Cocke's command hit on the trace cut by Jackson from Fort Deposit to Fort Strother, and it then made better progress.

On Sunday the twelfth, Cocke and his men marched into Jackson's camp. Jackson saluted the welcome arrivals with three blasts from a cannon. In their honor he had also drawn up on the parade ground several lines of his soldiers. To the newcomers they were not an encouraging sight. One of Cocke's officers, with only rudimentary spelling abilities, observed that Jackson's soldiers "Loocked verey bad In general." Cocke's men soon found that the situation at the camp mirrored the appearance of Jackson's men. Confusion reigned supreme—"ther could hardeley bee aney think bee Dune for Cursing and Swearing amongst the men." Cocke's men, too, began to suffer from a lack of food. "We have nothing Cuck in but one tine bucket for all my Companey, and we Sufer much at this time. I Seeme much Disturbed in my mind to See So much Raskality Caried on and men Sufering on account of it."[46]

But the arrival of Cocke and his army was a cruel tease for Jackson. Cocke informed a dismayed Jackson that one of Cocke's regiment's enlistments expired on December 23 and another's on December 29, and the enlistments of Cocke's remaining men, the 2nd Regiment of East Tennessee Volunteers under Colonel William Lillard, expired on January 14, 1814.[47] Jackson ordered his adjunct general, Francis Huger, to provide him with a tally of the troops under Jackson's command. As of December 13, Huger reported 876 men in General Roberts's brigade, 48 men in the artillery company, and 47 spies, for a total of 971 men. Coffee's brigade of cavalry and mounted soldiers was listed at 1,000 men. Cocke's division totaled 1,608 infantry and 300 mounted men. All of these units totaled 3,879 soldiers, more than enough troops to protect the forts while concomitantly invading the Creek Nation. Huger's report, however, also contained some ominous notations. Roberts's brigade was supposed to be "engaged for six months"; the enlistments of all of Major General Cocke's Division were supposed to expire by January 14, 1814.[48]

On December 15, to replace these coming losses, Jackson ordered Cocke to return to east Tennessee, recruit one thousand five hundred men, and arrange for substantial supplies to be forwarded downriver to Jackson.[49] He also instructed Cocke to order General White and his two regiments under Colonels Ware and Brown to return to Tennessee as soon as they were ready to march. Some weeks earlier, Jackson had taken the precaution of sending the reliable Colonel Carroll to the west Tennessee settlements to try his hand at recruitment. By early December, the diligent Carroll was advertising in the local papers for recruits and promising pardons for deserters who rejoined the militia.

It was fortunate for Cocke, who departed Fort Strother for Tennessee on the fifteenth, that he left when he did. Several days later, Jackson received a copy of the order Cocke wrote to White before the Battle of Talladega countermanding Jackson's order to White to join him at the Ten Islands and directing White to return to Fort Armstrong. From that moment on, Cocke joined the long list of the unforgiving Jackson's mortal enemies. That letter, as far as Jackson was concerned, fully solved the mysterious retrograde of White on the eve of the Battle of Talladega. But Jackson's manifold present difficulties required him to postpone for now his vengeance on Cocke for his "underhanded efforts" to sabotage Jackson's campaign against the Creeks. Sounding like a Mafia don, Jackson wrote William Berkeley Lewis, his deputy quartermaster, on December 19 that Cocke's treachery "is noted and will in due time be attended to."[50]

Late that same evening, as the light from the taper on his camp desk faded, Jackson wrote Blount begging the governor to raise additional troops. In that letter Jackson also expressed his concern to Blount that Coffee's brigade of cavalry and mounted men would be "infected" with the mutinous spirit of General Hall's brigade of volunteer infantry as that unit marched through the Huntsville region on its way back to Tennessee and that he would lose those men as well. Nonetheless, Jackson vowed to the governor, he would not desert his post no matter how few men remained to him unless General Pinckney ordered it.[51]

Shortly after the first of Cocke's troops left Fort Strother for Tennessee, Jackson began to receive complaints from his Cherokee allies about various depredations the homebound east Tennesseans were committing on Cherokee property as they marched through Cherokee lands. Path Killer wrote Jackson on December 28 that the returning troops took eight horses from a Cherokee warrior named the Whooping Boy who had fought with the Americans at Tallushatchee and at Talladega, where he was seriously wounded. When other of Cocke's men passed through the farm of John Ratliff, the mixed-blood Cherokee at whose home David Crockett spent the night in the first weeks of the war, the soldiers stole his slaves and around twenty horses, and for good measure took Ratliff prisoner on suspicion of conspiring with the Red Clubs. At the home of John Brown, a prominent Cherokee war leader, the Tennesseans killed his hogs, stole money from his wife, burned down his chimney, and made campfires with his fence rails and various lumber they found on his property.[52] Less prominent Cherokees likely suffered even worse indignities and depredations at the hands of Cocke's troops.

When Jackson received this news, which further fueled his animosity against Cocke, he exploded with outrage. He immediately wrote a lengthy letter to Cocke demanding that Ratliff be released, his property returned to him, and everyone involved in the depredations against the Cherokees be arrested and tried. Jackson, who admired bravery in whatever color it came, was particularly incensed at the treatment accorded the Whooping Boy. His letter also conveyed a practical concern: the short-handed Americans could not risk alienating the powerful Cherokee Nation, which had proved many times over to be loyal and effective allies.[53]

Christmas Eve had brought further, if minor, trials on the beleaguered general. Late that night and contrary to orders, all but one company of soldiers began discharging their guns in celebration. No doubt alcohol was involved, because even the officers participated in the frolic. The firing began two hours before dawn, with cannons briefly joining in, and continued until the sun rose. Jackson was furious at the waste of powder and the undisciplined behavior of his army, but all he could do was fume and threaten to cashier officers who were beyond caring. On Christmas morning, the men were rewarded for their behavior with hours of drill. But there was some cheer in the day. After drill, a group of officers organized a game of "town ball"—a crude precursor of modern baseball—as entertainment.[54]

With Jackson's army evaporating around him, he received some welcome news from Colonel Carroll on December 23. Twenty days earlier, Jackson had dispatched Carroll to west Tennessee to recruit a body of new troops. The task had not been easy. Jackson's political enemies, men of "influential character," as Carroll put it, as well as members of the public whose minds had been "poisoned" by the returning volunteers, had hampered Carroll's best efforts to obtain enlistments.[55] However, on December 23, Carroll was able to write Jackson from Huntsville that he had procured the services of around six hundred mounted men, mostly well equipped. That was the good news. The bad news was that the men had only enlisted for sixty days, not much time to organize and mount a campaign against the Red Clubs.[56] Jackson was, of course, furious at this condition, but there was nothing he could do but complain to Blount and Pinckney, neither of whom were able to provide any remedy.

New Year's Eve ushered in even more troubles for the beleaguered general, who by now must have been close to his tipping point. He had perhaps found a way to persuade his last remaining body of militia to remain in service. It depended on his friend Willie Blount. Jackson's view was that because the militiamen had "been accepted" on their enlistment into the service of the United States, under federal law they must serve six months; the men insisted they had been called by the state of Tennessee for three months. Jackson, and with Jackson's permission the commanders of the brigade's two regiments, Colonel John Wynne and Major Anthony Turner, had earlier put the question to Governor Blount for his decision.[57]

In the waning days of perhaps the longest December through which Jackson had ever lived, his friend Blount hit him with several body blows in the form of letters that left Jackson reeling. Jackson had written to Blount seeking to obtain the governor's official opinion on whether the militia had been called out for three months or six months. The squirming Blount, who was beset by returning soldiers and their friends complaining about Jackson's manifold tyrannies, evasively parried Jackson's question by proclaiming that he had no authority to discharge the militiamen because they served under the authority of the United States.[58] Finally in a letter dated December 26, 1813, which Jackson received late in the afternoon of December 31, the cornered Blount admitted that assuming he had the authority to decide the question (which he iterated with comic repetitiveness throughout his correspondence that he did not), he believed the soldiers should be discharged from duty after three months subject to a ruling on the question from Secretary of War Armstrong.[59]

Blount's answer to the question of the militias' term of service was an unexpected betrayal, but it was the second of two letters that Blount wrote Jackson on December 22 that almost ruined their friendship and certainly rocked Jackson to his core.[60] In that letter, Blount foolishly advised Jackson to abandon Fort Strother and return to Tennessee, where he could build a new army; it was tantamount to asking Jackson himself to become a deserter. Jackson exploded. In his lengthy, angry, and anguished reply to Blount's suggestion, he roundly castigated the governor for inaction in raising troops for Jackson's projected campaign into the Creek Nation and in listening to a "dastardly and designing crew" of "wretches" who would desert Blount and hang the blame on him when their schemes resulted in disaster. Jackson exhorted Blount to act like a man. There are times in political life, Jackson lectured Blount, "when it is highly criminal to shrink from responsibility, or scruple about the exercise of our powers. There are times, when we must disregard punctilious etiquette, and think only of serving our country."[61] As for Blount's suggestion that Jackson abandon his line of forts and retreat to Tennessee to regroup, the general's refusal was both emphatic and melodramatic: "What! Retrograde under such circumstances! I will perish first. No, I will do my duty: I will hold the posts I have established, until ordered to abandon them by the commanding general, or die in the struggle;—long since I have determined, not to seek the preservation of life, at the sacrifice of reputation."[62] It remained to be seen what effect Jackson's letter would have on the cautious Blount, but, at the moment, the governor probably felt he had just had his ears roundly boxed.

When Colonel Wynn and Major Turner read the governor's letter to the militia, the men decided to march home on January 4, 1814.[63] But before that happened, a tragedy among the brigade was averted only by the narrowest of margins.

Much like Benjamin Hawkins's experience the previous spring in trying to control the Creeks, when Jackson had dealt with one crisis among his soldiers, another immediately popped up. On January 4, 1814, Major William Bradley of the 2nd Regiment of General Roberts's brigade who was officer of the day, was walking the lines occupied by the 1st Regiment of that brigade. Bradley observed that not only was the officer of the guard of that regiment absent from his post but that no sentinels were present either. He reported this egregious breach of standard military protocol to Jackson. Jackson ascertained that Lieutenant William M. Kirby was the responsible officer of the guard that day. Viewing the matter as a serious one, Jackson ordered his adjutant general, William Sitler, to take Jackson's life guard and the ever-useful and reliable Lieutenant Gordon and his company of spies to find and arrest Kirby.[64]

Sitler and his troops rode to Kirby's quarters, but he was gone. They searched the lines and found him at the head of his company, marching his men for home. Sitler drew up his men before Kirby and commanded him to halt. Kirby ignored Sitler's command and kept his men marching. Sitler then ordered his troops to stop Kirby and his men. Outnumbered and facing veteran troops, Kirby and his company halted. Sitler then demanded the lieutenant's sword. Kirby refused. He needed the sword to protect him on his march to the Tennessee River, he told Sitler. Moreover, echoing the great seventeenth century English leveller "Free Born" John Lilburne, Kirby impertinently informed Sitler that he was not under General Jackson's command but was a "free man."

Outraged at this effrontery, Sitler ordered his men to fire on the rebels if Kirby did not hand over his sword. In response, the infuriated Kirby pulled his pistol from his holster, cocked it, and pointed it at Sitler. Many of the lieutenant's company also cocked their rifles and pointed them at Sitler's men. Amid this standoff, a furious Jackson and his staff arrived. Quickly spying the troublemaker, Jackson went up to Kirby and demanded his sword. To Jackson's astonishment, Kirby refused. At that insolence, Jackson unholstered his pistol, pointed it at Kirby, and declared that if he refused to surrender, Jackson would blow him through. Sitler bravely pushed between the two men and again demanded the lieutenant's sword, explaining to Kirby that he wanted to avoid bloodshed.[65]

At that moment, Kirby's friend, a Dr. Taylor of Gordon's company, rushed up between Sitler and Kirby and pulled Kirby's sword from its scabbard. The doctor then tried to hand the sword to Sitler, but he refused to accept it from anyone but Kirby. By this time the lieutenant seemed to have come to his senses. He took his sword back from Taylor and handed it over to Sitler, submitted quietly to arrest, and was marched off to the stockade, where he awaited a court-martial that never came.[66] Kirby's friends employed the tried and true "devil made me do it" defense to persuade Jackson to release the lieutenant. The young and impressionable Kirby, Jackson was told, had fallen under the malign influence of bad men with political motives and was acting out of a deluded sense of personal honor. At this point in the campaign, Jackson was still understanding of and willing to forgive the failings of young men. He graciously accepted this thin explanation for Kirby's outrageous conduct and the lieutenant's subsequent apology and let the matter drop.[67] A few more months into the campaign and Kirby would not have been so lucky, in fact he might well be dead.

With the departure on January 4 of General Roberts's 2nd Brigade of west Tennessee militia, "except one small company," and the departure on the fourteenth of Colonel Lillard's east Tennessee regiment from General Cocke's command, except for Captain William Hamilton and three of his men, Jackson was left at Fort Strother with only two companies of spies and a company of artillery. Soon, however, he was joined by his protégé, Colonel Carroll, and about 850 newly recruited mounted men. Particularly welcome was the arrival of Jackson's great friend John Coffee, whom Jackson rightly called his "best prop." Accompanying Coffee, who had sufficiently recovered from his illness to take the field, was a handful of men, mostly veteran officers loyal to Jackson, whom Coffee had been able to scrape together for the coming campaign. Coffee also brought with him several hundred mounted troops to reinforce Carroll's new men.[68] Coffee, however, had had his own serious trouble with his men and two senior officers.

On December 27, Jackson, who was desperate to begin his campaign against the Creeks, ordered General Coffee to bring the new recruits down to Fort Strother.[69] Coffee was now almost fully recovered from his illness, writing his wife, Mary, that he had recently ridden the ten miles from Huntsville to the Tennessee River and back.[70] But when Coffee transmitted Jackson's order to the commanding officers of the two regiments of the brigade of troops—Colonels Nicholas Perkins of the 1st Regiment West Tennessee Mounted Volunteers and William Higgins of the 2nd Regiment West Tennessee Mounted Volunteers—it touched off a fracas over the prerogatives of command among Coffee and the two colonels. The volunteers were under the direct command of Cocke, but he was back in Tennessee on Jackson's orders, supposedly finding new recruits for Jackson. Coffee was in command of Camp Carroll, where the brigade was in residence. On January 6, 1814, Coffee had one of his officers deliver to Perkins a letter somewhat peremptorily instructing the brigade to begin its march to Fort Strother under the command of Coffee.[71]

Perkins, who apparently thought that Coffee meant to assume command of the brigade, did not bother to forward the letter to Higgins. Instead he promptly sent Coffee a reply. The letter was signed by himself, as commander of the 1st Regiment, by Colonel Higgins, commanding the 2nd Regiment, and by the officers of both regiments. That letter informed Coffee that these officers had not chosen him to lead them and that they wished to be marched to Fort Strother by Colonel Carroll of Jackson's general staff. Once there, they informed Coffee, they intended to place themselves directly under Jackson's command.[72]

Coffee took Perkins's ill-advised letter as a personal insult. The general's lengthy confinement had not improved his temper; by now he was describing Huntsville to Mary as a "loathsome place."[73] The following morning the incensed Coffee dashed off a note to Jackson requesting that the beleaguered general order the arrest of Perkins for "disobedience of orders and ungentlemanly and unofficer like conduct." In addition, Coffee asked Jackson to order the immediate arrest of Higgins, who Coffee plainly thought less culpable, on a single charge of disobeying orders.[74]

Higgins, who was by this time—January 13—at Fort Strother, sensibly realized the danger of antagonizing Jackson's best friend and wrote Coffee, placing the blame on Perkins. Higgins explained to Coffee that he had no objection to being commanded by him and that he had never received Coffee's order or even been officially advised of it until January 13. Rather he had been led to believe by an unidentified someone that "the intermediate general who should command us, must be chosen by ourselves."[75] This explanation satisfied Coffee, who wrote Jackson the following day asking that the requested charges against Higgins be withdrawn. Jackson, who had enough troubles on his hands, endorsed Coffee's request on the letter.[76]

Perkins now found himself isolated and took immediate steps to save himself. On the day Coffee withdrew his charges against Higgins, Perkins wrote Coffee a grudging apology in which he implausibly ascribed his conduct to the failure of anyone to instruct him that the general was to take command of the volunteers coupled with the usual "council of wicked & designing men." Coffee reluctantly accepted Perkins's apology, notwithstanding that he was "able to establish by competent proof" the charges against Perkins. He explained to Jackson that he was willing to put aside his personal feelings for the good of Perkins's "Public Service," which otherwise would be interrupted if Coffee's charges were acted on. Jackson

honored Coffee's request, which extricated Jackson from yet another difficult situation.[77] Possibly he and Coffee had talked over the entire matter
beforehand and arranged a solution that was conveyed to Higgins and
Perkins by intermediaries. As John Reid points out, the volunteers, who
were the only substantial force Jackson now had under his command, were
raw recruits with no experience of military service. To deprive them of
their commanders before they had been even tested in battle would most
likely undermine their effectiveness if not touch off yet another mutiny.[78]
Certainly, at this point, Jackson had more important matters to attend to.
His long-delayed campaign against the Creeks was slated to begin the next
day.

But the tireless imps of war had yet another trick to play on Andrew
Jackson. He had been counting on the arrival of around two hundred militia under General Roberts. Roberts had indeed obtained the men and at
Jackson's order was bringing 191 of them to Fort Strother to be paraded
before Jackson at 9 A.M. December 29. On December 28, Roberts got the
militia to within two miles of that fort when yet another length-of-service
dispute broke out among the men. To resolve this dispute, Roberts decided to obtain Jackson's assurance that the men's term of service would be
for three months and that they would be paid for this period. He left his
men where they were and rode the two miles to Fort Strother.[79]

When Roberts placed his men's unwelcome demands before Jackson, the
latter refused to consider them. These men owed their country six months'
service, he declared. Roberts tried to reason with Jackson, explaining what
Jackson surely knew, that the men were poor farmers and needed to be
home at spring planting time. Roberts's explanation only infuriated
Jackson. Although he did not believe his intended campaign against the
Creeks would take nearly six months, he stubbornly insisted that Roberts's
men must serve for that entire period. Roberts replied that the men would
only serve for three months and that if Jackson would not agree, Roberts
would send them home. Their discussion became increasingly heated until
both men reportedly drew their swords and threatened to cut the other
down.[80] Given Jackson's debilitating illness and the severe injury to his
sword arm from the Benton fracas, it was fortunate for him that the officers present were able to separate the enraged generals before any injury
ensued.

The morning's excitement over, the two combatants retired to their tents
for the night. From the safety of their respective corners, the generals
exchanged correspondence but still were unable to reach a resolution.
Finally, the following evening, Roberts went to Jackson's tent in an attempt
to resolve the dispute in person. Jackson's compromise was to accept a
three-month term of service but without a guarantee of pay. Roberts
agreed to have Jackson's terms read to his men and rode out to their

encampment on December 29. The result was predictable. Without an assurance from Jackson that they would be paid, the men left camp and headed for home.

When Roberts returned to Fort Strother and reported to Jackson the results of Jackson's message to the troops, a furious Jackson ordered Roberts to pursue and jail the renegades, with the help of whatever troops he could find. Ominously, Jackson later wrote General Pinckney, "It has become indispensably necessary that the most energetic measures should be adopted in regard to these citizen soldiers."[81] Eventually many of the disgruntled soldiers returned to the ranks.[82] The others made it home. For the moment, Jackson's incessant problems with mutinous troops was over, and he could turn his attention to the enemy he had originally been tasked with subduing. But predictably, Jackson did not forget the incident with Roberts and his mutinous troops, and Roberts was added to Jackson's long list of enemies.

Over the previous two months, Jackson had endured one of the most trying ordeals not involving combat of any commander in military history. Unlike the uniformed, carefully trained and professionally led men who soldiered for his contemporaries—Napoleon, Wellington, Blucher, and Suvorov—the men Jackson had at his disposal constituted a virtual mobocracy—products of a frontier democracy who viewed government and the laws it issued as a threat to their liberties and personal honor. Jackson himself was a product of this environment and undoubtedly had a good understanding of the temper of the men under his command. This common background goes a good way toward explaining the leniency Jackson showed one mutinous unit of soldiers after another over the past tumultuous months. What divided him from them was his overweening ambition and his willingness to sacrifice every material and physical comfort on the altar of that ambition.

Nonetheless, Jackson's achievement was indeed remarkable. He had maintained his position at a remote fortification many miles within enemy territory for months under nearly impossible conditions of supply and transport. Sickness and hunger were rampant among his troops, who were constantly on the brink of mutiny. Jackson's own physical ailments—his wounded shoulder was so painful he could not even put on his coat, and his gastrointestinal tract was savaged with dysentery—would have destroyed the command fitness of an ordinary man.[83]

Historians have generally attributed Jackson's achievement to his indomitable will. Unquestionably, Jackson had a preternaturally strong will and an enormous capacity for physical suffering, but he was also extremely fortunate to have the support of an unusually talented group of officers in the field and a competent and loving wife at home. The subsequent careers of men like John Coffee, William Carroll, Richard Keith Call,

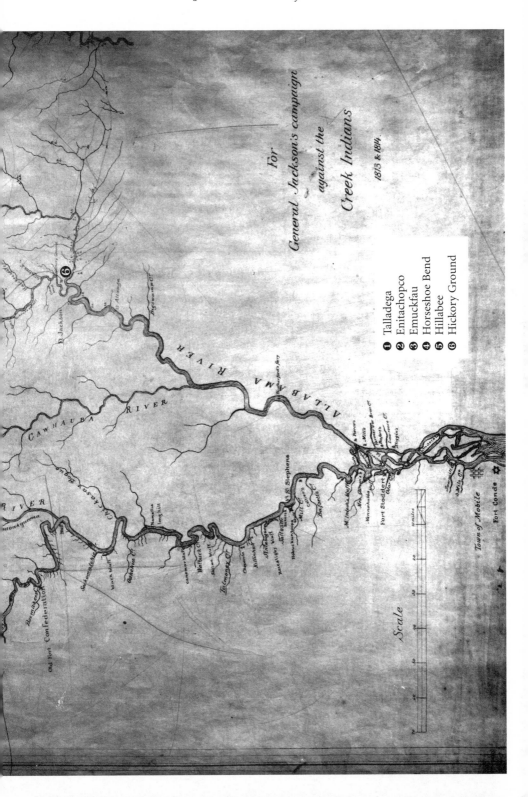

For
General Jackson's campaign
against the
Creek Indians
1813 & 1814

1 Talladega
2 Enitachopco
3 Emuckfau
4 Horseshoe Bend
5 Hillabee
6 Hickory Ground

the immensely promising but sadly short-lived John Reid, and others of his military family evidence the extraordinary talents of the individuals to whom Jackson could fall back on for support.[84] At home, Jackson's beloved Rachel managed his prosperous plantation and cared for Jackson's much-loved son, Andrew, removing a potential source of concern from Jackson's life. In other words, although Jackson's achievements during the hard months of November, December, and January of 1813–14 were utterly remarkable, he did not overcome this difficult and challenging period in his life by his preternatural will alone. Throughout these hard days, Jackson was fortunate to have propping him up several remarkable men and one remarkable woman.

But at last he had an army of sorts: fewer than one thousand mostly inexperienced soldiers with a sixty-day term of service, but an army nonetheless. He could have been patient and waited until he received more and higher-quality reinforcements—a regiment of regular US infantry and two thousand five hundred militiamen were on their way—and spent time training them. But in a moment of extraordinarily bad judgment—perhaps the prophets' "physic" was still at work on him—the impetuous and impatient Jackson decided to use the untempered metal of the raw troops he had at hand to strike at the Creeks.

The Battle of Emuckfau Creek

ON January 14, 1814, Colonel Lillard's regiment, the last unit of General Cocke's army still with Jackson, marched out of Fort Strother for Tennessee. Ordinarily this departure would have infuriated Jackson. Nonetheless, his spirits were high for the first time since Talladega—"the prospects began to brighten," he wrote a friend.[85] They would have been brighter still for the general had he known that on that very same day, Colonel John Williams's 39th Infantry Regiment of US regulars had marched south out of Nashville to join Jackson's army. After several months in purgatory, Jackson was at last on the move. On January 15, he began his campaign against the Red Clubs by ordering his brigade of eight hundred newly arrived, and very raw, sixty-day west Tennessee mounted volunteers to ride out of the encampment of Fort Strother and ford the Coosa to its eastern shore. Once there they were to graze their horses and wait for Jackson's arrival. The following day Jackson and the remainder of his command crossed the Coosa and joined the volunteers. With Jackson was a veteran infantry company of forty-eight men, Gordon's and Russell's companies of spies consisting of thirty men each, and a company of volunteer officers led by General Coffee.[86] Jackson also brought an artillery company with a single six-pound cannon because his spies had informed him that the hostiles were gathered in a strongly fortified town.[87] The cannon would be employed to batter down walls.

Essentially, Jackson now had in his army only around 125 soldiers, out of a total 930 officers and men, whom he could rely on—a meager and untested force with which to invade the nation. Jackson was also joined in the expedition by a contingent of two hundred to three hundred Creeks and Cherokees wearing white feathers in their hair or deer tails hanging from their waists to distinguish them from the Red Clubs. Major John Reid dismissed their usefulness to the campaign, writing his father that these Indians could be little counted on for gaining a victory, although, as Reid wryly remarked, they were of considerable service after victory in cutting down the fleeing Red Clubs.[88]

Nonetheless, despite the serious deficiencies in the number and quality of his troops, after months of idleness, a severe gastrointestinal illness, the constant pain of his unhealed and deep shoulder wound, ceaseless battles with incompetent or venal contractors and mutinous soldiers, Jackson seized eagerly on the opportunity to get back into the field. He was well aware that his latest instrument for visiting destruction on the Red Clubs was an imperfect one. The officers of the volunteers were undisciplined and unskilled in military operations, and the men they were leading were of the same insubordinate and independent-minded stripe as the troops who had recently abandoned Jackson.[89]

Jackson had several reasons for embarking on a dangerous campaign with largely untested men through a deep forest and toward an objective none in the army had ever seen. Among the foremost was the need to immediately employ the men or lose them back to their lives in Tennessee. Their term of service was only two months, and although they seemed eager to meet the enemy, Jackson knew that if he did not occupy their minds with an expedition against the Creeks soon, the always-lurking idea of mutiny would spread like a virus among them. Moreover, there was the rumored Red Club attack on Fort Armstrong. If Jackson could strike the "emboldened" Red Clubs before they mobilized, he could thwart that threatened attack.[90] In addition, according to Jackson, an expedition to the upper Tallapoosa towns would prevent them from reinforcing the Red Club army facing General Floyd several hundred miles southeast. General Pinckney was not so sure of this benefit.

He had foreseen the restless and impulsive natures of both commanders. Floyd, he believed, he had somewhat in hand, but Jackson he tried to keep on a tighter leash. On January 9, 1814, Pinckney wrote a letter to Jackson from Pinckney's temporary headquarters in Milledgeville, Georgia. In his letter, Pinckney cautioned Jackson against a new expedition into the nation until the Tennessean was fully prepared. According to Pinckney's best information, the Red Clubs had begun the war with four thousand men and now, after five months of battle, were down to about three thousand effective fighters who were badly supplied with arms and munitions. Together with their Creek, Choctaw, and Chickasaw allies, the armies of Georgia, Tennessee, and Mississippi were more than a match for any force the Red Clubs could muster—if the allies were able to act in reasonable concert.

Accordingly, Pinckney recommended that Jackson not "embarrass" himself with the "60 day mounted men." The problem of finding forage for their voracious mounts in winter and the men's limited period of service would only allow for a short incursion into the nation and necessitate a prompt return to their base at Fort Strother after battle. This course of action, Pinckney bluntly told Jackson, "would render the advantages obtained of comparatively little importance, as has been already proved by the victories gained by the Tennessee & Georgia troops not having been attended with more decisive consequences." Instead, Jackson should remain patient a little longer until the arrival of the six-month state militia, Williams's 39th Infantry, and ample stores of provisions before embarking on another military campaign against the Red Clubs.[91] In addition, urged on by the hot poker of Jackson's recent letters, Governor Blount roused himself from his political inertia and, on January 3, 1814, issued a call for two thousand five hundred volunteers to reinforce his friend.[92] Jackson need only wait a few months and he would have an overwhelming force at this disposal.

Pinckney's good advice went unheeded by Jackson. It was like trying to coax a suddenly uncaged lion back into its enclosure. Jackson had little, if any, respect for the military abilities of the Creeks or any Indians for that matter, and after Tallushatchee and Talladega, any such respect he might have grudgingly harbored was gone. This attitude appears to have been shared by his officers. As Coffee wrote his wife, Mary, after his murderous victory at Tallushatchee, "I don't expect after this the enemy will ever meet us—they have no kind of chance—our men will drive them where ever they find them." With this kind of attitude toward the enemy, it is not surprising that Jackson ignored Pinckney's good advice and rode off on his madcap adventure.[93]

On January 18, Jackson's army reached Talladega. The fields and forests of the old battlefield were still littered with the rotting, but otherwise strangely intact, corpses of several hundred Red Club warriors. As unpleasant as the sight was, it must also have lifted the confidence and spirits of the untested volunteers, who were doubtless treated to a tour of the field along with embellished tales of the battle from the few veterans of that fight still with the army. The volunteers were further encouraged by the arrival of some 235 Creeks and 65 Cherokees.[94] The friendly Indians had stuck white plumes in their head wrappings to distinguish them from the Red Club warriors. In the distance these ornaments must have made them look like a flock of egrets.

After an unsettling night camped among the dead Creeks, the army struck off the next morning toward the southeast through a wilderness of bare hardwoods, brush, and troublesome mountains cut by swift creeks. It was led by a party of axmen who hacked a road through the forest for the army's wagons and its single cannon. An advance guard followed the pioneers, and another detachment guarded the army's rear. In the surrounding woods rode the usual flankers. Jackson's two companies of spies, and a number of the friendly Creeks and Cherokees, ranged farther ahead looking for Red Club ambushes.

That night, as Jackson's army slept, a war party led by Old Chenibee's son, Selocta, surprised yet another unfortunate Hillabee village. Unhappily for the Tennesseans' Indian allies, these Hillabees were not so surprised that they were unable to fight back, and fight back with ferocity. Selocta's brother was killed, and Selocta missed death by a literal hair when a Red Club bullet cut his white plume off at the scalp. Soon, however, Selocta's men visited a "terrible retribution" on the village and its inhabitants.[95] This retribution no doubt included the standard looting and burning of the village, the "accidental" death of noncombatants, the capture of women and children, and the lifting of scalps from the dead and dying. Some Hillabees, however, managed to escape the attack and make their way through the forest to warn their neighbors.

As Jackson's army moved deeper into hilly and heavily wooded country, he learned that his guides appeared to have little knowledge of the remote land into which they were heading. Perhaps more ominously, after only a few days on the march, the volunteers were already showing signs of the insubordination that had left Jackson stranded for months at Fort Strother. And the volunteers' barely trained officers were of little use in managing the men under their command.[96] On a positive note, Jackson found that the men were still eager to fight. Jackson just needed to quickly find an enemy to pit them against before he and his friends assumed that role in the men's eyes.

The next morning, January 21, the army resumed its march through the hilly terrain along a pretty little stream known as Enitachopco Creek. Around two o'clock that afternoon, spies located two hostiles who had been shadowing Jackson's army, but in the rough country they were unable to capture them. Not long thereafter, the army came across a large trail that soon turned into a well and recently traveled road. Believing that he was now close to a large number of the enemy, and having traveled a good number of miles, Jackson decided to find a place to camp for the night.[97]

Just before dusk, the army reached a likely spot on a rise in the ground above yet another fine stream called Emuckfau Creek near its junction with the Tallapoosa River. The place selected for camp was described by Richard Call as "a beautiful eminence, near Emuckfau Creek, where in our front the ground was level for more than half a mile with an open pine forest without undergrowth. On our right and left it was equally favorable for more than two hundred yards, while in our rear it was also level and favorable for the same distance, when it commenced descending to a deep valley through which a stream flowed, bearing on its margin a dense growth of cane."[98] They were just two miles from the reported fortified Indian town on the Tallapoosa River.

Jackson ordered his men to entrench themselves in the typical hollow square employed by armies in the field at that time. The horsemen covered the internal perimeter, while in the center of the square Jackson placed the baggage, the artillery company and its little canon, the friendly Indians, and the horses. Sentinels were posted in the piney woods about two hundred yards from the camp and were assigned the watchword "stick to it." Mindful of the possibility of attack, as a further precaution Jackson put out pickets, doubled the sentinels, and sent the spies into the woods for a nighttime reconnaissance of the surrounding countryside. Jackson or some other officer also ordered that campfires be built and kept burning outside the perimeter of the camp. If the enemy came at night, the men were trained to form a battle line about ten to fifteen feet behind the fires. Once assembled, the front line of soldiers would kneel on their left knees and be concealed by the fires. When the Creeks emerged from the black woods, the light from those fires would make them easy targets while blinding them to the soldiers' positions.[99] It remained to be seen, however, whether the raw recruits would follow their rudimentary training in the face of a Red Club attack.

From reports of his spies, Jackson knew the Red Clubs had a substantial settlement a few miles east. But Jackson had no idea that this settlement was a veritable hornet's nest of hostile Creeks determined to slaughter everyone in his army. There were hundreds of warriors there from the Okfuskee, Eufaula, and Hillabee towns, led by the famous horse thief Menawa.[100] They were massed in another newly built and sacred refuge town like the now-destroyed Holy Ground but substantially larger and protected by skillfully constructed fortifications as well as the requisite invisible magic circles and incantations. The town was built just downstream on the opposite bank from the town of Neuyakau that General Adams had burned the previous month. Here the Tallapoosa formed a great loop that resembled the footprint of a colossal horse. Because of that resemblance, the Creeks called the peninsula formed by this quirk of geology Tohopeka, and the whites, Horseshoe Bend.

Jackson estimated the bend covered eighty to one hundred acres. Across the open end of the peninsula, several hundred yards below a quick rise in the ground, the Indians with great labor and skill had constructed a formidable wall of pine logs and earth about five to eight feet high.[101] This ingenious structure was built in a zigzag form so as to provide enfilading fire on any attackers and had a double row of portholes cut along its length. At the opposite end of the peninsula, near the river, the Red Clubs had built a substantial town. The lack of European or American trade goods in the town, noted by archeologists who 150 years later excavated the site, indicated that this was a town that took seriously the message of the prophets that the Indian people must rid themselves of such white-manufactured material.[102]

That night, at his army's encampment across Emuckfau Creek, Jackson received the first solid news of this fortification and the settlement that it guarded. Around 11:00 P.M., a contingent of spies he had sent to explore the surrounding countryside returned to a camp full of tense and nervously alert men. Earlier that night, around ten, the new recruits had experienced a brief taste of battle when the sentinel on duty fired on three hostile warriors scouting the camp. Another Creek, who had foolishly gone to harvest corn from a nearby field, was on his way back to the Indian camp when he was killed by a picket stationed near a small path in the forest.[103] Given these alarms, the spies were fortunate that the jumpy soldiers did not shoot at them as they approached the camp.

The news from Jackson's spies only heightened the tension produced by the little skirmishes. Several miles northeast, along the Tallapoosa, they had discovered a large town filled with numerous fighters singing their war songs and dancing their war dances—surely the Shawnee "dance of the lakes"—as if preparing for battle. One of the friendly Indians among the spies, in whom Jackson "had great confidence," reported that the Red Clubs were shepherding their women and children out of the town. This precaution, the spy believed, was the prelude to a possible assault on the American camp. Jackson took the man's warning seriously and had his men ready and alert all night for just such an event.[104]

It came around 6:00 A.M. Painted scarlet and black and howling their war cries, the Red Clubs poured out of the black woods like demons from the pit. The pickets met the initial Creek onslaught by firing one shot at the shadows coming at them out of the trees and then skedaddled for the camp pursued by a yowling mob of Red Clubs. The terrified pickets only just reached the American lines when the Red Clubs smashed into Jackson's left flank. They were met there by the 2nd Battalion of the 2nd Regiment of east Tennessee volunteers, commanded by Coffee's recent antagonist, Colonel Higgins. Higgins's men stood their ground, but in a short time the Red Clubs fought their way around the battalion's flank to its rear. This crisis was met by the veteran officers in the camp who had lost their commands during the various mutinies. Led by General Coffee,

Colonel Sitler, and Colonel Carroll, they mounted their horses and gal-loped to the point of greatest danger. For thirty minutes these officers kept the novice soldiers steady amid the terrifying sights and hellish sounds coming toward them in the dark and hard at work killing the phantas-magorical figures bursting from the trees.[105]

Like General Floyd's Georgians at Camp Defiance, the Tennesseans held the Red Clubs in check until dawn. By then, Jackson had reinforced his left flank with Captain Larkin Ferrell's reserve company of forty raw infantry-men. Once these men were in position, Coffee gave the welcome order to charge and, at the head of Ferrell's company himself, led the men into the midst of the startled warriors. The hostiles quickly broke off their attack and fled through the lightening dawn into the woods. The Tennesseans' giddy but deadly pursuit was joined by the friendly Indians, keen for blood and booty. The chase went on for nearly two miles before Jackson pru-dently ordered the by-then exhausted pursuers to return to camp; he was afraid of a Red Club ambush. Jackson later reported with satisfaction that his men had executed "considerable slaughter" among the fleeing Red Clubs. The Americans lost five killed and several wounded in the melee. Their Indian allies' losses, if any, were not reported.[106]

For some reason, at this moment in the campaign, Jackson expressed a curious solicitude for his handful of wounded that purportedly caused him to drastically alter his plans. Instead of following up the morning's repulse and rout of the Red Clubs' attack with an assault of his entire army on their stronghold, Jackson chose to remain in his unnamed camp and let the loyal Coffee and a detachment of four hundred Tennesseans and all the friendly Indians try their fortunes against the mysterious Red Club town. Jackson's explanation to Pinckney for this half-measure against a force he had journeyed many hard, personally painful miles to destroy was the need to protect his wounded men from the Indians.[107] Curiously, when he left Fort Strother for Talladega, he did not see fit to leave over half of his avail-able force to guard the sick and wounded in that place. After his easy vic-tory at Talladega, he may have been surprised by the Red Clubs' audacious and fierce attack on his Emuckfau camp that morning and, for the first time in the war, recognized that this foe was a serious one, his expedition was in peril, and his ability to extricate it from the many miles of deep and enveloping wilderness with it and his reputation intact was in jeopardy.

Coffee and his men set off for the town in the late morning. Although Jackson knew from his spies that the place was strongly fortified and must have realized that the cannon would be needed to reduce it, he neverthe-less insisted that Coffee first reconnoiter the town. If the town's fortifica-tions were too stout, only then should Coffee send for the cannon.[108]

The town was just two miles away, and in a short while led by the scouts, Coffee and his men emerged from the forested, low-hill country and stopped on a small, pine-covered knoll just above the mouth of the peninsula. From that eminence he looked down on Horseshoe Bend. A few hundred feet below him, and across several hundred yards of cleared ground covered with fresh pine stumps, he could see a surprisingly solid and formidable wall of timber pierced by two rows of portholes stretching across the mouth of the peninsula. Given the strength of the fortifications, as Jackson had ordered, Coffee would have to send for the cannon. But then, contrary to the urgings of Colonel Carroll, who wanted to immediately attack the stronghold, Coffee did a prudent and fortunate thing. Instead of dispatching a strong squad of men to Jackson's camp to retrieve the cannon, the usually audacious and aggressive Coffee set off for the American camp with his entire force to escort the weapon back to the Indian fortress.[109]

What Coffee did not know was that Menawa and the other Red Club leaders had only placed part of their forces within the peninsula. Confident that the wall could withstand any assault Jackson could mount, they had regrouped the bulk of the hostile forces in the forests surrounding Jackson's encampment. Now they were placing their companies in position for another attack on the place. During their first attack, despite Jackson's boast that his men had whipped them, the Red Club leaders had apparently seen something about the organization of the camp and the character of the troops stationed there that they thought they could exploit.

Their plan was to feign an attack on the right side of the camp as a diversion for the main attack on the left side. A third contingent of warriors from the Chealegran tribe was to simultaneously assault the extreme right of the American front line. While their comrades were maneuvering into position, however, the Chealegrans were busy making their escape from the battlefield. As they stole through the woods toward their assigned position, they simply kept going in the direction of their homes to the south, undetected by the Americans or their fellow Creeks.[110]

Meanwhile, around 1:00 P.M., as the bulk of the Red Club forces crept through the woods into position, Coffee and his large contingent of volunteers and Indians returned to camp for the cannon. While transportation of the piece was being organized, Coffee provided Jackson with a report of the situation of the town of Tohopeka and its impressive fortifications. Less than half an hour had passed since Coffee's return when the Red Clubs struck.[111] At the time, a group of Gordon's spies were combing the woods outside the encampment, like hunters in search of downed game, for the corpses of Indians they believed they had killed in the earlier fight.[112] A party of about fifty concealed warriors tasked with conducting the feint on the right side of the American lines watched as the searchers approached their hiding place. When the Americans came within range, the Red Clubs fired on the Tennesseans, precipitating a sharp fight.

Faced with the threat that had suddenly materialized among the trees, Coffee reacted immediately and violently. While Gordon and his men fled for their lives toward the American lines, Coffee quickly took in the situation and thought he saw an opportunity to turn the left flank of the Red Club party. He asked Jackson's permission to take two hundred men and attempt the maneuver. Jackson granted Coffee's request, and Coffee's staff scurried about to round up the soldiers. Unfortunately for Coffee, only fifty-four men followed him. These included many of the veteran but commandless officers and his aide-de-camp, Sandy Donaldson, Coffee's brother-in-law and Jackson's nephew. In the ensuing confusion, the other men of the detachment following behind dropped away from the charge either because of a mistake (as Jackson later claimed) or fear (as Jackson's aide Reid later wrote). [113] The Americans, however, had taken the Red Club bait.

As Coffee's mounted riflemen rode through the woods toward the Creeks, the Indians fell back to positions along a low ridge covered with pine and thick brush, their movements directed by the loud cries of a chief sitting on his horse out of range and wearing a bearskin cap fantastically adorned with cow horns protruding from either side. When the Red Clubs reached their assigned position they concealed themselves in the rough terrain and waited for the Tennesseans to come within effective gun range. As he advanced his mounted command toward the waiting Red Clubs, Coffee realized that the men presented excellent targets for the enemy. Just out of range, Coffee ordered them to dismount and attack through the woods on foot. But they made little forward progress in the face of the fire from the hidden Red Clubs on the ridge. Coffee's attack quickly bogged down, and Jackson decided to reinforce Coffee with 150 of the friendly Indians. Just as Jackson sent them toward Coffee's position, the Red Club's main attack exploded out of the woods on Jackson's left. Jackson's several accounts of the friendly Indians' subsequent conduct are somewhat contradictory, but what is clear is that they abandoned their movement toward Coffee's position and turned to the sound of firing on Jackson's left. [114]

Jackson later claimed he had anticipated that the main Indian attack would occur on his left and had warned his men stationed there to be ready. He gathered up Captain Ferrell's reserve and rode immediately to the point of attack, apparently forgetting the embattled Coffee and his men. When Jackson reached the threatened part of his line, he was surprised to see the volunteers facing the Red Club assault with "astonishing intrepidity." Elated by this development, Jackson ordered his reinforced soldiers, with one of his favorite officers, Colonel Carroll at their head, to launch a counterattack against the Red Clubs. Carroll's furious charge on the startled Red Clubs broke up the hostiles' attack and sent them running for their lives through the woods. This triumph of arms, as at the Battle of Talladega, was followed by a pursuit of the hostiles for several miles by the Tennesseans and Jackson's Indian allies. These warriors were supposed to be assisting Coffee but were unable to resist the prospect of easy kills and the precious scalps.[115]

John Reid, who was at Jackson's side, describes what more likely happened in this attack. According to Reid, the volunteers did indeed repulse the Red Clubs' "sudden and violent" assault by their main force on the left side of Jackson's line. However, rather than the easy rout and pursuit of the Creeks that Jackson describes, the fight settled down on the left to a mode of warfare familiar to the defenders of Tuckabatchee and Fort Sinquefield months earlier: "The battle was now maintained by the assailants, by quick and irregular firing, from behind logs, trees, shrubbery, and whatever could afford concealment: behind these, prostrating themselves after firing, and, reloading, they would rise and again discharge their guns."[116]

After a protracted exchange of gunfire over an hour's time, the Red Clubs' rate of fire diminished as they ran low on ammunition. It was then that Carroll ordered the Tennesseans to charge the enemy. And it was then that the Red Clubs broke and were pursued by the Tennesseans and their Indian allies over several miles of countryside, during which a large but unknown number of Red Clubs were slaughtered.

While the fight on Jackson's left was evolving, Coffee and an equal number of Red Clubs were engaged in a slugfest in which neither side was able to prevail. According to Reid, Coffee decided to break the stalemate by feigning retreat, thereby hoping to lure the overconfident Creeks from their concealed positions. As Coffee's troops turned and hustled back toward the camp, the excited Red Clubs rose from cover and ran down the ridge in pursuit. Now able to contend with his enemy on "equal terms," Coffee ordered an about face.[117] His ruse was a classic Indian maneuver and demonstrates how the resourceful Coffee had learned to adapt his tactics to those of his foe.

The Red Clubs may have been surprised at this maneuver, but they did not run. If anything, the fight reached a new crescendo of violence. Coffee was shot in his right side, and a few minutes later his brother-in-law, Donaldson, was mortally wounded with a bullet to the head. Donaldson was brought into camp seated upright on a horse supported from behind by a friend of Lieutenant Keith Call's named McCleary. Donaldson was pale from the loss of the blood that streamed down his face. Jackson rode up and saw that the stricken soldier was his favorite nephew. Controlling his emotions, Jackson muttered sadly, "well it is the fortunes of war," and rode back to the battle. Donaldson never regained consciousness and died several hours later.[118]

Further casualties mounted on both sides, and after an hour's struggle, Tennesseans and Indians alike were about to drop from exhaustion. Still they fought on, including the painfully wounded General Coffee. At this point, having defeated the main Red Club force, Jackson turned his attention to the plight of Coffee and his steadily diminishing command, which Jackson mistakenly believed was facing "superior numbers." Jackson rounded up a hundred Creeks under the Natchez *micco* Jim Fife and sent them against the flank of the Red Clubs fighting Coffee. Joined by these welcomed reinforcements, Coffee ordered a charge, and the inevitable rout of the outnumbered and outgunned hostiles ensued. By every American account, the Tennesseans and their Indian allies killed all the hostiles, around fifty Red Clubs in total.[119]

The tally of casualties among the volunteers was four dead and at least twenty-three wounded. The known casualties among their Indian allies was not reported other than the fact that one of the Big Warrior's men, known as the Elk, shepherded nine wounded friendly Creeks back to Fort Strother.[120] Unexplained by any of the accounts of the battle is why Jackson, unlike Floyd at Autossee and Calebee Creek, did not get his precious cannon into action, particularly at the main point of the Red Club attack. He claimed to have foreseen that attack and had his men ready for it. Yet the cannon remained useless in the center of his encampment. As Reid wrote, it took over an hour for the volunteers to break the Red Stick attack, so Jackson's artillerymen had ample time in which to haul the cannon to that spot. Then, with the cannon loaded with grapeshot and employed like a gigantic shotgun, it could have swept the field of the enemy much more readily than soldiers with muskets alone. Jackson may have been holding it in reserve in case the enemy broke through his lines, but, as he later wrote, when he reached the point of attack on his left flank, he could see that his men would hold their ground. Compared with Floyd's management of the similar battle at Camp Defiance several days later, it appears that Jackson's generalship at Emuckfau Creek left much to be desired.

The fight ended late in the afternoon, and whatever Jackson later wrote about the battle, it was clear he was seriously disconcerted by the situation in which he found himself.[121] Unlike General Floyd, whose battle had taken place just off of the well-known and well-traveled Federal Road forty-five miles over relatively gentle countryside from his base, Jackson's position was altogether different and exceedingly more perilous. He had just lost the badly wounded General Coffee, his best commander. He was seventy miles from his base at Fort Strother, linked only by the rough and narrow path his axmen had been able to hack through the hilly wilderness, where any one of the many rocky and steep folds of land along the way could conceal hundreds of hostile warriors. The volunteers, who had been so eager to meet the Red Clubs, now wished never to see another Indian again and in fact were dangerously close to panic. To bolster their confidence, Jackson ordered breastworks of timber to be constructed around the camp, an order that the semimutinous troops enthusiastically obeyed. Nonetheless, the poor sentinels who were ordered to their posts outside the breastworks were so terrified that they fired their weapons in the direction of the least noise from the woods and then fled to the camp.[122] Only the threat from their officers of certain death forced them back to their posts. The hostiles on watch around Jackson's camp must have enjoyed great sport in spooking the volunteers.

Jackson, however, could not accept the fact, at least officially, that his campaign to date had been a disaster. In a letter written to General Pinckney, Jackson dredged up every reason he could think of why his retreat from his camp at Emuckfau to Fort Strother was the logical course following a successful campaign. The prime objective of Jackson's campaign, as envisioned by Pinckney and made explicit by Pinckney to Jackson, had been to link up Jackson's forces with Floyd's army at the Tuckabatchee towns. In his after-action report, however, Jackson claimed he had a more limited objective in mind: to forestall a possible attack against Fort Armstrong and to divert Creek forces from Floyd's campaign. Jackson also explained away his failure to destroy the Red Clubs' fortress at Tohopeka by dismissing it as an "empty encampment" that presumably was not worth the trouble to torch, even though Jackson had shown no hesitation to burn abandoned Creek settlements before.[123]

Jackson further attempted to mask the reason for his retreat by claiming improbably that it was part of his plan to destroy the Creek army. According to Jackson, his retrograde march home was a ruse to bring what was left of the beaten Red Clubs out of hiding to attack his army.

Jackson's excuses to Pinckney just kept coming. Jackson was concerned that the defeated Red Clubs would receive reinforcements from the hostile lower towns along the Tallapoosa and Coosa. As the shameless Jackson well knew, Floyd was at that very moment scheduled to attack these towns, and these Red Clubs would need every warrior they could muster to defeat the Georgians. In the same breath, however, Jackson boasted to Pinckney that his expedition against the Upper Tallapoosa Creeks had prevented those hostiles from reinforcing the southern hostiles facing Floyd.

Finally, Jackson pulled from his bag of excuses one that had the ring of truth. His return to his base of operations, he explained to Pinckney (whose head by now must have been spinning) was necessitated by his supply situation. His horses, which had had no corn or cane for two days, were starving, as were his imprudent Indian allies, who had not brought sufficient provisions to sustain a lengthy campaign and were now "destitute."[124]

In truth, as the astute Pinckney clearly realized, when Jackson decided to return to his base, he had achieved little and was simply trying to save his novice, and by now thoroughly spooked, army from utter destruction. But Pinckney also wisely realized that Jackson's weaknesses—his overconfidence, obsession with honor, and recklessness—were also part of his strength. To paraphrase Abraham Lincoln's remark fifty years later about General Ulysses S. Grant, Pinckney could not spare a man like Andrew Jackson—"he fights."

The Battle of Enitachopco Creek

A ROUND 10:30 on the cold morning of January 23, 1814, Jackson's army broke its camp on Emuckfau Creek. With great relief and no little trepidation, the men began the long journey home. After the two hard fights at Emuckfau, their spirits had begun to falter. They were worn out with the prior day's fighting and an anxious and sleepless night, expecting at any moment another attack. Jackson's plan was to march that day to their former base at the village of Enitachopco, about ten miles north, and camp there. It would take all day over rough country, slowed as the army was by twenty-three sick and wounded comrades who could neither walk nor ride and, thus, had to be transported by horse litter.[125] The litter was actually a blanket suspended on poles attached to a leading and a trailing horse; the patient was slung hammock-style between the animals. One soldier was assigned to manage the lead horse, another, the trailing horse. A third soldier was assigned to attend to the needs of the wounded passenger, particularly to ensure he did not tumble out as the horse litter went up and down the frequent hills.[126] General Coffee occupied one such litter.

It was not until late afternoon that the lumbering army stopped to camp for the night about a quarter of a mile from a ford over Enitachopco Creek. The journey had been one of hardship and, for many of the volunteers, one of utter terror. Like Lewis Sewell's parody of Colonel Caller's travails in the swamps of the Tensaw Delta the previous summer, Jackson's fearful soldiers saw an Indian behind every tree.[127] And not without reason. Reports from the spies indicated that the Red Clubs were shadowing the Tennesseans' line of march.

Along the route even Jackson had his anxious moments. At one place the army found its way blocked by what Jackson described as a "harycane" but was in fact an area of land where one of the enormous and frequent tornados of an Alabama spring had touched down.[128] Here enormous trees were scattered about the landscape like matchsticks spilled from a giant's box. It was an ideal spot for an ambush, as it provided concealment for the enemy while forcing Jackson to constrict his forces to a narrow column in order to negotiate the downed trees. Jackson was greatly relieved when his army safely threaded its way through this obstacle.

To compound the men's hardships, it was raining when the army stopped for the night. However exhausted the men were, fear of attack provided them sufficient energy to promptly construct a breastwork of logs around the encampment. This structure gave the men some measure of comfort against their fear of another night attack by the Creeks, whom the soldiers, with good cause, believed were lurking just outside their encampment. Nonetheless, even with the erection of the breastworks, so great was the men's terror that the sentinels posted outside the camp could only be kept at their stations by threats of extreme punishment by their officers. Even so, the most innocuous sound from the forest about them immediately elicited shots from their muskets in its direction followed by their flight to the breastworks. The officers would then be forced to round them up again and, with threats and curses, send them back out to face the night's terrors.[129] As with Jackson's camp on Emuckfau Creek, the hostiles outside the encampment must have delighted in the poor sentinels' antics and with provocative sounds alone kept them scurrying back to the breast-works all night. All this constant commotion, of course, kept the soldiers inside the breastworks on edge and sleepless through the night.

Although irritated by the jumpy sentinels' behavior, Jackson nonetheless acknowledged that he heard sounds of Indians prowling around the camp throughout the night, but it was not the threat of another night attack that most concerned Jackson. He was convinced that the Red Clubs intended to attack his army the next morning while it was fording Enitachopco Creek.[130] On its march into the nation, Jackson's army had crossed the creek in a place that was ideal for an ambush. The approach to the ford across the creek from its southern bank entered a deep and rugged ravine that ran between two hills all the way to the water.[131] The narrow path down this defile was lined with thick brush and, as it approached the stream, thick stands of reeds in which the Red Clubs, as masters of con-cealment, could easily hide. In fact, Jackson was convinced that the Red Clubs were even now waiting along both sides of the ravine to entrap his army as it made its slow way down to the creek.

His instincts and judgment were correct. In a tactic that closely mirrored the one proposed by William Weatherford a day later at Calebee Creek, Menawa and the other major chiefs were that evening putting their war-riors in place well within musket range of the ford along the heights lining the defile. From these concealed positions the warriors would enjoy the advantage of firing unseen down into the mass of soldiers below. Constricted by the rain-slickened ravine walls on either side and the high winter waters of the creek to its front, and encumbered by its sick and

wounded on litters as well as its baggage, Jackson's army would have virtually no room to maneuver. Their horses would be useful only to present
their riders as easier targets, and their little cannon could not be deployed.
Their line of retreat would be back up the muddy slope of the gulch and
into the very tough country from which they were trying to escape.
Although this way had the advantage of being on the path the Tennesseans'
had cut into the countryside, only an idiot would send his soldiers into
such an obvious trap. Certainly, whatever his defects as a commander,
Jackson was no idiot.

Consulting with his officers that night, Jackson decided to turn his
dilemma to his advantage. He would foil the Indians' plan by crossing the
creek farther downstream of the nearby ford in more open country where,
if the Indians attacked, he "could slaughter the whole of them." To that
end, early the next morning he sent a detachment of pioneers (the nineteenth-century equivalent of modern combat engineers) downstream to
locate the appropriate ford and associated killing ground.[132]

As luck would have it (Napoleon's *sine qua non* for every successful general), they found such a place some six hundred yards away. The approach
to the new ford was across a slope of open woodland where Jackson could
deploy his cannon and his superiority in firepower if necessary. The crossing place itself was in an area of sparse vegetation—mostly a fringe of the
ever-present reeds along the creek bank.[133] Jackson was elated with the
news and immediately put his pioneers to the task of cutting a path to the
ford while he assembled the remainder of his army for the march.

Some hours later, with the hostiles looking on with dismay, Jackson's
army marched out of its sodden quarters into the morning cold and
turned south, away from the waiting ambush at its former crossing point
on the creek. His vanguard, screened by the friendly Indians and Gordon's
company of spies, followed closely behind the pioneers. Next came the
main body of Jackson's army arrayed in three columns. In the center column were the sick and wounded on their horse litters and the precious
cannon. Behind the main columns came the rear guard, whose command
Jackson wisely entrusted to the steady and redoubtable Colonel Carroll.
This formation was also arranged in three columns: Carroll commanded
the center column, Colonel Stump commanded the left column, and the
right column, the position of honor, was commanded by Colonel Perkins.
The rear guard was mounted and, if attacked, was under orders to dismount and form a battle line against the enemy. Finally, lurking like a trip-
wire at the very rear of the army was Major Russell and his company of
spies. Jackson prudently had ordered them to linger awhile around the
camp and watch for hostiles trailing the army.[134]

Remarkably, General Coffee had somehow risen from his litter and
mounted his horse to ride with Jackson. Despite the pain from his wound,

Coffee, like Jackson, was certain the Red Clubs would attack the army on its way to the creek. For all of his outward confidence, Coffee realized the peril facing the army in its attempt to escape the nation and, ever the warrior, wanted to be there for his friend Jackson and the men.[135]

The march was slow but pleasant. The route to the creek covered six hundred yards over a "handsome ridge" dropping down to the reed-fringed creek. The land hereabout was "open woodland" that presented the Red Clubs with no opportunity to conceal their forces in ambush. When the army reached Enitachopco Creek, however, the terrain became more dangerous. The creek was small and shallow but swollen with rain, its waters purling over a rocky bed that provided firm footing for man and beast. The danger lay in the limitation on movement imposed by the narrow path down which the army had to funnel to reach the stream crossing marked by the pioneers.[136]

A strangely relaxed Jackson, his ubiquitous aide-de-camp, John Reid, at his side, rode leisurely down the defile and splashed through the shallow water to the opposite shore where they halted to the side to watch the crossing. The vanguard crossed without incident, then a good portion of the main army and the litter-borne sick and wounded. The cannon and its limber, pulled by heavy draft horses, were about to enter the stream when the alarm gun sounded and all hell broke loose at the rear of the army.[137]

Initially, the sudden pop of the alarm gun followed by a crescendo of firing weapons and the cries of embattled men elated Jackson. The hostiles had fallen into his trap. Now was his chance to destroy them, provided the rear guard held together long enough for Jackson to organize his counterattack. His plan was for the right and left columns of his main force to turn about, flank the Creek army, and draw together in its rear. Jackson and the cannon in the center column would move forward; when the two wings of the army met behind the Red Clubs, the hostiles would be encircled and, as at Tallushatchee and Talladega, the slaughter could begin. Unfortunately for Jackson, this plan required the portion of his army that had already crossed to the far bank of the creek to face about and recross the stream. Jackson did not yet know it, but he did not have that much time.

When the firing commenced, Jackson dispatched the indispensable Reid to assemble a line of men to protect the wounded and to convey Jackson's order to the army's right wing to turn on the enemy. Jackson himself galloped off to turn the left wing against the Creeks.[138] But the battle had already escaped Jackson's control. Several hundred yards from the crossing, while the three columns of the rear guard waited their turn to ford the creek, as Jackson had hoped, the Red Clubs had attacked his army. At first the startled soldiers could only hear the sudden explosions of gunfire and the high sounds of human voices coming toward them from the forest to their rear. Then, all at once, like game flushed from cover by beaters, Major

Russell and his men came pounding out of the woods on horseback. In pursuit were several hundred fantastically painted and feather-bedecked Red Club warriors singing out their war cries.

The commander of the rear guard, Colonel Carroll, immediately sent his aides to the various columns with instructions for each column to dismount its horses and form battle lines. But after two days of constant fighting and marching in miserable weather and through hard country, the ill-trained militiamen had had enough. Their initial shock from the attack was quickly replaced with unreasoning panic that dictated flight. Both the left and right columns ignored Carroll's orders to dismount, turned their horses as one, and rode helter-skelter for the creek, in the process also carrying most of Carroll's center column with them. The crossing at Enitachopco Creek quickly became clotted with terrified soldiers from the rear guard, while upstream and downstream of the crossing other guardsmen drove their horses across the creek and into the shelter of the woods on its north bank.[139]

Time for reacting to the Creek attack was measured in seconds. On the right, amid the growing noise, smoke, and utter confusion, Colonel Perkins ordered his men of the 1st Regiment to dismount and form a firing line. Several obeyed, but the rest, overcome by a plague of terror, simply ignored his orders and fled across the creek from the frightful mob of warriors coming at them through the trees. In moments, Perkins and the handful of his men who had followed his orders were all that was left of his command to face the Creeks. Bowing to the maxim that discretion is the better part of valor, Perkins's remaining men soon joined the flight of their comrades to the north side of the creek, followed by the frantic colonel vainly attempting to halt their retreat. When he reached the far bank of the creek, Perkins continued to endeavor to rally those of his command within the sound of his voice, but without success. There he remained, a solitary and distraught figure attempting to restore order, shouting commands to his scattered command to reform, and, waving his sword about him, loudly threatening to cut down men unhearing and already beyond his reach. Suddenly, upstream of the fleeing rear guard, a cannon boomed.[140]

The situation of the left rear column was no better, if not worse. It is unclear what attempts, if any, Colonel Stump made to form his men into a battle line. He claimed he tried but that his attempts were thwarted by a cry of "Retreat" from Perkins's right column. Whatever he did to control his men was not enough to prevent their flight to the rear and his subsequent court-martial.[141]

As for Carroll's center column, although there was never any question about the colonel's competence or bravery—to the contrary—nonetheless, most of his command also joined the flight of the other two columns for the north bank of the creek. Unlike their comrades of the rear guard, however, and much to Jackson's delight and admiration, twenty-five hardy soldiers and their commander, Captain John B. Quarles, remained with the undaunted Carroll on the south bank to face the Creek attack.[142] Also remaining with Carroll's tiny command were Russell and his veteran company of spies—in total about one hundred men. They faced several times their number of Red Clubs, now greatly energized by their initial success.[143]

Meanwhile, the panic that had seized the rear guard had spread to the main body of the army directly under Jackson's command. Incredulous and crazed with rage—his soldiers disgracefully fleeing from the enemy, his chance of a crushing victory over the Creeks evaporating from the scene like his troops—Jackson quickly rode to the creek bank where almost his entire rear guard was making its precipitous escape. Here, in his blue jacket, with gold epaulets, head crowned with a black hat, and astride his horse, he made an enticing target to the Creek marksmen. But the fearless Jackson took no notice of the danger, all consumed as he was with alternately issuing commands to his aides and raging at his fleeing men to turn about and face the enemy.[144] His orders had no more effect on his men than Canute's command to the ocean to still its waves. If possible, they paid even less attention to their general than they had to their officers when on the opposite and more dangerous shore.

His soldiers' conduct appeared to momentarily unhinge the general. Beside himself, Jackson attempted to pull with his left hand his sword from its scabbard, intending to saber the fugitives into obedience. But the sword was stuck in its scabbard, and no matter how hard Jackson pulled at the sword's hilt—he claimed the effort almost broke his arm—the weapon would not come free.[145] Meanwhile, his panic-stricken rear guard continued to flow past the general—frantic in his impotence—like the clamorous waters of rapids around a rock.

At this point, Jackson was in danger of not only losing the battle to the Red Clubs but his army as well. Carroll and his men and Russell and his spies still held out on the opposite bank, but they were few and on the verge of being overwhelmed by the Creek warriors; in the front line, Quarles had been killed with a ball to the head.[146] Fortunately, help was near at hand. Perhaps barely noticed by Jackson in the roiling chaos at the outset of the battle was a small band of artillerymen. They and their single six-pound gun also remained on the south bank of the creek, and they were about to go into action against daunting odds.

This company was composed of the cream of Nashville society—Reid complimentarily described them as "men of the first families"—and commanded by an appropriately named Lieutenant Robert Armstrong, an incredibly tough and brave soldier. When the Red Club attack began,

Armstrong was preparing to send his cannon across the creek. Quickly turning and taking in the terrain behind him, Armstrong spied a nearby hill from which, if he could get it there, his gun could control the rapidly developing battlefield. He ordered a group of his men to form on top of the bare hilltop and provide covering musket fire while he and his remaining men ran to unhitch the cannon from the draft horses. Joining Armstrong in this effort was a former member of the artillery, Adjutant General Sitler, now an aide to Jackson. Recognizing the importance of Armstrong's plan, Sitler impulsively splashed back across the shallow creek to assist his former comrades in getting the cannon in place on the little hill.[147]

Like Floyd's fight at Fort Defiance a few days later, the outcome of the battle now centered on the artillery. Armstrong and his fellow socialite cannoneers were in a particularly perilous situation. The crown of the hill on which they had gathered was almost bare of vegetation. On either side of it, however, lay brush-filled ravines, while the country to its front was filled with trees—ideal concealment for Red Club marksmen. Indeed, while the cannon was being wrestled into position, some warriors already had found a firing position behind a large tree that had fallen near the hill. Jackson saw the artillerists' dilemma and, from the far side of the creek, attempted to send help to the isolated artillerymen. However, no one would obey him, and he was forced to look impotently on as Armstrong and his men fought against seemingly overwhelming odds.[148]

Before long Creek marksmen began to take a toll on Armstrong's band. Among the first to fall was Armstrong. After ordering the detachment of his men to seize the hilltop, he and several others of his company, including gunner Constantine Perkins, had attempted to follow with the cannon. At the creek they unhitched the gun from the draft horses and separated the cannon from its limber. Then, under fire, Armstrong and his men somehow managed to drag the piece up the hill and wrestle it into place. Shortly thereafter, Armstrong, stationed beside a wheel of the cannon, was struck in the groin by a Creek ball, and he fell beside the gun. As he lay in agony from his wound, he exhorted his men that whatever happened, they must not lose the cannon to the Red Clubs. Soon after Armstrong was wounded, his friend Bird Evans fell at his side with a mortal gunshot wound. Joining Evans in death was the loyal Captain Hamilton. Like Coffee and other veteran officers, Hamilton had been abandoned at Fort Strother by his men. Nonetheless, Hamilton enlisted as a private in Armstrong's artillery company, where he was joined by his father and brothers. Now the young man died before their horrified eyes in the struggle for the gun. Adding to the rapidly mounting casualties list among the artillerists were the wounded Hiram Bradford and Jacob McGivock.[149]

With the cannon now in position and ready to be charged with grapeshot, gunners Craven Jackson and Constantine Perkins discovered to their dismay that in their hurry to get the cannon to the top of the hill they had left behind, attached to the limber, two critical pieces of equipment for firing the gun: the rammer and the picker. The rammer was used to push the powder charge, wad, and shot down the barrel of the gun. The picker was an ice-pick-like device used to clear the gun's vent and pierce the powder bag so it could be ignited by the flame from the primer. Now these crucial items lay downhill beside the creek across many yards of open ground easily swept by enemy fire. The hostiles, running from cover to cover up the hillside, were also closing fast on the remaining artillerymen. At any moment the two gunners, who made wonderful targets, could be shot. Braving almost certain death, they hastily improvised a means for firing the cannon. Perkins pulled the ramrod from his musket and used it as a picker while Jackson yanked the bayonet from his musket and used the gun as a rammer to charge the cannon with canister shot. When Craven Jackson finally ignited the piece, the Red Clubs were only yards away. The effect of the grapeshot fired at point-blank range against the warriors was devastating and momentarily halted their attack, giving the gunners enough time to load and fire the gun a second time.[150]

By now Jackson and his aides, scurrying frantically among the panicked troops, had begun to restore some order to their main force. All niceties of rank and duties were abandoned. Even the proud Jackson, ever sensitive to the prerogatives of his position and protective of his special dignity, stooped to perform staff work. The wounded Coffee, seated prominently on horseback at the core of the battle, set an example that the frightened men began to emulate. As Jackson and his officers restored sufficient order among the troops to prepare a counterattack, the aggressive Captain Gordon led his veteran company of spies back across the creek and hard into the left flank of the Red Clubs.[151] Remarkably, Colonel Carroll and his ad hoc unit were still fighting. Also still in the fight were Major Russell and his company of spies.

At this critical point in the battle, the Americans' Cherokee allies entered the contest. When the Red Club attack began, a unit of Cherokee warriors commanded by Colonel Richard Brown had been out of gunshot range of the fighting. From his vantage point on the northern bank of the creek, however, Brown could see the American rout and Jackson's inability to organize an effective resistance. He also saw that a particularly galling fire on the Tennesseans was coming from a stand of cane along the creek in which Red Clubs marksmen had concealed themselves. Gathering his men around him, Brown began hollering out commands in the Cherokee language. At the end of his harangue he rode his horse, a particularly fleet animal, pell-mell toward the cane from which the unseen Red Clubs were firing. At the last possible moment, Brown turned the animal away from the cane and rode parallel to it, drawing the fire of the astonished Red Club warriors. As the smoke from the Creek guns disclosed their positions, they were slain by Brown's men before they could reload.[152]

But the turning point of the battle came on the exposed hilltop. Gunners Jackson and Perkins blasted the Red Clubs with the cannon a second time, and the warriors' attack on the hill broke apart. When the rest of the artillery company saw the Red Club attack falter, they suddenly and improbably charged the hostiles with fixed bayonets, completing their rout aided by Gordon's company's attack against the Red Clubs' left flank. Seeing his opportunity, Colonel Carroll also ordered his small command to charge. This charge was joined by Russell and his spies. Jackson now launched a belated counterattack from the northern bank of the creek with a group of soldiers he and his officers had managed to corral in flight; a Red Club rout was on once again.[153]

It was the usual murderous scenario after a Jackson victory. According to Reid, the Red Clubs, in their newfound terror, fled several miles over hill and dale from the pursuing Tennesseans and their Indian allies, who slaughtered them along the way. As evidence of their terror, Reid notes that the defeated Creeks threw down "their blankets, and whatever was likely to retard their flight." Why on this occasion the Creeks, who even in the coldest weather fought almost naked, would be wearing blankets is unexplained. Pickett, echoing Reid, also says the Indians threw away their "packs."[154]

Whatever the truth, it appears that at this point in the fight, the Red Clubs had lost heart and retreated into the countryside in disorder, pursued like game by Jackson's now animated main force of soldiers and their Indian allies. Among those joining the chase with "youthful ardor" was a sixty-five-year-old judge and Jackson friend, William Cocke (not to be confused, as some have done, with Jackson's latest mortal enemy, General John Cocke). Judge Cocke was one of those soldiers whom Jackson singled out for meritorious conduct in his official report of the battle to General Pinckney, citing the judge for saving "the life of a fellow soldier [a Lieutenant Moss] by killing his savage antagonist."[155] If this notable event happened during the chase of the Red Clubs, it indicates that not all the retreating Indians fled from Jackson's army like frightened game.

The battle now over, the Tennesseans began tallying the losses on both sides, as if to find victory among those numbers if not in the battle itself. Jackson informed Pinckney that twenty-six Indian dead were found on the battlefield; in a letter to his wife, however, Jackson numbered the Indian dead at twenty-five. Jackson also estimated, perhaps from information extracted from Red Club prisoners, that two hundred of their dead had been removed by their companions from the field of battle. Jackson reported as unknown the number of Red Club wounded.[156]

As for the American losses, Jackson informed Pinckney that in the Emuckfau Creek and Enitachopco Creek battles collectively, the Americans lost twenty-four killed and seventy-five wounded. He did not break out for Pinckney the figures for each battle, but he did inform Rachel that "in this last affair we lost four killed and several wounded, some of whom is since dead." Not unexpectedly, Jackson does not in his reports of the battles note the losses suffered by his Indian allies in these affairs. Nor does he say much about their roles in the two fights.[157] However, in a letter to Georgia governor Peter Early, penned several days after the battle, Judge Cocke reported that the "Cherokees have distinguished themselves & some of the friendly Creeks have done well." He singled out several Cherokees—Colonel Richard Brown and Captain John Brown—for bravery. And Cocke was in a position to know of what he wrote, because during the battle he fought side by side with Bear Meat, the son of Path Killer, and ten other Cherokees. Another prominent Tennessean, Richard Keith Call, later governor of Florida, in a letter to General Coffee, also praised Colonel Brown for helping to turn back the Red Club attack.[158]

The Battle of Enitachopco Creek was not the finest hour in Jackson's military career to date. In his biography of Jackson written several years after the war, the worshipful John Reid lionized his hero for his conduct of the battle and contended that "but for him, everything must have gone to ruin."[159] No one can seriously question Jackson's considerable personal bravery during this affair, but Reid appears to conflate personal bravery with good generalship. Reading between the lines of the several accounts of the battle, including Jackson's and Reid's, it is apparent that when the Creeks attacked, Jackson quickly lost control of his army and was only belatedly able to restore some order to his troops. But for the extraordinary bravery and improvisation by small units of Jackson's veterans, the Red Clubs might have destroyed his army or, at the very least, gotten control of his wagons with their treasure of badly needed ammunition and captured, trophy of trophies, Lieutenant Armstrong's pesky cannon.

Fortunately for Jackson, men such as Lieutenant Armstrong, Colonel Coffee, Colonel Carroll, captains Quarles and Russell, and Colonel Brown, although greatly outnumbered and separated from the main force of a disintegrating army by Enitachopco Creek, were able to operate independently of Jackson and halt the Red Club advance before Jackson could even get the part of the soldiers under his direct command into the fight. According to David Crockett, "if it hadn't been for Carroll, we should all have been genteely licked that time."[160] Crockett's depiction of Carroll's key role in stopping the Red Club attack is repeated in Reid's and Jackson's reports of the battle. Curiously, Coffee, in a letter to the father of John Donaldson, Coffee's young aide who died at Coffee's side at Emuckfau Creek, makes no mention of his friend Andrew Jackson's role in the battle at all.

Perhaps more than Carroll or any other participant in the battle, the socially prominent Lieutenant Armstrong deserves credit as the savior of Jackson's army and military reputation. Armstrong's coolness and courage under fire, while many of the soldiers about him were carried away by panic, is long forgotten, the tale of his backwoods valor in this little known war all but vanished with the deaths of family and friends. Well might Andrew Jackson have said of Armstrong what Robert E. Lee said of another artilleryman, Captain John Pelham, at the Battle of Fredericksburg: "It is glorious to see such courage in one so young."[161]

Another forgotten incident, almost a coda to the battles Jackson's army had fought with the Creeks over the past several days, was a raid that a group of Tennesseans and Cherokees made the day after the Enitachopco Creek affair on the nearby Okfuskee towns, which Jackson may have ordered to secure his rear from further assaults. On the night of January 25, a contingent of the Tennesseans and their Cherokee allies crept up on an Okfuskee settlement and raced out of the dark on the sleeping Creeks.[162] Unfortunately for the attackers, not all of the Okfuskees were asleep, and a vicious battle ensued with ten men lost on each side. After incurring this painful check, the Americans retreated into the dark to their main encampment. The next morning the Okfuskees assembled a strong war party and hurried off in pursuit of their enemies.

The Okfuskees quickly found their assailants in an entrenched position a few miles away. The Americans were just breaking camp to renew their assault on the Okfuskee towns when the Okfuskee war party hit them. The fighting was hand to hand, and the Okfuskees were counting on the arrival of reinforcements from the nearby neutral towns of Kialegee and Eufaula to support them. These towns had been roused from their neutrality by an Okfuskee threat to destroy them if they did provide the Okfuskees with warriors when called on. Animated by this threat, the neutral towns sent warriors toward the battle, but before they could enter the fight the majority of them decided to turn back for home.[163] Apparently, by the time the war parties from the neutral towns arrived at the battlefield, the Okfuskees were in control of the situation, or their putative allies would not dared have deserted. If nothing else, the defeated raiders unsettled the Okfuskees' sense of safety in their homeland and perhaps dissuaded them from further attacking General Jackson's retreating column.

While his detachment of raiders stole toward the Okfuskee towns, Jackson and his battered legions set off for their base at Fort Strother. After many miles of sloughing over rough, hilly country, shepherding their numerous wounded, they arrived at the fort on the twenty-seventh. There Jackson discharged the sixty-day volunteers. He also gave Reid permission to return to his family on a month furlough. On January 30, he also sent his great friend, the sorely wounded John Coffee, back to Nashville to recuperate.[164]

For all the glowing press accounts of Jackson's "victories" at Emuckfau and Enitachopco, not everyone agreed with the popular sentiment that Jackson's army had emerged from this campaign victorious. As Crockett colorfully put it in his autobiography:

> I will not say exactly that the old general was whip'd; but I will say, that if we escaped it at all, it was like old Henry Snider going to heaven, 'mita tam tite squeeze'. I think he would confess, that he was nearer whip'd this time than he was at any other, for I know that all the world couldn't make him acknowledge that he was *pointedly* whip'd. I know I was mighty glad when it was over and the savages quit us, for I had begun to think there was one behind every tree in the woods.[165]

The Red Clubs, with good reason, also had a different view of the outcome of Jackson's campaign of January 1814 against the upper Tallapoosa River towns. Years later, some prominent Red Club chiefs and warriors who had participated in the battles of Emuckfau and Enitachopco boasted to the historian Albert Pickett that they had "whipped Captain Jackson, and run him to the Coosa River."[166] Indeed they had, and with a force half the size of Jackson's army.

9. TWILIGHT OF THE GODS

Colonel Russell's Alabama River Campaign

N OT long after General Claiborne's army had reached the safety of Fort Claiborne at the end of its grueling retreat from the Holy Ground, Colonel Russell began planning another expedition up the Alabama River valley against the Red Clubs. Claiborne departed with his Mississippi troops to cantonment Mount Vernon, where he would soon discharge them and retire from the service, the expedition to the Holy Ground having wrecked his health.[1] Claiborne had left Russell in charge at Fort Claiborne, and the colonel now seized the opportunity to assume command of operations in this theater.[2]

In Claiborne's absence, Russell had recently received important news from two friendly Creeks who had traveled all the dangerous way from the Chattahoochee towns to Fort Claiborne. General Floyd had defeated the Creeks at Autossee, they told him, but a lack of provisions had forced him to retreat to Fort Mitchell. Around this time, Russell also learned from another source that supply problems had compelled General Jackson to break off his campaign against the Creeks and to retreat to Fort Strother. This situation made it evident to Russell that he alone was left in the field to "subdue" the hostile Creeks.[3]

Looking ahead strategically, he surmised that unless supplies from Tennessee were free to travel down the Coosa and onward down the Alabama River, the Americans could not take and hold Pensacola, because the British navy could easily block supplies from New Orleans from reaching the town. Russell's solution to this dilemma was to lead an expedition to the Hickory Ground near the juncture of the Coosa and Alabama rivers. There he would post his soldiers in the heart of Creek Country and, "like the Goths & Vandals," lay the Creek land to "waste & make it a wilderness."[4] Civil War Union general William Tecumseh Sherman could not have expressed it better.

Russell believed that a force of eight hundred or nine hundred men would be sufficient to implement his strategy. He proposed sending some of his marauders up the Alabama River in armored boats capable of transporting two hundred men and one thousand five hundred barrels of provisions. Concurrently, the remainder of his command would follow the track of the boats by land, destroying any Creek settlements it encountered. Along the way, the land and naval components would coordinate their positions by means of periodic fire from an artillery piece mounted on one of the boats. Meanwhile, Russell's amphibious forces would destroy any Creek settlements they discovered along the river. The land and naval units would then unite at the point where the Cahaba River flowed into the Alabama River. From there, Russell's combined command would proceed upstream to the legendary Hickory Ground and establish a fort for his "Goths & Vandals."[5]

On January 12, 1814, in a letter shot through with insincerity and provocatively addressed from the "Alabama Heights," Russell wrote Claiborne at Mount Vernon. In his letter he outlined his plan for conquering the Creek Nation and ostensibly sought Claiborne's permission to put it into effect under the general's command. However, if the seriously ill and exhausted Claiborne declined to command the expedition, as Russell knew he must, Russell graciously volunteered to do so with the condition that Claiborne give Russell command of the militia. By now the personal relations between the two officers had deteriorated to such a degree that Russell felt obliged to assure Claiborne that his proposal was not "actuated by sinister motives" but rather in obedience to the iron call of duty. Russell's protestations, however, did not prevent him from high-handedly informing Claiborne that on his way to ostensibly consult with him at Mount Vernon, Russell planned to stop off at Peirce's Mill to initiate construction of boats for his proposed but as-yet-unapproved expedition.[6]

Several days later, on January 16, while still at the "Alabama Heights," Russell took the precaution of writing his superior in the regular army, who he did not yet know was General Pinckney, about his plan to attack up the Alabama River valley all the way to the Hickory Ground, an expedition he advised would take thirty days to ready. He also advised his commander that he intended to execute his plan with or without the consent of General Claiborne, unless he heard otherwise from the officer in overall command of the Creek War. Before he left on the expedition he would provide army command headquarters several days' notice via his messenger, James Cornells. That was plainly insufficient time in which to return a reply countermanding Russell's campaign. Russell also advised that he had learned that Peter McQueen, with one hundred mounted men, was in Pensacola procuring more munitions from the Spanish and confidently assured his superior that he would intercept McQueen's party on its way back to the nation "and take away his goods."[7]

When Pinckney received Russell's letter, which was forwarded to him by General Floyd, stopping the expedition until Claiborne was heard from did not enter Pinckney's mind. He was delighted with Russell's plan, which was similar in form to the one he had urged on his generals as soon as he assumed command of the war, sourly noting to Russell that General Flournoy had ignored his advice on this subject. In fact, Pinckney was so enthused with Russell's plan that he not only gave him permission to implement it and authorization to requisition from the quartermaster any materials needed for construction of the boats and other supplies, but the general went even further and provided Russell specific instructions on how to conduct the campaign.

The nautical-minded Pinckney, perhaps influenced by his deep Charleston port-town roots, preferred that Russell place his entire force on boats, each of which was to be armored by whatever appropriate materials were available. In the event that Russell could not obtain sufficient vessels to implement this plan, Pinckney instructed him to place part of his force on whatever boats were available and take up a march parallel to the river with the remainder of his men "in concert with the boats." Communication between the land and naval forces was to be realized by cannon fire from both parties at regular intervals. Russell was also to obtain good guides for his land forces, preferable Choctaws and friendly Creeks. Further, Pinckney warned Russell against encumbering his land forces with too much cavalry—"those devourers of provisions." Sixty to one hundred should be sufficient, Pinckney advised, complaining that too large a contingent of cavalry had impeded the movements of Jackson's and Floyd's campaigns. To make sure that Claiborne did not interfere in Russell's campaign, Pinckney prudently provided Russell a letter addressed to Claiborne in which Pinckney ordered him to cooperate with Russell in all things, particularly the requisition of militiamen for the expedition.[8]

It was not until the first week of February that Russell was finally prepared to embark on a scaled-back campaign up the Alabama River. He had plainly overestimated his capacity to marshal in a few weeks the resources required for the scope of the expedition Pinckney desired and Russell had originally planned. However, rather than postpone the campaign, Russell recast his and Pinckney's ambitious plans to ascend the Alabama River to the Hickory Ground into a reconnaissance in force designed to scour the Alabama River valley of hostile Creeks from Fort Claiborne to their towns along the Cahaba River. On his return from destroying the Cahaba towns and any Creek settlements or hunting camps along the way, Russell left open the option to invade the Black Warrior River country to the northwest and scourge the Creek settlements there.[9] In this way he would secure his rear against attack when he later commenced the more ambitious campaign to the Hickory Ground for which Pinckney hoped.

On February 1, Russell's campaign to the Cahaba towns began. The colonel had hoped to commence the expedition a few weeks earlier but had been delayed by the construction of the boats and, although he later denied it, by his abortive attempt in mid-January to intercept McQueen's and Weatherford's party on its return from Pensacola. Now deep into winter, he led the 3rd Regiment and two companies of mounted local militia—six hundred men in all—out of Fort Claiborne and across the Alabama River to its north bank against a reported three hundred to seven hundred Red Clubs. Almost all the militiamen were veterans of Claiborne's expedition to the Holy Ground. The militia was still commanded by Sam Dale, recently promoted from captain to major. Directly under Dale, however, as captain of one of the militia companies, was an addition to the men who had fought at the Holy Ground: Dale's old associate from the Fort Madison militia, Captain Evan Austill, had joined this newest campaign up the Alabama River valley. His intrepid son Jeremiah, of the famous Canoe Fight and the winter excursion across the Alabama at the Holy Ground, had stayed behind at Fort Madison to look after the Austill clan. Apparently father and son took turns risking their lives in the field and watching over their people at home. Also in Dale's company was Lieutenant Creagh, a veteran of the Burnt Corn Creek and Holy Ground engagements as well as the Canoe Fight expedition. Another veteran of the Canoe Fight expedition, Captain Arthur Foster, commanded the militia cavalry.[10]

Russell's expedition by land was shadowed by his little navy commanded by his trusted subordinate, Captain James E. Dinkins. On this campaign, Russell would not repeat the mistake Claiborne had made on the Holy Ground expedition by relying on incompetent, if not corrupt, civilian contractors for overland transport of the army's critical supplies. Russell ordered the construction at Peirce's Mill, several miles downstream of Fort Claiborne, of vessels to ferry the bulk of his army's provisions up the Alabama River. His builders eventually produced two sizable bateaux propelled by oars. Together they carried seventy "chosen" soldiers and sixty-nine barrels of supplies. As Pinckney had suggested, the vessels were protected with makeshift armor, probably wooden planks covered with cowhides, that Russell outlandishly claimed was sufficient "to secure the men from the fire of 10,000 rifles." One of the boats mounted a swivel gun.[11]

Dinkins was ordered to proceed up the Alabama River to the mouth of the Cahaba River, which entered the Alabama on its north bank, and to arrive there by February 8. On arrival, Dinkins was to anchor the boats and lead an amphibious assault on the hostile settlement that Cornells had told Russell was there. After destroying the town and any of its inhabitants who resisted the assault, Dinkins would then take his supply boats fifteen miles up the Cahaba River to the Creek settlements there and rendezvous with Russell's forces. The colonel planned to reach that spot by February 8 as well and, with his Vandals and Goths, spend the day thoroughly ravaging the Creek towns.[12] Timing was everything.

Russell had selected a route along the north bank of the Alabama that was trackless and largely uninhabited. Without a road, the army would have to dispense with its wagons and carry its supplies by pack horses and in the troops' knapsacks, as living off the wintered land was not possible. Russell's "land pilot" told him that to reach the Cahaba towns was a three-day journey of seventy miles. The actual distance was closer to ninety miles, over rough ground. The local expert on water travel, Cornells, opined that it was a hundred-mile journey over four days to the mouth of the Cahaba; Cornells was short in the distance by twenty-two critical miles. On the assumption that both his army and Dinkins's boat would be at the Cahaba River by February 8, Russell calculated that the army could safely get by on six days' rations for a journey that purportedly would take four days.[13] This appeared to be the maximum amount of provisions the army could reasonably transport by pack horse and in the men's personal knapsacks. Although this amount of provisions gave the army a two-day cushion, it was nonetheless critical to the success of the operation and, indeed, to the lives of the soldiers, that Dinkins and his supply boats and Russell arrive by February 8 at the appointed place up the Cahaba River.

Russell's plan for transporting supplies for his army by boat appeared sound and even innovative on paper. In practice it was a disaster. The Alabama proceeds northeast from Fort Claiborne in an unbroken series of enormous, sweeping loops not readily followed by land. Russell's guides had misinformed him as to the true distances to the Cahaba towns both by land and by water. Moreover, as Russell could plainly see, whatever the correct mileage, the winter rains had swollen the already powerful Alabama River, and even the most muscular oarsmen would be challenged to make progress against its strong current.

When Russell and his men left Fort Claiborne on February 1, they crossed the Alabama River and camped at a place known as the Crossroads, four miles north of modern-day Suggsville, Alabama, near Fort Madison. On February 2, they were joined by a company of the 3rd Infantry Regiment commanded by Lieutenant Joseph Wilcox, a twenty-three–year-old West Point graduate. Wilcox had joined the army at seventeen and was the son of a Revolutionary War veteran, General Joseph Wilcox. The young officer was a rising star in the regular army, smart, brave, honorable, and personable. He would be sorely tested in the coming days.[14]

The army marched out of the Crossroads camp on February 4. After several days of slogging through the wilderness, it still had not reached any of the Cahaba towns. By the fifth day of the journey, if not sooner, Russell was ready to string up the guides and abandon the expedition. But he knew his old comrade in arms, Captain Dinkins, would at all costs obey orders, attack the town at the mouth of the Cahaba, then head upstream to find

Russell. If Dinkins did not find Russell at the Cahaba towns, Russell knew Dinkins would wait until Russell arrived and maintain that position against any number of Indians.[15] Russell refused to leave Dinkins and his men to the mercy of the hostile Creeks and reluctantly plodded onward.

When Russell's command finally reached the Cahaba towns around midday February 10, the men had been twenty-four hours without food. The hostiles had been shadowing the army along its journey. Thus, when Russell's army came to the Indian town perched on a bluff on the Cahaba, they found that it was deserted and had been so for at least a day. Russell also learned that Creeks from the Black Warrior country had been there but had fled across the Cahaba when they discovered the approaching American army. In any event, it was not much of a town: only fifteen or twenty cabins to loot and burn. But even worse, there was no Captain Dinkins and his boatload of supplies to greet them.

Reminiscent of the aftermath of the Holy Ground fight, that evening the officers held a council to determine what to do next. They were eighty-six long miles from Fort Claiborne, with no Indians in sight, no food to eat, and not the slightest idea where Dinkins and his fleet were. The council decided the best way to salvage the campaign was to attempt to locate Dinkins, who they thought had probably been detained by the heavy current. If they could join up with him in the next day or so, they would have the supplies needed to continue their hunt for Indian towns.[16]

Russell's soldiers had found a small canoe at the Creek town. The colonel asked for volunteers to paddle it down the Cahaba that night in search of Dinkins and his boats. Lieutenant Wilcox; a Corporal Simpson; one other 3rd Regiment regular; a Private Armar; and one of Sam Dale's militia, apparently a Matthew Wilson, volunteered for this very hazardous assignment. Russell estimated that it was about a three-to-four-hour paddle to the mouth of the Cahaba; it would take Wilcox and his men twenty hours. If they did not encounter Dinkins that evening, they would surely find him by daybreak. Wilcox was to guide Dinkins to Russell's position by firing the swivel gun from time to time to announce the boat's location. If it took Wilcox more than twenty-four hours to find Dinkins, he was to instruct the captain to return to Fort Claiborne; Russell and his men would wait twenty-four hours at the Cahaba towns and then try to make it back to Fort Claiborne as best they could. To this end, as a precaution, Russell wisely ordered twenty of his mounted soldiers to ride back to Fort Claiborne and return with provisions for the main army as it was traveling back to the fort.[17]

Wilcox and his men set off in the canoe from the army's encampment on the banks of the Cahaba late that night. The water was running high and fast and very cold. The turbulence pushed up small waves from the dark surface of the river. The men had not traveled far when an unseen log flipped their canoe. Somehow they managed to swim the craft to shore, empty it of water, and wrestle it up the bank to safety. Wet and cold, the men took stock of their situation. It was not good. One gun was lost, and most of their powder was ruined by the water. Only a bag of cartridges and a small gourd filled with powder remained. If they happened on any hostiles, they were in a world of trouble. Nonetheless, they dried themselves and their guns as best they could and continued their journey in the river darkness in search of Dinkins.

Near dusk the following evening, the canoeists came on a point in the growing river. Since turning over their canoe the previous night they had seen no one. That was about to change. As they rounded the point, just downstream they saw a sizable encampment of Indians along the western bank of the river. They were now near the town Dinkins was supposed to assault and destroy. Dinkins and his boats were not there, but plenty of Red Clubs were. The shore below the town was lined for half a mile with beached canoes. The Creeks had been collecting food for the Tallapoosa towns upstream, and a number of the vessels were already loaded for the journey. The hostiles soon spied the paddlers, who had little choice but to rely on the Cahaba's rapid current and their own efforts to get past the Indian encampment now quickly mobilizing to intercept them. As their leaders shouted orders, some of the Creeks rushed for their canoes while others ran along the shore of the narrow river hoping for a clear shot at the Americans. The fast-running waters and furious paddling of the men drove them safely through the Indian gunfire. After fifteen or twenty of the longest minutes of their lives, Wilcox and his companions shot out of the mouth of the Cahaba River onto the safety of the broad and rapidly moving waters of the Alabama River.[18]

The paddlers slumped their aching shoulders with welcome relief, but that relief was short lived. They knew that the Indians had sent large boats with many strong paddlers after them. Hoping to outdistance their pursuers and reach Dinkins's expedition before the Red Clubs reached them, the Americans paddled steadily all night and the next day. Unfortunately, their exertions were for naught. As dusk lit the waters around them, they sighted two Indian pirogues, each filled with ten warriors, bearing steadily down on them. When the Indians realized they had been seen, they raised their war cries and sped up after their quarry. Wilcox ordered his men to paddle for their lives toward the nearest shore, in this case the northern one. His best chance, he believed, was to fight his pursuers from solid ground as they came at him from the water. But the odds against him increased by a fourth when, as they drove the canoe onshore, the militiaman sprang out of the boat, scrambled up the bank, and disappeared into the woods, ignoring Wilcox's cries to return and fight.[19]

The Indian boats were now upon them. Although they were under fire from Wilcox and his two men, the Creeks had nonetheless managed to reach the riverbank. But the Americans' fire was so steady and accurate, killing two of them, that it halted the Indians' attack.[20] At this moment the impetuous Wilcox did the unthinkable: he ordered his men to charge the Creeks. This tactic was so surprising and the charge so ferocious (Simpson broke his bayonet during the attack) that the astonished Indians clambered back into their boats and fled down the darkening river, unfortunately taking the Americans' canoe with them.[21]

That night, Wilcox and his remaining two men took stock of their perilous situation. They climbed up the riverbank and concealed themselves in the heavy brush leading back from its edge. Although the night was very cold, they lit no fires. In this condition, while listening for the slightest night noise and speaking in whispers, they decided that their best chance to escape the Indians was to cross the river the next night to the southern shore and from there move downriver along the bank. It was not clear why they chose this escape plan, unless they thought by slipping away at night down the opposite shore they could fool the Indians as to their true position on the river.

The next morning, February 13, in full sight of the Indians, they began constructing a raft from logs and the plentiful cane they found along the riverbank. That night they slipped the crude vessel into the freezing water. When the raft was afloat, they slithered aboard and, using the butt ends of their guns as paddles, angled it to the other shore. With some difficulty handling the makeshift craft in the turbulent and fast-moving water, they soon made the crossing, but the effort cost them dearly. One of their three guns and all of their munitions, except the powder in the gourd, fell overboard during the crossing; most likely one of the soldiers had fastened the gourd to his belt by a strip of rawhide.[22]

Strangely, rather than proceed downstream along the opposite shore under the cover of night, the Americans pulled their raft onto a sandbar at the mouth of a small creek opening onto the apex of one of the Alabama River's great, geometrical loops. There they spent the night. The next morning, February 14, they began constructing a larger and sturdier raft of logs that could better handle the river's rough waters, intending to float downstream once night fell. The Indians were not so easily fooled. At dusk, the three Americans were dismayed to see ten of them paddle past the American position and presumably take up their own position just downstream. The famished soldiers, who were now without food, spent another long and anxious night on shore, debating what to do. By this time Wilcox and his men had had enough of the vagaries of travel by water and decided to hazard their lives by land.[23]

On the morning of February 15, Wilcox and his two companions left their new-built raft and the unpredictable Alabama River for the forested high ground along its southern shore. The Federal Road that General

Claiborne had traveled to the Holy Ground back in December lay in this direction, and perhaps the lieutenant hoped to reach it. Unfortunately, the sky was cloudy and the position of the sun uncertain; without a compass, the Americans had no better luck navigating by land than by water. At this point, the men had been without food three days.[24] Famished, they wandered aimlessly and laboriously through heavy cover for hours. Finally, his men exhausted and weak from hunger, Wilcox decided to return to the sandbar where he had left the raft and try once again to make his escape downriver under cover of night. Wilcox prudently concealed his little party among the brush and cane lining the riverbank, with the raft in sight below, and waited for night. At this point, given the party's physical condition, it would be surprising if everyone's judgment was not impaired.

For Wilcox, night never came. With the patience of professional hunters, the Creeks were waiting. In the space of minutes, a canoe filled with six Creeks landed at the sandbar where the raft rested. While some of them stayed with the raft, the others climbed the riverbank where the Americans were hiding, their two guns charged with their remaining shot. The parties exchanged fire, and men on both sides were hit. Corporal Simpson fell with a ball through the knee, while Wilcox was shot through the body. Somehow, Wilcox managed to keep fighting. Amid the black powder smoke and the screams from the closing Indians, Wilcox ordered the unhurt Private Armar to help Simpson to the sandbar at the mouth of Pursley's Creek, where the Indians had beached their canoe. Wilcox then grabbed his rifle by the barrel, slid down the riverbank, and attacked the Indian guarding the canoe. Lacking any weapons, the powerless Armar took advantage of Wilcox's charge and fled up the riverbank and into a cane thicket, abandoning poor Simpson. Remarkably, by then Wilcox had fought his way into the Creek canoe and was now struggling hand to hand with one of the warriors. The remaining Creeks were closing in on him and Simpson, tomahawks in hand. After a brief struggle, the Indians subdued the two Americans and bound their hands, clearly hoping to take them back to the Creek encampment for display and terrible amusement. Then the Creeks saw the outlines of two large boats on the horizon. A curtain of spray rising from their oars, the vessels were fast approaching and not Indian; undoubtedly they had been attracted by the gunfire from the recent skirmish. It was Captain Dinkins.[25]

At this point both Americans were badly injured but alive. Ironically, the appearance of Dinkins's boats, which had been the objective of their expedition, was also their death warrant. The startled Indians risked the brief time necessary to scalp and tomahawk Wilcox and Simpson, toss their dead comrades into the river, and push off in their canoe downstream. The Creeks' flight was so panicked that when Dinkins reached the sandbar, he found that along with the two Americans the Indians had left behind their scalp knives and tomahawks, edges brightly stained with Wilcox's and Simpson's fresh blood, and even their precious guns. Wilcox was unconscious but still alive when Dinkins reached him. Tragically, the monumentally courageous lieutenant, and Corporal Simpson, drew breath only several minutes more. Saddened and chastened, Dinkins and his men loaded their shattered bodies onto one of the boats and prepared to row for Fort Claiborne. But Dinkins was able to salvage something from his rescue attempt. To everyone's surprise, Armar, probably somewhat tentatively and shamefaced, had crept out of the lordly stand of cane from whose safety he had watched in horror as the Creeks butchered his comrades. Once he identified himself, he climbed into one of the boats, where he was doubtless immediately peppered with questions. Dinkins's fleet reached Fort Claiborne the night of February 16, and the Americans buried their comrades the following day. The Creeks had obtained some measure of revenge for their defeat at the celebrated Canoe Fight.[26]

But where in the world had Dinkins and the fleet been the last ten days? Although they left on February 4, Dinkins and his boats, even with the men pulling on the oars virtually day and night, did not reach what Cornells told him was the mouth of the Cahaba River until February 11—three days behind an unforgiving schedule. By this point, Dinkins must have been as crazed with frustration and worry on the water as was Russell on the land. To make matters worse, the watercourse Cornells pointed out to Dinkins as the Cahaba was actually a large creek; the Cahaba was twenty miles upstream. Dinkins should have been strongly suspicious of Cornells's information, for tellingly there was no Creek town at the mouth of the purported Cahaba River. Ignoring this fact, Dinkins proceeded to have his men pull the boats two miles up the creek until it shallowed such that they could go no farther. Although this development should have further alerted Dinkins that he was on the wrong stream, it apparently had little or no effect on the man. His water ascent thwarted, Dinkins ordered an officer to take half of the ad hoc sailors in Dinkins's command and march them off upstream in search of Russell while he and the other men waited at anchor.

Dinkins waited forty-eight hours for the detachment's return while it traveled twenty miles upstream in search of Russell, who was by this time desperately attempting to get his starving army to Fort Claiborne intact. When the little band returned on the thirteenth, Dinkins set his course upriver on the Alabama. After endless hours of arduous rowing against the heavy current, by noon February 14, Dinkins concluded that he had passed the mouth of the Cahaba River and reluctantly turned his boats downstream. It was on this return journey that he spied Wilcox's melee with the Creeks.[27]

As for Russell and his main force, two days had passed at their camp on the Cahaba River with no sign of Dinkins and his supply boats. Russell's command was now in an even more desperate situation than it had been six weeks earlier in the rain-sodden fields of Weatherford's destroyed plantation. The men had not eaten a regular meal for days, and already the Creeks had killed one soldier in an ambush. Russell ordered a return march to Fort Claiborne. As Lieutenant Creagh, the hardened veteran of several campaigns in southwestern Alabama, put it, "then commenced more suffering than it had been my lot to witness in my life."[28]

Russell set an example for his men by killing his fattest horse and distributing its flesh among the troops. Before the march was done, the men went through twelve horses, supplementing this diet with acorns, hickory nuts, rats, and mice. The tasty rodents were captured by setting fire to the Indian cabins and catching the frantic animals as they scurried out of cover from the flames. Even with their meals of horseflesh, so great was the soldiers' hunger that the price for a single rat rose to ten dollars before journey's end. The army's ordeal finally ended at a place known as Bradford's pond, where the starving soldiers were met with wagons loaded with supplies brought back by the men Russell had wisely dispatched from the Cahaba towns to Fort Claiborne.[29]

On February 18, the day after Wilcox and his comrade were buried, Russell and his long-suffering Goths and Vandals reached Fort Claiborne; the starving, and now infamous, militiaman who had deserted Wilcox's expedition came in the next day. Russell immediately began looking for someone to blame for an expedition for which he had presciently already provided an apt description in his January 16, 1814, letter describing the Holy Ground campaign: "[T]he project failed & after killing a few Indians, burning a few towns, & committing some capital blunders, we contented ourselves with what we had done, & marched back." This time there was no venal contractor to blame for this most recent disaster and, as Dinkins was one of Russell's own, he blamed the guides, James Cornells, and the unnamed "land pilot."[30]

With the return of Russell's command to Fort Claiborne, the war in the Alabama River valley effectively came to an end. Dale and his militia were disbanded, and Colonel Russell and the 3rd Regiment went into quarters at Fort Claiborne, where the colonel frittered away his time waiting for General Flournoy to provide him with the tools and materials to build a fleet of boats.[31] It was not until after the first of April, when Russell had received reinforcements at Fort Claiborne of 671 Chickasaws and Choctaws, that he contemplated another combined land and water expedition into the nation. Aside from the problem with building boats, Russell explained that until the arrival of the Indian legion, "a movement to the fork of the river with the few regulars and militia I have would be too hazardous."[32] However, by the time the colonel's new fleet was completed and he was ready to launch his belated expedition up the Alabama to the Hickory Ground, the war was essentially over.

With the retreat of Russell's army from the Cahaba River towns, and against all odds and reason, the nation had survived multiple attacks by armies from Mississippi, Tennessee, and Georgia, most of whom were aided by Creek, Cherokee, Chickasaw, and Choctaw auxiliaries. All of the commanders of these armies—Floyd, Claiborne, Adams, Flournoy, and Russell—had retired from the field. Of the field commanders present at the start of the war, only the otherworldly and long-suffering Andrew Jackson, with his pit-bull-like ferocity and tenacity, remained.

The Battle of Horseshoe Bend

J ACKSON had at last learned a little patience. After his retreat from the nation, he remained at Fort Strother for six weeks, building a new army composed of several thousand militia around a core of his veterans and a US infantry regiment. But most of his energies were devoted to assuring an abundance of supplies for his men and the implementation of a transportation system to timely deliver them to troops in the field. As Jackson confessed to a senior supply officer, Colonel Robert Steele, in a letter as close to pleading for help as Jackson ever came, the "source of all my fears are the want of supplies."[33] Jackson had learned from hard experience that hunger and mutiny go hand in hand, and he was determined to prevent that evil from afflicting his coming campaign. To that end, in makeshift dockyards below the Ten Islands, he had a fleet of boats constructed sufficient to transport over 650 men and plentiful supplies for the army down the Coosa River to a new base of operations against the Red Clubs to be built sixty miles south. He had also set three hundred fatigue troops to work improving the road from Fort Deposit to Fort Strother. Nonetheless, somehow amid all this activity, and suffering from another excruciating bout of dysentery,[34] Jackson found the strength to pursue his vendetta against General Cocke, obtaining permission from General Pinckney to institute court-martial proceedings against Cocke for allegedly enticing soldiers to desert.[35] The charges—disobedience of orders, inciting mutiny, and neglect of duty—were set forth in a lengthy document signed by Jackson's acolyte, William Carroll, acting as special judge advocate.[36]

In planning his third expedition into the nation, Jackson wisely decided to incorporate Pinckney's ideas into his planning, at least to some extent. His newly built fleet of boats would provide an alternate supply route as well as ferry Colonel John Williams and his regiment down the Coosa River. Jackson and the rest of the army, with their supply wagons and pack horses, would move overland along the east bank of the Coosa. The land and water forces would meet fifty-nine miles south at the mouth of Cedar Creek on the eastern shore of the Coosa. At the point of land formed where creek and river meet, Jackson planned to build a fort to be used as a depot for supplies and a place to care for his sick and wounded.

According to the plan favored by Pinckney, after constructing and garrisoning the fort, Jackson would march down the Coosa Valley to the fabled Hickory Ground, just above the juncture of the Coosa River with the Tallapoosa River, where he would rendezvous with his supply boats. At roughly the same time, Colonel Homer Milton and his command of South and North Carolinians, designated the army of the Centre, would move west along the Federal Road to the Hickory Ground. A third army, led by Colonel Russell and carrying extra supplies for the other two, would travel by boat up the Alabama River from its base at Fort Claiborne to the Hickory Ground. Once this flotilla joined with Jackson and Milton, the war would soon be over.[37]

However, as always, Jackson had his own ideas about how the campaign against the Creeks should be conducted. He did not reject Pinckney's cherished plan of uniting the American forces at the Hickory Ground, but on February 16, he had learned from the chief of the Kialegees that a large number of hostiles from the towns in the upper Tallapoosa watershed had gathered at the fortified peninsula near the Emuckfau battlefield.[38] Jackson proposed that he first proceed to the Red Club fort and destroy the hostiles concentrated there. At the same time, Colonel John McKee, Andrew Jackson's liaison with the Choctaws, and his Choctaw and Chickasaw warriors would attack the Black Warrior River towns and from there move east to the Cahaba River towns, where a large contingent of Creeks were purportedly gathered. In conjunction with McKee's attack, Jackson would send a contingent of mounted troops against the Cahaba River towns where they would meet up with McKee's forces. With the region west of the Coosa River secure and the Okfuskees and their allies defeated, Jackson would march his army south to the lower Tallapoosa towns. There he would link up with Milton and proceed to the nearby Hickory Ground, where they would be met by Russell and his fleet of supply boats.[39]

Pinckney approved of Jackson's plan with some delicately worded provisos. In particular, Pinckney wished to avoid the fiasco of Jackson's and Floyd's prior forays into Creek country in which they enjoyed Pyrrhic victories and were sent limping home by the unobliging Creeks. Accordingly, Pinckney advised Jackson that he should establish a strong base below Fort Strother from which to launch his attack against the Okfuskee towns. Thus, if Jackson were compelled to retreat "for want of provisions" or casualties, supplies and a refuge for his wounded would be obtained "so much sooner." With a gentle dig aimed at both Jackson and Floyd,

Pinckney also noted a further advantage of an advance fortification deep in Creek country: "you will not have the mortification of giving up so much territory."[40]

The reason for Jackson's departure from Pinckney's original plan—he was turning his army at a right angle away from the line of march to the Hickory Ground—was probably a strange mix of Jackson' military acumen and his desire to retrieve his all-important honor. It would have been militarily foolhardy to leave a large and aggressive Red Club contingent on his left flank as he toiled his way to the Hickory Ground. But Jackson's obsession with revenge and honor also must have played some part in his decision. Jackson and his supporters had portrayed his recent campaign into the Okfuskee country as victorious. In truth, Jackson had been forced to abandon the campaign by a rude confederation of untutored savages who were seemingly thumbing their noses at him from the sanctuary of their sacred fortress. The death-before-dishonor Jackson may have found irresistible the opportunity to wash clean this perceived stain on his military record with the blood of his Emuckfau and Enitachopco tormentors.

What Jackson believed would be the campaign that would finally end the war began under bizarre and macabre circumstances. On March 14, 1814, the day before Jackson's army departed from its quarters at Fort Strother, the general staged a spectacle before the army that haunted his presidential campaign a decade later but at the time appeared to be good policy. It involved the public execution of a teenaged militia private before a firing squad under dubious charges of mutiny.

The would-be mutineer was an illiterate private named John Woods who, along with an elder brother, had made the singular mistake of enlisting in an infamous company of volunteers. Woods was seventeen at the time and not required to serve, but he enlisted as a substitute for a soldier who wished to leave the service. Unfortunately, the company he joined was the one General Isaac Roberts had raised the previous fall to serve for three months but, when Jackson refused to accept this term of service, had turned about several miles from Fort Strother and marched for home. Desperate for men, Jackson eventually allowed Roberts to issue pardons to those mutineers who agreed to remain with the company. The company was then reformed in Fayetteville, Tennessee, where young Woods first joined its ranks, and marched back to Fort Strother. Thus Woods was no part of December's mutiny, but he became fatally tarred with it nonetheless.[41] However, Woods was not entirely blameless in the series of events that ended in his death. He, like so many of his kind, did not respond well to arbitrary authority, and this characteristic led to his downfall.

On a miserable February morning, twinned with cold and rain, Woods found himself on guard duty on the picket lines around Fort Strother. He had apparently been running late for this duty, because he left his blanket

in his tent and also missed breakfast. The miserable weather soon reminded him of the forgotten blanket, and he asked permission of his superior
to retrieve it. Permission was granted, and Woods trotted back to his tent
to get his blanket. When he arrived, the famished Woods was delighted to
find that food was still laid out on the table. He joined the men at the table
and, with a teenager's rapacious appetite, began wolfing down food.

While Wood and the other men were enjoying their breakfast, an officer
entered the tent. Glancing about, he found the floor littered with chicken
bones and other detritus from an earlier morning's meal. The officer
ordered the breakfasting soldiers to clean up the mess. Woods ignored the
order and continued eating. Incensed by Woods's behavior, the officer
barked out an order at Woods in a manner Woods found insufferable. The
two soldiers were soon engaged in a violent argument that finally prompted the officer to order Woods's breakfast companions to arrest the private.
At this order, Woods snatched up his gun, reprimed it, and threatened to
shoot the first man who laid a hand on him.[42]

While a standoff in Woods's tent ensued, word reached Jackson that one
of his soldiers had mutinied. After all of these months of quelling constant
unrest among his troops, this report was the final straw that broke
Jackson's capacity to address the situation with at least a modicum of reason.[43] Infuriated, he reportedly screamed out an order to no one in particular to shoot the "villain" down and raced for Woods's tent. By the time
Jackson arrived, Woods's companions had persuaded him to hand over his
gun and submit to arrest. Typically, Woods would have been taken into
custody by his own militia unit. Ominously, however, Jackson ordered him
placed in the charge of the 39th Infantry Regiment. A squad from that regiment was called up, and Woods, who by now had turned eighteen, was led
away in irons to its encampment.[44]

Woods was tried for mutiny on March 12. The trial took place between
two tents in the woods around the camp. Five militia officers constituted
the tribunal. The young man sat on a log before his judges while the evidence against him was introduced. His manner was defiant, and given the
usual severe but not terminal punishments in such cases, he apparently
was not anxious about the verdict. To Woods's astonishment, not only was
he found guilty of mutiny, but his sentence was death before a firing
squad.[45] It was carried out on March 14. At high noon, Jackson had the
entire army paraded onto an elevated section of ground in front of Fort
Strother.[46] Private Woods was then escorted to his place of execution by a
squad of soldiers from the 39th Infantry. There, "Divine service" was
held.[47] Then, when the religious service was over, Jackson read to the
assembled troops the order sentencing the private to death. While the
army looked on, a firing squad from the 39th Infantry stepped forward,
presented arms, and, as the command to fire faded away, discharged their

guns at poor John Woods. It is said that every shot "told," and that Woods died instantly.[48] Jackson had delivered his lesson.[49]

The reasons Jackson gave for this unheard-of punishment in his army were patently untrue. Jackson found that Woods had mutinied twice, first as a member of General Roberts's command in December and second in the recent breakfast incident, a squabble between an officious officer and a hot-headed teenager that hardly rose to the level of mutiny. In his order of execution, Jackson noted that he had demonstrated mercy to the prisoner by pardoning Woods for his mutinous conduct on the first occasion but that it was not in the interest of the service to pardon him for the second transgression. The company muster rolls plainly showed that Woods was a not member of Roberts's mutinous command in December, when the so-called first of Woods's mutinies occurred. Woods or his brother or their company commander or Roberts could have told the court-martial that seemingly critical fact. But no evidence has been found that the court-martial was ever aware of, or ever gave consideration to, such irrefutable evidence.[50]

It appears Jackson seized on Woods's misbehavior as a means for instilling a chilling lesson in his army. So important was it to Jackson to gain control of his unruly soldiers before embarking on what he believed was the campaign against the Creeks that would win the war that he was willing to sacrifice the young private to achieve that end. At the time, Jackson's drastic step was praised for purging the army of sedition, discord, and mutiny and thus creating a military climate "from which the most salutary effects may reasonably be expected to result."[51] The judicial murder of Private Woods, however, would be a tonic that had only a temporary effect on the seemingly inveterate mutinous disposition of Jackson's soldiers. But the general's newfound constraints on the quality of his mercy did not bode well for the Muskogee Nation in the coming months.

The day following the "salutary" execution of Private Woods, the army left Fort Strother for Creek country. Brigadier General Thomas Johnson's brigade led the way after drawing food and ammunition from the quartermaster sufficient to supply the anticipated week's march to the mouth of Cedar Creek on the Coosa River. Johnson's command crossed the Coosa from Fort Strother just upstream of the Ten Islands at the ford General Coffee had discovered in October on his way to Tallushatchee. On March 16, Johnson resumed his march south to the mouth of a little creek emptying into the river. There he camped for the night and waited for Jackson and his men to join them.[52] Jackson arrived on the eighteenth, and the next morning the combined force took up the march for Cedar Creek.

While Johnson made his way to Cedar Creek from Fort Strother, Colonel Williams's regiment and the flotilla of supply boats embarked on their journey down the Coosa. In his order to Williams, Jackson was quite particular in specifying the measures for avoiding an ambush by the Red Clubs and the loss of critical supplies. Every evening the fleet was to beach itself on the eastern shore of the Coosa at a piece of land well suited for defense. Scouts were then to be sent out into the forest to search for hostiles. And in each boat, Williams was to place two sentinels—one at each end. Jackson also warned that a significant shoal obstructed the river just upstream of Cedar Creek.[53] Despite the dangers, in being chosen for the journey down the Coosa to Cedar Creek, the novice aquanauts of the 39th Infantry seemed to have drawn the longest straw. Lounging on sacks of flour, playing cards, pulling in the fish they could see in their teeming multitudes off the sides of the boats—while the more diligent of them cleaned their guns and sharpened their bayonets—they enjoyed an effortless tour of the magnificent Coosa Valley just coming into flower as they floated over water as clear as the moonshine whiskey a number of them were skilled at producing.

Bringing up the expedition's rear was Coffee and his mounted riflemen. Jackson ordered him to remain at Fort Strother until Colonel Robert Dyer arrived with his company of horsemen. Once united, the officers were to cross the river and follow in Jackson's wake. On Coffee's arrival at Fort Williams, he was to organize all the mounted men into a brigade and take command. Dyer and Coffee left Fort Strother on March 18.[54] So far, Jackson's campaign appeared to be off to a promising start.

Unfortunately, the ever-surprising Alabama countryside had a way of frustrating the Americans' plans. The water in the Coosa had mysteriously dropped at a time of year when it usually ran its highest. Although the river in this section of its course flowed fairly straight through long stretches of countryside, the current low state of its waters slowed the supply flotillas' progress and finally ended it altogether a mile and a half above the mouth of Cedar Creek. Here, on March 21, the boats became lodged on a rocky line of shoals across the river that was just the first of many such obstacles to navigation on the lower reaches of a river Williams described as "extremely difficult and dangerous."[55] The amateur aquanauts' vacation was over.

Jackson was not happy at the report that the boats with their crucial supplies were stuck on the shoals and that the river below was choked with even greater obstacles, although he may have secretly been pleased that Pinckney's pet scheme for water transport had foundered on the shoals as well. His army had taken a leisurely and uneventful six days to reach its destination. Spring was coming on with breathtaking beauty but at a relaxed pace—John Reid termed it a "backward" spring.[56] A mist of bright, shimmering green covered the branches of the hardwoods through which they moved. Among the trees rose the soft and subtle glory of solitary redbud trees. The ground was firm underfoot, and the cold was wrung out of the winter's hard air; breath now came easily, with the air unusually cool and refreshing for this time of year. Their journey was also gentled by the perfume and blossoms of countless flowering trees and bushes and the varied sounds of spring songbirds. Their spirits lifted with every mile farther away from the noisome encampment at Fort Strother. In raucous counterpoint to spring's melodies, however, was the incessant thwack of ax against wood that sounded from the head of the columns as the army cut its way farther south through the forest. And although the kingdom of insects had not yet arisen in its summer fullness to torment man and beast, the men had to be ever watchful for spring rattlers emerging famished and ill-tempered from their winter burrows.

These responsibilities Jackson accomplished in short order with his usual manic energy and dogged determination in spite of the fact that he was suffering from another of his recurrent bouts of dysentery. Construction of a fort housing four hundred soldiers and named for Colonel Williams was begun. As for the colonel himself, his time was filled supervising the crossing of the shoals blocking his passage to his eponymous fort. To the sounds of groans, curses, and sudden cries of pain as bone met river rock, men and supplies were off-loaded from the foundered boats. When the vessels were lightened enough they were dragged across the rocks and reloaded below the shoals. The 39th Infantry then floated to the mouth of Cedar Creek, which it reached on March 22, putting the campaign a day behind schedule.[57] The preceding afternoon, not long after Jackson arrived, he dispatched a detachment of soldiers to burn an abandoned hostile village six miles downstream. He also found time to promote a group of officers, including a Major Howell Tatum, who was to replace the retiring Major Strother as topographical engineer.[58]

Jackson's attention, however, was primarily focused on the vital issue of supplies for his army. Accordingly, he sent a string of letters to his supply officers at Fort Strother badgering them to push down supplies from there by boat and wagon as fast as they were able. Looking into future operations toward the Hickory Ground to the south, Jackson sent scouts down the Coosa River to explore its potential for navigation by large supply boats. They reported that the Coosa's course downstream was broken by enormous rapids whose tormented waters could be heard in the distance for miles and whose rapids later acquired such appropriately fearsome names as the Devil's Race, Butting Ram, Hell's Gap, and the Devil's Staircase by the brave boatmen who attempted to run them.[59] The last and worst of these death traps, the Devil's Staircase, was of particular interest to Jackson since it ended just above the Hickory Ground, where his army was eventually headed. The scouts confirmed the existence of these horrendous obstacles to navigation.

Also of concern to Jackson was his alternative supply route by wagon road. While his river route was frustrated by low water and ferocious rapids, his land route faced a human threat. In the early morning hours of March 24, a band of Creeks attacked one of his wagon trains on its way with supplies from Fort Deposit on the Tennessee River to Fort Strother on the Coosa. On the evening of March 23, the convoy had pulled over to the side of the road for the night. About an hour before dawn, a group of five or six far-afield Red Clubs stole within fifty yards of the camp and opened fire. One guard, Denny Weeks, had a ball pass clear through a hip and a second ball lodge in his side; he soon died. The Creeks then charged out of the darkness toward the camp, preceded by the sound of their hideous war cries. Before they reached the camp, however, they broke off the attack and vanished back into the night without further loss to either side. Eventually the alarmed Americans organized a pursuit. Fourteen or fifteen Cherokee warriors and a few whites were dispatched from the wagon camp to hunt down the Red Club marauders, who by then were long gone.[60] Nonetheless, the incident underscored the vulnerability of the wagon route and the precarious nature of this vital supply line. With insufficient forces to guard the supply depots and at the same time protect the wagons, Jackson's army risked being cut off landward from their base of supplies if the also undermanned Creeks were able to mount systematic attacks along the wagon road.

That same day, to protect his rear and to smooth the way to Horseshoe Bend, Jackson ordered two short-term raids into the nation with orders to rid the countryside of hostiles: one party to the lands east of the Coosa River and the other to the lands on its western side.

Not long after he had arrived at his destination, the restless Jackson penned an order directing his adjutant general to assemble a force of two hundred "healthy, stout and well armed men" from Johnson's brigade, two hundred similarly qualified soldiers from Brigadier General George Doherty's brigade, four hundred of the "best mounted and armed men from the cavalry mounted gunmen and spies," and all well-armed Indians for an expedition to set out the following morning under the command of Johnson.[61] Jackson also delivered an order to Johnson describing the objectives of this expedition. Because Jackson intended to leave for Emuckfau on the twenty-fourth and place Johnson in command of Fort Williams, Jackson intended Johnson's excursion to be a short one designed merely to sweep his immediate front of hostiles. Accordingly, he instructed Johnson to allot only one day's provisions for each man and to return by the twenty-third. In particular he ordered Johnson to burn a hostile village said to lie ten miles west, "killing all the warriors, and making prisoners of all women and children." When that murderous task was accomplished, Johnson was to march to the next village and repeat the process. With his experience at Emuckfau and Enitachopco still fresh in his mind, Jackson spelled out very precisely to Johnson the order of march by which his command was to proceed and the precautions he was to take to avoid an ambush by day and a surprise attack by night.[62]

Johnson and his large contingent of infantry and mounted men left early on the morning of March 22, heading southwest into a forestland of rolling and just-greening hills laced by many clear and lively streams. Six miles on they came to the small village of Woccoccoie, which a detachment of Jackson's men had burnt earlier that week. Near that village, Johnson's scouts discovered a trail leading into the deeper forest. Johnson ordered Major Gibson and his spies to see where it led. Gibson's men quickly discovered signs that indicated a number of hostiles were in the neighborhood and that the trail led to a town about thirteen to fourteen miles away just above "the mouth of a small creek emptying into the Coosa." Gibson reported this information to Johnson waiting back at the burnt village. On receipt of Gibson's report, Johnson immediately ordered him to follow the trail to the vicinity of the town.[63]

Gibson's spies were on horseback, and Johnson quickly found himself alone at the destroyed village without the important eyes and ears of his force that Gibson and his men provided. Apparently feeling exposed in his current position and ignorant of the way to the Okfuskee towns, Johnson and the infantry took off at a quick pace along the trail down which Gibson had disappeared. Along the way, Johnson's flankers discovered a number of bushels of corn and some beef jerky to which they helped themselves.

Johnson eventually met up with Gibson about a mile from the town. Gibson advised Johnson that his men had discovered "considerable" Indian signs in the area, although he had not approached near enough to the town to examine its defenses. Nonetheless, after fruitless miles of wandering, Gibson's report ignited Johnson's martial spirits at the prospect of a fight at last with the enemy. Accordingly, Johnson arrayed his soldiers in the Americans' typical battle formation for an attack on the town. He positioned the infantry in the center of his lines and sent columns of mounted men on either flank to encircle the town. However, when the Americans approached the town, Johnson's dreams of martial glory evaporated when he saw that the place had been abandoned and burnt by its inhabitants.

Although he was greatly disappointed, Johnson's blood was now up, and he believed he was on the eve of a sweet victory. It was only two o'clock in the afternoon, and his guides had reported that the major Creek town of Okfuskee was only six miles away. Johnson put his army in motion for that new objective. But before he had gone far, the inconstant country turned on him. The way grew increasing rugged and mountainous as the tail end of the Appalachians played out onto the piedmont. Six difficult miles on and the army still had not reached the reported location of Okfuskee, which actually lay thirty more miles east. The eager Johnson pressed his army forward toward their objective. At last, six miles farther on, around sunset, the soldiers reached a sizable Creek settlement of one hundred houses surrounded by swampy ground. Once again Johnson's hopes were frustrated. This town, too, was deserted.

Night was now coming on fast and cold, and Johnson sensibly decided to use the abandoned Creek homes to shelter his troops, who were exhausted after their rapid march over difficult ground. Unfortunately for the men's rest, their Cherokee allies could not resist a good burning, and a number of houses were in flames before Johnson and his men could get the rampaging Cherokees, and with them the fires, under control.[64]

The next morning, with the army's one day's ration of food all but gone (a number of his men had even neglected to obtain any rations before the army set out), Johnson decided to return to Fort Williams. Along the route of the march, a group of the irrepressible and largely ungovernable Cherokees and several unruly whites on the army's right flank, including an adventuresome physician named Napier, took off for a frolic through the countryside in search of hostiles and opportunities to put more hous-es to the torch. These men were not seen again until that evening, when they straggled into Fort Williams with little to show for their exertions. They did find a deserted town of sixty to seventy houses to ransack and torch. In their search for booty they also found a sizable collection of scalps, which the adventuresome Dr. Napier gathered up and presented to Jackson and Johnson at Fort Williams. This settlement may have been the village of Wehoofka.[65]

Other than alerting every Indian within thirty miles of Fort Williams of Jackson's arrival, Johnson's expedition had accomplished little beyond some small-scale plundering and burning designed to make more of the hostile population miserable and the Americans' Indian allies happy. (The only live thing the expedition apparently encountered was a "small hog," which a soldier promptly shot and brought back to camp.)[66] The Red Clubs residing in this region of the nation were nowhere to be found, but Jackson was sure where he could find them: in the upper Tallapoosa lands where two months earlier he had almost lost his army.

On the day Johnson's command returned from its brief foray into the Creek lands to the east, Jackson determined to send a smaller force of two hundred men of the 1st Regiment of the Tennessee Militia across the Coosa to scour the western countryside of hostiles. Under the command of Colonel Evan Allison, the men did not depart camp until late in the afternoon of March 24 because of the difficulty they had in drawing rations from the commissary. Once the men had crossed the river, Allison led the way into the interior in search of Indians, leaving behind a group of soldiers near the river crossing to secure his line of communication.

As the evening wore on, the men back at Fort Williams were suddenly startled by a crescendo of gunfire coming from across the river. As they anxiously listened, the sound of firing not only continued but rose in intensity, as if more men were rushing to the scene of what the listeners were sure was an ambush by the Creeks. Johnson's closest source of reinforcements for Allison's small command was a cavalry unit. Unfortunately, it was on the opposite shore of the Coosa from where the battle was raging and where most of the army's canoes were beached. But before Johnson could determine how to send help, the firing diminished, fell off more, and then ceased altogether except for the isolated crack of a gun. Many of the soldiers at Fort Williams feared the worst, and Johnson sent scouts across the river to determine the outcome of the battle.[67]

Allison first heard the firing along the river on his return to the position where he had left part of his command. He and his men had penetrated about ten miles into the wilderness but discovered no sign of Indians. Discouraged and hampered by the dark, Allison decided to abandon the search until morning. He was still several miles from the Coosa when he heard the faint then increasingly intense sound of gunfire from the direction of the river. Urging his men to speed forward and shouting out the password as they neared the encampment, he was astonished to burst on the demented scene of a riotous crowd of his soldiers firing at the numerous light grey squirrels hopping in panic through the branches of the trees along the riverbank.[68]

The soldiers' officers appeared impotent to stop their men's sport, which violated strict orders given the men as well as the very "rules and articles of war." What was worse, when Allison's men came on the scene they proceeded to join the fun. Although Allison desperately attempted to restore order, only the men within the sound of his voice obeyed his command to stop firing.[69] Eventually, their ranks decimated, the defeated squirrels retreated into the forest, and the soldiers rushed forward to police the battlefield of the succulent dead now headed for roasting spits and stew pots.

When a furious Johnson finally learned the reason for the gunfire, he was all for arresting Allison and charging him with a laundry list of military crimes. At this point, one or more of his officers sensibly informed the general that if he took such action against the popular colonel he stood a good chance of having a serious mutiny on his hands. It appears animosity already existed between the troops under Allison and the troops who had remained in camp because Allison's men believed the army's high command treated their rival soldiers more favorably.

This situation had escaped Johnson's, as well as Jackson's, attention, but now the affair of the squirrels threatened to bring the simmering animosity out into open violence between the two groups of soldiers. Johnson initially was inclined to initiate court-martial proceedings against Allison. Being no Andrew Jackson, however, Johnson did the prudent thing and suspended any action against Allison until Jackson returned.[70]

When the battle with the squirrels erupted, Jackson was well on his way to Horseshoe Bend. He had left Fort Strother around five o'clock on the morning of March 24, with a motley army of almost three thousand men comprising US regulars, Tennessee militia, Cherokees, and friendly Creeks. The latter were principally Cowetas led by William McIntosh, Menawa's old adversary; the remainder were Tuckabatchees under the Big Warrior's son. Shortly after the Battle of Calebee Creek, McIntosh and seventy-five of his Coweta warriors somehow traveled unmolested across the breadth of the Red Clubs lands and joined Jackson at Fort Strother around January 29.[71]

As Jackson confided to Pinckney in a letter dated March 23, he was not pleased with the inclusion of these Creeks and Cherokees among his expedition forces. Traitors are rarely trusted by their employers, and Jackson, who had suffered under such men during the Revolutionary War, was no different in this respect. Additionally, at least in Jackson's eyes, his ungovernable Indian allies had hardly distinguished themselves during his last expedition to Emuckfau Creek. Perhaps most importantly, as he noted in his letter to Pinckney, the friendly Indians were devouring his precious supplies at an alarming rate. As soon as he could rid himself of his troublesome allies, "with a good grace, & without leaving improper impressions on their minds," Jackson intended to do so. He thought this objective could best be achieved once the army reached Emuckfau. There he would "find or make a pretext for discharging the greater part of them; & perhaps the whole, except my guides."[72] Fortunately for Jackson, the opportunity to do so did not present itself.

Leaving its encampment at Fort Williams, for the next fifty-two miles Jackson's army hacked its way through forests, trudged over hills, and forded melodiously named streams like the Weogefka, the Socapatoy, and the Hillabee. The main body of the army followed a company of pioneers wielding axes and other implements against the forest in order to widen existing Indian trails sufficient to accompany the army's supply wagons and its two cannon: a three pounder and a six pounder. Amazingly, the militia marched in good order, perhaps inspired by the example of the recently executed Private Woods. Spies spread out in the woods ahead of and to the rear of his army. Groups of flankers roamed the woods to both sides of the army, and a strong rear guard under a trusted officer followed. There would be no Enitachopco on this march.

The route of the army took it over the ridge that separated the Coosa and Tallapoosa drainages and roughly followed a slightly southeastern direction through a countryside now drained of human beings.[73] On the evening of March 24, the army camped near present-day Sylacauga, Alabama. The following day it camped near present-day Hollins, Alabama, at the edge of an immense forest. By the afternoon of the twenty-sixth, the army was only six miles northeast of Horseshoe Bend. Here, around the Pinckneyville area, the artillerymen apparently paused to engage in a little target practice to sight in their guns and make sure they were in proper working order, for many years later, in 1946, a lumberman found a six-pound shot lodged in one of the trees he was felling.[74] The sound of the cannon firing may have also been intended as a form of psychological warfare on an enemy who had recently suffered from the fire of this fearsome weapon at Enitachopco Creek.

On the evening of the twenty-sixth, Jackson's army set up camp near the old Emuckfau battlefield. After supper, Jackson and his senior officers met in Jackson's tent to plan the coming battle. From their earlier expedition to the region, and the more recent reports of their scouts, the Americans had a good idea of the terrain and disposition of the Red Clubs embraced by the loop in the Tallapoosa River known as Horseshoe Bend.[75]

At the toe of the horseshoe lay a sizable and recently constructed town. Like the Alabamans and the tribes in the lower Tallapoosa River had done, the Red Clubs living on the upper Tallapoosa River had built a sacred refuge to which they could retreat should the war turn against them. Jackson estimated the size of the peninsula to be eighty to one hundred acres. To the northwest the land at the mouth of the Horseshoe rose in a line of small hills no more than two hundred feet high. As the hills neared the peninsula's mouth, they dropped smoothly into a swale of land that had been shorn of its timber. At first glance this area of cleared forestland riddled with stumps appeared to have been prepared by the Creeks as a field for crops. It was only when one saw at the field's far end the enormous wooden barricade that zigzagged across the mouth of the peninsula several hundred yards from the hill line that it became clear that the Red Clubs had prepared the place as a killing ground.[76]

With great labor and ingenuity, the Creeks had built the barrier to seal off the landward side of the peninsula, leaving the Tallapoosa River to guard the remainder of this fortress. A few hundred yards behind the barrier, almost in the center of the peninsula, the land rose into a curious and thickly forested hump of biting stone, then fell away again to a plateau of slightly undulating land that rose no more than fourteen feet above the river. On twenty acres of this spot at the toe of the horseshoe, one-half mile from the barrier, the Creeks had built a town of several dozen hastily constructed houses. As was typical of Creek towns, the houses were arranged around an open square. Atypically, however, as befits the village's function as a temporary refuge, the houses were very large, each able to hold twenty to thirty-three people.[77] A thicket of trees and brush lined both banks of the river. Two islands lay on the north side of the river downstream from the town: a small islet just off the tip of the peninsula and, one thousand feet downstream, a much larger island of several wooded acres. The river ranged from 100 to 150 yards wide and up to 20 feet deep at points, a significant obstacle if properly defended. Directly overhanging the far side of the Tallapoosa was the same craggy ridge of timber-covered rock that General Adams encountered in December when he attacked the town of New Yaucau a few miles upstream.[78] The whole peninsula was greening with spring, but the thick green that would blanket it was a few weeks away, and the land was still largely brown and gray and bare with winter.

Within the refuge were approximately one thousand warriors and several hundred old men, women, and children from the nearby towns of Okfuskee, Oakehoga, New-yaucau, Fish Ponds, Hillabee, and Eufaula.[79] The warriors were battle-hardened veterans of many fights with the Americans but were poorly armed with a mixture of rifles, old muskets, and bows and arrows. Among them was the young warrior Santo, the savior of Vicey McGirth and her seven children at Fort Mims. The Red Clubs were assembling an army at Horseshoe Bend from the Coosa and upper Tallapoosa towns to await an anticipated attack by Jackson, and Santo was leaving to fight there. Before he left, he took Vicey McGirth aside and explained the situation. He was off to fight Jackson at a place called the Horseshoe, he told her, and well may not return. In that event she and her family must escape his village as best she could and make their way to the white settlements. She watched as he rode from the town with the other warriors and made her plans.[80]

Perhaps Santo had a premonition of his own death, but if so it was most likely informed by the fate of the denizens of Fort Mims who had carelessly penned themselves up in a tiny, ill-built fort. Horseshoe Bend, however, was not Fort Mims. The barricade across the neck of the peninsula was stout and cleverly engineered to allow a killing fire to be brought to bear against any assailants. It was manned not by a ragtag assemblage of barely trained citizen soldiers but by hundreds of seasoned Creek warriors. The Tallapoosa to their back and sides was running swift, cold, and high. The interior of the peninsula was rough and hilly, and furnished excellent concealment to cover a retreat from the barricade. Moreover, their prophets, particularly the noted Monahee, had assured them that Jackson's army would be destroyed at the barricade while the waters of the Tallapoosa would shield them from other avenues of attack. Just in case this set of prophets was as misinformed as their brothers on other fields of battle, however, the inhabitants of Tohopeka had assembled a flotilla of approximately one hundred large canoes along the banks of the Tallapoosa River near the town.

The primary military leader of the Creeks at the Horseshoe was Menawa, the mixed-blood Okfuskee chief who most likely commanded the warriors who had attacked Jackson the past January at Emuckfau and Enitachopco creeks. At the time, Menawa was about the same age as Jackson, forty-seven. He was a large, powerful, and imposing man with pecan-colored skin, a massive head, a long, straight nose, and a thin upper lip. In his youth he had been the most famous horse thief in the nation, noted for his daring raids on the Tennessee settlements in the Cumberland River valley. He was something of a dandy even among warriors who fancied extravagant, bright-colored dress. And when he wore a colored turban with a plume, he looked much like a seventeenth-century Turkish nobleman. Like many Red Club leaders, he was wealthy, with a large plantation, huge numbers of hogs and cattle, and many African slaves. Like his peers, he had much to lose if the Americans won the war. He was, Menawa declared, as if describing a characteristic as mundane as eye color, "a man of blood." [81]

Although like most of his people Menawa was sufficiently superstitious to give some credence to the words of the prophets, when the chief learned of the size and composition of Jackson's army, now only a few days' march from Tohopeka, and compared it to his own force and the position he had to defend, he must have been dismayed. With insufficient room for his warriors to maneuver and no place to retreat to other than the dubious avenue of the Tallapoosa and the rocky interior of the peninsula, his people faced annihilation if Jackson breached the wall. Unlike the Alabama River at the Holy Ground or the lower Tallapoosa at the Battle of Autossee, the Tallapoosa here was not broad enough to prevent a crossing by Jackson's forces or to cover an escape under the guns of any Americans waiting on the river's opposite bank. Menawa has been criticized for overestimating the utility of the river as a barrier to the Americans. But given that he had insufficient numbers of warriors to both man the barricades and repel a potential American crossing of the river, he was forced to gamble that the battle would be won or lost at the barricade. The canoes waiting below the town were perhaps his sop to assuage his people's fears that, regardless of whatever their prophets promised them, their enemies would breach their natural and man-made defenses. [82]

Unlike Menawa, Jackson must have been delighted at the prospect before him. As he wrote Pinckney, he was "[d]etermined to exterminate" the hostiles. [83] Incredibly, his adversaries, who fought best employing concealment, surprise, and quick movement, had facilitated that objective by obligingly penning themselves within this discrete thumb of land where their ability to maneuver was limited and the opportunity for escape even more so. This time, unlike the Emuckfau expedition, Jackson believed he had the men and the artillery to take the place.

Foremost among the infantry available to him were Colonel Williams's 39th Infantry Regiment of 650 US regulars. Among their ranks were some tough young fighters, including the future president of the Republic of Texas, the twenty-one-year-old, six-foot-eight ensign Sam Houston, and Houston's superior officer, Major Lemuel P. Montgomery, a brilliant, twenty-eight-year-old lawyer turned soldier. With his auburn hair, dark eyes, and well-proportioned six-foot-two-inch frame, Montgomery was said to be "the finest looking man in the army."[84]

The mounted arm of Jackson's force was seven hundred men strong and led by his old warhorse and natural soldier, John Coffee.[85] Included in Coffee's command were five hundred Cherokees. They were led by a real killer, a white man, Colonel Gideon Morgan. He had been in command of the Cherokees who massacred the unsuspecting Hillabees during General White's foray into their country the previous November. Among Morgan's warriors was a more cerebral and perhaps gentler soul who would become the most famous Cherokee in that tribe's long history. His name was Sequoyah, and he was the son of a Cherokee mother and a white soldier. In later years he would develop the first Cherokee written language. In addition to Morgan's Cherokee contingent, Coffee also had in his command a hundred friendly Creeks, mostly Cowetas, under William McIntosh, the personal enemy of Menawa and a tough fighter in his own right. Jackson may have disparaged these Indians' worth to Pinckney before the coming battle, but these men and their leaders were proven warriors who had fought in most of the battles in the Creek War. Coffee was also reinforced by one of Jackson's hard-hitting companies of spies, led by the veteran of many fights, Captain William Russell.[86]

The largest unit Jackson had in his army was the one-thousand-five-hundred-man newly recruited militia, of the brigade of east Tennessee militia commanded by General Doherty. Based on his experience with militiamen over the last several months, Jackson did not have great confidence in this unit. He did expect great things from his artillery company in which Rachel's nephew, Private John Caffery Jr., served. The artillery company's strength was boosted by the addition of a three-pound cannon to the six-pound piece Jackson had employed at Enitachopco Creek. Thus, Jackson had with him over triple the number of Red Club warriors gathered at the Horseshoe, as well as a second cannon; the general was confident of a complete and easy victory.

Jackson's plan was the standard one he employed for destroying Creek towns and their defenders. Encircle the town with mounted men, attack from the front with the infantry, and meet in the center over heaps of dead Indians. Toward that end, early on the morning of Sunday, March 27, Jackson ordered Coffee to encircle that portion (the toe) of the Horseshoe protected by the river. In accordance with that order, at 6:30 A.M., Coffee

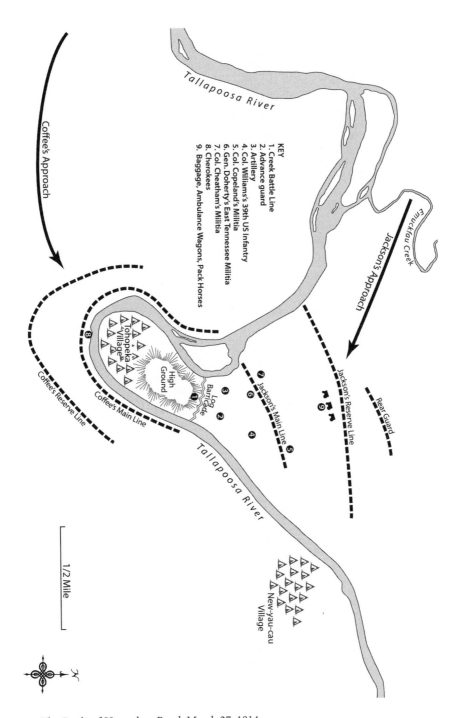

KEY
1. Creek Battle Line
2. Advance guard
3. Artillery
4. Col. Williams's 39th US Infantry
5. Col. Copeland's Militia
6. Gen. Doherty's East Tennessee Militia
7. Col. Cheatham's Militia
8. Cherokees
9. Baggage, Ambulance Wagons, Pack Horses

The Battle of Horseshoe Bend, March 27, 1814.

and his command forded the Tallapoosa two and a half miles below the town. Once his men had assembled on the other side, he sent them through the woods sloping upward from the eastern bank of the Tallapoosa until they ringed the peninsula from one end of the barricade to the other. In order to secure his rear from an attack by Red Clubs from the Okfuskee towns six miles below the Horseshoe, he placed his mounted volunteers on the high ground of the low ridge overlooking the Horseshoe and established his command post on the very top of the ridge. From there he could monitor the developments in the Horseshoe fight and at the same time protect his rear from an attack by any Red Club forces from the downstream Okfuskee towns approaching up the other side of the ridge.[87] This precaution was unnecessary as to the Okfuskee because virtually all of their warriors were behind the barricade. But it would have been critical, however, had the Creeks in the lower Tallapoosa towns not fallen into that strange lassitude described by historian George Stiggins and failed to come to the assistance of their brothers.[88]

Coffee stationed his Indian allies in a battle line close to the river's edge to seal off an escape of the hostiles by water. Once Jackson and his force had breached the barrier and driven the Creeks toward the river, Coffee's men would be in position to shoot any Red Clubs who tried to cross. To the same end, Coffee also detached a company of forty spies under Lieutenant Jessie Bean to the large island splitting the downstream stretch of the river near the barricade's western (downstream) end, which the Red Clubs, probably because of a shortage of fighters, had left unmanned.[89] If any fugitive hostiles made it past Coffee's men and the friendly Indians, the soldiers on the island could pick the Red Clubs off as they floated past or attempted to swim to the island.

While Coffee headed his forces into position, Jackson marched his men from the Emuckfau campsite to the high ground overlooking the Creek barricade. He was in no hurry to engage the Red Clubs, because he needed to give Coffee time to get into position and seal off all avenues of escape across the Tallapoosa. Once Coffee was in position, Jackson intended to employ his two cannons to batter down the barrier and then attack across the ruined wall with his troops. Thus it was not until 10 A.M. that Jackson was ready.[90]

From the small eminence near the barrier, Jackson gazed through his spyglass, inevitably and mercilessly indifferent as death, at the obstacle that had the past January led a daunted Coffee to return to their camp at Emuckfau Creek. He was duly impressed with what he saw below him writing, "[i]t is difficult to conceive a situation more eligible for defence than the one they had chosen, or one rendered more secure by the skill with which they had erected their breast work." It was a wooden wall that zigzagged in a curious fashion for 350 yards across the mouth of the

Horseshoe from one bank of the Tallapoosa to another.[91] The structure rose from five to eight feet along its length and was built of roughhewn pine logs cut from the woods between the barrier and the gentle hill several hundred yards away, leaving a clear field of fire between. The center of the wall, where the entrance was located, was concave. The entrance was a gap in the wall formed by overlapping sections of wall, so that one entered at an angle into a corridor that ran between the two sections and thus was subjected to fire from both sides.[92]

The Creeks had begun construction of this structure by laboriously excavating a trench several feet deep and several feet wide running at angles across the mouth of the Horseshoe. They floored the trench with timber, which gave them a steady platform from which to fire on their enemies. On the north side of the trench, where Jackson's army now stood, they erected a wall by placing five logs one on the other horizontally; the logs were as long as forty feet and in diameter as wide as a foot and a half. These they supported with vertical posts running at regular intervals along the outer face of the barrier. The posts were supported at their upper ends by other posts planted at a forty-five-degree angle into the earth. This interpretation, based on archeological records, contemporaneous drawings, and written descriptions of the barrier, as well as similar constructions by Native American people at other sites, provides the most accurate depiction of the barricade's architecture we are ever likely to have.[93]

To further confound an attacker, the Red Clubs had cut an upper and lower tier of portholes along the length of the wall. From these positions the defenders could fire in relative safety at an enemy charging across the wide clearing from which the wall's builders had obtained their logs; now it was filled with tree stumps, which would break up any cohesive troop formation assaulting the barrier. And although this arrangement made an attack on the barrier a formidable proposition in and of itself, it was the zigzag architecture of the structure that made it a truly dangerous position to attack. The genius of the structure's design was to expose an attacker, from whatever direction he approached, to fire from both sides of the angled wall.

For some reason, perhaps concealment, the wall's builders had daubed the chinks between the rows of logs with clay much like a pioneer or Indian cabin. But the face of the barrier was far from smooth, for the builders had left sharpened branches projecting outward from the row of logs, creating a wooden predecessor, known as fraising, to the barbed wire of the next century's wars. To protect themselves against an attack from the rear of the wall, the Red Clubs had erected another, although lower, log wall along the opposite side of the trench. They had also felled large trees with untrimmed branches in the area that lay between the wall and the rocky hillock set like a rough stone in a ring in the center of the peninsu-

la. These obstacles, which were covered by brush, provided fighting positions that allowed concealed communication with one another.[94]

Despite the barrier's formidable appearance, Jackson was unperturbed
by the Creek breastwork. No savages could construct a wall that could
withstand cannon fire, and this time he had brought two guns with him.
He would simply batter the Creek barricade down with his cannon and
unleash his troops on what remained of the hostile forces. Coffee would
snare the remainder who tried to flee by the river.

While the Red Clubs behind the wall jeered at Jackson's troops, led on by
several prophets bedecked with "the plumage of many birds about their
heads and shoulders" and the de rigueur cowtails flopping about their
painted bodies, Jackson arranged his forces carefully to exploit the break-
through he believed would come once his cannon breached the fortification. He had positioned these weapons and their limbers on a small knoll
that rose, not far beyond the left, or downstream side, of the wall. At that
point the wall was only eighty yards from the cannon; the distance of the
remainder of the wall from the guns ranged from 150 to 250 yards.[95]

To his army's left, Jackson positioned an advance guard of chosen men
within gunshot of the wall. Behind this company he placed Williams's 39th
Infantry, backed by a Colonel Copeland's regiment of 660 militiamen. On
the backside of the hill on which he had placed his cannon, Jackson stationed General Doherty's brigade of east Tennessee militia, and behind
this unit Colonel John Cheatham's regiment of 520 militiamen. The army's
supply wagons and pack horses were stationed between the 39th Infantry
and Copeland's regiment. In back of all of these formations, Jackson stationed a rear guard. He was finally ready to initiate his plan of extermina-
tion against the men who had forced him to retreat from this place two
months earlier.[96]

Around 10:30 A.M., Coffee signaled to Jackson that his men were in
place. Immediately following Coffee's signal, Jackson ordered the firing of
his two cannon against the center of the barricade behind which the Red
Clubs now prudently crouched. To Jackson's surprise and consternation,
the balls seemed to have no effect on the wall. They either lodged in the
soft pine logs or passed through them. Although the fire from the cannon
that pierced the wall occasionally killed or maimed a Red Club, it failed to
shake the wall's integrity.[97] The elated Red Clubs resumed their jeering,
and their spirits rose as their wall continued over the course of the morning to withstand the fire from the feared cannon. Jackson was so stubborn
that he did not trust what his own eyes told him—his cannon could not
breach the wall—and, resisting calls from some of his officers to storm the
barricades, ordered his artillerymen to keep firing.

Adding to their confidence, Red Club marksmen also began picking off
Jackson's men. The artillerymen on the little hill naturally drew special

attention from the Creeks. Among the cannon crew, eleven men were eventually wounded, one of whom later died. The advance infantry contingent also began to suffer casualties from the Red Clubs firing through the portholes in the wall. Several of these men were wounded, and one was killed.[98] In response, a frustrated Jackson encouraged his cannoneers to increase their rate of fire. He also ordered his advance guard to lie prone behind the sheltering stumps in the clearing and pick off any Red Club foolish enough to show himself above the logs of the barricade.

This contest continued, with brief interruptions to cool the cannon barrels and to replenish their ammunition from the limbers, for almost two hours. Jackson had figured that by this point in the cannonade, the wall would have been largely destroyed. But his artillerists had fired seventy rounds against the structure and yet there it stood, as strong as ever.[99] Jackson now had to decide whether to continue the fruitless cannonade or order his men to assault the intact wall across more than a hundred yards of open ground against an enemy that was almost completely protected from return fire. Ironically, acting on their own initiative, the Americans' Indian allies that Jackson so disdained solved Jackson's dilemma and saved the lives of many American soldiers.

While Jackson was attempting to breach the Creek barricade, Coffee was positioning his troops along the shore of the Tallapoosa opposite the Indian village. When he was within a half mile of the town, the Red Clubs detected his approach and set up a frightful howling. In response, Coffee arrayed his men in a line of battle and cautiously approached the village along the upper slopes of the ridge. When he was within a quarter of a mile from the town, Coffee heard the firing of Jackson's cannon and many small arms. He earlier had ordered his Indian allies to move stealthily up to the riverbank below him to cut off any attempt by the hostiles to escape across the river. They had done so carefully and orderly and now ringed the toe of the peninsula. However, after waiting there for some time, the sound of the cannon and gunfire from the Red Club breastworks barrier, which had now reached a crescendo, and the hundreds of women and children running about the village in terror, so excited them they could stand the waiting no more and, essentially ignoring Coffee's order, decided to attack the village.

The attack began in an ad hoc fashion. On reaching the river's edge, a group of Cherokees spied a line of canoes on the opposite shore. The vessels were tethered beneath the thick brush overhanging a section of the riverbank just downstream of the Red Club settlement. In the village, among the women and children scurrying about, the Cherokees could see about one hundred Red Club warriors forming for battle. Three of the more impulsive Cherokees hit on the idea of swimming across the rain-swollen river under covering fire from their comrades along the bank and retrieving some of the canoes. Once they had possession of enough canoes, they could ferry their comrades across the stream and attack the town.[100]

The idea of swimming more than one hundred yards across a chilly, fast-moving stream under fire was insane, but that is exactly what three of the Cherokees did. A private named the Whale, whose great size explained his name; his nephew, Corporal Charles Reese; and a third, unidentified man plunged into the Tallapoosa and began swimming for their lives while bullets from their friends zinged overhead and bullets from their enemies splattered the waters around them. Before they had reached the other shore, the Whale was shot in the shoulder. With the Whale in tow, his nephew and their other companion managed to reach the canoes unscathed. They secured two of the canoes, helped the Whale into one, and, again under fire, paddled furiously to the opposite shore amid the cheers of their fellows. Using those canoes, more Cherokees braved the Creek fire and captured additional canoes. They soon began ferrying warriors to the opposite shore, where they had established a fast-growing beachhead under the cover of the riverbank. Taking in the situation, Colonel Morgan rode hard for the left (upstream) side of Jackson's line. There he met with Major Montgomery and informed him of developments at the toe of the Horseshoe. On his return to the Cherokee position, Morgan discovered that not only had 150 to 200 of his warriors crossed the river and engaged in heavy fighting about the village with the beleaguered and grossly outnumbered Red Clubs, but that the friendly Creeks had joined them.[101]

On the upstream side of the town, where the Red Clubs had assembled another group of canoes, the friendly Creeks had begun crossing the river. Within a short time, Jackson's Indian allies managed to transport under fire over two hundred men to the rear of the Creek town, including Captain Russell's veteran company of spies. Morgan commanded the Cherokee landing party, William McIntosh the landing party of friendly Creeks. Once safely across the river, these men organized their warriors for an attack on the Red Club positions. When the Cherokees and friendly Creeks vacated their positions along the riverbank, Coffee ordered one-third of his mounted riflemen to move down and take their places. From this new position the Americans could cover the amphibious assault of the friendly Indians and shoot any Red Clubs they caught trying to escape.[102]

The Red Club warriors at first fought back from positions near the riverbank, but as additional canoes filled with their enemies landed, they were driven back to the shelter of their houses where their families huddled in terror. Those positions soon became untenable, so the Creek warriors herded the women and children together and led them toward the rocky eminence in the center of the Horseshoe where the prophets were stationed. Not far behind them, the Cherokees, friendly Creeks, and Russell's spies entered the town. While the majority of the attackers pursued the fleeing Red Clubs into the heart of the peninsula, some of the less-impulsive or bloodthirsty of these men began to loot and torch the Creek town. In the confusion of the hostiles' retreat, an old Indian, nearing the century mark, deaf, and probably in the latter stages of dementia, was left behind. He was seated on the ground near one of the houses calmly grinding corn in a mortar, oblivious to the storm about him. He was sighted by one of the Americans, who coldly raised his rifle and shot the ancient Indian dead. He was determined, he told his astonished comrade, to be able to tell his family and friends back home that he had killed an Indian.[103]

As the hostiles fled to the refuge on the knoll behind the burning town, they began to regroup among the rock-studded terrain. The fighting between the Red Clubs and the Americans' Indian allies grew more ferocious by the minute. The Red Clubs attempted to encircle their attackers and cut them off from the reinforcements crossing the river in the captured canoes, while the attackers sought hard to keep this line of communication open. After an hour's savage combat, the attackers finally reached the summit of the rough hill at the center of the peninsula. Here they managed to retain their position although assaulted by Red Club warriors on all sides. After an hour's combat, the Cherokees' commander, Colonel Morgan, was shot in the right side of the head, near the eye. The blow left him insensible for a time, but amazingly, he soon recovered and resumed leading his men.[104]

Not long before noon, both Jackson and Menawa heard the first sound of gunfire coming from the Creek town and saw clouds of smoke rising from the burning houses. Menawa's warriors behind the breastworks had held off Jackson's army almost two hours and were growing more confident by the minute that they could hold off any attack Jackson might muster against them. But the sound of firing to their rear was soon followed with news that must have shaken the confidence of all but the fanatics among them. Runners from the Creeks defending the town appeared at the breastworks and informed Menawa of the crisis that had developed at the toe of the peninsula. Reluctantly, the Okfuskee chief was forced to send a significant detachment of warriors from the barricade to the center of the Horseshoe in an attempt to counter the growing threat behind his lines. But after a sharp fight with the invaders, these warriors returned, along with what remained of their comrades formerly guarding the town, and took shelter in the trench within the breastworks. Behind them came the Cherokees, turncoat Creeks, and Russell's spy company.[105]

The Red Clubs in the breastworks now faced assault from two sides, but the combination of the trench and the rear wall of the barricade provided sufficient protection from the attack by Coffee's men. Once the guns of the defenders manning the rear of the fortification had their range the friendly Indians began falling, their attack soon faltered, and they fell back. It was now just after 12:00 P.M. From his vantage point on the hill, where his artillery was stationed, a frustrated Jackson realized that his Indian allies and Russell's spy company did not have sufficient manpower to take the barricade from the rear and were in fact taking a beating from the Red Club warriors firing from the protection of the trench behind the wall. Jackson decided to hazard a direct assault on the barricade. After consulting his senior officers, at 12:30 P.M. he gave the order for his eager men to storm the breastworks.[106]

Jackson chose Williams's 39th Infantry of regulars and one of General Doherty's regiment of militia led by Colonel Samuel Bunch to lead the attack. A fierce drumroll sounded, signaling the advance. In a letter to his wife Betsy, John Reid described his feelings as the soldiers moved to their jumping-off positions beneath the loud roll of drums: "This was a moment of feeling and not of reflection. I never had such emotions as while the long roll was beating, and the troops in motion. It was not fear, it was not anxiety nor concern of the fate of those who were so soon to fall but it was a kind of enthusiasm that thrilled through every nerve and animated me with the belief that the day was ours, without adverting to what it must cost us."[107]

After a final barrage from the cannon, the lead elements of Jackson's army stepped off into hell in style, the hard roll of the drums and the cheers of their comrades urging them on.

The Creeks waiting behind the wall as the soldiers formed their ranks a hundred yards to their front must have experienced many of the same emotions young Reid described. Added to these emotions was doubtless curiosity that many of them had about the American soldiers forming up to their right. As the Red Clubs looked out through their portholes, with some less-cautious souls peeping over the parapet, they noticed something strange about these men. They moved with more precision, and were dressed with more flair, than the awkward and motley attired militia with which they were familiar forming up on their left. The new men were all dressed identically. Their dark hats were tall and shaped like a stovepipe in the kitchen of a rich white man. Their coats were dark blue, open in the front, tight about the torso, and dropped with a slight flair just below the waist. Their shirts were white and their tight woolen trousers dark gray. By his right side, each held a heavy musket with a long, pointed, metal shaft at the end that gleamed portentously in the sunlight.

At the head of each company of these strange soldiers was a man with an even more elaborate uniform than the men about him. Each of these soldiers wore fringed trays of gold on his shoulders and a scarlet sash about his waist. They also held an elaborate sword in one hand that they were excitedly waving about. The Red Club leaders knew that these more colorful and lively figures were the officers and that their men relied heavily on them for direction in a fight. Menawa ordered word passed down the line of warriors massed behind the barricade for their best shots to concentrate on these conspicuous targets.

But could these strange soldiers with the spearguns fight? Buoyed by their success in withstanding the fire of the terrible cannons and the promises of their prophets of the coming destruction of the American army, many of the Red Clubs waiting behind the wall no doubt saw these fancy soldiers as an opportunity, not a threat. With their fondness for colorful and curious outfits, many a defender must have greedily anticipated stripping the uniforms, as well as the scalps, from the bodies of the impressively attired solders of the 39th Infantry, who would shortly fall in heaps before the invulnerable wall.

And then it was time. The soldiers in the attacking regiments answered the drum calls with a roar from hundreds of voices. They were answered in return by the war cries of the Red Clubs behind the wall, urged on by the antics of their cowtail- and feather-bedecked prophets leaping to and fro to ready themselves for the kill. All at once, with officers in the lead, the soldiers of the 39th Infantry and the Tennessee militia started off at a run, dodging stumps as they advanced toward the great barrier now obscured behind the puffs of gunsmoke flowering along its length. Overcome with excitement, Colonel Carroll and even a wounded artilleryman, James Lewis, raced to the head of the assault. Soldiers, particularly among the 39th, who had the longest distance to go, were dropped by the Red Clubs as they ran, but the pace of their comrades' charge did not diminish. Heartened by this advance, the Americans' Indian allies resumed their attack on the rear of the fortification.[108]

Dark and acrid-smelling smoke from the guns firing on both sides soon obscured both field and fort. The noise from the guns and the voices of two thousand men was so deafening it was like a tangible presence to be pushed through as the soldiers rushed the breastworks. A number of Americans fell dead and wounded in the several minutes it took to cross the field. Suddenly the wall itself emerged out of the smoke and rose just over their heads, rough and formidable and spitting fire and smoke along its length.

As at Fort Mims, a fierce struggle for command of the portholes ensued. The fight was at such close quarters that balls from the Creek guns were welded to the tips of the soldiers' bayonets. Major Montgomery, stationed at the left of the 39th Infantry, sprang forward, his outstretched sword high above him. With his long and eager stride he was one of the first men to reach the barricade. Arriving at one of the portholes in the barrier, he pulled his pistol and shot a Creek through the opening.[109] In turn another Creek thrust his gun into the porthole and shot the major in the head. By the time Montgomery fell, other soldiers from the 39th followed the young major's lead and were now up and over the rough wall and into the mass of Creeks below. The fighting was close and furious, with no time to reload musket or rifle. One soldier, reputedly the first man to surmount the wall, received a nasty face wound from the blade of a tomahawk hurled by a Red Club defender.[110]

Ensign Sam Houston, farther down the line to the right of the place where Montgomery fell, was also one of the first over the wall. As he topped the barrier, a Creek defender shot a barbed arrow into his thigh. For a moment adrenaline kept him hacking at the nearest Red Clubs with his sword, but he soon fell to the ground among the warriors. By then a lieutenant, named Francher, and other comrades had reached him and drove back the advancing Red Club warriors. Meanwhile, Houston endeavored to pull the arrow from his thigh. After several painful and futile tries, he yelled to Francher to extract it. The lieutenant failed also. Maddened by pain, Houston brandished his sword at the man, a court-martial offense, and threatened to cut him down if he did not get the arrow out of his leg. Encouraged by Houston's threat, which Francher rightly took seriously, he succeeded in wrenching the object from Houston's thigh, bringing with it a hunk of flesh and letting forth a torrent of blood. Houston's companions did their best to stanch the flow of blood and hauled him along to an aid station for treatment. While the surgeon was binding up the ugly wound, Jackson walked over to see who of his soldiers had been hurt. He knew Houston, and perhaps something of his character, and over his protests ordered him not to return to the battle.

While Houston lay in the aid station having his wound dressed, the fight turned quickly against the outnumbered and outweaponed Red Clubs. Of particular advantage in this close-quarters fighting were the bayonets wielded by the trained soldiers of the 39th. The Creeks' war clubs and tomahawks simply did not have the reach, however skillful the Indians were in the use of those weapons. Moreover, the Red Clubs were now squeezed in their trench between the two American forces. It was utter chaos along the length of the breastworks, which was rapidly filling with Creek dead. As Houston, who had disobeyed Jackson's order and returned to the battle, described the scene: "[t]he action had now become general, and more than two thousand men were struggling hand to hand. Arrows, and spears, and balls were flying; swords and tomahawks were gleaming in the sun; and the whole Peninsula rang with the yell of the savage, and the groans of the dying."

Not long after this clash described by Houston, the Americans took the hostiles' breastworks, with the militiamen, who had only seventy-five yards of ground to cross to the works, securing their section of the barrier before the regulars. The Creeks now began desperately racing away from their former refuge to find cover. Many Red Clubs made their way along the trench out the far ends of the barrier and fled down both sides of the Tallapoosa River until they found cover among the heavy vegetation along its banks. Others found fighting positions about the rocky face of the timbered hump of ground in the middle of the Horseshoe or in the prepared fighting positions about the peninsula formed from brush and downed trees. One group of Red Clubs fortified themselves in a curious structure the Indians had erected along the south bank of the river. At that point their trench line fell off into a ravine running down into the river. The defenders had covered this avenue with heavy logs pierced with narrow portholes. It was a strong, bunkerlike position and would have to be taken by direct assault because the cannon barrels could not be depressed enough to strike it with anything better than a glancing blow. Other bands of Creeks gathered hopefully about their prophets on the high ground, waiting for the storm that the prophets assured them would soon appear to sweep their enemies away. From this position the Red Clubs stubbornly continued to resist the Americans and their Indian allies.[111]

Nonetheless, however hard the Red Clubs resisted or their prophets prayed, once the barrier was taken, the battle, for all intents and purposes, was over. As the afternoon wore slowly on, the Red Clubs continued to disperse throughout the peninsula in increasingly diminished and isolated groups. They were still fighting hard, which Jackson attributed to desperation. Many hundreds, however, now sought an opportunity to cross the Tallapoosa where an illusionary safety beckoned. But there on the far shore death waited. General Coffee's men were lined thickly along the riverbank, waiting eagerly for the turkey shoot that was about to begin.

Years later, when Jackson was running for president, his political rivals charged that his great victory at the Horseshoe was nothing more than a "cold-blooded massacre." In response to this charge, Coffee wrote a letter rebutting this accusation. He claimed that after the breastworks fell, Jackson went with his interpreter, George Mayfield, for many years a white captive of the Creeks, to one of the remaining Red Club fighting positions to attempt to convince the hostiles to surrender.[112] The two groups met at a distance but within gun range. Initially the meeting went well. When Mayfield began speaking in their language, the Red Clubs ceased fighting to listen to his words. Mayfield told them that in return for their surrender, Jackson offered them "pardon and protection," but first they must come forth from their hiding places and "lay down their arms." After this offer was made, something went wrong—the ineptitude of the Americans' interpreter was suggested as the culprit—and the Red Clubs replied to Jackson's overtures with gunfire. One shot, aimed at Jackson's head, ricocheted off the side of the tree against which he was standing and into poor Mayfield's shoulder.[113]

It was said that what remained of the prophets were the cause of the failed negotiations. As both sides were discussing an end to hostilities, a sudden cloud appeared overhead. The prophets pointed to this phenomenon as a harbinger of their prediction that a terrible storm would descend on the Horseshoe and selectively sweep their enemies from the land. So it was that the hopes of the mighty Muskogee Confederation devolved into an unremarkable cloud in a spring sky. But seeing this sign, what was left of the Creeks at Horseshoe Bend renewed the struggle. By the time the cloud had resolved itself into a mild spring shower, any hope of supernatural succor vanished and the methodical slaughter of the Red Clubs continued.

Sometime around this point in the battle, the Americans commenced what Reid called their "work of destruction," or what an early Jackson biographer memorably described as a "slow, laborious slaughter."[114] Even Jackson was impressed: "The carnage was dreadful," he wrote. Similarly, Coffee told his wife that "this is the greatest defeat we have ever given them." Not only was the destruction of the Red Clubs apocalyptic, but it lasted five hours or more until nightfall and, in some parts of the Horseshoe, until 10:00 P.M.[115] The blood fever infected the troops like a virus. As at Tallushatchee, but on a vaster, if not nastier scale, the Americans and their Indian allies gave no quarter and the Creeks purportedly asked for none. So intense was the bloodlust that even prominent officers of high rank, like Colonel Carroll, went out hunting small coveys of Creek warriors concealed about the peninsula.[116] The fever only passed for Carroll when a Red Club shot him in the side, about half an hour before nightfall, forcing him to retire from the field.

Hundreds of Creeks who made it to the river never reached the other side as Coffee's men vied with each other to notch the most kills. Captain Eli Hammond's ranger company stationed on the riverbank near the downstream side of the town particularly enjoyed the bloody sport of shooting the desperate Creeks flailing about in the frigid Tallapoosa. One soldier, quartermaster Joshua Haskell, a future Tennessee circuit judge, was said to have fired "not less than fifty rounds" against the Indian warriors flailing through the waters.[117]

Killing Creeks was even less of a challenge than Colonel Allison's men enjoyed in the battle with the squirrels. Unlike the grey shadows flitting through the trees, the heads of the swimming Creeks presented targets the size of melons. It took little effort for men who had hunted game since childhood to pop open the heads of the swimming warriors with a single shot and then riddle their floating corpses for the simple hell of it. Within no time, the river was filled with several hundred dead Creeks and reportedly dyed red by Creek blood.[118]

Farther upstream, the fight became hand to hand between the fleeing Creeks and the Americans' pursuing Indian allies. One of the Cherokee warriors, a Major Ridge, gained particular renown in this vicious, close-quarters combat. In all he is said to have killed six Creeks. To cap off his killing spree, he engaged a particularly stout Creek warrior in an epic hand-to-hand contest in the shallows of the Tallapoosa. During this fight, in which the two opponents appeared equally matched, Ridge managed to snatch the knife from his unnamed opponent's belt and wound him with it. Nonetheless, the Creek fought on with great ferocity, and the contest was only terminated when another Cherokee drove his spear through the Red Club's back.[119]

On the peninsula, the massacre was proceeding apace as Jackson's men chivied Red Club by Red Club out of their hiding places. Ever gracious when his men comported themselves to his standards, once the defeat of the Creeks was assured, Jackson loosed from his leash to hunt the enemy every man who could carry a weapon. Even some of the artillerymen, when their cannon were no longer in danger of capture, were allowed to join the slaughter of the defeated Red Clubs. To the general's delight, his wife's nephew, Jack Caffery, who was an artilleryman, won his battle spurs with Jackson by killing an Indian.[120] Another soldier used the butt of his musket to crush the skull of a little boy of five or six who, in his terror and confusion, had made the mistake of wandering into a group of Jackson's soldiers. He killed the child, the soldier laconically explained to a horrified officer, because the little tyke would become a grown Indian someday.[121]

As the afternoon wore on, the fighting—and with it the noise and acrid clouds of smoke—spread all about the Horseshoe as discrete clusters of Red Club warriors fought back in numerous small actions across the wooded land and on the muddy banks of the Tallapoosa, where, as at Autossee, they had excavated shelters in the riverbank. Amazingly, several Creek strong points still bedeviled the American soldiers, particularly within the labyrinth of artfully arranged downed timber and brush between the barricade and the rocky knoll at the center of the peninsula. Jackson was now eager to bring to a close what had begun as a glorious assault on a heavily fortified position, assisted by an amphibious landing, but had disintegrated into a tedious yet still dangerous campaign of exterminating what many of the Americans apparently considered little more than noisome vermin.

He decided to resolve the situation by calling up his cannon to pepper the Red Club works with grapeshot. But the cannon had no more effect in dislodging these Creeks in their ad hoc strongholds than they did in dislodging the Creeks behind the more formally built wall earlier in the day. Finally someone hit on the obvious, and the Americans decided to burn the recalcitrant hostiles from their positions. Dozens of torches were lit, and the men vied with each other for the opportunity to toss them into the tinderbox of wood and brush that was the Red Clubs' hideout. If the Red Club prophets ever had the power to call down a storm of rain on the Horseshoe, now was the time to exercise it. But no rain came, and fire soon whipped maniacally about the area. Before long the scorched hostiles exploded from their hideouts like small game from cover, and like small game, were shot as they ran by Jackson's soldiers.

But the burning tangle of brush and trees was not the only stronghold still left on the Horseshoe. As Jackson and his staff rode over the battle-field, their horses stepping delicately over the Red Club corpses littering it, his attention was directed to a particularly tough hostile strongpoint. This Red Club position was at the end of the barrier where a ravine contiguous with the trench emptied into the Tallapoosa. The Creeks had incorporat-ed the ravine into their breastworks by roofing it with logs and cutting portholes through the wood arranged in such a way that every approach to the structure was covered. The barrels of Jackson's two cannon could not be sufficiently depressed to harm this burrow, which was arranged somewhat like a modern bunker or pillbox.[122]

After Jackson rode up and investigated the Creek position, he realized that it would have to be taken by infantry. The task was so dangerous that rather than order an assault by a particular unit, he turned to his soldiers and asked for volunteers. Not one man stepped forward and accepted the honor of being a forlorn hope—not one except the grievously wounded Houston. He hesitated at first, not of out fear but out of deference to his betters of higher rank. But when no such man stepped forward, the brave and ambitious Houston did, and, to the horror of his platoon, volunteered it for the dangerous assignment.[123] For some reason, perhaps because no one else had volunteered, the rule-bound Jackson let the young man who had disobeyed his order to remain in the rear lead this crazy attack on the Indian fortification.

The best approach to taking the position required the attacking party to drop quickly down into the ravine and then rush the portholes of the Indian fort from whose rough mouths a nasty assortment of gun muzzles and arrowheads poked their snouts. The gigantic Houston possessed a commanding presence to say the least, but when he ordered his men to "follow me," not a one stirred from his position. Aiming to set an example, Houston snatched a musket from one of his soldiers and, injured thigh be damned, leaped down into the ravine. But this bold, brave, and idiotic maneuver did not have the desired effect on his men, and Houston found himself alone in the bottom of a ditch with all sorts of deadly weapons aimed at him. Houston's insane stunt must have momentarily frozen the defenders, for Houston had time to level his musket at a porthole in the bunker and, before firing, turn to his platoon and scream out at his men to join him in the ravine. These antics were finally enough for one defender, who blasted Houston with a doubled-shotted gun. One ball lodged deep in his right shoulder, the other shattered his arm. Amazingly, Houston somehow managed to keep on his feet as blood poured from his new wounds and continued to cajole his more-than-ever-terrified troops to join him in this death pit. His men were having none of it. Not one moved to assist him as he abandoned his assault and painfully crawled his way up the ravine and out of range of the Indian weapons. There Houston sank to the ground in a puddle of his own blood, awaiting aid.[124]

Eventually, several other young heroes attempted to assault the Indian position, with equally bad if not worse results than Houston's. The day was drawing to a close when soldiers of a more practical bent of mind decided the best way to eliminate the Indian position was to burn them out. Quickly they gathered piles of brush, which they rolled or shoved down the ravine onto the Creek fort, then tossed in lighted torches. The brush caught fire, and not long after so did the logs of the Creek refuge. Smoke began to roil out of the ravine as dozens of soldiers waited about the place, guns primed, for the sport to begin. It was the rat-killing tactics employed by Colonel Russell's starving soldiers all over again. Like those creatures hiding in the Indian huts along the Alabama River, eventually, the heat and smoke became too great for the warriors to endure, and one by one, then in groups, they began scurrying out of the burning bunker in all directions. The far larger Indians made easier targets than Sam Dale's rats, and the Tennesseans shot them down like the vermin of Colonel Russell's expedition. Every Red Club was killed, some many times over, and scalped. Those few souls who made it to the river were cut down by Coffee's men on the opposite bank.

The unceasing movement of the heavens finally brought an end to the slaughter. The pale light of the sun winked out, and the dead stone of the moon, with its crescent of borrowed light, rose in its place. As Jackson explained to his wife, with the weary tone of a man who had just finished ridding his barn of vermin: "It was dark before we finished killing them."[125] Whatever was left of the Red Club warriors on the Horseshoe had gone to ground in the black places of the peninsula; the weary victors could ferret at their leisure the remaining warriors out of their hiding places the next morning. The several hundred terrified women and children taken prisoners were herded together in a hollow of land where they could be easily guarded.[126] From recent experience, the Hillabee prisoners among them must have thought that the whites would surely loose the Cherokees on them and that all would be massacred by morning. Sated with killing and with a great victory in hand, Jackson made sure to protect his political flanks by placing the more disciplined regulars of the 39th Infantry at guard over the innocents. But their ordeal was far from over.

After the battle, on Jackson's orders, the prisoners were escorted to Fort Lashley, at Talladega. There they were to be collected by a David Smith from Fort Strother and taken to Huntsville. But when Smith arrived at Fort Lashley, he found no one to collect except "8 or 10 and those the most helpless and indifferent." Others had been there before him, notably Old Chenibee, who took some of his fellow Creeks as slaves, and the Cherokees "who had carried off most of the prisoners and had picked them over leaving none but the most indifferent behind." Smith did learn that two Creek boys had been sold to an American lieutenant for twenty dollars and was able to rescue the boys and take him into his care. The remaining prisoners he left at the fort.[127]

For some among the whites and their Indian allies, there was work to be done before they could celebrate their victory. The many wounded were tended to with the crude medical techniques of the time, which basically consisted of sharp instruments, bandages, and booze, attended with great effusions of blood and greater effusions of pain. Houston was among these patients triaged by the army surgeons. They were able to extract the ball from his arm but as an act of mercy ended the excruciating process of retrieving the other ball from his shoulder. The surgeons decided he was as good as dead, and it was senseless and even cruel to cause him further pain.[128] He was carried to the side of the medical tent and laid out on the ground to die.

The white and friendly Indian dead were gathered together and placed under guard to preserve their scalps from any vengeful Red Clubs still alive on the Horseshoe. Tents were pitched away from the Creek dead on the high ground above the barricade from which the American infantry had launched its attack. Food was cooked around mess fires, the corks pried from barrels of rum, and liquor spread freely among those of the men not on duty. Coffee and his legion had crossed the ford above New-yaucau around 7:00 P.M. and arrived on the peninsula to join in the last hours of slaughter.[129] Now it was time to celebrate Jackson's greatest triumph. Happily reunited with his best friend, Jackson and his officers gathered in the commander's large tent, where servants passed around food and wine and then brandy and cigars after dinner. The usual ornate toasts were made, and one man was especially mourned, Major Montgomery—the hero whom a weeping Jackson described, as he stood over his body, as "the flower of my army."[130]

The next morning Jackson ordered a tally of the Creek dead. In a letter, he assured Governor Blount that he had assigned several officers of "great respectability" to supervise the task. That toll was reckoned by a counting mechanism perhaps unique in the annals of war. One of these respectable gentlemen with a bureaucratic bent of mind came up with the novel idea that the most accurate and efficient way to tally the Creek dead was by slicing off their noses. This atrocity was ordered done, and the dirty work of obtaining the count was assigned to the less-respectable enlisted men.[131]

No description of the counting process has been found, but the men probably went about the peninsula, like fieldworkers stooping to pick cotton, removing the noses, placing them in sacks, and delivering them to a collection station for counting. What is known is that the day after the battle, Jackson penned a report to General Pinckney in which he proudly informed his superior that precisely 557 Red Clubs "were left dead on the peninsula." [132] Prudently, however, Jackson omitted from his report to the gentlemanly Pinckney an explanation of how so precise a figure was obtained. As for the number of Creeks whose bodies rested beneath the waters of the Tallapoosa, the Americans were reduced to relying on a rough estimate Coffee obtained from his commanders, Hammond, Russell, Bean, and Gibson. In a statement signed by each of these officers on the night of the battle, they estimated that 250 to 300 hostiles had either been killed in the river or thrown there by their comrades.[133]

The number of Creek dead counted apparently included sixteen warriors dispatched the morning after the battle. This final pocket of resistance was discovered by Coffee's men as they patrolled the battlefield looking for Red Club holdouts. The hostiles were forted up beneath an overhanging riverbank out of effective musket or rifle range from the opposite shore. So cleverly had their refuge been designed that it defied all attempts of the Americans to dislodge them. Some of Jackson's soldiers endeavored to creep up to the edge of the bank and shoot down on the Indians, but these efforts failed to dislodge the Creeks. Finally, some clever soul hit on the idea of burying them alive. One group of soldiers dug a ditch about three feet deep in the soft earth several yards behind the length of the overhanging bank sheltering the Red Clubs. Other soldiers constructed a number of long wedges from the abundant logs of the Indian breastworks. These stakes were then driven into the bottom of the ditch eighteen inches apart. Working in terrible concert, the soldiers managed to use the wedges to lever the ledge of overhanging earth loose from the riverbank. To the whoops of delight from participants and spectators alike, tons of earth slid down on the heads of the Creeks below, entombing them in their refuge and sending a bow wave across the Tallapoosa River as the ledge crashed into it.[134]

After an appropriate period of time had passed to ensure the warriors' suffocation, their bodies were exhumed from their fatal refuge and their heads washed clean enough in the river for nose slicing and scalping. Whether this last clutch of victims was included in Jackson's total or not, the number of Red Clubs killed by Jackson's army constituted the greatest losses any Indian tribe had ever suffered in a single battle against whites on the North American continent.[135]

Jackson's several accounts of the battle also noted the number of prisoners taken, varying from 250 to 350 women and children plus two or three men.[136] Among the women, the Cherokees found one of their own. She had been captured by the Red Clubs and made prisoner. Brought before Jackson, who described her as an "intelligent Cherokee Squaw," she informed him that the Red Clubs had assembled about one thousand warriors at the Horseshoe. As for the several men who were captured, they were probably of the age of the demented old Indian who had senselessly been murdered as he squatted in the yard outside his home in the early stages of the battle, or they were badly wounded warriors.

There is some evidence that a few males of fighting age were taken prisoner and allowed to live. Coffee claimed that the day after the battle, two young Indians were found hiding on the peninsula and brought before Jackson, who took them under his protection and eventually brought them to Nashville where he had them educated as mechanics.[137] Another heartwarming story is told that a badly wounded Red Club was brought by his captors to an aid station for treatment. Jackson just happened to be there at the time. When the surgeons began to treat the wounded man, indicative of what the Creeks' understood of American policy, the warrior laconically observed, "Cure him, kill him again." Impressed by the man's courage, Jackson assured the man that this was not the Americans' intent. When the warrior recovered from his wounds, Jackson took him, too, to Tennessee, where the fellow married a "colored" woman and lived happily ever after.[138]

Whatever the truth of these stories, the tiny figure Jackson gave for captured adult males betrays the fact that virtually every Creek male on the peninsula, except for the very young children, was killed by the Americans or their Indian allies. No quarter was the silent watchword of that bitter day.[139]

Jackson also reported that nineteen Red Clubs, all wounded, had escaped that night by river. This information he gleaned from a single prisoner who had been a member of this group and probably too badly wounded to join the escape.[140] Like Coffee after the Battle of Tallushatchee, Jackson also regretfully reported that several children had been accidentally killed in the confusion of the fray. When he reported these accidental deaths, he apparently had not seen the corpse of the child whose skull had been crushed by the rifle butt of one of his soldiers.

But there was a particular gruesome atrocity reportedly perpetrated on the bodies of the Red Club warriors that Jackson in his tour of the battlefield could not have failed to observe, or to at least have knowledge of. Long after the war, an elderly gentleman, Warren Wilbanks, told historian Henry Halbert that "many of the Tennessee soldiers" fashioned bridle reins from the skin of dead warriors, an outrage also said to have been inflicted on the corpse of the great Tecumseh after the Battle of the Thames. Apparently the atrocity was still vivid in the old man's memory, because he was able to describe the process in great detail. According to Wilbanks, starting at the victim's heel, the artificer first made parallel incisions three to four inches apart. From there he ran "the incisions up the leg and along the side of the back to the shoulder blade and thence across to the other shoulder and from there down the other side of the back and down the other leg to the heel." Once these incisions had been made, if done correctly, it was a simple task to peel back "a long strap of human skin" that could then be dried and tanned for a bridle rein. Wilbank's story was only hearsay—he got it from veterans of the battle—but the careful and conscientious Halbert appeared to believe very strongly that it was true.[141]

Notably, none of Jackson's reports about the battle mentions the fate of his principal adversary, Menawa, who once said of himself, "I have been a man of blood all my life."[142] Almost certainly, Jackson ordered William McIntosh and his troop of friendly Creek warriors to scour the battlefield for the body of the prominent Okfuskee chief, a man they would have known well, because the general thought it sufficiently noteworthy to report that the body of a principal prophet named Monahee had been found, and to include the delicious irony that Monahee had been shot through the mouth by grapeshot. As Jackson sanctimoniously explained to Blount, it was "as if Heaven designed to chastise his impostures by an appropriate punishment."[143] Even if Jackson had not looked for Menawa among the hundreds of Creek bodies littering the peninsula, the friendly Creek leader William McIntosh, on his own initiative, would certainly have instructed his warriors to search for his enemy's corpse with its precious scalp. But Menawa was not among the dead identified on the field of battle, and the victors may well have considered him among the hundreds of other Red Clubs sunk beneath the waters of the Tallapoosa.

It was not so, however. Although terribly wounded in at least seven places, including the face, this remarkable man survived the battle, exacted a deadly revenge against McIntosh, and lived long enough to be cheated out of his lands and deported across the Mississippi River. There are several versions of his escape. One has him dressing in women's clothing, as Jefferson Davis was falsely said to have done in an attempt to escape his Yankee pursuers, and hiding among the dead. When night fell, the half-dead Menawa crawled to the river and escaped downstream in a canoe. Albert Pickett, who interviewed an aged Menawa years later and particularly noted the scars from his horrible wounds, also claimed that after the battle, Menawa was able to make his way to a stand of cane along the riverbank. But Pickett's tale takes an improbable turn. According to him, the enterprising chief fashioned a primitive snorkel from a cane stalk, submerged himself beneath the water, and, breathing through the cane, waited for darkness. When at last night fell, he rose from the river and, leaking blood, made off through the forest.[144]

Yet another and more plausible version of Menawa's escape from the Horseshoe, given his terrible wounds, is found in Indian agent Thomas McKenney's short history of Menawa's life in *History of the Indian Tribes of North America*. According to McKenney, although horribly wounded, Menawa was able to crawl to the riverbank and ease himself down to the margin of the water. There he discovered an abandoned canoe beached on the muddy shore. By rocking the craft to and fro, he was able to loosen it from the mud's grip and ease it into the water. Once he had the craft afloat, he somehow managed to plop over its side into its bottom. Half-conscious, he let the current float him some twelve miles down the river. After hours drifting under the stars, he arrived at the swamp formed where Elkahatchee Creek entered the Tallapoosa. There his craft was spied by some Creek women who were anxiously waiting for news from the battle upstream and hauled to shore. He was then taken upstream to the village of Elkahatchee, where the Creeks had secreted a number of their women and children.

Menawa somehow survived his wounds and lived long enough to avenge himself on McIntosh in 1825, when he led the Creek party that executed McIntosh for selling Creek lands in Georgia without tribal authorization.[145] But although he lived nearby the Horseshoe, the old warrior never returned to the battlefield. It was said he believed an evil spirit inhabited the place, but as McKenney speculated, it may simply have been that Menawa had no desire to return to the site of his great defeat.[146]

As for the American losses, Jackson reported that 26 were killed and 106 were wounded, a number of them mortally. Of the losses, not surprisingly, far and away the largest number were found among Colonel Williams's 39th Infantry: seventeen killed and fifty-five wounded, two of whom soon died. According to Jackson's aide John Reid, the bodies of the dead whites were sunk in the Tallapoosa to prevent the Red Clubs from committing outrages on their corpses.[147]

Out of the allied Indians who fought at the Horseshoe and so mightily contributed to the victory there, Jackson reported that the Cherokees lost eighteen killed and thirty-six wounded and that the Creeks lost five killed and eleven wounded. Thus, at least in men killed, the allied Indian numbers closely approximated the white number, evidencing how hard the allies had fought against their Native American brothers.[148]

One of the more prominent Cherokee warriors who was missing after the battle and thought killed was fifty-seven-year-old Shoe Boots. He was a famous Cherokee fighter, around six feet two inches tall and between 180 and 200 pounds with a hair-trigger temper. He is said to have beaten a man to death because the fellow refused to accompany the music-loving Shoe

Boots' dancing with a song. Shoe Boots was also among the new breed of Cherokees with aspirations of becoming a planter. Among his small property holdings was an African American woman named Doll with whom he cohabited and by whom he had three children, placing Shoe Boots in the anomalous but soon-to-be-common position of owning his own children.[149]

Shoe Boots was said to have been a particular favorite of Andrew Jackson's, who had nicknamed him "the Old Cock" for his fondness for crowing like a rooster in the midst of a battle. Now Jackson lamented the passing of the old warrior, as did a group of Shoe Boots's Cherokees taking their leisure in the woods of the battlefield. "[T]he old cock has got to the end of his crowing," one man reportedly sighed.[150] About that point in their conversation the men were startled by the sound of a cock crowing a biblical three times. Suddenly there was a great commotion coming from the bushes and out leaped old Shoe Boots onto a stump. He was wounded in several places but somehow managed to perch on the stump like a proud bird, proclaiming that he would live to continue his crowing for many a long year.[151]

According to Cherokee tradition, at least one Cherokee hero lived to rue the day that he ever fought for Jackson. He was Junaluska, a prominent Cherokee leader who early in the war had raised a large contingent of warriors to fight for the Americans. The story goes that Junaluska was present at the Horseshoe with Jackson in his tent for the interrogation of the few Red Club warriors taken prisoner by the Americans. As Jackson's officers questioned the Creeks, one of the Red Clubs broke free from his guards, snatched up a knife he had spied upon a table, and attempted to stab the general. Fortunately for Jackson, Junaluska was too quick for the assailant, sticking out a leg and tripping the man at Jackson's feet, thus saving the general's life.

After the battle, an apparently grateful Jackson told his Cherokee savior that "[as] long as the sun shines and the grass grows, there shall be friendship between us, and the feet of the Cherokee shall be toward the East." Some years later Jackson, now President Jackson, ordered the forceful expulsion of the loyal Cherokee Nation from its ancient lands to lands across the Mississippi River. Aptly named the Trail of Tears, this terrible journey cost the lives of many Cherokee men, women, and children before they reached its end. Jackson's betrayal of his Cherokee allies infuriated the man who had saved his life. "If I had known that Jackson would drive us from our homes," Junaluska reportedly said, "I would have killed him that day at the Horseshoe."[152]

It was not until evening of the day after the battle that Jackson's men finished dispatching the few surviving Red Club warriors remaining on the peninsula, counted noses, consigned their own dead to the waters of the

Tallapoosa, and gathered scalps and additional battlefield souvenirs; Jackson himself obtained a bow and quiver for little Andrew.[153] Nonetheless, despite the onset of darkness, Jackson immediately marched his army back toward Fort Williams and away from the peninsula where hundreds of scalped and otherwise mutilated Red Club corpses lay rotting.[154] Already the skies were clouded with circling buzzards and vultures—their wildest dreams realized—eyeing the banquet of slain Red Clubs below. Because of its many wounded, the army necessarily slowly retraced its route to Fort Williams. Nonetheless, it made steady progress, because the road had already been cut. Remarkably, among the wounded transported with the army, lying on a blanket slung between two horses was the given-up-for-dead Sam Houston. His long and painful ordeal was only just beginning; his shoulder wound would never heal during his long and eventful life.

With the end of the Americans' slow, deliberate, and relentless butchery at the Horseshoe, which came close to achieving Jackson's goal of "exterminating" its defenders, the Red Clubs' capacity for further resistance appeared to be nearing an end. Not without reason, Colonel Carroll called the battle "the most complete victory that has ever been obtained over the Indians in America." Certainly it was the bloodiest. John Coffee wrote Mary shortly after the Horseshoe battle that the Red Clubs "cannot hold out, they are already nearly starved to death." But, as if remembering that he had been wrong many months before about the military resilience of his foe, Coffee acknowledged to his wife that they might have one last fight in them.[155] John Reid, on the other hand, was sure there would be a battle and that it would be "severe."[156] Indeed, as both men well knew, several thousand Red Club warriors; their principal prophets, Paddy Walsh and Josiah Francis; and proven military leaders such as William Weatherford and Peter McQueen were still at large in the heavily populated upper Alabama River and lower Tallapoosa River towns. That is where Jackson and his army headed next.

The Campaign for the Hickory Ground

J ACKSON'S army arrived at Fort Williams around 3:00 P.M. March 31, doubtless to the cheers of their comrades, who had been informed by Jackson's outriders of the great victory at the Horseshoe. The next morning, the indefatigable Jackson began issuing orders discharging with honor a number of his best commanders and their companies, such as the spy companies led so capably by captains Russell and Gordon, and the contingent of Cherokee warriors led by the hard-fighting Gideon Morgan. He also found time to communicate with his quartermasters about supplies and to write a lengthy letter to Rachel describing the battle of Tohopeka.[157] And of course, he instituted a string of courts-martial in yet another attempt to tame his half-disciplined soldiers.

The courts-martial were of questionable value. Several days had passed since Jackson had arrived at Fort Williams. He was enjoying, as much as possible for him, a sorely needed respite from battles with the Red Clubs and the Alabama wilderness. But during this brief lull in the war, that serpent Mutiny once again began spreading its poison through the contumacious east Tennessee militiamen who apparently had forgotten the "lesson" of Private Woods. On April 4, Jackson felt compelled to issue an order to his army advising it that he knew that a "seditious and mutinous disposition has begun to manifest itself" among the ranks of these troops. Of particular concern and great disappointment to Jackson was the fact that officers aware of the situation had "withheld" the names of the guilty parties from him. Thus, not only did Jackson cite that section of the Articles of War that provided death as a penalty for any soldier involved in mutinous conduct, he also pointedly cited the section that provided for death to officers who failed to report mutinous conduct among the troops.[158] Given the recent example Jackson had made of Woods, the men could have little doubt that Jackson was deadly serious on this subject.

But Jackson had also learned from hard experience that the best remedy for discontented soldiers was action. Thus, at 6 A.M. on April 7, Jackson departed Fort Williams with a depleted and disgruntled army and headed south down an unknown and particularly rugged section of the eastern side of the Coosa Valley. The army comprised the stalwarts of Colonel Williams's 39th Infantry Regiment, 653 cavalry and mounted men commanded by General Coffee, around 1,700 soldiers from General Doherty's and General Johnson's brigades, and a contingent of friendly Indians, probably Creek. Jackson's objective was the Creek towns clustered along a ten-mile stretch of the Tallapoosa below Tuckabatchee. His plan, worked out with Pinckney beforehand, was to form a juncture with Colonel Milton's army in an attack on the large Creek town of Hoithlewaulee, about seventy-five miles southwest, where the main body of Red Clubs was said to be gathered for a fight.[159]

On April 5, Jackson wrote Colonel Milton and ordered Milton to meet him on April 11 for an attack on Hoithlewaulee or, at the very least, have his soldiers prepared to make a diversion in the area. He also ordered Milton to deliver to Jackson the supplies earmarked for Jackson's army purportedly stored at the colonel's base at Fort Decatur. Jackson's army had been furnished with sufficient rations to last only through April 14 and was counting on the supplies he understood from Pinckney were being kept for Jackson's army at that fort.[160] To Jackson's irritation, however, he could not find any Indian runners willing to deliver the dispatch into the teeth of the nation. Finally, after suitable persuasion, Jackson found two men either brave enough, greedy enough, or foolish enough to deliver the message, each proceeding by a separate route in the hope that one would get through to Milton.[161]

The march to the lower Tallapoosa was a nightmare. The terrain was an endless series a sharp, thickly wooded hills cut with numerous creeks. Then the rains began. They were unlike any Jackson had experienced during the war: cold, relentless, and heavy. Soon the pleasant streams that crossed the army's path were transformed into swift and dangerous rivers. The pace of Jackson's march slowed to a miserable slog through mud and high water, interspersed with long, wet waits while Jackson's engineers figured out ways to cross the turbulent streams blocking their path.[162]

By April 11, the day scheduled for the attack on Hoithlewaulee, Jackson's army had managed to travel only thirty miles from Fort Williams to the Creek village of Weoka, which it promptly burned. The army was now about forty-five rainy and rough miles northwest of Hoithlewaulee. On the following day, Jackson again sent a letter to Milton, advising him of his progress and once again ordering him to prepare for an attack on the town. On April 13, as Jackson approached his objective, he received an acknowledgement from Milton of his receipt of Jackson's letters. By then it was too late. The Red Clubs had plainly learned of the approach of the terrible Jackson and his victorious army. By April 9 they had abandoned Hoithlewaulee and camped three miles down the Tallapoosa at Coolomee.[163] By April 11, they were well on their way to Pensacola.

That day Jackson virtually willed his army to the town of Fooseehatchee, or Bird Creek town. This important town lay sprawled along the northern bank of the Tallapoosa River several miles downstream from Hoithlewaulee and opposite the mouth of Line Creek. There an infuriated Jackson learned that on April 11, Milton, stationed at Fort Decatur about six miles upriver of Hoithlewaulee, had allowed the main body of Indian warriors gathered at that town to flee across the Tallapoosa in the direction of Pensacola. Jackson also learned, however, that the Big Warrior's men had taken into custody one of the most prominent Red Club leaders, ninety-four-year-old Hoboheilthle, whom the whites also called the Tame King or Tallassee King, and had turned him over to Milton.[164] They had also captured Peter McQueen and Josiah Francis. However, the tough McQueen soon managed to escape and flee to Pensacola, as did the cunning prophet Francis.[165]

The ancient Tallassee King, Hoboheilthle, however, languished as a prisoner at Milton's camp. Hailing the chief's "capture" and concomitantly betraying his ignorance of Creek governance, John Reid described him as "the ringleader of the War, and in reality the King of the Nation."[166] If the "King" was captured, however, it was by his own subjects. Around April 11, a party of Red Clubs who had had their fill of war learned that Benjamin Hawkins was with Milton's army. A year earlier their faction had wanted to kill the agent. Now they saw him as their salvation. Seizing the Tallassee King, they bound his arms, placed him on a horse, and led him to Milton's camp as a peace offering, prudently displaying before them a flag of surrender. As it approached the camp, the Red Club party was met by a company of its Creek enemies attached to Milton's army. These sent for Hawkins and with great delight took one of their foremost enemies into custody, eagerly anticipating inflicting a sweet and terminal revenge on the old man. They were to be disappointed.[167]

When Hawkins arrived, he greeted his old friend in a respectful manner and ordered the chief to be untied. Initially, and naively, Hawkins placed the chief in charge of the friendly Creeks. Later that evening, Hawkins learned that these Indians planned to put Hoboheilthle to death. Over the protests of his Indian allies, Hawkins had Hoboheilthle removed from their custody and placed under the care of Milton's troops. The friendly chiefs argued that Hoboheilthle should be handed back over to them for trial. Hawkins ignored them and, although the old chief was one of the men most responsible for destroying his life's work, the agent nonetheless set about trying to save his friend's life.[168]

The frustrated Jackson sent a detachment of horsemen in a futile pursuit of the escaping Red Clubs and turned his troops loose to loot and burn Fooseehatchee and the town of Coolomee just downstream. Among the possessions the Red Clubs left behind at those towns were 150 scalps, most of which Jackson was told came from the Fort Mims massacre.[169] They also captured some prisoners, mostly women and children, but got little information from them about the location of the main body of the hostiles.

Having inflicted what small injury it could on the panicked Red Clubs, Jackson's army camped a mile upstream of the destroyed town of Fooseehatchee on a beautiful plain along the Tallapoosa at a place surprisingly named Camp Milton. There, wrapped in the uncertain glory of an April day, John Reid spent several hours resting from the rigors of the wet march from Fort Williams, lounging in "the most beautiful encampment in the world" and enjoying the novel *The Royal Captives*. His pleasant afternoon, however, was tempered by the army's lack of rations, and he was looking forward to the tardy Colonel Milton's arriving with the first load of the plentiful foodstuffs Reid had heard were stored at Fort Decatur.[170] Reid was temporarily disappointed in his anticipation of a full meal when the dilatory Milton, who, on April 14, was camped three miles above Jackson at Hoithlewaulee, foolishly refused to immediately turn over his warehoused supplies to the general's army, impertinently advising Jackson that "he felt himself under no obligation to furnish any."[171]

In responding to Jackson this way, Milton must have been temporarily bereft of his senses, or, like the foolish man who does not know a snake is poisonous snatches it from the ground. Milton soon changed his mind, however, when Jackson demanded the supplies, as Reid delicately put it, "in a tone which they knew not how to refuse."[172] Perhaps part of the problem between the two commanders was that Colonel Milton was regular US Army and Jackson, although a major general, was not. In any event, Jackson was taking no chances of having hunger work its evil on the morale of his troops. The next day he ordered Coffee to dispatch to Fort Decatur all of his men with "horses capable of service" and armed with bags suitable for transporting as much meat and flour as the horses could carry back to Jackson's camp.[173]

At Camp Milton, Jackson pondered the reason for his failure to entrap and destroy the remaining Creek army. Initially he had blamed the heavy rains and rugged terrain for his failure to reach Hoithlewaulee by April 11 and prevent the Red Club army's escape.[174] Unable to effectively vent his anger at nature, however, Jackson found a human target to attack: the man for whom his very encampment was named. In a letter to Secretary of War Armstrong, Jackson asserted that the inexplicably inactive Colonel Milton could easily have prevented the Creek army from escaping across the rain-swollen Tallapoosa but did not even try.[175] Jackson's pique was justified. As we have seen, Milton had arrived on the east bank of the Tallapoosa with the North and the South Carolina militiamen and regulars on April 3, not far from Tuckabatchee. There he and his regiment constructed an earthen fortification and boats to transport supplies down the Tallapoosa to Jackson's army. Inexplicably, even though he knew of Jackson's plan to entrap the Creeks between their respective forces and that Jackson's army was on its way to execute that plan, Milton, through his passivity, allowed the Creek forces to escape.[176]

His human quarry having fled, Jackson was reduced to venting his spleen on the nation's material remains. Marching out of his camp below Hoithlewaulee, he embarked on a Shermanesque destruction of every Creek settlement in his immediate reach. From the already destroyed towns of Hoithlewaulee, Fooseehatchee, and Coloome, Jackson's army continued downstream and burned every Creek settlement it could find along the lower Tallapoosa.[177] On April 15, it burned the towns of Ecanhatke, Mucklassa, and Sauwanogee. For miles along the shores of the Creeks' "beloved river" the fiercely burning towns could be seen, their agitated flames reflected on the surface of its pellucid waters.

There was frost on the banks of the Tallapoosa on the morning of April 16 when Jackson's army woke at its encampment at the recently burnt town of Mucklassa. The army was now about seven miles upstream from the juncture of the Coosa and Tallapoosa rivers where the old French Fort Toulouse had been and where the ancient town of Taskigi lay. Several miles upstream, on the eastern bank of the Coosa, lay the fabled Hickory Ground. Jackson's luck in terrain had changed, and he wrote Pinckney that the roads to Taskigi were good.[178]

By now Jackson had interrogated several Red Clubs taken by his men at Fusihatchee. Among them was a black woman who had previously escaped her master at Pensacola. She informed Jackson that Pensacola merchant John Innerarity had provided the Creeks ammunition some weeks earlier.[179] The woman's report is a curious statement given the merchant's brave resistance to the threats of Peter McQueen in July 1813. Perhaps Innerarity had provided the supplies at the behest of his British masters, who were in the early stages of implementing their plan to attack the American southwestern territories. But the woman was certainly correct in her assertion that the Red Clubs had expended their ammunition at the Battle of Calebee Creek, and it is hardly surprising that they had returned to Pensacola to replenish their store.

The other prisoners interrogated by Jackson reported that the Red Clubs had long departed for Pensacola and safety among the Spanish there. Jackson, however, discounted their story. Based on the slave woman's information, he believed that a "considerable portion" of the hostiles were still in the region, probably gathered at the juncture of the Coosa and Tallapoosa rivers near the Hickory Ground.[180] This surmise was probably wishful thinking on Jackson's part. The best information he had indicated that every hostile Creek within miles had fled south.

This situation was confirmed on April 17 when he reached old Fort Toulouse. Passing for once over good roads, Jackson's army marched to the rich peninsula of black earth at the fork of the Coosa and Tallapoosa. Along the way he found only Indians ready to surrender, not fight. As the army proceeded toward the old fort, it was even met by a number of *miccos* from the Hickory Ground bearing a flag of truce.[181] When Jackson finally arrived at his destination, he found the ruins of old Fort Toulouse lying in a forlorn heap at a point where the Coosa and Tallapoosa approached six hundred yards from each other before ballooning away for several miles downstream where the rivers met to form the source of the Alabama River. Among the fort's ruins were a number of the old French cannon, unhorsed from their trunnions and laying like stubby black logs among the detritus of the old fort.[182] Several hundred yards west of the abandoned fort, near the toe of the peninsula, close by the high east bank of the Coosa River lay a large mound covered in vegetation and old trees— another relic of the Mississippian people who themselves lay hidden, crouched close in silence in great clay pots beneath the soil of a cemetery by their mound.[183]

There was nothing Jackson could do to the ancient mound or to the long-forgotten dead in their vanished cemetery; however, there was the ancient but still-inhabited town of Taskigi a short way up the peninsula. Jackson's men went gratuitously to work with their torches, and the town was soon in flames.

The Apotheosis of William Weatherford

Soon after Jackson arrived at this new encampment, prominent Red Clubs who had not run for Pensacola or been captured began coming into his camp to surrender. Foremost among these were the Fusihatchee King and, in Jackson's and the frontier peoples' eyes, the greatest Indian villain of them all: William Weatherford.[184] Like Weatherford's fabled leap into the Alabama River at the Holy Ground, his audacious appearance at Camp Jackson to surrender personally to the general almost instantly became a thing of legend. So much so that even a short time after his surrender, it became difficult to separate fact from fiction.

The most trustworthy accounts of the surrender are several letters Jackson wrote within hours of the event on April 18, 1814. That day, Jackson reported to Pinckney, who was on his way from Fort Decatur to assume command of the American forces, that hostiles from the Hickory Ground, several miles up the Coosa River on its east bank, were showing up hourly at the American encampment, "all thankful to be received upon unconditional submission." But Jackson was eager to get this process over and done with, just "[o]ne more interview will be sufficient to reduce the most stubborn of the Red Sticks to such a temper," he all but sighed, and then he would "have it over."[185] It appears that last "interview" Jackson was so eager to conclude was with the notorious Weatherford. Jackson laconically described to Governor Blount what happened next: "Weatherford has been with me & I did not confine him. He will be with me again in a few days."[186] Somewhat more informatively, he reported to Governor David Holmes of the Mississippi Territory, where Fort Mims had stood: "Since my arrival here, two of the principle Chiefs of the war party who were conspicuous characters in the affair at Fort Mimms have surrendered themselves. Fusihatchee, the Hickory Ground king Micco & William Weatherford have come in, they have brought in with them fifteen Negroes taken at Fort Mimms, & are under promises to bring in all that are in their power, together with such prisoners as they can get."

Jackson enclosed with this letter to Holmes a list of the slaves recovered and the names of their owners for repatriation. Jackson informed Holmes that until such time as master and slave could be reunited, he intended to send the slaves to his own lands in Tennessee for safekeeping—in this case meaning hard work on Jackson's plantation.[187]

Aside from Jackson's hastily penned descriptions of Weatherford's surrender, there is a plethora of versions of perhaps the most dramatic event of the Creek War. Jackson's aide-de-camp and early biographer John Reid, who was present at Weatherford's surrender, presents one account. A. B. Meek, writing in 1844, plainly obtained his account of the surrender from Reid's book on Jackson. Colonel Albert J. Pickett, writing over ten years after Meeks, presents a third account, based on his interviews of men to whom Weatherford recounted the surrender. Jackson biographer and antebellum author James Parton melds the Pickett and Reid accounts into a fourth story. Thomas Woodward, who was not present at the surrender but was in the vicinity of Fort Jackson at the time, also provided a description of the surrender, which, not surprisingly, is at variance with Pickett's account as well as with Reid's. Woodward claimed he took his account from his conversations after the war with Weatherford and Jackson, and that Pickett and Reid simply made up events out of whole cloth in order to create an interesting narrative. Further, shortly after the surrender, newspapers printed a laudatory eyewitness account that quotes Weatherford's surrender speech to Jackson under the headline "Indian Eloquence." Finally, there is a little-known account related by a soldier who was outside Jackson's tent when the general came out to meet Weatherford.[188]

The surrender story begins with Jackson ordering the Red Club chiefs who had surrendered to him to prove the sincerity of their professed desire for peace by capturing Weatherford, binding him closely, and delivering him like a wild animal to the general's tent. No one doubted that a swift hanging before Jackson's assembled troops would follow; as the reputed architect of the Fort Mims massacre, Weatherford was easily the most reviled Native American in the South.

Weatherford was not hard to find. At the time of Jackson's arrival at Fort Toulouse, he was with his Alabama people at Moniac's Island near the Holy Ground, less than half a day's ride away. Reid says a delegation of Weatherford's fellow chiefs convinced the war leader that his only option was to surrender to Jackson and seek mercy. Woodward writes that Weatherford prudently sent a man named Tom Carr to Jackson's camp to sound out whether he would accept Weatherford's surrender. When Carr arrived, he spoke with Weatherford's former brother-in-law, Sam Moniac, the Creek who was in great favor with the whites because of his wartime services to the American cause. Moniac most likely consulted with Hawkins about the matter, and Hawkins in turn sounded out Jackson. It appears the general gave a favorable reply, because Moniac informed Carr that it was safe for Weatherford to come in.[189] Whatever the case, Weatherford chose not to flee to Pensacola, as Peter McQueen, Josiah

Francis, and hundreds of other Red Clubs had done, but to face down the terrible General Jackson at Fort Toulouse.

Pickett's tale goes on to relate how, having decided to surrender, Weatherford saddled up his famous grey stallion—the animal that had carried him off the bluff into the Alabama River at the Battle of the Holy Ground—and rode to Jackson's camp.[190] Along the way, Weatherford spotted a plump deer and, inveterate hunter that he was, could not resist shooting it from horseback. After gutting the deer, he draped the carcass behind his saddle and continued on toward what was possibly the end of his life's road. Before he remounted his horse, however, he took care to charge his gun with two balls. They were intended not for Jackson but for the despised Big Warrior should that traitor dare to confront Weatherford at Jackson's camp.[191]

Weatherford rode onto the grounds of the old fort where long ago his famous grandmother, Sehoy, had met the French captain Marchand, Weatherford's grandfather. With both friendly and surrendering hostile Indians coming and going from Jackson's raucous camp, a lone Indian riding in with a fresh-killed deer probably excited nothing more among the soldiers than hunger. The bored sentries on duty gave him some rude replies when he asked the location of Jackson's headquarters—under other circumstances a deadly game to play with this man. Shortly, however, an old man, hair white with age, kindly pointed Weatherford in the right direction. Threading his way through soldiers' camps and work crews moving about with their tasks, Weatherford made it all the way over the muddy ground to Jackson's large tent before he was recognized.

Just as he pulled his horse up before the sentries at the tent's entrance, a gigantic, spotted Indian heaved himself up from the ground where he had been enjoying the new sunshine and cried out with delight, "Ah! Bill Weatherford, we have got you at last!" It was the Big Warrior, the man Weatherford most despised among the friendly Creeks, doubtless seeking some advantage from his proximity to Jackson's headquarters. Weatherford's hatred for the man welled up instantly, but at the same time he was careful not to let his hatred for the Big Warrior ruin his meeting with Jackson. He knew how to handle this spineless creature.

In the first flush of triumph, the otherwise cautious Big Warrior may not have noticed the gun Weatherford was now leveling at him from his horse. "You d—d traitor," Weatherford shouted, "if you give me any insolence, I will blow a ball through your cowardly heart." As the suddenly speechless Big Warrior backed away, an irritable Jackson, with Hawkins at his side, strode out of his tent demanding the cause of the disturbance.

Jackson had never seen Weatherford, but Hawkins knew him well from that long-ago time when, at Hawkins's bidding, a young Weatherford and Moniac had bravely snatched the renegade William Augustus Bowles from the midst of his followers. When someone pointed out the imposing man on the grey horse as Weatherford, the irascible Jackson went off like the little three-pound cannon that accompanied his army. "How dare you sir ride up to my tent, after having murdered the women and children at Fort Mims," Jackson demanded.[192]

Undaunted but certainly cognizant of the danger he was in, Weatherford, demonstrating grace under pressure, calmly and quietly replied in perhaps the only manner that could have disarmed the volatile Jackson's famous temper:[193]

> General Jackson, I am not afraid of you. I fear no man, for I am a Creek warrior. I have nothing to request in behalf of myself; you can kill me, if you desire. But I come to beg you to send for the women and children of the war party, who are now starving in the woods. Their fields and cribs have been destroyed by your people, who have driven them to the woods, without an ear of corn. I hope that you will send out parties, who will safely conduct them here, in order that they may be fed. I exerted myself in vain to prevent the massacre of the women and children at Fort Mims. I am now done fighting. The Red Sticks are nearly all killed. If I could fight you any longer, I would most heartily do so. Send for the woman and children. They never did you any harm. But kill me, if the white people want it done.[194]

Weatherford's speech, whether prepared beforehand or given extemporaneously, contained the perfect mixture of bravery, reasoned submission in the face of the inevitable, and concern for the helpless that appealed to a nineteenth-century romantic such as Jackson. Mingled in the talk were all the qualities of courage, honor, and chivalry toward women and children that were now coalescing among the upper classes of southerners as a code by which to live and die. Coming from a man he had considered little more than a murdering savage but who looked and acted like a cultured white, an astonished Jackson must have found Weatherford irresistible. But peering back from two centuries, the stamp that may have sealed Weatherford's safety is what Pickett says happened next.

A crowd of soldiers and hangers-on had gathered about Jackson's tent. Their numbers grew rapidly as word spread that the notorious Weatherford was there. One man, soon joined by many more, began shouting out in a rising and angrily repetitive chorus, "Kill him, kill him, kill him." By now Jackson, having endured mutiny upon mutiny, had long had his fill of the mob and its mindless rule. If there was any event that could wash away Weatherford's misdeeds and turn Jackson's attitude in Weatherford's favor it was the familiar scene being played out before him. At once Jackson silenced the mob. And when he extracted its silence, he admonished them, "Any man who would kill as brave a man as this would rob the dead!"[195]

Then, as the open-mouthed crowd looked on—the Big Warrior must have been consumed with rage—Jackson invited Weatherford to dismount and join him in his tent. Weatherford slid from his saddle, heaved the deer onto his shoulder, and followed the general inside.

Pickett's charming tale of Weatherford's encounter with Jackson ends with a pleasant conversation between the two men over a glass of brandy and Weatherford's gift to Jackson of the deer. But as we know from Jackson's letters to governors Blount and Holmes, there was more to it than that. Weatherford had not come to Jackson as the lone man on horseback bearing the gift of a deer for the general. He had come to Jackson's camp bringing a group of fifteen slaves taken at Fort Mims; these unfortunates were certainly part of the group of slaves the Red Clubs had stashed at the Holy Ground and spirited off when Claiborne attacked. It is also unlikely that Weatherford by himself undertook to march these men from Moniac's Island back into slavery at Fort Jackson without an appropriate escort of his warriors. More likely when he arrived at Fort Jackson with his human cargo (a quite valuable token of good faith), he left the slaves guarded over by his men while he proceeded to Jackson's tent. It was still a brave act, for Weatherford had every reason not to trust Jackson, and, as Weatherford well knew, many people at Fort Toulouse besides Jackson, particularly among his own people, desired his death.

John Reid offers another version of Weatherford's entry into Jackson's presence.[196] In an account that smacks of hero worship, Reid writes that Weatherford voluntarily entered Jackson's encampment and made his way unannounced to his tent. After gaining admission, Weatherford introduced himself to the astonished general and informed him that he had come to sue for peace.[197] Jackson sternly replied to his uninvited guest that as a leader of the massacre at Fort Mims, Weatherford deserved to die and that Jackson had expected only to meet Weatherford as a prisoner. Jackson further made it clear to Weatherford that if he had been brought to Jackson as a prisoner, Weatherford's execution would soon have followed. But because Weatherford had come in voluntarily, Jackson was now unsure what to do with him. Jackson's hesitation gave Weatherford the opportunity to give the speech of his life. According to Reid's published account, Weatherford replied to Jackson: "I am in your power—do with me as you please. I am a soldier. I have done the white people all the harm I could; I have fought them, and I have fought them bravely: if I had an army I would yet fight, and contend to the last: but I have none; my people are all gone. I can now do no more than weep over the misfortunes of my nation."[198]

Reid has Weatherford say more, but the foregoing appears to be the true core of what the warrior said. After this final exchange, the victor and the defeated part amicably. Curiously, however, unlike Pickett's account, in neither of Reid's accounts (public or private) does Weatherford attempt to exonerate himself from responsibility of the Fort Mims massacre, something he spent the rest of his days among his neighbors in the Tensaw Delta country attempting to do.

Thomas Woodward says that his spare account of Weatherford's first meeting with Jackson was taken from his conversations with Jackson and Weatherford. Woodward writes that at their meeting, Weatherford explained to Jackson that he was not responsible for the Fort Mims massacre; that after the Red Clubs had been driven off by the defenders, particularly Dixon Bailey and his men, the chiefs held a conference to decide whether to continue the fight and that at that conference Weatherford counseled them to break off the battle. He said that when his advice was rejected, he left Fort Mims and traveled to his half-brother David Tate's plantation to save his brother's slaves from the rampaging Creeks. Woodward has Weatherford close his speech to Jackson in a manner common to other authors: "Now, sir, I have told the truth, if you think I deserve death, do as you please; I shall only beg for the protection of a starving parcel of women and children, and those ignorant men who have been led into war by their Chiefs."[199]

There is yet another account of Weatherford's surrender to Jackson that also has the decided ring of truth to it. It is contained in a letter written to the historian Henry Halbert by the grandson of South Carolina militiaman William Gates. Sergeant Gates claimed to have witnessed Weatherford's initial meeting with Jackson outside the general's tent. Gates was standing about "ten or fifteen" steps from the tent when an unarmed man dressed in buckskin breeches strode up and asked a soldier the location of the tent. Jackson emerged from it—plainly one of the soldiers informed him there was a man outside who was asking for him. On seeing Jackson, no doubt splendidly attired, Weatherford walked up to him and asked if he were General Jackson. Jackson replied, "Yes." Weatherford identified himself, and the two men shook hands—Jackson extending his first. Weatherford then said to Jackson that he had come to surrender. Jackson replied simply, "I am glad to hear of it." Weatherford then explained his decision to capitulate, in the manner reported by other writers on the subject: "Our warriors are killed and scattered, our ammunition is out. Our women and children are naked and starving. If we had warriors and something to eat we would fight on." According to Gates, Jackson replied, "You are a brave man and I glory in your spunk." The two men then entered Jackson's tent, and Gates heard no more.[200]

In the end, sweeping away the devil with the details, one is left with the remarkable story of a man who for the sake of his people was willing to risk death in an encounter with another man who, less than a month ago at Horseshoe Bend, had supervised the systematic and brutal killing of hundreds of those people. Equally as remarkable a story is that of the preternaturally ferocious and vengeful Jackson's capacity to befriend a man who shortly before their first meeting he had intended to put to death. As Woodward writes, the fact that Jackson did not have Weatherford executed, as he would later do to Josiah Francis, is the best evidence of Jackson's opinion of a man he described to Woodward after the war as "as high-toned and fearless as any man he had met with—one whose very nature scorned a mean action."[201]

Around this time and place, although long forgotten to history, there is another encounter between one of the Red Club principals in the war and an American leader that, although not as dramatic as the Jackson-Weatherford story, is almost as remarkable. That involves Hawkins's attempt to save the life of the ancient Tallassee King, Hoboheilthle, one of the main leaders in a war that had essentially destroyed Hawkins's life's work.

The Tallassee King had endured captivity for some two weeks when, on April 26, 1814, Hawkins wrote to General Pinckney asking him, in the indirect manner of address of the times, to free the old man. Describing Hoboheilthle as "a warm, decided, & useful friend to the U.S.," Hawkins recited to Pinckney the chief's many services to the United States. Foremost among these was Hoboheilthle's assistance against the British during the American War for Independence, a subject Hawkins must have known would speak directly to the deep sensibilities of Pinckney, a veteran of that war. Hawkins also cast the old chief as the victim of an internal power struggle with the Big Warrior and the Little Prince for control of the Creek Nation. The old chief, Hawkins wrote, had misguidedly attempted to harness the prophets' movement as an ally against these two enemies. However, Hoboheilthle had sadly underestimated the prophets' power and soon found they had escaped his control. For these and other reasons, such as the Tallassee King's critical help in bringing the Treaty of New York to pass, Hawkins thought the chief "a fit subject to be reported to you with this statement of facts for your decision."[202]

Hawkins and Pinckney, who were both at Fort Toulouse at the time, had probably worked together on a plan to save Hoboheilthle. For on the same day Hawkins wrote his letter to Pinckney, the general wrote a letter to Secretary of War Armstrong enclosing Hawkins's letter. In his letter, Pinckney asked Armstrong to pass Hawkins's letter along to President Madison for his "intentions" regarding the fate of the old chief. Happily for Hoboheilthle, Madison informed Armstrong in a letter dated May 20, 1814, that "[t]he treatment of the aged Telassia King may be safely trusted to the humanity of Col. Hawkins."[203]

Like Jackson with Weatherford, Hawkins was prepared to let his ancient friend, now around ninety-five years old, go in peace. For some reason it was not to be. Perhaps Madison's letter arrived too late. The old king remained a prisoner of the Americans until June 12, when he died of mistreatment he had received from his guards on May 30. Former Red Club warriors from Okfuskee, Wewoka, and Okchai buried Hoboheilthle with the "honors of war" on a bluff overlooking the Coosa River, only several hundred yards from Fort Toulouse.[204]

The few white prisoners taken by the Red Clubs at Fort Mims were more fortunate. Polly Jones and her three children, who had been taken captive at Fort Mims by Dog Warrior of Atasi, arrived at Fort Jackson on April 18. Even more remarkable was the story of the Creek wife of Zachariah McGirth, known as Vicey, who was also taken prisoner at Fort Mims. Just before her captor and adopted son Santo left to fight at Horseshoe Bend, he had urged her to make her way to the white settlements. Now she, too, had shown up at Jackson's camp, along with her five daughters. In the chaotic aftermath of Jackson's devastating march through the lower Tallapoosa towns, she had apparently walked down from the Hickory Ground with Creek women and children seeking food at Jackson's encampment.[205]

But her adventures were not yet over. From Fort Toulouse she and her family walked all of the dangerous two hundred miles down the Federal Road to the Tensaw settlements. When she arrived there with her children, worn out and half-starved, she found the region deserted. Fortunately, she stumbled on a "rude hut" in which they all could take shelter and a sweet-potato patch that provided food. She was found languishing there by Captain Blue's spy company and not long thereafter found transportation to Mobile, where her husband was staying. He had somehow managed to survive perhaps the most dangerous job in the war: express rider carrying dispatches between Fort Stoddert and the Georgia settlements. As the war wound down and McGirth could no longer outride the loss of his family, he made his way to Mobile, perhaps to start a new life in that city.[206]

One day a friend stopped him on the street and mysteriously informed him that someone was at the city wharf who wanted to see him. When McGirth arrived there he saw a piteous sight: an emaciated woman wrapped in a tattered blanket and several equally emaciated and half-naked children squatting in a canoe tied up to the quay. McGirth's friend seemed to be playing a strange and cruel game with him. For as the story goes, he asked McGirth whether he knew the pitiful group in the canoe. "No," he said, and looked again at the strangers but without recognition. At this point the woman in the boat, no doubt exasperated to her limits by the charade playing out before her, pulled off her blanket and "exposed her face and person." A stupefied McGirth at last recognized his wife and remaining children; his son James had been killed at Fort Mims.[207] No doubt, after McGirth regained his senses and tears of joy were shed by all, the reunited family headed off to obtain some clothes and afterward a robust meal, hopefully paid for by McGirth's odd friend.

A Land in Chaos

ON April 20, 1814, Major General Pinckney arrived at Fort Jackson and assumed command of the American forces there. The next day he ordered Jackson to return with his militia to Fort Williams. The victorious Jackson left that day in what for him must have been high spirits, and by April 24 he had reached Fort Williams. He wrote Pinckney on April 21 for instructions regarding his future duties and requested that Colonel Williams, whose 39th Infantry Regiment had been severely cut up during the Battle of Horseshoe Bend, be allowed to return to Tennessee to procure new recruits for his regiment.[208]

Pinckney responded promptly to Jackson's letter the following day, granting his request regarding Williams and instructing Jackson also to return to Tennessee with his army after he had scoured the Cahaba River region west of Fort Williams of any hostiles assembled there. On his arrival at Fort Jackson, Pinckney also wasted no time initiating a program for bringing the Creek War to a close. On the same day he ordered Jackson to Fort Williams, he also ordered that Colonel Milton's and Colonel Williams's commands of regular army troops be combined into one brigade. He further ordered that a second brigade, under the command of General Joseph Graham, be formed from the North and South Carolina militia troops, currently on the march to Pinckney's camp, and the creation of a corps of artillery. Pinckney also ordered his commanders to bind the entire Muskogee Nation with a chain of forts connected by roads that could accommodate wagons and cannon radiating from Fort Jackson down the Alabama River valley to Mobile and up the Coosa River valley into Tennessee.[209]

The dutiful Pinckney, who along with Hawkins had been appointed back in March by the federal government as a commissioner to "negotiate" a treaty with the Creek Nation, also wasted no time in initiating those negotiations. On April 23, 1814, he set forth terms for resolution of the war in a letter to Hawkins and instructed the agent to convey the terms to the Creek leaders currently at Fort Jackson. The treaty terms outlined by Pinckney, which he was careful to emphasize to the Creeks could not be altered, contained a number of general provisions: (1) the Creeks were to indemnify the United States by a land cession for the expenses it had incurred in prosecuting the war; (2) the United States was to have the right to establish military posts and roads as it saw fit throughout the nation and was to be given free navigation of the nation's rivers; (3) the Creeks were to surrender to the United States all prophets and other instigators of the war and to prosecute any hostiles who refused to surrender; and (4) the friendly Indians were to be indemnified for their losses incurred in fighting the Red Clubs with Red Club lands. Unfortunately for the Muskogee Nation, however, the day before Pinckney wrote that letter he had resigned as a treaty commissioner because those duties conflicted with his new assignment of organizing the defense of the southeastern coast of the United States against the British.[210]

Nonetheless, Hawkins immediately conveyed these general treaty terms to the friendly chiefs and iterated Pinckney's injunction that the terms were nonnegotiable. Hawkins also instructed the chiefs to convey these terms to the hostile party, who by now had retreated to Pensacola for sanctuary under the tattered umbrella of Spanish sovereignty. In response, Alex Cornells, Hawkins's assistant agent and a Tuckabatchee chief, informed Hawkins that he did not believe that the hostile Creeks from the many wrecked towns along the lower Tallapoosa River would even now enter into a treaty with the United States. The forces of these Red Clubs presently in Spanish Florida were still largely intact, Cornells said, and they remained "proud, haughty, brave, and mad by fanaticism." Accordingly, Cornells believed, they would probably consider Pinckney's offer a sign of weakness. Cornells went on to advise that the Red Clubs would need to suffer a further defeat before they would agree to peace. The optimistic Hawkins, on the other hand, told the friendly chiefs that enough blood had been loosened in the war and that they should try to persuade the hostiles to make peace.[211]

Jackson had other ideas about the treaty conditions that should be imposed on the Creeks, friendly as well as hostile. He was infuriated to learn that Pinckney and Hawkins had been appointed treaty commissioners for the United States, leaving Jackson, who had done so much to defeat the Red Clubs, on the sidelines. On April 18, 1814, shortly after his arrival at Tuskegee, Jackson's senior officers sent a letter signed by each of them to George Washington Campbell, the US secretary of the Treasury and former US senator for Tennessee, complaining of this arrangement. Obviously, Jackson was behind this maneuver and probably dictated the letter. In it the signatories expressed their outrage that the United States had failed to consult with the Tennesseans about the terms of the treaty, despite the fact that Tennessee had contributed most to the conquest of the Red Clubs. As to Pinckney, who was described in the letter as a "genial" person, the Tennesseans had no objection. But the appointment of the notorious Indian lover Hawkins was another matter. His sympathies, the Tennesseans believed, lay with the hostile Creeks, and the Creek agent's past transgressions—unnamed—had forfeited the trust of Americans both on the frontier and in the East. Campbell was urged to place the letter before the president and to add any comments of his own to the protests of Jackson's officers.[212]

After his officers' letter was written, Jackson was quick to open a second front against the treaty negotiations. On April 25, shortly after Jackson arrived at Fort Williams, he wrote the secretary of war a letter in which he acknowledged that federal treaty commissioners had been appointed to deal with the Creeks but then went on to express his views as to the amount of land the nation should cede to the United States. The scope of Jackson's proposal was breathtaking: millions of the choicest acres possessed by the nation would be ceded to the United States. Essentially he proposed to divest the Creeks of all their lands west of the Coosa and Alabama rivers.[213]

That same day, Jackson departed from Fort Williams for home. Pursuant to Pinckney's orders, Jackson left behind General Johnson and his command to "scour" the Cahaba River country of hostiles and to then rendezvous with Jackson at Fort Deposit. He assigned General Doherty the task of keeping open the lines of communication between Tennessee and Fort Jackson.

By the evening of May 7, a slightly indisposed Jackson arrived at Huntsville, where he and his staff were feted by what passed for society in that small town with a "sumptuous dinner" and "elegant ball." During these festivities, Jackson was reunited with his adopted Indian son, Lyncoya. Maria Pope, the daughter of Huntsville's foremost citizen, Leroy Pope, presented the little Creek orphan, dressed like a "poppet" (a little doll), along with an "elegant stand of Coulours" to the general.[214]

Two days before his arrival in Huntsville, from a camp near the Cherokee leader Colonel John Brown's farm, Jackson had dispatched a company of rangers under Captain Hammond, together with twenty Cherokee spies, selected by Colonel Brown, to the Cahaba and Black Warrior regions. Their orders were to kill any warriors they found there and to make prisoners of any women and children they discovered. As Jackson made plain in his instructions, no Creeks or any other Indian tribe were to be allowed to settle west of the Coosa River or northwest of the Alabama River. This expedition was overkill for anyone but Jackson, since Johnson was already rampaging through the Cahaba region with 200 infantry and 270 mounted soldiers, killing, burning, and taking prisoners. Johnson's prisoners were escorted, under the supervision of the friendly chief, Old Chenibee, to lands in the nation that Jackson, on his own initiative, had selected for Creek resettlement. Jackson ordered this resettlement in furtherance of his own larger plan, which he recently had confided to Governor Blount, to reshape the entire frontier between whites and Native Americans in the southeastern United States.[215]

By May 14, Jackson was back in Nashville, where he received a tumultuous welcome from the citizens and was feted at a formal banquet on May
19 sponsored by the leading men of the town. Equally if not even more
gratifying to the victorious general was his reunion there with his beloved
Rachel and his adopted son, little Andrew. Mother and son had traveled
from the Hermitage to Nashville to greet him on his arrival. Jackson must
have been particularly delighted to introduce Andrew to his new playmate,
Lyncoya, whom the boy had been waiting months to meet. Along with
Lyncoya, Jackson brought more additions to his plantation family: a group
of "Fort Meams Negroes," some of the slaves William Weatherford had
turned over to the general. The arrival of these well-traveled slaves was
especially welcome to Jackson because a sickness among his own slaves
had prevented his overseer, a man named Fields, from planting sufficient
land on the general's plantation. Now Fields was instructed to employ the
men to plant every bit of land they could; the women were to be put to
work in the kitchen.[216]

Jackson did not allow the enjoyment of his family and the management
of his plantation to distract him from national interests, particularly the
Creek treaty negotiations. Clearly with Jackson pushing hard from the
wings, Tennessee's elected representatives lobbied the federal government
hard for Jackson's inclusion in those negotiations. On May 18,
Congressman John Rhea of Tennessee wrote Secretary Armstrong requesting that the general be appointed one of the treaty commissioners. Rhea
was a Revolutionary War veteran who had fought with the victorious colonials at the key Battle of King's Mountain and was presently a powerful
member of the House of Representatives. In his letter, Rhea came right to
the point. The citizens of Tennessee had "done the principal part of the
fighting business" in the Creek War and deserved a seat at the treaty table.
Given General Jackson's record in that war, he was "the man" to represent
Tennessee at that table. Congressman Rhea went on to not-so-subtly
advise Secretary Armstrong that such an appointment would not only be
"gratifying" to the people of Tennessee but "certainly will be to me." Rhea
would not have long to wait for a response.[217]

While Jackson was enjoying domestic bliss and the adulation of his fellow citizens, Pinckney and Hawkins were trying to wind up the Creek War.
Hawkins's most pressing concern was feeding the 5,257 famished Creek
men, women, and children who had flocked to Fort Jackson for food.[218]
Pinckney had a different concern. Peter McQueen, Josiah Francis, and other
hostile leaders had escaped Jackson's dragnet and, along with over a thousand of their adherents, had made their way to the safety of Spanish
Florida. By April 26, several hundred of them were encamped five or six
miles outside Pensacola, where they were being poorly fed from the limited
stores of the Spanish, while three hundred Creek warriors slept under the

walls of Fort George just outside of town. Not so the prophet Francis. The Spanish provided him with "a handsome suite of apartments" in town.[219]

Hundreds of other Red Clubs had established settlements along the Escambia River to the northeast of Pensacola. From these sanctuaries in Spanish territory, they launched raids, mostly for corn and cattle, into the American settlements to the north, making the abandoned Tensaw region a deadly place for settlers to return for the crucial spring planting. On April 26, 1814, a farmer named Gerald Byrne, mistakenly thinking the Creek War was over, left the protection of Mobile, where he and his family had been living since the Fort Mims debacle, and traveled with several of his slaves to his old farm in the Tensaw region to get a crop planted. Several days after his arrival, he was visited at his home by some acquaintances—Mr. Taylor and Mr. Hatcher and Colonel John House—all of whom spent the night there. House rose before dawn the next day and made a fortuitous departure from the Byrne farm. He had ridden only a few miles from Byrne's house when he was startled by the unsettling sound of a furious exchange of gunfire coming from the direction of the place. Shortly, the firing ceased and the prudent colonel rode on.

By then all the whites and one of Byrne's slaves lay dead. The remaining slaves and the Americans' horses were stolen. Before sunrise, a party of Creek warriors had secreted themselves in several outbuildings near Byrne's home. At first light they attacked the house, and in the exchange of gunfire killed Byrne, Taylor, and an unnamed slave who was said to have died protecting his master. During the fight, Hatcher made a break from the house and ran desperately for the woods. He made it three hundred yards before he, too, was shot down and then scalped. These sorts of attacks, word of which spread quickly through the small community of settlers, served to discourage the inhabitants from returning to their farms that spring.[220]

Into this tumultuous situation along the lower Alabama River, on April 22, Pinckney ordered Colonel Milton and the 39th Infantry Regiment to descend the Alabama River from Fort Jackson and bring back to Fort Jackson the curiously inactive Colonel Russell and the 3rd Infantry Regiment. Once that regiment had delivered the long-awaited supplies to Fort Jackson, it would then descend the river and unite with the 39th Infantry at Mobile, which, ironically, was to be commanded by General Jackson's old adversary, Thomas Hart Benton, while Colonel Williams was in Tennessee recruiting replacements for the depleted regiment.[221] Since Russell's abortive expedition to the mouth of the Cahaba River the past February, which, aside from burning a village or two, had essentially served only to get Lieutenant Wilcox and several of his companions killed, the 3rd Infantry had been cooling its heels at Fort Claiborne, waiting interminably for boats to be built to transport supplies to Fort Jackson.[222]

When Milton and his regiment arrived at Fort Claiborne on April 27, they found that Russell and several hundred men were on the march to the Florida line to drive the hostiles from the intervening countryside. Milton dispatched a messenger to Russell, peremptorily ordering him to halt his troops in position and to return in person to Fort Claiborne to explain his actions. Russell obeyed, returned to the fort, and reported his plans for scouring the hostiles all the way to the Florida line. Milton was not impressed with this exercise and demanded to know what Russell had done to execute Pinckney's long-outstanding orders to transport supplies to the Hickory Ground. Russell lamely explained that he still had boats being constructed sixty miles downstream but that progress had been thwarted because the never-helpful General Flournoy had failed to supply the necessary tools. Russell also advised Milton that even when the boats were completed, they would have to sail to Mobile and load supplies. The whole process, Russell said, would delay any expedition up the river until May 20.

After receiving Russell's home report, Milton turned his attention to the six hundred or so Choctaws and Chickasaws he had discovered "lounging" around the post, assiduously devoting their main energies to devouring every available provision in sight. Milton optimistically but naively ordered the warriors to divide into two companies, one to ascend the Alabama River and roust out any hostiles there, the other to scour the country of hostiles between Fort Claiborne and the Florida line. To Milton's consternation, the Indians responded that they would first have to convene a council to consider his plan, after which they would give him an answer.[223]

The frustrated Milton reported the situation at Fort Claiborne to Pinckney. But the messenger he selected was an unusual one. After William Weatherford parted from General Jackson at the headwaters of the Alabama River, he traveled to the Fort Claiborne area, where he had a plantation on the Little River tributary of the Alabama near the home of his half-brother David Tate. Unfortunately for the Creek leader, the survivors of Fort Mims and the many relatives of the victims of Weatherford's attack on that place also lived in the region. So great was the threat to Weatherford's life from his vengeful neighbors that he was forced to leave his plantation and seek the dubious protection of Fort Claiborne to the north.

On Weatherford's arrival at that post, Russell placed a guard over the warrior to ensure his safety.[224] According to one story, among the men assigned to this duty was the intrepid express rider and yaws-disfigured James Cornells. He hated Weatherford with an intense but misguided passion because he believed Weatherford was partially responsible for the violence done to his wife and property during Peter McQueen's expedition to

Pensacola the previous July. Accordingly, Cornells vowed to kill Weatherford at his first opportunity. Now he was pleasantly surprised to find that the opportunity had fallen unbeckoned into his lap.

Weatherford soon learned of Cornells's vow and immediately confronted the man, declaring that Cornells's hatred toward him made Cornells unfit to act as Weatherford's guard. Chivalrously, Cornells assured Weatherford that he would not take advantage of his position as Weatherford's guard to harm the refugee. But Cornells also made clear to Weatherford that when his guard duty was over, he intended to seek out Weatherford and kill him. Cornells's threat was not an idle one. Despite his horrible disfigurement, or perhaps because of it, Cornells was a tough character and when aroused was not averse to murder; after the war he killed a man named Jones in a dispute over title to a ferry. Fortunately, perhaps for both Cornells and Weatherford, Cornells later learned that Weatherford was not involved in the wrongs inflicted on the Cornells family, and the two men eventually became fast friends.[225]

Even with the danger from Cornells averted, Weatherford's safety at Fort Claiborne remained precarious. Shortly after his arrival at the fort, Milton met with the famous warrior and apparently succumbed to his charm. Apprehensive for the warrior's safety, on April 28, Milton decided to send him with a letter to the commanding general at Fort Jackson. There, some three hundred miles upriver, Milton felt Weatherford would at least be out of the immediate reach of his enemies in the Tensaw country.[226] The fact that Milton felt comfortable entrusting the architect of the Fort Mims massacre with an official report of the military situation in southern Alabama to his superior officer speaks volumes of the confidence that the upper echelon of the American military command reposed in the former renegade.

Pickett recounts a romantic version of Weatherford's departure from Fort Claiborne that he obtained from an interview with one of the participants in the reputed affair, a Major Laval. Laval, who was then a captain, was serving as officer of the guard at the fort one night. Around midnight he was approached by an aide to Milton accompanied by Weatherford. Following introductions, the aide pointed to a nearby tree to which a horse had been tethered. Invoking Milton's authority, the aide ordered Laval to walk Weatherford to the tree and give him the horse. Weatherford quickly mounted the animal, thanked Laval, and galloped away in the darkness to Fort Jackson.[227]

Following Weatherford's arrival at Fort Jackson, the commanding general there, John Graham, quickly found employment for the former Red Club leader in the lower Alabama River region. On May 20, 1814, on Graham's orders, Colonel Pearson and several hundred North Carolina militia marched from Fort Jackson down the west side of the Alabama

River while a fleet of boats crewed by fifty men loaded with the expedition's provisions proceeded in tandem down the river.[228] Pearson's command consisted of three hundred infantry and a company of South Carolina dragoons. With them were seventy-five Creek warriors at whose head he had placed the "famous Bill Weatherford." With the supply boats in regular contact with Pearson's land forces, the marauders soon found themselves in uncharted country where even the narrow Indian paths they had been following finally vanished into wilderness. Wilderness it may have been, but the countryside along the army's route was beautiful. Pearson, for instance, was struck by a "remarkable bend" in the Alabama River "encircling a body of the richest land I ever saw."[229]

Although there were several hundred Red Club warriors in the area — "stout likely young men, with fine intelligent countenances and a manly deportment," they were too dispirited to put up a meaningful resistance. A good number of their people were also starving in what before the war had been the granary of the Muskogee Confederation. In the course of the campaign, one body of Pearson's troopers encountered a group of Indians in canoes who had just entered the Alabama River from the mouth of the Cahaba River. The soldiers chased the Indians onto shore, where the Indians abandoned their canoes and most of their property and fled into the interior. As the troopers rummaged through the Creeks' abandoned possessions they found that the most valuable thing left behind "was the legs and thighs of a Colt," which they had not entirely consumed.[230] Brought to this sorry pass, the Alabamas were no doubt cursing the prophets who had persuaded them to destroy their crops and animals as the polluting spawn of the white man's culture.

For over ten days, Pearson's forces tore through the country of the Alabamas, damaging much property but doing little fighting. The campaign largely consisted of a town-by-town surrender of the hostiles—men, women, and children. Near the end of the campaign, Pearson's men received something of a scare when they met up as planned with a company of the US 39th Infantry Regiment from Fort Claiborne. As the troops from each command mingled, Pearson's men learned from the men of the 39th that the British had armed the hostile Creeks gathered in Pensacola and that war could break out again any day.

The source of this rumor was the by-now stale information Colonel Milton had recently received via Judge Toulmin now in Mobile, which led Milton to conclude that "the Creek War so far from being at an end—will range tenfold fury." In the same grandiloquent prose style in which the past April he had assured General Pinckney that he would level Hoithlewaulee, Milton now dramatically declared to General Graham that he would pursue the Red Clubs to the gates of Pensacola "or die in the attempt." [231] Of course, he said, Graham and his troops would have to join him in this insane enterprise, which, aside from the danger, amounted to invading a sovereign nation with whom the United States was not at war. Milton was rescued from his foolishness when he received information from a reliable source that Toulmin had sounded a false alarm.[232] The crisis over, several weeks later, Milton marched the 3rd Infantry to Fort Jackson as previously planned.

As Pearson wisely recognized, the men of the 39th had no doubt embellished the reports of slavering Creek hordes about to descend on the frontier, but nonetheless the rumors had a dispiriting effect on his soldiers. On May 30, 1814, one of Pearson's officers relayed to him the disturbing news that most of those in his command were so concerned for their safety that they were for breaking camp and heading for home at once. Pearson persuaded his soldiers to wait a few days to see what developed. Matters were taken out of the colonel's hands, however, when the wagon train his army was depending on for supplies turned back and returned to base. At this news, Pearson decided to abandon his encampment and take his troops back to Fort Jackson.[233]

Despite its premature end, Pearson's expedition was largely successful. During their sweep through the Alabama country, Pearson's forces took five hundred prisoners, of whom two hundred were warriors. However, for all the results he achieved in ridding the Alabama country of the hostiles, Pearson suffered a galling failure. One of the most prominent and dangerous of the Creek prophets, Paddy Walsh, who the Creek historian George Stiggins claimed was among the party of warriors who attacked Lieutenant Wilcox, still stalked the region, intent on inflicting as much evil on the Americans as he could.[234] And for a short while he did, until betrayed by his own people into the hands of the Americans who promptly imprisoned him at Fort Claiborne. Even there Walsh continued to torment the whites, escaping from that place with a fellow prisoner. Unfortunately for Walsh, his fellow Creeks were by now so cowed by the Americans that they took him back to Fort Claiborne. There he received a trial of sorts for killing two whites; he did kill them, but he was convicted without evidence, other than the lies of an interpreter who claimed that Walsh proudly admitted the crime. Walsh was sentenced to hang. This time the prophet was out of magic, and he spent his last moments on Earth gazing out on a no-doubt large and raucous crowd eager to see the little monster die, before swinging off into the baleful spotlight of an Alabama summer sun.[235]

As for William Weatherford, in his official report of his expedition, Pearson praised Weatherford's integrity and "great usefulness" during the mission. According to Pearson, "I cannot speak in too high terms [of Weatherford] and whom, I am induced to believe evil reports has said more than he deserves."[236] Weatherford would go on in the coming months to assist the Americans in bringing to heel other renegade Creeks, but it would be years before his neighbors in the Tensaw Delta, where he settled after the war, accepted him into their company.[237] During the first years at his Little River plantation, Weatherford had a number of encounters with people who bore him grudges for his role at Fort Mims.[238] After a while, however, these incidents became less frequent, and the irresistible charm of the man converted foes to friends. Within five years after Weatherford surrendered to Jackson, the Tensaw Delta people even looked to him for protection from the numerous evil characters whose depredations kept the region in turmoil. One such incident involved a particularly vicious murder in which one of the culprits was a man named James Caller, almost certainly the miscreant colonel of Burnt Corn Creek fame.[239]

One day Caller and a companion named George Fisher turned up at an estate sale in what is now lower Monroe County, Alabama. Some of the crowd was reported to be intoxicated; probably most of them were, particularly Caller and Fisher. Present at the sale was an elderly blacksmith named Bradberry. He was the father of Captain William Bradberry who had fought a heroic rearguard action at Burnt Corn Creek and later lost an arm, from which he eventually died, in the fighting that occurred during General Claiborne's expedition to Fort Easley the previous October. For some reason, Fisher took a dislike to old Bradberry and began bullying him. The situation turned deadly after Fisher insisted that Bradberry fetch him a pitcher of water from a nearby spring. Bradberry good-naturedly complied, but when he returned from the spring with the pitcher of water, Fisher broke the crockery over the old man's head.[240]

Bradberry fled for safety into a nearby kitchen where several women were cooking food for the crowd and asked for their protection. Fisher followed the bloody-headed old man into the room. The women began upbraiding the ruffian for picking on the old fellow. Fisher left. At that point, Caller entered the kitchen and ordered Bradberry outside. Perhaps intimidated by the imposing Caller, Bradberry complied. Fisher was waiting by the door, and when Bradberry emerged, he attempted to brain the old man with a length of wood. Bradberry somehow avoided the blow and ran for the nearby woods followed by Caller, who was brandishing "an immense knife." Caller soon caught up with Bradberry and drove the knife blade so forcefully into the old man's back that the point came out his chest.

Murder was not uncommon on that turbulent frontier, but this one was so senseless, brutal, and cowardly that the onlooking crowd, even drunk as many of them undoubtedly were, was horrified. A justice of the peace named Henderson who was in the crowd cried out for the people to capture Caller and Fisher, who stood about forty feet away, chests puffed up, waving their knives and threatening to kill the first man who dared try to apprehend them. Shamefully, no person in the crowd moved toward the killers—except one.

Because of his peculiar situation in regard to Fort Mims, William Weatherford tended to dissociate himself from the affairs of white men and made it his practice to keep to the fringes of white gatherings. But this outrage was too much for the former war chief. He upbraided the crowd for its timidity and declared that if the murdered Bradberry had possessed one drop of Indian blood in his veins, he would have killed the murderers then and there. Encouraged by Weatherford's bold talk, Henderson pleaded with Weatherford to capture Caller and Fisher. Weatherford hesitated, not out of fear of the two men but of the white man's laws should he make the attempt. Henderson assured the warrior that he was in no danger from the law whatever occurred.

That was sufficient for Weatherford, who immediately drew out a long dirk with a silver handle and strode quickly toward Caller and Fisher, now perhaps not so energetically waving their fearsome knives in the air. He approached the quaking Caller first and raised his dirk above his head to strike the creature. Caller immediately dropped his bloody knife to the ground and allowed Weatherford to seize him by the collar and drag him over to the spectators for them to secure. He then turned his attention to Fisher, who must have been frozen in terror, for he had made no attempt to escape while Weatherford was dealing with Caller. When Weatherford aimed his dirk at the man, Fisher surrendered. "I will not resist you Billy Weatherford," he said.[241]

As for the local white citizenry, even after the crowd had tied up the murderers for transport to the nearest jail at the new town of Claiborne, no one dared take them there. Finally, Weatherford and another prominent mixed-blood, William Sizemore, carried the two prisoners to jail. Weatherford's distrust of the white man's law was well founded. The case against Caller and Fisher was promptly tried by a jury, but despite the overwhelming evidence of their guilt, the jury acquitted the two culprits.[242] Weatherford, however, had done much to rehabilitate himself in the eyes of his neighbors.[243]

Following Pearson's success, and the prior capitulation on May 18 of the Hillabee, Okfuskee, and Fish Pond tribes to General Graham, Benjamin Hawkins pronounced the country down to the Florida line free of hostile activity.[244] Then, in early June, Colonel Milton received two letters dated back to back that cast the whole situation in Florida in a dangerously different light. The first, dated June 7, was from Colonel McKee at Fort Saint Stephens. In that letter he advised Milton that Peter McQueen and his followers were on their way to Fort Claiborne to sue for peace.[245] The second letter, dated June 8, from an anonymous "gentleman" in Pensacola to a friend at Fort Stoddert, contained information that the writer characterized as a "great change" in Indian affairs in the region. According to the author, rather than traveling to Fort Claiborne to surrender, McQueen and his followers had abruptly left Pensacola to join the British, who had landed a large number of troops and supplies down the coast to the east of Pensacola.[246] This news was not necessarily inconsistent with McKee's letter. McQueen may at one point have become frustrated with his treatment by the Spanish and decided to surrender to the Americans. On the arrival of the British, however, McQueen apparently abruptly changed his mind. He would not be coming to Fort Claiborne now, at least not to surrender.

The second letter further reported the arrival on June 1 at Apalachicola Bay of a forty-four-gun British frigate known as the *Orpheus* along with its tender.[247] Apalachicola Bay was a remote place on the Gulf Coast located approximately 140 miles east of Pensacola. To its north, inland swamps and an immense pine forest stretched for many difficult miles through Georgia. To its south, the bay was not easily navigated, particularly by large ships, because its inviting waters were dangerously shallow. Nonetheless, the Apalachicola River, with its access to the Lower Creek Nation via the Chattahoochee and Flint rivers, had great advantages that offset the risk. For that reason, John Forbes & Company had established a trading post there. This connection with the Indian settlements in the interior and its remote location also made it a good place for mischief-makers to gather, particularly those from a foreign nation who needed a staging ground for an invasion of the southern coast of the United States. It was the land where William Augustus Bowles had made his headquarters.

The arrival of the *Orpheus* at Apalachicola was the first step in the British government's plan for just such an invasion. The ship was commanded by a Captain Pigot and carried ample arms and ammunition for the hostile Creek forces, as well as a large contingent of British soldiers and their officers. Some 300 to 350 of these men embarked on shore along with a reported, but clearly exaggerated, 20,000 stands of guns for the Creeks. The British and the elated Indians then went to work building a fort on a nearby island known as Saint Georges, a long and slender barrier of sand fencing off the south end of the bay. McQueen soon joined them, having been secretly transported in a Forbes company ship to Apalachicola.[248] Thus the report of his imminent surrender to Colonel Milton at Fort Claiborne may well have been a nice piece of disinformation.

Heartened by the influx of British weapons and troops, which would have been enormously more useful to the hostiles had they been delivered several months earlier, the Red Clubs sent out runners to their former enemies, the Lower Creeks, with an invitation to join them.[249] Astonishingly, the Red Clubs even approached the Big Warrior, who less than a year earlier they had tried to murder, and attempted to induce him to subscribe to their cause. Apparently his former enemies had unbounded confidence in the chief's bottomless capacity for cupidity and treachery, and at their instigation, the newly appointed British Indian agent, Brevet Captain Woodbine of the Royal Marines, sent an Indian known as Young Chief Yellow Hair to meet with the Big Warrior "and doubt not succeeding in gaining every Indian over from the Americans."[250]

Nor was such confidence entirely misplaced. Rather than rejecting the British proposals outright, the cagey chief replied that because he had been deceived by British words in the past, he required more substantial proof of their "sincerity" before he could commit to their propositions.[251] The old reprobate was wise to hedge his bet, given that a veritable cornucopia of military supplies and foodstuffs had landed on the Red Club shores backed by a strong contingent of British troops. In light of these hopeful developments, it appears that the demise of the Red Club movement had been greatly exaggerated. Andrew Jackson's sledgehammer touch was needed once more.

The Return of the General: The Treaty of Fort Jackson

THE domestic comforts of the Hermitage and the responsibilities of a husband and father were insufficient to absorb the demonic energies and ambitions of Andrew Jackson. Fortunately for those within his immediate reach, Jackson was not required to endure the role of a gentleman farmer for long. In the space of a week, in a rapid series of remarkable coincidences that appeared almost supernatural, Jackson was elevated to a position of power and recognition of which his orphaned self had long dreamed.

Not long after he had settled back into his home, Jackson received a letter from Secretary of War Armstrong dated May 22, 1814, informing a delighted Jackson that General Wade Hampton had resigned from the regular US Army and offering Jackson a commission as brigadier general, with a brevet to major general, in the regular army. Hard on the heels of this letter, on May 24, Armstrong wrote Jackson another welcomed letter, instructing him to proceed to Fort Jackson and consummate the treaty negotiations with the Creeks initiated by General Pinckney. Then came the best letter of all from Armstrong. Dated May 28, it informed Jackson that Major General William Henry Harrison, the victor over Tecumseh at the Battle of the Thames, had just resigned his commission and that President Madison, subject to Senate confirmation, had appointed Jackson to the permanent rank of major general in the US Army. One of the first to congratulate him was his friend Treasury Secretary Campbell, who doubtless had had much to do with Jackson's recent appointments and Creek treaty responsibility.[252]

On June 26, Jackson left the Hermitage for Fort Jackson, where he arrived July 10. Not unexpectedly, conditions at the post were not to the major general's liking, and with good reason. He found that the fort was not even half-finished, the work that was done was shoddy, and even the undergrowth around the site that was present when Jackson was last at the place had not been removed. In sum, while the British were arming the Red Clubs in Apalachicola Bay, the fort's defenses were all but nonexistent and the troops indifferent to security. Jackson had summoned the leaders of the Creek Nation to meet him at Fort Jackson on August 1 to conclude a treaty between their nation and the United States, and he planned to have the fort and the troops manning it in top condition. To correct the shortcomings he found at this post, Jackson immediately instituted "rigid discipline" and "aroused" the men to put the fort in a state capable of defense. The good news about the place was that it at least appeared to be a healthy one for the troops and was furnished with fine springs of waters.[253]

While his officers implemented his new regime at the fort, Jackson turned his attention to the various rumors filtering up from Pensacola of preparations for war among the remaining hostile Indians. Not only did Jackson dispatch spies to every "quarter" of the region to ascertain the situation, but, characteristically, he also went directly to the individual responsible for all local activities in Spanish Florida—Governor Manrique—to ascertain the truth of the disturbing reports about British and Indian machinations in that territory. On July 14, Jackson dispatched his trusted subordinate, the immensely capable Captain Gordon, to Pensacola with a letter from Jackson for Manrique. In the letter, Jackson demanded to know whether the British had landed arms and ammunition in Spanish territory to enable the hostile Creeks to prosecute war against the United States and whether the governor was harboring and feeding the Red Clubs. He also demanded that if Peter McQueen and Josiah Francis were at Pensacola they immediately be confined until such time as they could be delivered over to US authorities.[254]

On July 29, Gordon returned to Fort Jackson and submitted a written report to the general. The information it contained was unlikely to raise Jackson's opinion of the Spanish. Gordon had dutifully delivered Jackson's letter to Manrique on his arrival July 20. Soon afterward, Manrique summoned Gordon to his office and began berating him about the contents of the letter. Manrique claimed it was "impertinent" and insulting. Jackson's demand that Manrique turn McQueen and Francis over to the United States particularly incensed the governor, and he dramatically and implausibly declared that he would rather die than allow that to happen.[255]

During his stay at Pensacola, Gordon also observed the Indians meeting in the town plaza for hours and learned that as soon as he left, Manrique intended to furnish them with arms and ammunition. Gordon's sources further informed him that the British had indeed landed at Apalachicola Bay and had furnished the Indians in the neighborhood with between two thousand and three thousand guns, as well as a large quantity of ammunition. The British plan, Gordon learned, was to land six hundred troops in Florida and, together with as many Indians as they could assemble, attack key American military installations in the lower Alabama River region. Gordon further discovered that to support themselves, as the murders at the Byrne homestead demonstrated, the Red Clubs were raiding the Tensaw settlements. He even witnessed a group of Red Clubs driving a herd of stolen cattle into Pensacola for sale.[256]

Gordon's report was substantially confirmed by other reports that had made their way to Jackson, including one by Jackson's old enemy Thomas Hart Benton. Jackson further received information from his spies in Pensacola that indicated that the British also intended to foment a slave insurrection throughout the region.[257] Meanwhile, Jackson dispatched another spy to Apalachicola Bay to report on the rumored Indian and British activities there. In addition to confirming what other sources had reported, this man presented Jackson with a brand new musket as evidence of the arms the British were delivering to the Indians. Even more alarming was the spy's news that the British had sailed into the bay with three large vessels containing four thousand soldiers.

Jackson's growing apprehensions that the detested British were planning a major offensive against the American southwest in league with the Red Clubs and black slaves were not soothed by the politely oleaginous letter dated July 26 he received from Manrique in response to his letter to the governor delivered by Gordon. Manrique informed Jackson that even if McQueen and Francis and other Red Club chiefs were at Pensacola, the laws of humanity and nations, as well a Spanish treaty with the Creeks, forbade that Spain should comply with Jackson's demand to turn the Indians over to the United States. Manrique then cleverly threw in Jackson's face the fact that the United States was presently giving sanctuary to Spanish filibusterers who had unsuccessfully attacked Mexican territory.[258]

Jackson now had sufficient proof that the British, aided by Spain, were planning a serious incursion into the American southwest—probably with attacks on both Mobile and New Orleans—in furtherance of which they intended to enlist Indian and African American aid. When he had first arrived at Fort Jackson, he had written Rachel that he thought the treaty negotiations with the Creeks would take no more than five days and then he would depart for home. Now, on July 31, the day before those negotiations were to begin, Jackson was forced to write the long-suffering Rachel and explain that the situation in Spanish Florida with the British and the hostile Creeks was such that on the conclusion of the treaty with the

Creeks, he would have to leave for Mobile to organize its defense against a British invasion.[259]

These developments also affected Jackson's approach to the treaty negotiations. Well before they began Jackson's goal had been to extract as much land as he could from the defeated Creeks under the guise of an indemnity payment for the United States' cost of prosecuting the war. Consistent with this goal was his determination to create a land barrier between the Creek Nation and Spanish Florida to cut off foreign involvement in the nation's affairs. The recent British landings in Apalachicola had given him an even more compelling argument by which to achieve both goals. Thus, the friendly Creeks, who understandably believed the negotiations were to concern a discussion of the treaty conditions outlined in Pinckney's letter of April 23, were in for a terrible surprise.

The treaty negotiations formally opened August 1, 1814, but the Creeks took their time to begin actual negotiations. They were held on the sweltering grounds of the peninsula on which Fort Jackson stood rooted in the ruins of old Fort Toulouse. Nearby—a black and silent warning to the Creek negotiators—lay the ruins of the recently burned town of Taskigi. Jackson established his camp outside the new fort. Some distance away, the Creeks set up a temporary village of lightly constructed summer houses built around the traditional square. All but perhaps one of the chiefs who attended the conference belonged to the friendly party. The rest of the nation was in Florida with McQueen and Francis. In a separate village were the Cherokees and their agent, Return Meigs. They had come to the treaty convention to protect their territorial interests.[260]

Even though Jackson's resolve had been steeled by the British intrigue in Spanish Florida, he was still not a well man—among other things, his arm had yet to heal—and, as he confessed to Rachel, he found the back and forth with the Indians a "disagreeable and fatigueing business." Jackson also reported to his wife that the consequences to the starving Creeks—who before his eyes were picking up from the ground the corn spilled from horses' mouths and even those kernels trod into the mud—if he failed in the negotiations had wracked him with anxiety.[261] Given that the future of the United States' security and its territorial ambitions in the southwest were also at stake, at least some of the general's anxiety might fairly be ascribed to those considerations as well. The Creeks' delay in starting actual negotiations must have further added to his cares. Whatever the difficulties facing him, however, as he had done time and again in all sorts of highly stressful situations, Jackson mastered his physical and emotional disabilities and carried on.

One of Jackson's first tasks before the negotiations could begin was to address the chiefs' complaint that the United States had failed to feed their starving people as it promised to do. Jackson had visual proof of the truth of this assertion, as he had written Rachel, and immediately ordered the contractor to increase the Indians' rations. Not only was this the humane thing to do, Jackson told the contractor, but it was also good policy. If the Americans did not feed the Creeks, Jackson said, they would turn to the British for food. As Jackson colorfully put it, "where the carcass is, there will the fowls be gathered together."[262]

The Creeks were in no hurry to commence negotiations. However, on the morning of Thursday, August 4, the Cherokee agent, Colonel Meigs; along with the tribal leaders Colonels Brown and John Lowry; the Path Killer; and around sixty other Cherokee chiefs and warriors arrived at Fort Jackson. The arrival of this contingent of Cherokees appeared to goad the Creeks to begin treaty discussions. On August 5, with the help of Colonel Hawkins, Jackson finally was able to get their leaders assembled in council.[263]

In his first meeting with the Indian leaders, Jackson was no doubt dressed in the impressive formal regalia of a major general in the regular US Army: cockaded hat, blue coat with brass buttons and gold epaulettes, riding breeches and highly polished riding boots with spurs, sword in an ornate scabbard at his side. His audience, squatting on blankets or on the bare earth of the council ground, loved finery and would have appreciated the display. What they did not appreciate was the manner in which Jackson conducted the meeting. They had anticipated that the treaty negotiations would proceed as a series of the leisurely and lengthy debates they so enjoyed. Instead, Jackson brusquely advised the Creek leaders of the terms of their surrender, which, he made plain, brooked no debate. The scope of Jackson's demands was breathtaking. The Creek Nation was to cede to the United States as a war indemnity an astonishing 21 million acres of land. More incredibly, the Creek lands Jackson had singled out for cession made no distinction between lands occupied by the hostiles and those that belonged to the friendly Creeks. Of the 21-million-acre indemnity, the friendly Creeks were to contribute 8 million acres.[264]

At the start of the war, the Big Warrior had voluntarily offered up to Hawkins the lands of the hostile Alabama tribe as payment for the US expenses incurred in prosecuting the war, and he expected the United States to cash that particular check. Now, to his utter astonishment, he found that the loyal towns of the Lower Creeks would be giving up much of their land as well, and worse—that Jackson intended to settle the dispossessed Lower Creeks, together with the hostile Creeks, on land belonging to the Big Warrior's Upper Creeks. According to the shameless Jackson, this arrangement was for their own good. The cession to the United States of the Lower Creeks' lands in Georgia, Jackson explained, would separate the Creeks from the dangers attendant on foreign nations meddling in Indian affairs.[265] The United States would further protect the Creeks from foreign enemies (of which they had none) by the establishment of additional federal roads and forts throughout the nation. In any event, given that most of the game in the nation had been hunted out, the Creeks did not need their former extensive lands. Now they must become farmers, just like their American brothers, on what land remained to them. Only by taking this path would the Creeks "become a happy people," Jackson lectured.[266]

Following his oration, Jackson read the United States' complete peace terms through an interpreter to his shocked and somber audience. Finished, he studied the reaction of the assembled chiefs. From what he saw on their troubled faces, he had grave doubts whether they would sign the treaty or join their tribesmen in Florida instead.[267]

It was raining that evening, and the mood among the Creek chieftains as they sat in council was well matched to the weather. Jackson's talk had particularly unsettled the Big Warrior, who had no real experience of the man. From Pinckney's letter to them of April 23, 1814, the Big Warrior and the other friendly chiefs expected to be rewarded for their loyalty to the United States and compensated for the losses they had suffered at the hands of the Red Clubs during the war. Now, to their astonishment, they found that Jackson had placed them on the same footing as the very hostiles who had attacked the United States. Oblivious to the shift of power among the American leaders, the chiefs decided that night to bypass the intimidating general and make their case to their old friend Benjamin Hawkins.

The next morning, August 6, the anxious chiefs summoned Colonel Hawkins and his interpreter, Alex Cornells, to their encampment; Jackson was not invited. When Hawkins arrived, the agent already found them assembled in council, where the Big Warrior announced he would deliver the chiefs' reply to Jackson's talk of the previous day. The predictable thesis of that reply was the gross unfairness of the treaty proposed by Jackson to the friendly Creeks. As the Big Warrior reminded Hawkins, they had abided by the Treaty of New York and had executed the hostiles who had killed the whites in spring 1813. By so honoring their obligations under that treaty they had brought on themselves the Red Club war, a war that was not yet over. At this very moment, the Red Clubs were gathered with the British to the east of Pensacola, and, the Big Warrior slyly reminded Hawkins, they were attempting to convince the friendly Creeks to join them. How could Jackson demand land from the nation to indemnify the United States for its costs incurred in an ongoing war? The time to talk of the amount of land necessary to fairly indemnify the United States for those costs, the Big Warrior argued, was at the war's conclusion. Then the United States could present the Creek Nation with its bill for those costs, and the parties could discuss fair payment in lands belonging to the Red Clubs.[268]

Hawkins was well aware of why he alone had been called to the Creek council to receive the nation's reply to Jackson's talk and was too honorable a man not to have advised Jackson immediately what the Big Warrior, for whom Hawkins had little or no respect, was scheming. Hawkins had already advised Jackson the afternoon of the previous day that the British had recently sent two letters into the nation; one to Hawkins expressing their desire for peace, the other to the friendly chiefs advising them that the British, and the coalition of nations who had conquered France, intended to invade the United States and conquer it. Thus, the two men together most likely crafted the response that Hawkins now gave in response to the Big Warrior's talk.[269]

In addressing the Indian assembly, the agent feigned surprise that their talk had been addressed to him and not to Jackson, but informed them that he knew the general's mind well enough to respond. At that he launched into a harangue that was vintage Jackson. First he chided the chiefs for siding with the British during the Revolutionary War, for welcoming the renegade Bowles into their midst, and, more recently, for accepting Tecumseh and his British-inspired schemes into the nation. Hawkins then reminded the chiefs that when the Red Clubs rose against them, they had fled to Coweta, where they pleaded with Hawkins for American help against their enemies. Jackson had delivered them from those enemies and had come back before them to make peace. Yet on his return, he found that while the Americans were feeding the starving Creeks, the Lower Creeks were conspiring with the British and Red Clubs in Florida to attack the Americans.[270]

Jackson knew, Hawkins told the chiefs, of the letter from the British boasting to the chiefs that the coalition of European powers that beat the French would now attack the United States. It was all lies. The British were alone. As he had done so often before, Hawkins reminded the chiefs of the crushing defeat the Americans had visited on the British 30 years earlier, when the Americans were much weaker. Nonetheless, Hawkins said, any Creeks who were so foolish as to want to join the British were welcome to do so. Jackson would even provide them with food and ammunition for the journey. But, Hawkins sternly warned them, the general had established a "line of conquest" to separate the Indians from the British troublemakers, and any Indian who crossed that line would be destroyed.

In closing, Hawkins promised the chiefs that he would promptly advise Jackson of their position on the treaty and that Jackson would give them his response the following day. Apparently fed up with the inconstant Creeks, Hawkins further told them that he wanted to add a personal note to the official response he had just delivered, one that came not from Jackson but from him alone. The chiefs should know, he said, that the Americans had recently beaten the British badly up north on both the land and the water. The import to be drawn from that information Hawkins left unsaid.

The chiefs and the Americans met the next day, August 7, at the Creek encampment. It was not a happy occasion for the Creek leaders. If anything, the recent machinations of the British to lure the friendly Creeks to their side had hardened Jackson's resolve not to deviate from his outrageous demand for Creek land. His address to them was blunt and to the point. He immediately expressed his surprise that the chiefs had chosen to deliver their reply to his talk of August 5 to Colonel Hawkins rather than to him face to face. But he knew what Hawkins had said to them, and it was exactly what Jackson would have said himself.

Nonetheless, Jackson said, he had a few words of his own to add to what Hawkins had said. Contrary to their assertion, it was not their punishment of the hostiles for killing the whites that caused the war. The war was caused by the hostiles killing the whites. These murders had been prompted by Tecumseh, whom the Creeks had welcomed into their nation and had followed not long after his talk that the Americans should be destroyed. By the terms of the Treaty of New York, the chiefs were required at once to turn this enemy of the United States over to the American authorities or to kill him themselves. The Creeks, however, had mistakenly thought that the United States was weak and could not stand against the Indians and the British. That is why they ignored their treaty obligations and did not inform the Americans of Tecumseh's plot against them.[271] All of that was disingenuous on Jackson's part. Hawkins, through his spies, knew exactly what Tecumseh was about. He could have alerted US authorities or urged the Creek leaders to arrest Tecumseh. He did neither, because he had underestimated Tecumseh and the power of the anti-American sentiments that were fast gaining currency among the Creeks.

Jackson next turned his lawyerly skills on the Creeks' argument that the land indemnity he demanded was premature because the war with the Red Clubs was not over. I know the war is not over, Jackson told them. That is precisely why the Creeks must cede the designated lands—to stop the current intercourse between the British and the Red Clubs assembling in Florida to attack the United States. At that point Jackson dramatically held up the treaty before his audience and told the chiefs they had a choice: either sign the document and enjoy the protection of the United States or join the hostiles in Florida. In this way the United States would be able to distinguish between those Creeks who are their friends and those who are their enemies, making it easier to know whom to destroy.[272]

Following this threat, Jackson sensibly closed his talk with an offer he knew would appeal to the avarice of men such as the Big Warrior. He was well aware, he said, that the chiefs had personal claims against the United States for expenses associated with the war. If they would submit these claims to Hawkins, the agent would see that they were paid. Those who had crops growing on lands ceded to the Americans would be allowed to remain there until the crops were harvested. And finally, the United States would see to it that those Creeks who lacked food and clothing would be cared for.

The friendly Creeks persisted, however, in their attempt to convince Jackson to withdraw, at least as to them, the harsh terms of the proposed treaty. The Big Warrior urged Jackson to follow the terms set forth in Pinckney's letter read to the chiefs by Hawkins, an argument that only irritated the general.[273] Then another chief rose who, unlike the Big Warrior, had a soldier's claim on Jackson. It was Selocta, the son of the prominent Creek chieftain and longstanding American friend Chenibee. Selocta had fought in every one of Jackson's battles of the war, from the killing fields of Talladega on through that terrible day at the Horseshoe. Now Selocta tried before the treaty council to cash his claim on his general.[274]

The loyal chief reminded Jackson of the hardships and dangers the two men had shared for many months and many battles. Selocta also shrewdly attempted to counter Jackson's purported reason for the harsh land terms he sought to impose on the Creeks. Take the Alabama tribe's lands, Selocta told Jackson. Their possession by the Americans would fully satisfy Jackson's goal of severing communications between the Spanish and the Creeks. As for the Creek lands west of the Coosa River, they did not provide the Spanish with a route into Creek territory, Selocta argued, and should remain with the nation.

Selocta had sadly misjudged the worth Jackson placed on his and the other friendly Creeks' service to the Americans during the war. Jackson nimbly replied to Selocta that, contrary to Selocta's assertion concerning the cession of the lands west of the Coosa River, it was necessary to ensure the peace between the Creeks and the United States by eliminating another corridor of outside influence on the nation. It was through these lands, Jackson said, that Tecumseh and his allies from the Great Lakes had entered the Creek Nation and incited the Creeks to war. This avenue of egress between the southern and northern Indians must be eliminated to prevent future warfare.

At this point, Jackson stopped speaking and wisely allowed the Indians time to vent their displeasure with the proposed treaty. Eventually, however, he lost patience with them. He brought the council to an abrupt close by handing the Big Warrior the treaty. Either sign the document by tomorrow and prove they were the Americans' friends, he told the chiefs, or depart at once for Pensacola and show they were their enemies. It was their choice; he would not coerce them to sign the document.[275]

Of course, everything Jackson did at the treaty convention was designed to coerce the friendly Creeks into granting his wishes. He could see with his very eyes that they were a beaten people. In a letter to Rachel on August 10, he described the Creeks as "many of the most distressed wretches you ever saw."

The next morning, August 8, the chiefs assembled in their council square and sent for Jackson and Hawkins. The Big Warrior tried again to preserve for the nation some lands west of the Coosa. Jackson was unmovable. The land the Creeks demanded, Jackson told them, was land that had been used by the Little Warrior and his band of killers to travel between the Creek Nation and the Indians on the Great Lakes. On their way through these lands, they had cruelly murdered innocent white settlers. For the sake of peace between the United States and the Creek Nation, this route must be closed to the Indian people forever.[276]

The Big Warrior once more addressed the Americans. He advised that the chiefs would sign the treaty, but, before they gave over their land, he had something to say. To show that they were yet masters of the land Jackson had demanded, and perhaps to shame the shameless general, the Big Warrior announced that out of the land to be signed over to the United States, they were giving to Jackson, in gratitude "for his distinguished services," and to Hawkins, "to whom they owed much," each a three-square-mile parcel of land to be chosen where they wished. The chiefs also made grants of one square mile of land to the interpreters: Alex Cornells, who had lost all of his property, and George Mayfield, who had been wounded at Horseshoe Bend. Hawkins reported that the offer surprised and impressed Jackson. Jackson, who never really understood Indian culture, replied to the Creeks' generous offer with what he surely considered an equally magnanimous gesture. He would accept the chiefs' offer, he told them, but with the condition that if their offer met the president's approval, the land should be sold "to clothe their poor naked women and children" of the Creek Nation.[277]

Hawkins's eloquent response to the chiefs' gift, in contrast to Jackson's, was graciously sensitive to the spirit of the gift:

> I have been long among you, and grown gray in your service. I shall not much longer be your agent. You all know me, that, when applied to by red, white, and black, I looked not to color, but to the justice of the claim. I shall continue to be friendly and useful to you while I live, and my children, born among you, will be so brought up as to do the same. I accept your present, and esteem it the more highly by the manner of bestowing it, as it resulted from the impulse of your own minds, and not from any intimation from the General or me.

Hawkins's speech sounded the right note with the Creeks. Not so Jackson's. In a meeting with Hawkins later that day, the chiefs indignantly told him they did not give Jackson the land to have him give it back to them and would not sign anything to that effect. They also expressed their dismay and outrage that the United States was taking their land under the pretense that it was a war indemnity; the amount taken was well in excess of any costs the United States had incurred. But as Jackson had demanded the land, and Hawkins had advised that they sign the treaty, they would do so. But, they told Hawkins, they still held out hope that the United States, when its leaders in Washington City saw the harsh terms of the treaty, would act justly.[278]

With Major McIntosh and Alex Cornells interpreting, on August 9, 1814, the chiefs drew up an instrument that set forth their gifts of land to Jackson, Hawkins, and the two interpreters. The document also contained a preamble that expressed their dissatisfaction with the unfairness of the enormous amount of Indian land demanded by Jackson's treaty. In addition, it contained a condition that Pinckney's April 23 letter to Hawkins outlining the terms of a treaty with the Creeks, and Hawkins's reply to that letter, be sent to the president with the treaty. The chiefs then signed the document in their council square and appended to it the Pinckney and Hawkins letters. That afternoon around 2:30, the chiefs met with Jackson and reluctantly signed the hated treaty.[279] One of the signatories was the ex-sorcerer and all-around villain Captain Isaacs. Jackson had burned his town of Coosada and taken his people's lands, yet still he signed.

At least Hawkins emerged from Jackson's naked heist of Creek land with a clear conscience. The principled colonel, who appears to have shaken off the influence of Jackson's personality, had privately urged the general to respect the terms of Pinckney's letter, believing that Jackson possessed only the authority to take the lands conquered from the Red Club tribes as the indemnity to the United States for its costs of prosecuting the war. Jackson shamelessly replied that he had no authority to limit the treaty cession to the hostiles' land, which Hawkins must have known was a bald-faced lie. Hawkins then suggested that if Jackson's reason for taking the land of the friendly chiefs was to prevent intercourse between the Creeks and the British and Spanish, he might find a "reasonable equivalent" among other Creek lands and suggested some Creek territory in Georgia. Jackson considered this alternative but eventually rejected it by repeating the lame excuse that he had not the power to effect Hawkins's suggestion.[280]

On August 11, 1814, the sickly, but indefatigable Jackson, accompanied by his topographer, Major Howell Tatum, and a contingent of regular army troops departed Fort Jackson by keel boat down the Alabama River for Mobile, which was threatened by a British and Indian alliance. Their horses followed along on the Federal Road. Like the final scene in a classic American Western movie, but by boat, not horse or wagon, the general sailed into the western sun toward, as an early biographer put it, immortality.[281] In his wake he left, now coming inexorably on the land, a disaster of biblical proportions.

On this day of Jackson's journey toward further blood and destruction, he traveled on a "magnificent river, abounding in fish; with delicious and cool fountains, gushing out from the foot of the hills; with rich lands, that produced without cultivation; and with vast forests, abounding in fame of every description."[282] In the mind's eye, one envisions Captain Isaacs on this trip. The chief is lounging on sacks of flour stuffed in the stern of the boat, eyeing Jackson and his staff in the bow enjoying the passing vistas. He has situated himself as far away from the terrifying Jackson as he can, thinking and watching. Over the past years the ever resourceful captain has escaped burning as a witch, suffered through a savage beating by Dixon Bailey, and survived the war to put his mark to a document that disinherited his Coosada people. Now he has somehow finagled a ride on Jackson's boat, which he is certain is sailing toward opportunity. It is dusk, and he is enjoying the light bleeding away from the river sky and the dark shapes of birds flitting against the low horizon as they seek out their night's roosts. He has a half-emptied bottle of tafia comfortably close at hand, and the rotgut rum is beginning to roar in his brain as the raucous day slides into the evening quiet. It is a magical time, a time when visions come to the anointed.

Then, his peace at day's end is gone. Suddenly, like a grip from a bear's paws, he is seized by so strong a compulsion to kill Andrew Jackson that it threatens to overwhelm his well-honed instinct for self-preservation. But how kill the man? Jackson seems protected by a power beyond Isaacs's ken. He suddenly feels cold and begins to shiver in the fading heat. He takes a long drink of the burning tafia against the inner chill and looks toward the sternward waters. Then he sees it; a startling flash of gold beneath the moonshine-clear waters. He rises slowly and unsteadily to his feet. There it is, a flash, again and yet again. His eyes adjust to the dimming light and he sees, or seems to see, in the silvered water playing out behind the boat, golden scales each as large as a war shield. They are undulating just above the riverbed like the skin of an enormously thick hawser cut loose from the anchor of a gigantic warship. They are following. The impulse for the general's blood mysteriously passes. Isaacs's heart grows glad, and he stares at the water until the golden vision disappears with the last light. As he settles himself back on the sacks of flour, he does not bother to reflect whether the thing is shepherding him or Jackson down the river.[283]

Thirty years later, the Arcadian landscape through which Jackson, his Tennesseans, and all the American armies had raged had undergone a dramatic transformation, wistfully and regretfully reflected on by the antebellum historian Albert J. Pickett. Not long after the Creek War, while still a child, Pickett had moved from North Carolina with his well-to-do parents to the lovely and wild countryside near Montgomery, Alabama. The beauty of the land and the culture of its Native American people quietly took hold on the boy. By the time he entered manhood, he had fallen deeply and irredeemably in love with the land and its tragic history. Comparing those early days with the present cotton culture in which he lived and prospered, a forlorn Pickett sadly wrote:

> The country is no longer half so beautiful; the waters of Alabama begin to be discolored; the forests have been cut down; steamers have destroyed the finny race; deer bound not over the plain; the sluggish bear has ceased to wind through the swamps; the bloody panther does not spring upon his prey; wolves have ceased to howl upon the hills; birds cannot be seen in the branches of the trees; graceful warriors guide no longer their well-shaped canoes; and beautiful squaws loiter not upon the plain, nor pick the delicious berries. Now, vast fields of cotton, noisy steamers, huge rafts of lumber, towns reared for business, disagreeable corporation laws, harassing courts of justice, mills, factories, and everything else that is calculated to destroy the beauty of a country and to rob man of his quiet and native independence, present themselves to our view.
>
> The heart yearns to behold, once more, such a country as Alabama was the first time we saw it, when a boy. But where can we now go, that we shall not find the busy American, with keen desire to destroy everything that nature has made lovely.[284]

Left conspicuously unmentioned in Pickett's reverie decrying the horrors of civilization that accompanied the clamorous land rush into Alabama after the Creek War and destroyed his childhood Eden was the infamous "peculiar institution." It had traveled like a second skin among the train of settlers that roared into the Creek land; an insidious evil far worse than the brash, passing evil that was de Soto's *entrada*; an evil that spread and grew as powerful in the fertile lands of the dispossessed Creeks as the cotton with which it was inexorably entwined; the shadow that fell from the wondrous white fiber, clothing king and commoner alike, that so ruled the world's economy it was rightly called King Cotton.[285]

And so it was, as Andrew Jackson sailed on, borne west by the as-yet-unsullied and uncertain waters of the Alabama River, that the fine country through which he traveled began its quick and raucous fall from grace. Another paradise was lost, and a new, peculiarly American, hell was born.

NOTES

ABBREVIATIONS

ADAH	Alabama Department of Archives and History
FSA	Florida State Archives
GDAH	Georgia Department of Archives and History
LOC	Library of Congress
MDAH	Mississippi Department of Archives and History
NCDCR	North Carolina Department of Cultural Resources
TSLA	Tennessee State Library and Archives

PROLOGUE

1. There are four primary sources for de Soto's *entrada*, scholars' term for the first major European invasion of the southeastern United States. They are known as the De Soto Chronicles and have been helpfully collected by a group of Alabama scholars in a two-volume book by that name: *The De Soto Chronicles: Expedition of Hernando De Soto to North America 1539–1543*, ed. Lawrence A. Clayton, Vernon James Knight Jr., and Edward C. Moore (Tuscaloosa: University of Alabama Press, 1993). Three of the four chronicles were written by members of de Soto's expedition. The fourth and most literary chronicle was written by Garcilaso de Vega. His father was a prominent conquistador under Francisco Pizarro. His mother was the granddaughter of an Incan emperor. De Vega's account was taken largely from a prominent member of the expedition. There also exists a one-page fragment of an account written by a priest who accompanied the expedition. Known as the Canete Fragment, it is reproduced in the De Soto Chronicles. The most complete and certainly the most entertaining account of the *entrada* that I have encountered is David Ewing Duncan's *Hernando de Soto, A Savage Quest in the Americas* (New York: Crown, 1995). This work weaves the chronicles and other source materials into a classic adventure story, albeit with sound scholarly underpinnings. Unless another source is cited, my brief account of the *entrada* is taken from these sources.

2. Edward E. Baptist, *The Half Has Never Been Told: Slavery and the Making of American Capitalism* (New York: Basic Books, 2014), 22.

3. Clayton et al., *De Soto Chronicles*, 1:93.

4. Ned Jenkins, e-mail message to author, August 20, 2012.

5. John R. Swanton, *Early History of the Creek Indians & Their Neighbors* (Washington, DC: Smithsonian Institution Press, 1922; repr., Gainesville: University Press of Florida, 1998), 231.

1. A ROPE OF SAND

1. Albert James Pickett, *The History of Alabama, and Incidentally of Georgia and Mississippi, from the Earliest Period* (Charleston, SC: Walker and James, 1851).

2. Governor Blount to the Secretary of War, Knoxville, November 10, 1792, *American State Papers: Indian Affairs*, 1:536.

3. For more on the French expeditions against the Chickasaws, see H. B. Cushman, *History of the Choctaw, Chickasaw, and Natchez Indians*, ed. Angie Debo (Norman: University of Oklahoma Press, 1999 [1899]), 363–86.

4. John Reed Swanton, *Early History of the Creek Indians and Their Neighbors*, Bureau of American Ethnology, Bulletin 73 (Washington, DC: Government Printing Office, 1922), 440–52.

5. Ibid., 215.

6. The quote "a rope of sand" was reprinted in John Walton Caughey, *McGillivray of the Creeks*, with new introduction by William J. Bauer Jr. (Columbia: University of South Carolina Press, 2007), 54, but originally published in Theodore Roosevelt's *The Winning of the West* (New York: Putnam, 1889), 1:67.

7. Swanton, *Early History*, 26–27. In the literature of the Creeks stretching back into the eighteenth century, the same towns are given differently spelled names, in a number of cases ten or more. I have standardized the names in the narrative, but retained the original spellings as they occur in any quoted primary sources. I have also taken this approach with the multiple spellings as well as the multiple names given the Native Americans in this narrative.

8. Ibid., 251–52.

9. Ibid., 315.

10. Marvin T. Smith, *Coosa: The Rise and Fall of a Southeastern Mississippian Chiefdom* (Gainesville: University Press of Florida, 2000), 117.

11. For further reading on Okfuskee, see Joshua Piker, *Okfuskee: A Creek Indian Town in Colonial America* (Cambridge, MA: Harvard University Press, 2004).

12. Swanton, *Early History*, 242–44.

13. Ibid., 243.

14. Peter A. Brannon, *Handbook of the Alabama Anthropological Society* (Montgomery: Alabama Department of Archives and History, 1920), 43.

15. Swanton, *Early History*, 254.

16. Thomas H. Foster II, ed., *The Collected Works of Benjamin Hawkins, 1796–1810* (Tuscaloosa: University of Alabama Press, 2003), 33s–35s.

17. For more on the Cussetahs, see Foster, *Collected Works*, 57s–59s, and Swanton, *Early History*, 216–25. For more on the Coweta see Foster, *Collected Works*, 52s–55s, and Swanton, *Early History*, 225–30.

18. For a discussion of the Uchee language, see Swanton, *Early History*, 287.

19. Swanton, *Early History*, 312–13.

20. Reference to the nickname Savannah Jack in Foster, *Collected Works*, 169.

21. Foster, *Collected Works*, 31s. Hawkins writes "the Indian women from there too, are capable of and willing to become instrumental in civilising the men." Ibid., 40.

22. C. L. Grant, ed., *Letters, Journals and Writings of Benjamin Hawkins* (Savannah, GA: Beehive Press, 1980), 2:551.

23. For a map of Hawkins's Creek agency, see Robbie Ethridge, *Creek Country: The Creek Indians and Their World* (Chapel Hill: University of North Carolina Press, 2003), 66–67.

24. Grant, *Letters*, 2:607.

25. Ibid., 2:451.

26. Ibid., 2:551.

27. Ibid., 2:563.

28. Ibid., 1:199.

29. For further reading on gender roles among the Creeks, see Kathryn E. Holland Braund, "Guardians of Tradition and Handmaidens to Change: Women's Roles in Creek Economic and Social Life during the Eighteenth Century," *American Indian Quarterly* 14:3 (1990): 239–285.

30. Ferdinand L. Claiborne, "Letter from Ferdinand L. Claiborne at a 'Soldier's Retreat' to Colonel James Caller in Washington County of the Mississippi Territory," June 23, 1812, James Caller Papers 1795–1824, SPR554, Alabama Department of Archives and History (ADAH).

31. The Creek term for "the Dirt King" was *Fusse Mico.* Benjamin Hawkins, "Letters of Benjamin Hawkins, 1796–1806," *Collections of the Georgia Historical Society,* vol. 9 (Savannah, GA: Morning News, 1916), 248–50.

32. Robert V. Remini, *Andrew Jackson and the Course of American Empire, 1767–1821* (New York: Harper and Row, 1977), 1:102–5.

33. Ibid., 1:103–4.

34. Hawkins wrote to US senator George Walton, "Mr. Blount did not disguise his apprehensions, and he urged his agent to get me removed because 'he can and will do great injury to our plan.'" Grant, *Letters,* 1:220.

35. Ibid., 2:623–24. The Tennessee congressional delegation was "instructed and requested" to seek the removal of Hawkins after a resolution critical of the agent was introduced by General John Cocke and adopted by the Tennessee legislature.

36. Letter from the Commissioners of Georgia to the Secretary of War James McHenry, Coleraine, June 15, 1796, *American State Papers: Indian Affairs,* 1:597.

37. Louise Frederick Hays, comp., *Unpublished Letters of Timothy Barnard: 1784–1820* (Atlanta: Georgia Department of Archives and History, 1939), 285.

38. Commissioners to McHenry, 1:597.

39. Pickett, *History of Alabama,* 2:144.

40. Amos J. Wright Jr., *Historic Indian Towns in Alabama, 1540–1838* (Tuscaloosa: University of Alabama Press, 2003), 106–7.

41. Edward J. Cashin, *Lachlan McGillivray, Indian Trader: The Shaping of the Southern Colonial Frontier* (Athens: University of Georgia Press, 1992), 72; Stewart Mitchell, ed., *New Letters of Abigail Adams, 1788–1801* (Boston: Houghton Mifflin, 1947), 57.

42. John Pope, *A Tour through the Southern and Western Territories of the United States of North-America; the Spanish Dominions on the River Mississippi, and the Floridas; the Countries of the Creek Nations; and Many Uninhabited Parts* (Richmond, VA: John Dixon, 1792), 48.

43. Cashin, *McGillivray,* 72–76.

44. Ibid., 297.

45. William S. Coker and Thomas D. Watson, *Indian Traders of the Southeastern Spanish Borderlands: Panton, Leslie & Company and John Forbes & Company, 1783–1847* (Pensacola: University of West Florida Press, 1986), 53.

46. Coker and Watson, *Indian Traders,* 53; Caughey, *McGillivray,* 16.

47. Pickett, *History of Alabama,* 2:61.

48. Caughey, *McGillivray,* 75–76, 77, 119.

49. Ibid., xxii; Major Caleb Swan, "Position and State of Manners and Arts in the Creek Nation, in 1791," in *Information Respecting the History, Condition and Prospects of the Indian Tribes of the United States,* ed. Henry R. Schoolcraft (Philadelphia: Lippincott, 1855), 5:281.

50. Paper presented by [Benjamin] Hawkins at Council Meeting Between the Creek Chiefs, Commissioners of the United States, and the Commissioners of Georgia on June 24, 1796, *American State Papers: Indian Affairs,* 1:603.

51. Caughey, *McGillivray,* 103, 140.

52. Ibid., 140, 153, 160–61, 165.

53. Ibid., 34–35.

54. Pickett, *History of Alabama,* 2:112–15.

55. Francis Paul Prucha, *The Sword of the Republic: The United States Army on the Frontier, 1783–1846* (Lincoln: University of Nebraska Press, 1987), 75–78.

56 See Caughey, *McGillivray,* 39, 251–52, for biographical sketches of the commissioners.

57. Instructions to the Commissioners for treating with the Southern Indians, August 29, 1789, *American State Papers: Indian Affairs,* 1:65–68.

58. Caughey, *McGillivray,* 243.

59. Ibid., 260. In a letter to Panton on May 8, 1790, McGillivray describes Humphreys as "that puppy." In an earlier letter to Panton, on October 8, 1789, McGillivray writes "they pitted that Gentleman against me, being fluent of Speech, and a great boaster of his political knowledge." Ibid., 253.

60. Caughey, *McGillivray*, 253.

61. For more about the treaty negotiations, see The Address of White Bird King to the Commissioners and Subsequent Correspondence between McGillivray and the Commissioners, *American State Papers: Indian Affairs*, 1:74–75.

62. Henry Knox, "Instructions Regarding Willet's Mission to the Creek Nation," March 12, 1790, Henry Knox Papers, Chicago Historical Society.

63. William M. Willett, *A Narrative of the Military Actions of Colonel Marinus Willett, Taken Chiefly from His Own Manuscript* (New York: G. & C. & H. Carvill, 1831), 95–108.

64. David Tate modified his last name apparently because "Taitt" was notorious in those days when the American Revolution was still fresh in people's minds.

65. Ibid., 110; Lou Vickery and Steve Travis, *The Rise of the Poarch Band of Creek Indians* (Atmore, AL: Upword Press, 2009), 46.

66. Willett, *Narrative*, 110–11.

67. Henry Knox, "Keep an Attentive Eye on the Said Captain Howard," July 3, 1790, Henry Knox Papers, Chicago Historical Society.

68. Caughey, *McGillivray*, 276; Willett, *Narrative*, 112.

69. James Schouler, *History of the United States of America, Under the Constitution* (New York: Dodd, Mead, 1880), 1:157.

70. Willett, *Narrative*, 112–13.

71. Caughey, *McGillivray*, 273.

72. Mitchell, *New Letters*, 57.

73. For the sketches, see Emma L. Fundaburk, ed., *Southeastern Indians Life Portraits: A Catalogue of Pictures, 1564–1860* (Luverne, AL: Emma Lila Fundaburk, 1958), plate 132; Caughey, *McGillivray*, 279.

74. Caughey, *McGillivray*, 261, 263, 267.

75. Ibid., 282; 264, 270; 276–77, 279.

76. Ibid., 276–77.

77. US Congress, *Journal of the Executive Proceedings of the Senate of the United States of America*, 1st Cong., 2nd sess., August 7, 1790, 58, Library of Congress (LOC); Communication to the Senate from President George Washington, August 7, 1790, *American State Papers: Indian Affairs*, 1:81.

78. A Treaty of Peace and Friendship Made between the President of the United States of America and the Creek Nation, *American State Papers: Indian Affairs*, 1:81–82.

79. US Congress, *Journal of the Executive Proceedings of the Senate of the United States of America*, 1st Cong., 2nd sess., August 4, 1790, 55–56, LOC.

80. Pickett, *History of Alabama*, 2:110.

81. Caughey, *McGillivray*, 275.

82. Improbably, and eerily, the watch Washington gave McGillivray to commemorate the Treaty of New York surfaced on the two hundredth anniversary of the War of 1812 on the reality television program *Cajun Pawn Stars*. The timepiece was similar in quality to Washington's personal watch and was essentially in its original condition. How this unique and well-traveled timepiece got from McGillivray's pocket to a twenty-first century television show is a mystery, but its authenticity was verified by an expert, who also appraised its value at somewhere north of $1 million.

83. Pope, *Tour*, 51.

84. Pickett, *History of Alabama*, 2:256.

85. US Congress, *Journal of the Executive Proceedings of the Senate of the United States of America*, 1st Cong., 2nd sess., August 6, 1790, 57 LOC.

86. Mitchell, *New Letters*, 57.

87. Swan, "Position and State of Manners," 5:251–54; Caughey, *McGillivray*, 44.

88. In a letter dated October 8, 1788, the Spanish Governor of East Florida, Vincent Manuel Zépedes, warned McGillivray of "that villain Bowles." Caughey, *McGillivray*, 202. George Handley, the governor of Georgia, referred to Bowles as "a vile, infamous character" in a letter to Zépedes dated November 25, 1788. Ibid., 203n158. William Panton called on the Creeks on February 19, 1792, to bring him "that Villain that Prince of Liars Bowles" dead or alive. Ibid., 309. Panton wrote

to McGillivray on February 9, 1792, that the nation had "Joined with a Scoundrel to destroy me" and demanded Bowles's life. Ibid., 308. In a talk to the Spanish commissioner on July 3, 1792, the Lower Creeks pleaded for the return of "Our Beloved Friend & Father." Ibid., 314.

89. For McGillivray's first impression of Bowles and quotes, see ibid., 192. Governor Zépedes informs McGillivray that Bowles was never a captain in a letter dated October 8, 1788. Ibid., 202.

90. J. Leitch Wright Jr., *William Augustus Bowles: Director General of the Creek Nation* (Athens: University of Georgia Press, 1967), 13.

91. Benjamin Baynton, *Authentic Memoirs of William Augustus Bowles, Esquire, Ambassador from the United Nations of Creeks and Cherokees, to the Court of London* (London: R. Faulder, 1791), 47–48.

92. Caughey, *McGillivray*, 192, 195.

93. Ibid., 197, 204. For more on Charles Weatherford as informant, see ibid., 205, 212.

94. Ibid., 37.

95. Ibid., 296–97.

96. Extract of a letter from Mr. James Seagrove, addressed to Major General Henry Knox, Secretary of War, Rock Landing, on the Oconee River, May 24, 1792, *American State Papers: Indian Affairs*, 1:296.

97. James Seagrove to the President of the United States, Rock Landing, on the Oconee, in Georgia, July 27, 1792, *American State Papers: Indian Affairs*, 1:306.

98. For more on Spanish suspicions of McGillivray, see Caughey, *McGillivray*, 316; McGillivray's illness and Creeks' acceptance of Bowles, ibid., 300; and McGillivray's reminder to his countrymen, ibid., 301.

99. Ibid., 300.

100. The Following Information Delivered on Oath, by James Leonard, a Citizen of the United States, to James Seagrove, Agent of Indian Affairs, Southern Department, Rock Landing, on the Oconee, in Georgia, 24th July, 1792, *American State Papers: Indian Affairs*, 1:308.

101. Caughey, *McGillivray*, 312.

102. William S. Coker and Thomas D. Watson, *Indian Traders of the Southeastern Spanish Borderlands: Panton, Leslie & Company and John Forbes & Company, 1783–1847* (Pensacola: University of West Florida Press, 1986), 152–53.

103. Ibid., 162.

104. Caughey, *McGillivray*, 317.

105. Extract of a letter from Mr. James Seagrove, 1:296.

106. Caughey, *McGillivray*, 313.

107. Ibid., 341–42.

108. For more on the Georgians' objections, see The Following Information Delivered by Charles Weatherford To James Seagrove, Agent of Indian Affairs, at the Rock Landing, on the Oconee, the 10th day of July, 1792, *American State Papers: Indian Affairs*, 1:307.

109. The Secretary of War to James Seagrove, Esq., 11th August 1792, *American State Papers: Indian Affairs*, 1:257.

110. For more on McGillivray's death, see Caughey, *McGillivray*, 354, 363; Spanish refusal to bury McGillivray in the town cemetery, see Amos J. Wright Jr., *The McGillivray and McIntosh Traders on the Old Southwest Frontier, 1716–1815* (Montgomery, AL: New South Books, 2001), 257; McGillivray's burial in Panton's garden, see Vickery and Travis, *Rise of the Poarch*, 50.

111. John Romer, *Valley of the Kings* (New York: William Morrow, 1981), 138.

112. Hays, *Barnard*, 238.

113. Charles Weatherford, "Letter from Charles Weatherford to Creek Indian Agent James Seagrove on Confusion Since Death of General McGillivray," March 22, 1793, National Archives: 3rd Cong., House, Sec. War. Confidential Rep., RG233.

114. Hays, *Barnard*, 125, 128, 130, 159.

115. The Honorable Commissioners of the United States Reply to the Georgia Commissioners, Coleraine, June 1, 1796, *American State Papers: Indian Affairs*, 1:591–92.

116. Meeting between the Commissioners and the Chiefs, Coleraine, June 28, 1796, *American State Papers: Indian Affairs*, 1:606–7.

117. Hawkins's vote to ratify the Treaty of New York is found in U.S. Congress, *Journal of the Executive Proceedings of the Senate of the United States of America,* 1st Cong., 2nd sess., August 12, 1790, 62, LOC.

118. For Hawkins's reply, quotes, and Creeks argument of McGillivray not advising them of treaty terms, see The Commissioners of the United States Address to the Creek Nation, Coleraine, June 23, 1796, *American State Papers: Indian Affairs,* 1:602.

119. Commissioners Address to the Creek Nation, ibid., 1:602.

120. Meeting between the Commissioners and the Chiefs, ibid., 1:606–7.

121. Letter from The Commissioners of the United States to his Excellency Jared Irwin, Governor of the State of Georgia, Coleraine, July 1, 1796, 1:612.

122. The Protest of the Commissioners of Georgia to the Proceedings of the Treaty of Coleraine, Coleraine, June 28, 1796, 1:614.

123. Wright, *William Augustus Bowles,* 92–96.

124. Grant, *Letters,* 2:442.

125. Ibid., 437, 442, 445.

126. Ibid., 458.

127. Coker and Watson, *Indian Traders,* 241.

128. Wright, *William Augustus Bowles,* 166.

129. Ibid., 167–171.

130. Grant, *Letters,* 2:520.

131. Joseph G. Baldwin, *The Flush Times of Alabama and Mississippi: A Series of Sketches* (New York: D. Appleton, 1853), 88–89.

132. US Bureau of the Census, *Historical Statistics of the United States, Colonial Times to 1970, Bicentennial Edition, Part 1* (Washington, DC: Government Printing Office, 1975), 26, 35.

2. Rise of the Prophets

1. Henry S. Halbert and Timothy H. Ball, *The Creek War of 1813 and 1814* (Chicago: Donohue & Henneberry, 1895), 42.

2. Robert Burnham, *Great Comets* (Cambridge: Cambridge University Press, 2002), 182.

3. Foster, *Collected Works,* 37.

4. William Bartram, *William Bartram on the Southeast Indians,* eds. Gregory A. Waselkov and Kathryn E. Holland Braund (Lincoln: University of Nebraska Press, 1995).

5. Adair, *History,* 209.

6. Adair, *History,* 394–395.

7. *Wikipedia,* s.v. "Great Comet of 1811," accessed February 17, 2010, http://en.wikipedia.org/wiki/Great_Comet_of_1811; see generally, Robert Burnham, *Great Comets* (Cambridge: Cambridge University Press, 2002).

8. *Wikipedia,* "Great Comet of 1811"; Burnham, *Great Comets.*

9. John Sugden, *Tecumseh: A Life* (New York: Henry Holt, 1999), 23.

10. Extracts of Letters Addressed to the War Department, Vincennes, August 6, 1811, *American State Papers: Indian Affairs,* 1:800–1.

11. Sugden, *Tecumseh,* 241.

12. Extracts of Letters Addressed to the War Department, Vincennes, September 9, 1811, *American State Papers: Indian Affairs,* 1:801.

13. Halbert and Ball, *Creek War,* 41. The following discussion of Tecumseh relies principally on Halbert and Ball, *Creek War,* 40–57.

14. Sugden, *Tecumseh,* 5–6; Woodward, *Woodward's Reminiscences,* 85; George Cary Eggleston, *Red Eagle and the Wars with the Creek Indians of Alabama* (New York: Dodd, Mead, 1878), 14.

15. Reverend Lee Compere, letter to A. J. Pickett, April 6, 1848, LPR 185, box 2, Albert J Pickett Papers, ADAH; Woodward, *Woodward's Reminiscences,* 116.

16. Grant, *Letters,* 2:588.

17. Eggleston, *Red Eagle,* 56. Virginia Pounds Brown, ed., *Creek Indian History: A Historical*

Narrative of the Genealogy, Traditions, and Downfall of the Ispocoga or Creek Indian Tribe of Indians, by George Stiggins (Birmingham, AL: Birmingham Public Library Press, 1989), 86.

18. Benjamin W. Griffith Jr., *McIntosh and Weatherford: Creek Indian Leaders* (Tuscaloosa: University of Alabama Press, 1989), 3–4.

19. Grant, *Letters,* 1:290.

20. Ibid.

21. Ibid., 2:588.

22. Ibid., 2:562.

23. Woodward, *Woodward's Reminiscences,* 110; Grant, *Letters,* 1:290.

24. William E. Myer, "Indian Trails of the Southeast," *Bureau of American Ethnology Bulletin* 42 (Washington, DC: Government Printing Office, 1928): 727–857.

25. For more on the Federal Road, see Henry DeLeon Southerland Jr. and Jerry Elijah Brown, *The Federal Road through Georgia and the Creek Nation, and Alabama, 1806–1836* (Tuscaloosa: University of Alabama Press, 1989).

26. Ibid., 19–21.

27. Ibid., 33.

28. Hoboheilthlee Micco, "Talk to the President of the United States," May 15, 1811, National Archives, Record Group 75, 75.2.

29. Southerland and Brown, *Federal Road,* 33–35. Hampton was a Revolutionary War hero and father of the famous Civil War cavalry general of the same name.

30. Grant, *Letters,* 2:590.

31. Ibid.

32. Ibid., 2:657.

33. Angela Pulley Hudson, *Creek Paths and Federal Roads: Indians, Settlers, and Slaves and the Making of the American South* (Chapel Hill: University of North Carolina Press, 2010), 85.

34. Grant, *Letters,* 2:516–17, 2:527.

35. "Washington, (Geo.), October 12," *Republican and Savannah Evening Ledger,* October 17, 1811.

36. Grant, *Letters,* 2:593–94.

37. Ibid.; Extract of a Letter from Col. Hawkins, the Creek Agent, dated Sept. 20, 1811, to a Gentleman of Respectability near Columbia, *Republican and Savannah Evening Ledger,* November 5, 1811.

38. Grant, *Letters,* 2:591, 2:594.

39. Ibid., 2:591.

40. Ibid., 2:591.

41. "Washington, (Geo.), October 12," *Republican and Savannah Evening Ledger,* October 17, 1811.

42. Grant, *Letters,* 2:592; Eggleston, *Red Eagle,* 53.

43. Grant, *Letters,* 2:596.

44. Ibid., 2:594.

45. Woodward, *Woodward's Reminiscences,* 84.

46. Ibid.

47. Pickett, *History of Alabama,* 1:152; J. F. H. Claiborne, *Life and Times of General Sam Dale: The Mississippi Partisan* (New York: Harper & Brothers, 1860), 59–61.

48. Brown, *Creek Indian History,* 87.

49. Woodward, *Woodward's Reminiscence,* 95.

50. Ibid., 95.

51. Pickett, *History of Alabama,* 2:246.

52. Hawkins to General Thomas Pinckney, April 26, 1814, Letters Received by the Secretary of War, Registered Series, 1801–1860, M-221, National Archives.

53. Barbara W. Tuchman, *The March of Folly* (New York: Alfred A. Knopf, 1984), 4.

54. Hawkins to Armstrong, July 13, 1813, *American State Papers: Indian Affairs,* 1: 848.

55. Jay Feldman, *When the Mississippi Ran Backwards: Empire, Intrigue, Murder, and the New Madrid Earthquakes of 1811–12* (New York: Free Press, 2012), 9.

56. Feldman, *When the Mississippi,* 15.

57. Ibid.

58. "Georgia, Milledgeville, December 19 Earthquakes," *Rhode Island Republican*, January 15, 1812.

59. Margaret (Eades) Austill, "Memories of Journeying through Creek Country and of Childhood in Clarke County, 1811–1814," *Alabama Historical Quarterly* 6 (1944): 92–98.

60. Grant, *Letters*, 2:601.

61. Ibid., 2:604.

62. Halbert and Ball, *Creek War*, 40.

63. Pickett, *History of Alabama*, 2:245.

64. Manuel de Lanzos to Arturo O'Neill, March 21, 1793, cited in Karl Davis, "'Much of the Indian Appears': Adaptation and Persistence in a Creek Community, 1783–1854" (Ph.D. diss., University of North Carolina, 2003), 152, translation in Gregory A. Waselkov, *A Conquering Spirit: Fort Mims and the Redstick War of 1813–1814* (Tuscaloosa: University of Alabama Press, 2006), 300n48.

65. Pickett, *History of Alabama*, 2:544.

66. Brown, *Creek Indian History*, 91–93.

67. Report of Alexander Cornells, Interpreter, Upper Creeks, to Colonel Hawkins, Creek Agency, June 22, 1813, *American State Papers: Indian Affairs*, 1:845–46.

68. Benjamin Hawkins to General Armstrong, Creek Agency, June 28, 1813, *American State Papers: Indian Affairs*, 1:847.

69. Woodward, *Woodward's Reminiscences*, 36–37. Woodward was correct. In addition, Isaacs was a brutal bully with a bully's cowardly streak who ran his tribe like a gangster.

70. Waselkov, *Conquering Spirit*, 83.

71. Brown, *Creek Indian History*, 93–94.

3. The Red Clubs

1. Grant, *Letters, Journals and Writings*, 2:602.

2. Gary Burton, "Pintlala's Cold Murder Case: The Death of Thomas Meredith in 1812," *Alabama Review* 63:3 (2010): 163–64.

3. Ibid., 164.

4. Grant, *Letters, Journals, and Writings*, 2:605.

5. For more on Creek culture and lifeways, see Ethridge, *Creek Country*.

6. Grant, *Letters, Journals, and Writings*, 2:617.

7. Ibid., 2:606.

8. John C. Barron, "Early Immigration of the Lott Family to Mississippi," Ancestry.com, http://freepages.genealogy.rootsweb.ancestry.com/~jcbarron/lott/LottImmMS.htm.

9. Woodward, *Woodward's Reminiscences*, 34.

10. Ibid., 35.

11. Hawkins's account of murder, see Grant, *Letters, Journals, and Writings*, 2:606.

12. Grant, *Letters, Journals, and Writings*, 2:605, 2:609.

13. Ibid., 2:612–13.

14. We, chiefs, now in council, of the Upper Creeks, to Col. Hawkins, Tuckabatchee, April 26, 1813, *American State Papers: Indian Affairs*, 1:841.

15. "Indians," *Democrat Clarion and Tennessee Gazette*, May 19, 1812.

16. James P. Pate, ed., *The Reminiscences of George Strother Gaines: Pioneer and Statesman of Early Alabama and Mississippi, 1805–1843* (Tuscaloosa: University of Alabama Press, 1998), 53.

17. "Indians," *Democrat Clarion*, May 19, 1812; "Expedition Against the Creeks," ibid., June 10, 1812.

18. Blount to Eustis, June 25, 1812, *American State Papers: Indian Affairs*, vol. 4, part 2, 1832, 813.

19. Grant, *Letters, Journals, and Writings*, 2:612.

20. Extract from a letter from Col. Benjamin Hawkins, Creek Agency, July 1, 1812, *Democrat Clarion and Tennessee Gazette*, July 28, 1812.

21. Letter from George Colbert, May 24, 1812, in *Democrat Clarion and Tennessee Gazette*, June 2, 1812.

22. *Democrat Clarion and Tennessee Gazette,* June 2, 1812.

23. "Mrs. Crawley," *Nashville Clarion,* July 22, 1812.

24. Ibid.

25. Pate, *Reminiscences of George Strother Gaines,* 50–52.

26. Ibid., 53–54.

27. Grant, *Letters, Journals, and Writings,* 2:616.

28. Blount to Eustis, June 25, 1812, *American State Papers: Indian Affairs,* 1:813.

29. Benjamin Hawkins to Secretary of War John Armstrong, Creek Agency, March 1, 1813, *American State Papers: Indian Affairs,* 1:838.

30. William Henry Harrison to the Honorable W. Eustis, Vincennes, November 18, 1811, ibid., *American State Papers: Indian Affairs,* 1:776-79.

31. Ibid.; Sugden, *Tecumseh,* 271–75, 281.

32. Willie Blount to Brigadier General Thomas Flournoy, Nashville, October 15, 1813, *American State Papers: Indian Affairs,* 1:856.

33. Sugden, *Tecumseh,* 322.

34. Report of Alexander Cornells, interpreter, Upper Creeks to Colonel Hawkins, Creek Agency, June 22, 1813, *American State Papers: Indian Affairs,* 1:846; Benjamin Hawkins to General Armstrong, Creek Agency, June 28, 1813, ibid., 1:847. Willie Blount to Brigadier General Thomas Flournoy, Nashville, October 15, 1813, ibid., 1:855.

35. Colonel Hawkins, Agent for Indian Affairs, to Tustunnuggee, Oche Haujo, and every chief of the Upper Creeks, Creek Agency, March 29, 1813, ibid., 1:839.

36. Ibid.

37. Benjamin Hawkins to General Armstrong, Secretary of War, Creek Agency, March 25, 1813, ibid., 1:840; Handwritten copy of a letter from Big Warrior and Alex Cornells at Tuckabatchee, writing on behalf of the Creek Indians, April, 18, 1813, James Caller Papers, 1795–1824, SPR554, ADAH.

38. Handwritten copy of a letter from Big Warrior and Alex Cornells at Tuckabatchee, writing on behalf of the Creek Indians, April, 18, 1813, James Caller Papers, 1795–1824, SPR554, ADAH.

39. Benjamin Hawkins to General Armstrong, Secretary of War, Creek Agency, March 1, 1813, *American State Papers: Indian Affairs,* 1:838; Benjamin Hawkins to Alexander Cornells, Creek Agency, March 25, 1813, *American State Papers: Indian Affairs,* 1:839.

40. Benjamin Hawkins to Alexander Cornells, Creek Agency, March 25, 1813, ibid., 1:839.

41. Adair, *History of the American Indians,* 274.

42. Colonel Benjamin Hawkins to Secretary of War General Armstrong, Fort Hawkins, April 6, 1813, *American State Papers: Indian Affairs,* 1:840.

43. Big Warrior and Alexander Cornells to Colonel Benjamin Hawkins, Tuckabatchee, April 26, 1813, *American State Papers: Indian Affairs,* 1:843; Report of Nimrod Doyell, Assistant Agent for Indian Affairs, to Colonel Hawkins, the Agent, Creek Agency, May 3, 1813, *American State Papers: Indian Affairs,* 1:843.

44. The following account of the search for and execution of the Ohio River killers is from Report of Nimrod Doyell to Colonel Hawkins, May 3, 1813, *American State Papers: Indian Affairs,* 1:843.

45. Brigadier General Thomas Flourney, letter to Governor Mitchell, April 26, 1813, MS517, 192, Papers of Thomas Flournoy, William L. Clements Library, University of Michigan, Ann Arbor.

46. Letter from Benjamin Hawkins to General Armstrong, Creek Agency, June 7, 1813, *American State Papers: Indian Affairs,* 1:844.

47. "Journal, Milledgeville, April 13, 1814," *Georgia Journal,* April 14, 1813, 3.

48. Pickett, *History of Alabama,* 2:250.

49. Grant, *Letters, Journals and Writings,* 2:619 (October 12), 620 (October 30), 629 (February 15 and rheumatism).

50. Report of Alexander Cornells, interpreter, Upper Creeks, to Colonel Hawkins, Creek Agency, June 22, 1813, *American State Papers: Indian Affairs,* 1:846.

51. Ibid.

52. Benjamin Hawkins to the Secretary of War, Creek Agency, July 28, 1813, *American State Papers: Indian Affairs,* 1:850; Deposition by Sam Manac, a plantation owner in Alabama, and "a warrior of the Creek Nation," August 2, 1813, Samuel Manac Deposition, SPR26, ADAH.

53. Talosee Fixico, a runner from Tuckabatchee, to Colonel Hawkins, Creek Agency, July 5, 1813, *American State Papers: Indian Affairs,* 1:847; Foster, *Collected Works of Benjamin Hawkins,* 49s.

54. Cornells to Hawkins, June 22, 1813, *American State Papers: Indian Affairs,* 1:846.

55. Benjamin Hawkins to General Armstrong, Creek Agency, June 28, 1813, *American State Papers: Indian Affairs,* 1:847.

56. Cornells to Hawkins, June 22, 1813, *American State Papers: Indian Affairs,* 1:846.

57. Amos Wright, *Historic Indian Towns in Alabama, 1540–1838* (Tuscaloosa: University of Alabama Press, 2003), 121; Talosee Fixico to Hawkins, *American State Papers: Indian Affairs,* 1:847.

58. Cornells to Hawkins, June 22, 1813, *American State Papers: Indian Affairs,* 1:846.

59. Grant, *Letters, Journals and Writings,* 2:643; Big Warrior and Tustunnuggee Hopoie, head chiefs of the Upper and Lower Creeks, their talks to Col. Benjamin Hawkins, Agent for Indian Affairs, Coweta, August 4, 1813, *American State Papers: Indian Affairs,* 1:851.

60. Hawkins to Secretary of War, July 28, 1813, *American State Papers: Indian Affairs,* 1:849–50.

61. Talosee Fixico to Hawkins, July 5, 1813, *American State Papers: Indian Affairs,* 1:847.

62. John Ross to Colonel Return J. Meigs, July 30, 1813, MS557, folder 37, William C. Cook Collection: The War of 1812 in the South, Williams Research Center, Historic New Orleans Collection.

63. For more on Wilkinson, see Andro Linklater, *An Artist in Treason: The Extraordinary Double Life of General James Wilkinson* (New York: Walker, 2009).

64. Ibid., 285.

65. Ibid.

66. Gaines to James Wilkinson, St. Stephens, April 17, 1813, *Papers of Paton, Leslie, and Company,* ed. William S. Coker, microfilm, roll 19, University of South Alabama Library.

67. Deposition of James Curnels, August 1, 1813, Letterbook F, J. F. H. Claiborne Collection, Mississippi Department of Archives and History (MDAH); Linklater, *Artist in Treason,* 301.

68. For a collection of accounts written by those who traveled the road in the early nineteenth century, see Jeffery C. Benton, *The Very Worst Road: Travellers' Accounts of Crossing Alabama's Old Creek Indian Territory, 1820–1847* (Tuscaloosa: University of Alabama Press, 2009).

69. Linklater, *Artist in Treason,* 328.

70. Deposition of Curnels, Letterbook F, J. F. H. Claiborne Collection, MDAH.

71. A demand on the fanatical chiefs and their associates, for an explanation of their conduct, Creek Agency, July 6, 1813, *American State Papers: Indian Affairs,* 1:848.

72. Ibid.

73. Benjamin Hawkins to General Pinckney, Milledgeville, July 9, 1813, *American State Papers: Indian Affairs,* 1:848; Cussetah Micco to Colonel Hawkins, Agent for Indian Affairs, Cussetah, July 10, 1813, *American State Papers: Indian Affairs,* 1:849.

74. Woodward, *Woodward's Reminiscences,* 114; quotes in Hawkins to Secretary of War, July 28, 1813, *American State Papers: Indian Affairs,* 1:849.

75. Brown, *Creek Indian History,* 95; Grant, *Letters, Writings and Journals,* 2:648.

76. Woodward, *Woodward's Reminiscences,* 96; Grant, *Letters, Writings and Journals,* 2:648–49.

77. Grant, *Letters, Writings and Journals,* 2:648–49.

78. Brown, *Creek Indian History,* 95–96.

79. Wright, *Historic Indian Towns,* 46–50.

80. Hawkins to Secretary of War, July 28, 1813, *American State Papers: Indian Affairs,* 1:849–50.

81. Grant, *Letters, Journals and Writings,* 2:654; Benjamin Hawkins to the Secretary of War, Creek Agency, August 10, 1813, *American State Papers: Indian Affairs,* 1:851.

82. Grant, *Letters, Journals and Writings,* 2:655; Wright, *Historic Indian Towns,* 165–66; John Floyd to Mary H. Floyd, Camp Covington, December 28, 1814, in "Letters of John Floyd," *Georgia Historical Quarterly* 33, no. 4 (1949): 245.

83. Big Warrior and Tustunnuggee Hopoie to Hawkins, *American State Papers: Indian Affairs,* 1:851.

84. The terms *Red Club* and *Red Stick* are used interchangeably by historians and nonspecialists alike. I prefer *Red Club* to describe the hostile Creeks because that is the term Benjamin Hawkins uses. See, for example, Hawkins to Secretary of War, September 26, 1813, *American State Papers: Indian Affairs*, 1:854. It also more accurately describes the object itself: a nasty weapon often with a metal blade set in one end and used as a club by Creek warriors for close combat. Their word for this weapon in the Muskogee tongue, *atássa*, means war club. Anyone struck by this weapon who survived would hardly remark that he had been hit with a "stick." A comprehensive discussion of these terms is in Kathryn E. Holland Braund, "Red Sticks," in *Tohopeka: Rethinking the Creek War and the War of 1812*, ed. Kathryn E. Holland Braund (Tuscaloosa: University of Alabama Press, 2012).

85. Grant, *Letters, Journals and Writings*, 2:654–55.

86. Big Warrior and Tustunmuggee Hopoie to Hawkins, *American State Papers: Indian Affairs*, 1:851.

87. Benjamin Hawkins to the Secretary of War, Creek Agency, August 23, 1813, *American State Papers: Indian Affairs*, 1:851–52.

88. Grant, *Letters, Journals and Writings*, 2:659.

89. Ibid., 2:656–57.

90. Benjamin Hawkins to General Armstrong, Creek Agency, September 6, 1813, *American State Papers: Indian Affairs*, 1:852.

91. Andrew Jackson to His Excellency Willie Blount, Nashville, July 13, 1813, *American State Papers: Indian Affairs*, 1:850.

92. Robert P. Collins, "A Packet from Canada," in *Tohopeka: Rethinking the Creek War and the War of 1812*, ed. Kathryn E. Holland Braund (Tuscaloosa: University of Alabama Press, 2012), 54. One scholar has questioned the actual existence of such a letter, which, indeed, has never been found. He argues that the prophets used the fiction of the letter to impress the Americans with their power, and that American officials, in turn, used the rumored document to raise the frontier people against the Creeks.

93. David Tate Deposition, August 2, 1813, Letterbook F., Claiborne Collection, MDAH; John Innerarity, "A Prelude to the Creek War of 1813–1814, in a Letter of John Innerarity to James Innerarity," *Florida Historical Quarterly* 18 (April 1940): 247–66; Deposition by Sam Manac, a plantation owner in Alabama, and "a warrior of the Creek Nation," August 2, 1813, Samuel Manac Deposition, SPR26, ADAH.

94. Deposition by Sam Manac, Samuel Manac Deposition, ADAH.

95. Brown, *Creek Indian History*, 98; Big Warrior to Colonel Hawkins, William McIntosh's, August 4, 1813, *American State Papers: Indian Affairs*, 1:851; Harry Toulmin to Brigadier General Ferdinand L. Claiborne, Fort Stoddert, July 23, 1813, Harry Toulmin Letters, SPR234, ADAH.

96. Brown, *Creek Indian History*, 98–99.

97. Toulmin to Claiborne, July 23, 1813, Toulmin Papers, ADAH.

98. Deposition by Sam Manac, Samuel Manac Deposition, ADAH.

99. Toulmin to Claiborne, July 23, 1813, Toulmin Papers, ADAH; Deposition by Sam Manac, Samuel Manac Deposition, ADAH.

100. Woodward, *Woodward's Reminiscences*, 87.

101. "Journal, Milledgeville, April 13, 1814," *Georgia Journal*, April 14, 1813, 3; Interesting Papers in relation to the Indian Hostilities in 1813–1814, the destruction of Fort Mims, furnished Pickett by Col. John H. F. Claiborne found among his Father's Papers (Gen. Ferdinand H. Claiborne), Albert J. Pickett Papers, LPR185, box 2, ADAH; Claiborne, *Life and Times*, 68–69.

102. Toulmin to Claiborne, July 23, 1813, Toulmin Papers, ADAH; David Tate Deposition, Claiborne Collection, MDAH.

103. Toulmin to Claiborne, July 23, 1813, Toulmin Papers, ADAH; David Tate Deposition, Claiborne Collection, MDAH; Captain James Jones to Jackson, July 4, 1814, reel 10, Jackson Papers, LOC.

104. Coker and Watson, *Indian Traders*, 279–80.

105. Innerarity, "Prelude to the Creek War," 256. David Tate Deposition, Claiborne Collection, MDAH.

106. One scholar contends that following the surrender of Mobile to General Wilkinson, the Spanish authorities in Cuba, to whom Manrique reported, believed, not unreasonably, that Pensacola would be the American's next target. Unwilling and unable to involve the limited Spanish troops available, the captain general of Cuba, Juan Ruiz Apodaca, seized on Spain's former strategy in the late eighteenth century of employing the Creeks against the Americans. Frank Lawrence Owsley Jr., *Struggle for the Gulf Borderlands: The Creek War and the Battle of New Orleans, 1812–1815* (Tuscaloosa: University of Alabama Press, 2000), 24–27. The Spaniards' willingness to supply the Creeks in the following months confirms this view. Unfortunately for the Creeks, the Spanish themselves were woefully short on military supplies.

107. Toulmin to Claiborne, July 23, 1813, Toulmin Papers, ADAH; David Tate Deposition, Claiborne Collection, MDAH.

108. David Tate Deposition, Claiborne Collection, MDAH; Toulmin to Claiborne, July 23, 1813, Toulmin Papers, ADAH.

109. McQueen owed more than seven hundred dollars and Francis more than nine hundred dollars. Coker and Watson, *Indian Traders,* 280.

110. Ibid., 19.

111. The following account of McQueen's conference with Manrique is taken from Innerarity, "Prelude to the Creek War," 247–66, unless otherwise noted.

112. Toulmin to Claiborne, July 23, 1813, Toulmin Papers, ADAH; Collins, "'Packet from Canada,'" 66; Woodward, *Woodward's Reminiscences,* 97.

113. Innerarity, "Prelude to the Creek War," 256.

114. Toulmin to Claiborne, July 23, 1813, Toulmin Papers, ADAH.

115. Harry Toulmin to Brigadier General Ferdinand L. Claiborne, Fort Stoddert, July 23, 1813, Harry Toulmin Letters, SPR234, ADAH.

116. For a description of the forts, see Halbert and Ball, *Creek War,* 105–117.

117. Colonel Joseph Carson to General F. L. Claiborne, Mount Vernon, July 30, 1813, Joseph Carson Letter, SPR42, ADAH.

118. Toulmin to Claiborne, July 23, 1813, Toulmin Papers, ADAH.

119. Carter, *Territory of Mississippi,* 5:367.

120. W. Stanley Hoole, *Alias Simon Suggs: The Life and Times of Johnson Jones Hooper* (Tuscaloosa: University of Alabama Press, 1952), 51; Carter, *Territory of Mississippi,* 6:345, 367; Philip D. Beidler, *First Books: The Printed Word and Cultural Formation in Early Alabama* (Tuscaloosa: University of Alabama Press, 1999), 17.

121. Alan V. Briceland, "Ephraim Kirby: Mr. Jefferson's Emissary on the Tombigbee-Mobile Frontier in 1804," *Alabama Review* 24:2 (April 1971): 83–113.

122. Ibid., 109–111.

123. Carter, *Territory of Mississippi,* 6:432.

124. Pickett, *History of Alabama,* 2:236–239.

125. Carter, *Territory of Mississippi,* 6:98, 6:114.

126. Ibid, 6:157; Notes furnished by Doc Thos G. Holmes about the Kemper Party in Alabama in 1810 and other things, Albert J. Pickett Papers, LPR 185, ADAH.

127. Carter, *Territory of Mississippi,* 6:154.

128. Ibid., 6:157; Notes furnished by Dr. Holmes, Pickett Papers, ADAH.

129. Carter, *Territory of Mississippi,* 6:245–46.

130. Congress's decision to not proceed with charges against Toulmin, in US Congress, *Journal of the House of Representatives of the United States, 1811–1813,* 12th Cong., 1st sess., May 22, 1812, 347.

131. Toulmin to Graham, March 10, 1812, in Carter, *Territory of Mississippi,* 6:283–84.

132. Ibid., 6:297.

133. Ibid., 6:306–07.

134. James Caller to Ferdinand L. Claiborne, July 20, 1813, James Caller Papers, SPR554, ADAH.

135. Notes Furnished by General Patrick May of Greene County in Relation to the Battle of Burnt Corn and the Canoe Fight, Albert J. Pickett Papers, LPR185, ADAH; Halbert and Ball, *Creek War,* 309.

136. Halbert and Ball, *Creek War*, 130.

137. Toulmin to Claiborne, July 23, 1813, Toulmin Papers, ADAH; Caller to Claiborne, August 25, 1813, Letterbook F, Claiborne Collection, MDAH.

138. Carter, *Territory of Mississippi*, 6:275.

139. Lewis Sewall, *The Miscellaneous Poems of Lewis Sewall, Esq., Containing the Last Campaign of Col. J. Caller-Alias Sir John Falstaff the Second-Alias the Hero of Burnt Corn Battle; The Birth Progress, and Probable End of G.F. Mynheer Van Slaverchap's Grandson-Alias Doctor Furnace; The Battle for the Cow and Calf; The Canoe Fight; And Other Miscellaneous Matters* (Mobile, AL: 1833). For further reading on historical and literary frontiers, see Gregory A. Waselkov, *A Conquering Spirit: Fort Mims and the Redstick War of 1813–1814* (Tuscaloosa: University of Alabama Press, 2006), 179–84.

140. Notes from Dr. Holmes, Pickett Papers, ADAH.

141. Notes Furnished by Gen. May, Pickett Papers, ADAH; Foster, *Collected Works of Benjamin Hawkins*, 39–40.

142. Claiborne, *Life and Times*, 73.

143. Brown, *Creek Indian History*, 100; Woodward, *Woodward's Reminiscences*, 97–98; Halbert and Ball, *Creek War*, 131–133; Notes Furnished by Colonel G.W. Creagh, Albert J. Pickett Papers, LPR 185, ADAH.

144. Notes Furnished by Gen. May, Pickett Papers, ADAH.

145. Ibid.; Notes from Dr. Holmes, Pickett Papers, ADAH.

146. Carson to Claiborne, July 30, 1813, Joseph Carson Letter, ADAH.

147. Claiborne, *Life of Sam Dale*, 74; Halbert and Ball, *Creek War*, 136.

148. Notes Furnished by Col Creagh, Pickett Papers, ADAH; Halbert and Ball, *Creek War*, 135.

149. Notes from Dr. Holmes, Pickett Papers, ADAH.

150. Ibid; David Tate Deposition, August 2, 1813, Letterbook F, Claiborne Collection, MDAH.

151. Notes from Dr. Holmes, Pickett Papers, ADAH.

152. Caller to Holmes, August 15, 1813, Mississippi Territorial Papers, Series 488: Administration Papers, 1769, 1788–1817, MDAH.

153. Notes from Dr. Holmes, Pickett Papers, ADAH; Toulmin to Claiborne, July 31, 1813, Toulmin Papers, ADAH; Carson to Claiborne, July 30, 1813, Joseph Carson Letter, ADAH; Claiborne, *Life of Sam Dale*, 74.

154. Claiborne, *Life of Sam Dale*, 74.

155. Notes Furnished by Col. Creagh, Pickett Papers, ADAH.

156. Notes Furnished by Gen. May, Pickett Papers, ADAH.

157. Claiborne, *Life of Sam Dale*, 77.

158. Claiborne, *Life of Sam Dale*, 77–78; Halbert and Ball, *Creek War*, 138; Notes Furnished by Gen. May, Pickett Papers, ADAH; Notes Furnished by Col. Creagh, Pickett Papers, ADAH.

159. Notes Furnished by Gen. May, Pickett Papers, ADAH.

160. Notes Taken from Dr. Holmes, Pickett Papers, ADAH; Notes Furnished by Col. Creagh, Pickett Papers, ADAH.

161. Notes Furnished by Col. Creagh, Pickett Papers, ADAH; Notes Furnished by Gen. May, Pickett Papers, ADAH.

162. Notes Furnished by Gen. May, Pickett Papers, ADAH.

163. Pickett, *History of Alabama*, 2:260.

164. Woodward, *Woodward's Reminiscences*, 98.

165. Carson to Claiborne, July 30, 1813, Joseph Carson Letter, ADAH.

166. Captain James B. Wilkinson to General Ferdinand L. Claiborne, August 4, 1813, Letterbook F, Claiborne Collection, MDAH. Captain Wilkinson was General James Wilkinson's son and Judge Toulmin's son-in-law. Tragically, the promising young officer died of one of the many diseases that infested the region.

167. Notes Furnished by Gen. May, Pickett Papers, ADAH; Notes Taken from Dr. Holmes, Pickett Papers, ADAH.

168. Willis Brewer, *Alabama, Her History, Resources, War Record, and Public Men, from 1540 to 1872* (Montgomery: Barrett and Brown, 1872), 349; Claiborne, *Life of Sam Dale*, 81.

169. Claiborne, *Life of Sam Dale*, 81.

170. Carson to Claiborne, July 30, 1813, Joseph Carson Letter, ADAH.

4. RUN UP TO TRAGEDY

1. Claiborne, *Life and Times*, 90.

2. Clarence Edwin Carter, comp., *Territorial Papers of the United States*, vols. 5–6, *The Territory of Mississippi, 1798–1817* (Washington, DC: Government Printing Office, 1937–38), 5:368.

3. Claiborne, *Life and Times*, 86–87.

4. Ibid., 81.

5. Halbert and Ball, *Creek War*, 308.

6. Claiborne, *Life and Times*, 84.

7. Henry S. Halbert, Letters on Fort Mims, November 10, 1882, to March 3, 1887, Series YY: Tecumseh Papers (microfilm Reel 119), Lyman Draper Collection, Wisconsin Historical Society, Madison.

8. Richard S. Lackey, comp., *Frontier Claims in the Lower South: Records of Claims Filed by Citizens of the Alabama and Tombigbee River Settlements in the Mississippi Territory for Depredations by the Creek Indians During the War of 1812*, introduction by John D. W. Guice (New Orleans: Polyanthos, 1977), 31.

9. Margaret (Eades) Austill, "Memories of Journeying through Creek Country and of Childhood in Clarke County, 1811–1814," *Alabama Historical Quarterly* 6 (1944): 95.

10. Lackey, *Frontier Claims*, 21–67; Gregory A. Waselkov, *A Conquering Spirit: Fort Mims and the Redstick War of 1813–1814* (Tuscaloosa: University of Alabama Press, 2006), 116.

11. W. W. Osborne to Colonel Joseph Carson, July 28, 1813, Letterbook F, Claiborne Collection, MDAH.

12. Notes of Dr. Thomas G. Holmes, 1847, LPR185, Albert J. Pickett Papers, ADAH.

13. Waselkov, *Conquering Spirit*, 64–66; Halbert, Letters on Fort Mims, Draper Collection, Wisconsin Historical Society. For a more in-depth discussion of personal honor, see *Southern Honor: Ethics and Behavior in the Old South* (Oxford: Oxford University Press, 1982).

14. Waselkov, *Conquering Spirit*, 67–69.

15. Claiborne, *Life and Times*, 115.

16. Waselkov, *Conquering Spirit*, 70–71.

17. Daniel Beasley to General Ferdinand L. Claiborne, August 6, 1813, Letterbook F, Claiborne Collection, MDAH.

18. Beasley to Claiborne, August 7, 1813, Letterbook F, Claiborne Collection, MDAH.

19. Ibid.; Claiborne to Beasley, August 7, 1813, Letterbook F, Claiborne Collection, MDAH.

20. Ferdinand L. Claiborne, "To the Editor of the Mississippi Republican," *Mississippi Republican*, March 25, 1814.

21. Beasley to Claiborne, August 12, 1813, Letterbook F, Claiborne Collection, MDAH.

22. Beasley to Claiborne, August 14, 1813, Letterbook F, Claiborne Collection, MDAH.

23. Finding Aid to Thomas Flournoy Papers, 1799–1827, May 2010, William L. Clements Library Manuscript Division, University of Michigan, Ann Arbor.

24. Claiborne, *Life and Times*, 100–101.

25. General Claiborne to Governor David B. Mitchell, August 14, 1813, Letterbook F, Claiborne Collection, MDAH.

26. Thomas Flournoy to General Claiborne, August 10, 1813, Letterbook F, Claiborne Collection, MDAH.

27. Ibid., quoted in Claiborne, *Life and Times*, 93.

28. Ibid., 100–101.

29. Harry Toulmin to Claiborne, September 6, 1813, Letterbook F, Claiborne Collection, MDAH.

30. Big Warrior to Colonel Hawkins, William McIntosh's, August 4, 1813, *American State Papers: Indian Affairs*, 1:851.

31. Halbert and Ball, *Creek War*, 104; Brown, *Creek Indian History*, 102.

32. Benjamin Hawkins to General Armstrong, Fort Hawkins, October 18, 1813, *American State Papers: Indian Affairs*, 1:857.

33. Benjamin Hawkins to Judge Toulmin, Creek Agency, October 23, 1813, *American State Papers: Indian Affairs*, 1:857.

34. Ibid.; Brown, *Creek Indian History*, 102.

35. Halbert and Ball, *Creek War*, 121; Franklin L. Riley, ed., "Inaccuracies in Claiborne's History in Regard to Tecumseh," *Publications of the Mississippi Historical Society* 1 (1898): 102–3.

36. Gideon Lincecum, *Pushmataha: A Choctaw Leader and His People* (Tuscaloosa: University of Alabama Press, 2004), 90.

37. Pickett, *History of Alabama*, 1:220–21.

38. A. B. Meek, *Romantic Passages in Southwestern History* (New York: S. H. Goetzel, 1857), 271.

39. Woodward, *Woodward's Reminiscences*, 87.

40. Halbert, Letters on Fort Mims, Draper Collection, Wisconsin Historical Society, Madison.

41. Waselkov, *Conquering Spirit*, 94; Vickery and Travis, *Rise of the Poarch*, 55.

42. J. Anthony Perkins and Judith Knight, eds., *Red Eagle's Children: Weatherford vs. Weatherford et al* (Tuscaloosa: University of Alabama Press, 2012), 56–57.

43. Vickery and Travis, *Rise of the Poarch*, 57.

44. For more in-depth discussion of how and when Weatherford joined the Red Club party, see Brown, *Creek Indian History*, 103–6; Meek, *Romantic Passages*, 270–73; and Woodward, *Woodward's Reminiscences*, 95–96.

45. Woodward, *Woodward's Reminiscences*, 95–96.

46. Brown, *Creek Indian History*, 104; Foster, *Collected Works*, 81j.

47. Brown, *Creek Indian History*, 104–5.

48. Woodward, *Woodward's Reminiscences*, 96.

49. Wayne Curtis, "Clarifying an Historic Event," *American Archaeology* 11:3 (Fall 2007): 12–17.

50. Waselkov, *Conquering Spirit*, 118.

51. Ferdinand Leigh Claiborne, Map of Fort Mims and Environs [1813], LPR185, Box 2, Albert J. Pickett Papers, ADAH.

52. Claiborne, Map of Fort Mims, Pickett Papers, ADAH; Waselkov, *Conquering Spirit*, 119.

53. Claiborne, Map of Fort Mims, Pickett Papers, ADAH.

54. Ibid.

55. Ibid.; Waselkov, *Conquering Spirit*, 119.

56. Beasley to Claiborne, August 14, 1813, Letterbook F, Claiborne Collection, MDAH; Dr. Marion Elisha Tarvin, "The Muscogees or Creek Indians, 1519 to 1893," *Alabama Historical Quarterly* 17 (Fall 1955): 136.

57. W. R. Chambliss Certificate, July 16, 1814, Letterbook F, Claiborne Collection, MDAH.

58. Peter Brannon, "Spruce McCall Osborne," *Alabama Historical Quarterly* 5 (Spring 1943): 68–70.

59. Halbert and Ball, *Creek War*, 113.

60. Hugh Cassity, a Choctaw Indian, statement, signed by Joseph Carson, August 23, 1813, Letterbook F, Claiborne Collection, MDAH.

61. Ibid.; James F. Doster, "Letters Relating to the Tragedy of Fort Mims: August–September, 1813," *Alabama Review* 14:4 (April 1961): 269–85. Beasley to Claiborne, August 30, 1814, Letterbook F, Claiborne Collection, MDAH.

62. Claiborne to Kennedy, August 25, 1813, Letterbook F, Claiborne Collection, MDAH.

63. Chambliss Certificate, July 16, 1815, Letterbook F, Claiborne Collection, MDAH.

64. Claiborne to Kennedy, September 22, 1813, Letterbook F, Claiborne Collection, MDAH; Lackey, *Frontier Claims*, 36.

65. One such slave, called Hannah, belonged to Margret Eades's family. Hannah was a tall and "handsome" woman, and was a terror to the Indians. From Eades's refuge at Fort Carney, the fearless Hannah routinely and voluntarily traveled on errands to their plantation in the countryside. Although Indian moccasin tracks were often seen on the path to the plantation, Hannah was never

molested. Perhaps it was her startling blue eyes glowing in her blue-back face and her fearless and commanding demeanor that kept her safe. Austill, "Memories," 96–97.

66. Notes of Dr. Holmes, Pickett Papers, ADAH.

67. Fletcher N. Hale collection of field notes and maps, 1938–1950, SPR375, ADAH.

68. Beasley to Claiborne, August 30, 1813, Letterbook F, Claiborne Collection, MDAH. Beasley writes that Randon owned both slaves.

69. Vickery and Travis, *Rise of the Poarch,* 49.

70. Pickett, *History of Alabama,* 2:268–69; Beasley to Claiborne, August 30, 1813, Letterbook F, Claiborne Collection, MDAH.

71. Notes of Dr. Holmes, Pickett Papers, ADAH; Pickett, *History of Alabama,* 2:269.

72. Ibid.

73. Waselkov, *Conquering Spirit,* 123–24, 225–26.

74. Brown, *Creek Indian History,* 105–8; Waselkov, *Conquering Spirit,* 309n37.

75. Brown, *Creek Indian History,* 112.

76. Woodward, *Woodward's Reminiscences,* 98; Waselkov, *Conquering Spirit,* 310n41; Pickett, *History of Alabama,* 2:268; Notes of Dr. Holmes, Pickett Papers, ADAH.

77. Brown, *Creek Indian History,* 109.

78. Ibid., 109–10; Waselkov, *Conquering Spirit,* 112.

79. In at least one instance, they succeeded beyond all expectations: during the battle, a soldier named Rishbury reportedly "died from pure fear" at the sight of the savages. Notes of Dr. Holmes, Pickett Papers, ADAH.

80. Waselkov, *Conquering Spirit,* 127; Notes of Dr. Holmes, Pickett Papers, ADAH; Meek, *Romantic Passages,* 247.

81. Halbert and Ball, *Creek War,* 166–67.

82. Notes of Dr. Holmes, Pickett Papers, ADAH; Waselkov, *Conquering Spirit,* 122; Benjamin Hawkins, Creek Agency, September 17, 1813, *American State Papers: Indian Affairs,* 1:853; Halbert and Ball, *Creek War,* 165.

83. The story of the fort's inhabitants partying at the fort on the night before the Red Club attack comes from an interview in 1884 with Judge Toulmin's slave Tony Morgan, who said he was at the fort when it fell and was taken by the Red Clubs to the Holy Ground. Francois L. Diard, "A Slave Interviews a Slave, April 20, 1937," WPA Slave Narrative Project, Alabama Narratives, Federal Writers Project, Works Projects Administration, LOC.

84. Beasley to Claiborne, August 30, 1813, Letterbook F, Claiborne Papers, MDAH.

85. Halbert, Letters on Fort Mims, Draper Collection, Wisconsin Historical Society; Woodward, *Woodward's Reminiscences,* 98.

86. Beasley to Claiborne, August 30, 1813, Letterbook F, Claiborne Papers, MDAH; Pickett, *History of Alabama,* 2:269.

87. Notes from the lips of Dr. Thomas Holmes, Pickett Papers, ADAH.

88. Halbert, Letters on Fort Mims, Draper Collection, Wisconsin Historical Society; Grant, *Letters, Journals and Writings,* 2:532; Pickett, *History of Alabama,* 2:269–70.

89. Drum at 10:00 A.M., see Extract of a communication from the chiefs at Coweta to Col Hawkins, Creek Agency, September 16, 1813, *American State Papers: Indian Affairs,* 1:853; Montgomery reports 11:00, see Claiborne to General Flournoy, October 22, 1813, Letterbook F, Claiborne Papers, MDAH; Toulmin, see *Washington Republican,* September 16, 1813; Dr. Holmes reports noon, in Notes of Dr. Holmes, Pickett Papers, ADAH; Halbert and Ball, *Creek War,* 153, and George Stiggins in Brown, *Creek Indian History,* 111, say noon as well.

90. Claiborne, *War in the South,* 21–22.

91. Halbert and Ball, *Creek Indian War,* 166–67.

92. Claiborne, *Life and Times,* 109; Harry Toulmin, "Indian Warfare, Mobile, September 7," *Weekly Register* 5 (October 16, 1813):105–7, referenced in Waselkov, *Conquering Spirit,* 128.

93. Halbert, Letters on Fort Mims, Draper Collection, Wisconsin Historical Society.

94. Claiborne to Flournoy, September 3, 1813, in John Brannan, *Official Letters of the Military and Naval Officers of the United States during the War with Great Britain in the Years 1812, 13, 14, & 15*

(Washington, DC: Way and Gideon, 1823), 203. Pickett, *History of Alabama,* 2:272. Halbert, Letters on Fort Mims, Draper Collection, Wisconsin Historical Society, referenced in Waselkov, *Conquering Spirit,* 342n91.

95. Pickett, *History of Alabama,* 2:270; Notes of Dr. Holmes, Pickett Papers, ADAH.

96. Notes of Dr. Holmes, Pickett Papers, ADAH.

97. Halbert, Letters on Fort Mims, Draper Collection, Wisconsin Historical Society.

98. Hawkins to Secretary of War, Creek Agency, October 11, 1813, *American State Papers: Indian Affairs,* 1:852. The Wewocau tribe, which Benjamin Hawkins lauded as "always the foremost in battle" among the Red Clubs, would pay dearly in casualties for their bravery and aggressiveness. Hawkins to Pinckney, May 17, 1814, in Grant, *Letters, Journals and Writings,* 2:681.

99. Halbert, Letters on Fort Mims, Draper Collection, Wisconsin Historical Society; Hawkins to Secretary of War, Creek Agency, October 11, 1813, *American State Papers: Indian Affairs,* 1:852; Claiborne to Flournoy, September 3, 1818, in Brannan, *Official Letters,* 203.

100. Notes of Dr. Holmes, Pickett Papers, ADAH.

101. Ibid.; Waselkov, *Conquering Spirit,* 129.

102. Waselkov, *Conquering Spirit,* 146; Brown, *Creek Indian History,* 114.

103. Brown, *Creek Indian History,* 110.

104. Woodward, *Woodward's Reminiscences,* 99; Brown, *Creek Indian History,* 110.

105. Brown, *Creek Indian History,* 114–15.

106. Notes of Dr. Holmes, Pickett Papers, ADAH; Waselkov, *Conquering Spirit,* Appendix 1, 229.

107. "Toulmin to Joseph Gales, Sr. editor," *Raleigh Register and North Carolina Gazette,* September 7, 1813, printed in the *Dailey National Intelligencer,* October 12, 1813.

108. Waselkov, *Conquering Spirit,* 131; Extract of a communication from the chiefs at Coweta to Colonel Hawkins, Creek Agency, September 16, 1813, *American State Papers: Indian Affairs,* 1:853.

109. Notes of Dr. Holmes, Pickett Papers, ADAH; Pickett, *History of Alabama,* 2:272.

110. Meek, *Romantic Passages,* 253.

111. Notes of Dr. Holmes, Pickett Papers, ADAH.

112. Benjamin Hawkins, Creek Agency, September 17, 1813, *American State Papers: Indian Affairs,* 1:853.

113. Curtis, "Clarifying an Historic Event," 12–17.

114. Pickett, *History of Alabama,* 2:272–73.

115. Ibid.

116. Pickett, *History of Alabama,* 2:273.

117. "Toulmin to Joseph Gales, Sr. editor," *Raleigh Register and North Carolina Gazette,* September 7, 1813, printed in the *Daily National Intelligencer,* October 12, 1813; Notes taken from the Lips of Col Robert James of Clarke County Ala relative to Zachariah McGirth and Weatherford, Pickett Papers, ADAH.

118. Notes of Dr. Holmes, Pickett Papers, ADAH.

119. Brown, *Creek Indian History,* 112.

120. Notes of Dr. Holmes, Pickett Papers, ADAH; Pickett, *History of Alabama,* 2:272; Eggleston, *Red Eagle,* 111; Woodward, *Woodward's Reminiscences,* 92.

121. Woodward, *Woodward's Reminiscences,* 92.

122. Ibid., 99; Harry Toulmin to James Madison, September 11, 1813, in John Charles Anderson Stagg, *The Papers of James Madison: Presidential Series* (Charlottesville: University of Virginia Press, 2008), 6:616.

123. Notes of Dr. Holmes, Pickett Papers, ADAH; Pickett, *History of Alabama,* 2:272; Claiborne to Flournoy, September 3, 1813; Brannon, *Official Letter,* 203; Halbert and Ball, *Creek War,* 156, place end of fighting at 5:00 P.M.; "Toulmin to Joseph Gales, Sr. editor," *Raleigh Register and North Carolina Gazette,* September 7, 1813, printed in the *Daily National Intelligencer,* October 12, 1813, "an hour, or an hour and a half before sunset"; Brown, *Creek Indian History,* 112, "an hour of sun setting."

124. Halbert, Letters on Fort Mims, Draper Collection, Wisconsin Historical Society.

125. Halbert and Ball, *Creek War,* 158n; Grant, *Letters, Journals and Writings,* 2:667.

126. Dr. Holmes identifies the woman as Mrs. Daniel Bailey, which cannot be correct as fifteen-year-old Daniel was not married. Notes of Dr. Holmes, Pickett Papers, ADAH. The only other Bailey women at the fort were Dixon's wife, Sarah; his sister, Elizabeth Fletcher; and James Bailey's wife, Nancy. Waselkov, *Conquering Spirit*, 51.

127. Notes of Dr. Holmes, Pickett Papers, ADAH. After the war, Tom was recaptured by the Americans and recognized. Reportedly, he excused his conduct at Fort Mims with the suspect explanation that he returned to the fort in hopes of bartering the boy for his freedom and did not believe the hostiles would harm the child. Nonetheless, coupled with his protestations that he was truly remorseful for the mistake he had made, Tom persuaded his captors to spare his life. He was placed back in bondage and allowed to live out his life on the mixed-blood Arthur Sizemore's plantation, not far from the ruins of Fort Mims. Ibid.

128. Halbert, Letters on Fort Mims, Draper Collection, Wisconsin Historical Society.

129. Claiborne, *Life and Times*, 102n; Halbert, Letters on Fort Mims, Draper Collection, Wisconsin Historical Society.

130. Notes of Dr. Holmes, Pickett Papers, ADAH; Halbert, Letters on Fort Mims, Draper Collection, Wisconsin Historical Society.

131. David Pierce Mason, *Massacre at Fort Mims* (Mobile, AL: Greenberry, 1975), 124.

132. Notes of Dr. Holmes, Pickett Papers, ADAH; Meek, *Romantic Passages*, 254; Benjamin Hawkins, Creek Agency, September 17, 1813, *American State Papers: Indian Affairs*, 1:853. If Mrs. Bailey indeed uttered these words, she must have been referring to her brother-in-law Daniel. As the wife of James Bailey she was related to the Bailey family by marriage not blood.

133. Notes of Col James, Pickett Papers, ADAH; Halbert and Ball, *Creek War*, 158–59.

134. Halbert and Ball, *Creek War*, 158–59.

135. Meek, *Romantic Passages*, 256.

136. Halbert and Ball, *Creek War*, 164.

137. One of those who made it to safety was the young hostler Nehemiah Page. He was last seen running for his life as William Weatherford and his men charged the east gate of the fort. Something pursued him, but it was not an Indian—it was a little Indian dog. As Page fled through the woods to the Alabama River, the dog followed close behind. When Page leaped into the river, the dog leaped after him and swam up onto his back. With great difficulty, Page swam several hundred yards through the warm waters to the far shore with his canine passenger clinging about his shoulders. From there the two companions made their way to the nearest settlement. Page became so attached to the little animal that for the rest of the dog's life, he and Page never parted. The fortunate hostler had kept not only his life but had gained the friendship of one of the rare and wondrously good spirits in an evil world. Halbert, Letters on Fort Mims, Draper Collection, Wisconsin Historical Society; Halbert and Ball, *Creek War*, 166–67. The unmasking involved forcing the sergeant to lower his trousers, thus revealing the bayonet wounds on his buttocks that the female defender in the bastion had inflicted on him.

138. Waselkov, *Conquering Spirit*, 225.

139. Extract of a communication from the chiefs at Coweta to Colonel Hawkins, Creek Agency, September 16, 1813, *American State Papers: Indian Affairs*, 1:853; Benjamin Hawkins, Creek Agency, September 17, 1813, *American State Papers: Indian Affairs*, 1:853.

140. Waselkov, *Conquering Spirit*, 148.

141. Notes from Col James, Pickett Papers, ADAH; Grant, *Letters, Journals and Writings*, 2:667.

142. Waselkov, *Conquering Spirit*, Appendix 1, 243.

143. The following description of McGirth's visit to Fort Mims is taken from the notes of his interview with Albert J. Pickett.

144. Pickett, *History of Alabama*, 2:280–81.

145. Notes of Dr. Holmes, Pickett Papers, ADAH.

146. Meek, *Romantic Passages*, 254; Waselkov, *Conquering Spirit*, 147.

147. Waselkov, *Conquering Spirit*, 147.

148. Benjamin Hawkins to the Secretary of War, Creek Agency, October 11, 1813, *American State Papers: Indian Affairs*, 1:852.

149. Benjamin Hawkins, Creek Agency, September 17, 1813, *American State Papers: Indian Affairs*, 1:853.

150. Waselkov, *Conquering Spirit*, 146–47.

151. Brown, *Creek Indian History*, 115.

152. Halbert and Ball, *Creek War*, 177.

153. Ibid., 177–78.

154. Ibid., 178–79.

155. Eggleston, *Red Eagle*, 122–23; Halbert and Ball, *Creek War*, 180.

156. Halbert and Ball, *Creek War*, 180–81.

157. Ibid., 185–89.

158. Notes Furnished by Col. Jeremiah Austill, Albert J. Pickett Papers, LPR 185, ADAH; Notes Furnished by Colonel G. W. Creagh, Albert J. Pickett Papers, LPR 185, ADAH.

159. Halbert and Ball, *Creek War*, 188–197.

160. There is a remarkable and wonderful coda to the story of the mutilated Sarah Merrill. Under the care of a nineteen-year-old apprentice physician named Jeremiah Austill, who was to become one of the heroes of the war, Sarah Merrill and her infant son survived their terrible wounds. Yet the cruelty of fate was not yet through with her. While recovering from her wounds, she learned that her husband had been killed in a battle with the Red Clubs at a place called the Holy Ground. Happily, however, this indomitable woman eventually married a man named Holtham and raised a large family on the Alabama frontier. One night some years later, a family traveling from Tennessee stopped at the Holtham farm seeking food and shelter for the night. As was customary in those times, the strangers were invited to stay. The two families had just seated themselves around the supper table when to everyone's astonishment, Sarah recognized her former husband among her guests. He had been badly wounded and left for dead at the Holy Ground fight. He, too, had survived his wounds, and having heard that Sarah had been murdered by the Red Clubs, he, too, remarried and raised a family. Once the former spouses got past their initial shock and awkwardness, one can only imagine how the two families received their miracle. But they parted as friends and went on with their new lives. At this late remove it is all but impossible to confirm this story, but if it is not true, it should be. Eggleston, *Red Eagle*, 124; Meek, *Romantic Passages*, 301.

161. "Lieutenant Montgomery to Samuel Montgomery, September 4, 1813," *Washington Republican*, September 29, 1813.

162. Ibid.; "An Old Soldier," *Washington Republican*, October 27, 1813.

163. "A letter to the editor from an anonymous veteran praising Lieutenant Montgomery's conduct," *Washington Republican*, 1813.

164. "Montgomery to Montgomery," *Washington Republican*, September 4, 1813.

165. Waselkov, *Conquering Spirit*, 140.

166. Doster, "Letters Relating to the Tragedy, 283; Toulmin to Joseph Gales, Sr. editor," *Raleigh Register and North Carolina Gazette*, September 7, 1813, printed in the *Dailey National Intelligencer*, October 12, 1813.

167. Ibid.; Toulmin to Madison, September 11, 1813, in Stagg, *Papers of James Madison*, 6:616.

168. Claiborne to Flournoy, September 3, 1813, in Brannan, *Official Letters*, 204.

169. J. F. H. Claiborne to Albert J. Pickett, August 23, 1847, Pickett Papers, ADAH.

170. Walter Johnson, *River of Dark Dreams: Slavery and Empire in the Cotton Kingdom* (Cambridge: Harvard University Press, 2013), 18–22.

171. Governor David Holmes to Madison, September 11, 1813, in Stagg, *Papers of James Madison*, 6:617–18.

172. Holmes to Wilkinson, July 22, 1812, in Carter, *Territorial Papers*, 6:299.

173. Halbert and Ball, *Creek War*, 258.

174. Toulmin to Claiborne, September 6, 1813, Letterbook F, Claiborne Collection, MDAH.

175. Holmes to Secretary of War, Washington, Mississippi Territory, September 14, 1813, Papers of the Mississippi Territory, Executive Journal of David Holmes, MDAH.

176. Claiborne to Flournoy, September 3, 1813, in Brannan, *Official Letters*, 203.

177. Major Joseph Kennedy and Captain Uriah Blue to General Claiborne, September 9, 1813, in Interesting Papers in relation to the Indian Hostilities in 1813–1814, the destruction of Fort Mims, furnished Pickett by Col. John H. F. Claiborne found among his Father's Papers (Gen. Ferdinand H. Claiborne), Albert J. Pickett Papers, LPR185, box 2, ADAH.

178. Ibid.; The Burial of the Dead at Fort Mims, March 3, 1887, in Henry S. Halbert, Letters on Fort Mims, November 10, 1882, to March 3, 1887, Series YY: Tecumseh Papers (microfilm Reel 119), Lyman Draper Collection, Wisconsin Historical Society.

179. Toulmin to Madison, September 11, 1813, in Stagg, *Papers of James Madison*, 6:616.

180. Notes of Doctor Thomas G. Holmes, Albert J. Pickett Papers, LPR185, box 2, ADAH; Claiborne to Kennedy, September 22, 1813, Letterbook F, Claiborne Collection, MDAH; Halbert, Letters on Fort Mims, Draper Collection, Wisconsin Historical Society. For Embree's military services during the Creek War, his master eventually emancipated him, but only after extracting thirty-four more years of labor out of this slave turned soldier.

181. Halbert, Letters on Fort Mims, Draper Collection, Wisconsin Historical Society; Notes of Doctor Holmes, Pickett Papers, ADAH.

182. Notes of Doctor Holmes, Pickett Papers, ADAH; Halbert, Letters on Fort Mims, Draper Collection, Wisconsin Historical Society; Notes taken from the Lips of Col Robert James of Clarke County Ala Relative to Zachariah McGirth and Weatherford, Pickett Papers, ADAH.

183. Notes of Doctor Holmes, Pickett Papers, ADAH; Halbert, Letters on Fort Mims, Draper Collection, Wisconsin Historical Society.

184. Robert W. Mann, William M. Bass, and Lee Meadows, "Time Since Death and Decomposition of the Human Body: Variables and Observations in Case and Experimental Field Studies," *Journal of Forensic Sciences* 35:1 (January 1990): 105–8.

185. Kennedy to Claiborne, September 26, 1813, Letterbook F, Claiborne Collection, MDAH.

186. Kennedy and Blue to Claiborne, September 9, 1813, in Papers furnished by John H. F. Claiborne, Pickett Papers, ADAH.

187. Halbert and Ball, *Creek War,* 206–10.

188. Meek, *Romantic Passages*, 309.

5. The Lion Upon the Fold

1. "Don't all rivers flow south . . . " R. H. W. Dillard, *News of the Nile: A Book of Poems* (Chapel Hill: University of North Carolina Press, 1971), 26.

2. Anne Newport Royall, *Letters from Alabama on Various Subjects: To Which is Added an Appendix, containing Remarks on Sundry Members of the 20th and 21st Congress, and other high Characters at the Seat of Government* (Washington: 1830), 43–44.

3. James Parton, *Life of Andrew Jackson in Three Volumes* (New York: Mason Brothers 1861), 1:389.

4. Ibid.

5. Ibid., 1:390.

6. Ibid., 1:394.

7. "Important!," *Nashville Whig*, September 14, 1813.

8. Pate, *Reminiscences of George Strother Gaines*, 62.

9. "Fellow Soldiers," *Nashville Whig*, September 14, 1813.

10. Parton, *Life of Andrew Jackson*, 3:610.

11. Ibid.

12. Statement of Certain Tennessee Volunteers who served under General Jackson in the Creek War, in Parton, *Life of Andrew Jackson*, 1:631 (Appendix 3).

13. John R. Elting, *Amateurs, to Arms: A Military History of the War of 1812* (Chapel Hill, NC: Algonquin Books, 1991), 8.

14. Brannan, *Official Letters*, 236.

15. John Pitchlynn to Willie Blount, September 18, 1813, Jackson Papers, reel 6, LOC. In a similar vein, the credulous John Coffee wrote his wife, Mary, while camped on the south side of the Tennessee that he had "news that the whole creek nation" was moving "in one body" toward his

position. Coffee to Mary Coffee, October 13, 1813, John Coffee Papers, Dyas Collection, box 13, reel 6, Tennessee State Library and Archives (TSLA).

16. John McKee to Pitchlynn, September 14, 1813, Jackson Papers, reel 6.

17. Pitchlynn to Blount, September 18, 1813, Jackson Papers, reel 6; Extract of a Letter Dated Choctaw Trading House, St. Stephens, MT, September 17, 1813, from Gen. Gaines to Gov. Blount, Jackson Papers, reel 6.

18. Jackson to the Tennessee Volunteers, September 24, 1813, in Harold D. Moser and Sharon MacPherson, eds., *The Papers of Andrew Jackson, Vol. 2, 1804–1813* (Knoxville: University of Tennessee Press, 1984), 428–29.

19. Brannan, *Official Letters*, 215.

20. Royall, *Letters from Alabama*, 45.

21. Mateo Gonzalez Manrique to Gentlemen, September 29, 1813, Letterbook F. Claiborne Collection, MDAH; Jackson to Coffee, September 29, 1813, in Moser and MacPherson, *Papers of Andrew Jackson*, 2:431.

22. Coffee to Jackson, October 6, 1813, Jackson Papers, reel 5, LOC.

23. Sugden, *Tecumseh*, 379–80.

24. John Reid and John H. Eaton, *The Life of Andrew Jackson, Original 1817 Edition*, ed. Frank L. Owsley Jr. (Tuscaloosa: University of Alabama Press, 1974), 56.

25. Richard Keith Call Journal, Richard Keith Call Collection, N2013-5, Florida State Archives (FSA).

26. John Coffee to Mary Coffee, October 13, 1813, John Coffee Papers, Dyas Collection, box 13, reel 6, TSLA.

27. Parton, *Life of Andrew Jackson*, 1:428; David Crockett, *A Narrative of the Life of David Crockett of the State of Tennessee* (Philadelphia: E. L. Cary and A. Hart, 1834), 34.

28. Crockett, *Narrative*, 36.

29. Ibid., 39–40; Parton, *Life of Andrew Jackson*, 1:427–28.

30. Coffee to Mary Coffee, October 13, 1813, Coffee Papers, Dyas Collection, TSLA; Crockett, *Narrative*, 39; Parton, *Life of Andrew Jackson*, 1:428.

31. Parton, *Life of Andrew Jackson*, 1:428; Crockett, *Narrative*, 39–40.

32. Coffee to Mary Coffee, October 13, 1813, Coffee Papers, Dyas Collection.

33. Crockett, *Narrative*, 40.

34. Royall, *Letters from Alabama*, 58.

35. Crockett, *Narrative*, 40.

36. John Coffee to General Jackson, Indian Lands, October 22, 1813, Andrew Jackson Papers, reel 7, LOC.

37. Jackson's military secretary, Major John Reid, reported that the mountains were "more tremendous than the Alps," a mountain range he had obviously never seen. John Reid to William B. Lewis, October 24, 1813, quoted in Parton, *Life of Andrew Jackson*, 1:432.

38. Wright, *Historic Indian Towns*, 165–66.

39. Path Killer to Andrew Jackson, October 22, 1813, in Moser and MacPherson, *Papers of Andrew Jackson*, 2:439.

40. Brown, *Creek Indian History*, 37–44; Swanton, *Early History of the Creek Indians*, 312–13.

41. Jackson to Fellow Soldiers, October 24, 1813, Andrew Jackson Papers, reel 7, LOC.

42. John Reid and John Coffee were the men closest to Jackson. Their letters to their wives—who, to both men's annoyance, were indifferent correspondents—provide a candid and intimate look into Jackson's mind as he directed the campaign against the Creeks.

43. Reid to Betsy Reid, October 24, 1813, John Reid Papers, LOC; Wright, *Historic Indian Towns*, 100; Reid to Betsy Reid, October 29, 1813, John Reid Papers, LOC.

44. T. R. Henderson, "The Destruction of Littafuchee, and a Brief History of American Settlement," *Alabama Review* 67, no. 3 (July 2014): 233, 238, 242.

45. Reid to Betsy Reid, October 29, 1813, John Reid Papers, LOC.

46. Jackson to Blount, October 28, 1813, in Moser and MacPherson, *Papers of Andrew Jackson*, 2:442–43.

47. Reid to Betsy Reid, November 1, 1813, John Reid Papers, LOC.

48. Marvin T. Smith, "Woods Island Revisited," *Journal of Alabama Archaeology* 41:2 (December 1995): 100–103.

49. General Order, October 30, 1813, Presidential Papers Microfilm, Andrew Jackson Papers, reel 7, LOC; General Order, November 2, 1813, Jackson Papers, reel 7, LOC.

50. John Coffee to Andrew Jackson, November 2, 1813, Jackson Papers, reel 7, LOC.

51. Path Killer to Friend and Brother, October 28, 1813, Jackson Papers, reel 7, LOC.

52. Coffee to Jackson, November 4, 1813, in Brannan, *Official Letters*, 255.

53. Ibid.

54. Crockett, *Narrative*, 75.

55. Reid to Father, November 6, 1813, John Reid Papers, LOC.

56. Nathaniel Herbert Claiborne, *Notes on the War in the South with Biographical Sketches of Montgomery, Jackson, Sevier, the Late Gov. Claiborne, and Others* (Richmond: William Ramsay, 1819), 30.

57. Coffee to Jackson, November 4, 1813, in Brannan, *Official Letters*, 256.

58. Crockett, *Narrative*, 76–77.

59. Ibid., 67.

60. Ironically, years later, when Crockett the Indian killer had become Crockett the congressman, he voted against President Andrew Jackson's bill to remove what was left of the tribes in the South to the Trans-Mississippi lands, describing the removal as a "wicked, unjust measure." Crockett, *Narrative*, 105.

61. Coffee to Jackson, November 4, 1813, in Brannan, *Official Letters*, 256.

62. Coffee to Mary Coffee, November 4, 1813, John Coffee Papers, Dyas Collection, box 13, reel 5, TSLA, Nashville.

63. William Berkeley Lewis to Jackson, November 12, 1813, Moser and MacPherson, *Papers of Andrew Jackson*, 2:450.

64. LeRoy Pope to Jackson, November 4, 1813, in Moser and MacPherson, *Papers of Andrew Jackson*, 2:444–45.

65. Moser and MacPherson, *Papers of Andrew Jackson*, 2:494–95.

66. Over the course of the war, Jackson acquired several such pets. T. R. Henderson, "The Destruction of Littafuchee, and a Brief History of American Settlement," *Alabama Review* 67, no. 3 (2014):243.

67. Ibid., 2:516, 2:444, 2:494–95; Harold D. Moser, David R. Hoth, Sharon MacPherson, and John H. Reinbold, eds. *The Papers of Andrew Jackson, Volume 3, 1814–1815* (Knoxville: University of Tennessee Press, 1991), 24.

68. Parton, *Life of Andrew Jackson*, 1:439–40.

69. Ibid., 1:441; Brigade Order, November 6, 1813, Presidential Papers Microfilm, Andrew Jackson Papers, reel 7, LOC.

70. Crockett, *Narrative*, 89.

71. Richard Keith Call Journal, Richard Keith Call Collection, FSA.

72. Reid to Betsy Reid, November 4, 1813, John Reid Papers, LOC.

73. John Lowrey to Jackson and John Strother, November 7, 1813, in Moser and MacPherson, *Papers of Andrew Jackson*, 2:445–46.

74. Jackson to Lowrey, November 7, 1813, in Moser and MacPherson, *Papers of Andrew Jackson*, 2:446.

75. James White to Jackson, November 7, 1813, in Moser and MacPherson, *Papers of Andrew Jackson*, 2:446–447.

76. Reid and Eaton, *Life of Andrew Jackson*, 59.

77. Reid to Betsy Reid, November 7, 1813, John Reid Papers, LOC.

78. "Extract of a letter from Mr. John P. Erwin to his friend in Nashville, dated Camp Strother, on Coose river, November 12, 1813," *Clarion and Tennessee State Gazette*, November, 16, 1813.

79. Parton, *Life of Andrew Jackson*, 442; Reid to Father, November 21, 1813, John Reid Papers, LOC; "Extract of a letter from Mr. John P. Erwin"; Mary Hardin McCown, ed., "The 'J. Hartsell

Memora': The Journal of a Tennessee Captain in the War of 1812," *East Tennessee Historical Society's Publications* 11 (1939): 110n79; Parton, *Life of Andrew Jackson,* 442.

80. Jackson to Blount, November 13, 1813, *Nashville Whig,* November 1813.

81. Parton, *Life of Andrew Jackson,* 442–43.

82. Tom Kanon, "Regimental Histories of Tennessee Units during the War of 1812," TSLA, http://www.tennessee.gov/tsla/history/military/1812reg.htm.

83. E. Grace Jemison, *Historic Tales of Talladega* (Montgomery, AL: Paragon, 1959), 38.

84. "Extract of a letter from Mr. John P. Erwin"; Path Killer to Jackson, October 23, 1813, Jackson Papers, reel 7, LOC.

85. John Cocke to Jackson, November 27, 1813, in Moser and MacPherson, *Papers of Andrew Jackson,* 2:462.

86. Jackson to Governor Willie Blount, *Nashville Whig,* November 21, 1813. The flag is in the collections of the Smithsonian Institute, which claims, not improbably, that Dederick risked his life to rescue the flag when its bearer fell in battle. http://collections.si.edu/search/results.

87. "Extract of a letter from Mr. John P. Erwin."

88. Crockett, *Narrative,* 92.

89. "Glorious News," *Nashville Whig,* November 17, 1813.

90. "Extract of a letter from Mr. John P. Erwin."

91. "Extract from a letter from Col. Wm Carroll to his brother in Nashville, brought by the express," *Clarion and Tennessee State Gazette,* November, 16, 1813.

92. Reid to Father, December 24, 1813, John Reid Papers, LOC.

93. Ewing to Jackson, November 24, 1813, Jackson Papers, reel 7, LOC.

94. "Extract of a letter from Mr. John P. Erwin."

95. Ibid.

96. Jackson to Rachel Jackson, November __, 1813, in Moser and MacPherson, *Papers of Andrew Jackson,* 2:451.

97. Reid and Eaton, *Life of Andrew Jackson,* 56–57.

98. Parton, *Life of Andrew Jackson,* 443–44.

99. "Extract of a letter from Mr. John P. Erwin."

100. Path Killer to Jackson, December 28, 1813, Jackson Papers, reel 8, LOC.

101. "Extract of a letter from Maj. General Jackson to his Excellency Gov. Blount, dated Fort Strother, Jan. 2, 1814," *Mississippian Republican–Extra,* February 12, 1814.

102. Willie Blount to Jackson, November 17, 1813, Jackson Papers, reel 7, LOC.

103. *Clarion and Tennessee State Gazette,* November, 16, 1813.

104. Willie Blount to Jackson, November 17, 1813, Jackson Papers, reel 7, LOC.

105. Crockett, *Narrative,* 93.

106. William Martin, *The Self Vindication of Colonel William Martin: Against Certain Charges and Aspersions Made Against Him by Gen. Andrew Jackson and Others, in Relation to Sundry Transactions in the Campaign Against the Creek Indians in the Year 1813* (Nashville: John Simpson, 1829), 27.

107. Wright, *Historic Indian Towns,* 87.

108. Robert Grierson to General Jackson, November 13, 1813, in Moser and MacPherson, *Papers of Andrew Jackson,* 2:451.

109. Jackson to Grierson, November 17, 1813, in Moser and MacPherson, *Papers of Andrew Jackson,* 2:456.

110. Grierson to Jackson, November 15, 1813, in Moser and MacPherson, *Papers of Andrew Jackson,* 2:452.

111. Jackson to Grierson, November 17, 1813, in Moser and MacPherson, *Papers of Andrew Jackson,* 2:456–57.

112. Willie Blount to General Jackson, November 24, 1813, in Moser and MacPherson, *Papers of Andrew Jackson,* 2:461; General Jackson to John Cocke, November 18, 1813, in Moser and MacPherson, *Papers of Andrew Jackson,* 2:457.

113. Brigadier General James White to Major General John Cocke, November 24, 1813, in Brannan, *Official Letters,* 281–82.

114. Ibid., 281.

115. Ibid., 281–82.

116. Brannan, *Official Letters,* 281–82; Colonel Morgan to Colonel Meigs, November 23, 1813, CIART, roll 6, and Gideon Morgan Papers, MS AC no.78–31, TSLA.

117. "Jackson's Army," *Nashville Whig,* December 8, 1813.

118. Morgan to Meigs, November 23, 1813, Morgan Papers, TSLA.

119. "Error Corrected," *Nashville Whig,* December 22, 1813.

120. Morgan to Meigs, November 23, 1813, Morgan Papers, TSLA.

121. Ibid.

122. McCown, "'J. Hartsell Memora,'" 110n79.

123. Morgan to Meigs, November 23, 1813, Morgan Papers, TSLA.

124. *Clarion & Tennessee State Gazette,* December 7, 1813.

125. "Jackson's Army," *Nashville Whig,* December 8, 1813.

126. Jackson to Grierson, November 17, 1813, in Moser and MacPherson, *Papers of Andrew Jackson,* 2:457.

6. Upon the Silver Plain

1. "General Orders, Milledgeville, July 30, 1813," *Milledgeville Georgia Journal,* August 4, 1813.

2. Benton, *Very Worst Road,* 70.

3. Benjamin Hawkins to John Armstrong, June 7, 1814, *American State Papers: Indian Affairs,* 1:858.

4. Hawkins to Armstrong, August 23, 1814, *American State Papers: Indian Affairs,* 1:852.

5. Ibid.

6. Hawkins to Floyd, October 4, 1813, *American State Papers: Indian Affairs,* 1:855; Hawkins to Armstrong, September 6, 1813, *American State Papers: Indian Affairs,* 1:852.

7. Extract of a communication from the chiefs at Coweta to Colonel Hawkins, September 16, 1813, *American State Papers: Indian Affairs,* 1:853.

8. Hawkins to Floyd, September 30, 1813, *American State Papers: Indian Affairs,* 1:854.

9. Hawkins to Armstrong, October 18, 1813, *American State Papers: Indian Affairs,* 1:857; Hawkins to Floyd, September 30, 1813, *American State Papers: Indian Affairs,* 1:854.

10. Peter A. Brannon, ed., "Journal of James A. Tait for the Year 1813," *Alabama Historical Quarterly* 2:4 (1940): 433.

11. Mary Floyd Hamilton, *A Little Family History* (Savannah, GA: Morning News Print, 1908), 10–11.

12. Brannon, "Journal of James A. Tait," 433.

13. Hawkins to Armstrong, September 14, 1813, *American State Papers: Indian Affairs,* 1:853.

14. Brannon, "Journal of James A. Tait," 434.

15. Hawkins to Armstrong, September 26, 1813, *American State Papers: Indian Affairs,* 1:854.

16. Hawkins to Floyd, September 30, 1813, *American State Papers: Indian Affairs,* 1:854.

17. Hawkins to Toulmin, October 23, 1813, *American State Papers: Indian Affairs,* 1:857.

18. Grant, *Letters, Journals and Writings,* 2:674; Journal of Occurrence at the Convention of the Creeks at Tookabatchee commencing September 9, 1815, *American State Papers: Indian Affairs,* 2:759.

19. Journal of Occurrence, 2:759.

20. Hawkins to Armstrong, June 7, 1814, *American State Papers: Indian Affairs,* 1:858.

21. Peter Brannon, "More about Mordecai," *Alabama Historical Quarterly* 20:1 (1958): 31, 29. The enterprising Mordecai had a history of bad luck in setting up business in the Creek Nation. In 1807, with Benjamin Hawkins's encouragement, he built the first cotton gin in Alabama. The project was off to a promising start until his neighbor, Captain Isaacs and his gang, burned down the establishment, beating Mordecai senseless in the process. Notes taken from the lips of Abraham Mordecai, Pickett Papers, ADAH.

22. Hawkins to Armstrong, June 7, 1814, *American State Papers: Indian Affairs,* 1:858.

23. Thomas Pinckney to Secretary of War, November 3, 1813, Record Group 107, Letters Received by the Secretary of War, Registered Series, 1801–1860, Microfilm Publication #221, National Archives, Washington, DC.

24. Thomas Pinckney to General Jackson, November 29, 1813, Presidential Papers Microfilm, Andrew Jackson Papers, reel 7, slide 465, LOC.

25. Ibid.

26. Grant, *Letters, Journals and Writings*, 2:674.

27. Southerland and Brown, *Federal Road*, 42.

28. Letter from Big Warrior, William McIntosh, Little Prince and Alex Cornells to General Floyd, November 18, 1813, in Southerland and Brown, *Federal Road*, 42–43.

29. Brannon, "Journal of James A. Tait," 435. John Floyd to Mary H. Floyd, November 18, 1813, "Letters of John Floyd," *Georgia Historical Quarterly* 33:4 (1949): 234. John Floyd to Andrew Jackson, December 18, 1813, Andrew Jackson Papers, Presidential Papers Microfilm, M221, reel 7, LOC.

30. Benjamin Hawkins to General Armstrong, Creek Agency, June 7, 1814, *American State Papers: Indian Affairs*, 1:858; Foster, *Collected Works of Benjamin Hawkins*, 168; "Letters of John Floyd," 261.

31. Floyd to Pinckney, December 4, 1813, in Brannan, *Official Letters*, 283–84.

32. Brannon, "Journal of James A. Tait," 436; Floyd to Pinckney, December 4, 1813, in Brannan, *Official Letters*, 283. Edmund Shackelford, one of Floyd's officers, says the march began at 2:00 A.M., E. Shackelford to "Girles," December 3, 1813, Society for Georgia Archeology, MSS 4911, Macon, Georgia.

33. William Bartram, *The Travels of William Bartram: Naturalist's Edition*, ed. Frances Harper (New Haven, CT: Yale University Press, 1967), 102, 105–6.

34. Foster, *Collected Works*, 31s; Floyd to Pinckney, December 4, 1813, in Brannan, *Official Letters*, 284–85.

35. Floyd to Mary Floyd, December 5, 1813, in "Letters of John Floyd," 235–36.

36. Floyd to Pinckney, December 4, 1813, in Brannan, *Official Letters*, 283–84.

37. Ibid., 283.

38. John McKee to Coffee, October 6, 1813, Jackson Papers, reel 6, LOC.

39. Floyd to Pinckney, December 4, 1813, in Brannan, *Official Letters*, 284.

40. Shackelford to "Girles," December 3, 1813.

41. Ibid.; Brown, *Creek Indian History*, 124–25. Floyd estimates two thousand warriors. Floyd to Mary Floyd, December 5, 1813, in "Letters of John Floyd," 235.

42. Shackelford to "Girles," December 3, 1813.

43. Floyd to Pinckney, December 4, 1813, Brannan, *Official Letters*, 283; Floyd to Pinckney, December 12, 1813, Secretary of War Letters, National Archives.

44. Brown, *Creek Indian History*, 125.

45. Floyd to Mary Floyd, December 5, 1813, in "Letters of John Floyd," 235.

46. Bartram, *Travels*, 106.

47. Brannon, "Journal of James A. Tait," 436; Brown, *Creek Indian History*, 126.

48. Shackelford to "Girles," December 3, 1813.

49. Floyd to Pinckney, December 4, 1813, in Brannan, *Official Letters*, 284.

50. Letters and Diaries of Charles Rinaldo Floyd, vol. 1, 54, unpublished manuscript, courtesy of a direct descendant, my friend Brooke Clagett.

51. Floyd to Mary Floyd, December 5, 1813, in "Letters of John Floyd," 237.

52. Letters and Diaries of Charles Floyd, vol. 1, 54.

53. Floyd to Mary Floyd, December 5, 1813, in "Letters of John Floyd," 236; Brannon, "Journal of James A. Tait," 436; "War of 1812," Ancestry.com, http://www.rootsweb.ancestry.com/~gataylor/regim.htm#officers.

54. "Heroism!" *Georgia Journal*, December 15, 1813.

55. Ibid.

56. Brown, *Creek Indian History*, 126.

57. Brannon, "Journal of James A. Tait," 436.

58. Ibid.

59. Brown, *Creek Indian History*, 127.

60. Floyd to Mary Floyd, December 5, 1813, in "Letters of John Floyd," 235.

61. Floyd to Pinckney, December 4, 1813, in Brannan, *Official Letters*, 284–85; Floyd to Mary Floyd, December 5, 1813, in "Letters of John Floyd," 236; Brannon, "Journal of James A. Tait," 436.

62. Floyd to Mary Floyd, December 5, 1813, in "Letters of John Floyd," 235–36.

63. Ibid., 235–37; Floyd to Pinckney, December 4, 1813, in Brannan, *Official Letters*, 284.

64. American calculation of dead and wounded in Floyd to Pinckney, December 4, 1813, in Brannan, *Official Letters*, 284; Creek calculation of wounded and dead in Brown, *Creek Indian History*, 127.

65. Floyd to Governor Early, December 12, 1813, in "Some Early Fort Mitchell References," *Alabama Historical Quarterly* 21 (1959): 3.

66. "War of 1812," Ancestry.com, http://www.rootsweb.ancestry.com/~gataylor/regim.htm#officers.

67. Ibid.

68. Benjamin Hawkins to General Armstrong, Creek Agency, June 7, 1814, *American State Papers: Indian Affairs*, 1:858.

69. Floyd to Jackson, December 18, 1813, Jackson Papers, reel 7, LOC.

70. Major General David Adams to Georgia governor Peter Early, December 24, 1813, "Georgia Military Affairs, Vol. 3., 1801–1813," unpublished, comp. J. E. Hays, Georgia Department of Archives and History (GDAH), 1940, 316–21.

71. General Floyd to Major General Jackson, December 18, 1813, Presidential Papers Microfilm, Andrew Jackson Papers, reel 7, slide 746, LOC.

72. Hawkins to Pinckney, February 12, 1814, Presidential Papers of Andrew Jackson, reel 7, LOC.

73. Floyd to Jackson, December 18, 1813, Andrew Jackson Papers, LOC; Adams to Early, December 24, 1813, "Georgia Military Affairs," GDAH, 320–21.

74. Adams to Early, December 24, 1813, "Georgia Military Affairs," GDAH, 320–21.

75. Wright, *Historic Indian Towns*, 118.

76. For more on New Yaucau, see Roy S. Dickens Jr., *Archeological Investigations at Horseshoe Bend, National Military Park, Alabama*, Alabama Archaeological Society, Special Publication 3 (Tuscaloosa: Alabama Archeological Society, 1979), 127–35.

77. Foster, *Collected Works*, 46a.

78. Adams to Early, December 24, 1813, "Georgia Military Affairs," GDAH, 318.

79. Ibid., 317.

80. Ibid.

81. Ibid., 318.

82. Ibid.

83. John Foshee, *Alabama Canoe Rides and Float Trips* (Huntsville, AL: Strode, 1975), 180–82.

84. Adams to Early, December 24, 1813, "Georgia Military Affairs," GDAH, 318–19.

85. Talk of the Friendly Chiefs, January 5, 1814, Records of the Office of the Secretary of War, Microfilm Publication 221, National Archives, Washington, DC.

86. Adams to Early, December 24, 1813, "Georgia Military Affairs," GDAH, 319–20.

87. Ibid., 320.

88. Foster, *Collected Works*, 46s–47s.

89. Adams to Early, December 24, 1813, "Georgia Military Affairs, GDAH, 319.

90. Ibid., 320.

91. Ibid.

92. Ibid.

93. Major Howell Tatum, "Topographic Notes and Observations on the Alabama River, August 1814," in *Transactions of the Alabama Historical Society* 2, 1897–1898, ed. Peter J. Hamilton and Thomas M. Owen, 1898: 168.

94. Andrew Jackson to Rachel Jackson, August 23, 1814, in Moser and MacPherson, *Papers of Andrew Jackson*, 1984), 3:117; Benjamin Hawkins to General Armstrong, Creek Agency, June 28, 1813, *American State Papers: Indian Affairs*, 1:847.

95. Claiborne, *Life and Times*, 116–18.

96. Henry Halbert, "Creek War Incidents," in *Transactions of the Alabama Historical Society, 1897–1898*, vol. 2, ed. Thomas McAdory Owen (Tuscaloosa, AL: n.p., 1898), 106.

97. Notes furnished by Col. Jeremiah Austill, Albert J. Pickett Papers, LPR185, ADAH.

98. Thomas Flournoy to F. L. Claiborne, October 12, 1813, Letterbook F. Claiborne Collection, MDAH.

99. Ibid.

100. Ferdinand Claiborne to Editor, Supplement to the *Mississippi Republican*, March 25, 1814.

101. Pickett, *History of Alabama*, 549.

102. Pate, *Reminiscences of George Strother Gaines*, 136.

103. Ibid.

104. Toulmin, et al., to Flournoy, September 28, 1813, in Lackey, *Frontier Claims*, 18–20.

105. Thomas Flournoy to Madison, October 6, 1813, in Stagg, *Papers of James Madison*, 6:680n4.

106. Pate, *Reminiscences of George Strother Gaines*, 57.

107. Ibid., 134.

108. Ibid., 59, 134.

109. Ibid., 61.

110. Notes taken from the Lips of Dr. Thos G. Holmes in relation to various expeditions made by Capt Blue, Col Benton & others in 1814, 1813, Albert J. Pickett Papers, LPR 185, ADAH..

111. Claiborne to Holmes, November 12, 1813, Letterbook F, Claiborne Collection, MDAH.

112. Flourney to Claiborne, November 9, 1813, Letterbook F, Claiborne Collection, MDAH.

113. J. F. H Claiborne, *Mississippi, as a Province, Territory and State* (Jackson, MS: Power & Barksdale, 1880), 328.

114. Claiborne, *Life of Sam Dale*, 132–33.

115. Dunbar Rowland, "Mississippi Territory in the War of 1812," in *Publications of the Mississippi Historical Society*, Centenary Series, vol. 4 (Jackson: Mississippi Historical Society, 1921), 57.

116. Waselkov, *Conquering Spirit*, 322n4.

117. Rowland, "Mississippi Territory," 157.

118. Claiborne to Flournoy, October 22, 1813, Letterbook F, Claiborne Collection, MDAH.

119. Ibid.; Claiborne to Peter Isler, October 29, 1813, Letterbook F, Claiborne Collection, MDAH.

120. Claiborne to Flournoy, October 22, 1813, Letterbook F, Claiborne Collection, MDAH.

121. Ibid.

122. Notes Furnished by Austill, Pickett Papers, ADAH.

123. Claiborne, *Mississippi*, 327.

124. Notes Furnished by Austill, Pickett Papers, ADAH.

125. Brown, *Creek Indian History*, 117.

126. Notes Furnished by General Patrick May of Greene County in Relation to the Battle of Burnt Corn Creek and the Canoe Fight, Albert J. Pickett Papers, LPR185, ADAH.

127. Ibid.; Notes Furnished by Austill, Pickett Papers, ADAH.

128. Notes Furnished by Austill, Picket Papers, ADAH.

129. Notes Furnished by Austill, Pickett Papers, ADAH; Flournoy to Claiborne, November 7, 1813, Letterbook F, Claiborne Collection, MDAH.

130. Flournoy to Claiborne, November 7, 1813, Letterbook F, Claiborne Collection, MDAH.

131. Claiborne to Flournoy, November 8, 1813, Letterbook F, Claiborne Collection, MDAH.

132. Claiborne, *Mississippi*, 327.

133. Holmes to Claiborne, November, 10, 1813, Letterbook F, Claiborne Collection, MDAH.

134. Claiborne to Holmes, November 12, 1813, Letterbook F, Claiborne Collection, MDAH.

135. Flournoy to Claiborne, November 10, 1813, Letterbook F, Claiborne Collection, MDAH.

136. Claiborne to Holmes, November 21, 1813, Letterbook F, Claiborne Collection, MDAH; Waselkov, *Conquering Spirit*, 161.

7. Invasion

1. F. L. Claiborne to Thomas Flournoy, November 12, 1813, Letterbook F, Claiborne Collection, MDAH; Tatum, "Topographic Notes," 159. Tatum refers to the bluff as Alabama Heights.
2. Claiborne to Holmes, November 21, 1813, Letterbook F, Claiborne Collection, MDAH; Claiborne to Isler, November 25, 1813, Letterbook F, Claiborne Collection, MDAH.
3. Extract of a letter from an officer of the volunteer corps, at Fort Claiborne, dated November 26, 1813, *Mississippi Republican*, December 15, 1813.
4. Claiborne to Holmes, November 21, 1813; Tatum, "Topographic Notes," 159; Claiborne to Jackson, November 29, 1813, Letterbook F, Claiborne Collection, Mississippi Department of Archives and History.
5. Claiborne to Jackson, November 29, 1813, Letterbook F, Claiborne Collection, MDAH.
6. Willis Brewer, *Alabama, Her History, Resources, War Record, and Public Men, from 1540 to 1872* (Montgomery: Barrett and Brown, 1872), 394–95.
7. Thomas Danisi, *Uncovering the Truth about Meriwether Lewis* (Amherst, NY: Prometheus, 2012), 160–62, 238.
8. Pickett to Lyman P. Draper, September 20, 1854, Draper Papers, Wisconsin Historical Society.
9. Claiborne to Jackson, December 6, 1813, Presidential Papers Microfilm, Andrew Jackson Papers, reel 7, LOC.
10. Notes furnished by Col. G. W. Creagh, 1847, Section 2, Notes, LPR185, Albert J. Pickett Papers, ADAH.
11. Claiborne, *Life and Times*, 118–19
12. Halbert and Ball, *Creek War*, 226; Pickett, *History of Alabama*, 2:304–5.
13. Pickett, *History of Alabama*, 2:306.
14. Ibid.; Notes furnished by Creagh, Pickett Papers, ADAH; Claiborne, *Life and Times*, 130–31.
15. Notes furnished by Col Jeremiah Austill, Section 1, Notes, LPR185, Albert J. Pickett Papers, ADAH; Jeremiah Austill, "Autobiography," *Alabama Historical Quarterly* 6 (Spring 1944): 84.
16. Hand drawn map showing Canoe Fight in Notes furnished by Austill, Pickett Papers, ADAH; Notes furnished by Austill, Pickett Papers, ADAH; Claiborne, *Life and Times*, 120.
17. Claiborne, *Life and* Times, 120–21; R. Jones to F. L. Claiborne, November 13, 1813, Letterbook F, J. F. H. Claiborne Collection, MDAH; Claiborne, *Life and Times*, 120.
18. Claiborne, *Life and* Times, 121.
19. Notes furnished by Austill, Pickett Papers, ADAH. Austill refers to Captain Jones as Johnson.
20. Claiborne, *Life and Times*, 122; R. Jones to F. L. Claiborne, November 13, 1813, Letterbook F, J. F. H. Claiborne Collection, MDAH; Notes furnished by Creagh, Pickett Papers, ADAH; Jones to Claiborne, November 13, 1813, Letterbook F, Claiborne Collection, MDAH; Austill, "Autobiography," 84–86; Notes furnished by Austill, Pickett Papers, ADAH.
21. Notes furnished by Austill, Pickett Papers, ADAH.
22. Claiborne, *Life and Times*, 126.
23. Notes furnished by Austill, Pickett Papers, ADAH; Austill, "Autobiography," 85.
24. Notes furnished by Austill, Pickett Papers, ADAH.
25. Ibid.; Woodward, *Woodward's Reminiscences*, 109.
26. Notes furnished by Austill, Pickett Papers, ADAH; Austill, "Autobiography," 85; Claiborne, *Life and Times*, 123–24.
27. Notes furnished by Austill, Pickett Papers, ADAH; Austill, "Autobiography," 85.
28. Austill, "Autobiography," Notes furnished by Creagh, Pickett Papers, ADAH.
29. Notes furnished by Creagh, Pickett Papers, ADAH; Claiborne, *Life and Times*, 125.
30. Claiborne, *Life and Times*, 125; Notes furnished by Austill, Pickett Papers, ADAH.
31. Austill, "Autobiography," 86.
32. Ibid.; Notes furnished by Austill, Pickett Papers, ADAH.
33. The official notice of the action was a brief note in Captain Jones's report to General Claiborne about the results of the expedition from Fort Madison. In it Jones mentions that Dale's men fired "with certainty" from the east bank of the Alabama River on a canoe filled with hostiles passing

by, "killing eight Indians, some in the boat and others as they attempted to swim to safety." Jones to Claiborne, November 18, 1813, Letterbook F, Claiborne Collection, Mississippi Department of Archives and History. That debunker of great tales, Thomas Woodward, claims from conversations he had with all four American participants in the fight that the story was embellished to portray the American victors "to the best advantage." Although the old countryman does admit that "the canoe fight was reality." Woodward, *Woodward's Reminiscences*, 86. What Woodward does not acknowledge or perhaps did not know is that Dr. Thomas Holmes, then a surgeon's mate with Colonel Russell's 3rd Infantry, says that a "flotilla" of watercraft bound up the Alabama River with supplies for Fort Claiborne discovered along the way nine Creek bodies from the Canoe Fight. Notes taken from the lips of Dr. Thos. G. Holmes in relations to various expeditions by Capt. Blue, Col. Benton & others in 1814, 1813, Albert J. Pickett Papers, LPR 185, ADAH.

34. F. L. Claiborne to Andrew Jackson, December 6, 1813, Presidential Papers Microfilm, Andrew Jackson Papers, reel 7, LOC.

35. "Truth to the Editor," *Washington Republican*, June 29, 1814.

36. Tatum, "Topographic Notes," 139–40.

37. Woodward, *Woodward's Reminiscences*, 100,

38. Claiborne, *Mississippi*, 328–29; Claiborne, *Life and Times*, 139.

39. Claiborne, *Life and* Times, 140.

40. Claiborne to Jackson, November 12, 1813, Jackson Papers, reel 7, LOC; Halbert and Ball, *Creek War*, 246.

41. Claiborne, *Mississippi*, 328–29; "Truth to the Editor," *Washington Republican*, June 29, 1813.

42. Gregory Waselkov, "Return to the Holy Ground: The Legendary Battle Site Discovered," *Alabama Heritage* 101 (2011): 31–32; "Truth to the Editor," *Washington Republican*, June 29, 1813. Another source claims that only 110 warriors engaged Claiborne's army. Editor Note, *Washington Republican*, February 3, 1814.

43. Mateo Gonzalez Manrique to My Friend and Brother, November 15, 1813, Letterbook F, Claiborne Collection, MDAH..

44. Nathaniel Claiborne, "Notes on the War," 24.

45. Caesar Statement, January 16, 1814, Jackson Papers, reel 8, LOC.

46. Claiborne, *Life and Times*, 140; Halbert and Ball, *Creek War*, 246; Austill, "Autobiography," 86. Austill calls the place "big swamp creek." Waselkov, "Return to the Holy Ground," 29–30; Austill, "Autobiography," 86.

47. "Truth to the Editor," *Washington Republican*, June 29, 1814.

48. Claiborne to Armstrong, January 1, 1814, in Brannan, *Official Letters*, 295.

49. Russell to Gen. James Robertson, January 9, 1814, *Clarion*, March 1, 1814.

50. Halbert and Ball, *Creek War*, 248–50; Claiborne to Armstrong, January 1, 1814, in Brannan, *Official Letters*, 295; Austill, "Autobiography," 86; Brown, *Creek Indian History*, 118–19.

51. Halbert and Ball, *Creek War*, 248–50; "Truth to the Editor," *Washington Republican*, June 29, 1814. A venomous letter to the editor, highly critical of General Claiborne, from someone called "**TRUTH**," claimed the town consisted of only fifty houses. Given the importance of the town to the Alabamas, and the number housed there, that figure appears far too low.

52. Gregory Waselkov, e-mail message to author, April 14, 2012.

53. Halbert and Ball, *Creek War*, 248–49.

54. Halbert and Ball, *Creek War*, 248–51. Holy Ground Creek is now known as House Creek; McKee to Jackson, January 6, 1814, Jackson Papers, reel 8, LOC; Certificate of Major Benj. S. Smoot, July 5, 1814, *Washington Republican*, August 24, 1814; Waselkov, "Return to the Holy Ground," 32.

55. Claiborne to Armstrong, January 1, 1814, in Brannan, *Official Letters*, 29; Halbert and Ball, *Creek War*, 251–52.

56 Brown, *Creek Indian History*, 118.

57. Russell to Gen. James Robertson, January 9, 1814, *Clarion*, March 1, 1814.

58. "Truth to the Editor," *Washington Republican*, June 29, 1814.

59. "To the Editor of the Washington Republican, Colonel Joseph Carson, July 30, 1814; Captain

Benjamin Smoot, July 25, 1814; and Captain Joseph Lister, July 23, 1814," *Washington Republican*, August 24, 1814.

60. Halbert and Ball, *Creek War*, 251–52; "Russell to Robertson, January 9, 1814," *Clarion*, March 1, 1814; Waselkov, "Return to the Holy Ground," 33–34 and Pickett, *History of Alabama*, 2:325–26 (deception by Cassel's pilot Sam Moniac, court-martial found Moniac at fault).

61. Halbert and Ball, *Creek War*, 252.

62. Brown, *Creek Indian History*, 119–20.

63. Dr. Neal Smith to James Smiley, January 8,1814, Dr. Neal Smith Letter, SPR8, ADAH; Caesar Deposition, January 16, 1814, Jackson Papers, reel 8, LOC (difficult to read, this could say eight "Negroes" rather than "eighteen"); Claiborne to Armstrong, January 1, 1814, in Brannan, *Official Letters*, 295; "Truth to the Editor," *Washington Republican*, June 29, 1814.

64. Halbert and Ball, *Creek War,* 258; Claiborne, *Mississippi*, 329; Henry S. Halbert, The Battle of the Holy Ground, Series YY: Tecumseh Papers (microfilm reel 119), Lyman Draper Collection, Wisconsin Historical Society.

65. "Russell to Robertson, January 9, 1814," *Clarion*, March 1, 1814.

66. Halbert and Ball, *Creek War*, 258.

67. Ibid., 256–57.

68. Ibid.; Claiborne to Armstrong, January 1, 1814, in Brannan, *Official Letters*, 295.

69. Austill, "Autobiography," 86–87.

70. "Russell to Robertson, January 9, 1814," *Clarion*, March 1, 1814.

71. Austill, "Autobiography," 87; Halbert and Ball, *Creek War*, 259; "Russell to Robertson, January 9, 1814," *Clarion*, March 1, 1814.

72. Pinckney to Jackson, January 9, 1814, Jackson Papers, reel 8, LOC. General Pinckney wrote General Jackson that some Indians had reported that a town of sixty houses had been destroyed by the "army of Mobile." Amos Wright concludes, rightly, that these towns were one and the same. Wright, *Historic Indian Towns*, 38. Claiborne to Armstrong, January 1, 1814, in Brannan, *Official Letters*, 295; A harsh critic of Claiborne's January 1, 1814, report of the Holy Ground expedition claims implausibly that the town did not exist, Truth to the Editor, *Washington Republican*, June 29, 1814.

73. Truth to the Editor, *Washington Republican*, June 29, 1814.

74. Halbert and Ball, *Creek War*, 260.

75. Robertson to Armstrong, February 1, 1814, Secretary of War Letters, National Archives.

76. Claiborne to Armstrong, January 1, 1814, in Brannan, *Official Letters*, 296.

77. Claiborne, *Life and Times*, 141; Claiborne to Secretary of War, January 14, 1814, in Claiborne, *Mississippi*, 340. However, it may well be that by now General Claiborne had achieved all he had planned to accomplish. Two weeks before he embarked on his expedition to "Weatherford's town," he wrote Andrew Jackson that "for want of support" for his army, he intended to return to Fort Claiborne "as soon as we have destroyed the villages in that Quarter." Claiborne to Jackson, December 6, 1813, Jackson Papers, reel 7, LOC. That he had done.

78. Claiborne, *Life and Times*, 141.

79. Austill, "Autobiography," 87.

80. Vaughn to Claiborne, December 31, 1813, in Halbert and Ball, *Creek War*, 262; Smith to Smiley, January 8, 1814, Dr. Neal Smith Letter, ADAH.

81. Claiborne to Armstrong, January 1, 1814, in Brannan, *Official Letters*, 295; Claiborne to Armstrong, January 24, 1814, Letterbook F, Claiborne Collection, MDAH.

82. Claiborne to Armstrong, January 24, 1814, Letterbook F, Claiborne Collection, MDAH.

83. Captain R. B. Moore to Claiborne, January 1, 1814, Letterbook F, Claiborne Collection, MDAH.

84. Ibid.

85. Claiborne, *Mississippi*, 330.

86. Soldiers to Brigadier-General Claiborne, March 22, 1813 [1814], in Claiborne, *Mississippi*, 331n1; Claiborne to Armstrong, January 24, 1814, Letterbook F, Claiborne Collection, MDAH.

87. Russell to the Officer commanding the Forces in the service of the U.S. destined to act against the Creeks, January 15, 1814, Secretary of War Papers, National Archives.

88. It may be that Moniac did deceive Cassels in order to save his family, who had joined the Red

Clubs and were at the Holy Ground. Waselkov, *Conquering Spirit*, 93–94. If so, he doesn't appear to have suffered any repercussions. Indeed, his son David became the first Native American graduate of West Point.

89. Pickett, *History of Alabama*, 2:325–26.

90. Russell to Claiborne, January 15, 1814, Letterbook F, Claiborne Collection, MDAH.

91. Ibid.

92. Russell to the Officer commanding the Forces, January 15, 1814, Secretary of War Papers, National Archives.

93. Notes from the lips of Dr. Thomas G. Holmes, Picket Papers, ADAH.

94. Ibid.

95. Claiborne, *Mississippi*, 340.

96. Pickett, *History of Alabama*, 2:324

97. Halbert and Ball, *Creek War*, 259.

98. Remini, *Andrew Jackson*, 1:163; Parton, *Life of Andrew Jackson*, 1:352–53.

99. Remini, *Andrew* Jackson, 163–64.

100. Pate, *Reminiscences of George Strother Gaines*, 163.

101. Ibid.; Pickett, *History of Alabama*, 2:235.

102. It is said that in summer 1813, in the Choctaw Nation, Moshulitubbee met with William Weatherford, who attempted to persuade the chief to join the Red Clubs, but that the cautious Choctaw declined the invitation. Waselkov, *Conquering Spirit*, 95.

103. John McKee to John Pitchlynn, September 14, 1813, Presidential Papers Microfilm, Andrew Jackson Papers, reel 6, LOC.

104. McKee to Pitchlynn, September 20, 1813, Jackson Papers, reel 6, LOC.

105. Governor Blount to the General Assembly, September 28, 1813, Jackson Papers, reel 6, LOC.

106. John Coffee to Mary Coffee, October 14, 1813, John Coffee Papers, Dyas Collection, box 13, reel 6, TSLA; Resolution of John McKee, Jackson Papers, reel 6, LOC.

107. McKee to Coffee, October 15, 1813, Jackson Papers, reel 7, LOC.

108. Resolution of McKee, Jackson Papers, reel 6, LOC.

109. Willie Blount to Jackson, November 23, 1813, Jackson Papers, reel 7, LOC; Smith to Jackson, November 23, 1813, Jackson Papers, reel 7, LOC.

110. Resolution of McKee, Jackson Papers, reel 6, LOC.

111. Ibid.; McKee to Coffee, October 21, 1813, Jackson Papers, reel 7, LOC.

112. Resolution of McKee, Jackson Papers, reel 6, LOC.

113. Blount to Jackson, November 9, 1813, quoting extract from Robertson to Blount, November 6, 1813, Jackson papers, reel 7, LOC.

114. Adam James to head Chiefs in the Creek Nation, November 29, 1813, Adam James Letter, SPR54, ADAH. After the war, Pushmataha, with the concurrence of other Choctaw leaders, granted the request of these warriors to return home from the Creek Nation. As the party of renegade Choctaws traveled toward the Choctaw Nation, Pushmataha's warriors ambushed them in a ravine and killed everyone. Halbert, "Creek War Incidents," 113.

115. Adam James to head Chiefs in the Creek Nation, November 29, 1813, Adam James Letter, SPR54, ADAH.

116. Resolution of McKee, Jackson Papers, reel 6, LOC.

117. Smith to Jackson, November 23, 1813, Jackson Papers, reel 7, LOC.

118. Claiborne to Jackson, November, 29, 1813, Jackson Papers, reel 7, LOC.

119. Resolution of McKee, Jackson Papers, reel 6, LOC.

120. Resolution of McKee, Jackson Papers, reel 6, LOC.

121. Ferdinand L. Claiborne to Jackson, December 6, 1813, Jackson Papers, reel 7, LOC.

122. Resolution of McKee, Jackson Papers, reel 6, LOC.

123. McKee to Jackson, January 6, 1814, Jackson Papers, reel 8, LOC.

124. Ibid.

125. James Allen to Jackson, January 9, 1814, Jackson Papers, reel 8, LOC.

126. George and James Colbert to Jackson, January 10, 1814, Jackson Papers, reel 8, LOC.

127. Resolution of McKee, Jackson Papers, reel 6, LOC.

128. Ibid.

129. McKee to Jackson, January 26, 1814, Jackson Papers, reel 8, LOC.

130. Resolution of McKee, Jackson Papers, reel 6, LOC.

131. John Durant to Alickander Durant, n.d., Ferdinand Leigh Claiborne Papers, ADAH; Waselkov, *Conquering Spirit*, 167–68.

132. Brown, *Creek Indian History*, 123.

133. Savannah Jack, by consensus the most bloodthirsty man in the nation, was also present. J. D. Dreisback, "A Man of Blood—One-Handed 'Savanna Jack,'" *Alabama Historical Reporter* 3, no. 7 (July 1885). He famously boasted that he and his warriors had killed so many women and children on the Tennessee and Georgia frontiers that if their blood were collected in a pool he could swim in it. Peter Brannon, "Through the Years, 'Old Augusta,'" *Montgomery Advertiser*, No. 6, August 30, 1931; Woodward, *Woodward's Reminiscences*, 90–91.

134. Brown, *Creek Indian History*, 129; Thomas Pinckney to Andrew Jackson, January 9, 1814, Presidential Papers Microfilm, Andrew Jackson Papers, reel 8, LOC.

135. Brown, *Creek Indian History*, 127–28. Andrew Jackson, however, reported to General Pinckney that the Creeks he had recently encountered had plenty of ammunition. Jackson to Pinckney, February 1814, Record Group 107, Letters Received by the Secretary of War, Registered Series, 1801–1860, Microfilm Publication #221, National Archives; John Floyd to Jackson, January 2, 1814, Jackson Papers, reel 8, LOC.

136. Gilbert Russell to Ferdinand Claiborne, January 15, 1814, Letterbook F., J. F. H. Claiborne Collection, MDAH; Russell to Pinckney, February 21, 1814, Secretary of War Letters, National Archives; Brown, *Creek Indian History*, 128.

137. John Floyd to Mary Floyd, December 24, 1813, in "Letters of John Floyd," *Georgia Historical Quarterly* 33:4 (1949): 238.

138. Pinckney to Secretary of War, December 10, 1813, SOW Letters, National Archives.

139. Floyd to Jackson, January 2, 1814, Jackson Papers, reel 8, LOC; Peter Early to David Blackshear, January 4, 1814, Secretary of War Letters, National Archives; Pinckney to Floyd, January 5, 1814, Secretary of War Letters, National Archives.

140. Benjamin Hawkins to Pinckney, January 14, 1814, Secretary of War Letters, National Archives.

141. Floyd to Pinckney, January 3, 1814, Secretary of War Letters, National Archives.

142. Talk of the friendly Chiefs, January 5, 1814, Secretary of War Letters, National Archives, reel 221.

143. Floyd to Pinckney, January 11, 1814, Secretary of War Letters, National Archives.

144. Ibid.

145. Floyd to Pinckney, January 14, 1814, Secretary of War Letters, National Archives; Pinckney to Floyd, January 17, 1813, Secretary of War Letters, National Archives.

146. Floyd to Pinckney, January 18, 1814, Secretary of War Letters, National Archives.

147. Ibid.

148. Caesar Statement, January 16, 1814, Jackson Papers, reel 8, LOC.

149. Woodward, *Woodward's Reminiscences*, 115, Caesar Statement, January 16, 1814, Jackson Papers, reel 8, LOC.

150. Pinckney to Jackson, January 26, 1814, Secretary of War Letters, National Archives; Floyd to Jackson, February 4, 1814, Jackson Papers, reel 8, LOC.

151. Floyd to Pinckney, January 23, 1814, Secretary of War Letters, National Archives; Floyd to Pinckney, January 27, 1814, Secretary of War Letters, National Archives.

152. Floyd to Pinckney, January 21, 1814, Secretary of War Letters, National Archives; Pinckney to Jackson, January 23, 1814, Secretary of War Letters, National Archives.

153. Floyd to Pinckney, January 27, 1814, Secretary of War Letters, National Archives.

154. Floyd to Jackson, January 24, 1814, Secretary of War Letters, National Archives.

155. Peter Brannon, ed., "Journal of James A. Tait for the Year 1813," *Alabama Historical Quarterly* 2:4 (1940): 438.

156. Floyd to Pinckney, January 27, 1814, Secretary of War Letters, National Archives; Brannon, "Journal of James Tait," 438.

157. Floyd to Pinckney, January 27, 1814, Secretary of War Letters, National Archives; Brannon, "Journal of James Tait," 438.

158. Floyd to Pinckney, January 27, 1814, Secretary of War Letters, National Archives.

159. "Camp Defiance," Alabama Forts, http://www.northamericanforts.com/East/al.html#defiance, accessed September 3, 2015.

160. Floyd to Jackson, February 4, 1814, Jackson Papers, reel 8, LOC.

161. Brannon, "Journal of James Tait," 438.

162. Brown, *Creek Indian History*, 128–29; Floyd to Pinckney, January 27, 1814, Secretary of War Letters, National Archives.

163. Brown, *Creek Indian History*, 129.

164. Woodward, *Woodward's Reminiscences*, 101–2. This plan had the support of Savannah Jack, by consensus the most evil man in the nation. Shortly before the meeting of the Creek leaders, he had simply and directly advised Weatherford that Creek strategy should be to kill as many Americans as they could. Ibid., 90.

165. Brown, *Creek Indian History*, 128; Woodward, *Woodward's Reminiscences,* 101–2. Stiggins claims, in contrast to Woodward, that Weatherford proposed that a forlorn hope of three hundred warriors, led by Paddy Walsh, rush the American officers who Weatherford knew typically gathered in the center of camp and slaughter them in close-quarters fighting. While this attack took place, the remaining Creeks would assault the rest of the camp. Once the American officers were dispatched, the private soldiers would be like a snake without a head, easy to chop apart as it writhed blind and directionless about the grounds of the camp. Walsh, not entirely without reason, saw this plan as one designed by Weatherford to get him (Walsh) killed, and said so, foolishly adding that Weatherford himself would not dare lead such an attack. The discussion from that point on degenerated into an increasingly bitter exchange of insults between Weatherford and Walsh.

166. Woodward, *Woodward's Reminiscences*, 101–2.

167. Brown, *Creek Indians History*, 131.

168. Ibid., 131–32; Woodward, *Woodward's Reminiscences*, 102.

169. Henry S. Halbert, Letters on Fort Mims, November 10, 1882, to March 3, 1887, Series YY: Tecumseh Papers (microfilm Reel 119), Lyman Draper Collection, Wisconsin Historical Society.

170. Floyd to Pinckney, January 27, 1814, Secretary of War Letters, National Archives. At the same time, at a place a mile or so from the Red Club encampment called Pole Cat Springs, a still-fuming Weatherford and his companions heard the commotion but continued riding toward home. Woodward, *Woodward's Reminiscences*, 102.

171. Halbert, Letters on Fort Mims, Draper Collection, Wisconsin Historical Society.

172. Floyd to Pinckney, January 27, 1814, Secretary of War Letters, National Archives.

173. "Journal, Milledgeville," *Georgia Journal*, March 16, 1814.

174. Floyd to Pinckney, January 27, 1814, Secretary of War Letters, National Archives.

175. Halbert, Letters on Fort Mims, Draper Collection, Wisconsin Historical Society.

176. Floyd to Pinckney, January 31, 1814, Secretary of War Letters, National Archives.

177. William J. Northern, *Men of Mark in Georgia: A Complete and Elaborate History of the State from Its Settlement to the Present Time, Chiefly Told in Biographies, and Autobiographies of the Most Eminent Men of Each Period of Georgia's Progress and Development, Vol. 2* (Atlanta: A.B. Caldwell, 1910), 379.

178. Floyd to Pinckney, January 27, 1814, Secretary of War Letters, National Archives.

179. Floyd to Pinckney, January 31, 1814, Secretary of War Letters, National Archives; Charles Williamson, Hospital Surgeon, List of Killed and Wounded appended to Floyd to Pinckney, January 27, 1814, Secretary of War Letters, National Archives.

180. Floyd to Pinckney, January 31, 1814, Secretary of War Letters, National Archives; Woodward, *Woodward's Reminiscences*, 48.

181. Floyd to Pinckney, January 31, 1814, Secretary of War Letters, National Archives.

182. Halbert, Letters on Fort Mims, Draper Collection, Wisconsin Historical Society.

183. Woodward, *Woodward's Reminiscences,* 102; Floyd to Pinckney, January 27, 1814, Secretary of War Letters, National Archives.

184. Floyd to Pinckney, January 27, 1814, Secretary of War Letters, National Archives.

185. Ibid.; Floyd to Pinckney, January 31, 1814, Secretary of War Papers, National Archives.

186. Henry S. Halbert, The Battle of Calabee Swamp, Series YY, Tecumseh Papers, microfilm reel 119, Lyman Draper Collection, Wisconsin Historical Society.

187. Floyd to Pinckney, February 2, 1814, Secretary of War Papers, National Archives.

188. Floyd to Pinckney, January 31, 1814, Secretary of War Letters, National Archives.

189. Williamson, see List of Killed and Wounded, Floyd to Pinckney, January 27, 1813, Secretary of War Letters, National Archives.

190. Brannon, "Journal of James Tait," 438–39.

191. Floyd to Pinckney, February 1, 1814, Secretary of War Letters, National Archives.

192. Floyd to Pinckney, January 31, 1814, Secretary of War Letters, National Archives; Floyd to Pinckney, February 1, 1814, Secretary of War Letters, National Archives.

193. Floyd to Pinckney, February 2, 1814, Secretary of War Letters, National Archives.

194. Floyd to Pinckney, January 27, 1814, Secretary of War Letters, National Archives.

195. Floyd to Pinckney, February 1, 1814, Secretary of War Letters, National Archives; Floyd to Pinckney, January 31, 1814, Secretary of War Letters, National Archives.

196. Floyd to Pinckney, February 2, 1814, Secretary of War Letters, National Archives.

197. Steven Earl Coulter, *Our Quaker Kin and Allied Families: Ancestors and Descendants of Adam Davis (1781–1861) and His Wife, Lydia Commons (1781–1841)* (Des Moines: Coulter, 1977), 137.

198. Woodward, *Woodward's Reminiscences,* 90.

199. Halbert, Battle of Calabee Swamp.

200. *Georgia Journal,* March 16, 1814.

201. Ibid.

202. Brown, *Creek Indian History,* 132.

203. Floyd to Pinckney, February 6, 1814, Secretary of War Letters, National Archives.

204. Brown, *Creek Indian History,* 132.

205. "Extract of a letter from Col. Benj. Hawkins to Maj. Gen. Pinckney, dated Camp near Fort Mitchell, Feb. 16," *Georgia Journal,* February 23, 1814.

8. Jackson Overreaches

1. Parton, *Life of Andrew Jackson,* 1:446.

2. Ibid., 446–47.

3. McCown, "'J. Hartsell Memora,'" 127.

4. Reid and Eaton, *Life of Andrew Jackson,* 62–63.

5. Jackson to the Commanding General of Division, November 12, 1813, Presidential Papers Microfilm, Andrew Jackson Papers, reel 7, LOC.

6. 2nd Regiment of Volunteers to Jackson, November 13, 1813, Jackson Papers, reel 7, LOC.

7. Parton, *Life of Andrew Jackson,* 1:459–60.

8. Jackson to Willie Blount, November 14, 1813, in Moser and MacPherson, *Papers of Andrew Jackson,* 2:453–54.

9. William Martin to Jackson, November 14, 1813, Jackson Papers, reel 7, LOC.

10. William Martin, *The Self Vindication of Colonel William Martin: Against Certain Charges and Aspersions Made Against Him by Gen. Andrew Jackson and Others, in Relation to Sundry Transactions in the Campaign Against the Creek Indians in the Year 1813* (Nashville: John Simpson, 1829), 38–40.

11. Ibid.

12. John Coffee, Brigade Orders, November 15, 1813, Jackson Papers, reel 7, LOC.

13. Jackson to John Cocke, November 18, 1813, in Moser and MacPherson, *Papers of Andrew Jackson,* 1:457; William Carroll to Jackson, November 20, 1813, in Moser and MacPherson, *Papers of Andrew Jackson,* 1:458–59.

14. Reid and Eaton, *Life of Andrew Jackson*, 69–70.

15. Ibid., 70.; Royall, *Letters from Alabama*, 69, 115.

16. One officer wrote in his diary that men were swearing to kill Jackson if he tried to make them stay three months. McCown, "'J. Hartsell Memora,'" 131.

17. Parton, *Life of Andrew Jackson*, 463–64.

18. Ibid.

19. Royall, *Letters from Alabama*, 116.

20. Jackson to Blount, December 15, 1813, in Moser and MacPherson, *Papers of Andrew Jackson*, 2:489.

21. Reid to Father, November 21, 1813, John Reid Papers, LOC.

22. Jackson to Thomas Pinckney, December 13, 1813, Jackson Papers, reel 7, LOC.

23. Carroll to Jackson, November 20, 1813, in Moser and MacPherson, *Papers of Andrew Jackson*, 2:458–59.

24. Martin to Jackson, December 4, 1813, in Moser and MacPherson, *Papers of Andrew Jackson*, 2:467; Martin, *Self Vindication*, 10–14.

25. Reid to Betsy Reid, November 21, 1813, John Reid Papers, LOC.

26. Reid and Eaton, *Life of Andrew Jackson*, 83–84.

27. Martin, *Self Vindication*, 32.

28. Ibid., 14–15.

29. Jackson to Rachel Jackson, December 14, 1813, in Moser and MacPherson, *Papers of Andrew Jackson*, 2:486.

30. Statement of certain Tennessee Volunteers, Parton, *Life of Andrew Jackson*, 632.

31. Reid and Eaton, *Life of Andrew Jackson*, 84–85.

32. Ibid.; Parton, *Life of Andrew Jackson*, 471–72.

33. Jackson to Blount, December 12, 1813, in Moser and MacPherson, *Papers of Andrew Jackson*, 2:479–80; Jackson to the 1st Brigade, Tennessee Volunteer Infantry, December 13, 1813, in Moser and MacPherson, *Papers of Andrew Jackson*, 2:482–84.

34. Parton, *Life of Andrew Jackson*, 632.

35. Jackson to Rachel Jackson, December 19, 1813, in Moser and MacPherson, *Papers of Andrew Jackson*, 2:494.

36. Given Jackson's Scottish-Irish heritage, John Coffee voiced an odd view of the matter. As he remarked to his wife, Mary, about General Hall's command's departure from camp, "thus we are clear of the Scotch Irish in that quarter." Then, as if he had said too much in writing, Coffee added a postscript to his letter, cautioning his wife not to show his letter to anyone else but a Captain Parks. Coffee to Mary Coffee, December 19, 1813, John Coffee Papers, Dyas Collection, box 13, reel 5, TSLA.

37. Brigade Orders, November 22, 1813, Jackson Papers, reel 6, LOC.

38. Coffee to Mary Coffee, December 19, 1813, John Coffee Papers, Dyas Collection, box 13, reel 5, TSLA.

39. Jackson to Coffee, December 16, 1813, John Coffee Papers, Dyas Collection, box 13, reel 5, TSLA; Brigade Orders, December 17, 1813, John Coffee Papers, Dyas Collection, box 13, reel 5, TSLA.

40. Jackson to Coffee, December 16, 1813, John Coffee Papers, Dyas Collection, box 13, reel 5, TSLA; Coffee to Jackson, December 20, 1813, John Coffee Papers, Dyas Collection, box 13, reel 5, TSLA; John Alcorn to Coffee, December 20, 1813, John Coffee Papers, Dyas Collection, box 13, reel 5, TSLA; Robert Allen to Coffee, December 20 1813, John Coffee Papers, Dyas Collection, box 13, reel 5, TSLA.

41. Coffee to Jackson, December 22, 1813, in Moser and MacPherson, *Papers of Andrew Jackson*, 2:497.

42. Jackson to Rachel Jackson, December 19, 1813, in Moser and MacPherson, *Papers of Andrew Jackson*, 2:494.

43. Alcorn to Coffee, December 20, 1813, John Coffee Papers, Dyas Collection, box 13, reel 5, TSLA; Allen to Coffee, December 20 1813, John Coffee Papers, Dyas Collection, box 13, reel 5, TSLA.

44. Coffee to Jackson, December 20, 1813, John Coffee Papers, Dyas Collection, box 13, reel 5, TSLA.

45. Jackson to Coffee, December 23, 1813, John Coffee Papers, Dyas Collection, box 13, reel 5, TSLA; Jackson to Coffee, December 25, 1813, John Coffee Papers, Dyas Collection, box 13, reel 5, TSLA.

46. McCown, "'J. Hartsell Memora,'" 123–26.

47. Andrew Jackson to Willie Blount, December 15, 1813, in Moser and MacPherson, *Papers of Andrew Jackson*, 2:488.

48. Francis Huger, Troops under the Command of Maj. Gen'l Jackson, December 13, 1813, Secretary of War Papers, National Archives.

49. Jackson to Pinckney, December 26, 1813, Jackson Papers, reel 8, LOC.

50. Jackson to William Berkeley Lewis, December 19, 1813, in Moser and MacPherson, *Papers of Andrew Jackson*, 2:495–96.

51. Jackson to Blount, December 19, 1813, Jackson Papers, reel 7, LOC.

52. Path Killer to Jackson, December 28, 1813, Jackson Papers, reel 8, LOC.

53. Jackson to John Cocke, December 28, 1813, in Moser and MacPherson, *Papers of Andrew Jackson*, 2:511–12.

54. McCown, 'J. Hartsell Memora,' 133–34.

55. William Carroll to Jackson, December 23, 1813, in Moser and MacPherson, *Papers of Andrew Jackson*, 2:500. Carroll singled out for particular scorn, and warned Jackson about, a Colonel Stump who had claimed he had raised a troop of forty men but delivered none of them. In a critical moment in the upcoming campaign, Carroll's evaluation of the man would be proven all too correct. Ibid., 2:501–502.

56. William Carroll to Jackson, December 23, 1813, in Moser and MacPherson, *Papers of Andrew Jackson*, 2:500–502.

57. Jackson to Blount, January 2, 1814, in Moser and MacPherson, *Papers of Andrew Jackson*, 3:4–5.

58. Jackson had put this question to the governor back on November 20, and Blount had replied on November 24 with the evasive answer that he lacked authority to decide the issue. Blount's letter, however, was mislaid in Huntsville and did not reach Jackson until December 31. Jackson to Pinckney, December 31, 1813, in Moser and MacPherson, *Papers of Andrew Jackson*, 1:518–20.

59. Blount to Jackson, December 26, 1813, Jackson Papers, reel 7, LOC.

60. Remini, *Andrew Jackson*, 1:203.

61. Jackson to Blount, December 28, 1813, in Reid and Eaton, *Life of Andrew Jackson*, 101–6.

62. Ibid., 105–6.

63. Jackson to Hugh Lawson White, January 6, 1814, in Moser and MacPherson, *Papers of Andrew Jackson*, 3:9. Hugh White was the son of General James White, the leader of the murderous attack on the Hillabee towns.

64. Reid and Eaton, *Life of Andrew Jackson*, 110; William Sitler to Jackson, January 4, 1814, Jackson Papers, reel 8, LOC. Reid and Eaton use the name Kearley rather than Kirby. Kirby is used here because that was the name used in contemporary documents describing the incident.

65. William Sitler to Jackson, January 4, 1814, Jackson Papers, reel 8, LOC.

66. Ibid.

67. Reid and Eaton, *Life of Andrew Jackson*, 112.

68. Jackson to White, January 6, 1814, in Moser and MacPherson, *Papers of Andrew Jackson*, 3:9; Jackson to Blount, January 2, 1814, in ibid., 3:4–5; Jackson to Rachel Jackson, December 19, 1813, in ibid., 2:494.

69. Jackson to John Coffee, December 27, 1813, Jackson Papers, reel 7, LOC.

70. Coffee to Mary Coffee, December 27, 1813, John Coffee Papers, Dyas Collection, box 13, reel 5, TSLA.

71. Brigade Order, January 6, 1814, Jackson Papers, reel 8, LOC.

72. Nicolas Perkins to Coffee, January 6, 1814, Jackson Papers, reel 8, LOC.

73. Coffee to Mary Coffee, January 3, 1814, John Coffee Papers, Dyas Collection, box 13, reel 5, TSLA.

74. Coffee to Jackson, January 7, 1814, Jackson Papers, reel 8, LOC.

75. Higgins to Coffee, January 13, 1814, John Coffee Papers, Dyas Collection, box 13, reel 5, TSLA.

76. Coffee to Jackson, January 14, 1814, Jackson Papers, reel 8, LOC.

77. Coffee to Jackson, January 15, 1814, Jackson Papers, reel 8, LOC.

78. Reid and Eaton, *Life of Andrew Jackson*, 122–23.

79. Jackson to Pinckney, December 31, 1813, in Moser and MacPherson, *Papers of Andrew Jackson*, 2:519.

80. McCown, "'J. Hartsell Memora,'" 135.

81. Jackson to Pinckney, December 31, 1813, in Moser and MacPherson, *Papers of Andrew Jackson*, 2:519–20.

82. Reid and Eaton, *Life of Andrew Jackson*, 116.

83. Jackson to Rachel Jackson, December 29, 1813, in Moser and MacPherson, *Papers of Andrew Jackson*, 2:515; Remini, *Andrew Jackson*, 1:224.

84. Reid died suddenly in 1819, probably of pneumonia, while visiting his family home in Bedford, Virginia.

85. Andrew Jackson to Hugh Lawson White, January 6, 1814, in Moser and MacPherson, *Papers of Andrew Jackson*, 3:9.

86. This group was a curious and unique band of brothers. It consisted of a number of Jackson's officers, including General Coffee, whose men had earlier abandoned them and gone home. Although they had no troops to command, they refused to abandon Jackson. One of these men, Captain Hamilton, had even joined the artillery company as a private soldier. Moser and MacPherson, *Papers of Andrew Jackson*, 3:300, 3:304.

87. Jackson to Thomas Pinckney, January 29, 1814, in Brannan, *Official Letters*, 300; Jackson to John Coffee, January 4, 1814, Andrew Jackson Papers, reel 8, LOC.

88. Brannan, *Official Letters*, 299; Jackson to Coffee, October 7, 1813, Jackson Papers, reel 6, LOC; Reid to Nathan Reid, January 14, 1814, Reid Papers, LOC.

89. Reid to Nathan Reid, January 14, 1814, Reid Papers, LOC; David Crockett, in his autobiography, baldly claimed that he had joined Jackson's new campaign as one of Russell's company of spies. Lately equipped with winter clothes and fresh mounts, Crockett wrote that he was ready to resume his aborted military career. And, as he boasted, there was something in him that liked to be in the thickest danger. Crockett, *Narrative*, 96. Unfortunately for this teller of tall tales, there is no record of his rejoining Jackson's army for this expedition. James Atkins Shackford, *David Crockett: The Man and the Legend* (Lincoln: University of Nebraska Press, 1994), 28. Shackford surmises that Crockett relied on the accounts of others, such as Reid and Eaton.

90. Reid to Nathan Reid, January 14, 1814, Reid Papers, LOC.

91. Pinckney to Jackson, January 9, 1814, Jackson Papers, reel 8, LOC.

92. Blount to the brigadier Genl Oldest in commission, January 3, 1814, Jackson Papers, reel 8, LOC.

93. Quotes in Coffee to Mary Coffee, November 4, 1813, John Coffee Papers, Dyas Collection, box 13, reel 5, TSLA. John Reid was not so sanguine about the outcome of the expedition. He feared that the fighting would cause severe losses on both sides, and because of the size of the American army, it would eventually have to make a dangerous retreat from Creek country to Fort Strother. Journal entry, January 9, 1814, Reid Papers, LOC.

94. Jackson to Pinckney, January 29, 1814, in Brannan, *Official Letters*, 299.

95. Richard Keith Call Journal, Richard Keith Call Collection, N2013-5, FSA.

96. Jackson to Pinckney, January 29, 1814, in Brannan, *Official Letters*, 300.

97. Ibid.

98. Call Journal, Call Collection, N2013-5, FSA.

99. Ibid.

100. Here, as in the other battles in the Creek War, the exact number of Red Club participants remains elusive. Albert Pickett, who interviewed several former Red Clubs who fought in the battles of Emuckfau and Enitachopco creeks, states "with confidence" that no more than five hun-

dred Red Clubs were involved. Pickett, *History of Alabama*, 2:336. Pickett's opinion is supported by a report received by General Floyd after the battle of Calebee Creek, which took place the same week as the Jackson battles, that a number of Okfuskees had participated in Floyd's battle. Floyd to Pinckney, February 6, 1814, Record Group 107, Letters Received by the Secretary of War, Registered Series, 1801–1860, Microfilm Publication #221, National Archives.

101. Jackson to Blount, March 28, 1814, in Brannan, *Official Letters*, 322.

102. Dickens, *Archeological Investigations*, 198.

103. Jackson to Pinckney, January 29, 1814, in Brannan, *Official Letters*, 300.

104. Ibid.

105. Ibid.; Reid to Nathan Reid, February, 14, 1814, Reid Papers, LOC.

106. Jackson to Pinckney, January 29, 1814, Brannan, *Official Letters*, 301; Jackson to Rachel Jackson, January 28, 1814, in Moser and MacPherson, *Papers of Andrew Jackson*, 3:18. As a window into Andrew Jackson's priorities in his life, it is notable that after the expedition ended, he wrote to his wife, Rachel, about the fight a day before he wrote to his superior, General Pinckney.

107. Jackson to Pinckney, January 29, 1814, Brannan, *Official Letters*, 302.

108. Ibid., 301.

109. Call Journal, Call Collection, N2013-5, FSA; Jackson to Pinckney, January 29, 1814, Brannan, *Official Letters*, 301.

110. Ibid.; John Reid to Nathan Reid, February 14, 1814, Reid Papers, LC. Reid and Eaton, *Life of Andrew Jackson*, 128–30. Also known as the Kealedji, the Chealegran people lived at the mouth of a creek that emptied into the Tallapoosa River fifteen miles upstream of Tuckabatchee. Theoretically neutral in the war, they were quietly at odds with their Red Club neighbors, who had probably forcibly conscripted them into the Red Club army. This uneasy relationship may explain why the Kealedji abandoned the fight at their first opportunity. In any event, their desertion materially compromised the Red Club's plan of attack. As John Reid tersely put it, had the Kealedji not slipped off, "the contest might have terminated less advantageously."

111. Reid and Eaton, *Life of Andrew Jackson*, 127.

112. Jackson to Rachel Jackson, January 28, 1814, in Moser and MacPherson, *Papers of Andrew Jackson*, 3:18.

113. Jackson to Pinckney, January 29, 1814, in Brannan, *Official Letters*, 301; Reid and Eaton, *Life of Andrew Jackson*, 127–28.

114. Call Journal, Call Collection, N2013-5, FSA; Reid to Nathan Reid, February 14, 1814, Reid Papers, LOC; Reid and Eaton, *Life of Andrew Jackson*, 128–129.

115. Jackson to Pinckney, January 29, 1814, Brannan, *Official Letters*, 301–2.

116. Reid and Eaton, *Life of Andrew Jackson*, 128.

117. Ibid., 129.

118. Coffee to Mary Coffee, January 30, 1814, Coffee Papers, TSLA; Call Journal, Call Collection, N2013-5, FSA.

119. Jackson to Pinckney, January 29, 1814, Brannan, *Official Letters*, 302.

120. Jackson to Floyd, January 30, 1814, Jackson Papers, reel 8, LOC.

121. Jackson to Pinckney, January 29, 1814, Brannan, *Official Letters*, 300–302. One participant in the expedition, Ephraim Foster, wrote his father several days later that after this second battle, the army was "too much weakened to protect our wounded, & advance any further into the enemy's country." Ephraim Foster to Robert C. Foster, January 29, 1815, Horseshoe Bend Historical Files, Dr. Kathryn H. Braund Papers, Horseshoe Bend National Military Park.

122. Reid and Eaton, *Life of Andrew Jackson*, 130; Reid to Nathan Reid, February 14, 1814, Reid Papers, LOC.

123. Jackson to Pinckney, January 29, 1814, Brannan, *Official Letters*, 302.

124. Ibid.

125. Reid and Eaton, *Life of Andrew Jackson*, 131–32.

126. Call Journal, Call Collection, N2013-5, FSA.

127. During the battle, Crockett describes Indians hidden behind a large tree. Crockett, *Narrative*, 99.

128. Jackson to Rachel Jackson, January 28, 1814, in Moser and McPherson, *Papers of Andrew Jackson*, 3:19.

129. Call Journal, Call Collection, N2013-5, FSA. At one point in the long night, the Creeks ceased their devilment. At last men began to drift off to a much-needed sleep. Suddenly the frantic cry of "Indians within the encampment" drove them terrified to their feet, hands clutching muskets, heads twisting frantically about searching for the enemy. It was a false but comedic alarm. A soldier gripped by a nightmare believed that the Creeks were within the walls and, still sleeping, ran about the camp shouting the alarm until a sharp encounter with a tree knocked him senseless, ending his cries. Ibid.

130. Jackson to Pinckney, January 29, 1814, in Brannan, *Official Letters*, 302.

131. Reid and Eaton, *Life of Andrew Jackson*, 132.

132. Jackson to Rachel Jackson, January 28, 1814, Moser and MacPherson, *Papers of Andrew Jackson*, 3:19.

133. Reid and Barton, *Life of Andrew Jackson*, 132.

134. Call Journal, Call Collection, N2013-5, FSA; Jackson to Pinckney, January 29, 1814, in Brannan, *Official Letters*, 302–3. Perkins's appointment was somewhat of a surprise given that less than two weeks earlier, he and Jackson's favorite, John Coffee, had been embroiled in an ugly spat.

135. Reid and Eaton, *Life of Andrew Jackson*, 135.

136. Jackson to Pinckney, January 29, 1814, in Brannan, *Official Letters*, 302; Reid and Eaton, *Life of Andrew Jackson*, 132.

137. Call Journal, Call Papers, N2013-5, FSA.

138. Reid to Nathan Reid, February 14, 1814, John Reid Papers, LOC.

139. Jackson to Pinckney, January 29, 1814, in Brannan, *Official Letters*, 303.

140. Record of Court Martial Proceedings Against Colonel Perkins, January 29, 1814, Jackson Papers, reel 8, LOC.

141. John Stump to Jackson, January 31, 1814, Jackson Papers, reel 8, LOC. After the battle, Jackson wasted no time initiating court-martial proceedings against Colonel Stump and Colonel Perkins for desertion of their posts and cowardice. The army arrived at Fort Strother on January 27, 1814, and the trial of the two colonels was held two days later. Perkins was acquitted and returned to his command. Stump was found guilty and cashiered from the service. In light of what happened, Colonel Carroll turns out to have been prescient in warning Jackson about Stump's character. In fairness to Stump, he alleged that the chief witness against him at trial had lied. Court Martial Proceedings Against Perkins, January 29, 1814, Jackson Papers, reel 8, LOC; Stump to Jackson, January 31, 1814, Jackson Papers, reel 8, LOC.

142. Pickett, *History of Alabama*, 2:333; Jackson to Pinckney, January 29, 1814, in Brannan, *Official Letters*, 304.

143. Reid and Eaton, *Life of Andrew Jackson*, 134.

144. Ibid., 136.

145. Jackson to Rachel Jackson, January 28, 1814, in Moser and MacPherson, *Papers of Andrew Jackson*, 3:19–20.

146. Reid and Eaton, *Life of Andrew Jackson*, 134.

147. Ibid., 134, 136.

148. Call Journal, Call Collection, N2013-5, FSA; Crockett, *Narrative*, 98; Jackson to Rachel Jackson, January 28, 1814, in Moser and MacPherson, *Papers of Andrew Jackson*, 3:20.

149. Call Journal, Call Collection, N2013-5, FSA; Jackson to Pinckney, January 29, 1814, in Brannan, *Official Letters*, 303–4.

150. Jackson to Pinckney, January 29, 1814, in Brannan, *Official Letters*, 303–04, Call Journal, Call Collection, N2013-5, FSA. Richard Keith Call, who was a member of the artillery company and in a good position to know, claimed that the cannon blasts had little effect on the Red Clubs, who "fought behind trees" and that the cannoneers were saved by a horseback charge of riflemen. Call, who had every reason to tout the importance of his and his comrades' contribution to the battle, may be correct. But other participants in the battle, from Jackson on down, credited the artillerymen with saving the army. (As one soldier later said, it is "impossible to bestow too much praise

on the Artillery Boys.") Ephraim Foster to Robert C. Foster, January 29, 1813, Horseshoe Bend Historical Files, Braund Papers, Horseshoe Bend National Military Park.

151. Reid and Eaton. *Life of Andrew Jackson,* 136.

152. Susan Marie Abram, *"Souls in the Treetops": Cherokee War, Masculinity, and Community, 1760–1820* (Ann Arbor, MI: UMI Dissertation Publishing, 2009), 139.

153. Jackson to Pinckney, January 29, 1814, in Brannan, *Official Letters,* 303–4.

154. Reid and Eaton, *Life of Andrew Jackson,* 135; Pickett, *History of Alabama,* 2:334. Jackson also wrote that the Indians dropped their packs in the retreat, an account that is also at odds with the Creeks' usual mode of fighting: stripped to a breechcloth, painted, and carrying only their weapons. Jackson to Pinckney, January, 29, 1814, in Brannan, *Official Letters,* 304.

155. Jackson to Pinckney, January, 29, 1814, in Brannan, *Official Letters,* 304.

156. Ibid., 304; Jackson to Rachel Jackson, January 28, 1814, in Moser and MacPherson, *Papers of Andrew Jackson,* 3:20.

157. Jackson to Pinckney, January 29, 1814, in Brannan, *Official Letters,* 304; Jackson to Rachel Jackson, January 29, 1814, in Moser and MacPherson, *Papers of Andrew Jackson,* 3:20.

158. John Cocke to Peter Early, January 28, 1814, Telamon Cuyler Collection, box 77, folder 30, Hargrett Rare Book and Manuscript Library, University of Georgia Libraries; Call Journal, Call Collection, N2013-5, FSA.

159. Reid and Eaton, *Life of Andrew Jackson,* 136.

160. Crockett, *Narrative,* 98–99.

161. Shelby Foote, *The Civil War: A Narrative* (New York: Random House, 1963), 2:34.

162. Floyd to Pinckney, January 27, 1814, Record Group 107, Letters Received by the Secretary of War, Registered Series, 1801–1860, Microfilm Publication #221, National Archives.

163. Ibid.

164. Jackson to Pinckney, January 29, 1814, Jackson Papers, reel 8, LOC; Reid to Nathan Reid, February 14, 1814, Reid Papers, LOC; Jackson to Coffee, January 30, 1814, Jackson Papers, reel 8, LOC.

165. Crockett, *Narrative,* 99.

166. Pickett, *History of Alabama,* 2:335.

9. Twilight of the Gods

1. General Claiborne would spend the short remainder of his life defending his military reputation and attempting to remain solvent. The last of his funds were spent on an illumination of his home—Soldier's Retreat—celebrating the American victory over the British at the Battle of New Orleans.

2. Gilbert C. Russell to Ferdinand Claiborne, January 15, 1814, Letterbook F, Claiborne Collection, MDAH; Claiborne, *Mississippi,* 340.

3. Russell to Claiborne, January 12, 1814, Record Group 107, Letters Received by the Secretary of War, Registered Series, 1801–1860, Microfilm Publication #221, National Archives.

4. Ibid.

5. Ibid.

6. Ibid. According to the letter Russell had written to Claiborne the day before, the colonel planned to forego his inspection of the boat-building operation at Fort Peirce and lead the hunt for Peter McQueen and his party. Russell to Claiborne, January 15, 1814, Letterbook F, Claiborne Collection, MDAH.

7. Russell to the Commander of the U.S. forces in the Creek War, January 16, 1814, Secretary of War Letters, National Archives.

8. Thomas Pinckney to Russell, February 1, 1814, Secretary of War Letters, National Archives.

9. Russell to Pinckney, February 21, 1814, Secretary of War Letters, National Archives.

10. Claiborne, *Life and Times,* 143; Notes furnished by Col G. W. Creagh, 1847, Section 2, Notes, LPR185, Albert J. Pickett Papers, ADAH; soldier counts in Russell to Pinckney, February 21, 1814, Secretary of War Letters, National Archives; Austill, "Autobiography," 87.

11. Russell to Pinckney, February 21, 1814, Secretary of War Letters, National Archives; Austill, "Autobiography," 87; Notes furnished by Creagh, Pickett Papers, ADAH.

12. Russell to Pinckney, February 21, 1814, Secretary of War Letters, National Archives.

13. Ibid.

14. Notes furnished by Creagh, Pickett Papers, ADAH; Russell to Pinckney, February 21, 1814, Secretary of War Letters; Anonymous, *A Narrative of the Life and Death of Lieut. Joseph Morgan Wilcox, Who was Massacred by the Creek Indians, On the Alabama River, (Miss. Ter.) on the 15th of January, 1814* (Marietta, OH: R. Prentiss, 1816), 5. The foregoing documents provide the most reliable and trustworthy accounts of Wilcox's tragic expedition to find Captain Dinkins. They were written shortly after the events in question from information provided by eyewitnesses.

15. Claiborne, *Life and Times*, 143; Russell to Pinckney, February 21, 1814, Secretary of War Letters, National Archives.

16. Ibid.

17. Ibid.; Claiborne, *Life and Times*, 143–44; Pickett, *History of Alabama*, 2:327. In Pickett's account, Wilcox leads the Dinkins expedition with five men, including two Wilsons (who escape the Indian encounter unharmed). Wilcox and his other three companions are tomahawked and scalped; Russell to Pinckney, February 21, 1814, Secretary of War Letters, National Archives.

18. Claiborne, *Life and Times*, 143–44; Pickett, *History of Alabama*, 2:327.

19. Ibid.; Claiborne, *Life and Times*, 144. Surprisingly, Sam Dale, in his account of this event, does not censure his soldier for fleeing. Colonel Russell, in his February 21 letter to General Pinckney, simply reports the flight but does not characterize it. In contrast, an anonymous author whose "communication" was published in the March 16, 1814, edition of the *Washington Republican* describes the militiaman's conduct as "dastardly." This author was most likely Wilcox's brother officer and good friend Walter Bourke, who wrote an account of the expedition to the lieutenant's father.

20. Russell to Pinckney, February 21, 1814, Secretary of War Letters, National Archives; Bourke to General Joseph Wilcox, January 19, 1814; Anonymous, *Narrative*, 9.

21. Bourke to General Wilcox, January 19, 1814; Anonymous, *Narrative*, 9; Communication, *Washington Republican*, March 16, 1814.

22. Russell to Pinckney, February 21, 1814, Secretary of War Letters, National Archives.

23. Ibid.

24. Ibid.; Bourke to General Joseph Wilcox, January 19, 1814; Anonymous, *Narrative*, 10.

25. Russell to Pinckney, February 21, 1814, Secretary of War Letters, National Archives.

26. Ibid.; Claiborne, *Life and Times*, 144–45.

27. Russell to Pinckney, February 21, 1814, Secretary of War Letters, National Archives.

28. Pickett, *History of Alabama*, 2:328; Notes furnished by Creagh, Pickett Papers, ADAH.

29. Notes furnished by Creagh, Pickett Papers, ADAH; Claiborne, *Life and Times*, 145.

30. Russell to Pinckney, February 21, 1814, Secretary of War Letters, National Archives; Pickett, *History of Alabama*, 2:328; Russell to Commander of US Forces in the Creek War, January 16, 1814, Secretary of War Letters, National Archives; Russell to McKee, April 1, 1814, Secretary of War Letters, National Archives.

31. Russell to Pinckney, March 17, 1814, Secretary of War Letters, National Archives.

32. Russell to McKee, April 1, 1814, Secretary of War Letters, National Archives.

33. Andrew Jackson to Robert Steele, March 22, 1814, Jackson Papers, reel 9, LOC.

34. Jackson to Rachel Jackson, March 4, 1814, in Avery O. Craven and Andrew Jackson, "Letters of Andrew Jackson," *Huntington Library Bulletin* 3 (1933): 115.

35. Thomas Pinckney to Jackson, March 13, 1814, Jackson Papers, reel 9, LOC.

36. Charges of Specifications exhibited against John Cocke Maj Genl of the first division of the Militia of the State of Tennessee, late in the service of the militia, March 3, 1814, Jackson Papers, reel 8, LOC.

37. Pinckney to Jackson, February 26, 1814, Jackson Papers, reel 9, LOC.

38. On February 15, a group of 113 Kialegee warriors and their women and children had turned up at Talladega seeking refuge from the Red Clubs. Jackson was suspicious of this tribe and rebuffed their entreaties for peace with conditions the Kialegees could not possibly meet.

39. Jackson to Pinckney, February 16, 1814, Jackson Papers, reel 9, LOC.

40. Ibid.

41. Parton, *Life of Andrew Jackson*, 1:506–7.

42. Ibid., 1:507–8.

43. One historian persuasively argues that Jackson's response to Woods's outburst was a "contest of wills" between Jackson and Woods's friends in the army who wanted to defy Jackson because of the general's stance on terms of service. Jackson had offered to pardon Woods if the private would enlist in the regular army. Encouraged by his friends, Woods refused, giving Jackson no choice but to proceed with the sentence. Steve Inskeep, *Jacksonland: President Andrew Jackson, Cherokee Chief John Ross, and a Great American Land Grab* (New York: Penguin, 2015), 18–21.

44. Ibid., Parton, *Life of Andrew Jackson*, 1:508.

45. Ibid., 1:509.

46. "Headquarters, Fort Strother, March 15, 1814," *Nashville Whig*, April 6, 1814.

47. General Order, John Woods, March 14, 1814, in Moser et al., *Papers of Andrew Jackson*, 3:48–49.

48. "From our Correspondent, Headquarters, Fort Strother, March 15, 1814," *Nashville Whig*, April 6, 1814.

49. John Reid's reaction to the execution of young Woods was characteristically sympathetic and nonjudgmental. He was particularly concerned about the impact of the boy's death on his parents, "who are said to be very respectable." Reid to Betsy Reid, March 14, 1814, John Reid Papers, LOC.

50. Editor's Note, Moser et al., *Papers of Andrew Jackson*, 3:48. An early Jackson biographer, James Parton, claims that Jackson did not know "and never learned" that Woods had not been an original member of Roberts's command and that a secretary had included that assertion in the order of execution to bolster the case against Woods. Parton asserts that Woods's death sentence was just under "the laws of war of every nation." Parton, *Life of Andrew Jackson*, 1:508–11. Strictly speaking, perhaps it was, given that Woods had threatened an officer. But just a month earlier Jackson had pardoned Lieutenant Kirby for far worse conduct.

51. "From our Correspondent, Headquarters, Fort Strother, March 15, 1814," *Nashville Whig*, April 6, 1814.

52. General Order, March 14, 1814, Jackson Papers, reel 9, LOC.

53. Ibid.

54. General Order, March 17, 1814, Jackson Papers, reel 9, LOC; Brigade Order, March 18, 1814, Jackson Papers, reel 9, LOC.

55. Colonel John Williams' Report, March 22, 1814, Jackson Papers, reel 9, LOC.

56. Reid to Betsy Reid, March 21, 1814, Reid Papers, LOC.

57. Jackson to Pinckney, March 22, 1814, Reid Papers, LOC.

58. Jackson to Pope and Brahan, March 22, 1814, Jackson Papers, reel 9, LOC; Jackson to Pinckney, March 23, 1814, Jackson Papers, reel 9, LOC; General Orders, March 21, 1814, Jackson Papers, reel 9, LOC.

59. Harvey H. Jackson, *Rivers of History: Life on the Coosa, Tallapoosa, Cahaba, and Alabama* (Tuscaloosa: University of Alabama Press, 1995), 144.

60. Thomas D. Creable to Jackson, March 24, 1814, Jackson Papers, reel 9, LOC; The Cap't of the guard Statement concerning the attack, March 24, 1814, Jackson Papers, reel 9, LOC; Steele to Jackson, March 26, 1814, Jackson Papers, reel 9, LOC.

61. General Order, March 21, 1814, Jackson Papers, reel 9, LOC.

62. Jackson to Johnson, March 22, 1814, Jackson Papers, reel 9, LOC.

63. Johnson to Jackson, March 23, 1814, Jackson Papers, reel 9, LOC.

64. Ibid.

65. Ibid.; Gregory A. Waselkov and Brian M. Wood, "The Creek War of 1813–1814: Effects on Creek Society and Settlement Pattern," *Journal of Alabama Archeology* 32, no. 1 (June 1986): 13.

66. Johnson to Jackson, March 23, 1814, Jackson Papers, reel 9, LOC.

67. Johnson to Jackson, April 1, 1814, Jackson Papers, reel 9, LOC.

68. Ewen Allison to Johnson, March 27, 1814, Jackson Papers, reel 9, LOC.

69. Johnson to Jackson, April 1, 1814, Jackson Papers, reel 9, LOC; Allison to Johnson, March 27, 1814, Jackson Papers, reel 9, LOC.

70. Johnson to Jackson, April 1, 1814, Jackson Papers, reel 9, LOC.

71. Jackson to John Floyd, January 30, 1814, Jackson Papers, reel 8, LOC.

72. Jackson to Pinckney, March 23, 1814, Jackson Papers, reel 9, LOC.

73. Jackson to Blount, March 28, 1814, in Brannan, *Official Letters*, 321–22.

74. Ball stuck in tree, see Don C. East, *A Historical Analysis of the Creek Indian Hillabee Towns: And Personal Reflections on the Landscape and People of Clay County* (New York: iUniverse, 2008), 152–53.

75. John Cheatham, Battle Map of Horseshoe Bend, March 27, 1814, President William H. Harrison Papers, Record Group 77, CWMF, Misc. II-2, National Archives.

76. Jackson to Blount, March 28, 1814, Brannan, *Official Letters*, 322.

77. Dickens, *Archeological Investigations*, 47–48. This article of over two hundred pages constitutes the most comprehensive description of the topography and the archeology of the Horseshoe Bend area yet written.

78. Ibid.; Leonard Tarrant, Map of the Battle of Horseshoe Bend, A-44, ADAH.

79. Jackson to Pinckney, March 28, 1814, in Moser et al., *Papers of Andrew Jackson*, 3:52.

80. Notes taken from the Lips of Col Robert James of Clarke County Ala relative to Zachariah McGirth and Weatherford, Pickett Papers, ADAH.

81. Thomas L. McKenney and James Hall, *History of the Indian Tribes of North America, with Biographical Sketches and Anecdotes of the Principal Chiefs* (Philadelphia: D. Rice, 1838), 2:191.

82. John A. Tures, "Hell Comes to Horseshoe Bend," *Napoleon Series: The War of 1812 Magazine* 9 (May 2008), http://www.napoleon-series.org/military/Warof1812/2008/Issue9/c_HorseShoeBend.html.

83. Jackson to Pinckney, March 28, 1814, in Moser et al., *Papers of Andrew Jackson*, 3:52.

84. Pickett, *History of Alabama*, 2:346.

85. On Coffee's staff was a Yale University graduate and wastrel named Alexander McCulloch. McCulloch hailed from a socially prominent and wealthy North Carolina family. Despite his character flaws (McCulloch drank himself to death in later life), the young man fought well in the coming struggle. He also sired a son, Benjamin, who fought with Sam Houston's army at the battle of San Jacinto, became a lieutenant in the Texas Rangers, and, years after that, a brigadier general in the Confederate army.

86. John Coffee to Jackson, April 1, 1814, in Moser et al., *Papers of Andrew Jackson*, 3:55–56.

87. Ibid.; Tarrant, Map of the Battle of Horseshoe Bend, ADAH.

88. Twenty-five years after the battle, one of a group of general militia officers visiting the battlefield opined that if the Red Clubs had fortified the heights overlooking the toe of the peninsula, the Horseshoe would have been impregnable. "Messrs. Editors," *Wetumpka Argus and Commercial Advertiser*, June 26, 1839, Dadeville, Alabama. Unfortunately, Menawa did not have sufficient warriors to man this position. The veteran warriors who had fought General Floyd at Autossee and Calebee Creek were available for that assignment, but they were huddled in the lower Tallapoosa towns, disheartened and indecisive.

89. Coffee to Jackson, April 1, 1814, in Moser et al., *Papers of Andrew Jackson*, 3:56.

90. Jackson to Pinckney, March 28, 1814, in Moser et al., *Papers of Andrew Jackson*, 3:52.

91. Ibid.; Tarrant, Map of the Battle of Horseshoe Bend, ADAH; Cheatham, Battle Map of Horseshoe Bend, National Archives.

92. Anonymous, Map of the Battle of Horseshoe Bend, 27th March, 1814, Historical Map Archive, University of Alabama.

93. Interpretation based on Gregory A. Waselkov, "A Reinterpretation of the Creek Indian Barricade at Horseshoe Bend," *Journal of Alabama Archeology* 32, no. 2 (December 1986): 94–104. For other interpretations of the barricade, see Dickens, *Archeological Investigations*, 18–46, and George C. Mackenzie, *The Indian Breastwork in the Battle of Horseshoe Bend: Its Size, Location and Construction* (Washington, DC: US Department of Interior, Office of Archaeology and Historic Preservation, 1969): 38–47b.

94. Mackenzie, *Indian Breastwork*, 47–47b; "Gideon Morgan to Blount, April 1, 1814," *Clarion and Tennessee State Gazette*, April 12, 1814.

95. Reid and Eaton, *Life of Andrew Jackson*, 153; Reid to Nathan Reid, April 5, 1814, Reid Papers, LOC.

96. Jackson to John Armstrong, April 2, 1814, Jackson Papers, reel 10, LOC; Reid to Nathan Reid, April 5, 1814, Reid Papers, LOC; Reid and Eaton, *Life of Andrew Jackson*, 158–59. To the horror and outrage of the American soldiers, some of the Creeks behind the barrier were dressed in the clothes of their comrades the Red Clubs had killed and exhumed from their graves on the Emuckfau. Ibid., 166.

97. Jackson to John Armstrong, April 2, 1814, Jackson Papers, reel 10, LOC; Jackson to Rachel Jackson, April 1, 1814, Moser et al., *Papers of Andrew Jackson*, 3:54.

98. Reid to Betsy Reid, April 1, 1814, Reid Papers, LOC.

99. Jackson to Officer, April 1, 1814, in Parton, *Life of Andrew Jackson*, 1:517.

100. "Morgan to Blount, April 1, 1814," *Clarion*, April 12, 1814; Coffee to Jackson, April 1, 1814, in Moser et al., *Papers of Andrew Jackson*, 3:55–56.

101. "Morgan to Blount, April 1, 1814," *Clarion*, April 12, 1814; Abram, "'Souls in the Treetops,'" 145; Alexander McCulloch to Francis L. McCulloch. April 1, 1814.

102. Coffee to Jackson, April 1, 1814, in Moser et al., *Papers of Andrew Jackson*, 3:55–56.

103. Ibid.; Halbert and Ball, *Creek War*, 277.

104. "Morgan to Blount, April 1, 1814," *Clarion*, April 12, 1814.

105. Anonymous, *The Life of Sam Houston* (New York: J. C. Derby, 1855), 31.

106. Reid to Betsy Reid, April 1, 1814, Reid Papers, LOC; Jackson to Officer, April 1, 1814, in Parton, *Life of Andrew Jackson*, 1:517.

107. Reid to Betsy Reid, April 1, 1814, Reid papers, LOC.

108. Jackson to Officer, April 1, 1814, in Parton, *Life of Andrew Jackson*, 1:517.

109. Jackson to Blount, March 28, 1814, Brannan, *Official Letters*, 322; Reid to Betsy Reid, April 1, 1814, Reid Papers, LOC.

110. Tom Kanon, *Tennesseans at War 1812–1815: Andrew Jackson, The Creek War, and the Battle of New Orleans* (Tuscaloosa: University of Alabama Press, 2014), 101. It is said that before his death, Major Montgomery managed to pull himself up on top of the barricade near its center. As he stood tall and turned, waving his hat and crying out for his troops to follow him, a Creek musket ball punched through his skull and he toppled, instantly dead, from the rampart among his comrades. Alexander McCulloch to Francis McCulloch, April 1, 1814, reprinted in Thomas W. Cutrer, "'The Tallapoosa Might Truly be Called the River of Blood': Major Alexander McCulloch and the Battle of Horseshoe Bend," *Alabama Review* 43, no. 1 (1990): 38.

111. Anonymous, *Life of Sam Houston*, 31–32, 34–35.

112. Coffee to Sam Houston, April 25, 1828, Coffee Papers, TSLA.

113. Kanon, *Tennesseans at War*, 103.

114. Parton, *Life of Andrew Jackson*, 1:518.

115. Reid to Betsy Reid, April 1, 1814, Reid Papers, LOC; Parton, *Life of Jackson*, 1:518; Coffee to Mary Coffee, April 2, 1814, John Coffee Papers, Dyas Collection, box 13, reel 5, TSLA.

116. "Carroll to friend, April 1, 1814," *Clarion*, April 12, 1814.

117. Coffee to Jackson, April 1, 1814, Moser et al., *Papers of Andrew Jackson*, 3:56–57.

118. McCulloch to Francis, April 1, 1814, in Cutrer, "Tallapoosa," 38.

119. McKenney and Hall, *History of the Indian Tribes*, 1:420.

120. Jackson to Rachel Jackson, April 1, 1814, in Moser et al., *Papers of Andrew Jackson*, 3:55.

121. Halbert and Ball, *Creek War*, 277.

122. Anonymous, *Life of Sam Houston*, 34–35.

123. Ibid.

124. Ibid., 35; Parton, *Life of Jackson*, 1:519.

125. Jackson to Rachel Jackson, April 1, 1814, in Moser et al., *Papers of Andrew Jackson*, 3:54.

126. Jackson to Pinckney, March 28, 1814, in Moser et al., *Papers of Andrew Jackson*, 3:53.

127. David Smith to Jackson, April 4, 1814, Jackson Papers, reel 10, LOC.

128. Anonymous, *Life of Sam Houston*, 35.

129. Coffee to Jackson, April 1, 1814, in Moser et al., *Papers of Andrew Jackson*, 3:57.

130. Pickett, *History of Alabama*, 2:345.

131. "Jackson to Blount, March 31," *Clarion*, April 12, 1814; Halbert and Ball, *Creek War*, 277.

132. Jackson to Pinckney, March 28, 1814, in Moser et al., *Papers of Andrew Jackson*, 3:53.

133. Hammond, Bean, Gibson, and Russell, Report of the Creek Dead, March 27, 1814, Jackson Papers, reel 9, LOC.

134. Jackson to Pinckney, March 28, 1814, in Moser et al., *Papers of Andrew Jackson*, 3:55; Henry S. Halbert, Incidents of the Battle of Horseshoe Bend, November 10, 1882, to March 3, 1887, Series YY: Tecumseh Papers (microfilm Reel 119), Lyman Draper Collection, Wisconsin Historical Society.

135. Reid and Eaton, *Life of Andrew Jackson*, 164.

136. Jackson to Pinckney, March 28, 1813, in Moser et al., *Papers of Andrew Jackson*, 3:53; Jackson to Rachel Jackson, April 1, 1814, in Moser et al., *Papers of Andrew Jackson*, 3:55.

137. Coffee to Sam Houston, April 25, 1828, Coffee Papers, TSLA.

138. Parton, *Life of Jackson*, 1:520.

139. So much did the Americans later protest that the Creeks refused to surrender that one wonders whether it was true.

140. Jackson to Rachel Jackson, April 1, 1814, in Moser et al., *Papers of Andrew Jackson*, 3:55.

141. Halbert and Ball, *Creek War*, 276–77; Halbert, Incidents of the Battle of Horseshoe Bend, Wisconsin Historical Society.

142. McKenney and Hall, *History of the Indian Tribes*, 2:191.

143. Jackson to Blount, March 28, 1814, in Brannan, *Official Letters*, 322.

144. Pickett, *History of Alabama*, 2:343–44. Hawkins tells a similar story. Three months after the battle, he wrote that a formerly affluent Indian family showed up at Fort Jackson looking for food. Among the supplicants was a man who had fought at the Horseshoe and been wounded in several places. The chief had only escaped the battlefield, Hawkins wrote, by secreting himself beneath the waters of the Tallapoosa with only his nose above the surface to draw breath. When night fell, the man, who was doubtless Menawa, floated downstream to safety. Hawkins to Armstrong, June 21, 1814, in Grant, *Letters, Journals and Writings*, 2:685.

145. Benjamin W. Griffith Jr., *McIntosh and Weatherford: Creek Indian Leaders* (Tuscaloosa: University of Alabama Press, 1988), 248–51.

146. McKenney and Hall, *History of the Indian Tribes*, 2:184–86. Tellingly, shortly before being deported to the trans-Mississippi lands, Menawa expressed the wish never to lay eyes on a white man again. Ibid., 191.

147. Jackson to Blount, March 28, 1814, in Brannan, *Official Letters*, 322; Reid and Eaton, *Life of Andrew Jackson*, 155. Given this rationale, it is puzzling why the body of the battle's greatest hero, Major Montgomery, did not receive the same treatment. Instead, he was buried on the battlefield and, like the men interred at Emuckfau, a fire was set over his grave to conceal it from the Creeks. This precaution had been ineffective at that place, but, strangely, it apparently worked for Montgomery. In 1839, a committee of local citizens guided by a former slave who had drummed at the major's battlefield internment located his unmarked grave, exhumed his body, and reinterred it in a local cemetery. Perhaps the Creeks were too spooked by the national disaster at Horseshoe Bend to set foot on that cursed ground to look for the body themselves.

148. Jackson to Blount, March 28, 1814, in Brannan, *Official Letters*, 322.

149. Tiya Miles, *Ties that Bind: The Story of an Afro-Cherokee Family in Slavery and Freedom* (Berkeley: University of California Press, 2005), 15.

150. Ibid., 81.

151. True to his boast, Shoe Boots lived fifteen more years, until 1829. Ibid., 129. In 1824, he petitioned the Cherokee National Council to free his three children. Ibid., 115. The council granted the petition, and the line that he and Doll began lives on to this day. Ironically, a grandson enlisted in the Confederate army as a member of a group of Cherokee mounted volunteers: the son and grandson of slaves fighting to preserve a way of life under which two generations of his immediate ancestors had suffered. Ibid., 189.

152. Thomas' Legion: The 69th North Carolina Regiment, http://thomaslegion.net/index.html.

153. Jackson to Pinckney, March 28, 1814, in Moser et al., *Papers of Andrew Jackson*, 3:53.

154. Memorandum Book of Joseph Huffmaster, James Taylor Huffmaster Papers, 1814–1850, MSS #04-0007, Galveston and Texas History Center, Rosenberg Library.

155. "Carroll to friend, April 1, 1814," *Clarion*, April 12, 1814; Coffee to Mary Coffee, April 2, 1814, Coffee Papers, TSLA.

156. Reid to Father, April 5, 1814, Reid Papers, LOC.

157. Andrew Jackson to Rachel Jackson, April 1, 1814, in Moser et al., *Papers of Andrew Jackson*, 3:54; Order to Colonel Morgan, April 3, 1814, Jackson Papers, reel 10, LOC.

158. General Order, April 4, 1814, Jackson Papers, reel 10, LOC.

159. General Order, April 5, 1814, Jackson Papers, reel 10, LOC; Jackson to Pinckney, April 14, 1814, Record Group 107, Letters Received by the Secretary of War, Registered Series, 1801–1860, Microfilm Publication #221, National Archives.

160. Jackson to Colonel Milton, April 5, 1814, Jackson Papers, reel 10, LOC; General Order, April 5, 1814, Jackson Papers, reel 10, LOC.

161. Reid and Eaton, *Life of Andrew Jackson*, 159–60.

162. Jackson, Notes, April 13, 1814, Jackson Papers, reel 10, LOC.

163. Milton to Pinckney, April 9, 1814, Secretary of War Letters, National Archives.

164. Milton to Pinckney, April 14, 1814, Secretary of War Letters, National Archives.

165. Reid to Unnamed Friend, undated (ca. April 1814), Reid Papers, LOC.

166. Reid to Unnamed Friend, undated (likely in April 1814), Reid Papers, LOC.

167. Milton to Pinckney, April 14, 1814, Secretary of War Letters, National Archives; Hawkins to Pinckney, April 26, 1814, Secretary of War Letters, National Archives.

168. Hawkins to Pinckney, April 26, 1814, Secretary of War Letters, National Archives.

169. Jackson to Governor Holmes, April 18, 1814, Jackson Papers, reel 10, LOC.

170. Reid to Unnamed Friend, undated (likely in April 1814), Reid Papers, LOC.

171. Jackson to Pinckney, April 14, 1815, Secretary of War Letters, National Archives.

172. Reid to Betsy Reid, undated extract, probably April 14, 1814, Reid Papers, LOC.

173. Coffee Order, April 15, 1814, Jackson Papers, reel 10, LOC.

174. Jackson to Pinckney, April 14, 1814, Jackson Papers, reel 10, LOC.

175. Jackson to Armstrong, April 25, 1814, Jackson Papers, reel 10, LOC.

176. Reid to Betsy Reid, April 14, 1814, Reid Papers, LOC.

177. Jackson to Pinckney, April 14, 1814, Jackson Papers, reel 10, LOC.

178. Wright, *Historic Indian Towns*, 114; Jackson to Pinckney, April 18, 1814, Jackson Papers, reel 10, LOC.

179. Jackson, Notes, April 14, 1814, Jackson Papers, reel 10, LOC.

180. Ibid.

181. Jackson to Pinckney, April 18, 1814, Jackson Papers, reel 10, LOC; Reid to Betsy Reid, April 18, 1814, Reid Papers, LOC.

182. One of these cannons found new life several years later in the infant city of Montgomery, Alabama, just down the river. It was reconditioned and fired in town celebrations for a number of years before it exploded in 1825 during the celebration of John Quincy Adams's election as president and horribly maimed the civilian artilleryman, Ebenezer Pond. Pickett, *History of Alabama*, 1:221–22.

183. Daniel H. Thomas, *Fort Toulouse: The French Outpost at the Alabamas on the Coosa*, with a new introduction by Gregory A. Waselkov (Tuscaloosa: University of Alabama Press, 1989), viii.

184. Andrew Jackson to Willie Blount, April 18, 1814, Jackson Papers, reel 10, LOC.

185. Jackson to Thomas Pinckney, April 18, 1814, Jackson Papers, reel 10, LOC.

186. Jackson to Blount, April 18, 1814, Jackson Papers, reel 10, LOC.

187. Jackson to David Holmes, April 18, 1814, Jackson Papers, reel 10, LOC.

188. Reid and Eaton, *Life of Andrew Jackson*, 176–80; Meek, *Romantic Passages*, 284–86; Pickett, *History of Alabama*, 2:348–51; Parton, *Life of Andrew Jackson*, 1:532–35; Woodward, *Woodward's Reminiscences*, 91–93; "Indian Eloquence," *Washington Republican*, June 8, 1814.

189. Woodward, *Woodward's Reminiscences*, 91; Reid and Eaton, *Life of Andrew Jackson*, 165.

190. The spoilsport Woodward says Weatherford borrowed a horse from a mixed-blood Creek named Barney Riley for the journey because he was without one. Woodward, *Woodward's Reminiscences*, 83.

191. Pickett, *History of Alabama*, 2:348; Woodward, *Woodward's Reminiscences*, 93.

192. Pickett, *History of Alabama*, 2:348–49.

193. Meek, *Romantic Passages*, 285.

194. Pickett, *History of Alabama*, 2:349.

195. Ibid.

196. Reid's version of Weatherford's surrender is dismissed by Pickett as "camp gossip" (ibid., 2:350) and by Woodward as lies (Woodward, *Woodward's Reminiscences*, 93). Reid's version is lent credibility by the fact that during the war he was Jackson's secretary/aide-de-camp, virtual shadow, and very good friend. Reid, like his commander, was clearly impressed with Weatherford, who, despite being a "barbarian," preserved all the manliness of sentiment, all the heroism of soul, all the comprehension of intellect calculated to make an able commander. Parton believes that Reid might have embellished the tale somewhat to aid Jackson's political ambitions, but for the most part, he accepts its general accuracy. Parton, *Life of Andrew Jackson*, 1:533. Both Pickett and Parton wrongly assume that the source of this story was a "Major" John Eaton. Unlike Reid, Eaton was not a major nor was he even in Jackson's army. He was chosen by Jackson to complete Reid's unfinished life story of the general when it was interrupted after chapter 4 by Reid's untimely death in 1816. The error probably occurred because Pickett and Parton were referencing the 1824 edition of *The Life of Andrew Jackson*, whose title page listed only John Eaton as its author, in contrast to the exceedingly rare 1817 first edition, which gave authorial credit to both men and described Reid as a "brevet major." Reid and Eaton, *Life of Andrew Jackson*, x.

197. Reid and Eaton, *Life of Andrew Jackson*, 177.

198. Ibid., 165.

199. Woodward, *Woodward's Reminiscences*, 93.

200. William Gates Orr to H. S. Halbert, February 22, 1813, in W. G. Orr, "The Surrender of Weatherford," *Transactions of the Alabama Historical Society, 1897–98*, ed. Thomas McAdory Owen (Tuscaloosa, AL: Printed for the Society, 1898), 57–58.

201. Woodward, *Woodward's Reminiscences*, 102.

202. Benjamin Hawkins to Pinckney, April 26, 1814, Record Group 107, Letters Received by the Secretary of War, Registered Series, 1801–1860, Microfilm Publication #221, National Archives.

203. Pinckney to John Armstrong, April 26, 1814, Secretary of War Letters, National Archives; James Madison to Armstrong, May 20, 1814, James Madison Papers, 1723–1836, LOC.

204. Gregory Waselkov, "Fort Jackson and the Aftermath," in Braund, ed., *Tohopeka*, 162; Joseph Graham to Pinckney, June 14, 1814, Joseph Graham Papers, 1769–1864, Southern Historical Collection, University of North Carolina.

205. Waselkov, *Conquering Spirit*, 135; Jackson to Blount, April 18, 1814, Jackson Papers, reel 10, LOC.

206. Notes taken from the Lips of Col Robert James of Clarke County Ala relative to Zachariah McGirth and Weatherford, Pickett Papers, ADAH; Grant, *Letters, Journals and Writings*, 2:681. McGirth knew that his family had been taken prisoner after the fall of Fort Mims. Benjamin Hawkins was informed of that fact by the friendly chiefs on September 16, 1813. Chiefs at Coweta to Hawkins, Creek Agency, September 16, 1813, *American State Papers: Indian Affairs*, 1:853. McGirth was with the agent by October 23, 1813, having delivered mail from the Fort Stoddert area several days before. Hawkins to Toulmin, Creek Agency, October 23, 1813, *American State Papers: Indian Affairs*, 1:857. What McGirth had done to locate his family, if anything, after they arrived at Jackson's camp is unknown.

207. Notes taken from the Lips of Col Robert James of Clarke County Ala relative to Zachariah McGirth and Weatherford, Pickett Papers, ADAH.

208. Andrew Jackson to William Blount, April 25, 1814, Jackson Papers, reel 10, LOC; General Order, April 21, 1814, Jackson Papers, reel 10, LOC; Jackson to Thomas Pinckney, April 21, 1814, Jackson Papers, reel 10, LOC.

209. Pinckney to Jackson, April 22, 1814, Jackson Papers, reel 10, LOC; General Order, April 21, 1814, Jackson Papers, reel 10, LOC.

210. Secretary of War to Major General Pinckney, War Department, March 17, 1814, *American State Papers: Indian Affairs*, 1:837; Pinckney to Benjamin Hawkins, April 23, 1814, Secretary of War Letters, National Archives; Pinckney to John Armstrong, April 22, 1814, Secretary of War Letters, National Archives.

211. Hawkins to Pinckney, Fort Toulouse, April 25, 1814, *American State Papers: Indian Affairs*, 1:858.

212. Officers to George W. Campbell, April 18, 1814, Jackson Papers, reel 10, LOC.

213. Jackson to Armstrong, April 25, 1814, Jackson Papers, reel 10, LOC.

214. Jackson to Rachel Jackson, May 8, 1814, in Moser et al., *Papers of Andrew Jackson*, 3:70–71.

215. Jackson Orders to Captain Hammond, May 5, 1814, Jackson Papers, reel 10, LOC; Thomas Johnson to Jackson, May, 8 1814, Jackson Papers, reel 10, LOC ; Jackson to Blount, April 25, 1814, Jackson Papers, Jackson Papers, reel 10, LOC.

216. A Tribute to Merit, Invitation, May 12, 1814, Jackson Papers, reel 10, LOC; Jackson to Rachel Jackson, May 8, 1814, in Moser et al., *Papers of Andrew Jackson*, 3:71.

217. John Rhea to Armstrong, May 18, 1814, Secretary of War Letters, National Archives.

218. Benjamin Hawkins to Armstrong, July 13, 1814, in Grant, *Letters, Journals and Writings*, 2:689.

219. Benton to Flournoy, July 5, 1814, in Moser et al., *Papers of Andrew Jackson*, 3:84.

220. Notes taken from the Lips of Col Robert James of Clarke County Ala relative to Zachariah McGirth and Weatherford, Pickett Papers, ADAH.

221. John Williams to Flournoy, May 2, 1814, Jackson Papers, reel 10, LOC.

222. Homer Milton to Pinckney, April 28, 1814, Jackson Papers, reel 10, LOC.

223. Ibid. Eventually the Choctaw and Chickasaw agreed to attack the Red Clubs in the lower Cahaba River lands and along the US border with Spain. These forays were unsuccessful, and by the end of May, the warriors returned home. Milton to Joseph Graham, May 17, 1814, Joseph Graham Papers, North Carolina Department of Cultural Resources (NCDCR), Division of Archives and History.

224. Pickett, *History of Alabama*, 2:350.

225. Halbert, "Creek War Incidents," 102.

226. Pickett, *History of Alabama*, 2:350; Milton to Pinckney, April 28, 1814, Jackson Papers, reel 10, LOC.

227. Pickett, *History of Alabama*, 2:350. David Tate's grandson asserts that to protect Weatherford from his enemies, Jackson sent the Creek leader on to the Hermitage, where Weatherford stayed for several months before returning to his Little River plantation. Tarvin, "Muscogees," 142. A pleasant story but untrue. At that time, Weatherford was with the American soldiers pursuing fugitive Creeks in the Escambia River country. Waselkov, *Conquering Spirit*, 327n29.

228. Graham to Pinckney, May 21, 1814, Graham Papers, NCDCR.

229. Report of Col Pearson's Expedition Against the Hostile Creeks on the Alabama, June 1, 1814, enclosure in letter from Pinckney to Armstrong, June 28, 1814, Secretary of War Letters, National Archives.

230. Ibid.

231. Milton to Graham, May 17, 1814, Graham Papers, NCDCR.

232. Milton to Pinckney, May 20, 1814, Jackson Papers, reel 10, LOC.

233. Report of Col Pearson, June 1, 1814, Secretary of War Letters, National Archives.

234. Brown, *Creek Indian History*, 135.

235. Ibid.; Hawkins to Graham, July 5, 1814, in Grant, *Letters, Journals and Writings*, 2:688.

236. Report of Col Pearson, June 1, 1814, Secretary of War Letters, National Archives.

237. Waselkov, *Conquering Spirit*, 175.

238. Halbert and Ball, *Creek War*, 175–76.

239. Pickett, *History of Alabama*, 2:351–52. Albert Pickett's source for the story claims the incident occurred "About the year 1820," when Caller, who died in February 1819, was in his grave. But Pickett heard the story long after the event, and the teller of the tale may be excused if he was off

by less than a year. That the murderer was indeed Colonel Caller is evidenced by Pickett's published account in which he identifies Caller, and his accomplice, George Fisher, solely by the first and last letters of their surnames, graciously omitting even their Christian names. But in Pickett's interview notes from which the published story was taken, the full names of both men are given. In those days, given the seriousness of the affair, the historian would not have taken this step unless the reputation of a prominent Alabama family was involved. Ibid.

240. Ibid.; Notes taken from the Lips of Col Robert James of Clarke County Ala relative to Zachariah McGirth and Weatherford, Pickett Papers, ADAH.

241. Pickett, *History of Alabama*, 2:351–53; Notes taken from the Lips of Col Robert James of Clarke County Ala relative to Zachariah McGirth and Weatherford, Pickett Papers, ADAH.

242. Notes taken from the Lips of Col Robert James of Clarke County Ala relative to Zachariah McGirth and Weatherford, Pickett Papers, ADAH. Caller was up to no good until the day he died, November 27, 1819 ("old and highly respectable"), and the results of his mischief lived on years after him. "Mortuary Notice," *St. Stephens (AL) Halcyon and Tombeckbe Public Advertiser*, December 1, 1819. In 1818, three ships carrying 109 contraband Africans endeavored to run the US slave embargo along the Gulf Coast. They were captured by the US Navy, and the ships and their cargo were taken to Mobile and impounded under US law. Never one to pass up a main chance, Caller and his sometime associate, former major Benjamin Smoot, and a Mr. David posted a $100,000 bound for safekeeping of the Africans until the admiralty court could dispose of them. Caller's share of the captives promptly found their way to his plantation outside of St. Stephens, where they remained even after his death. When Caller's widow evidenced a disinclination to have them returned to the court's jurisdiction, former colonel Gilbert Russell, who had bought the rights of the slaves' captors, attempted to bring them back. After no little effort, given that the Callers had dispersed their charges about the countryside, Russell was able to recover all of the Africans except for ten (most of whom were under age twelve) who had "escaped." Apparently Robert Caller, the colonel's son, sold four of these to a man named Kimbro who took them to Tennessee. The remaining six were said to have been "stolen." Russell offered a reward of $1,000 each for the missing Africans as well as a $500 bounty for the capture of Kimbro and any others who had stolen Russell's human property. "1000 Dollars REWARD, Gilbert C. Russell, District of Alabama, Blakeley, 6th April, 1821," *Augusta Chronicle*, May 24, 1821.

243. William Weatherford died on March 4, 1824, three days after falling ill (perhaps from pneumonia) on returning home from a rigorous bear hunt. It is said that just before he died, he had a vision of his recently deceased second wife, Sapoth Thlaine. She was standing beside his sick bed calling to him to join her in the afterworld. J. D. Driesback, "Weatherford—'The Red Eagle,' Addendum to the Paper Furnished by the Writer on June 28th, 1877," *Alabama Historical Reporter* 2:3 (February 1884). Driesback was the son-in-law of Weatherford's half-brother David Tate; Griffith, *McIntosh and Weatherford*, 253–54. Weatherford is buried beside his mother, Sehoy III, on David Tate's former Brickyard Plantation near the mouth of Little River in Baldwin County. Lynn Hastie Thompson, *William Weatherford: His Country and His People* (Bay Minette, AL: Lavender, 1991), 620. A dozen miles to the south lies the site of Fort Mims. Waselkov, *Conquering Spirit*, 262–63.

244. Hawkins to Graham, July 5, 1814, in Grant, *Letters, Journals and Writings*, 2:688.

245. McKee to Milton, June 7, 1814, Jackson Papers, reel 10, LOC.

246. Gentleman in Pensacola to Friend, June 8, 1814, Jackson Papers, reel 10, LOC.

247. Ibid.

248. Ibid.; Holmes to Jackson, June 19, 1814, Moser et al., *Papers of Andrew Jackson*, 3:82.

249. Hawkins to Graham, July 5, 1814, in Grant, *Letters, Journals and Writings*, 2:688–89.

250. Gentleman in Pensacola to Friend, June 8, 1814, Jackson Papers, reel 10, LOC.

251. William H. Robertson to Brigadier Thomas Flournoy, Bay St. Louis, June 17, 1814, *American State Papers: Indian Affairs*, 1:859.

252. John Armstrong to Andrew Jackson, May 22, 1814, Jackson Papers, reel 10; Armstrong to Jackson, May 28, 1814, Jackson Papers, reel 10, LOC; George W. Campbell to Jackson, May 29, 1814, Jackson Papers, reel 10, LOC.

253. Jackson to John Coffee, July 17, 1814, Jackson Papers, reel 11, LOC.

254. Jackson to Armstrong, July 14, 1814, in Moser et al., *Papers of Andrew Jackson*, 3:87; Jackson to Manrique, July 12, 1814, in Moser et al., *Papers of Andrew Jackson*, 3:85–86.

255. Enclosure: Report by John Gordon to Jackson, July 29, 1814, in Moser et al., *Papers of Andrew Jackson*, 3:98–99.

256. Ibid.

257. Jackson to William Charles Cole Claiborne, July 21, 1814, in Moser et al., *Papers of Andrew Jackson*, 3:91.

258. Manrique to Jackson, July 26, 1814, in Moser et al., *Papers of Andrew Jackson*, 3:95–96.

259. Jackson to Rachel, July 31, 1814, in Moser et al., *Papers of Andrew Jackson*, 3:101.

260. Jackson to the Cherokee and Creek Indians, August 5, 1814, in Moser et al., *Papers of Andrew Jackson*, 3:103–4.

261. Jackson to Rachel Jackson, August 10, 1814, in Moser et al., *Papers of Andrew Jackson*, 3:114.

262. Jackson to John Prior Hickman, August 2, 1814, in Moser et al., *Papers of Andrew Jackson*, 3:102.

263. Jackson to the Cherokee and Creek Indians, August 5, 1814, in Moser et al., *Papers of Andrew Jackson*, 3:103–4; Jackson to Rachel Jackson, August 5, 1814, in Moser et al., *Papers of Andrew Jackson*, 3:105.

264. Jackson to the Cherokee and Creek Indians, August 5, 1814, in Moser et al., *Papers of Andrew Jackson*, 3:103–4; Benjamin Hawkins to George Graham, August 1, 1815, in Grant, *Letters, Journals and Writings*, 2:744.

265. Jackson's intention was to fill these new lands between the Creeks and Spanish Florida with American settlers, thus creating a legal and practical barrier between foreign nations and all the southeastern Indians. Jackson to Williams, May 18, 1814, in Moser et al., *Papers of Andrew Jackson*, 3:74; Jackson to the Cherokee and Creek Indians, August 5, 1814, in Moser et al., *Papers of Andrew Jackson*, 3:103.

266. Moser et al., *Papers of Andrew Jackson*, 3:104.

267. Jackson to Rachel Jackson, August 5, 1814, in Moser et al., *Papers of Andrew Jackson*, 3:105.

268. Hawkins to Jackson, August 6, 1814, Observations made by Col. Hawkins on the reply of the Chiefs to the speech of General Jackson addressed to him on the 5th, in Grant, *Letters, Journals and Writings*, 2:691–93; Hawkins to Graham, August 1, 1814, in Grant, *Letters, Journals and Writings*, 2:744.

269. Hawkins to Jackson, August 6, 1814, Report of Fullaapau Haujo and Noocossa Haujo at Headquarters, August 6, 1814, in Grant, *Letters, Journals and Writings*, 2:690–91. By this time Hawkins, like so many before him, had also fallen under Jackson's curious spell; the day after the treaty negotiations were completed, Jackson wrote John Coffee that "Colo. Hawkins was of great service to me in bringing to a close the convention—he is certainly a man of fine understanding, of great experience." Jackson to John Coffee, August 10, 1814, in Moser et al., *Papers of Andrew Jackson*, 3:113.

270. Hawkins to Jackson, Observations made by Col. Hawkins, in Grant, *Letters, Journals, and Writings*, 2:691–92.

271. Jackson to Big Warrior, August 7, 1814, in Moser et al., *Papers of Andrew Jackson*, 3:109–11.

272. Ibid.

273. Jackson to Coffee, August 10, 1814, in Moser et al., *Papers of Andrew Jackson*, 3:113.

274. Reid and Eaton, *Life of Andrew Jackson*, 189.

275. Ibid., 190–91.

276. August 8, 1814, *American State Papers: Indian Affairs*, 1:837.

277. Ibid.; Hawkins to Graham, August 1, 1815, in Grant, *Letters, Journals, and Writings*, 2:745.

278. August 8, 1814, *American State Papers: Indian Affairs*, 1:837.

279. Ibid., 1:838; Hawkins to Graham, August 1, 1815, in Grant, *Letters, Journals and Writings*, 2:745; Jackson to Coffee, August 10, 1814, in Moser et al., *Papers of Andrew Jackson*, 3:112.

280. Hawkins to Graham, August 1, 1815, in Grant, *Letters, Journals and Writings*, 2:743–44. Even after the suspect treaty reached Washington City, Hawkins did not abandon the Creeks. In letters

to the secretary of war, he continued to assail the harsh terms of the treaty. Hawkins's actual letters are missing from the secretary's file, probably removed by Jackson's cronies. But the thieves overlooked the entries in the registry of letters received denoting and briefly describing Hawkins's submissions to the secretary. Owsley, *Struggle for the Gulf Borderlands*, 90–91.

281. Parton, *Life of Andrew Jackson*, 1:560.

282. Pickett, *History of Alabama*, 1:368.

283. In 1816, Captain Isaacs was one of the leaders of a Creek contingent that assisted Jackson in taking what was called the "Negro Fort." This structure was an earthen fortification lying in Spanish territory constructed and manned largely by fugitive slaves. It had been built in 1814, on a bluff above the Apalachicola River fifteen miles upstream from the Gulf Coast. The slaves had been recruited and armed by the British to fight the Americans. But after the War of 1812, British honor gave way to necessity and the British abandoned them. Nonetheless, for several years, the former bondsmen maintained the post as a refuge for themselves and their families. Griffith, *McIntosh and Weatherford*, 172–77.

284. Ibid.

285. Gene Dattel, *Cotton and Race in the Making of America: The Human Costs of Economic Power* (Lanham, MD: Ivan R. Dee, 2009), 35–37.

BIBLIOGRAPHY

MANUSCRIPTS

ALABAMA DEPARTMENT OF ARCHIVES AND HISTORY, MONTGOMERY
Adam James to head Chiefs in the Creek Nation. November 29, 1813.
Caller, James. Papers, 1795–1824. SPR554.
Carson, Joseph. Letter, 1813. SPR42.
Claiborne, Ferdinand Leigh. "Map of Fort Mims and Environs" 1813, CB-23.
Colonel Joseph Carson to General F. L. Claiborne, Mount Vernon. July 30, 1813.
Hale, Fletcher. Collection of Field Notes and Maps. SPR375.
Interesting Papers . . . by Col John F. H. Claiborne, Section 7, Notes.
James, Adam. Letter, 1813. SPR54.
Manac, Samuel. Deposition, 1813. SPR26.
Notes furnished by Col G. W. Creagh, 1847, Section 2, Notes.
Notes furnished by Col Jeremiah Austill, Section 1, Notes.
Notes furnished by Doct Thos G. Holmes, Section 22, Notes.
Notes furnished by Gen Patrick May, Section 3, Notes.
Notes of Doctor Thomas G. Holmes, 1847, Section 4, Notes.
Notes taken from the lips of Abram Mordecai, 1847, Section 15, Notes.
Notes taken from the lips of Col Robert James, 1848, Section 12, Notes.
Notes taken from the lips of Dr Thos G. Holmes, 1848, Section 25, Notes.
Notes taken from the lips of Mr. Thos Malone, 1848, Section 27. Notes.
Pickett, Albert J. Papers. Pickett Family Papers, 1779–1904. LPR185.
Reverend Lee Compere, letter to A. J. Pickett, April 6, 1848.
Tarrant, Leonard. Map of the Battle of Horseshoe Bend. A-44.
Toulmin, Harry. Letters, 1813–1818. SPR234.
CENTER FOR HISTORY AND NEW MEDIA, GEORGE MASON UNIVERSITY, FAIRFAX, VIRGINIA
Knox, Henry. Instructions Regarding Willet's Mission to the Creek Nation. March 12, 1790.
Papers of the War Department, 1784–1800.
Weatherford, Charles. Letter from Charles Weatherford to Creek Indian Agent James Seagrove on Confusion since Death of General McGillivray. March 22, 1793.

FLORIDA STATE ARCHIVES, TALLAHASSEE
Call, Richard Keith. Papers. N2013-5.
GALVESTON AND TEXAS HISTORY CENTER, ROSENBERG LIBRARY, GALVESTON
Huffmaster, James Taylor. Papers, 1814–1850. MSS 04-0007.
GEORGIA HISTORICAL SOCIETY, SAVANNAH
Cuyler, Telamon. Collection, 1780–1832. MS 1131.
LIBRARY OF CONGRESS, WASHINGTON, DC
Jackson, Andrew. Papers, 1775–1874. MSS 27532.
Madison, James. Papers, 1723–1836. MSS 31021.
Reid, John. Reid Family Papers, 1795–1970. MSS 65491.
US Congress, *Journal of the Executive Proceedings of the Senate of the United States of America,* 1st Cong., 2nd sess., August 7, 1790.
US Congress, *Journal of the House of Representatives of the United States, 1811–1813,* 12th Cong., 1st sess., May 22, 1812.
MISSISSIPPI DEPARTMENT OF ARCHIVES AND HISTORY, JACKSON
Claiborne, J. F. H. Collection. Letterbook F: Letters and Papers Relating to the Indian Wars, 1812–1816.
NATIONAL ARCHIVES, WASHINGTON, DC, AND SILVER SPRING, MARYLAND
RG 77: Harrison, William H. Papers. John Cheatham, Battle Map of Horseshoe Bend, March 27, 1814.
RG 107: Records of the Office of the Secretary of War, Letters Received by the Secretary of War, Registered Series (1801–1870). M 221.
NORTH CAROLINA DEPARTMENT OF CULTURAL RESOURCES, DIVISION OF ARCHIVES AND HISTORY, RALEIGH
Graham, Joseph. Papers, 1759–1836.
TENNESSEE STATE LIBRARY AND ARCHIVES, NASHVILLE
Coffee, John. Papers, 1770–1917. Dyas Collection. THS 38, 211.
Morgan, Gideon. Papers. MS 78-31.
UNIVERSITY OF ALABAMA, HISTORIC MAP ARCHIVE, TUSCALOOSA
Anonymous. Map of the Battle of Horseshoe Bend, 27th March, 1814.
UNIVERSITY OF SOUTH ALABAMA LIBRARY, MOBILE
Papers of Paton, Leslie, and Company. Edited by William S. Coker (microfilm edition). Woodbridge, CT: Research Publications, 1986.
UNIVERSITY SYSTEM OF GEORGIA, DIGITAL LIBRARY OF GEORGIA, ATHENS
Southeastern Native American Documents, 1730–1842.
WILLIAM L. CLEMENTS LIBRARY, UNIVERSITY OF MICHIGAN, ANN ARBOR
Flournoy, Thomas. Papers. MS517.
WILLIAMS RESEARCH CENTER, HISTORIC NEW ORLEANS COLLECTION, NEW ORLEANS
The William C. Cook War of 1812 in the South Collection. MS 557.
WISCONSIN HISTORICAL SOCIETY, MADISON
Draper, Lyman. Manuscript Collection.
Halbert, Henry S. Letters on Fort Mims, November 10, 1882, to March 3, 1887. Series YY: Tecumseh Papers (microfilm reel 119).

NEWSPAPERS

Augusta Chronicle and Georgia Gazette
Daily National Intelligencer, Washington, DC
Georgia Journal, Milledgeville
Mississippi Republican, Natchez, Mississippi Territory
Nashville Clarion and Tennessee State Gazette
Nashville Democrat Clarion and Tennessee Gazette
Nashville Whig
Raleigh Register and North Carolina Gazette
Republican and Savannah (GA) Evening Ledger
Rhode Island Republican, Newport
St. Stephens Halcyon and Tombeckbe Public Advertiser, Alabama
Washington Republican, Washington, Mississippi Territory
Weekly Register, Baltimore

PRINTED SOURCES

Abram, Susan Marie. "'Souls in the Treetops': Cherokee War, Masculinity, and Community, 1760–1820." PhD diss., Auburn University, 2009.

Adair, James. *The History of the American Indians.* Edited by Kathryn E. Holland Braund. Tuscaloosa: University of Alabama Press, 2005 [1775].

Anonymous. *The Life of Sam Houston.* New York: J. C. Derby, 1855.

———. *A Narrative of the Life and Death of Lieut. Joseph Morgan Wilcox, Who was Massacred by the Creek Indians, On the Alabama River, (Miss. Ter.) on the 15th of January, 1814.* Marietta, OH: R. Prentiss, 1816.

Austill, Jeremiah. "Autobiography." *Alabama Historical Quarterly* 6, no. 1 (Spring 1944): 81–91.

Austill, Margaret Eades. "Memories of Journeying Through Creek Country and of Childhood in Clarke County, 1811–1814." *Alabama Historical Quarterly* 6, no. 1 (Spring 1944): 92–98.

Baldwin, Joseph G. *The Flush Times of Alabama and Mississippi: A Series of Sketches.* New York: D. Appleton, 1853.

Baptist, Edward E. *The Half Has Never Been Told: Slavery and the Making of American Capitalism.* New York: Basic Books, 2014.

Bartram, William. *The Travels of William Bartram: Naturalist's Edition.* Edited by Frances Harper. New Haven, CT: Yale University Press, 1967.

———. *William Bartram on the Southeastern Indians.* Edited by Gregory A. Waselkov and Kathryn E. Braund. Lincoln: University of Nebraska Press, 1995.

Baynton, Benjamin. *Authentic Memoirs of William Augustus Bowles, Esquire, Ambassador from the United Nations of Creeks and Cherokees, to the Court of London.* London: R. Faulder, 1791.

Beidler, Philip D. *First Books: The Printed Word and Cultural Formation in Early Alabama.* Tuscaloosa: University of Alabama Press, 1999.

Benton, Jeffery C. *The Very Worst Road: Travellers' Accounts of Crossing Alabama's Old Creek Indian Territory, 1820–1847*. Tuscaloosa: University of Alabama Press, 2009.

Brannan, John. *Official Letters of the Military and Naval Officers of the United States during the War with Great Britain*. Washington, DC: Way and Gideon, 1823.

Brannon, Peter A. *Handbook of the Alabama Anthropological Society*. Montgomery: Alabama Department of Archives and History, 1920.

———. "Journal of James A. Tait For the Year 1813." *Alabama Historical Quarterly* 2, no. 4 (1940): 431–40.

———. "More about Mordecai." *Alabama Historical Quarterly* 20, no. 1 (1958): 31.

———. "Samuel Baines Letter, Fort Deposit, November 25, 1813." *Alabama Historical Quarterly* 19 (Fall/Winter 1957): 405–06.

———. "Some Early Fort Mitchell References." *Alabama Historical Quarterly* 21 (1959): 3–7.

———. "Spruce McCall Osborne." *Alabama Historical Quarterly* 5 (Spring 1943): 68–70.

———. "Through the Years, 'Old Augusta.'" *Montgomery Advertiser* 6, August 30, 1931.

Braund, Kathryn E. Holland. "Guardians of Tradition and Handmaidens to Change: Women's Roles in Creek Economic and Social Life during the Eighteenth Century." *American Indian Quarterly* 14, no. 3 (1990): 239–285.

Brewer, Willis. *Alabama, Her History, Resources, War Record, and Public Men, from 1540 to 1872*. Montgomery, AL: Barrett and Brown, 1872.

Briceland, Alan V. "Ephraim Kirby: Mr. Jefferson's Emissary on the Tombigbee-Mobile Frontier in 1804." *Alabama Review* 24, no. 2 (April 1971): 83–113.

———. "Land, Law, and Politics on the Tombigbee Frontier, 1804." *Alabama Review* 33 (1980): 92–124.

Brown, Virginia Pounds, ed. *Creek Indian History: A Historical Narrative of the Genealogy, Traditions, and Downfall of the Ispocoga or Creek Indian Tribe of Indians, by George Stiggins*. Birmingham, AL: Birmingham Public Library Press, 1989.

Burnham, Robert. *Great Comets*. Cambridge: Cambridge University Press, 2002.

Burton, Gary. "Pintlala's Cold Murder Case: The Death of Thomas Meredith in 1812." *Alabama Review* 63, no. 3 (2010): 163–191.

Carter, Clarence Edwin, comp. *Territorial Papers of the United States*. Vols. 5–6, *The Territory of Mississippi, 1798–1817*. Washington, DC: Government Printing Office, 1937–38.

Cash, W. J. *The Mind of the South*. New York: Vintage Books, 1991.

Cashin, Edward J. *Lachlan McGillivray, Indian Trader: The Shaping of the Southern Colonial Frontier*. Athens: University of Georgia Press, 1992.

Caughey, John Walton. *McGillivray of the Creeks.* Introduction by William J. Bauer Jr. Columbia: University of South Carolina Press, 2007.

Chappell, Gordon T. "The Life and Activities of General John Coffee." PhD diss., Vanderbilt University, 1941.

Claiborne, J. F. H. *Life and Times of General Sam Dale: The Mississippi Partisan.* New York: Harper & Brothers, 1860.

———. *Mississippi, as a Province, Territory and State.* Jackson, MS: Power & Barksdale, 1880.

Claiborne, Nathaniel Herbert. *Notes on the War in the South with Biographical Sketches of Montgomery, Jackson, Sevier, the Late Gov. Claiborne, and Others.* Richmond, VA: William Ramsay, 1819.

Coker, William S., and Thomas D. Watson. *Indian Traders of the Southeastern Spanish Borderlands: Panton, Leslie & Company and John Forbes & Company, 1783–1847.* Pensacola: University of West Florida Press, 1986.

Collins, Robert P. "'A Packet from Canada': Telling Conspiracy Stories on the 1813 Creek Frontier." In *Tohopeka: Rethinking the Creek War and the War of 1812,* edited by Kathryn E. Holland Braund. Tuscaloosa: University of Alabama Press, 2012.

Coulter, Steven Earl. *Our Quaker Kin and Allied Families: Ancestors and Descendants of Adam Davis (1781–1861) and His Wife, Lydia Commons (1781–1841).* Des Moines, IA: Coulter, 1977.

Craven, Avery O., and Andrew Jackson. "Letters of Andrew Jackson." *Huntington Library Bulletin* 3 (1933): 109–134.

Crockett, David. *A Narrative of the Life of David Crockett of the State of Tennessee.* Philadelphia: E. L. Cary and A. Hart, 1834.

Curtis, Wayne. "Clarifying an Historic Event." *American Archaeology* 11, no. 3 (Fall 2007): 1–17.

Cushman, H. B., *History of the Choctaw, Chickasaw, and Natchez Indians.* Edited by Angie Debo. Norman: University of Oklahoma Press, 1999 [1899].

Cutrer, Thomas W. "'The Tallapoosa Might Truly be Called the River of Blood': Major Alexander McCulloch and the Battle of Horseshoe Bend." *Alabama Review* 43, no. 1 (1990): 35–39.

Danisi, Thomas. *Uncovering the Truth about Meriwether Lewis.* Amherst, NY: Prometheus, 2012.

Dattel, Gene. *Cotton and Race in the Making of America: The Human Costs of Economic Power.* Lanham, MD: Ivan R. Dee, 2009.

Davis, Karl. "'Much of the Indian Appears': Adaptation and Persistence in a Creek Community, 1783–1854." PhD diss., University of North Carolina, 2003.

Dickens, Roy S., Jr. *Archeological Investigations at Horseshoe Bend, National Military Park, Alabama.* Alabama Archaeological Society, Special Publication 3. Tuscaloosa: Alabama Archaeological Society, 1979.

Dillard, R. H. W. *News of the Nile: A Book of Poems.* Chapel Hill: University of North Carolina Press, 1971.

Doster, James F., ed. "Letters Relating to the Tragedy of Fort Mims: August–September." *Alabama Review* 14 (October 1961): 269–85.

Driesback, J. D. "Weatherford—'The Red Eagle,' Addendum to the Paper Furnished by the Writer on June 28th, 1877." *Alabama Historical Reporter* 2, no. 3 (1884): n.p.

East, Don C. *A Historical Analysis of the Creek Indian Hillabee Towns: And Personal Reflections on the Landscape and People of Clay County.* New York: iUniverse, 2008.

Eggleston, George Cary. *Red Eagle and the Wars with the Creek Indians of Alabama.* New York: Dodd, Mead, 1878.

Elting, John R. *Amateurs, to Arms: A Military History of the War of 1812.* Chapel Hill, NC: Algonquin Books, 1991.

Ethridge, Robbie. *Creek Country: The Creek Indians and Their World.* Chapel Hill: University of North Carolina Press, 2003.

Feldman, Jay. *When the Mississippi Ran Backwards: Empire, Intrigue, Murder, and the New Madrid Earthquakes of 1811–12.* New York: Free Press, 2012.

Floyd, John. "Letters of John Floyd." *Georgia Historical Quarterly* 33, no. 4 (1949): 228–69.

Foote, Shelby. *The Civil War: A Narrative in Three Volumes.* New York: Random House, 1963.

Foshee, John. *Alabama Canoe Rides and Float Trips.* Huntsville, AL: Strode, 1975.

Foster, H. Thomas, II, ed. *The Collected Works of Benjamin Hawkins, 1796–1810.* Tuscaloosa: University of Alabama Press, 2003.

Fundaburk, Emma L., ed. *Southeastern Indians Life Portraits: A Catalogue of Pictures, 1564–1860.* Luverne, AL: Emma Lila Fundaburk, 1958.

Gallay, Alan. *The Indian Slave Trade: The Rise of the English Empire in the American South, 1670–1717.* New Haven, CT: Yale University Press, 2002.

Grant, C. L., ed. *Letters, Journals and Writings of Benjamin Hawkins.* 2 vols. Savannah, GA: Beehive Press, 1980.

Griffith, Benjamin W., Jr. *McIntosh and Weatherford: Creek Indian Leaders.* Tuscaloosa: University of Alabama Press, 1989.

Halbert, Henry S. "Creek War Incidents." *Transactions of the Alabama Historical Society* 2 (1897–98): 95–119.

———. "Inaccuracies in Claiborne's History in Regard to Tecumseh." *Publications of the Mississippi Historical Society* 1 (1898): 101–03.

Halbert, Henry S., and Timothy H. Ball. *The Creek War of 1813 and 1814.* Chicago: Donohue & Henneberry, 1895.

Hamilton, Mary Floyd. *A Little Family History.* Savannah, GA: Morning News Print, 1908.

Hawkins, Benjamin. "Letters of Benjamin Hawkins, 1796–1806." *Collections of the Georgia Historical Society,* vol. 9. Savannah: Morning News, 1916.

Hays, J. E., comp. "Georgia Military Affairs, Vol. 3, 1801–1813." Unpublished. Georgia Department of Archives and History, 1940.

Hays, Louise Frederick, comp. *Unpublished Letters of Timothy Barnard: 1784–1820*. Morrow: Georgia Department of Archives and History, 1939.

Henderson, T. R. "The Destruction of Littafuchee, and a Brief History of American Settlement." *Alabama Review* 67, no. 3 (2014): 233–253.

Hoole, Stanley W. *Alias Simon Suggs: The Life and Times of Johnson Jones Hooper*. Tuscaloosa: University of Alabama Press, 1952.

Hooper, Johnson J. *Some Adventures of Captain Simon Suggs, Late of the Tallapoosa Volunteers; Together with "Taking the Census," and Other Alabama Sketches*. Philadelphia: Carey and Hart, 1845.

Hudson, Angela Pulley. *Creek Paths and Federal Roads: Indians, Settlers, and Slaves and the Making of the American South*. Chapel Hill: University of North Carolina Press, 2010.

Innerarity, John. "A Prelude to the Creek War of 1813–1814, in a Letter of John Innerarity to James Innerarity." *Florida Historical Quarterly* 18 (April 1940): 247–66.

Inskeep, Steve. *Jacksonland: President Andrew Jackson, Cherokee Chief John Ross, and a Great American Land Grab*. New York: Penguin, 2015.

Jackson, Harvey H. *Rivers of History: Life on the Coosa, Tallapoosa, Cahaba, and Alabama*. Tuscaloosa: University of Alabama Press, 1995.

Jemison, E. Grace. *Historic Tales of Talladega*. Montgomery, AL: Paragon, 1959.

Johnson, Walter. *River of Dark Dreams: Slavery and Empire in the Cotton Kingdom*. Cambridge: Harvard University Press, 2013.

Kanon, Tom. *Tennesseans at War 1812–1815: Andrew Jackson, the Creek War, and the Battle of New Orleans*. Tuscaloosa: University of Alabama Press, 2014.

Lackey, Richard S., comp. *Frontier Claims in the Lower South: Records of Claims Filed by Citizens of the Alabama and Tombigbee River Settlements in the Mississippi Territory for Depredations by the Creek Indians during the War of 1812*. Introduction by John D. W. Guice. New Orleans: Polyanthos, 1977.

Lincecum, Gideon. *Pushmataha: A Choctaw Leader and His People*. Tuscaloosa: University of Alabama Press, 2004.

Linklater, Andro. *An Artist in Treason: The Extraordinary Double Life of General James Wilkinson*. New York: Walker, 2009.

Lowrie, Walter, and Matthew St. Clair Clarke, eds. *American State Papers, Indian Affairs*. 2 vols. Washington, DC: Gales and Seaton, 1832.

Mackenzie, George C. *The Indian Breastwork in the Battle of Horseshoe Bend: Its Size, Location and Construction*. Washington, DC: US Department of Interior, Office of Archaeology and Historic Preservation, 1969.

Mann, Robert W., William M. Bass, and Lee Meadows. "Time Since Death and Decomposition of the Human Body: Variables and Observations in

Case and Experimental Field Studies." *Journal of Forensic Sciences* 35, no. 1 (January 1990): 103–11.

Martin, William. *The Self Vindication of Colonel William Martin: Against Certain Charges and Aspersions Made Against Him by Gen. Andrew Jackson and Others, in Relation to Sundry Transactions in the Campaign Against the Creek Indians in the Year 1813.* Nashville: John Simpson, 1829.

Mason, David Pierce. *Massacre at Fort Mims.* Mobile, AL: Greenberry, 1975.

Mauelshagen, Carl, and Gerald H. Davis, eds. *Partners in the Lord's Work: The Diary of Two Moravian Missionaries in the Creek Indian Country, 1807–1813.* Atlanta: Georgia State College, 1969.

McCown, Mary Hardin, ed. "The 'J. Hartsell Memora': The Journal of a Tennessee Captain in the War of 1812." *East Tennessee Historical Society's Publications* 11 (1939): 118–145.

McKenney, Thomas, L., and James Hall. *History of the Indian Tribes of North America, with Biographical Sketches and Anecdotes of the Principal Chiefs.* 3 vols. Philadelphia: D. Rice, 1838.

Meek, A. B. *Romantic Passages in Southwestern History.* New York: S. H. Goetzel, 1857.

Miles, Tiya. *Ties that Bind: The Story of an Afro-Cherokee Family in Slavery and Freedom.* Berkeley: University of California Press, 2005.

Milford, Louis LeClerc. *Memoirs: Or, a Cursory Glance at my Different Travels & My Sojourn in the Creek Nation* [1802]. Translated by Geraldine de Courcy, edited by John Francis McDermott. Chicago: R. R. Donnelley & Sons, 1956.

Mitchell, Stewart, ed. *New Letters of Abigail Adams, 1788–1801.* Boston: Houghton Mifflin, 1947.

Moser, Harold D., David R. Hoth, Sharon MacPherson, and John H. Reinbold, eds. *The Papers of Andrew Jackson Volume 3, 1814–1815.* Knoxville: University of Tennessee Press, 1991.

Moser, Harold D., and Sharon MacPherson, eds. *The Papers of Andrew Jackson Volume 2, 1804–1813.* Knoxville: University of Tennessee Press, 1984.

Myer, William E. "Indian Trails of the Southeast." In *Bureau of American Ethnology Bulletin* 42. Washington, DC: Government Printing Office, 1928.

Northern, William J. *Men of Mark in Georgia: A Complete and Elaborate History of the State from Its Settlement to the Present Time, Chiefly Told in Biographies, and Autobiographies of the Most Eminent Men of Each Period of Georgia's Progress and Development, Vol. 2.* Atlanta: A. B. Caldwell, 1910.

Orr, W. G. "The Surrender of Weatherford." In *Transactions of the Alabama Historical Society, 1897–98,* edited by Thomas McAdory Owen, 57–58. Tuscaloosa, AL: Printed for the Society, 1898.

Parton, James. *Life of Andrew Jackson in Three Volumes.* New York: Mason Brothers, 1860.

Pate, James P., ed. *The Reminiscences of George Strother Gaines: Pioneer and Statesman of Early Alabama and Mississippi, 1805–1843.* Tuscaloosa: University of Alabama Press, 1998.

Pickett, Albert James. *History of Alabama, and Incidentally of Georgia and Mississippi, from the Earliest Period.* 2 vols. Charleston, SC: Walker and James, 1851.

Piker, Joshua. *Okfuskee: A Creek Indian Town in Colonial America.* Cambridge, MA: Harvard University Press, 2004.

Pope, John. *A Tour through the Southern and Western Territories of the United States of North-America; the Spanish Dominions on the River Mississippi, and the Floridas; the Countries of the Creek Nations; and Many Uninhabited Parts.* Richmond, VA: John Dixon, 1792.

Prucha, Francis Paul. *The Sword of the Republic: The United States Army on the Frontier, 1783–1846.* Lincoln: University of Nebraska Press, 1987.

Reid, John, and John H. Eaton. *The Life of Andrew Jackson, Original 1817 Edition.* Edited by Frank L. Owsley Jr. Tuscaloosa: University of Alabama Press, 1974.

Remini, Robert V. *Andrew Jackson and the Course of American Empire, 1767–1821.* New York: Harper and Row, 1977.

Roosevelt, Theodore. *The Winning of the West, Volume 1: From the Alleghanies to the Mississippi, 1769–1776.* Lincoln: University of Nebraska Press, 1995.

Rowland, Dunbar. "Mississippi Territory in the War of 1812." In *Publications of the Mississippi Historical Society, Centenary Series Volume 4.* Jackson: Mississippi Historical Society, 1921.

Royall, Anne Newport. *Letters from Alabama on Various Subjects: To Which is Added an Appendix, containing Remarks on Sundry Members of the 20th and 21st Congress, and other High Characters at the Seat of Government.* Washington, DC: 1830.

Schouler, James. *History of the United States of America, Under the Constitution.* 6 vols. New York: Dodd, Mead, 1880.

Sewall, Lewis. *The Miscellaneous Poems of Lewis Sewall, Esq., Containing the Last Campaign of Col. J. Caller—Alias Sir John Falstaff the Second—Alias the Hero of Burnt Corn Battle; The Birth Progress, and Probable End of G.F. Mynheer Van Slaverchap's Grandson—Alias Doctor Furnace; The Battle for the Cow and Calf; The Canoe Fight; And Other Miscellaneous Matters.* Mobile, AL: 1833.

Shackford, James Atkins. *David Crockett: The Man and the Legend.* Lincoln: University of Nebraska Press, 1994.

Smith, Marvin T. *Coosa: The Rise and Fall of a Southeastern Mississippian Chiefdom.* Gainesville: University Press of Florida, 2000.

———. "Woods Island Revisited." *Journal of Alabama Archaeology* 41, no. 2 (December 1995): 93–106.

Southerland, Henry DeLeon, Jr., and Jerry Elijah Brown. *The Federal Road through Georgia and the Creek Nation, and Alabama, 1806–1836.* Tuscaloosa: University of Alabama Press, 1989.

Stagg, John Charles Anderson. *The Papers of James Madison: Presidential Series.* 7 vols. Charlottesville: University of Virginia Press, 2008.

Sugden, John. *Tecumseh: A Life.* New York: Henry Holt, 1991.

Swan, Major Caleb. "Position and State of Manners and Arts in the Creek Nation, in 1791." In *Information Respecting the History, Condition and Prospects of the Indian Tribes of the United States,* 6 vols. Edited by Henry R. Schoolcraft. Philadelphia: Lippincott, 1855.

Swanton, John Reed. *Early History of the Creek Indians and Their Neighbors.* Bureau of American Ethnology, Bulletin 73. Washington, DC: Government Printing Office, 1922.

———. *Final Report of the United States De Soto Expedition Commission.* Washington: Smithsonian Institution Press, 1985.

Taitt, David. "David Taitt's Journal of a Journey through the Creek Country, 1772." In *Travels in the American Colonies,* edited by Newton D. Mereness. New York: Macmillan, 1916.

Tarvin, Dr. Marion Elisha. "The Muscogees or Creek Indians, 1519 to 1893." *Alabama Historical Quarterly* 17 (Fall 1955): 125–45.

Tatum, Major Howell. "Topographic Notes and Observations on the Alabama River, August 1814." In *Transactions of the Alabama Historical Society,* vol. 2, 1897–1898, edited by Peter J. Hamilton and Thomas M. Owen, 130–177.

Thomas, Daniel H. *Fort Toulouse: The French Outpost at the Alabamas on the Coosa,* with a new introduction by Gregory A. Waselkov. Tuscaloosa: University of Alabama Press, 1989.

Thompson, Lynn Hastie. *William Weatherford: His Country and His People.* Bay Minette, AL: Lavender Publishing, 1991.

Tures, John A. "Hell Comes to Horseshoe Bend." *Napoleon Series: The War of 1812 Magazine* 9 (May 2008). http://www.napoleon-series.org/military/Warof1812/2008/Issue9/c_HorseShoeBend.html.

US Bureau of the Census. *Historical Statistics of the United States, Colonial Times to 1970, Bicentennial Edition, Part 1.* Washington, DC: Government Printing Office, 1975.

Vickery, Lou, and Steve Travis. *The Rise of the Poarch Band of Creek Indians.* Atmore, AL: Upword Press, 2009.

Waselkov, Gregory A. *A Conquering Spirit: Fort Mims and the Redstick War of 1813–1814.* Tuscaloosa: University of Alabama Press, 2006.

———. "Fort Jackson and the Aftermath." In *Tohopeka: Rethinking the Creek War and the War of 1812,* edited by Kathryn E. Holland Braund. Tuscaloosa: University of Alabama Press, 2012.

———. "A Reinterpretation of the Creek Indian Barricade at Horseshoe Bend." *Journal of Alabama Archaeology* 32, no. 2 (December 1986): 94–107.

————. "Return to the Holy Ground: The Legendary Battle Site Discovered." *Alabama Heritage* 101 (2011): 28–37.

Waselkov, Greg, and Raven Christopher. *Archeological Identification of Creek War Sites, Part 2, Technical Report on Grant Agreement No. GA-2255-11-025.* Mobile: University of South Alabama Center for Archaeological Studies, 2012.

Waselkov, Gregory A., and Brian M. Wood. "The Creek War of 1813–1814: Effects on Creek Society and Settlement Pattern." *Journal of Alabama Archaeology* 32, no. 1 (June 1986): 1–24.

Willett, William M. *A Narrative of the Military Actions of Colonel Marinus Willett, taken Chiefly from His Own Manuscript.* New York: G. & C. & H. Carvill, 1831.

Woodward, Thomas S. *Woodward's Reminiscences of the Creek, or Muscogee Indians, Contained in Letters to Friends in Georgia and Alabama.* Montgomery, AL: Barrett & Wimbish, 1859.

Wright, Amos J., Jr. *Historic Indian Towns in Alabama, 1540–1838.* Tuscaloosa: University of Alabama Press, 2003.

————. *The McGillivray and McIntosh Traders on the Old Southwest Frontier, 1716–1815.* Montgomery, AL: New South Books, 2001.

Wright, Leitch J., Jr. *William Augustus Bowles: Director General of the Creek Nation.* Athens: University of Georgia Press, 1967.

Wyatt-Brown, Bertram. *Southern Honor: Ethics and Behavior in the Old South.* Oxford: Oxford University Press, 1982.

ACKNOWLEDGMENTS

❖

The genesis of this book goes back to 1964 when I was an eighth grade student at Mountain Brook Junior High School located in a suburb of Birmingham, Alabama. At this late remove I remember learning two things that year: (1) "a body at rest tends to stay at rest, and a body in motion tends to stay in motion;" and (2) the remarkable but tragic history of the state of Alabama. I do not remember the name of the science teacher who taught me that core principle of physics, but I do remember the name of my history teacher—Stuart Harris. Mr. Harris had the remarkable ability to grab the attention of a classroom of young teenagers reeling under the relentless onslaught of profound hormonal change. Without being the least pedantic or condescending he would breathe startling life into the dry husks of the words in our state-issued "History of Alabama." When he spoke heads would pop up or stop swiveling. Even today I can still hear his enthralling tales of a number of the incidents related in this book. In the telling of these stories I hope that I have done justice to his high standard of discourse.

Of course a number of people have given me aid and comfort along this journey through a wilderness of long-forgotten words and deeds of long-forgotten people. Even now I am not sure I am out, but at least I have reached a clearing. As this has somewhat been a family affair I would like first to thank my son, Howard, my nephew Howard ("Buck") O'Leary and my wife Anne for bearing many heavy loads. Of those not of my blood but who probably bloodied themselves helping me through the thickets and quick sands I encountered, I would particularly like to thank the archeologist, teacher, and historian Dr. Gregory Waselkov, his student, the archeologist and historian Raven Christopher, my meticulous and remarkably patient editor Ron Silverman, whose knowledge of grammar and punctuation has yet to be overtaken by the COMPUTER, and neither last nor least my friend and professional computer wrangler, Ruth Davis, who pointed me in the right direction whenever I lost the way.

Finally I would like to express my gratitude to Bruce H. Franklin, the publisher of Westholme Publishing, for inviting me to join the family.

INDEX

❖